International Business Law and Lex Mercatoria

To Annelies, Hannelore & Lieselotte

T.M.C. ASSER INSTITUUT – THE HAGUE

International Business Law and Lex Mercatoria

by

Filip De Ly

LL.M. Harvard Law School
Dr.Iur. Faculty of Law, University of Ghent
Professor of Law
Faculty of Law, Erasmus University, Rotterdam

1992
NORTH-HOLLAND
AMSTERDAM – LONDON – NEW YORK – TOKYO

ISBN 0 444 88971 X

North Holland
Elsevier Science Publishers B.V.
Sara Burgerhartstraat 25
P.O. Box 211
1000 AE Amsterdam, The Netherlands

T.M.C. Asser Instituut — Institute for Private and Public International Law, International Commercial Arbitration and European Law
20-22 Alexanderstraat, 2514 JM The Hague, the Netherlands — tel. (0)70-3420300 — telex: 34273 asser nl, telefax: (0)70-3420359
Director: C.C.A. Voskuil
The T.M.C. Asser Instituut was founded in 1965 by the Dutch universities offering courses in international law to promote education and research in the fields of law covered by the departments of the Institute: Private International Law, Public International Law, including the Law of International Organisations, Law of the European Communities and International Commercial Arbitration. The Institute discharges this task by the establishment and management of documentation and research projects, in some instances in co-operation with non-Dutch or international organisations, by the dissemination of information deriving therefrom and by publication of monographs and series.

PRINTED IN THE NETHERLANDS

PREFACE

This book is in part based on a dissertation for which I obtained, on March 14, 1989, the degree of "doctor iuris", "summa cum laude", at the Faculty of Law of Ghent State University (Belgium).

The original text of the dissertation and the Dutch edition (Maklu Publishers, Antwerp/Apeldoorn, 1989, xxiii + 389 + LXIII p.), concentrated on the theory of the *lex mercatoria*. In contrast, this book places *lex mercatoria* in the broader perspective of the sources of international business law. The Dutch edition, then, was only a starting point and has been rewritten and reorganized substantially in order better to reflect the importance of the subject for day-to-day international business life and to make the text more readily accessible to practitioners. Furthermore, the text had to be updated; as such, it states the law as of March 1, 1992.

My sincere thanks go to Professors Eddy Wymeersch and Hubert Bocken of Ghent Law Faculty who respectively acted as promotor and co-promotor of the dissertation. Secondly, I have to thank Professor D. Kokkini-Iatridou of Utrecht Law Faculty (The Netherlands) for encouraging me to embark on this venture and for her continuous support during this project. Thanks also to the T.M.C. Asser Instituut (The Hague) and particularly to Marjolijn Bastiaans for her patience, as well as to the publisher for adding this title to their co-publication series. Also and once again, Ann and Johan Viaene-De Ly made the final touches to the original manuscript; the fine lay-out would not have been possible without their help and assistance. Last and not the least, Peter Bienenstock (J.D. 1981, Columbia Law School, Partner at the Brussels office of the law firm of Loeff Claeys Verbeke) is thanked for his loyalty in doing a superb and invaluable language review.

IJsselstein, April 1992 Filip De Ly

TABLE OF CONTENTS

LIST OF PERIODICALS

A.C.	Law reports appeal cases
AcP	Archiv für die civilistische Praxis
AG	Die Aktiengesellschaft
All E.R.	All England law reports
AM.J.COMP.L.	American journal of comparative law
Ann.Dr.	Annales de droit
Ann.Dr.Com.	Annales de droit commercial
Ann.Dr.Liège	Annales de droit de Liège
Ann.Fac.Dr.Liège	Annales de la Faculté de droit, d'économie et de sciences sociales de Liège
Ann.fr.dr.int.	Annuaire français de droit international
Ann.suisse Dr.Int.	Annuaire suisse de droit international
ARB.	Arbitration
ARB.INT'L	Arbitration international
ARB.J.	Arbitration journal
Arch.Phil.Dr.	Archives de philosophie du droit
ASA Bull.	Bulletin de l'association suisse de l'arbitrage
ATF	Arrêts du tribunal fédéral
AWD	Außenwirtschaftsdienst der Betriebs-Beraters
B.J.	Belgique judiciaire
Brit.Y.B.Int.L.	British Yearbook of international law
B.U.INT'L L.J.	Boston University international law journal
Bull.Ass.	Bulletin des assurances - De verzekering
Bull.Cass.	Bulletin des arrêts de la Cour de Cassation (Belgium)
BUS.LAW.	Business lawyer
Cah.Dr.Eur.	Cahiers de droit européen
Clunet	Journal du droit international
COL.J.TRANSNAT'L L.	Columbia journal of transnational law
D.	Recueil Dalloz
DB	Der Betrieb
D.P.C.I.	Droit et pratique du commerce international
Dr.mar.fr.	Droit maritime français
E.T.L.	European transport law
Gaz.Pal.	Gazette du palais
GEO.WASH.J.INT'L L. & EC.	George Washington journal of international law and economics
HARV.INT'L L.J.	Harvard international law journal
ICSID REV.	ISCID review - foreign investment law journal
I.L.M.	International legal materials
Int.Fin.Law Review	International financial law review
INT'L & COMP.L.Q.	International and comparative law quarterly
INT'L LAW.	International lawyer
IPRax.	Praxis des internationalen Privat- und Verfahrensrecht
J.BUS.L.	Journal of business law

J.C.B.	Jurisprudence commerciale de Belgique - Belgische rechtspraak in handelszaken
J.C.P.	Jurisclasseur périodique (édition générale)
J.C.P. éd. C.I.	Jurisclasseur périodique (édition commerce et industrie)
J.INT.ARB.	Journal of international arbitration
J.J.P.	Journal des juges de paix - Tijdschrift van de vrede- en politierechters
J.MAR.L. & COM.	Journal of maritime law and commerce
J.P.A.	Jurisprudence du port d'Anvers - Rechtspraak van de haven van Antwerpen
J.T.	Journal des tribunaux (Belgium)
Jura Falc.	Jura falconis
Jur.Liège	Jurisprudence de la Cour d'Appel de Liège et des jurisdictions de son ressort
JW	Juristische Wochenschrift
JZ	Juristenzeitung
KTS	Konkurs-, Treuhand- und Schiedsgerichtswesen
LA.L.REV.	Louisiana law review
LAW & CONTEMP.PROBS.	Law and contemporary problems
Lloyd's Mar. & COM.L.Q.	Lloyd's maritime and commercial law quarterly
Lloyd's Rep.	Lloyd's law reports
L.Q.R.	Law quarterly review
McGill L.J.	McGill law journal
Mod.L.Rev.	Modern law review
N.I.L.R.	Netherlands international law review
N.J.	Nederlandse jurisprudentie
N.J.B.	Nederlands juristenblad
NJW	Neue juristische Wochenschrift
N.T.I.R.	Nederlands tijdschrift voor internationaal recht
Nw.J.INT'L L. & BUS.	Northwestern journal of international law and business
N.Y.B.Int.L.	Netherlands Yearbook of international law
O.J.	Official Journal of the European Communities
Pas.	Pasicrisie belge
RabelsZ	Zeitschrift für ausländisches und internationales Privatrecht
R.B.D.I.	Revue belge de droit international - Belgisch tijdschrift voor internationaal recht
R.C.D.I.P.	Revue critique de droit international privé
R.C.J.B.	Revue critique de jurisprudence belge
R.D.A.I.	Revue du droit des affaires internationales
R.D.C.	Revue de droit commercial belge -Tijdschrift voor Belgisch handelsrecht
Rev.Arb.	Revue de l'arbitrage
Rev.Banque	Revue de la banque - Bank- en financiewezen
Rev.Crit.Lég.Jur.	Revue critique de législation et de jurisprudence
Rev.Dr.Int.Comp.	Revue de droit international et de droit comparé
Rev.Dr.Int.Lég.Comp.	Revue de droit international et de législation comparée
Rev.fr.dr.aér.	Revue français de droit aérien

Rev.Int.Dr.Comp.	Revue internationale de droit comparé
Rev.Interd.Jur.	Revue interdisciplineaire d'études juridiques
Rev.Liège	Revue de jurisprudence de Liège, Mons et Bruxelles
Rev.Prat.Soc.	Revue pratique des sociétés civiles et commerciales
Rev.Soc.	Revue des sociétés
Rev.Trim.Dr.Com.	Revue trimestrielle de droit commercial
R.G.D.C.	Revue générale de droit civil
R.I.D.E.	Revue internationale de droit économique
Riv.Dir.Int.Priv.Proc.	Rivista di diritto internazionale privato e processuale
RIW	Recht der internationalen Wirtschaft
R.W.	Rechtskundig Weekblad
Scan.Stud.L.	Scandinavian studies in law
S.Ct.	Supreme court reporter
S.E.W.	Sociaal economische wetgeving
TEX.INT'L L.J.	Texas international law journal
T.P.R.	Tijdschrift voor Privaatrecht
Trav.com.fr.dr.int.privé	Travaux du comité français de droit international privé
TUL.L.REV.	Tulane law review
T.V.V.S.	Maandblad voor ondernemingsrecht en rechtspersonen
UNIF.L.REV.	Uniform law review - Revue de droit uniforme
U.S.	United States reports
VA.J.INT'L L.	Virginia journal for international law
VAND.J.TRANSNAT'L L.	Vanderbilt journal of transnational law
VersR	Versicherungsrecht
WM	Wertpapier-Mitteilungen
W.P.N.R.	Weekblad voor privaatrecht, notarisambt en registratie
Y.B.COM.ARB.	Yearbook commercial arbitration
ZaöRV	Zeitschrift für ausländisches öffentliches Recht und Völkerrecht
ZfRV	Zeitschrift für Rechtsvergleichung
ZHR	Zeitschrift für das gesamte Handelsrecht und Wirtschaftsrecht
ZöffentlR	Zeitschrift für öffentliches recht
ZSchwR	Zeitschrift für schweizerisches Recht
ZVglRWiss	Zeitschrift für vergleichende Rechtswissenschaft

LIST OF ABBREVIATIONS

ABGB	Allgemeines Bürgerliches Gesetzbuch
AGBG	Allgemeine Geschäftbedingungengesetz
AHGB	Allgemeines Handelsgesetzbuch
AIBD	Association of international bond dealers
BGB	Bürgerliches Gesetzbuch
Cc	Code civil
CISG	Vienna Convention on contracts for the international sale of goods
C.M.I.	Comité maritime internationale
C.S.I.D.	Convention on the settlement of investment disputes between states and nationals of other states
E.C.E.	Economic commission for Europe
EEC	European Economic Community
EEIG	European economic interest grouping
EGBGB	Einführungsgesetz zum Bürgerlichen Gesetzbuch
F.I.D.I.C.	Fédération internationale des ingénieurs-conseils
GAFTA	Grain and feed trade association
HGB	Handelsgesetzbuch
IATA	International air transport association
I.C.C.	International chamber of commerce
I.C.S.I.D.	International center for the settlement of investment disputes
Incoterms	International rules for the interpretation of trade terms - International commercial terms
ISMA	International securities market association
N.B.W.	New civil code - Nieuw burgerlijk wetboek (The Netherlands)
N.C.P.C.	Nouveau code de procédure civile
N.I.E.O.	New international economic order
S.W.I.F.T.	Society for worldwide interbank financial telecommunications
UCC	Uniform commercial code
U.C.P.	Uniform customs and practice for documentary credits
ULIS	Uniform law on the international sales of goods
ULFIS	Uniform law on the formation of contracts for the international sales of goods
Uncitral	United Nations commission for international trade law
ZPO	Zivilprozeßordnung

INTRODUCTION

1. The importance of international trade for the world economy and the livelihood of millions of people cannot be denied. Since World War II, international trade has seen explosive growth, in a climate of political, economic and monetary stability. Lawyers also have been confronted often with problems relating to international business transactions and, consequently, with the legal rules applicable to such transactions.

From a traditional perspective, the answer to legal questions raised by international trade is relatively simple. The dispute should, according to this view, be resolved through the conflict of law rules applicable in the jurisdiction seized of any dispute (be it a judge sitting in a national court or an arbitration panel). These rules should refer to a given *national* legal system in which one should look for treaties, statutes, case law and scholarly writings relevant to the problem at hand.

In the mid-fifties, scholars began to contest this traditional theory. Their criticism focused around the argument that national legal rules are, to a large extent, inappropriate to regulate international business transactions. In turn, they have proposed alternatives based upon broad contractual autonomy of the parties, international trade customs and usages which were to be enforced through international commercial arbitration. At a later stage, they also added uniform law, general principles of law and arbitral case law as sources of international business law. Thus, the proponents of these alternatives aimed not only at a regulation of international business transactions by national law, but also at creating possibilities for applying legal rules of the international business community itself and rules which did not originate in national legal systems. This theory has become known under the Latin expression *lex mercatoria*, reflecting that international business transactions have historically been regulated by rules developed by the business community.

Finally, substantive and comparative methods also have been proposed in order to replace the traditional conflict of laws theory.

2. The above theories have been discussed at length in contemporary writings. In particular, the theory of the *lex mercatoria* has, more than any other theory, received considerable attention. It has been quite successful in France and, to a certain extent, influential in Belgium, Switzerland and The Netherlands. More importantly, the theory of the *lex mercatoria* also has had a considerable impact on recent arbitration laws and arbitral case law and, to a lesser extent, on international conventions and the case law of national courts. These developments will be discussed below, primarily from the perspective of uniform laws and of English, French, German, Swiss, Belgian and Dutch law; other legal systems will incidentally also be discussed.

3. As the sources of international business law are a central issue in the law of international trade, understanding the mechanisms of international business law depends upon conceptions about its sources and their interplay. From a practical perspective, it is essential to know whether and to what extent, self regulatory rules developed by the international business community may be enforced and to begin to identify and analyze such rules.

4. A description of the sources of international business law will only show part of the international regulatory efforts in the field of international economic relations. International business law may thus be distinguished from other forms of regulation, such as domestic public laws and public international law. This implies that only private law relations stemming from international business transactions will be dealt with in this book.

However, distinguishing between private and public law has proven to be very difficult in international business because states, state organizations and state affiliated companies have come to play an important role in international business transactions. This is particularly so with regard to centrally planned economies, developing countries and some western countries in which parts of the economy have been placed in the public sector. These developments have raised interesting issues whether and to what extent transactions with state controlled enterprises remain, or can be brought within the scope of private or public law. These issues are especially acute in relation to contracts between foreign investors and state controlled enterprises from developing countries.

Fierce debates have divided arbitral case law and scholarly writings over the question of the legal system which should control these so-called *State contracts*. Basically, three opinions have emerged. The first view would refer these State contracts through conflict rules to a given national legal system. A second opinion favors the application of public international law to these contracts. Finally, a third opinion would give autonomous status to these contracts: specific rules, apart from those of national laws or public international law, would apply to state contracts.

These problems will not be discussed in this book. First, these issues are quite specific and, therefore, cannot be considered a fundamental part of a study on sources of international business law. Second, since literature on the subject is abundant[1] and research would necessitate an interdisciplinary approach, discussion of State contracts would deflect attention from a study on the sources of international business law. The analyses of this book and its conclusions, however, may not be without importance in the debate on State contracts[2].

---

1. For instance : VAN HECKE, G., Les accords entre un Etat et une personne privée étrangère, Institute of international law, 57 Annuaire, II, 1977, 106-107; VAN HECKE, G., Contracts between States and foreign private law persons, Encyclopedia of public international law, Volume 7, 1984, 54-59; VERHOEVEN, J., Contrats entre Etats et ressortissants d'autres Etats, in Le contrat économique international, Travaux des VIIes Journées d'études juridiques Jean Dabin, Brussels, Bruylant, 1975, 115-150; VERHOEVEN, J., Droit international des contrats et droit des gens, R.B.D.I., 1978-79, 209; VERHOEVEN, J., Arbitrage entre Etats et entreprises étrangères : des règles spécifiques ?, in Hommage à Jean Robert, Les Etats et l'arbitrage international, Rev.Arb., 1985, 609-640; LEBOULANGER, P., Les contrats entre Etats et entreprises étrangères, Paris, Economica, 1985, 354 pp.; WEIL, P., Problèmes relatifs aux contrats passés entre un Etat et un particulier, Academy of international law, 128 Collected courses of the Hague, 1969, III, 95-240; KOKKINI-IATRIDOU, D. and DE WAARDT, P., Economic disputes between States and private parties, some legal thoughts on the institutionalization of their settlement, N.I.L.R., 1986, 289-333; BÖCKSTIEGEL, K.H., Der Staat als Vertagspartner ausländischer Privatunternehmen, Frankfurt, Athenäum Verlag, 1971, 432 pp.; BÖCKSTIEGEL, K.H., Arbitration and state enterprises, Survey on the national and international state of law and practice, Deventer, Kluwer, 1984, 113 pp.; KIPP, H., Verträge zwischen staatlichen und nichtstaatlichen Partnern, Berichte der deutschen Gesellschaft für Völkerrecht, Volume 5, 1964, 133-188; STOLL, J., Vereinbarungen zwischen Staat und ausländischem Investor, Berlin, Springer, 1982, 166 pp.; WENGLER, W., Nouveaux aspects de la problématique des contrats entre Etats et personnes privées, R.B.D.I., 1978-79, 415-424; SCHANZE, E., Investitionsverträge im internationalen Wirtschaftsrecht, Frankfurt, Metzner, 1986, 305 pp.; LALIVE, J.F., Contrats entre Etats ou entreprises étatiques et personnes privées, Academy of international law, 181 Collected courses of the Hague, 1983, III, 9-283; LIPSTEIN, K., International arbitration between individuals and governments and the conflict of laws, Contemporary problems of international law : Essays in honour of Georg Schwarzenberger on his eightieth birthday, London, Stevens & Sons, 1988, 177-195.
2. See DELAUME, G., The proper law of State contracts and the lex mercatoria : a reappraisal, 3 ICSID REV. 1988, 82. This author argues that the practice of State contracts teaches that these contracts remain largely within classical conflict of laws methodology, because of the choice of law clauses contained in most contracts.
   Finally, article 6 of the 1989 Santiago de Compostela resolution of the Institute of International Law on arbitration between states, state enterprises or state entities and foreign enterprises has provided parties and arbitrators great freedom in determining legal rules applicable to such arbitrations. In this regard, reference to lex mercatoria was considered, but finally replaced by a reference to usages of international commerce (JAYME, E. in IPRax, 1990, 70 with the text of the resolution on pp. 70-71).

5. It is obvious that a discussion of sources of international business law and the power of private parties to create their own law touches on jurisprudential issues, such as definitions of law, legal systems and law-creating sources[3]. In this book, the sources of international business law will be discussed from a legal rather than a jurisprudential perspective[4]. Since the analysis is then not exclusively based upon jurisprudential postulates, differences of opinion concerning these postulates should not lead scholars to accept or reject the analyses of this book. Consequently, rather than providing comprehensive definitions, concepts have been stated, to the extent necessary, in an operational and pragmatic way setting out minimum conditions.

6. The structure of this book may be summarized as follows. First, the introductory chapter discusses historical antecedents for current international business law. The same chapter then continues to describe the scope of international business law. Three elements are at the heart of the analysis: 1) what makes a business transaction international ?; 2) when does an international transaction take on a business character ?; and 3) what is the territorial scope of international business law ?

The second chapter discusses conflict of laws issues in relation to litigation before national courts and arbitral dispute resolution in order to analyze to what extent non-national rules or methods, other than the conflict of laws method, may be applied to international business transactions.

The third chapter analyzes the various sources of substantive international business law (general conditions, customs and usages, professional rules, technical rules, codes of conduct, general principles of law, arbitral case law, international conventions, including uniform law).

The last chapter discusses the various theories developed with regard to the sources of international business law. In this respect, the theory of the *lex mercatoria* and substantive and comparative methods are analyzed.

---

3. However, some authors have denied any such link and stated that scholarly writings on lex mercatoria were aimed only at a more adequate description of the real world of international business transactions (KAHN, P., Lex mercatoria et euro-obligations, in Law and international trade, Festschrift für Clive Schmitthoff, FABRICIUS, F. (ed.), Frankfurt, Athenäum Verlag, 1973, 240; FOUCHARD, P., La loi régissant les obligations contractuelles en droit international privé français, in Basle symposium on the law governing contractual obligations, KLEIN, F.E. and VISCHER, F. (ed.), Basle, Helbing & Lichtenhahn, 1983, 105).
4. References to the jurisprudential perspective may be found in Nos. 73, 332, 338, 351, 365 and 449.

Finally, these theories are assessed and conclusions are drawn as to the future of international business law.

CHAPTER I

Introduction to International Business Law : Definition, History and Scope of Application

I.1 Definition

7. First, the concept of *international business law* should be explained. In this regard, one may note that the expression has not been used often. Traditional writings have cited the notion of *international trade law*[1]. However, this approach mainly paid attention to international trade transactions, without analyzing the players of international trade. Taking the latter into account, one may speak of international business law, also covering international legal issues involving companies and other legal entities active in international trade.

On the other hand, some authors have introduced more novel terminology by speaking of *transnational law*[2]. This concept adequately

---

1. See SCHMITTHOFF'S EXPORT TRADE, The law and practice of international trade, ninth edition, London, Stevens & Sons, 1990, 798 pp.; DAY, D.M., The law of international trade, London, Butterworths, 1981, 254 pp.; HOYLE, M., The law of international trade, second edition London, CCH, 1985, 518 pp.; TIPLADY, D., Introduction to the law of international trade, BSP Professional books, 1989, 214 pp.
2. HORN, N., Das Recht der internationalen Anleihen, 513-515; LANGEN, E., Transnationales Handelsrecht, 2230; HINSCH, C. and HORN, N., Das Vertragsrecht der internationalen Konsortialkredite und Projektfinanzierungen, 196; SCHMITTHOFF, C., Nature and evolution of the transnational law of commercial transactions, 20; GOLDMAN, B., Une bataille judiciaire autour de la lex mercatoria, 409; GOLDMAN, B., intervention during the discussions, in Basle symposium on the law governing contractual obligations, KLEIN, F.E. and VISCHER, F. (ed.), Basle, Helbing & Lichtenhahn, 1983, 194; RIGAUX, F., Droit public et droit privé dans les relations internationales, 366-372; VERHOEVEN, J., Contrats entre Etats et ressortissants d'autres Etats, 142; VERHOEVEN, J., Arbitrage entre Etats et entreprises étrangères: des règles spécifiques ?, 626; MAYER, P., La neutralisation du pouvoir normatif de l'Etat en matière de contrats d'Etat, Clunet, 1986, 22-23; LOQUIN, E., L'amiable composition en droit comparé et international, Contribution à l'étude du non-droit dans l'arbitrage commercial, 311; PFAFF, D., International licensing contracts, transfer of technology and transnational law, in The transnational law of international commercial transactions, HORN, N. and SCHMITTHOFF, C. (ed.), Deventer, Kluwer, 1982, 209; DUNNWEBER, I., Vertrag zur Erstellung einer schlüsselfertigen Industrieanlage im internationalen Wirtschaftsverkehr, 167; *contra* FOUCHARD, P., L'arbitrage commercial international, 401.

expresses the cross-border nature of international business law and avoids the word "international" which, in this context, does not refer to relations between states. However, the term transnational law covers a far broader arena than simply commercial or business transactions and relations[3]. The term *transnational business law* may therefore be more appropriate.

This book speaks of international business law in order to avoid confusion about the concepts and to conform to a traditional, albeit mistaken, use of the word international. This is not to imply, however, that the adjective "transnational" should never be used.

I.2 Historical antecedents of present-day international business law

8. An analysis of historical antecedents to present-day sources of international business law is particularly relevant because proponents of *lex mercatoria* have argued that the traditional conflict of laws answer to international business problems dates back only to the emergence of national states in Europe, which created the necessity to refer international problems to a given national system. Goldman has, for instance, stated that *lex mercatoria* may be seen as a revival of much older traditions, such as the *ius gentium* of Roman law and the medieval law merchant[4]. Schmitthoff, on the other hand, does not argue in favor of a revival, because in his opinion fundamental differences exist between the medieval law merchant and present-day *lex mercatoria*. However, Schmitthoff has accepted the view that *lex mercatoria* goes back to the law merchant as known in medieval European cities.

Since classical conflict answers to the sources of international business law have been challenged by prominent scholars based on historical arguments, one cannot study sources of international business law without looking into these historical antecedents. They have been discussed by

3. Furthermore, the concept of *transnational law* also has been used in other contexts such as the law of transborder relations (JESSUP, P., Transnational law, New Haven, Yale University Press, 1956, 2-4; STEINER, H. and VAGTS, D., Transnational legal problems, third edition, Mineola, New York, Foundation Press, 1986, xix and 2), principles common to various states and as the law applicable to state contracts (HORN, N., Das Recht der internationalen Anleihen, 513-515; SIEHR, Sachrecht im IPR, transnationales Recht und lex mercatoria, 108-112; RIGAUX, F., Droit public et droit privé dans les relations internationales, 369-372).
4. GOLDMAN, B., Lex mercatoria, 3.

many authors, but have rarely been subject to thorough analysis[5]. Notable exceptions in this regard are Schmitthoff, Bärmann, Honnold, Berman and Trakman. So far, discussion of historical antecedents has been limited to the Roman law's *ius gentium* and the medieval law merchant[6]. Therefore, only these two aspects are discussed below.

I.2.1 *The ius gentium of Roman law*

9. In the debate about the sources of international business law, only Goldman drew attention to a relation between present-day *lex mercatoria* and the *ius gentium* as it was known in ancient Rome[7]. However, his analysis is quite short and rather confusing. At first, Goldman qualified *ius gentium* as a part of Roman law[8]. In later writings, Goldman stated that *ius gentium* contained a set of customary rules applicable to relations between Roman citizens and non-Romans and was autonomous in relation to traditional Roman law[9]. Other authors looking into *lex mercatoria* have

---

5. DABIN, J., Théorie générale du droit, 26; LEVEL, P., Le contrat dit sans loi, Trav.com.fr.dr.int.privé, 1964-66, Paris, Dalloz, 1967, 212-213; PADIS, P., L'affrontement des économies socialistes et capitalistes dans le monde ou l'arbitrage international en 1972, 6; PEYREFITTE, L., Le problème du contrat dit "sans loi", 114; RUBELLIN-DEVICHI, J., L'arbitrage, nature juridique, droit interne et droit international privé, 127; SANDERS, P., Ecafe Rules for international commercial arbitration, 254; SANDERS, P., International commercial arbitration, 485; HOYLE, M., The law of international trade, first edition, 2; RABEL, E., Das Recht des Warenkaufs, I, Berlin, de Gruyter, 1936, 35; RABEL, E., L'unification du droit de la vente internationale, ses rapports avec les formulaires ou contrats-types des divers commerces, in Introduction à l'étude du droit comparé, Recueil d'études en l'honneur d'Edouard Lambert, II, Paris, LGDJ, 1938, 694; BEGUIN, J., Le développement de la lex mercatoria menace-t-il juridique international ?, 487-488; HORSMANS, G. and VERWILGHEN, M., Stabilité et évolution du contrat économique international, 445.
6. For commercial transactions among Greek city-states see WIEACKER, F., Historische Bedingungen und Paradigmen supranationaler Privatsrechtsordnungen, Festschrift für K. Zweigert, Tubingen, Mohr, 1981, 581 and 591; WIEACKER, F., On the history of supranational legal system of commerce, in The legal organization of commerce and its relation to the social conditions, Aarhus, Provinsbanken, 1979, 7-15.
7. The Roman law concept of *ius gentium* should clearly be distinguished from *ius gentium* in the sense of public international law.
8. GOLDMAN, B., intervention during the discussions, in LEVEL, P., Le contrat dit sans loi, 242.
9. GOLDMAN, B., Lex mercatoria, 3; *cf.* GOLDMAN, B., La lex mercatoria dans les contrats et l'arbitrage internationaux: réalité et perspectives, 475.

doubted whether *ius gentium* had independent status in regard to Roman law. They rather argued that *ius gentium* formed a part of Roman law[10].

10. These controversies may be resolved only if one looks into the nature, the sources and the scope of application of *ius gentium*. Within the scope of this book, it seems sufficient to indicate how trade relations among Romans and with foreigners were regulated, and to what extent *ius gentium* may be considered autonomous vis-à-vis Roman *ius civile*.

11. The emergence of *ius gentium* cannot be traced back to ancient Roman law. In that period, trade relations took place only if a foreigner was protected by a Roman citizen[11] or treaty protection could be invoked. With regard to treaty protection, special trade tribunals had to resolve trade disputes between citizens of the treaty states[12].

A climate favorable to adaptation of traditional Roman law and leaving room for the development of *ius gentium*, was created only after the second Punic war (218-201 B.C.) when Rome became a dominant political power and trade could flourish.

12. As a starting point, one should note that legal writings unanimously state that *ius gentium* is a part of Roman law and that its binding character is, therefore, to be found in Roman law itself[13]. Consequently, it is hard

---

10. SCHINNERER, E., Um ein Recht des internationalen Handels, 192-193 and BAXTER, I., International conflict of laws and international business, INT'L & COMP.L.Q., 1985, 545.
11. LABORDERIE, P., Essai sur l'histoire du droit international privé. L'application des droits pérégrins dans le monde romain, Revue générale du droit, de la législation et de la jurisprudence en France et à l'étranger, 1910, 41; FUSINATO, G., Le droit international de la république romaine. Les étrangers, les récupérateurs, les fétiaux, Rev.Dr.Int.Lég.Comp., 1885, 279-280; BIERZANEK, R., Quelques remarques sur le statut juridique des étrangers à Rome, IVRA, Rivista internazionale di diritto romano e antico, 1962, 89-91.
12. BIERZANEK, R., Quelques remarques sur le statut juridique des étrangers à Rome, 106; SCHWIND, F., Römisches Recht, I, Vienna, Springer, 1950, 48-49; WALTON, F.P., Historical introduction to the Roman law, second edition, Edinburgh, Green & Sons, 1912, 364; SCHILLER, A., Roman law, The Hague, Mouton Publishers, 1978, 527; SOHN, R., Institutionen, 65-66.
13. SCHWIND, F., Römisches Recht, I, 49; MAY,G., Eléments de droit romain, fourteenth edition, Paris, Sirey, 1922, 41; DULCKEIT/SCHWARZ, Römische Rechtsgeschichte, fifth edition, Munich, Beck, 1970, 138; DECLAREUIL, J., Rome et l'organisation du droit, Paris, Albin Michel, 1924, 31; VON CZYHLARZ, K., Lehrbuch der Institutionen des römischen Rechts, eighteenth edition by SAN NICOLO, M., Vienna, Hölder, 1924, 35; KUNKEL, W., Römische Rechtsgeschichte, sixth edition, Cologne, Böhlau Verlag, 1972, 75; SIBER, H., Römisches Recht, II, Berlin, Verlag Sack, 1928, 7; CROOK, J.,

to defend the aforementioned proposition of Goldman and to conceive of *ius gentium* as a precedent for a present-day autonomous law of international trade.

13. Furthermore, one may question whether *ius gentium* may be considered as a separate set of rules of Roman law dealing with trade relations and whether any such rules are of Roman or transnational origin. In this regard, controversies about the field of application and the sources of *ius gentium* should be discussed.

14. The first dispute concerns whether *ius gentium* originally applied only between foreigners and to relations between Romans and foreigners[14], or whether from its inception it also applied between Roman citizens as advocated by Von Savigny[15]. It is obvious that the specificity of international business law is confirmed only by the first theory which holds that

---

Law and life of Rome, Ithaca, Cornell University Press, 1967, 29-30; BUCKLAND, W., The main institutions of Roman private law, Cambridge, University Press, 1931, 19; VAN WETTER, P., Cours élémentaire de droit romain, I, third edition, Paris, Maresq Aîné, 1893, 25; WENGER, L., Der heutigen Stand der römischen Rechtswissenschaft, second edition, Munich, Beck, 1970, 4-5; WEISS, E., V° Ius Gentium, in Paulys Real-Encyclopädie der classischen Altertumswissenschaft, Volume 19, Stuttgart, J.B. Metzler, 1917, 1226; JÖRS, P., Römisches Privatrecht, 60.

14. PUCHTA, G., Institutionen, I, tenth edition, Leipzig, Von Breitkopf, 1893, 206-207; JÖRS, P., Römisches Privatrecht, 60; LABORDERIE, P., Essai sur l'histoire du droit international privé. L'application des droits pérégrins dans le monde romain, 43; FUSINATO, G., Le droit international de la république romaine. Les étrangers, les récupérateurs, les fétiaux, 284; CHAUVEAU, A., Le droit des gens dans les rapports de Rome avec les peuples de l'antiquité, Nouvelle revue historique de droit français et étranger, 1891, 408-411; KASER, M., Das römische Privatrecht, I, Munich, Beck, 1955, 179; KASER, M., Mores maiorum und Gewohnheitsrecht, 59 Z.Savigny-Stiftung, Romanistische Abteilung, 1939, 67; HUVELIN, P., Etudes d'histoire du droit commercial romain, 18; HUVELIN, P., Cours élémentaire de droit romain, I, Paris, Sirey, 1927, 226; GIRARD, P.F., Manuel élémentaire de droit romain, sixth edition, Paris, Rousseau, 1918, 2; LEE, R., The elements of Roman law, London, Sweet & Maxwell, 1952, 84; GAUDEMET, J., Institutions de l'Antiquité, Paris, Sirey, 1967, 604; DECLAREUIL, J., Rome et l'organisation du droit, 30; GOLDSCHMIDT, L., Universalgeschichte des Handelsrechts, I, Aalen, Scientia, 1957, 75-76.

15. VON SAVIGNY, F., Traité de droit romain, I, Paris, Didot, 1840, 405-406; KARLOWA, O., Römische Rechtsgeschichte, I, Leipzig, Verlag Von Veit, 1885, 454 and 456; BARON, J., Peregrinenrecht und ius gentium, 39-40; DULCKEIT/SCHWARZ, Römische Rechtsgeschichte, 138; BÖGLI, H., Beiträge zur Lehre vom ius gentium der Römer, Burgdorf, Eggenweiler, 1913, 5 and 53-60; WALTON, F.P., Historical introduction to the Roman law, 366; SCHÖNBAUER, E., Studien zum Personalitätsprinzip im antiken Rechte, 49 Z.Savigny-Stiftung für Rechtsgeschichte, Romanistische Abteilung, 1929, 389.

Roman law provided specific answers for trade relations with and among foreigners.

Assuming the validity of this first theory, one may still question whether it can be transposed to present-day international business law. First, specificity of *ius gentium*, if any, should not be explained by transnationalization of Roman commerce, but rather by technical factors such as the absence of conflict rules[16], the restricted application of *ius civile* to Roman citizens[17] and the formalism of *ius civile*, which made inappropriate its application to transnational commerce. In this regard, there are fundamental differences between *ius gentium* and present-day international business law. Consequently, there are no compelling historical reasons to conclude from *ius gentium* that present-day international business law necessarily should be governed by specific rules different from those applied for purely internal transactions. Second, even if so, there seems to be little historical evidence that *ius gentium* evolved into a coherent and autonomous set of rules within Roman law[18]. Of course, this does not support the proposition that *ius gentium* was an antecedent of a present-day autonomous set of substantive rules within national legal systems. Finally, one should also keep in mind that the distinction between *ius civile* and *ius gentium* slowly has lost its significance. *Ius civile*, through the influence of *ius gentium*, became less formal and less procedural while some institutions of *ius civile* were opened to foreigners[19]. As more tribes

---

16. SCHWIND, F., Internationales Privatrecht und römisches Recht, Labeo. Rassegna di diritto romano, 1965, 314; KASER, M., Römisches Privatrecht, twelfth edition, Munich, Beck, 1981, 26; SIMON-DEPITRE, M., Les règles matérielles dans le conflit de lois, R.C.D.I.P., 1974, 592; STURM, F., Comment l'Antiquité réglait-elle ses conflits de lois, Clunet, 1979, 260-261, 265 and 270; YNTEMA, H., The historic bases of private international law, AM.J.COMP.L., 1953, 300-301.
17. BIERZANEK, R., Quelques remarques sur le statut juridique des étrangers à Rome, 92-93.
18. However, the following citation of Kaser may be mentioned (Das römische Privatrecht, I, 179): "...eine besondere, selbständige Masse von Einrichtungen und Grundsätzen, die für die Rechtsbeziehungen zwischen römischen Bürgern und Peregrinen (außerhalb des commercium und conubium) sowie unter Peregrinen galten,..."; other authors in this regard speak of *ius gentium* as a legal system (JOLOWICZ, H. and NICHOLAS, B., Historical introduction to the study of Roman law, third edition, Cambridge, University Press, 1972, 103; MAY,G., Eléments de droit romain, 41).
19. KASER, M., Das römische Privatrecht, I, 180; HUVELIN, P., Etudes d'histoire du droit commercial romain, 35-36; VON CZYHLARZ, K., Lehrbuch der Institutionen des römischen Rechts, 37; KRÜGER, P., Geschichte der Quellen und Literatur des römischen Rechts, second edition, Munich, Duncker & Humblot, 1912, 48; WILINSKI, A., Das römische Recht, Leipzig, Teubner Verlag, 1966, 21; VAN WETTER, P., Cours élémentaire de droit romain, I, 28; MITTEIS, L., Römisches Privatrecht, I, Leipzig, Duncker & Humblot, 1968, 69-70.

obtained Roman citizenship and the Constitutio Antoniana of 212 A.C. finally granted citizenship to all inhabitants of the Roman empire, the distinction largely disappeared[20].

15. Controversy also exists regarding the sources of *ius gentium*. In this respect, one can discern three different views, which find the origin of *ius gentium* in natural law, customary law and case law respectively.

The proposition that *ius gentium* was based upon a set of natural law principles common to then-existing legal systems is hardly defended. It is now recognized that this concept is a creation of classical Roman writers, influenced by the Greek Stoa. It was then adopted by post-classical authors[21]. Therefore, it is hard to accept the view that *ius gentium* should be placed outside the Roman legal system, and that it consisted of general principles of law based upon natural justice.

16. The French author Huvelin has defended the view that *ius gentium* was based upon customs developed in Roman market places and applied by the *praetor peregrinus*. *Ius gentium* in his view was really transnational law[22], as the customs were neither of Roman[23] nor of foreign[24] origin, but were developed specifically for transactions with foreigners.

17. Finally, a third view traces *ius gentium* back to the law-making by the *praetor peregrinus*, who created this body of law in the course of adjudicat-

---

20. HUVELIN, P., Etudes d'histoire du droit commercial romain, 49.
21. KASER, M., Das römische Privatrecht, I, 183; LEE,R., The elements of Roman law, 86; DULCKEIT/SCHWARZ, Römische Rechtsgeschichte, 139; ACCARIAS, C., Précis de droit romain, I, Paris, Pichon, 1886, 16; PRICHARD, A., Leage's Roman private law, third edition, London, Macmillan, 1961, 58-59; BUCKLAND, W. and McNAIR, A., Roman law & common law, Cambridge, University Press, 1936, 18-19; BUCKLAND, W., A text-book of Roman law from Augustus to Justinian, third edition by STEIN, P., Cambridge, University Press, 1975, 54; JÖRS, P., Römisches Privatrecht, 60.
22. HUVELIN, P., Cours élémentaire de droit romain, I, 227; HUVELIN, Etudes d'histoire du droit commercial romain, 16-17; also SAUTEL, G., Essai sur la notion romaine de "Commercium" à l'époque ancienne, in Varia, Etudes de droit romain, I, Paris, Sirey, 1952, 92-93 and NETTLESHIP, H., Ius gentium, The Journal of Philology, 1885, 178-179; *contra* KASER, M., Mores maiorum und Gewohnheitsrecht, 67 who argues that *ius gentium* cannot be based upon customary law. One might in this regard note that Huvelin was a colleague of Edouard Lambert at the University of Lyon and referred to Lambert's jurisdictional theory about customs (see infra No. 224).
23. *Contra* SCHÖNBAUER, E., Studien zum Personalitätsprinzip im antiken Rechte, 389.
24. *Contra* MONIER, R., Manuel élémentaire de droit romain, I, Montchrestien, Domat, 1945, 50 who insists on the influence of foreign customs for the development of *ius gentium*.

ing international disputes[25]. The analogy with present-day transnational arbitration is obvious. The existence of a specific jurisdiction in this respect opens up the possibility of creating specific rules with regard to disputes falling within the competence of these jurisdictions.

18. One may wonder whether *ius gentium* consisted of substantive rules of transnational origin. However, little information is available to support such a proposition[26]. On the contrary, it seems that the *praetor peregrinus* also applied Roman and foreign rules[27]. Furthermore, the transnational character of any such rules was affected by the fact that a Roman judge had to apply them. Consequently, Roman legal concepts had a distinct influence on the *ius gentium*[28].

19. One may conclude from the preceding paragraphs that *ius gentium* can hardly be considered as having been an autonomous legal system apart from Roman law. Also, the natural law concept of *ius gentium* should be rejected. Therefore, *ius gentium* cannot be invoked as a historical precedent for a present-day *lex mercatoria*, if the latter is defined as an autonomous legal system apart from national legal systems[29].

Also, it is unlikely that *ius gentium* evolved within Roman law into a separate set of rules of transnational origin specifically designed for transactions with foreign merchants. In this regard, it is doubtful whether *ius gentium* merely consisted of rules of transnational origin. Rather, *ius gentium* probably was a set of pragmatically developed rules without a strict hierarchy. Again, it is hard to argue that *ius gentium* constitutes a precedent

---

25. BUCKLAND, W., A manual of Roman private law, second edition, Aalen, Scientia Verlag, 1981, 9; see also SCHILLER, A., Roman law, 529-530. Laborderie (Essai sur l'histoire du droit international privé. L'application des droits pérégrins dans le monde romain, 43) only accepts this law making by the praetor to the extent that gaps in the *ius gentium* had to be filled.
26. LEE, R., The elements of Roman law, 84-85; MAYER-MALY, T., Das ius gentium bei den späteren Klassikern, Rivista internazionale di diritto Romano e antico, 1983, 102.
27. WIEACKER, F., Historische Bedingungen und Paradigmen supranationaler Privatsrechtsordnungen, 582-584; JOLOWICZ, H. and NICHOLAS, B., Historical introduction to the study of Roman law, 103; VON CZYHLARZ, K., Lehrbuch der Institutionen des römischen Rechts, 35; KIPP, T., Das römische Recht, 103; according to Dulckeit/Schwarz (Römische Rechtsgeschichte, 138) and Kunkel (Römische Rechtsgeschichte, 75), the praetor applied primarily Roman law rules.
28. PUCHTA, G., Institutionen, 207; WILINSKI, A., Das römische Recht, 21; WEISS, E., Ius gentium, 1226-1227.
29. See infra Nos. 325-331.

for *lex mercatoria*, defined as a set of rules of transnational origin which exists within national legal systems[30].

Finally, if international business law is seen as a set of substantive rules - irrespective of their national or transnational origin - which govern transnational commercial relations within national legal systems[31], one might find in *ius gentium* a historical precedent. However, this position implies a rejection of Von Savigny's theory that *ius gentium* also applied among Roman citizens[32].

I.2.2 *The medieval law merchant*

20. The similarities between the medieval law merchant[33] and present-day *lex mercatoria* have been stressed particularly by Schmitthoff. In this respect, Schmitthoff notes that in the period before the seventeenth century, there were hardly any conflict rules relating to transnational commercial transactions. The absence of conflict rules should, according to Schmitthoff, be explained by the existence of the *law merchant*, a cosmopolitan mercantile law based upon customs and applied to transnational disputes by the market tribunals of the various European trade centers[34]. This law merchant had many harmonizing effects. First, merchants met in the market places where their transactions were regulated by market practices and customs. Second, uniform customs developed in maritime trade (*e.g.*, the *Consolato del mare*, the scrolls of Oléron, the maritime law of Wisby, the judgments of Damme or the laws of Westkapelle). Thirdly,

---

30. See infra Nos. 322-324.
31. See infra No. 355.
32. See supra No. 14.
33. The medieval law merchant is also referred to as lex mercatoria, ius mercatorum, ius mercatorium, ius mercati, ius fori, ius forense, ius negotiatorum, ius negotiale, stilus mercatorum or ius nundinarum; *cf.* VON CAEMMERER, E., The influence of the law of international trade on the development and character of the commercial law in the civil law countries, 88; LEYMARIE, F., Les usages commerciaux, 6; DUPOUY, C., Le droit des faillites en France avant le Code de commerce, Paris, LGDJ, 1960, 33; HUVELIN, P., Essai historique sur le droit des marchés et des foires, Paris, Rousseau, 1897, 218; REHME, P., Geschichte des Handelsrechtes, in EHRENBERG, V., Handbuch des gesamten Handelsrechts, I, Leipzig, O.R.Reisland, 1913, 119.
34. SCHMITTHOFF, C., The English conflict of laws, 25; SCHMITTHOFF, C., Modern trends in English commercial law, in Tidskrift, Utgiven av Juridiska Föreningen in Finland, 1957, 351-352; SCHMITTHOFF, C., International trade law and private international law, 261; SCHMITTHOFF, C., The unification of the law of international trade, J.BUS.L.,1968, 105; SCHMITTHOFF, C., Commercial law in a changing economic climate, 3-4 and 19; see also BERMAN, H. and KAUFMAN, C., The law of international commercial transactions (lex mercatoria), 225-226; TRAKMAN, L., The evolution of the Law Merchant : our commercial heritage, 4-5.

all commercial disputes were entrusted to special courts such as the English *Court of Piepowder*. Finally, as of the thirteenth century, the notaries began to develop deeds which soon were copied and served as models for similar transactions[35]. Other authors have added a number of other factors such as the medieval guild-system[36] and the influence of Roman law on the law of the Italian city-states[37], which might explain the uniform patterns of the law merchant.

21. Authorities soon recognized, and for economic and tax purposes[38] encouraged, self-regulation by merchants with regard to transnational commercial transactions. The English *Carta Mercatoria* of 1303, for instance, assured certain foreign merchants of a fast dispute settlement mechanism and the application of the law merchant to their disputes[39]. Similarly, the *Statute of the Staple* of 1353 stated that disputes arising out of transactions in market places that had received monopoly status as to import and export trade, should be resolved according to the principles of the law merchant and not according to feudal law or city law[40]. There have been discussions as to whether the law merchant originally applied only to transnational transactions, and whether in a later stage of its

---

35. SCHMITTHOFF, C., International business law : a new law merchant, 132-134; SCHMITTHOFF, C., Das neue Recht des Welthandels, 49; SCHMITTHOFF, C., The unification of the law of international trade, J.BUS.L., 1968, 106; REHME, P., Geschichte des Handelsrechtes, 88 and 97; GOLDSCHMIDT, L., Universalgeschichte des Handelsrecht, 131; HOLDSWORTH, W., A history of English law, V, London, Methuen, 1924, 78-79 and 112-113.
36. VON CAEMMERER, E., The influence of the law of international trade on the development and character of the commercial law in the civil law countries, 88; LEYMARIE, F., Les usages commerciaux, 4; DEL MARMOL, C., Le droit corporatif de la vente commerciale, 603; DAVID, R., L'arbitrage dans le commerce international, 21; POHLMANN, H., Die Quellen des Handelsrecht, 813-815; HOLDSWORTH, W., A history of English law, V, 62-63 and 69-72.
37. GOLDSCHMIDT, L., Universalgeschichte des Handelsrecht, 131; REHME, P., Geschichte des Handelsrechtes, 97; POHLMANN, H., Die Quellen des Handelsrecht, 810-813; HOLDSWORTH, W., A history of English law, V, 62-63 and 75.
38. CREMADES, B. and PLEHN, S., The new lex mercatoria and the harmonization of the laws of international commercial transactions, 318.
39. SCHMITTHOFF, C., International trade law and private international law, 262-263; HOLDSWORTH, W., A history of English law, I, 541.
40. BÜLCK, H., Betrachtungen über ein Völkerhandelsrecht, 159; GÜTERBOCK, K., Zur Geschichte des Handelsrecht in England,, 20; HOLDSWORTH, W., A history of English law, I, 542; GROSS, C., Select cases concerning the law merchant, Selden Society, I, London, Quaritch, 1908, XXVII; TUDSBERY, F., Law merchant and the common law, L.Q.R, 1918, 396-397; BRODHURST, B., The merchants of the staple, in Select essays in Anglo-American legal history, III, London, Wildy & Sons, 1968, 16-33.

development it was extended to domestic commercial transactions[41]. In the long run, the law merchant was integrated into the common law. This process began between 1606 and 1640 when local courts, the High Court of Admiralty and the Court of Chancery gradually lost ground in favour of the courts of King's Bench and the courts of Common Pleas. From a substantive point of view, the absorption of the law merchant by the common law would start only as of 1756 under Chief Justice Mansfield, who began to qualify trade customs as legal rules and made them applicable to all citizens[42].

22. It emerges from the preceding paragraphs that any question as to the existence of a medieval law merchant has been raised primarily in England and other common law countries. This debate has hardly been analyzed on the European continent, and the few authors, such as Goldschmidt and Huvelin, who have tackled the problem, discuss it in broad terms. Therefore, analysis and conclusions will primarily be restricted to the common law.

23. As a preliminary point, one should note that the existence of a medieval law merchant has received little attention and, therefore, the subject has largely remained obscure[43]. However, the following positions regarding the medieval law merchant can be distinguished. First, some authors have taken the position that the medieval *lex mercatoria* had taken a universal and uniform character[44]. According to other authors, local

---

41. SCHMITTHOFF, C., Modern trends in English commercial law, 351-354; SCHMITTHOFF, C., Commercial law in a changing economic climate, 5-6; GÜTERBOCK, K., Zur Geschichte des Handelsrecht in England, 15; *contra* HOLDSWORTH, W., A history of English law, I, 535 and 568-570.
42. BERMAN, H. and KAUFMAN, C., The law of international commercial transactions (lex mercatoria), 226; BERMAN, H., The law of international trade, 11; TRAKMAN, L., The evolution of the Law Merchant : our commercial heritage, 158-159; HONNOLD, J., The influence of the law of international trade on the development and character of English and American commercial law, 72; HAYES, L., A modern lex mercatoria : political rhetoric or substantive progress ?, 215.
43. See also DAVID, R., Unification du droit et arbitrage, 350-351; GUTTERIDGE, H., Le droit comparé, Introduction à la méthode comparative dans la recherche juridique et l'étude du droit, Paris, LGDJ, 1953, 33.
44. MALYNES, G., Consuetudo vel lex mercatoria or the ancient lex mercatoria, 1622, cited by SCHERNER, K.O., Die Wissenschaft des Handelsrechts, in Handbuch der Quellen und Literatur der neueren Europäischen Privatrechtsgeschichte, II/1, COING, H.(ed.), Munich, Beck, 1977, 858-859 and 862-863 (Scherner and Holdsworth (A history of English law, V, 133) have rightly pointed to the natural law concepts which have influenced the book of Malynes); DEL MARMOL, C., Le droit corporatif de la vente commerciale, 604; SCHAPIRA, J., Le droit international des affaires, 7.

differences existed within the medieval law merchant, but this did not prevent the law merchant from acquiring a fairly uniform character[45]. Finally, some authorities claim that a medieval law merchant never existed[46].

24. Assuming that a law merchant did exist in the Middle Ages, its character still is debatable. It is in any event obvious that any law merchant has developed spontaneously and that the natural law interpretations which may be found since the seventeenth century do not correspond with historical reality[47]. Again, it is, therefore, hard to support the view that the medieval law merchant is based upon natural law.

25. Furthermore, there is hardly any evidence to determine whether the medieval law merchant had autonomous standing apart from local law or

---

45. HUVELIN, P., Essai historique sur le droit des marchés et des foires, 595-596; HUVELIN, P., Etudes d'histoire du droit commercial romain, 80; MITCHELL, W., Essay on the early history of the law merchant, New York, Franklin, 1904, 1-9 and 20; CARTER, A., Early history of the law merchant in England, L.Q.R., 1901, 232; BEWES, W., The romance of the law merchant, Being an introduction to the study of international and commercial law, London, Sweet & Maxwell, 1923, VI and 8-9; HILAIRE, J., Introduction historique au droit commercial, 41-43; BERMAN, H., The law of international trade, 5; BERMAN, H., Law and revolution : the formation of the Western legal tradition, Cambridge, Mass., Harvard, 1983, 342-434; TRAKMAN, L., The evolution of the Law Merchant : our commercial heritage, 9 and 20-22; TRAKMAN, L., book review of KURKELA, M., Letters of credit under international trade law: UCC, UCP and law merchant, AM.J.COMP.L., 1986, 146; BAXTER, I., International conflict of laws and international business, 547.
46. HOLDSWORTH, W., A history of English law, I, 528 and 543, IV, 240 and V, 60-61 but see V, 99-100; REHME, P., Geschichte des Handelsrechtes, 119-120; BAKER, J.H., The law merchant and the common law before 1700, Cambridge Law Journal, 1979, 295-322; STUART SUTHERLAND, L., The law merchant in England in the seventeenth and eigthteenth centuries, Royal Historical Society's Transactions, 4th series, XVII, 1934, 150-153; BÄRMANN, J., Ist internationales Handelsrecht kodifizierbar ?, 570; HONNOLD, J., The influence of the law of international trade on the development and character of English and American commercial law, 71; HAYES, L., A modern lex mercatoria : political rhetoric or substantive progress ?, 214; OLY, G., Algemene beschouwingen over de eenvormige wet op de internationale koop van goederen in historisch perspectief, 35; VAN DELDEN, R., Lex mercatoria of ius commune ?, 5.
47. BAKER, J.H., The law merchant and the common law before 1700, 321-322; RODGERS, C., Continental literature and the development of the common law by the King's Bench : c. 1750-1800, in The courts and the development of commercial law, PIERGIOVANNI, V. (ed.), Berlin, Duncker & Humblot, 1987, 166 and 168-169; SCHERNER, K.O., Allgemeine Rechtsgrundsätze und Rechtsvergleichung im europäischen Handelsrecht des 17. und 18. Jahrhunderts, in Ius commune, Volume VII, 1978, 128.

whether it derived its binding character from local law. The English *Carta Mercatoria* and the *Statute of the Staples* tend, however, to show that the latter proposition has more merit. The organization of medieval markets, harbours and guilds was indeed largely controlled by local laws which, consequently, also determined whether and to what extent self regulation was permitted[48]. For instance, economic regulation, taxation and the organization of the courts remained with local or central authorities. Also, these authorities could intervene in private relations through legislation, or by upper courts reversing decisions of lower courts[49].

For the reasons set forth above, it may be doubted whether the medieval law merchant evolved into a legal system largely independent from local laws. Again, there is hardly any historical evidence for the proposition that a precedent for present-day *lex mercatoria* existed.

26. The theory of Schmitthoff regarding the medieval law merchant also merits discussion. According to this theory, the medieval law merchant was a set of transnational customs applicable to transnational trade relations. In this respect, three issues should be discussed. First, one might wonder whether the law merchant was a set of rules clearly distinguishable from the rules of common law, or whether there was no such clear substantive distinction, but only a formal one stemming from the existence of separate courts for commercial and for other disputes[50].

Second, one should note the aforementioned discussion about the scope of application of the law merchant, which shows that there is some doubt about whether the law merchant was exclusively applicable to transnational trade disputes. Consequently, the law merchant might also be conceived as the expression of the general distinction between common law and mercantile law, rather than as a specific regulation for transnational trade problems[51]. It is true that local courts in England disappeared in the

---

48. HUVELIN, P., Essai historique sur le droit des marchés et des foires, 474, 483, 524 and 541-542; HILAIRE, J., Introduction historique au droit commercial, 33-35; COOPMANS, J.P.A., De jaarmarkten van Antwerpen en Bergen op Zoom als centra van rechtsverkeer en rechtsvorming, in Handelsrecht tussen "koophandel" en Nieuw BW, Deventer, Kluwer, 1988, 4-5.
49. CARTER, Early history of the law merchant in England, 234-235; HOLDSWORTH, W., A history of English law, V, 538-539; HUVELIN, P., Essai historique sur le droit des marchés et des foires, 395-410 and 426.
50. *Cf.* BEWES, W., The romance of the law merchant, 14; HOLDSWORTH, W., A history of English law, I, 63*; BAKER, J.H., The law merchant and the common law after 1700, 299-301 and 321-322.
51. *Cf.* GILISSEN, J., Introduction historique au droit, Brussels, Bruylant, 1979, 185; BLUMENWITZ, D., Einführung in das Anglo-Amerikanische Recht, second edition, Munich, Beck, 1976, 15.

sixteenth century, causing domestic mercantile disputes to be adjudicated by national courts according to common law. However, transnational trade disputes would follow suit in the seventeenth century, when courts for transnational commercial disputes disappeared[52]. Therefore, there is some doubt as to the original existence of a specific dispute settlement mechanism for transnational disputes. The sixteenth century's separation between domestic and transnational commercial disputes is in this regard not due to the nature of the dispute but to historical factors of English law (*i.e.*, the increasing royal power and the expansion of the common law).

Finally, the sources of the medieval law merchant were not limited to transnational custom or other sources of transnational origin since local custom[53], guild rules and city law were constituent parts of the law merchant.

One might therefore conclude from this paragraph that the theory of Schmitthoff about the medieval law merchant fails to support the view that it might be considered a precedent for present-day *lex mercatoria*, defined as a set of rules of transnational origin which exists within national legal systems.

I.2.3 *Conclusion*

27. From this subchapter, one may conclude that the Roman law concept of *ius gentium* and the medieval law merchant provide little evidence as historical precedents for a present-day *lex mercatoria*. Also, both *ius gentium* and law merchant were barely defined bodies of law within Roman law and local medieval laws.

I.3 Scope of application

28. An examination of the sources of international business law also requires a description of its scope. In this respect, three issues should be discussed in relation to transnational business law: 1. its transnational character; 2. its business law character; and 3. its territorial scope.

---

52. HOLDSWORTH, W., A history of English law, I, 539-540 and 568-572.
53. STUART SUTHERLAND, L., The Law Merchant in England in the seventeenth and eighteenth centuries, 153.

I.3.1 *The transnational character of international business law*

29. The concept of transnationality has been discussed thoroughly by Fontaine, who distinguishes between transnationality under domestic laws, under uniform law and under public international law[54]. Hereinafter, only the first two distinctions will be used[55]. Furthermore, the use of transnationality definitions as found in practice will be added.

I.3.1.1 Transnationality as defined in domestic laws

30. Private law[56] in domestic legal systems knows various definitions of transnationality. First, traditional conflict of laws analysis works with a transnationality concept, according to which situations or transactions are transnational, if points of connection with more than one legal system exist[57]. One then looks at the point which is most closely connected with

---

54. FONTAINE, M., Introduction, in Le contrat économique international, Travaux des VIIes Journées d'études juridiques Jean Dabin, Brussels, Bruylant, 1975, 23.

55. As public international law in principle is excluded from this study, definitions from public international law have not been analyzed.

56. Private law refers to the distinction known in some legal systems between private and public law. Public law definitions of transnationality as may be found in some statutes on economic regulation, trade regulation or tax laws have not been analyzed.

 Sometimes, definitions also may be found in statutes providing mandatory rules for transactions between subjects of private law (*e.g.*, § 26 and 27 (1) English "Unfair Contract Terms Act 1977" or § 12 German "Allgemeine Geschäftsbedingungengesetz"). Because of the regulatory purposes of these acts, they also have been excluded.

57. LOUSSOUARN, Y. and BREDIN, J.D., Droit du commerce international, 593-594; KAHN, P., La vente commerciale internationale, 3-5; SCHAPIRA, J., Le droit international des affaires, 20-21; JACQUEMONT, A., L'émission des emprunts euro-obligataires, 24-25; Count of Appeal Paris, June 19, 1970, Clunet, 1971, 833, case note OPPETIT, B.; FIRSCHING, K., Internationales Schuldrecht, I, 343-344; NEUHAUS, P., Die Grundbegriffe des internationalen Privatrechts, second edition, Tubingen, Mohr, 1976, 1-2; SANDROCK, O., Die Bedeutung des Gesetzes zur Neuregelung des internationalen Privatrechts für die Unternehmenspraxis, RIW, 1986, 846; CHESHIRE and NORTH, Private international law, tenth edition, London, Butterworths, 1979, 5; MORRIS, J., The conflict of laws, London, Stevens and Sons, 1984, 3; Belgian Supreme Court, September 4, 1975, Bull.Cass., 1976, 20, R.W., 1975-76, 1561, case note VAN HOUTTE, H. (implicit solution); VAN HECKE, G. and RIGAUX, F., Examen de jurisprudence (1976 à 1980), Droit international privé (conflit de lois), R.C.J.B., 1982, 424; VANDER ELST, R., L'autonomie de la volonté en droit international privé français et belge, in Liber amicorum L.Frédéricq, Volume II, Ghent, 1965, 986. According to some Swiss authors, only relevant connecting points should be taken into account (LALIVE, P., Les règles de conflit de lois appliquées au fond du litige par l'arbitre international siégeant en Suisse, 59; LALIVE, P., Sur une notion de "contrat international", 137; DUTOIT, B., KNOEPFLER, F., LALIVE, P. and MERCIER, P., Répertoire de droit international privé suisse, Volume 1, Bern,

the situation or transaction, and the connecting point thus chosen (connecting factor) is then used in the formulation of a conflict rule which finally leads to the applicable law. As such, this method links transnational transactions to a given domestic legal system thus nationalizing transnational transactions[58].

31. One might also look at transnationality as defined in conventions in the field of conflict of laws. Again, one notes that connection with more than one country should be present. For instance, article 1, first sentence of the Hague Convention on the law applicable to international sales of goods of June 15, 1955[59] provides that it is applicable to international sales of goods. This is somewhat clarified by the last sentence of the same article, providing that the mere existence of a choice of law clause, a jurisdiction clause or an arbitral clause does not suffice to give the sales contract an international character. By analogy, the EEC Convention on the law applicable to contractual obligations signed at Rome on June 19, 1980, provides in article 1 (1) that it applies when a choice between the laws of different countries should be made[60].

However, some recent conventions have departed from the approach set forth above. For instance, article 1 of the Hague Convention of December 22, 1986 on the law applicable to contracts for the international sale of goods[61] provides that it applies between parties having their places of business in different states or in all other cases involving a choice between the laws of different states. However, a reservation against the latter proviso may be made according to article 21 (1)(a) of the Convention. The derogation from the traditional conflict approach is to be explained by the fact that Eastern European states have or had specific regulations for foreign trade transactions[62]. They only agreed not to apply these regulations if the scope of the sales conflicts convention was

---

Stämpfli, 1982, 17 and 244).

58. LEMHÖFER, B., Die Beschränkung der Rechtsvereinheitlichung auf internationale Sachverhalte, RabelsZ, 1960, 421; JACQUET, J.M., Principe d'autonomie et contrats internationaux, 249.
59. This Convention is applicable between Belgium, Denmark, Finland, France, Italy, Niger, Norway, Sweden and Switzerland.
60. OJ L 266, October 9, 1980, 1-19. This Convention has entered into force on April 1, 1991 and has been introduced by national implementing acts in Belgium, Denmark, Germany, France, Greece, Italy, Luxemburg, The Netherlands and the United Kingdom. One should read article 1 (1) in conjunction with article 3 (3) regarding choice of law.
61. Not yet entered into force.
62. See infra No. 485.

determined in an objective way[63]. The convention has therefore also provided for a substantive criterion leaving Eastern European states with the option of making a reservation regarding the conflictual definition of the convention's scope.

32. Since the second half of the 1920's, French case law departed to some degree from the traditional conflict approach mentioned above and developed an *economic* definition of transnationality. At first, this development took place in respect of gold clauses in international loans. The French Supreme Court held that the prohibition of French law regarding gold clauses did not apply to international payments. In this respect, a criterion was developed in order to define international payments[64]. According to this criterion, a payment is deemed to be international if at two occasions, goods or capital are to be moved across frontiers in opposite directions[65]. Several decisions of the French Supreme Court have subsequently applied[66] and broadened this criterion[67].

33. In the same period, the French Supreme Court also began to take economic factors into account in the field of international commercial arbitration. First, there were some cases in which the validity of the arbitral clause was challenged on the ground that, until 1925, the French Code of Civil Procedure did not allow parties to provide for arbitration before a dispute had arisen. The Supreme Court held, however, that this prohibition did not apply in relation to international commercial arbitration[68]. The Court based its decision on the *interest of international commerce* and

---

63. LOUSSOUARN, Y., La Convention de La Haye d'octobre 1985 sur la loi applicable aux contrats de vente internationaux de marchandises, R.C.D.I.P., 1986, 273-274; COHEN, D. and UGHETTO, B., La nouvelle Convention de La Haye relative à la loi applicable aux ventes internationales de marchandises, D., 1986, 150; McLAGHLAN, C., The new Hague sales convention and the limits of the choice of law process, 603 and 608.
64. Matter, the "Procureur-Général" at the Supreme Court was the spiritual father of this criterion.
65. MATTER, P., opinion preceding French Supreme Court, May 17, 1927 (D., 1928, 28-31) and French Supreme Court, June 3, 1930 (D., 1931, 12).
66. French Supreme Court, May 17, 1927, D., 1928, 25, case note CAPITANT, H.; French Supreme Court, February 14, 1934, S., 1934, 296, case note MESTRE, A.; French Supreme Court, June 21, 1950, D., 1951, 749, case note HAMEL, J., Clunet, 1950, 1196.
67. French Supreme Court, July 9, 1930, D., 1931, 18, opinion MATTER, P. and case note SAVATIER, R.
68. French Supreme Court, February 19, 1930 and January 27, 1931, S., 1933, 41 and 43, case note NIBOYET, J.P.

concluded that arbitral clauses contained in international contracts were valid[69].

The French Supreme Court, in its decision in the *Impex*-case of May 18, 1971, also used the criterion of the interest of international commerce as a basis for its decision concerning the severability of the arbitral clause from the contract which contained it. However, the Court also referred to some connecting factors[70].

The economic criterion has been quite influential in French arbitration law, since it was adopted at the time of the 1980/1981 reform of French arbitration law. This law makes a distinction between domestic and international arbitration. In respect of the definition of the latter, article 1492 of the Code of Civil Procedure (*Nouveau Code de Procédure Civile* - "N.C.P.C.") provides that arbitration is international if the interests of international commerce are affected[71].

34. The aforementioned criteria reject a legal approach of transnationality on the basis of connecting factors such as nationality, domicile, residence, place of conclusion or place of performance. In this perspective, one may note that there was a clear intention to limit the scope of domestic rules to domestic transactions and to emphasize the specific nature of transnational commercial relations. Of course, the conflict method could not serve this purpose since it leads to application of domestic rules to transnational relations. Thus, a specific rule for transnational relations was created. Since

69. However, in a more recent case of the French Supreme Court of October 7, 1980 (*Tardieu*, J.C.P., 1980, 19480, R.C.D.I.P., 1981, 313, case note MESTRE, J., Rev.Arb., 1982, 36, case note LEVEL, P.), the Court preferred not to follow the economic definition. It stated that a contract of agency for the territory of Columbia between French contracting parties did not have an international character. Therefore, the arbitral clause contained in the agency contract under French law was null and void since it was related to disputes which according to French law are deemed non-commercial. Writers have been very critical of this decision of the Court (FOUCHARD, P., L'arbitrage international en France après le décret du 12 mai 1981, 379-380; MAYER, P., case note Court of Appeal Paris, January 18, 1983, Rev.Arb., 1984, 94; PONSARD, A., La jurisprudence de la Cour de cassation et le droit commercial international, in Le droit des relations économiques internationales, Etudes offertes à Berthold Goldman, Paris, Litec, 1982, 246).

70. R.C.D.I.P., 1972, 124, case note MEZGER, E., Clunet, 1972, 62, case note OPPETIT, B., Rev.Arb., 1972, 2.

71. GOLDMAN, B., La nouvelle réglementation française de l'arbitrage international, 155; ROBERT, J., L'arbitrage en matière internationale, 209; FOUCHARD, P., Le nouveau droit français de l'arbitrage, 43; FOUCHARD, P., L'arbitrage international en France après le décret du 12 mai 1981, 379; CARBONNEAU, T., Arbitral adjudication : a comparative assessment of its remedial and substantive status in transnational commerce, TEX.INT'L L.J., 1984, 77.

no conflict rule was used, one may speak of *substantive transnational rules*[72]. In this context, the relation between substantive transnational rules and economic criteria becomes apparent[73]. Because no connecting factors were identified in order to apply these rules, French case law and legal writing based the scope of these rules on an economic definition of transnationality.

35. The economic approach does have some merits. It may fill some gaps created by the legal approach. In this regard, transactions which from a legal point of view are deemed domestic, may under the economic approach be considered transnational. For instance, string contracts or related contracts (*e.g.*, subcontracts or guarantees) which do not have connecting factors with other legal systems, may still be considered transnational provided they are economically connected to transnational projects. Also, transactions with domestic subsidiaries or branches of foreign companies may, under some conditions, be qualified as transnational[74].

However, the economic approach must overcome major obstacles which hardly makes it suitable as the main criterion for defining transnationality. First, the application of the economic approach has basically been limited to France[75], where it has been used little in fields other than arbitration and monetary law[76]. Regarding the latter, application of the criterion ultimately led to protection of French bondholders against fluctuations in the currency of account of international bonds[77] or against restrictive foreign currency regulations[78]. In the law of arbitration, the

72. See infra IV.2.1.

73. GOLDMAN, B., case note Court of Appeal Paris, June 19, 1970, J.C.P., 1971, 16927; FOUCHARD, P., case note French Supreme Court, January 11, 1972, R.C.D.I.P., 1973, 125; OPPETIT, B., case note Court of Appeal Paris, June 20, 1969, Clunet, 1971, 129-130; LOQUIN, E., case note Court of Appeal Paris, November 9, 1984, Clunet, 1986, 1044-1046.

74. KAHN, P., L'essor du non-droit dans les relations commerciales internationales et le contrat sans loi, 234-235; Court of Appeal Paris, April 26, 1985, Rev.Arb., 1985, 311, case note MEZGER, E., Clunet, 1986, 175, case note JACQUET, J.M.

75. JACQUEMONT, A., L'émission des emprunts euro-obligataires, 24-25; VAN HECKE, G., Problèmes juridiques des emprunts internationaux, second edition, Leyden, Brill, 1964, 197 and 200.

76. DELAUME, G., What is an international contract ?, An American and a Gallic dilemma, INT'L & COMP.L.Q., 1979, 259.

77. VAN HECKE, G., Principes et méthodes de solution des conflits de lois, 441; HORN, N., Das Recht der internationalen Anleihen, 273; JACQUET, J.M., Principe d'autonomie et contrats internationaux, 52.

78. VAN HECKE, G., Problèmes juridiques des emprunts internationaux, 199-200.

criterion's application served to liberalize international commercial arbitration, because a number of restrictions of the Code of Civil Procedure were held no longer applicable in relation to international commercial arbitration. Therefore, the economic criterion in both cases served specific purposes which may not be generally applicable.

Second, the economic criterion has been criticized for its vagueness and the consequent difficulty of drawing clear lines between domestic and transnational relations[79]. Contrary to the legal criterion, application of economic criteria is less predictable and therefore uncertain.

From these arguments, one may conclude that the economic approach is not an appropriate alternative to the legal approach and should be considered rather a corrective mechanism[80].

36. In recent arbitration laws, one may also find a determination as to their transnational scope. In § 3 of the English *Arbitration Act 1979*, judicial review of arbitral awards may be excluded by agreement under arbitration agreements to which at least one party is (a) an individual who is a national of, or habitually resident in, any state other than the United Kingdom; or (b) a body corporate which is incorporated in, or whose central management and control is exercised in any state other than the United Kingdom. By contrast, the Belgian Act of March 27, 1985, on setting aside of arbitral awards has excluded setting aside awards if neither party is a Belgian national or resident nor a body corporate incorporated in Belgium or having a Belgian branch or center of activities[81]. Finally, article 176 of the Swiss Act of December 18, 1987, on Conflict of Laws provides that the Act's rules on international arbitration apply if at least one party has its domicile or habitual residence in a state other than Switzerland. According to article 192 of the Act, parties may exclude judicial review of awards provided neither party has its domicile, its habitual residence or a business center in Switzerland. The above acts have brought about a definition of transnational arbitration because the legislators moved to liberalize transnational arbitration. In these countries, a personal criterion was used

---

79. LEVEL, P., case note French Supreme Court, October 7, 1980, Rev.Arb., 1982, 37; Court of Appeal Paris, February 21, 1984, Rev.Arb., 1986, 65, case note FOUCHARD, P.

80. *Contra* FOUCHARD,P., L'arbitrage international en France après le décret du 12 mai 1981, 380 who argues that connecting factors may be manipulated and that an economic definition may avoid any such abuses.

81. See further DE LY, F., De liberalisering van de internationale arbitrage, 1034-1037.

to define transnational arbitration[82] because it was considered appropriate to maintain some control over arbitral awards rendered in cases where domestic parties were involved. It seems that under this approach cases have been forgotten in which foreign parties connected to the same foreign country would come to arbitrate in England, Belgium or Switzerland under the liberalized rules although no transnational element is involved[83].

37. It follows from the preceding paragraphs that important differences exist as to the definition of transnationality. These differences may be explained by two factors. First, transnationality is determined by the nature of the problem at hand. For instance, conflict of laws, monetary law and arbitration have shown different notions of transnationality. Second, the definition also depends upon the method which has been followed. As we have seen, the transnationality notion may vary depending upon the use of a conflict analysis or a substantive method.

I.3.1.2 Transnationality and uniform law[84]

38. Many uniform laws have limited their scope to transnational relations, thus excluding domestic relations from the intended unification[85]. This paragraph will discuss the border lines which uniform law has drawn between transnational and domestic relations.

As a preliminary point, one may try to find a justification for a distinction between the unification of international situations and the non-unification of domestic situations. This distinction is primarily based upon arguments of political pragmatism. The unification is considered to have

---

82. DE LY, F., De liberalisering van de internationale arbitrage, 1035. Derains (Le choix du lieu de l'arbitrage, R.D.A.I., 1986, 109) has rightly noted that the Belgian reform of 1985 did not translate the transnational character of arbitration to the same extent as the French law. For a criticism regarding the transnationality definition of the English Arbitration Act 1979, see CARBONNEAU, T., Arbitral adjudication : a comparative assessment of its remedial and substantive status in transnational commerce, 62-63.
83. DE LY, F., De liberalisering van de internationale arbitrage, 1035.
84. In this context conventions regarding uniform law will be discussed irrespective of the fact whether these conventions have entered into force or not. Draft conventions have, however, not been covered.
85. LEMHÖFER, B., Die Beschränkung der Rechtsvereinheitlichung auf internationale Sachverhalte, 401-455.

more chances of success if it is limited to international situations and does not interfere with domestic situations and thus, with domestic policies[86].

Yet, the distinction between international and domestic situations seems to be a gradual one. In some cases, it is obvious that unification cannot be extended at all to domestic situations to the extent that national legislatures insist on maintaining different rules for domestic situations. However, there are also situations in which any such extension to domestic relations creates no problems[87].

39. First, uniform law regarding international sales has used different definitions of transnationality. Both Hague Uniform Sales Laws, ULIS and ULFIS[88], provide that sales are international if the contracting parties have their places of business in different countries[89] *and* either (a) the goods are in the course of carriage or will be carried from one country to another country; (b) the acts constituting offer and acceptance have been effected in different countries; or (c) delivery has to be made in a country other than that in which offer and acceptance have been effected[90]. ULIS and ULFIS thus combine a personal criterion with an objective element[91].

40. More recent conventions on international sales have dropped the objective element[92] because of the uncertainties it might have created and

---

86. VAN HECKE, G., Principes et méthodes de solution des conflits de lois, 472; HONNOLD, J., Uniform law for international sales under the 1980 United Nations Convention, Deventer, Kluwer, 1982, 58.
87. *Cf.* LEMHÖFER, B., Die Beschränkung der Rechtsvereinheitlichung auf internationale Sachverhalte, 416-420.
88. Conventions relating to a uniform law on the international sale of goods, made at The Hague, July 1, 1964 and Convention relating to a uniform law on the formation of contracts for the international sale of goods, made at The Hague, July 1, 1964. These Uniform Laws still apply in Belgium, Gambia, Israël, Luxemburg, San Marino and the United Kingdom.
89. According to article III of the Conventions, their scope may be limited to contracting parties with place of business in convention states.
90. Application of ULIS and ULFIS may under article IV of the Conventions still depend upon conflict rules contained in international conventions on the law applicable to sales contracts.
91. FREDERICQ, L., La vente en droit international privé (quelques conventions récentes), Academy of international law, 93 Collected Courses of The Hague, 1958, I, 22-26; LOUSSOUARN, Y. and BREDIN, J.D., Droit du commerce international, 651-652; HERBER, R., Anwendungsbereich des Gesetzes, 8; MERTENS, H.J. and REHBINDER, E., Internationales Kaufrecht, Frankfurt, Metzner, 1975, 95-99.
92. See also article 2 of the Unidroit Convention on International Factoring (Ottawa, May 28, 1988, not yet entered into force) and article 3 of the Unidroit Convention on International Leasing (Ottawa, May 28, 1988, not yet entered into force).

the fact that the objective criterion of ULIS and ULFIS had become outdated due to developments in international trade and transport[93]. This process first took place in the United Nations Convention on the Limitation Period in the International Sale of Goods (New York, June 14, 1974) and was affirmed in the United Nations Convention on Contracts for the International Sale of Goods ("CISG")(Vienna, April 11, 1980)[94]. Both Conventions provide that a sales contract is international if the contracting parties have their places of business in different contracting states[95]. As a result of the deletion of the objective element, the scope of these Conventions has been broadened. In some cases, this may lead to application of the Conventions although domestic transactions are involved[96]. Finally, both Conventions may also apply between parties whose places of business are in different states when conflict rules lead to the application of the law of a Contracting State[97].

---

93. HONNOLD, J., Uniform law for international sales under the 1980 United Nations Convention, 78; WINSHIP, P., The scope of the Vienna Convention on international sales contracts, in International sales, The United Nations convention on contracts for the international sale of goods, GALSTON, N. and SMIT, H. (ed.), New York, Matthew Bender, 1984, 1-18.
94. See also article 2 Unidroit-Convention of February 17, 1983 on Agency in the International Sale of Goods (UNIF.L.REV., 1983, 161-174; not yet entered into force) which was clearly modelled after CISG. The Sales Limitation Period Convention has entered into force on August 1, 1988 and on June 1, 1991, it was applicable between eleven countries. CISG entered into force on January 1, 1988 and on June 1, 1991, it was applicable between thirthy two countries (Uncitral document A/CN.9/353, June 5, 1991).
95. FARNSWORTH, E., The Vienna Convention: history and scope, INT'L LAW., 1984, 19; SONO, K., Uncitral and the Vienna Sales Convention, INT'L LAW., 1984, 12. The Sales Limitation Period Convention at first did not restrict its scope to parties from contracting States; the Convention was in this respect amended by a Protocol signed at the Vienna Conference in order to adapt the Sales Limitation Period Convention to CISG.
96. VOLKEN, P., Champ d'application, interprétation, lacunes, usages, in Convention de Vienne de 1980 sur la vente internationale de marchandises, Zurich, Schulthess, 1985, 29.
97. Application by virtue of national conflict rules was originally also absent from the Sales Limitation Period Convention. At the time of the Vienna Conference, the aforementioned Protocol amended the Sales Limitation Period Convention in order to avoid differences between both sales conventions. Article 95 CISG provides for a reservation against the extension of CISG in application of conflict rules. *Cf.* HONNOLD, J., Uniform law for international sales under the 1980 United Nations Convention, 82-83 and HERBER, R., Wiener UNCITRAL-Übereinkommen über den internationalen Kauf beweglicher Sachen, Cologne, Bundesstelle für Außenhandelsinformation, 1981, 8.

41. Uniform law in the field of transportation was also limited to transnational relations. First, article 10 of the International Convention for the unification of certain rules of law relating to bills of lading (Brussels, August 25, 1924 - *The Hague Rules*) as amended by article 5 of the Protocol of February 23, 1968 (*The Hague-Visby Rules*)[98] provides that the convention applies to every bill of lading relating to the carriage of goods between ports in two different states if (a) the bill of lading is issued in a contracting state; (b) the carriage is from a port in a contracting state; or (c) the contract contained in or evidenced by the bill of lading provides that the rules of the convention or legislation of any state giving effect to them are to govern the contract. Furthermore, the nationality of the ship, the carrier, the shipper, the consignee or any other interested person is irrelevant as to the determination of the convention's scope. Thus, the convention primarily covers outbound transport and does not encompass all transnational sea transport[99].

Article 2 of the United Nations Convention on the Carriage of Goods by Sea (*Hamburg Rules* - May 30, 1978)[100] provides that it applies to all contracts of carriage by sea between two different states if (a) the port of loading as provided for in the contract of carriage by sea is located in a contracting state; (b) the port of discharge as provided for in the contract of carriage by sea is located in a contracting state; (c) one of the optional ports of discharge provided for in the contract of carriage by sea is the actual port of discharge and such port is located in a contracting state; (d) the bill of lading or other document evidencing the contract of carriage by sea is issued in a contracting state; or (e) the bill of lading or other document evidencing the contract of carriage by sea provides that the provisions of this convention or the legislation of any state giving effect to them are to govern the contract. The Hamburg Rules have a broader scope than the Hague-Visby Rules because inbound transport is also brought within its scope. The Hamburg Rules are also applicable without regard to the nationality of the ship, the carrier, the actual carrier, the shipper, the consignee or any other interested person.

42. A description of transnationality may also be found in article 1 of the Uniform Rules concerning the contract for international carriage of

98. As of January 1, 1991, the Hague Rules apply as between 76 states. The Hague-Visby Rules apply as of the same date between 20 states.
99. In some countries (*e.g.*, article 91, A, of the Belgian Maritime Act), the convention's scope has been extended to inbound traffic.
100. E.T.L., 1979, 471. As of June 1, 1991, this Convention has been ratified or acceded to by nineteen countries and needs one more ratification or accession before it can enter into force (Uncitral document A/CN.9/353, June 5, 1991).

passengers and luggage by rail ("*C.I.V.*") and article 1 of the Uniform Rules concerning the contract for international carriage of goods by rail ("*C.I.M.*")[101]. These articles provide that the Uniform Rules apply to carriage under international transport documents or a through consignment note made out for a route over the territories of at least two States and exclusively over rail lines or services designated and registered for direct international carriage[102] respectively. The limitation of the Rules' scope to specifically designated lines is typical for the COTIF-regulatory framework and rail transport. These features have therefore had a substantial impact on the definition of international carriage by rail[103].

43. Road transport also has its own definition of transnationality. Article 1 of the Convention on the contract for the international carriage of goods by road ("*C.M.R.*")[104] provides that the convention shall apply to every contract for the carriage of goods by road in vehicles for pay when the place of transfer of the goods and the place designated for delivery, as specified in the contract, are situated in two different countries, of which at least one is a contracting country, irrespective of the place of residence and the nationality of the parties. It follows from article 1 that border crossing is as such not a condition for the application of the Convention.

44. Transnationality also has been defined in air transport law. In this respect, Article 1 of the Warsaw Convention for the unification of certain rules relating to international carriage by air[105] as amended by the Hague Protocol of September 28, 1955[106] provides that carriage is international when, according to the agreement between the parties, the place of departure and the place of destination, whether or not there is a break in the carriage or a transhipment, are situated either within the territories of two contracting states, or within the territory of a single contracting state

---

101. These uniform rules are respectively Annex A and B of the Convention concerning International Carriage of Goods by Rail ("COTIF") dated May 9, 1980. This convention goes back to the nineteenth century's unification of the law on international carriage by rail. The convention entered into force on May 1, 1985 and as of January 1, 1991, 33 states were bound by it.
102. *Cf.* WICK, J., Le droit international des transports par chemins de fer, Neuchâtel, Chave, 1976, 21-28.
103. SCHAPIRA, J., Le droit international des affaires, 110.
104. Signed at Geneva on May 19, 1956. This convention applies as of January 1, 1991 between 24 countries.
105. Signed at Warsaw on October 12, 1929. This Convention is as of January 1, 1991 applicable as between 132 states.
106. This protocol has as of January 1, 1991 been adopted by 113 states.

if there is an agreed stopping place within the territory of another state, even if that state is not a contracting state[107].

45. Finally, article 1 of the United Nations Convention on International Multimodal Transport of Goods[108] defines international multimodal transport as the carriage of goods by at least two different modes of transport on the basis of a multimodal transport contract from a place in one country where the goods are put into the hands of the multimodal transport operator, to a place of delivery situated in a different country. According to article 2, either the place of shipment or the place of delivery as provided in the multimodal transport contract should be located in a contracting state.

46. Unification instruments in the field of international commercial arbitration also contain definitions of the transnationality of arbitration. In this regard, Article I, 1, a) of the European Convention on International Commercial Arbitration[109] provides that it applies to arbitration agreements concluded for the purpose of settling disputes arising from international trade between physical or legal persons having, at the time the agreement is concluded, their habitual places of residence or their seats of business in different contracting states. The Convention has thus formulated a requirement as to the transaction involved and as to the persons involved[110]. The drafters of the convention have preferred not to give a definition of "international trade" but one may conclude from the convention's drafting process that it refers to import or export transactions regarding goods, services or capital[111]. This may still not solve all interpretation problems. According to Klein, the lex fori should answer any

107. In some countries (*e.g.*, Belgium) the scope of the Warsaw Convention and The Hague Protocol has been extended to domestic air transport.

108. E.T.L., 1980, 487-521. This Convention was signed in Geneva on May 24, 1980 and has not yet entered into force as of January 1, 1991.

109. Done at Geneva on April 21, 1961. As of January 1, 1991, 20 states were bound by this Convention. However, European countries which are well known as arbitration centers as for instance the United Kingdom, The Netherlands, Sweden or Switzerland are not contracting states to this Convention.

110. ROBERT, J., La convention européenne sur l'arbitrage commercial international signée à Genève le 21 avril 1961, D., 1961, 175-176; GOLDMAN, B., Les conflits de lois dans l'arbitrage international de droit privé, 362; MEZGER, E., Das Europäische Übereinkommen über die Handelsschiedsgerichtsbarkeit, RabelsZ, 1965, 239.

111. Arbitral award, November 18, 1983 (Benteler v. Belgian State), J.T., 1984, 230, Y.B.COM.ARB. X-1985, 37. The ambiguity of the term has been criticized by David (DAVID, R., L'arbitrage dans le commerce international, 237).

remaining questions[112]. A recent arbitral award and Gentinetta have, however, argued that the convention should be interpreted autonomously[113].

47. The Uncitral Model Law on International Commercial Arbitration[114] has also defined international arbitration. Article 1 (3) provides that arbitration is international if (a) the parties have their places of business in different states; (b) the states in which the parties have their places of business are different from the place of arbitration as determined in or pursuant to the arbitration agreement, any place where a substantial part of the obligations of the commercial relationship is to be performed or the place with which the subject-matter of the dispute is most closely connected; or (c) the parties have expressly agreed that the subject-matter of the arbitration agreement relates to more than one country[115]. Here, transnationality is defined by various factors, such as the place of business, the place of arbitration, the place of performance, the place which is most closely connected or the parties' will.

48. Finally, the recent United Nations Convention on International Bills of Exchange and International Promissory Notes[116] also has been limited to international transactions. Bills of exchange and promissory notes will

---

112. KLEIN, F.E., La Convention européenne sur l'arbitrage commercial international, R.C.D.I.P., 1962, 626.

113. Arbitral Award, November 18, 1983, J.T., 1984, 230, Y.B.COM.ARB. X-1985, 37; GENTINETTA, J., Die lex fori internationaler Handelsschiedsgerichte, 310.

114. Adopted by Uncitral on June 21, 1985; I.L.M., 1985, 1302. Legislation based on this model law has been enacted by the Canadian Federation and all Canadian Provinces and Territories, Cyprus, Australia, Nigeria, Bulgaria, Hong Kong, Scotland and by the American state legislators of California, Connecticut and Texas (Uncitral document, A/CN.9/353, June 5, 1991).

115. DORE, I., Arbitration and conciliation under the Uncitral rules : a textual analysis, Dordrecht, Nijhoff, 1986, 92-96; REDFERN, A. and HUNTER, M., Law and practice of international commercial arbitration, first edition, 13-14. For criticism regarding this provision, see KERR, M., Arbitration and the courts : the Uncitral model law, INT'L & COMP.L.Q., 1985, 16.

116. Adopted by the UN General Assembly on December 9, 1988 in New York. The Convention has not yet entered into force. Three states have signed the Convention (Canada, the U.S.A. and the former U.S.S.R.) and Guinea has acceded to it (Uncitral document, A/CN.9/353, June 5, 1991). For a discussion, see VOLKEN, P., Das UNO-Übereinkommen vom 9. Dezember 1988 über internationale Wechsel, Schweizerische Zeitschrift für Wirtschaftsrecht, 1990, 100-108; HERRMANN, G., International bills of exchange and promissory notes : legal problems and disparities overcome by new United Nations Convention, The law of international trade finance, HORN, N. (ed.), Deventer, Kluwer, 1989, 259-274.

be deemed international for the application of the Convention if two places listed in article 2 of the Convention and specified in the bill or note are situated in different States. For bills of exchange, these places are the place of drawing, the place of payment and the places indicated next to the signature of the drawer, to the name of the drawer and to the name of the payee.

49. Some general observations may be deduced from the analysis set forth above. First, one may note that in many cases the scope of the uniform texts is not determined by reference to a conflict rule but defined in an autonomous way[117]. This seems to be related to the fact that these unification efforts relate to substantive law and not to conflict of laws. Second, it stems from the analysis that a wide variety of definitions may be found. A substantive determination of the scope of uniform law requires at least two criteria[118] which, if satisfied, lead to application of uniform law and not to domestic law applicable by virtue of a conflict rule. The criteria are determined by a process of selection, in which many factors (including the subject matter of the unification[119], the organization responsible for the unification, the motives for unification) may influence the choice. The variety of these factors may thus explain the varying definitions which have been found in uniform law.

I.3.1.3 Transnationality in transnational practice

50. Article 1 of the I.C.C. Conciliation Rules and article 1 (1) of the I.C.C. Arbitration Rules[120] provide that business disputes of an international character may be submitted to conciliation by a sole conciliator or settled by arbitration[121]. Article 1 (1) of the I.C.C. Technical Expertise Rules[122] limits the scope of these rules to transnational commercial transactions,

---

117. VAN HECKE, G., Principes et méthodes de solution des conflits de lois, 468; HAAK, K., De aansprakelijkheid van de vervoerder ingevolge de CMR, 42-45; KROPHOLLER, J., Internationales Einheitsrecht, Allgemeine Lehren, 190-191.
118. LEMHÖFER, B., Die Beschränkung der Rechtsvereinheitlichung auf internationale Sachverhalte, 422; KROPHOLLER, J., Internationales Einheitsrecht, 192.
119. See also RODIERE, R., Les domaines comparés des conventions d'unification du droit en matière de transports de marchandises, in Miscellanea W.J.Ganshof Van Der Meersch, Brussels, Bruylant, II, 1972, 904.
120. I.C.C. publication No. 447, Paris, I.C.C., 1987.
121. Article 1 of the Internal Rules of the International Court of Arbitration of the I.C.C. provides however that the Court may accept jurisdiction over business disputes not of an international business nature, if it has jurisdiction by reason of an arbitration agreement (see JARVIN, S., case note of I.C.C. case No. 5423, Clunet, 1987, 1048).
122. I.C.C. publication No. 307, Paris, I.C.C., 1977.

while the powers of the I.C.C. Committee on Contract Adaptation are, under article 1 (1) of the I.C.C. Adaptation Rules[123], limited to international economic relations. However, no further definition of transnationality may be found in the rules set forth above. The explanatory note to the Conciliation and Arbitration Rules states that the parties involved need not be of different nationalities and that the mere presence of one foreign element in a domestic situation might be sufficient for application of the rules[124]. The explanatory note illustrates this by referring to cases where a contract involves parties from the same country but performance takes place abroad or where a state contract is concluded with a domestic subsidiary of a foreign parent company. I.C.C. arbitral case No. 3880 provides another example. In this case, two Belgian parties were involved in a dispute concerning a sale of shoes. Since the shoes were supplied by a Romanian seller, the dispute was held to be international and subject to I.C.C. arbitration[125].

51. Other arbitration rules also have clauses on the transnationality of the dispute. For instance, the preamble of the Conciliation, Arbitration and Expertise Rules of the Euro-Arab Chambers of Commerce[126] states that the rules apply to international commercial disputes arising in transactions with Arab countries. Article 1 (g) of the Arbitration Rules of the Netherlands Arbitration Institute defines international arbitration as arbitration in which at least one party is domiciled or has its seat or actual residence outside the Netherlands. Similarly, article 1 of the International Arbitration Rules of the Zurich Chamber of Commerce provides that these rules are available if at least one party has its registered or actual seat, its domicile or its habitual residence outside Switzerland[127]. The Supplementary Procedures for International Commercial Arbitration of the American Arbitration Association provide that these procedures are applicable to parties of a different nationality or residents of different countries. Similarly, the introductory text to the Arbitration Rules of the Cairo

---

123. I.C.C. publication No. 326, Paris, I.C.C., 1978.

124. I.C.C. publication No. 301, Paris, I.C.C., 1977, 10 and 19. At the occasion of the 1927 amendments to the I.C.C. arbitration rules, the present text was preferred above a nationality or domicile-criterion (ARNAUD, R., L'arbitrage de la Chambre de Commerce Internationale, L'économie internationale, 1929, 126; EISEMANN, F., The Court of arbitration : outline of its changes from inception to the present day, 393).

125. I.C.C. case No. 3880, Clunet, 1983, 897; see also I.C.C. case No. 5910, Clunet, 1988, 1216, case note DERAINS, Y.

126. Paris, 1982.

127. International Arbitration Rules of the Zurich Chamber of Commerce, 1989 edition, Zurich, 36 pp.

Regional Centre for International Commercial Arbitration states that the Centre's facilities may be used for disputes having an international character (i.e., if the parties to the dispute belong to, or are resident in two or more different jurisdictions)[128]. The Arbitration Rules of the U.N. Economic Commission for Asia and the Far East ("*ECAFE*") may be available to parties having their residences in different countries of the region or in countries both within and outside the region. If neither party has its residence in the region, the dispute may still be settled under the ECAFE Rules provided the contract is to be performed in, or is somehow connected to, the region.

52. It thus appears that no uniform definition of transnationality can be found in transnational practice. Both a very broad concept (I.C.C. Rules) and more narrow concepts, based upon more specific criteria and situations, have been identified.

I.3.1.4 Transnationality and sources of international business law

53. The preceding paragraphs have shown that it is hard to arrive at a single uniform definition of transnationality as it is determined by many factors[129]. In addition, the method used is particularly relevant. Conflict of law methodology will work with transnational connecting points, while a substantive method will need less neutral and unilateral criteria to distinguish between domestic and transnational situations.

54. Post-war legal doctrine on the sources of international business law has rarely addressed the transnationality issue explicitly. The opinions of legal writers must be deduced from the positions they take with respect to related issues. For Goldman, international business law exists largely outside national legal systems. In this regard, Goldman seems to use the traditional conflict of law methodology in order to determine whether *lex mercatoria* applies. However, Goldman has also argued that *lex mercatoria* consists of substantive norms, the scope of which is unilaterally determined. In defining the scope of these rules, Goldman relies on the aforementioned criteria developed in French case law and legislation. One may thus

128. Arbitration under the auspices of the Cairo Regional Centre, Regional Centre for International Commercial Arbitration, Cairo, s.d.

129. Therefore, some authors have proposed a case-by-case approach to the transnationality issue (DELAUME, G., What is an international contract ?, An American and a Gallic dilemma, 279; BRABANT, A., Le contrat international de construction, Brussels, Bruylant, 1981, 77-78).

conclude that two distinct definitions are used to determine the transnationality of the *lex mercatoria* and that these definitions are by and large inspired by concepts of French law.

In the opinion of Schmitthoff, international business law is a diffuse complex of substantive rules of transnational origin which apply to international business transactions. The main sources of this *lex mercatoria* are international conventions on the unification of law and international trade usages. One may recall the variety of transnationality definitions which have been found in unification conventions. As to international usages, it remains uncertain how Schmitthoff conceives their application. One may assume that the applicable law will determine whether and to what extent these usages apply. Thus, a conflict of law approach would be chosen. Again, both substantive and conflict of law definitions of transnationality are used.

Finally, substantive methods are also used in international business law. In many cases, these methods will be applied directly, *i.e.*, without passing through a conflict of laws rules.

Thus, the definitions of the internationality of business law depend in great measure on the conceptions of authors regarding the sources, methods and autonomy of international business law.

I.3.2 *The limitation of international business law to business transactions*

55. The application of international business law to all kinds of business transactions has often been affirmed, but hardly ever described or analyzed, even by writers on the sources of international business law.

As a starting point, research on the sources of international business law has primarily been limited to business contracts and commercial arbitration. More exceptionally, company law has received attention[130], while other fields of business law such as commercial paper law[131] or bankruptcy law have never been discussed systematically. This leads to the conclusion that commercial contracts are at the center of any theory on the sources of international business law. Furthermore, one may refer to the

---

130. GOLDMAN, B., Le droit des sociétés internationales, 320-389; MANN, F.A., International corporations and national law, 42 Brit.Y.B.Int.L., 1967, 145-174; KAHN, P., International companies, Journal of world trade law, 1969, 498-521.

131. *Cf.* FOUCHARD, P., Foreword, in BLOCH, P., Les lettres de change et billets à ordre dans les relations commerciales internationales, Paris, Economica, 1986, II; BLOCH, P., Les lettres de change et billets à ordre dans les relations commerciales internationales, Paris, Economica, 1986, 9-10, 212 and 262; VAN RYN, J. and HEENEN, J., Principes de droit commercial, I, second edition, Brussels, Bruylant, 1976, 53; ROWE, M., Sham promissory notes : an international fraud, Int.Fin.Law Rev., November 1982, 25.

influence of contractual constructions in other fields of business law, such as regarding pre-incorporation agreements or contracts between shareholders in company law, bank contracts[132] in commercial paper law or contractual devices in bankruptcy law aimed at avoiding complications arising from application of the intricacies of national bankruptcy laws[133].

The analysis of fields other than commercial contracts and commercial arbitration, has basically focussed on company law. In this respect, Goldman was the first to examine the status of transnational companies[134]. He started from the observation that some companies are no longer governed by national law but are created through international agreements. Examples of this development are the "Bank for International Settlements", the "European Company for the Financing of Railroad Rolling Stock" (Eurofima), the "European Company for the Chemical Processing of Irradiated Fuels" (Eurochemic), the "Scandinavian Airlines Systems" (SAS), the "International Bank for Reconstruction and Development" (IBRD), the "International Finance Corporation" (IFC) and the "European Investment Bank" (EIB)[135]. Goldman further noted that the functioning of these companies had been organized in such a way that national law and national courts were rarely called upon to solve any disputes. In this regard, Goldman wondered whether these companies could not exist outside national legal systems. Referring to the then existing drafts of a Statute for a "European Company", Goldman stated that detachment from domestic laws is practically sound and theoretically justified as far as the internal organization of the company is concerned. However, Goldman recognized the need for a company charter based on domestic law for the company's relations with third parties (*e.g.*, the description of the corporate

---

132. *Cf.* DAL, G.A., L'Eurochèque, in La banque dans la vie quotidienne, Brussels, Jeune barreau, 1986, 331; KAHN, P., L'essor du non-droit dans les relations commerciales internationales et le contrat sans loi, 260; BLAISE, J.B. and FOUCHARD, P., La valeur juridique de la syndication, in Les Euro-crédits, un instrument du système bancaire pour le financement international, BLAISE, J.B., FOUCHARD, P. and KAHN, P. (ed.), Travaux du centre de recherche sur le droit des marchés et des investissements internationaux, Volume 8, Paris, Librairies Techniques, 1981, 168; SIMONT, L., Les garanties indépendantes, Rev.Banque, 1983, 579.
133. *Cf.* PRICE, J. and HENDERSON, S., Currency and interest rate swaps, London, Butterworths, 1984, 98; VAN HOUTTE, H., Internationaal faillissementsrecht, J.C.B., 1978, 394.
134. See infra No. 326.
135. GOLDMAN, B., Le droit des sociétés internationales, 328-355; *cf.* MARTY, G., Les sociétés internationales, RabelsZ, 1962-63, 78-82.

purpose, the powers of the directors)[136]. Finally, gaps in the rules applicable to these companies might, according to Goldman, be filled by using general principles of law applicable to transnational companies, or customary rules[137].

56. Goldman's opinion, however, is open to criticism. First, the transnational companies cited by Goldman are quite atypical, which prevents generalizations as to the possibility of denationalizing transnational company law[138]. Furthermore, some of these companies are chartered under public international law and are therefore detached from domestic law only to be governed by public international law[139]. Finally, company law contains many mandatory provisions from which, even in transnational relations, no derogation is possible. Consequently, in the field of company law, one may anticipate that conflicts with domestic laws may arise more frequently than in fields which are largely controlled by party autonomy[140]. In relation to third parties, national law will thus frequently be

---

136. GOLDMAN, B., Le droit des sociétés internationales, 372-382; *cf.* GOLDMAN, B., case note Court of Appeal Paris, March 19, 1965, Clunet, 1966, 136-137; GOLDMAN, B., case note under Court of Appeal Paris, October 3, 1984, Clunet, 1986, 167.

137. GOLDMAN, B., Le droit des sociétés internationales, 384-387; see also FOUCHARD, P., L'arbitrage commercial international, 429-430.

138. LOUSSOUARN, Y. and BREDIN, J.D., Droit du commerce international, 344; LOUSSOUARN, Y., Cours général de droit international privé, Academy of international law, Collected Courses of The Hague, 1973, II, Leyden, Sijthoff, 1974, 314; BATIFFOL, H., Conflict avoidance in European law, 577-579; BATIFFOL, H., Aspects philosophiques du droit international privé, 96-102; HOLLEAUX, G., intervention during the discussions, in Les sociétés de type européen, Trav.com.fr.dr.int.privé, 1962-1964, Paris, Dalloz, 1965, 40; I.C.C. case No. 3879, March 25, 1984, Clunet, 1985, 238.

Originally, Vlas (Rechtspersonen in het internationaal privaatrecht, 147) preferred application of general principles of law to application of the law of the place of incorporation or the place of business; see also AUBERTIN, C., Les associations en droit international privé français, Clunet, 1983, 573; *contra* STRUYCKEN, A., Verenigingen als wereldburgers: "qua patet orbis", 289. Influenced by the forceful arguments of Struycken, Vlas has changed his mind (VLAS, P., "Apatride" associations, Aspects of private international law, N.I.L.R., 1990, 47-48 and 60).

139. MANN, F.A., International corporations and national law, 145-174; KAHN, P., International companies, 502 and 520; *cf.* COLLIER, J.C., The status of an international corporation, in Multum non multa, Festschrift für K. Lipstein, Heidelberg, Müller, 1980, 21-29.

140. BÄRMANN, J., Supranationale Aktiengesellschaften ?, AcP, 1957, 169-171; LOUSSOUARN, Y., Règles de conflit et règles matérielles dans le droit international des sociétés, in Le droit des relations économiques internationales, Etudes offertes à Berthold Goldman, Paris, Litec, 1982, 183; *cf.* KAHN, P., International companies, 501.

used which might also tempt the parties involved to have domestic law apply to other relations as well.

The above discussion may be illustrated by an analogous debate regarding the E.E.C. work on a Statute of a "*European Company*". Originally, the European Company was conceived as a supranational company based upon E.E.C. law and largely detached from the domestic laws of the Member States[141]. This conception has been criticized, and some authors have expressed preference for a company form originating in domestic laws, which should conform to a model set by E.E.C. Regulation and which may also achieve the desired harmonization[142]. In the latest proposal for a Statute for a European Company, a compromise has been reached between the autonomous-supranational and the domestic conceptions. Article 7 (1) now provides that the general principles on which the Regulation is based should control matters dealt with in the Regulation, but not expressly settled by it. Absent such principles, the law on public limited companies of the state in which the European Company has its registered office should apply[143]. This compromise might be interpreted as an indication that even in EEC Community law, it is hard to denationalize company law.

This is also confirmed by Council Regulation No. 2137/85 of July 25, 1985 concerning the "*European Economic Interest Grouping*" ("EEIG")[144]. Within the framework of this Regulation, EEC Member States have retained wide powers to regulate EEIG's[145]. Furthermore, article 2 (1) of the Regulation provides that, subject to the provisions of the Regulation, the contract of formation of an EEIG as well as its internal organization shall be governed by the internal law of the State in which the official

141. See article 7 of the proposal for a Council Regulation on the statute for a European Company, O.J., C 124, October 10, 1970.

142. DUDEN, K., Internationale Aktiengesellschaften, RabelsZ, 1962-63, 100-104; HOUIN, R., Les sociétés de type européen, Trav.com.fr.dr.int.privé, 1962-63, Paris, Dalloz, 1965, 30; VASSEUR, M., Quo vadis, Societas Europea ?, in Quo vadis, ius societatum ?, Liber amicorum Pieter Sanders, ZONDERLAND, P. (ed.), Deventer, Kluwer, 1972, 236-238.

143. Proposal for a Council Regulation on the statute for a European Company, O.J., C 263, October 16, 1989, 41; for a first comment on the proposed article 7, see LUTTER, M., Genügen die vorgeschlagenen Regelungen für eine "Europäische Aktiengesellschaft" ?, AG 1990, 416.

144. OJ, L 199, July 31, 1985, 1-9.

145. GLEICHMANN, K., Europäische Wirtschaftliche Interessenvereinigung, ZHR, 1985, 648-649.

address is situated[146]. Therefore, the EEIG can hardly be described as having supranational status[147].

57. In defining the scope of international business law, one is confronted with the distinction which is known in some legal systems, between civil law and commercial law. This distinction is not at all universal. Important jurisdictions such as common law countries, The Netherlands, Switzerland or Italy do not have any such distinction or have abolished it. Furthermore, the relevance of the distinction in countries where it exists, should not be overestimated. In many respects, so-called commercial rules also apply to civil law relations and the distinction only remains relevant to the extent that commercial law rules derogate from civil law[148]. Because the distinction is not universally accepted and is also questioned[149], it is doubtful whether it should be used at all in transnational business relations[150].

146. VAN GERVEN, D., Le groupement européen d'intérêt économique - (G.E.I.E.), Rev.Prat.Soc., 1986, 204-205; MEYER-LANDRUT, A., Europäische Wirtschaftliche Interessenvereinigung (EWIV), RIW, 1986, 108.

147. WOODLAND, P., Le groupement européen d'intérêt économique : le regain du modèle français offre aux entreprises de la C.E.E. un futur instrument de coopération, J.C.P. éd. C.I., 1986, 283; ABMEIER, K., Die Europäische wirtschaftliche Interessenvereinigung und nationales Recht, NJW, 1986, 2991; PETELAUD, A., La construction de la Communauté européenne et le groupement européen d'intérêt économique (GEIE), Rev.Soc., 1986, 192 and 207-208.

148. In this regard, some authors distinguish between commercial law rules which respectively supplement or contradict civil law rules; see FREDERICQ, S., De eenmaking van het burgerlijk recht en het handelsrecht, Ghent, Faculty of Law, 1957, 11-12 and 395; LIMPENS, J., De l'unification du droit civil et du droit commercial, J.T., 1953, 354; *cf.* GIERKE/SANDROCK, Handels- und Wirtschaftsrecht, Volume 1, Berlin, de Gruyter, 1975, 4; STAUB, Großkommentar, fourth edition, Berlin, de Gruyter, 1983, Einl., 5.

149. FREDERICQ, S., De eenmaking van het burgerlijk recht en het handelsrecht, 539-553; LIMPENS, J., De l'unification du droit civil et du droit commercial, 358-359; *contra* VAN RYN, J., Autonomie nécessaire et permanence du droit commercial, Rev.Trim.Dr.Com., 1953, 565.

150. VON HOFFMANN, B., Internationale Handelsschiedsgerichtsbarkeit, 52; LOUSSOUARN, Y. and BREDIN, J.D., Droit du commerce international, 6 and 652-653; SCHAPIRA, J., Le droit international des affaires, 18-19; BELLET, P. and MEZGER, E., L'arbitrage international dans le nouveau code de procédure civile, 618-619; FOUCHARD, P., L'arbitrage international en France après le décret du 12 mai 1981, 380.

Consequently, some legal writings have used the expression *transnational private law* rather than *transnational business law*[151].

58. The fading relevance of the distinction between civil law and commercial law is confirmed by developments in French arbitration law, international conventions and transnational practice.

First, French case law has refused to apply the prohibition on arbitral clauses which exists in civil law relations, with regard to transnational transactions between a merchant and a non-merchant (so-called "*mixed commercial acts*"). Although the arbitral clause would have been null and void in domestic transactions, case law of lower courts[152] and the *Hecht*-decision of the Supreme Court of July 4, 1972[153] have held that an arbitral clause in a transnational contract is severable, and therefore valid, irrespective of the law applicable to it. The *Hecht*-decision makes clear that in transnational arbitration, French case law is prepared to ignore civil law rules which tend to protect non-merchants.

French law offers another example of this trend. With regard to the interpretation of the definition of transnational arbitration[154], French writers unanimously argue that the domestic definition of commercial law should not be used[155].

---

151. SIEHR, K., Sachrecht im IPR, transnationales Recht und lex mercatoria, 125; RIGAUX, F. and VANDER ELST, R., Relations juridiques transnationales ou dialogue sur un autre droit, J.T., 1982, 231; VANDER ELST, R., Conflits de lois, 38 and 175.
152. Court of Appeal Paris, June 19, 1970, Clunet, 1971, 833, case note OPPETIT, B., R.C.D.I.P., 1971, 692, case note LEVEL, P., J.C.P., 1971, 16927, case note GOLDMAN, B.; Court of Appeal Paris, December 13, 1975, R.C.D.I.P., 1976, 507, case note OPPETIT, B., Clunet, 1977, 106, case note LOQUIN, E.; Court of Appeal Toulouse, October 26, 1982, Clunet, 1984, 603, case note SYNVET, H.; Court of Appeal Paris, November 9, 1984, Clunet, 1986, 1039, case note LOQUIN, E.; Court of Appeal Paris, October 26, 1962, R.C.D.I.P., 1965, 535, case note BATIFFOL, H.
153. R.C.D.I.P., 1974, 82, case note LEVEL,P., Clunet, 1972, 843, case note OPPETIT, B.
154. Article 1492 N.C.P.C. provides that arbitration is deemed international if it affects the interests of international trade.
155. FOUCHARD, P., L'arbitrage international en France après le décret du 12 mai 1981, 380; DERAINS, Y., Sources et domaine d'application du droit français de l'arbitrage international, in Droit et pratique de l'arbitrage international en France, Feduci, Paris, 1984, 9; LEVEL, P., La réforme de l'arbitrage international, J.C.P., éd.C.I., 1981, 244; ROBERT, J., L'arbitrage en matière internationale, D., 1981, 210; AUDIT, B., A national codification of international commercial arbitration : the French Decree of May 12, 1981, in Resolving transnational disputes through international arbitration, CARBONNEAU, T. (ed.), Charlottesville, University Press of Virginia, 1984, 123.

59. The importance which some states attach to the distinction between civil law and commercial law is sometimes reflected in international conventions. These conventions permit ratifying states to limit the scope of the convention to transactions which are deemed commercial by the law of that state. This technique enables states in which the distinction between civil and commercial law still exists, to apply these conventions only with regard to commercial law transactions. This approach may be found in the Geneva Protocol on Arbitration Clauses of September 24, 1923, in the Geneva Convention on the Execution of Foreign Arbitral Awards of September 26, 1927 and in article I (3) of the New York Convention of June 10, 1958 on the Recognition and Enforcement of Foreign Arbitral Awards[156]. One should note, however, that the commercial law reservation of these conventions has not been used by some states which preserve the distinction between civil and commercial law[157].

60. Moreover, recent conventions tend not to use any distinction between civil and commercial law, nor to provide for a commercial law reservation. Article 1 (8) ULFIS and article 7 ULIS state that they apply regardless of the commercial or civil character of the parties or of the contracts[158]. In a similar vein, article 1 (3) CISG, article 2 (e) of the Sales Limitation Period Convention and article 2 (3) of the Sales Agency Convention provide that the civil or commercial character of the parties or of the contract should not be taken into consideration in the application of these conventions. A commercial law reservation is also absent from the 1961 European International Commercial Arbitration Convention and from the Uncitral Model Law on International Commercial Arbitration. Furthermore, the commercial element has been defined very broadly in article I,

156. With regard to the problems which might arise in relation to this reservation, see DAVID, R., Arbitration in international trade, 149, L'arbitrage dans le commerce international, 208.

157. *E.g.*, Germany and Belgium. Originally, France had used the reservation based upon the argument that arbitral clauses were only valid in commercial law relations (LOUSSOUARN, Y. and BREDIN, J.D., Droit du commerce international, 112). Quite recently, however, France has dropped the reservation (Rev.Arb., 1990, 210; for a commentary see FOUCHARD, P., La levée par la France de sa réserve de commercialité pour l'application de la Convention de New York, Rev.Arb., 1990, 571-583).

158. RIGAUX, F., Le domaine d'application de la loi uniforme sur la vente internationale des objets mobiliers corporels et la loi uniforme sur la formation de ces contrats de vente, 70; LOUSSOUARN, Y. and BREDIN, J.D., Droit du commerce international, 6. To a certain extent, the distinction between civil and commercial law might still be relevant under ULFIS and ULIS (see VAN DER VELDEN, F., De eenvormige koopwetten van 1964, 34; MERTENS, H.J and REHBINDER, E., Internationales Kaufrecht, 108-109).

1 (a) of the 1961 Convention (disputes arising from international *trade*)[159]. Finally, the Uncitral Model Law has taken a pragmatic approach in defining commercial arbitration by referring in a footnote to some examples which might be considered commercial transactions. This indicates that the drafters of the Model Law intended the Law to have a broad scope[160].

61. Transnational practice also works with definitions of business law. For instance, article 1 of the I.C.C. Conciliation Rules and article 1 (1) of the I.C.C. Arbitration Rules have limited their scope to business disputes[161]. Both the English ("business disputes") and the French texts of these Rules ("tout différend d'ordre commercial" and "des différends intervenant dans le domaine des affaires") as well as the explanatory note[162] are arguments in favour of an autonomous interpretation which should not be influenced by notions of domestic legal systems. In other private rules such as article 1 (1) of the I.C.C. Technical Expertise Rules and article 1 (1) of the I.C.C. Adaptation Rules, references may be found to commercial or economic transactions in relation to the scope of these respective Rules. However, these notions have not been defined.

62. Notwithstanding these developments, problems may still exist in transnational practice with regard to the impact of the distinction between

---

159. In this respect, two opinions exist. A first school of thought argues to interpret *international trade* according to the *lex fori* (KLEIN, F.E., La Convention européenne sur l'arbitrage commercial international, 626). According to other authors and one arbitral award, *international trade* should be interpreted autonomously (DAVID, R., Arbitration in international trade, 157; L'arbitrage dans le commerce international, 217-218; MEZGER, E., Das Europäische Übereinkommen über die Handelsschiedsgerichtsbarkeit, 240; GENTINETTA, J., Die lex fori internationaler Handelsschiedsgerichte, 310; MAIER, H.J., Europäisches Übereinkommen über die internationale Handelsschiedsgerichtsbarkeit und UN-Übereinkommen über die Anerkennung und Vollstreckung ausländischer Schiedssprüche, Cologne, Deutscher Wirtschaftsdienst, 1966, 7-8; Arbitral Award, November 18, 1983, J.T., 1984, 230, Y.B.COM.ARB. X-1985, 37, J.INT.ARB., 1984, 184).

160. Here again, one opinion would refer interpretation issues to the applicable law (REDFERN, A. and HUNTER, M. Law and practice of international commercial arbitration, first edition, 14-16) while others argue in favour of an autonomous interpretation (Dore,I., Arbitration and conciliation under the Uncitral rules : a textual analysis, 91; JARVIN, S., La loi-type de la C.N.U.D.C.I. sur l'arbitrage commercial international, Rev.Arb., 1986, 514).

161. A similar restriction in relation to disputes with Arab countries may be found in the preamble of the Conciliation, Arbitration and Expertise Rules of the Euro-Arab Chambers of Commerce.

162. I.C.C. publication No. 301, Paris, I.C.C., 1977, 10 and 19.

civil and commercial law on transnational transactions. There is no general answer to these questions; specific answers should be sought depending on the issue involved. In those countries which still distinguish between civil and commercial law, commercial law has different rules from civil law on such varied issues as notice of default, joint liability, commercial pledge or statute of limitations[163], questions of evidence, court jurisdiction and bankruptcy law. Subject to substantive rules for transnational relations, there might be a problem of the law applicable to these issues[164]. Notwithstanding autonomous tendencies in post-war legal writing, it seems that domestic laws still might have their say regarding these issues.

63. Furthermore, one might wonder whether the scope of transnational business law might not be extended to all private law relations in their transnational setting[165]. Any such extension would, however, imply that many mandatory rules regarding protection of parties which are considered weaker from an economic or social point of view, would have to be taken into account. Because transnational business law scholars have claimed freedom of contract and room for application of trade usages, customs and general principles of law, they have never proposed extending the scope[166] of transnational business law[167]. One should note, however, that there have rarely been problems in practice regarding conflicts between international business law and these mandatory rules[168].

---

163. For these issues, see FREDERICQ, S., De eenmaking van het burgerlijk recht en het handelsrecht, 109-314.

164. For solutions of these problems in their conflict of laws context, see LOUSSOUARN, Y. and BREDIN, J.D., Droit du commerce international, 130-133 and 175-178.

165. See JUENGER, F., Afterword : the lex mercatoria and the conflict of laws, Lex mercatoria and arbitration, CARBONNEAU, T. (ed.), Dobbs Ferry, Transnational, 1990, 222-223; JUENGER, F., Lex mercatoria und Eingriffsnormen, Festschrift für Fritz Rittner, Munich, Beck, 1991, 245-249.

166. *E.g.* with regard to consumer law. For a sharp criticism on the theory of the lex mercatoria from the point of view of consumers, see KARNELL, G., Will the consumer law field be the Waterloo of the new Lex Mercatoria ?, Svensk Juristtidning, 1981, 427-437.

167. The problem has also been noticed by some French authors (BELLET, P. and MEZGER, E., L'arbitrage international dans le nouveau code de procédure civile, 634; SYNVET, H., case note Court of Appeal Toulouse, October 26, 1982, Clunet, 1984, 612).

168. For one such rare case, see I.C.C. case No. 2558 (Clunet, 1977, 951, case note DERAINS, Y.) where the arbitrator declined jurisdiction despite the transnational character of the employment contract because the arbitral clause was null and void according to the applicable French law.

64. Developments show, however, that some transactions, especially in the consumer, employment and insurance fields, are being excluded from the scope of international business law. In this regard, article 2 (a) CISG[169], article 4 (a) of the Sales Limitation Period Convention and article 2 (c) of the Hague Sales Conflict Convention of December 22, 1986 provide that they do not apply to sales of goods bought for personal, family or household use[170]. Other provisions which may protect consumers and which derogate from general principles for international business relations, may be found in article 5 of the 1980 EEC Convention on the law applicable to contractual obligations, article 3 (2) of the Sales Agency Convention, article 5 (2) ULIS and the articles 13-15 of the Brussels Jurisdiction and Enforcement Convention. A similar tendency exists with regard to individual employment contracts, where specific rules have been provided in article 6 of the 1980 E.E.C. Convention and, quite recently, in articles 5 (1) and 17 (5) of the Brussels[171] and Lugano Jurisdiction and Enforcement Conventions. Finally, articles 7-12 of the Brussels and Lugano Conventions also derogate from the general jurisdiction rules upon which these Conventions are based in relation to insurance contracts[172].

65. In domestic laws, there is also a tendency to stress the specific character of business law. In countries where no distinction exists between civil and commercial law, there still has been, in varying degrees, some need for specific rules for business transactions. However, the main problem has been to define the scope of such rules[173].

In countries which still know the distinction between civil and commercial law, this distinction has often been criticized and scholars have shown that commercial law is gradually developing to business law. This implies that the application of business law no longer depends upon narrow legal criteria such as the identity of the person ("merchant") or the type of transaction involved. Rather, one looks at the organization and methods of

---

169. *Cf.* HONNOLD, J., Uniform law for international sales under the 1980 United Nations Convention, 47; KAHN, P., Aspects récents du droit de la vente commerciale internationale, Trav.com.fr.dr.int.privé, 1980-81, Volume 2, Paris, Centre national de la recherche scientifique, 1983, 76.

170. An exception has been inserted for cases where the seller neither knew nor ought to have known that the goods were bought for any such use.

171. As amended by the San Sebastian Convention.

172. As to the Brussels, Lugano and San Sebastian Conventions, see infra No. 245.

173. In The Netherlands, the distinction between civil and commercial law was abolished in 1934, but to a certain extent, specific rules still exist in relation to business transactions. The definition of "business" has in this respect been challenged as too narrow because it does not encompass all professional activities (see WESSELS, B., Beroep, bedrijf en onderneming, Zwolle, Tjeenk Willink, 1989, 62 pp.).

businesses[174]. In this regard, scholars have questioned whether business law should depend at all upon businessmen's intentions to make profits[175].

66. Another problem which may arise in this context relates to the participation of states, governmental agencies and state enterprises in international trade. The problem is whether these entities may be subject to rules of international business law[176] and, consequently, no longer subject to domestic rules regulating their specific positions. In this regard, the *Galakis*-decision of the French Supreme Court should be mentioned. In this case, the Court held that a state could not invoke its incapacity under the applicable law to conclude an agreement to arbitrate in relation to contracts which conform to the needs and the practices of international trade. By way of analogy, one might argue that a state or state entity could not avoid liability for its obligations by raising defences relating to the non-commercial character of these obligations under the applicable law[177]. This position was taken by an arbitral award of November 18, 1983 in the *Benteler*-case[178] against the argument of the Belgian State that the arbitral

---

174. PIROVANO, A., Introduction critique au droit commercial contemporain, Rev.Trim.Dr.Com., 1985, 220 and 233-242; HAMEL, J., LAGARDE, G. and JAUFFRET, A., Droit commercial, Volume 1, second edition, Paris, Dalloz, 1980, 317-344; SCHMIDT, K., Handelsrecht, second edition, Cologne, Heymanns, 1982, 49-202; FREDERICQ, S., De eenmaking van het burgerlijk recht en het handelsrecht, 545-546; VAN GERVEN, W., Handels- en economisch recht, Volume 1, Ondernemingsrecht, in Beginselen van Belgisch privaatrecht, second edition, Antwerp, Standaard, 1978, 1-12 and 32-34; VAN RYN, J. and HEENEN, J., Principes de droit commercial, I, second edition, Brussels, Bruylant, 1976, 4-323; SCHRANS, G., Poging tot omschrijving van de onderneming als rechtssubject, 2393-2394; SCHRANS, G., Levend en herlevend recht rond het winstoogmerk, 694-700; VAN RYN, J. and HEENEN, J., Esprit de lucre et droit commercial, 334.

175. SCHRANS, G., Poging tot omschrijving van de onderneming als rechtssubject, 2392-2393; SCHRANS, G., Levend en herlevend recht rond het winstoogmerk, T.P.R., 1986, 670-676; VAN RYN, J. and HEENEN, J., Esprit de lucre et droit commercial, R.C.J.B., 1974, 326-334; VAN GERVEN, W., Handels- en Economisch recht, Volume 1, 65-68.

This, however, is not the position of the Belgian Supreme Court which held that intention to make profit is essential for the application of commercial law (Supreme Court, January 19, 1973, Bull.Cass., 1973, 315, R.W., 1972-73, 1381, R.C.J.B., 1974, 321, case note VAN RYN, J. and HEENEN, J.).

176. Two French authors have proposed to apply the *lex mercatoria* to these entities (KAHN, P., Droit international économique, droit du développement, lex mercatoria : concept unique ou pluralisme des ordres juridiques ?, 100; FOUCHARD, P., Quand un arbitrage est-il international ?, 60).

177. *Cf.* VAN DEN BERG, A.J., L'arbitrage commercial en Amérique latine, Rev.Arb., 1979, 126.

178. J.T., 1984, 230, Y.B.COM.ARB. X-1985, 37, J.INT.ARB. 184 (1984).

tribunal had no jurisdiction because of the state's incapacity under Belgian law to conclude agreements to arbitrate. This defence would have been barred according to article 1676 (2) of the Belgian Code of Civil Procedure in combination with article II of the 1961 European International Commercial Arbitration Convention, provided the dispute came within the scope of the 1961 Convention. In this regard, the Belgian State argued that there was no dispute arising from international trade, according to article I (1) a) of the 1961 Convention, because the state's intervention in the transaction was deemed to be non-commercial under Belgian law, since the state acted only in the course of its industrial policy and without any intention to gain profits from the transactions. The arbitral tribunal interpreted the 1961 Convention autonomously without seeing any need to have recourse to qualifications of Belgian law and, therefore, declared itself competent.

67. One may thus note a trend to solve some problems which arise in relation to state participation in international trade in a way different from the solution for analogous but domestic transactions. It may, however, be doubted whether this trend can be generalized, so that states can never invoke civil law rules. It seems that for these problems, the applicable domestic law might still have an important role to play[179]. This should not at all exclude the possibility that the applicable law contains rules to protect *bona fide* contracting parties, or that substantive rules provide corrections against states raising meritless defences. Also, one is faced with a situation where a transnational definition of state enterprises[180] can hardly be given without any reference to domestic law concepts.

68. Furthermore, acts relating to the core of governmental tasks ("acts *iure imperii*") will remain outside the scope of international business law. This will be defined by reference to domestic law[181]. On the other hand, international business law is faced with competition from public interna-

---

179. *Cf.* LOUSSOUARN, Y. and BREDIN, J.D., Droit du commerce international, 130-133 and 175-178.

180. See for instance the definition used by Böckstiegel (Arbitration and state enterprises, Survey on the national and international state of law and practice, Institute of international business law and practice of the International Chamber of Commerce, Deventer, Kluwer, 1984, 14).

181. If the jurisdiction of the court is involved, the *lex fori* might be applicable; *cf.* LOUSSOUARN, Y. and BREDIN, J.D., Droit du commerce international, 132; SUY, E., Immunity of States before Belgian courts and tribunals, ZaöRV, 1967, 660). If the question is related to the merits of the dispute, the applicable law will have to be sought.

tional law, where tendencies exist to apply it to some categories of contracts to which a state enterprise is a party[182].

69. One may conclude from this paragraph that defining international business law is not an easy task. First, its scope has primarily been limited to commercial contracts and commercial arbitration and other fields containing many mandatory rules rarely have been included in its scope. Second, any transnational definition of international business law is faced with problems relating to the distinction which still exists in some countries between civil and commercial law. On the other hand, since recent approaches to describing business law have not yet matured and may vary from country to country[183], they are also hardly useful in defining transnational business law. Finally, international business law is thought of as being restricted to business relations. This raises difficult questions as to its application to non-business transactions such as consumer or employment transactions or relations with state entities. In this respect, one may even question whether business law should have autonomous status, and whether it should not be part of general private law.

I.3.3 *The territorial scope of international business law*

70. Defining international business law also poses the question of its territorial scope. One may ask whether international business law has a universal or regional character, or whether it is limited to transactions between a limited number of countries. This problem has rarely been analyzed and is particularly relevant in relations where quite differing legal systems are involved[184]. From a political point of view, one may ask whether the ambitions of developing countries to build a *New International Economic Order* ("N.I.E.O.")[185] should not be taken into account in the

182. See supra No. 4.

183. Compare with the interpretation of article 1 of the Brussels Jurisdiction and Enforcement Convention in relation to "civil and commercial matters" in the judgment of the EEC Court of Justice of October 14, 1976 (E.C.R., 1976, 1541, contrary opinion Adv. Gen. G. Reischl) and the criticism of Rigaux (Le droit comparé comme science appliquée, Rev.Dr.Int.Comp., 1978, 75). In this case, the Court was particularly concerned about a uniform definition of the Brussels Convention's scope. Therefore, it is hard to draw conclusions from this case as to the possibility of a uniform concept of business law.

184. DAVID, R., Le droit du commerce international: une nouvelle tâche pour les législateurs nationaux ou une nouvelle "lex mercatoria" ?, 20; BELLET, P. and MEZGER, E., L'arbitrage international dans le nouveau code de procédure civile, 633.

185. *Cf.* BÖCKSTIEGEL, K.H., Besondere Aspekte der Wirtschaftsschiedsgerichtsbarkeit mit Parteien aus Entwicklungsländern, NJW, 1979, 1863 and 1867.

process of defining the territorial scope of international business law. These elements are discussed below.

71. The question of the application of international business law in relation to Central and Eastern European countries used to receive divergent answers. The conception of an autonomous *lex mercatoria* was particularly subject to criticism[186]. In practice, an autonomous *lex mercatoria* was for ideological reasons not acceptable to contracting parties from the former socialist countries[187]. Furthermore, these parties were also hesitant[188] because most of their domestic legal systems had detailed rules for foreign trade transactions[189]. Finally, transactions within Comecon

---

186. POPESCU, T., Le droit du commerce international : une nouvelle tâche pour les législateurs nationaux ou une nouvelle "lex mercatoria" ?, in New directions in international trade law, Acts and proceedings of the 2nd Congress on Private Law held by Unidroit, I, Dobbs Ferry, Oceana, 1977, 35 and 44-45; JAKUBOWSKI, J., The autonomy of international trade law and its influence on the interpretation and application of its rules, in Law and international trade, Festschrift für C. Schmitthoff, FABRICIUS, F. (ed.), Frankfurt, Athenäum Verlag, 1973, 209; GOLDSTAJN, A., International conventions and standard contracts as means of escaping from the application of municipal law - I, 106; GOLDSTAJN, A., The new law merchant reconsidered, 181; CAPATINA, O., Doctrine et pratique du droit socialiste roumain en matière de contrat international, 252-253.

187. *Cf.* SZASZ, I., The CMEA Uniform law for international sales, Dordrecht, Nijhoff, 1985, 71-72; TSCHIKVADSE, V. and RUBANOV, A., Some aspects of the unification of the law of sales, 345; CAPATINA, O., Doctrine et pratique du droit socialiste roumain en matière de contrat international, 252-253.

188. *Cf.* SKAPSKI, J., Les obligations en droit international privé dans le cadre du commerce extérieur des pays socialistes, 571; JAKUBOWSKI, J., Some legal aspects of industrial co-operation in East-West relations, Academy of international law, 163 Collected Courses of The Hague, 1979, II, 289 and 291-292.

189. Special rules for foreign trade transactions were drafted because domestic economic rules regulating state-planned economies were unfit for trade on world markets. For these special rules, see RAJSKI, J., Les principes du droit commercial international de certains pays socialistes européens, Academy of international law, Collected Courses of The Hague, 1982, I, 19-30; ENDERLEIN, F., La réglementation juridique des relations économiques internationales en République démocratique allemande, Clunet, 1977, 391; CAPATINA, O., Doctrine et pratique du droit socialiste roumain en matière de contrat international, 254.

These rules in general were applied if referred to by a conflict rule. Choice of law clauses were thus able to avoid their application (MASKOW, D., Organisation et droit du commerce extérieur de la République démocratique allemande, D.P.C.I., 1984, 93; RAJSKI, J., Les principes du droit commercial international de certains pays socialistes européens, 58-69; ENDERLEIN, F., La réglementation juridique des relations économiques internationales en République démocratique allemande, 393-395; KOPAC, L., Le Code tchécoslovaque du commerce international, Clunet, 1967, 795; MASKOW, D., La réglementation des accords de commerce extérieur en République

were governed by international conventions and directives[190] and not by rules of international business law applicable to world markets[191].

Recent political, economic and legal reforms in Central and Eastern Europe will drastically change this picture[192]. At this point, any predictions might be conjectural but one may assume that international business law will also apply in relation to transactions with many of these countries, if the present pace of change is maintained.

72. In some Latin American countries, one may still find a hostile attitude against some of the concepts on which international business law is built. In some of these countries, agreements to arbitrate are not accepted, leading to a refusal to sign the 1958 New York Convention[193]. A similar attitude may be found regarding choice of law and jurisdiction clauses in international contracts, in which contracting parties from these countries are involved[194].

---

démocratique allemande, Rev.Dr.Int.Comp., 1981, 41-42; KALENSKY, P., Les traits essentiels des nouvelles codifications tchécoslovaques du droit du commerce international et du droit international privé, Rev.Int.Dr.Comp., 1964, 568).

190. RAJSKI, J., Les principes du droit commercial international de certains pays socialistes européens, 89-90; JAKUBOWSKI, J., CMEA General conditions of contracts, in The transnational law of international commercial transactions, HORN, N. and SCHMITTHOFF, C. (ed.), Deventer, Kluwer, 1982, 158.

191. *Cf.* MASKOW, D., La réglementation des accords de commerce extérieur en République démocratique allemande, 42; SKAPSKI, J., Les obligations en droit international privé dans le cadre du commerce extérieur des pays socialistes, Academy of international law, 136 Collected Courses of The Hague, 1972, II, 564-570.

192. *E.g.*, MADL, F., Codification of commercial practice in Eastern European countries : lex mercatoria from a Hungarian perspective, in Lex mercatoria and arbitration, CARBONNEAU, T. (ed.), Dobbs Ferry, Transnational, 1990, 195-212.

193. GRIGERA NAON, H., Transnational enterprises under the Pacto Andino and national laws of Latin America, 267 and for recent developments GRIGERA NAON, H., Arbitration in Latin America : overcoming traditional hostility, ARB. INT'L 1989, 137-172; SIQUEIROS, J.L., Arbitral autonomy and national sovereign authority in Latin America, in Lex mercatoria and arbitration, CARBONNEAU, T. (ed.), Dobbs Ferry, Transnational, 1990, 183-193; BÖCKSTIEGEL, K.H., Besondere Aspekte der Wirtschaftsschiedsgerichtsbarkeit mit Parteien aus Entwicklungsländern, 1865; DAVID, R., L'avenir de l'arbitrage, in International arbitration, Liber amicorum for Martin Domke, SANDERS, P. (ed.), The Hague, Nijhoff, 1967, 57; SCHLOSSER, P., Entwicklungstendenzen in Recht und Praxis der internationalen privaten Schiedsgerichtsbarkeit, Karlsruhe, Müller, 1976, 12-13; *but see* VAN DEN BERG, A.J., L'arbitrage commercial en Amérique latine, 197-198.

194. GRIGERA NAON, H., Transnational enterprise under the Pacto Andino and national laws of Latin America, 267; REIMANN, T., Zur Lehre vom "rechtsordnungslosen" Vertrag, 1970, 45; *cf.* HORN, N., Normative problems of a new international economic order, Journal of world trade law, 1982, 344.

Similar hesitations exist in some North African[195] and Arab[196] states. In Asia, the Chinese Law on International Economic Contracts has in some instances excluded choice of law clauses (*e.g.*, mixed joint venture or co-operation agreements)[197] or restricts the freedom of choice to those legal systems which are connected to the contract[198]. The Chinese Law does, however, reserve room for application of transnational trade usages if Chinese law is silent as to the solution of the dispute[199].

73. Finally, attention should be paid to the impact on international business law of efforts, particularly from developing countries, to build a *New International Economic Order*[200]. Philippe Kahn has analyzed this problem and has come to the conclusion that an autonomous *lex mercatoria*

---

195. YAHIA-BACHA, M., Sociétés transnationales et nouvel ordre économique international, 287; FEUER, G. and CASSAN, H., Droit international du développement, 187.
196. KRÜGER, H., Internationales Recht in Kuwait nach den Gesetzes-reformen 1980-1981, RIW, 1983, 808; BÖCKSTIEGEL, K.H., Besondere Aspekte der Wirtschaftsschiedsgerichtsbarkeit mit Parteien aus Entwicklungsländern, 1865; HORN, N., Normative problems of a new international economic order, 344; KRÜGER, H., Verbot von Rechtswahl-, Schieds- und Gerichtsstandsklauseln nach saudi-arabischem Recht, RIW, 1979, 737-741; KRÜGER, H., Probleme des saudi-arabischen internationalen Vertrags- und Schiedsrechts, in Vertragspraxis und Streiterledigung im Wirtschaftsverkehr mit arabischen Staaten, BÖCKSTIEGEL, K.H. (ed.), Cologne, 1981, 61-81; KASSIS, A., Particularités et problèmes de l'arbitrage dans les droits des pays arabes, Rev.Dr.Int.Comp., 1986, 26.
197. BELLSTEDT, C., Das Außenwirtschaftsvertragsgesetz der Volksrepublik China, Zvglrwiss, 1985, 361.
198. REN JISHENG, The basic provisions of foreign contract law of the People's Republic of China, mimeographed paper, s.l., s.d., 17-18; *cf.* HEUSER, R., Die Schiedsgerichtsbarkeit im Wirtschaftsverkehr mit der Volksrepublik China, RIW, 1979, 446.
199. REN JISHENG, The basic provisions of foreign contract law of the People's Republic of China, 18; HORN, N., Das chinesische Außenwirtschaftsvertragsgesetz von 1985, 691.
200. For the official texts of the United Nations institutions on the N.I.E.O., see STERN, B., Le nouvel ordre économique international, Paris, Economica, 1983, 740 pp.

For literature on the N.I.E.O., see RIGAUX, F., Pour un autre ordre international, in Droit économique 2, Institut des hautes études internationales de Paris, Paris, Pedone, 1979, 283; HORN, N., Normative problems of a new international economic order, 338-351; VIRALLY, M., Où en est le droit international du développement ?, Revue juridique et politique, Indépendance et coopération, 1975, 279-290; MAHIOU, A., Les implications juridiques du nouvel ordre économique et le droit international, R.B.D.I., 1976, 421-450.

On the legal character of the N.I.E.O.-instruments, SEIDLHOHENVELDERN, I., International economic soft law, Academy of international law, 163 Collected Courses of The Hague, 1979, II, 185; STERN, B., o.c., XL-XLV; DIEUX, X., Le nouvel ordre économique international et le droit positif, Mélanges offerts à Raymond Vander Elst, Volume 1, Brussels, Nemesis, 1986, 201-207; BERMEJO, R., Vers un nouvel ordre économique international, Fribourg, Editions universitaires, 1982, 141-144.

and N.I.E.O. might be reconciled[201]. In his view, both *lex mercatoria* and N.I.E.O. are legal systems. In some cases, *lex mercatoria* might be preempted by rules of N.I.E.O., but the relationship between the systems should, in general, be one of coexistence and harmony rather than of conflict[202]. In this respect, Kahn seems to suggest that *lex mercatoria* is universally applicable[203]. This implies that Kahn denies the possibility of the N.I.E.O. jeopardizing the autonomy and the territorial scope of the *lex mercatoria*. Legal writing from developing countries seems to have contradicted Kahn's proposition[204]. This is confirmed by developing countries' distrust regarding transnational trade usages and their attempts to provide for restrictions on arbitral and jurisdiction clauses in drafts of codes of conduct[205].

74. One may conclude from this paragraph that the territorial scope of international business law has limits. In some parts of the world, and in varying degrees, there is opposition against universally conceived principles of international business law or a universal and autonomous *lex mercatoria*. Nevertheless, in some cases, factual patterns of uniformity among legal systems and application of international conventions may prove to be almost universal. One may wonder whether this would occur frequently as

---

201. Kahn is reconciling both theories on a jurisprudential basis (*i.e.*, the legal theory of *legal pluralism*). Under this theory, any social group creates legal rules. In this perspective, both the international community of states and the international business community are generating law.
202. KAHN, P., Droit international économique, droit du développement, lex mercatoria : concept unique ou pluralisme des ordres juridiques ?, 104-107.
203. KAHN, P., Droit international économique, droit du développement, lex mercatoria : concept unique ou pluralisme des ordres juridiques ?, 100; see also PAULSSON, J., Le tiers monde et l'arbitrage commercial international, Rev.Arb., 1983, 4-5 and 34-35.
204. GRIGERA NAON, H., Transnational enterprise under the Pacto Andino and national laws of Latin America, 261, 265 and 268-269; SORNARAJAH, M., International commercial arbitration, Singapore, Longman, 1990, 146.
205. HONNOLD, J., Uniform law for international sales under the 1980 United Nations Convention, 51; GRIGERA NAON, H., The UN Convention on contracts for the international sale of goods, in HORN, N. and SCHMITTHOFF, C. (ed.), The transnational law of international commercial transactions, Deventer, Kluwer, 1982, 102 and 123; BONELL, M., La nouvelle Convention des Nations-Unies sur les contrats de vente internationale de marchandises, D.P.C.I., 1981, 16-17; BEGUIN, J., Le développement de la lex mercatoria menace-t-il l'ordre juridique international ?, 509 and 514; HORN, N., Entwicklung des internationalen Wirtschaftsrechts durch Verhaltensrichtlinien, 439-442; FIKENTSCHER, W., United Nations codes of conduct : new paths in international law, AM.J.COMP.L., 1982, 596.

many international unification conventions have a regional character[206] and transnational trade usages are often also only of a merely local, domestic or regional nature.

I.4 Conclusions

75. From this chapter, the following conclusions may be drawn :

i) Roman law *ius gentium* and medieval law merchant may not be invoked as historical precedents of an autonomous system of international business law. Also, it is unlikely that their sources were only of a transnational nature. They were probably unsystematic rules relating to transnational business transactions.

ii) A definition of transnationality is hard to form. This is particularly troublesome for the theory of an autonomous *lex mercatoria*, which seems therefore unable to define its own scope and has to rely on varying definitions which are derived from domestic laws. Other authors also have used a variety of domestic definitions, which shows that even within domestic legal systems it is nearly impossible to define transnationality.

iii) A similar conclusion was reached at the end of the analysis on the business or commercial component of international business law. Here again, transnational definitions are absent and reference to domestic law is needed. This may be relevant in relation to domestic legal systems which still have a distinction between civil and commercial law and in relation to consumers and state-controlled entities. Furthermore, one must note that international business law is particularly detached from domestic laws in fields such as commercial contracts and commercial arbitration, where party autonomy is a guiding principle.

iv) International business law is limited in its territorial scope where it takes on a regional rather than a universal character. Some of its basic principles (*e.g.*, party autonomy) have not been recognized everywhere to the same extent, and have recently come under scrutiny by the proponents

206. See LIMPENS, J., L'étude du droit comparé envisagée comme moyen de rechercher les matières susceptibles d'unification sur le plan international, in Rapports des juristes belges, Vth International Congress of Comparative Law, Brussels, Bruylant, 1958, 95-96; LOUSSOUARN, Y. and BREDIN, J.D., Droit du commerce international, 22.

of a N.I.E.O. Furthermore, in most cases unification efforts at government and industry levels have at best only a regional character.

CHAPTER II

International Business Law and Conflict of Laws

76. Traditionally, international business law problems have been solved through domestic conflict rules applied by the court or the arbitral tribunal seized of the dispute. This approach has come under serious attack (II.1) and raises the question whether the traditional approach should still be the main technique for the resolution of international business law problems where domestic courts (II.2) or arbitral tribunals (II.3) have jurisdiction.

II.1 Criticism regarding the traditional conflict of laws approach

77. Since the end of the nineteen fifties, specialists on international business law have come to criticize traditional conflict of laws. Basically, this criticism is founded on the fact that conflict rules lead to application of national law to international problems. This idea is then often coupled with the postulate that national law has been developed for national and not for international situations and, therefore, may not provide the best answers to international business problems[1]. Some authors have argued, however, that there simply is no evidence that domestic laws are unfit to regulate international commercial transactions[2].

---

1. GOLDMAN, B., Le droit applicable selon la Convention de la B.I.R.D. du 18 mars 1965 pour le règlement des différends relatifs aux investissements entre Etats et ressortisssants d'autres Etats, Investissements étrangers et arbitrage entre Etats et personnes privées, la Convention B.I.R.D. du 18 mars 1965, Paris, Pedone, 1969, 133; KAHN, P., La Convention de La Haye du 1er juillet 1964 portant loi uniforme sur la vente internationale des objets mobiliers corporels, 690 and 698; KAHN, P., L'essor du non-droit dans les relations commerciales internationales et le contrat sans loi, 234; FOUCHARD, P., L'arbitrage commercial international, 544-545; LANGEN, E., Studien zum internationalen Wirtschaftsrecht, 1963, 12; LOUSSOUARN, Y. and BREDIN, J.D., Droit du commerce international, 9; LOUSSOUARN, Y., Cours général de droit international privé, 286; GOLDSTAJN, A., The new law merchant, 12; GOLDSTAJN, A., The new law merchant reconsidered, 171; REIMANN, T., Zur Lehre vom "rechtsordnungslosen" Vertrag, 23-26.
2. HEUZE, V., La réglementation française des contrats internationaux, Paris, GLN Editions, 1990, 102.

78. Criticism has also been expressed as to the technique of conflict of laws. As conflict rules look for connecting points in international situations, they remain blind to underlying policies and the contents of substantive law[3]. Furthermore, it may be not only difficult, but arbitrary to localize some complex international business transactions in one jurisdiction[4]. Finally, conflict of laws is sometimes seen as too complex and unpredictable for international business life[5].

79. Also, conflict rules should be seen in combination with rules on jurisdiction, since the conflict rule is dependent upon the *forum* having jurisdiction over the case. Since conflict of jurisdictions, including the problem of *forum shopping*[6], may be involved, uncertainty may arise over the ultimate outcome of the dispute. Furthermore, there clearly is a perception that judges, however unconsciously in most cases, tend to show some bias against foreign parties[7].

80. Clearly, the function of conflict of laws in resolution of international business disputes has been called into question by these criticisms. These problems will hereafter be discussed in relation to dispute settlement before national courts (II.2) and international commercial arbitration tribunals (II.3).

---

3. One may in this regard refer to the American conflicts revolution led by Currie, Cavers, Ehrenzweig and Leflar; adde KEGEL, G., The crisis of conflict of laws, Academy of international law, Collected Courses of The Hague, 1964, II, 95-268; STEINDORFF, E., Sachnormen im internationalen Privatrecht, Frankfurt, Klostermann, 1958, 288 pp.; RIGAUX, F., Les règles de droit délimitant leur propre domaine d'application, Ann.Dr., 1983, 298; SCHURIG,K., Kollisionsnormen und Sachrecht, 19-20.
4. KAHN, P., L'essor du non-droit dans les relations commerciales internationales et le contrat sans loi, 239; JACQUET, J.M., Principe d'autonomie et contrats internationaux, 121.
5. LOUSSOUARN, Y. and BREDIN, J.D., Droit du commerce international, 8 and 584; LOUSSOUARN, Y., Cours général de droit international privé, 284-285; KOPELMANAS, L., Quelques réflexions sur le colloque de Helsinki de l'Association internationale des sciences juridiques au sujet de la vente internationale, Problèmes de l'inexécution et la force majeure dans les contrats de vente internationale, Travaux du colloque de l'Association internationale des sciences juridiques à Helsinki du 20 au 22 juin 1960, Institutum Iurisprudentiae comparativae Universitatis Helsingiensis, Helsinki, 1969, 309; LUITHLEN, W., Einheitliches Kaufrecht und autonomes Handelsrecht, 17; REIMANN, T., Zur Lehre vom "rechtsordnungslosen" Vertrag, 23-26.
6. *I.e.*, manipulating jurisdictional rules in order to have the case heard in a jurisdiction where the law may be more favorable to the plaintiff.
7. MOTULSKY, H., L'évolution récente en matière d'arbitrage international, 295-296.

II.2 Conflict of laws and national courts

81. This paragraph examines whether, and to what extent, conflict of laws is still important for the resolution of disputes arising in connection to international business contracts. One may also invert this question and ask whether international business problems may be solved without the support of conflict rules.

82. With regard to contractual problems, a traditional distinction is made between choice of law by the parties and, absent such choice, the proper law applicable to the contract. This distinction has developed in two respects. First, choice of law is now quite generally accepted, but made conditional upon some indication that the parties have agreed upon the chosen law. Second, absent such choice, the proper law is determined on the basis of objective elements, without relying on the hypothetical or presumed will of the parties[8].

8. Article 3 (1) EEC Convention on the law applicable to contractual obligation; article 2, second paragraph of the Hague Convention on the law applicable to international sales of goods of June 15, 1955; article 7 (1) of the Hague Convention on the law applicable to international sales of goods of December 22, 1986; article 116 (2) Swiss Law on Conflict of Laws.

II.2.1 *Choice of law in international contracts*

II.2.1.1 Importance of choice of law clauses

83. Choice of law is of paramount importance in international trade[9]. Its main objective is to provide certainty and predictability as to the applicable law and, consequently, the outcome of a dispute[10]. On the other hand, one should not overestimate the importance of a choice of law clause. Since many international contracts do contain extensive clauses regulating a wide variety of problems, the role of the applicable law, apart from its mandatory rules, is fairly limited. The applicable law functions then more as the general framework for the contractual regulation. Choice of law then has a *residual* function[11].

II.2.1.2 Floating contracts

84. When analyzing choice of law, one must first face the question whether any law at all should be applied to an international contract and

---

9. There exists controversy over the question whether choice of law clauses have become more and more frequent during this century (BATIFFOL, H., Les conflits de lois en matière de contrats, Paris, Sirey, 1938, 17; *contra* GAMILLSCHEG, F., Rechtswahl, Schwerpunkt und mutmaßlicher Parteiwille im internationalen Vertragsrecht, AcP, 1958-59, 317-318).

   In relation to choice of law in the nineteenth century, see RANOUIL, V., L'autonomie de la volonté, Paris, PUF, 1980, 165 pp. Choice of law has only been accepted late in the nineteenth century. It was restricted in France under the influence of Niboyet (case note French Supreme Court, February 19, 1930 and January 27 1931, S., 1933, 42). Choice of law revived after the first world war in Germany; during the nineteen sixties it was discredited under the influence of theories on unilateralism and mandatory rules. From the seventies on, choice of law, provided some flexible conditions were met, was hardly contested.

   There is a general lack of data as to the frequency of choice of law clauses in international contracts (for one study, see VERWILGHEN, M. and RAVET-GOBBE, A., Une enquête sur la pratique du contrat international dans les milieux d'affaires belges, 315).

10. Gamillscheg (Rechtswahl, Schwerpunkt und mutmaßlicher Parteiwille im internationalen Vertragsrecht, 316) quite rightly pointed to the economic function of choice of law; it enables businessmen to calculate costs and prices taking into account the risks allocated to them under the applicable law. In this regard, Julian Lew may be cited (Applicable law in international commercial arbitration, 71): "Indeed it is sometimes suggested that a lawyer who fails to ensure that a contract contains a clear choice of law fails his client."

11. The expression comes from P. Kahn (Lex mercatoria et euro-obligations, 237; Etude de quelques problèmes juridiques de la vente internationale de gaz, 281 and Lex mercatoria et pratique des contrats internationaux : l'expérience française, 208).

whether the contract shouldn't be *self-regulatory*, only governed by the clauses of the contract. In jurisprudence, it has long been debated whether the will of the parties or the law was the origin of the binding nature of contract. In this book, this no-winner's debate will not be analyzed, all the more because it is hardly relevant with regard to the basic principles concerning choice of law which are generally accepted. One of these principles is the supremacy of the law over the will of the parties[12]. Although there had been arguments for an *absolute autonomy* of the parties[13], the possibility of *floating contracts* ("contrat sans loi") is now

---

12. For a convincing statement of this principle, see BÖCKSTIEGEL, K.H., Der Staat als Vertragspartner ausländischer Privatunternehmen, 133.

    Proponents of the *lex mercatoria*-theory also have accepted this principle, see GOLDMAN, B., Preface to KAHN, P., La vente commerciale internationale, VIII; GOLDMAN, B., Frontières du droit et "lex mercatoria", 185; GOLDMAN, B., Un "conflictualiste" d'esprit international: M.Henri Batiffol, 331; GOLDMAN, B., Preface to BERLIOZ, G., Le contrat d'adhésion, XVI; GOLDMAN, B., La lex mercatoria dans les contrats et l'arbitrage internationaux : réalité et perspectives, 504-505; KAHN, P., La vente commerciale internationale, 236; KAHN, P., Lex mercatoria et pratique des contrats internationaux : l'expérience française, 194 and 207; LOQUIN, E., L'amiable composition en droit comparé et international, 331; OPPETIT, B., L'engagement d'honneur, 107; DERAINS, Y., case note I.C.C. case No. 2291, Clunet, 1976, 989; LEVEL, P., Le contrat dit sans loi, 211; PEYREFITTE, L., Le problème du contrat dit "sans loi", 120; LALIVE, P., Problèmes relatifs à l'arbitrage international commercial, 649.

13. *E.g.*, Belgian Supreme Court, February 24, 1938, Pas., 1938, I, 66, B.J., 1938, 289, case note PHILONENKO, M., R.C.D.I.P., 1938, 661, critical note WIGNY, A.

generally rejected[14]. Contractual regulation, therefore, does not stand alone but is somehow anchored in the applicable law.

---

14. *International Conventions* : article 3 (4) read with article 8 EEC Convention on the law applicable to contractual obligations (see RIGAUX, F., Examen de quelques questions laissées ouvertes par la Convention de Rome sur la loi applicable aux obligations contractuelles, 316); article 2, third paragraph Hague Convention on the law applicable to international sales of goods of June 15, 1955 (see LOUSSOUARN, Y., La Convention de La Haye sur la loi applicable aux ventes à caractère international d'objets mobiliers corporels, Etudes juridiques offertes à Léon Julliot de la Morandière, Paris, Dalloz, 1964, 320); article 10 (1) Hague Convention on the law applicable to international sales of goods of December 22, 1986. *Case law* : Belgian Supreme Court, February 21, Bull.Cass., 1975, 705, R.W., 1974-75, 2552, R.C.J.B., 1976, 5, case note VAN HECKE, G., R.C.D.I.P., 1976, 660, case note GOTHOT, P.; German Supreme Court, May 28, 1936, JW, 1936, 2058, Clunet, 1936, 951, case note WOLFF, K.; Amin Rasheed Shipping Corp v Kuwait Insurance Co., [1983] 2 All E.R. 891 and 895, [1984] A.C. 50 (House of Lords). *Scholarly writings* : *Belgium* : VAN HECKE, G., Internationaal privaatrecht, first edition, 317; GOTHOT, P., case note Belgian Supreme Court, November 27, 1974 and February 21, 1975, R.C.D.I.P., 1976, 667; *France* : DEBY-GERARD, F., Le rôle de la règle de conflit dans le règlement des rapports internationaux, 176; JACQUET, J.M., Principe d'autonomie et contrats internationaux, 87; MAYER, P., Le mythe de l'"ordre juridique de base" (ou Grundlegung), Le droit des relations économiques internationales, Etudes offertes à Berthold Goldman, Paris, Litec, 1982, 205; LEQUETTE, Y., L'évolution des sources nationales et conventionnelles du droit des contrats internationaux, 193-194; LEBOULANGER, P., Les contrats entre Etats et entreprises étrangères, 203; *The Netherlands* : KOLLEWIJN, R., De conventies voor eenvormig internationaal kooprecht en het internationaal privaatrecht, 150; HONDIUS, E., Standaardvoorwaarden, 317; *Germany* : WENGLER, W., Immunité législative des contrats multinationaux, R.C.D.I.P., 1971, 649-650; ZWEIGERT, K., Verträge zwischen staatlichen und nichtstaatlichen Partnern, in Berichte der deutschen Gesellschaft für Völkerrecht, Volume 5, Karlsruhe, Müller, 1964, 198-199; MünchKomm-Sonnenberger, IPR Einleitung, Munich, Beck, 1983, 48-49; STOLL, J., Vereinbarungen zwischen Staat und ausländischem Investor, 33; SCHLOSSER, P., Das internationale an der internationalen privaten Schiedsgerichtsbarkeit, 857; MUNZBERG, R., Die Schranken der Parteivereinbarungen in der privaten internationalen Schiedsgerichtsbarkeit, 83-84; REIMANN, T., Zur Lehre vom "rechtsordnungslosen" Vertrag, 43; VON HOFFMANN, B., Internationale Handelsschiedsgerichtsbarkeit, 69-71; ROTH, W., Internationales Versicherungsvertragsrecht, Tubingen, Mohr, 1985, 553; *Switzerland* : SCHNITZER, A., Die Einordnung der internationalen Sachverhalte in das Rechtssystem, 299; LALIVE, P., Problèmes relatifs à l'arbitrage international commercial, 640-641; *England* : MANN, F., Lex facit arbitrum, 160 and Internationale Schiedsgerichte und nationale Rechtsordnung, 102; *contra* MERCADAL, B., Ordre public et contrat international, D.P.C.I., 1977, 457-460; MERCADAL, B. and JANIN, P., Les contrats de coopération inter-entreprises, Paris, Lefebvre, 1974, 44; VERHEUL, J.P., Rechtsvinding in het internationaal privaatrecht, Preadvies Calvinistische Juristenvereniging, 1973, 107-108.

II.2.1.3 Theories about choice of law

85. In order to understand choice of law, one should know something about its implications. In this regard, there is a fundamental difference between freedom of contract as it is known in contract law and choice of law in conflict of laws. In contract law, freedom of contract permits parties to depart from the otherwise applicable rules and to develop their own rules, provided their regulation does not conflict with mandatory rules. In conflict of laws, the choice which parties may make, does not relate to one single legal system but to several. Choice of law thus implies that the parties may choose the applicable law among several legal systems. Only the mandatory rules of the chosen law will be applicable; mandatory rules of other jurisdictions may thus be avoided[15]. Positively, choice of law indicates the applicable law; from a negative point of view, it avoids rules of other legal systems[16]. One may thus easily understand that choice of law may be subject to requirements other than freedom of contract[17].

---

15. WENGLER, W., Les principes généraux du droit en tant que loi du contrat, R.C.D.I.P., 1982, 487, also published under the title Allgemeine Rechtsgrundsätze als wählbares Geschäftsstatut ?, ZfRV, 1982, 28 ff.; MAYER, P., Droit international privé, second edition, 551-552; LOUSSOUARN, Y. and BOUREL, P., Droit international privé, 229-230.

    The statement in the text must be qualified in the sense that *lois d'application immédiate* might be applicable (see article 7 (1) of the EEC Convention on the law applicable to contractual obligations).

16. This was well stated in the Alnati-decision of the Dutch Supreme Court of May 13, 1966, N.J., 1967, No. 3, R.C.D.I.P., 1967, 522; see also HORN, N., Das Recht der internationalen Anleihen, 487-491; BRAECKMANS, H., Juridische aspecten van consortiumkredieten in Eurodeviezen, 1985, 367-369.

17. *E.g.*, application of the theory of *fraude à la loi*, application of foreign mandatory rules, the exception of public order and conflict rules which limit choice of law in order to protect consumers and employees (see PATOCCHI, M.P., Règles de rattachement localisatrices et règles de rattachement à caractère substantiel, 121).

    Because these elements had not sufficiently been taken into account, some Dutch authors had expressed criticism towards choice of law (JESSURUN D'OLIVEIRA, H., Preadvies, Internationaal overeenkomstenrecht, Mededelingen van de Vereniging voor internationaal recht, Deventer, Kluwer, 1975, 89-93 and De sluipweg van de partijwil, in Partijinvloed in het internationaal privaatrecht, Deventer, Kluwer, 1974, 13-16; BERVOETS, T., Rechtskeuze, Een rechtstheoretisch onderzoek van het beginsel der rechtskeuze in het internationaal privaatrecht, Deventer, Kluwer, 1974, 41).

86. In this respect, the distinction between *materiellrechtliche Verweisung* and *kollisionsrechtliche Verweisung* may be cited[18]. The latter authorizes parties to determine the applicable law; according to the former, within the applicable law parties may have freedom of contract including the possibility to *incorporate* provisions of foreign law into their contract to the extent permitted by the applicable law.

Having clarified the implications of choice of law, we may turn to its nature and ramifications. Basically, three theories have been proposed : A. The will of the parties as expressed in the choice of law clause as an exclusive connecting point (subjective theory); B. The will of the parties as expressed in the choice of law clause as one of the relevant connecting points; C. Choice of law as a transnational substantive rule. These theories will be discussed hereafter.

A. Subjective theory

87. This theory views the will of the parties, as indicated in the choice of law clause, as the *only* connecting point to localize an international contract[19]. Because of the exclusive importance attached to the parties' will, one may call this conception the subjective theory on choice of law. At present, this theory is dominant and had been accepted by the Supreme

---

18. *Germany* : MELCHIOR, G., Die Grundlagen des deutschen internationalen Privatrechts, Berlin, de Gruyter, reprint 1971, 499-500; NUSSBAUM, A., Deutsches internationales Privatrecht, Aalen, Scientia, reprint 1974, 247; NEUHAUS, P.H., Die Grundbegriffe des internationalen Privatrechts, 253; *France* : BATIFFOL, H., Subjectivisme et objectivisme dans le droit international privé des contrats, BATIFFOL, H., Choix d'articles, Paris, LGDJ, 1976, 255, originally in Mélanges Jacques Maury, Paris, Dalloz, 1960, I, 39 ff.; *Belgium* : VAN HECKE, G., Problèmes juridiques des emprunts internationaux, 62; *Switzerland* : SCHÖNENBERGER, W., Kommentar zum schweizerischen Zivilgesetzbuch, Volume V 1a, Allgemeine Einleitung, Zurich, Schulthess, 1973, 69-70; *The Netherlands* : STRUYCKEN, A., Internationaal privaatrecht, Contractenrecht, VI, Deventer, Kluwer, 353; *England* : DICEY, A. and MORRIS, J., The conflict of laws, Volume 2, 758-761; CHESHIRE, G. and NORTH, P., Private international law, 202-203; *Italy* : BONELL, M., The law applicable to international commercial contracts : the standpoint of Italian doctrine and case-law, 14.
19. JACQUET, J.M., Principe d'autonomie et contrats internationaux, 228; PATOCCHI, P.M., Règles de rattachement localisatrices et règles de rattachement à caractère substantiel, 120.

Courts of Belgium[20], France[21], Germany[22], The Netherlands[23], Switzerland[24] before it became statutory law[25] and endorsed by article 3 (1) of the EEC Convention on the law applicable to contractual obligations.

88. From a logical point of view, it is difficult to argue that an international contract only becomes binding under rules of law chosen by the parties in that same contract[26]. This circular objection was solved in Germany and Switzerland by making a distinction between the main contract and the choice of law clause. The main contract is then governed by the law indicated by the choice of law while the *lex fori* will determine whether and to what extent choice of law is possible[27]. In this respect, various issues

---

20. February 24, 1938, Pas., 1938, I, 66, B.J., 1938, 289, case note PHILONENKO, M., R.C.D.I.P.,1938, 661, case note WIGNY, A.
21. December 5, 1910, S., 1911, 129, case note LYON-CAEN, C.
22. See MARTINY, D., Bestimmung des Schuldstatuts, in REITHMANN, C., Internationales Vertragsrecht, third edition, Cologne, Schmidt, 1980, 14-15.
23. May 13, 1966, N.J., 1967, No. 3, opinion Adv.Gen. Minkenhof and case note H.B., R.C.D.I.P., 1967, 522, case note STRUYCKEN, A.
24. See PATOCCHI, P.M., Règles de rattachement localisatrices et règles de rattachement à caractère substantiel, 106.
25. Article 116 Swiss Law on Conflict of Laws; see PATOCCHI, P.M., Règles de rattachement localisatrices et règles de rattachement à caractère substantiel, 106.
26. In France and Belgium, the formation of contract has traditionally been connected to the same law as the laws applicable to its interpretation and performance (Belgian Supreme Court, February 21, 1975, Bull.Cass., 1975, 705, R.W., 1974-75, 2552, R.C.J.B., 1976, 5, case note VAN HECKE, G., R.C.D.I.P., 1976, 660, case note GOTHOT, P.; French Supreme Court, December 5, 1910, S., 1911, 129). In Switzerland, from 1906 till the *Chevalley*-decision of the Supreme Court of February 12, 1952 (ATF 78 II 74, Die Rechtsprechung des Bundesgerichts im internationalen Privatrecht, Volume II, Zurich, Schulthess, 1977, 37, Ann.suisse Dr.Int., 1953, 299), formation of contracts was governed by the law of the place where the contract was formed while the chosen law applied to other contractual problems (PATOCCHI, M.P., Règles de rattachement localisatrices et règles de rattachement à caractère substantiel, 58-59).
27. *Switzerland* : Supreme Court, August 31, 1953, ATF 79 II 295, Ann.suisse Dr.Int., 1954, 274; Supreme Court, May 18, 1965, ATF 91 II 248, Ann.suisse Dr.Int., 1965, 283, Clunet, 1970, 417; VISCHER, F., Internationales Vertragsrecht, Bern, Stämpfli, 1962, 24; PATOCCHI, P.M., Règles de rattachement localisatrices et règles de rattachement à caractère substantiel, 101; SCHWANDER, I., Zur Rechtswahl im IPR des Schuldvertragsrecht, Festschrift für Max Keller, Zurich, Schulthess, 1989, 474; SIEHR, K., Die Parteiautonomie im internationalen Privatrecht, Festschrift für Max Keller, Zurich, Schulthess, 1989, 486 and 493; *France* : LEVEL, P., Le contrat dit sans loi, 217-218; *Germany* : GAMILLSCHEG, F., Rechtswahl, Schwerpunkt und mutmaßlicher Parteiwille im internationalen Vertragsrecht, 306 and especially KRONSTEIN, H., The law of international cartels, Ithaca, Cornell University Press, 1973, 235; *Belgium* : WIGNY, P., La règle de conflit applicable aux contrats, 687-688; VAN HECKE, G., Contracts subject to international or transnational law, 304;

will be determined by the *lex fori* (*e.g.*, the conflict rule and its scope, the problem of qualification[28], the possibility of *renvoi*[29] and *dépeçage*[30], the problem of preliminary questions, application of *fraude à la loi*, the exception of public order, *ex officio*-application of conflict rules by the judge, evidence of foreign law). Thus, choice of law is generally embedded in the conflict of laws of the *lex fori*[31].

VANDER ELST, R., L'autonomie de la volonté en droit international privé français et belge, 986; *England* : PIERCE, D., Post-formation choice of law in contract, Mod.L.Rev., 1987, 192-193; THOMSON, A., A different approach to choice of law in contract, Mod.L.R., 1980, 652; *The Netherlands* : VAN BRAKEL, S., Grondslagen en beginselen van Nederlandsch internationaal privaatrecht, Zwolle, Tjeenk Willink, 1950, 214.

Some authors did consider the distinction as artificial (BATIFFOL, H., Les conflits de lois en matière de contrats, 46; HELLEMA, A., Beschouwingen over de aanknopingsleer in het internationaal privaatrecht, 71). However, it makes clear that the *lex fori* has a great impact upon choice of law and that there is no need to rely on notions such as *Grundlegung* and *ordre juridique de base* when national courts must determine the choice of law clause's ramifications.

28. See VISCHER, F., Internationales Vertragsrecht, 68.
29. Article 15 of the EEC Convention on the law applicable to contractual obligations as well as article 15 of the 1986 Hague Convention on the law applicable to international sales of goods have excluded *renvoi*. This is also the position of the Swiss Supreme Court (decision of October 21, 1955, ATF 81 II 391, Ann.suisse Dr.Int., 1957, 273; SCHÖNENBERGER, W., Kommentar zum schweizerischen Zivilgesetzbuch, Volume V, 1a, 71; PATOCCHI, M.P., Règles de rattachement localisatrices et règles de rattachement à caractère substantiel, 287).
30. The law chosen by the parties may relate to the whole or a part of the contract. The latter is called *dépeçage*. The validity and usefulness of *dépeçage* has been subject to debate. The 1955 Hague Convention on the law applicable to international sales of goods had rejected it (HELLEMA, A., Beschouwingen over de aanknopingsleer in het internationaal privaatrecht, 72 and 75-76; DE WINTER, L., De eenvormige wet inzake de internationale koop van roerende lichamelijke zaken en het internationaal privaatrecht, 840). More important, article 3 (1) of the EEC Convention on the law applicable to contractual obligations as well as article 7 (1) of the 1986 Hague Convention on the law applicable to international sales of goods have accepted it (see EKELMANS, M., Le dépeçage du contrat dans la Convention de Rome du 19 juin 1980 sur la loi applicable aux obligations contractuelles, Mélanges offerts à Raymond Vander Elst, Volume 1, Brussels, Nemesis, 1986, 243-253). The Swiss Law on Conflict of Laws has deliberately chosen not to regulate the problem (Message concernant une loi fédérale sur le droit international privé du 10 novembre 1982, 150). For a further discussion on *dépeçage*, see infra No. 110.
31. SCHULZE (Die Kodifikation des Vertragsstatuts im internationalen Privatrecht, 31-32) quite rightly makes the distinction between the law applicable to the choice of law clause and the requirements of the *lex fori* as to the possibility of choice of law. Similarly, Jacquet has introduced the concept of a *ordre juridique cadre* to express the same idea (Principe d'autonomie et contrats internationaux, 98 and 101).

89. Controversy exists as to the conflict rule of the *lex fori* which connects the choice of law clause to the applicable law[32]. A first theory would apply the *lex fori* to the choice of law clause[33]. The disadvantage of this theory is that it is too dependent on rules of jurisdiction determining which court may hear the case and, therefore, it may frustrate the intentions of the parties[34].

90. According to a second line of thought, the law applicable to the contract absent choice of law should be applied to the choice of law clause[35]. The disadvantage of this theory is that it leads back to the uncertainties which the parties, through their choice of law clause, wanted to avoid.

91. A third view would apply the chosen law to the choice of law clause[36].

---

32. For a summary, see OTTO, H.H., Allgemeine Geschäftsbedingungen und internationales Privatrecht, Göttingen, Verlagsgesellschaft für Wirtschafts- und Steuerrecht, 1984, 170-173; HAAK, W.E., Preadvies, in Internationaal overeenkomstenrecht, Mededelingen van de Nederlandse Vereniging voor internationaal recht, Deventer, Kluwer, 1975, 49.
33. Swiss Supreme Court, March 30, 1976, ATF 102 II 143; German Supreme Court, May 30, 1983, NJW, 1983, 2772, DB, 1983, 2759 (rev'd German Supreme Court, December 15, 1986, DB, 1987, 882, RIW, 1987, 215); WIGNY, P., La règle de conflit applicable aux contrats, 687-688; MOSER, R., Vertragsabschluß, Vertragsgültigkeit und Parteiwille im internationalen Obligationenrecht, St.Gallen, Verlag der Fehr'schen Buchhandlung, 1948, 182-183; RAAPE, L., Internationales Privatrecht, fourth edition, Berlin, Vahlen, 1955, 433-438; JAFFEY, A., Offer and acceptance and related questions in the English conflict of laws, INT'L & COMP.L.Q., 1975, 606 and 613.
34. BATIFFOL, H., Les conflits de lois en matière de contrats, 46; HELLEMA, A., Beschouwingen over de aanknopingsleer in het internationaal privaatrecht, 71.
35. SCHNITZER, A., Handbuch des internationalen Privatrecht, I, fourth edition, Basle, Verlag für Recht und Gesellschaft, 1957, 177-178; Chitty on contracts, I, twenty-fifth edition, London, Sweet & Maxwell, 1983, 1173.
36. Article 3 (4) read with article 8 EEC Convention on the law applicable to contractual obligations; article 2 (3) 1955 Hague Convention on the law applicable to international sales of goods; article 10 (1) and (3) 1986 Hague Convention on the law applicable to international sales of goods; also so article 116 (2) Swiss Law on Conflict of Laws; German Supreme Court, December 15, 1986, DB, 1987, 882, RIW, 1987, 215; VISCHER, F. and VON PLANTA, A., Internationales Privatrecht, second edition, Basle, Helbing & Lichtenhahn, 1982, 170; SIEHR, K., Die Parteiautonomie im internationalen Privatrecht, 493; MANN, F., Die Gültigkeit des Rechtswahl- und Gerichtsstandsklausel und das internationale Privatrecht, NJW, 1984, 2741; MünchKomm-Martiny, Volume 7, Munich, Beck, 1983, 537; FIRSCHING, K., Internationales Schuldrecht, I, 376-377; SOERGEL/KEGEL, Bürgerliches Gesetzbuch, Volume 8, Stuttgart, Verlag Kohlhammer, 1983, 229; SANDROCK, O. and STEINSCHULTE, F.P., Die Rechtswahl nach deutschem Kollisionsrecht, in SANDROCK, O., Handbuch der internationalen Vertragsgestaltung, Volume 1,

This conception has the advantage that the same law applicable to the main contract also applies to the choice of law clause[37]. However, this theory may lead to inequitable consequences if some doubt exists as to the consent of one of the parties regarding the chosen law. Recent international conventions have thus provided an exception to the rule stated above in order to protect one party against consent *by surprise*; a party may, although he is bound according to the chosen law, rely on the law of the country of his habitual residence to establish that he did not consent[38].

92. Since the rules of conflict of laws of the *lex fori* provide the general framework for choice of law, one may question whether the *lex fori* contains specific requirements as to choice of law. First, one may wonder whether the parties may choose a law that, but for the choice of law clause, has no relation to the contract. § 1-105 of the Uniform Commercial Code ("UCC") in this regard requires that there be a reasonable relation between the contract and the state whose law has been chosen[39]. The state of New York, however, has provided for a derogation from § 1-105 UCC regarding transactions having a value of more than $ 250.000[40]. The *reasonable relation*-requirement has particularly been addressed in Switzerland. In the *Adès*-case of March 23, 1965, the Swiss Supreme Court put forward the requirement that the parties, when choosing the applicable law, should have a legitimate interest[41]. However, the Swiss Law on Conflict of Laws has

---

Heidelberg, Verlagsgesellschaft Recht und Wirtschaft, 1980, 57-58; BATIFFOL, H. and LAGARDE, P., Droit international privé, Volume II, seventh edition, Paris, LGDJ, 1983, 271; BATIFFOL, H., Les conflits de lois en matière de contrats, 340; SCHÖNENBERGER, W., Kommentar zum schweizerischen Zivilgesetzbuch, Volume V, 1a, 71; LIBLING, D., Formation of international contracts, Mod.L.R., 1979, 172-181.

37. SANDROCK, O., Die Bedeutung des Gesetzes zur Neuregelung des internationalen Privatrechts für die Unternehmenspraxis, 850.

38. Article 3 (4) read with article 8 EEC Convention; article 10 (1) and (3) 1986 Hague Convention on the law applicable to international sales of goods; see also article 123 Swiss Law on Conflict of Laws.

39. See also § 187(2) Second Restatement, Conflict of laws.

40. Exceptions do exist for employment contracts, consumer transactions and the mandatory rules of § 1-105 (2) UCC; see further EBENROTH, C. and TSESCHLOCK, R., Rechtswahlklauseln in internationalen Finanzierungsverträgen nach New Yorker Recht, IPRax, 1988, 199.

41. Swiss Supreme Court, March 23, 1965, ATF 91 II 44, Ann.suisse Dr.Int., 1965, 281, Clunet, 1970, 415, RabelsZ, 1966, 329, RIW, 1965, 380; see AUBERT, J.F., Les contrats internationaux dans la doctrine et la jurisprudence suisse, 34; SCHÖNENBERGER, W., Kommentar zum schweizerischen Zivilgesetzbuch, Volume V, 1a, 70; DUTOIT, B., KNOEPFLER, F., LALIVE, P. and MERCIER, P., Répertoire de droit international privé suisse, Volume 1, 30; PATOCCHI, M.P., Règles de rattachement localisatrices et règles de rattachement à caractère substantiel, 59.

not codified this requirement and article 116 of the Law may be interpreted as an implicit abolition of this requirement[42]. In many other countries, no statutory or judicial restrictions on choice of law regarding a reasonable relation-test seem to exist, nor have any such restrictions been proposed[43]. The same position may be found in international conventions such as the EEC Convention on the law applicable to contractual obligations and the 1955 Hague Convention on the law applicable to international sales of goods[44].

To the extent that these discussions are relevant for international business practice, one may approve[45] of the development which does not permit a vague reasonable relation-requirement to create uncertainty as to the applicable law. Furthermore, since localization of the transaction is no longer to be understood in a purely geographical sense, this development permits a choice of law which is neutral to both parties, which has specific expertise regarding certain problems[46], which is generally conceived as

---

42. Message concernant une loi fédérale sur le droit international privé du 10 novembre 1982, 142; PATOCCHI, M.P., Règles de rattachement localisatrices et règles de rattachement à caractère substantiel, 75; SCHNYDER, A.K., Das neue IPR-Gesetz, 96.
43. *Belgium* : see LIENARD-LIGNY, M., L'autonomie de la volonté face aux lois impératives dans les contrats internationaux, Ann.Fac.Dr.Liège, 1968, 8-9; *contra* VANDER ELST, R., L'autonomie de la volonté en droit international privé français et belge, 989; *France* : JACQUET, J.M., Principe d'autonomie et contrats internationaux, 228; *Germany* : GAMILLSCHEG, F., Rechtswahl, Schwerpunkt und mutmaßlicher Parteiwille im internationalen Vertragsrecht, 309-312. In *England*, one may doubt whether any such restrictions exist; see Vita Food Products Inc. v. Unus Shipping Co.Ltd., [1939] A.C. 277, [1939] 1 All.E.R. 521 (Privy Council); COLLINS, L., Arbitration and the law governing contractual relations : an introductory report on the position in England, 60; Benjamin's sale of goods, third edition, London, Sweet & Maxwell, 1987, 1522; DICKSON, B., The "de-internationalizing" of private international law in the United Kingdom, Mélanges offerts à Raymond Vander Elst, Volume 1, Brussels, Nemesis, 1986, 190; but see CHESHIRE, G. and NORTH, P., Private international law, 202.

    Furthermore, the case where no reasonable relation exists between the chosen law and the transaction, seems to be rather exceptional (*cf.* MANN, F., The law governing state contracts, 21 Brit.Y.B.Int.L., 1944, 19).
44. VON CAEMMERER, E., Measures for unifying the rules on choice of law, Unification of the law governing international sales of goods, HONNOLD, J. (ed.), International Association of Legal Science, Paris, Dalloz, 1966, 315; PATOCCHI, M.P., Règles de rattachement localisatrices et règles de rattachement à caractère substantiel, 85.
45. SIEHR, K., Die Parteiautonomie im internationalen Privatrecht, 497-498; *contra* VISCHER, F., Internationales Vertragsrecht, 52-53.
46. *E.g.*, English law in relation to admiralty or insurance contracts, English law or the law of New York in relation to financial transactions.

well adapted to international contracts[47] or which is applicable to related contracts. Abuses eventually may be corrected through other mechanisms such as *fraude à la loi* or application of mandatory rules. Contracting parties acting in good faith should, however, be ensured that their choice of law will be upheld.

93. Second, the conflict of laws of the *lex fori* will determine whether and to what extent the parties may insulate the contract from any changes in the chosen law which take place after the formation of the contract. This phenomenon may be called *contract freeze* and contract clauses to that effect are being called *stabilization clauses*. As a matter of principle, the validity of contract freeze will be determined by transitory provisions of the applicable law as indicated by the conflict of laws of the *lex fori*[48].

94. Thirdly, the *lex fori* will determine whether the parties[49] may change the applicable law either by choosing the applicable law after the contract was formed without a choice of law or by substituting another law for the chosen law. This problem of *post-formation choice of law* has arisen primarily in Switzerland, Germany and recently also in England[50]. No

---

47. *E.g.*, Swiss contract law (KOPELMANAS, L., La procédure arbitrale dans les contrats internationaux de travaux publics, Arbitrage commercial, Essais in memoriam Eugenio Minoli, Rome, Associazione italiana per l'arbitrato, 1974, 276).
48. VISCHER, F., Internationales Vertragsrecht, 80-81; see also VISCHER, F., Veränderungen des Vertragsstatuts und ihre Folgen, Festschrift für Max Keller, Zurich, Schulthess, 1989, 552-553. Some authors have doubted the validity of stabilization clauses (VAN HECKE, G., Internationaal privaatrecht, first edition, 316-317; RIGAUX, F., Droit international privé, II, Brussels, Larcier, 1979, 375; KLEIN, F.E., intervention during the discussions, Basle symposium on the law governing contractual obligations, KLEIN, F.E. and VISCHER, F. (ed.), Basle, Helbing & Lichtenhahn, 1983, 167); *contra* LOUIS-LUCAS, P., La liberté contractuelle en droit international privé français, Mélanges en l'honneur de Jean Dabin, II, Brussels, Bruylant, 1963, 758; SANDROCK, O. and STEINSCHULTE, F.P., Grundfragen des internationalen Vertragsrecht : die kollisionsrechtliche Anknüpfung von Schuldverträgen, 17 and SANDROCK, O., "Versteinerungsklauseln" in Rechtswahlvereinbarungen für internationale Handelsverträge, Ius inter nationes, Festschrift für Riesenfeld, Heidelberg, 1983, 220-222; *compare* article 8 of the 1991 Basle Resolution of the Institute of international law (IPRax., 1991, 430).
49. This problem should be distinguished from contractual clauses which authorize one of the parties to change the applicable law. These clauses seem to be governed by the *lex contractus*.
50. *Switzerland* : Supreme Court, August 31, 1953, ATF 79 II, 295, Ann.suisse Dr.Int., 1954, 274; VISCHER, F., Internationales Vertragsrecht, 84-85; SIEHR, K., Die Parteiautonomie im internationalen Privatrecht, 500; *Germany* : GAMILLSCHEG, F., Rechtswahl, Schwerpunkt und mutmaßlicher Parteiwille im internationalen Vertragsrecht, 314-315; *England* : Armar Shipping Co. Ltd. v. Caisse Algérienne d'Assurance et Reassurance,

single answer to this issue existed in the EEC Member States party to the EEC Convention on the law applicable to contractual obligations[51]. Article 3 (2) of the Convention has given a uniform answer authorizing post-formation choice of law, provided it does not prejudice the formal validity of the contract and the rights of third parties[52].

95. Finally, it also will depend upon the *lex fori* whether legal systems or rules other than national ones may be chosen (*e.g.*, public international law, natural justice, no longer existing legal systems[53] or lex mercatoria)[54]. Furthermore, the validity and consequences of other choice of law techniques[55] are also determined by the *lex fori*.

B. Objective theory

96. A second theory on choice of law primarily developed by Batiffol[56], sees the will of the parties as expressed in their choice of law clause as an important, albeit not exclusive, element in the determination of the applicable law. According to this theory, a judge should take all elements into account, which implies that he may override the parties choice of law if other, more important, elements point in the direction of another law. This theory thus views the choice of law clause not as a legal act, but as a factual element in the process of searching for the applicable law[57]. Because one is also looking to objective elements to localize the contract, this theory may be called the objective theory on choice of law. Because of its approach, the objective theory has consequences different from the

---

[1981] 1 All.E.R. 498 (Court of Appeal); BRIGGS, A., The validity of "floating" choice of law and jurisdiction clauses, Lloyd's Mar.& Com.L.Q., 1986, 508-518; PIERCE, D., Post-formation choice of law in contract, Mod.L.Rev., 1987, 176-201; DANILOWICZ, V., "Floating" choice-of-law clauses and their enforceability, INT'L LAW., 1986, 1005-1013.

51. GIULIANO, M. and LAGARDE, P., Report on the Convention on the Law Applicable to Contractual Obligations, O.J., C 282, October 31, 1980, 18.
52. See also article 7 (2) of the 1986 Hague Convention on the law applicable to international sales of goods and article 116 (3) Swiss Law on Conflict of Laws.
53. ZWEIGERT (Verträge zwischen staatlichen und nichtstaatlichen Partnern, 196-197) has rejected such choice as too impractical.
54. See infra Nos. 108-111.
55. *E.g.*, cumulative clauses where the parties choose to apply two or more laws to their contract, alternative clauses where the one law in the absence of the other law is applicable, residual clauses where the chosen law only applies to the extent that the contractual regulation does not suffice.
56. In *The Netherlands*, this theory has been defended by Kollewijn (Handelingen Nederlandse Juristenvereniging, 1947, II, 108).
57. BATIFFOL, H., Les conflits de lois en matière de contrats, 340.

subjective theory. First, more emphasis will be placed on the requirement of a reasonable relation between chosen law and contract[58]. Furthermore, under the objective theory *renvoi* will more readily be accepted[59] and *dépeçage*[60] and contract freeze[61] rejected.

C. Choice of law as a transnational substantive rule

97. In France, some authors have departed from traditional conflict of laws analysis and have characterized choice of law as a *transnational substantive rule*. This means that choice of law is directly authorized, irrespective of rules of conflict, provided the contract is transnational[62]. The *lex fori* thus unilaterally[63] recognizes choice of law even if a conflict rule would lead to a legal system which forbids or restricts choice of law. In the view of the proponents of this theory, choice of law is not a legal act aimed at localizing a contract in a certain legal system, but rather an act which directly points to the applicable law[64]. The consequences of this theory may be as follows. First, it is clear that *renvoi* is excluded since the chosen law is directly applicable and not by virtue of a conflict rule. Second, the contract is not localized so that there will no requirement as

---

58. BATIFFOL, H., Les conflits de lois en matière de contrats, 52; BATIFFOL, H., La loi appropriée au contrat, Le droit des relations économiques internationales, Etudes offertes à Berthold Goldman, Paris, 1982, 4-5.
59. BATIFFOL, H., Les conflits de lois en matière de contrats, 47.
60. BATIFFOL, H., Les conflits de lois en matière de contrats, 66.
61. BATIFFOL, H., Les conflits de lois en matière de contrats, 68; BATIFFOL, H., Conflict avoidance in European law, 577-578.
62. DEBY-GERARD, F., Le rôle de la règle de conflit dans le règlement des rapports internationaux, 255 and 257; LEBOULANGER, P., Les contrats entre Etats et entreprises étrangères, 231-232; LEQUETTE, Y., L'évolution des sources nationales et conventionnelles du droit des contrats internationaux, 193; HEUZE, V., La réglementation française des contrats internationaux, 143. In *The Netherlands*, Lemaire endorsed this view (Nederlands internationaal privaatrecht (Hoofdlijnen), 255-256).

    Oppetit (Le développement des règles matérielles, Com.fr.dr.int.privé, meeting of November 23, 1985, mimeographed paper, Paris, 1985, 16) did state that choice of law may be qualified as a transnational substantive rule under article 3(1) of the EEC Convention on the law applicable to contractual obligations. This proposition is doubtful.
63. See GOTHOT, P., La méthode unilatéraliste face au droit international privé des contrats, Trav.Com.fr.dr.int.privé, 1975-1977, Parijs, Centre national de la recherche scientifique, 201-219.
64. See GAMILLSCHEG, F., Rechtswahl, Schwerpunkt und mutmaßlicher Parteiwille im internationalen Vertragsrecht, 315-316; DE BOER, T., Subjectieve verwijzing : anomalie of grondbeginsel ?, 56-57; MAYER, P., Droit international privé, second edition, 550-551.

to a relation between the chosen law and the contract[65]. Other implications of this theory remain unclear. The theory has been attacked by Patocchi on the basis that it leads to unlimited party autonomy and does not conform to the prevailing theory (*i.e.*, the subjective theory)[66]. This criticism does not attack the basis of the theory as much as its lack of completeness.

Quite recently, E. Lorenz made an analysis which is comparable to the conception of choice of law as a transnational substantive rule. In his opinion, choice of law has become much more substantive than localizing, since the parties tend to look to the content of the applicable rules rather than to the localization of the transaction. Therefore, choice of law should no longer depend upon the contract having an international character but should rather look to the consequences and scope of the contract[67].

D. Assessment

98. One may now try to assess the different theories on choice of law. The prevailing subjective theory really does not fit into the tradition of conflict of laws as developed by Von Savigny, as it can easily lead to the application of a law that is insufficiently related to the transaction[68]. Furthermore, the consequences of the subjective theory, are hardly compatible with its theoretical framework. It seems that the subjective theory is pursuing a liberal policy in favour of choice of law rather than consistently staying within the tradition of conflict of laws.

99. The objective theory, on the other hand, exhibits greater consistency between theoretical basis and its consequences. However, this theory simply is out of line with present-day conflict of laws as it has developed from international conventions, statutes, case law and legal literature.

---

65. DEBY-GERARD, F., Le rôle de la règle de conflit dans le règlement des rapports internationaux, 266-272.

66. PATOCCHI, P.M., Règles de rattachement localisatrices et règles de rattachement à caractère substantiel, 120.

67. LORENZ, E., Die Rechtswahlfreiheit im internationalen Schuldvertragsrecht, RIW, 1987, 569-571.

68. DE BOER, T., Subjectieve verwijzing : anomalie of grondbeginsel ?, 57 and 67-71; BERVOETS, T., Rechtskeuze, Een rechtstheoretisch onderzoek van het beginsel der rechtskeuze, 35; MINCKE, W., Die Parteiautonomie : Rechtswahl oder Ortswahl ?, IPRax 1985, 315-317; *contra* PATOCCHI, M.P., Règles de rattachement localisatrices et règles de rattachement à caractère substantiel, 120 and 232-233 who expands the notion of localization.

100. Moreover, both theories have an important drawback, in that they are based upon the proposition that parties choosing the applicable law try to localize the transaction rather than to choose the applicable substantive rules. From an intellectual point of view, choice of law as a transnational substantive rule is thus more appealing. However, the implications of this theory have not been sufficiently elaborated. As a result, respect for the parties' choice is given too much weight and the role of choice of law (*i.e.*, a legitimate technique to avoid mandatory rules of the law applicable absent such choice[69]) is underestimated. Therefore, the legal systems containing the transnational substantive rule will have to provide for the conditions of its existence and validity as well as its consequences.

101. By way of general conclusion, one may thus say that the subjective theory of choice of law is grounded in pragmatism[70]. A sounder theoretical basis might be found in the theory of transnational substantive rules, but the implications of this theory remain unclear.

II.2.2 *Proper law absent choice of law*

102. Absent an express choice of law[71], the conflict of law rules of the *lex fori* will determine the law applicable to international contracts[72]. National laws increasingly tend to localize contracts in an objective way and, thus, pay less attention to the hypothetical will of the parties[73]. Furthermore, one may note a development from *closed* to *open conflict rules*. Traditional closed conflict rules, such as the *lex loci conclusionis* (the law of the place of contract formation) or the *lex loci solutionis* (the law of the place of contract performance) which directly lead to the determination of the

---

69. See supra No. 85.
70. *Cf.* BERVOETS, T., Rechtskeuze, Een rechtstheoretisch onderzoek van het beginsel der rechtskeuze, 41; DE BOER, T., Subjectieve verwijzing : anomalie of grondbeginsel ?, 67 and 70-71; KEGEL, G., Internationales Privatrecht, 379; DEELEN, J., Rechtskeuze in het Nederlands internationaal contractenrecht, Amsterdam, Scholtema & Holkema, 1965, 242; SIEHR, K., Die Parteiautonomie im internationalen Privatrecht, 498 and 509.
71. Parties may forget to provide for a choice of law clause or may not agree on the applicable law.
72. Likewise regarding choice of law, the conflict of laws of the *lex fori* will provide answers to a variety of issues such as the scope of the applicable law, preliminary questions, *fraude à la loi*, the exception of public order, *dépeçage* (see article 4 (1), last sentence EEC Convention, *ex officio*-application of conflict rules by the judge, evidence on foreign law).
73. German Supreme Court, October 9, 1986, WM, 1987, 77,DB, 1987,267, RIW, 1987, 148, AG, 1987, 124.

applicable law, have been replaced by open rules. In case of open-ended conflict rules, further factual and circumstantial information is needed to determine the applicable law. One notable example of an open conflict rule is article 4 (1) of the EEC Convention on the law applicable to contractual obligations *(most closely connected test)*[74]. Generally, conflict rules in relation to contracts also apply to all kinds of contracts[75]. In this respect, open conflict rules, however, may create uncertainty as to the applicable law. Therefore, they sometimes are supplemented by presumptions which help to determine the applicable law[76]. Finally, *escape clauses*[77] should prevent these presumptions from resulting in the application of a law other than that of the country to which the contract is most closely connected.

103. It follows from the foregoing that, absent choice of law, conflict rules are used in determining the law applicable to contracts. Generally, no transnational substantive rules are being used. Only in exceptional cases has French case law used such rules[78].

II.2.3 *International business contracts and conflict of laws before national courts*

104. The foregoing sections have indicated that disputes arising before national courts in connection with international business contracts will be solved through the conflict of law rules of the *lex fori*. Traditional conflict of laws approaches would look to the laws with which the contract is most closely connected and would result in the application of national law. Recent theories on international business law, however, have tried to find

---

74. See also article 117 (1) Swiss Law on Conflict of Laws; this rule has primarily been developed in Swiss case law, see Swiss Supreme Court, March 19, 1949, ATF 75 II 57, Ann.suisse Dr.Int., 1950, 242; Swiss Supreme Court, February 12, 1952, ATF 78 II 74, Ann.suisse Dr.Int., 1953, 299; see also SANDROCK, O., Die Bedeutung des Gesetzes zur Neuregelung des internationalen Privatrechts für die Unternehmenspraxis, 851; PATOCCHI, P.M., Règles de rattachement localisatrices et règles de rattachement à caractère substantiel, 106 and 109; DE BOER, T., Objectieve verwijzing in het internationale overeenkomstenrecht, W.P.N.R., 1974, 6-8; DICEY, A. and MORRIS, J., The conflict of laws, Volume 2, 769-771; BATIFFOL, H., La loi appropriée au contrat, 1 ff.
75. *E.g.*, article 4 of the EEC Convention and article 117 (2) Swiss Law; see SCHÖNENBERGER, W., Kommentar zum schweizerischen Zivilgesetzbuch, Volume V, 1a, 78-80 and 89-90.
76. *E.g.*, article 4 (2), (3) and (4) of the EEC Convention.
77. *E.g.*, article 4 (5) EEC Convention and article 8 (3) 1986 Hague Convention on the law applicable to international sales of goods.
78. See supra Nos. 32-36 and IV.2.1.

answers in other conflict of laws techniques as well as in the non-exclusive application of national law (see Chapter IV). The issue to be analyzed here is whether and to what extent the conflict of laws of national states would accept these alternative approaches.

105. Where the parties choose the law, only minor problems arise. Since choice of law theories are pragmatic and liberal, the choice of non-national rules will largely be respected[79]. Some authors have proposed dropping the requirement that choice of law pertains to a national law[80]. Bucher, for instance, has argued that localization of a contract should not be exclusively geographic and, consequently, a contract may even be more closely connected to non-national legal rules than to a given system of national law[81]. Goldman has even gone so far as to predict that French case law would respect a parties' choice of non-national legal rules, such as the *lex mercatoria*[82].

106. In the absence of an express choice of law, there clearly are greater objections against new conflict of laws methods or application of non-national rules. Notwithstanding these objections, Goldman has proposed that non-national rules such as *lex mercatoria* be applied through a transnational substantive rule[83]. On the other hand, Lagarde has rejected, in the absence of an express choice of law, the application by national judges of non-national rules such as *lex mercatoria*[84].

---

79. *Contra* VON BAR, C., Internationales Privatrecht, Volume 1, Munich, Beck, 1987, 86.
80. FOUCHARD, P., intervention during the discussions, Basle symposium on the law governing contractual obligations, KLEIN, F.E. and VISCHER, F. (ed.), Basle, Helbing & Lichtenhahn, 1983, 163-164; BUCHER, A., Transnationales Recht im ipr, in Aktuelle Fragen aus der Sicht in- und ausländischer Gelehrter, SCHWIND, F. (ed.), Vienna, 1986, 43.
81. BUCHER, A., Transnationales Recht im ipr, 48.
82. GOLDMAN, B., intervention during the discussions, Basle symposium on the law governing contractual obligations, KLEIN, F.E. and VISCHER, F. (ed.), Basle, Helbing & Lichtenhahn, 1983, 129; also DIENER, M., Contrats internationaux de propriété industrielle, 72 and VIRALLY, M., Un tiers droit ? Réflexions théoriques, 385.
    Other authors have expressed doubts as to this prediction; see LOUSSOUARN, Y., intervention during the discussions, Basle symposium on the law governing contractual obligations KLEIN, F.E. and VISCHER, F. (ed.), Basle, Helbing & Lichtenhahn, 1983, 131 and LAGARDE, P., Approche critique de la lex mercatoria, 144-146; STOECKER, C., The lex mercatoria : to what extent does it exist ?, J.INT.ARB., 1990, 107-108.
83. GOLDMAN, B., intervention during the discussions, Basle symposium on the law governing contractual obligations, KLEIN, F.E. and VISCHER, F.(ed.), Basle, Helbing & Lichtenhahn, 1983, 129.
84. Approche critique de la lex mercatoria, 144.

107. As we have seen, conflict of law rules for international contracts stay within traditional limits when the parties do not provide a choice of law. Non-national rules might therefore apply only if they are most closely connected with the contract. One might argue that such a non-geographical localization is out of line with traditional conflict of laws, which requires localization in a national state. However, in cases which cannot be tied to any one country, localization in a transnational space might be theoretically proper and, therefore, does not appear contrary to conflict of laws tradition. This may also solve problems such as the localization of complex multi-party cases or transactions in outer space or on the high seas.

Absent choice of law, non-national rules might also apply through transnational substantive rules, as proposed by Goldman. However, the scope of such rules has barely been analyzed[85]. More important, transnational substantive rules have been created primarily in French case law and hardly in other jurisdictions, which might be more hesitant to create such rules. This could threaten international unification. Furthermore, the scope for creating transnational substantive rules may have been narrowed by international conventions, such as the EEC Convention on the law applicable to contractual obligations, or national statutes, which have followed a traditional conflicts approach (and not a substantive approach) to the question of the applicable law absent a choice of law.

108. Thus far, we have examined whether and to what extent alternative conflict of law or substantive approaches are available for disputes arising out of international business contracts. Now, one should ask when alternative conflict methods or non-national rules may be applicable to international business contracts.

For some authors, this is a non-question since international business contracts should be governed by national law through a national conflict rule[86]. According to Lagarde, Martiny and W. Lorenz, this is also the position of article 3 of the EEC Convention on the law applicable to

85. See infra Nos. 109-111.

86. VAN HECKE, G., Internationaal privaatrecht, first edition, 316; VON CAEMMERER, E., Measures for unifying the rules on choice of law, 323-324; VISCHER, F., Internationales Vertragsrecht, 62-63; FIRSCHING, K., Internationales Schuldrecht, I, 374; BRAECKMANS, H., Juridische aspecten van consortiumkredieten in Eurodeviezen, 1985, 431; EKELMANS, M., Le dépeçage du contrat dans la Convention de Rome du 19 juin 1980 sur la loi applicable aux obligations contractuelles, 251-252; HAAK, W.E., Preadvies, 7-11.

contractual obligations[87]. In Switzerland, there is the authority of Vischer for the proposition that article 116 of the Swiss Law on Conflict of Laws has taken the same stance[88]. Sometimes, case law is invoked to uphold this theory. First, the Permanent Court of International Justice in its decision of July 12, 1929 in the *Serbian-loan* case[89] stated that every contract should be submitted to national law, with the exception of contracts between states acting as subjects of international law. The *Messageries maritimes*-case, decided by the French Supreme Court on June 21, 1950 also held that every contract should be governed by national law[90]. Finally, judge Donaldson in his opinion before the Court of Appeal in the *Amin Rasheed Corp. v. Kuwait Insurance Co.*-case stated that the law applicable to a Lloyds insurance policy should be a national law[91]. On the other hand, the argument has been made that application of either national or international law is an outdated approach, since it denies the existence of non-national rules[92].

109. The conditions under which non-national rules might provide the applicable law have, but for a few authors, hardly been analyzed. In particular, Batiffol indicated this problem. He stressed that a contract does not stand isolated, but is embedded in the law, which also takes into account other interests (the public interest, the interests of weaker contracting parties and the interests of third parties). Any law that might be applicable to an international contract should, to a certain extent,

---

87. LAGARDE, P., Examen de l'avant-projet de convention C.E.E. sur la loi applicable aux obligations contractuelles et non-contractuelles, Trav.com.fr.dr.int.privé, 1971-73, Paris, Dalloz, 1974, 153; MARTINY, D., Bestimmung des Schuldstatuts, 24; LORENZ, W., Vom alten zum neuen internationalen Schuldvertragsrecht, IPRax, 1987, 272.

    Goldman has criticized this provision of the EEC Convention (La lex mercatoria dans les contrats et l'arbitrage internationaux : réalité et perspectives, 504-505).
88. Freiburger Kolloquium über den schweizerischen Entwurf zu einem Bundesgesetz über das internationale Privatrecht, Zurich, Schulthess, 1979, 49.
89. Case No.14, C.P.J.I., Recueil des arrêts, Série A, No. 20-21, 41.
90. D., 1951, 749, case note HAMEL, J., Clunet, 1950, 1196. From this case, Loussouarn and Bourel (Droit international privé, 1978, 493) have concluded that an international contract may not be governed by non-national rules.
91. [1983] 1 All E.R. 879. The House of Lords-decision in this case requires application of a legal system without mentioning explicitly that the applicable legal system should be a national one (*contra* MANN, F., England rejects "delocalized" contracts and arbitration, 197).
92. BÖCKSTIEGEL, K.H., Der Staat als Vertragspartner ausländischer Privatunternehmen, 111-112; STRUYCKEN, A., Verenigingen als wereldburgers: "Qua patet orbis", 287.

consider these interests[93]. Also, the applicable law should contain rules of sufficient precision. Absent such rules, moral and non-binding obligations would be created[94]. Similarly, Struycken has emphasized that the applicable law should have sufficient structure and sense of values, aside from those of the rule-making community itself[95]. Other authors have stressed the need for the applicable law to fill the gaps in the contract[96]. Finally, some authors have summarized all this by requiring that the applicable rules form a *legal system*[97].

110. By way of analogy to the problem discussed in the preceding paragraph, one may refer to *dépeçage*. The objection has been raised that *dépeçage* would threaten the unity of the contract. Quite rightly, Lagarde has shown that *dépeçage* may more readily lead to inconsistencies as to the applicable rules[98].

However, *dépeçage* may not be used only in order to escape mandatory rules[99] or to create a mixture of applicable rules from different legal

---

93. BATIFFOL, H., Réflexions sur la coordination des systèmes nationaux, Academy of international law, 120 Collected Courses of The Hague, 1967, I, 172; BATIFFOL, H., Les contrats en droit international privé comparé, 83-84; BATIFFOL, H. and LAGARDE, P., Droit international privé, Volume II, 263 and 288.

94. BATIFFOL, H., Les contrats en droit international privé comparé, 83-84.

95. STRUYCKEN, A., Verenigingen als wereldburgers: "Qua patet orbis", 287-288.

96. BÖCKSTIEGEL, K.H., Der Staat als Vertragspartner ausländischer Privatunternehmen, 100; ZWEIGERT, K., Verträge zwischen staatlichen und nichtstaatlichen Partnern, 199; SUMAMPOUW, M., case note Swiss Supreme Court, March 23, 1965, RabelsZ, 1966, 347 (mentioning "das Axiom der Lückenlosigkeit" regarding legal systems which would not apply to contracts). In this respect, Tunc has stated that international custom or, referring to article 1 Swiss Civil Code, law-making by arbitrators (and judges) may fill contractual gaps (TUNC, A., intervention during the discussions, reported by GODWIN SARRE, D., A note on the discussions of the colloquium, The sources of the law of international trade, SCHMITTHOFF, C. (ed.), International Association of Legal Science, London, Stevens & Sons, 1964, 277).

97. MARTINY, D., Bestimmung des Schuldstatuts, 23-24; WENGLER, W., Les principes généraux du droit en tant que loi du contrat, 496; BONELL, M., The law applicable to international commercial contracts : the standpoint of Italian doctrine and case-law, 16; KASSIS, A., Théorie générale des usages du commerce, 303-304, 408 and 423-424; JACQUET, J.M., Principe d'autonomie et contrats internationaux, 101.

    In this book, the concept of *legal system* or *legal order* is used pragmatically. For an approach which is much more influenced by jurisprudence, see KASSIS, A., Théorie générale des usages du commerce, 381-384; RIGAUX, F., Souveraineté des Etats et arbitrage transnational, 262.

98. Le "dépeçage" dans le droit international privé des contrats, Riv.Dir.Int.Priv.Proc., 1975, 666-669.

99. See German Supreme Court, May 28, 1936, JW, 1936, 2058, Clunet, 1936, 951, case note WOLFF, K.

systems[100]. In these cases, parties are not pursuing legitimate aims (*i.e.*, localizing their contract adequately) and are trying to avoid mandatory laws or are creating an unworkable system. The *lex fori* might then intervene with the *dépeçage*. Similarly, the *lex fori* might apply non-national rules if the conditions it imposes for applying such rules have not been met.

111. From the foregoing, one may conclude that alternative conflict of laws techniques and application of non-national rules before national judges may be possible if there is sufficient consistency and consideration for all interests involved. This implies that a gap-filling mechanism should be available and that mandatory rules have been developed guaranteeing public interests and certain private interests.

II.2.4 *Enforcement of foreign judgments*

112. In the preceding sections, we have analyzed the law applicable to international business contracts before national judges. In this section, the question is whether decisions of national judges on the law applicable to such contracts may be reviewed in the course of enforcement proceedings in other jurisdictions. This is all the more important because of development of new conflict and substantive methods in international business law.

Some recent international conventions on enforcement have excluded review on the merits including the question as to the conflict of laws issues. If review on the merits is possible, the enforcement judge generally will not review conflict of laws methodology since review in contractual matters is not aimed at substituting the enforcement jurisdiction's system to that of the origin state[101]. Eventually, an enforcement judge might apply the exception of public order. However, in that case, the application will be reviewed *in concreto*[102]. Application of conflict or substantive rules other than those of the enforcement forum generally will not be sufficient to trigger application of the exception. Rather, the concrete results of application of those rules will be reviewed.

100. RIGAUX, F., Droit international privé, Volume II, 374; RIGAUX, F., Examen de quelques questions laissées ouvertes par la Convention de Rome sur la loi applicable aux obligations contractuelles, 317.

101. *Cf.* VAN HECKE, G., Internationaal privaatrecht, first edition, 83-86.

102. See VANDER ELST, R., Ordre public international, lois de police et lois d'application immédiate, Mélanges offerts à Robert Legros, Brussels, Editions de l'Université de Bruxelles, 657-667.

II.2.5 *Conclusions*

113. This section made clear that the conflict of laws system of the *lex fori* may play an important role as to the application of new conflict methods or non-national rules. Application of non-national rules is, under current conflict of laws, most likely when parties have made a choice of law for these rules provided no mandatory rules are involved and gaps may easily be filled without reference to national law. If these conditions aren't met, the choice of law should be interpreted as a choice for substantive non-national rules to the extent permissible by the then applicable national law. Absent choice of law, it is less likely that new conflict methods or non-national rules will be applied since the jurisdiction seized of the dispute is bound by its conflict rules. Where these rules lead to unsatisfactory results, judges may be more tempted to look for alternatives within (*e.g.*, open conflict rules) or outside traditional conflict rules.

II.3 **Conflict of laws and arbitration tribunals**

114. Many international business disputes are submitted to arbitration. This section will analyze the application of conflict rules by arbitrators. Particular attention will be paid to the differences in the conflict of laws process before national judges and international commercial arbitrators. First, an attempt is made to define international commercial arbitration and discuss its importance[103].

II.3.1 *International commercial arbitration : definition*

115. For the discussion and analysis which follows, it may be helpful to define international commercial arbitration. Different definitions have been used due to different conceptions regarding international commercial arbitration. According to a first theory, an arbitration is international if conflict problems may arise. This is the case when relevant elements (*e.g.*, nationality or domicile of the parties or the arbitrators or the place of

103. In this book, obligatory arbitrations and public international law arbitration are not discussed. This is also the case for other forms of dispute resolution such as technical expertise, adaptation of contracts, mediation, conciliation or alternative dispute resolution. Also, the specific problem of arbitration with state enterprises warrants a more detailed analysis and discussion than is possible within the scope of this book (see supra No. 4).

arbitration) point to different countries[104]. This theory may be called the *conflict definition* of arbitration. One may also look to the substance of the dispute which has been submitted to arbitration, as has been done in France in article 1492 N.C.P.C., and in article I of the European International Commercial Arbitration Convention[105]. This definition may be called the *substantive definition* of international arbitration because it unilaterally determines the scope of application of substantive rules without considering other rules which might be applicable[106].

II.3.2 *Importance of international commercial arbitration as a dispute settlement method*

116. There is scant data on the number of international commercial arbitrations and the amounts involved. In London, the number of arbitrations is estimated at 7,000 a year[107]. More than 7,000 arbitrations have been held under the I.C.C.-arbitration system since its inception. Every year, some 300 new cases are filed[108].

---

104. VAN HOUTTE, H., La loi applicable à l'arbitrage commercial international, Rev.Dr.Int.Comp., 1980, 285-286.
105. See supra Nos. 33 and 46. A substantive definition has been advocated by GOLDMAN, B., Les conflits de lois dans l'arbitrage de droit privé, 356-362; DAVID, R., L'arbitrage dans le commerce international, 97; LOQUIN, E., Les pouvoirs des arbitres internationaux à la lumière de l'évolution récente du droit de l'arbitrage international, 300; LALIVE, P., Problèmes relatifs à l'arbitrage international commercial, 581; GENTINETTA, J., Die lex fori internationaler Handelsschiedsgerichte, 21; LEW, J., Applicable law in international commercial arbitration, 3-4.
106. The French rules on international arbitration have only partially succeeded in that goal because only a limited number of transnational substantive rules exist. In addition, one should note that the review of transnational awards rendered in France is the same as that for foreign awards rendered in purely domestic disputes. Of course, the specificity of international arbitration is hardly acknowledged under such an approach (MAYER, P., L'insertion de la sentence dans l'ordre juridique français, 101-104).
107. KERR, M., International arbitration v. litigation, J.BUS.L., 1980, 178. In this regard, maritime arbitration is important. For instance, during September 1969 and July 1970, some 2000 maritime arbitrations took place in London (BARCLAY, C., intervention during the discussions, 54 Conference International Law Association, Londen, 1971, 64).
108. DERAINS, Y. and JARVIN, S., Cour d'arbitrage de la Chambre de Commerce Internationale, Chronique des sentences arbitrales, Clunet, 1986, 1093, Clunet, 1987, 1010.

117. Generally speaking, it is unclear why parties often prefer to go to arbitration for international business disputes[109]. Many factors (*e.g.*, the type of industry or trade[110], the region, the parties[111] or the nature of the arbitral procedure or the dispute) may influence the choice between international commercial arbitration or court litigation.

118. Traditionally, it has been argued that arbitration is cheaper and quicker than court litigation and that arbitrators having greater expertise than judges in certain areas may be chosen. This may still be so for industry and trade arbitrations, but the statement is an unwarranted generalization as far as institutional arbitration is involved[112]. One rather sees that the relation between arbitration and litigation is dynamic; parties may reconsider their choice for arbitration or litigation in view of changes in costs, duration or expertise of these dispute settlement methods.

119. Other factors too may explain the importance of international commercial arbitration as a dispute settlement technique. One of these is confidentiality. For some disputes (*e.g.*, intellectual or industrial property rights), this may be very important.

120. In his study on transnational cartels, Kronstein did point out that arbitration is an important technique of self-regulation aimed at avoiding national laws[113]. This may be so particularly where national mandatory laws are involved. In other areas, this factor also may be present albeit not

---

109. Arbitration may have certain disadvantages when compared to court litigation. For instance, the competence of arbitration panels is restricted to those matters submitted to arbitration, enforcement needs the support of the court system and multi-party disputes are more difficult to handle in arbitration than before national courts. These disadvantages will not be discussed further.

110. *E.g.*, maritime law, commodities transactions, insurance law, for the latter, see SCHÜTTE, E., Schiedsklauseln und "transnationales Recht", VersR 1982, 223-225; CREMADES, B. and PLEHN, S., The new lex mercatoria and the harmonization of the laws of international commercial transactions, 325-326. In the banking and securities sectors, few disputes are submitted to arbitration (SIMONT, L., Les mécanismes financiers des contrats internationaux, 267-271).

111. *E.g.*, disputes arising under State Contracts.

112. DAVID, R., Jurisdictions arbitrales ou jurisdictions interétatiques ?, Arbitrage commercial, Essais in memoriam Eugenio Minoli, Associazione italiana per l'arbitrato, Rome, 1974, 109; EISEMANN, F., Le phénomène de l'arbitrage, son utilité, ses avantages et son rôle, Rev.Dr.Int.Comp., 1976, 111; KRONSTEIN, H., The law of international cartels, 379-383; KERR, M., International arbitration v. litigation, 176; but see SCHMITTHOFF, C., Extrajudicial dispute settlement, 6.

113. KRONSTEIN, H., The law of international cartels, 410.

to the same extent. In any event, it is not the only reason why parties may choose to go to arbitration.

121. Sometimes, it has been suggested that arbitration is chosen because one might expect that a party may be more willing to execute an arbitral award than a court judgment[114]. This is hardly a convincing argument. First, it does not guarantee voluntary compliance. Compliance depends indeed not only upon legal but even more upon commercial arguments. Second, one may note a general loss of the *spirit of arbitration*[115] implying, in relation to enforcement proceedings, a growing number of enforcement challenges.

122. The advantages of arbitration which have so far been discussed, may apply equally to domestic and international arbitrations. There is, however, one major difference between national and international arbitrations. In international commercial arbitrations problems relating to applicable law, international jurisdiction and enforcement abroad will almost always be present. The arbitral agreement is in this regard very effective because it does, under national law or international conventions, oust courts of jurisdiction with regard to the decision on the merits[116]. As such, in many cases, it is preferable to a *forum selection* or *jurisdiction clause* because international conventions on arbitration (especially the 1958 New York Convention on the Recognition and Enforcement of Foreign Arbitral Awards[117]) bind more states than conventions on jurisdiction. The same holds true for recognition and enforcement. While many states are parties to the 1958 New York Convention system regarding recognition and enforcement of foreign arbitral awards, there is no real network of

114. This expectation is based upon the high percentage of voluntary compliance with I.C.C. arbitral awards. 90 % of these awards would spontaneously be complied with (CARABIBER, C., L'évolution de l'arbitrage commercial international, Academy of international law, 99 Collected Courses of The Hague, 1960, I, 133; EISEMANN, F., L'arbitrage de la Chambre de Commerce Internationale, Ann.Fac.Dr.Liège, 1964, 107; DERAINS, Y., New trends in the practical application of the ICC Rules of arbitration, Nw.J.INT'L L. & BUS., 1981, 50).

115. DERAINS, Y., New trends in the practical application of the ICC Rules of arbitration, 44-45.

116. *Cf.* ROBERT, J., Exposé introductif et général sur l'arbitrage, Ann.Fac.Dr.Liège, 1964, 29-30; GAUDEMET-TALLON, H., Réflexions comparatives sur certaines tendances nouvelles en matière de compétence internationale des juges et des arbitres, Mélanges dédiés à Gabriël Marty, Université des sciences sociales de Toulouse, 1978, 563-564.

117. This Convention is of paramount importance for international commercial arbitration since, on June 1, 1991, it applied to 84 countries (Uncitral document A/CN.9/353, June 5, 1991).

international conventions regarding recognition and enforcement of foreign judgments. The absence of conventions and the lack of uniformity of national laws on recognition and enforcement of foreign judgments make it less attractive to enforce judgments than awards. Furthermore, review on the merits does not take place in relation to awards under the New York Convention while this may be possible under bilateral conventions or national law on enforcement of foreign judgments[118].

123. Finally, it has been argued that it might be easier to find a *transnational solution* to the dispute in international commercial arbitrations, than before national courts. This would imply that arbitrators have more freedom as to the application of conflict rules and would show more of a transnational reflex[119]. Arbitrators would not, to the same extent as judges, tend to take a *homeward trend* (*i.e.*, manipulating conflict rules so that the *lex fori* is applicable) and would, according to this argument, be more likely to have the specific transnational nature of the transaction reflected in their awards.

124. From the foregoing, one may conclude that many factors may determine whether or not to choose transnational commercial arbitration. A single answer cannot explain the frequent use of arbitral clauses in international business contracts.

---

118. ROBERT, J., Exposé introductif et général sur l'arbitrage, 29-30; EISEMANN, F., Le phénomène de l'arbitrage, son utilité, ses avantages et son rôle, 1976, 114.

119. See LAMBERT, E., Un parère de jurisprudence comparative, 213-214; MOTULSKY, H., L'évolution récente en matière d'arbitrage international, 295-296; LOUSSOUARN, Y., Arbitrage commercial international et droit du commerce international, 168; GAUDEMET-TALLON, H., Réflexions comparatives sur certaines tendances nouvelles en matière de compétence internationale des juges et des arbitres, 563-564; KAHN, P., Lex mercatoria et pratique des contrats internationaux : l'expérience française, 209; MATRAY, L., Rédaction d'une clause d'arbitrage et choix d'arbitres compétents en matière internationale, Rev.Dr.Int.Comp., 1979, 52; CARBONNEAU, T., Arbitral adjudication : a comparative assessment of its remedial and substantive status in transnational commerce, 36; LIONNET, K., ICC-Schiedsgerichtsbarkeit aus der Sicht einer Partei, Recht und Praxis der Schiedsgerichtsbarkeit der Internationalen Handelskammer, BÖCKSTIEGEL, K.H. (ed.), Cologne, Heymanns, 1986, 67.

II.3.3 *Conflict of laws before arbitral tribunals*

II.3.3.1 International commercial arbitration and national legal systems

125. First, one may ask whether and to what extent national legal systems want to get involved in international commercial arbitrations. No general answer may be given to that question because different attitudes may be found in different jurisdictions. Every legal system will thus provide its own answer[120]. This is sometimes called the nationality of arbitration; the nationality concept means that every legal system may decide how and when to intervene in, and exercise control over, the international commercial arbitration process.

126. Different conceptions exist as to the criteria which should be used to determine whether a legal system should intervene or control arbitrations. Most countries consider an arbitration to be domestic if the arbitral seat is located in that country[121]. A minority of countries such as Germany and, until recently, France[122], prefers to use the law applicable to the arbitral procedure[123]. Theoretically, application of these two criteria may result in arbitrations over which no country, or several countries, want to exercise control. In practice, this will rarely be the case since the law of the arbitral seat also will be applicable to the arbitral procedure.

When international commercial arbitration is not approached from a conflict of laws but from a substantive point of view, criteria are used not to localize the arbitration but to determine the scope of the substantive

---

120. VAN HOUTTE, H., Rechtsvinding bij transnationale handelsarbitrage, 117 and 121-122; LEW, J., Applicable law in international commercial arbitration, 14.

121. *Belgium* : articles 1719, 1 and 1723 Code of Civil Procedure (interpreted *a contrario*, zie DERMINE, L., L'exequatur des sentences arbitrales étrangères en Belgique, 415; VAN HOUTTE, H., La loi applicable à l'arbitrage commercial international, 292; HUYS, M. and KEUTGEN, G., L'arbitrage en droit belge et international, 395; *The Netherlands* : article 1073, first paragraph and 1074, first paragraph Code of Civil Procedure; VAN DEN BERG, A.J., Internationale arbitrage in Nederland en arbitrage buiten Nederland, Tijdschrift voor Arbitrage, 1987, 122; *Switzerland* : HABSCHEID, W., Das schweizerische Schiedskonkordat, der Entwurf zu einem Bundesgesetz über das Internationale Privatrecht und die internationale Schiedsgerichtsbarkeit, Beiträge zum internationalen Verfahrensrecht und zur Schiedsgerichtsbarkeit, Festschrift für H. Nagel, Münster, Aschendorff, 1987, 73; *England* : RUSSELL on the law of arbitration, London, Stevens & Sons, 1982, 377; MANN, F.A., Zur Nationalität des Schiedsspruchs, Festschrift für Oppenhoff, Munich, Beck, 1985, 215-225.

122. See GOLDMAN, B., v° Arbitrage (droit international privé), 112-114.

123. § 1044, II, 1 ZPO; German Supreme Court, September 26, 1985, NJW, 1986, 1436, JZ, 1986, 401, DB, 1986, 683.

provisions. This is for instance the case in article 1492 N.C.P.C. (*implicating the interests of international trade*). Consequently, France has two categories of arbitrations : French domestic arbitrations and French transnational arbitrations[124]. French transnational arbitrations are then subject to specific rules, different from those for domestic arbitration. Article 176 (1) of the Swiss law also has used a scope rule to determine the application of the provisions of the law regarding international arbitration. The law is thus applicable to arbitrations having their seat in Switzerland, provided at least one of the parties, at the time of the conclusion of the arbitration agreement, had neither its domicile nor its habitual residence in Switzerland.

127. The foregoing paragraph may raise the question whether arbitrations should be connected to any national law. Could one not authorize the parties, or find support in national law for disconnecting arbitration from any national law. This would imply that no national system would support or review the arbitral process nor intervene at the enforcement stage. This question is known as the problem of *denationalized*, *anational*, *floating* or *drifting* arbitrations[125]. From the outset, it should be clear that the parties themselves cannot denationalize arbitrations if no support for such construction can be found in the applicable law.

128. The phenomenon of floating arbitrations has been met in practice in the famous S.E.E.E.-, Gotaverken- and Aksa-arbitrations. In the *S.E.E.E.-arbitration*[126], the District Court of the Swiss Canton of Vaud in Lausanne held that an arbitral decision, under domestic law, could not be considered as an arbitral award and, therefore, the Court refused to review the decision[127]. The Dutch Supreme Court was on two occasions seized of this case. First, the Court held that the refusal in Switzerland to review the award did not jeopardize application of the New York Convention, since

---

124. AUDIT, B., A national codification of international commercial arbitration: the French Decree of May 12, 1981, in Resolving transnational disputes through international arbitration, CARBONNEAU, T. (ed.), Charlottesville, University Press of Virginia, 1984, 135.

125. See DAVID, R., Arbitrage international ou arbitrage étranger, Festschrift für H. Ficker, 1967, 121-137; MANN, F.A., Zur Nationalität des Schiedsspruchs, 224-226; NAGEL, H., Durchsetzung von Vertragsansprüchen im Auslandsgeschäft, 1978, Berlin, Berlin Verlag, 50-51.

126. Société européenne d'études et d'entreprises v. Federal Republic of Yugoslavia, Clunet, 1959, 1074.

127. February 12, 1957 aff'd Swiss Supreme Court, September 18, 1957, R.C.D.I.P., 1958, 358, case note AUBERT, J.F.

the award could not be considered to be floating[128]. Shortly thereafter, the Court was again seized of the case. Now it held that the arbitral decision needed some support in domestic law in order to be binding under article V, § 1 (e) of the New York Convention. Since the decision was not binding under Swiss law, leave for enforcement could have been refused[129].

French case law did not consider the Swiss decision to be so relevant; the Court of Appeal of Rouen ultimately held the New York Convention to be applicable to the arbitral decision[130].

129. Similarly, the Court of Appeal in Paris refused to intervene with regard to two arbitrations in the *Gotaverken*- and *Aksa-cases*. The Court held that setting aside was impossible since the awards could not be qualified as French awards because the parties and the arbitrators had chosen that the proceedings be governed solely by the I.C.C Arbitration Rules and not by French law. It was relevant that in one case, no party was French and in the other case the dispute did involve transnational commerce[131]. However, one may doubt whether the parties may, absent authorization by the applicable law, denationalize arbitration by Arbitration Rules alone.

The Gotaverken- and Aksa-decisions have to a certain extent been overruled by the provisions of the N.C.P.C. on international arbitrations, since parties may not exclude judicial review of awards rendered in France and article 1504 N.C.P.C. consequently introduced a minimal review of international awards rendered in France[132].

130. Writers are divided as to whether the New York Convention applies to floating awards[133]. Two theories have been developed on the basis of

---

128. October 26, 1973, N.J., 1974, No. 361.

129. November 7, 1975, N.J., 1976, No. 274.

130. Court of Appeal Rouen, November 13, 1984, R.C.D.I.P., 1985, 658, case note MAYER, P., Clunet, 1985, 473, case note OPPETIT, B.

131. Court of Appeal Paris, February 21, 1980, D., 1980, 568, case note ROBERT, J., J.C.P., 1981, 19512, case note LEVEL, P., R.C.D.I.P., 1980, 763, case note MEZGER, E., Clunet, 1980, 660, case note FOUCHARD, P. and Rev.Arb., 1980, 524, case note JEANTET, F.C.; Court of Appeal Paris, December 9, 1980, R.C.D.I.P., 1981, 545, case note MEZGER, E. and Rev.Arb., 1981, 306, case note JEANTET, F.C.

132. Report to the Prime Minister regarding Book III and IV N.C.P.C., supplement to J.C.P., June 3,1981; LEVEL, P., La réforme de l'arbitrage international, J.C.P., éd.C.I., 1981, 249-250.

133. See BÖCKSTIEGEL, K.H., Zu den Thesen von einer "delokalisierten" internationalen Schiedsgerichtsbarkeit, 6.

the obscure drafting history of article V, § 1, d) of the Convention[134]. A first theory holds that this provision creates *complete autonomy* which implies that the state of origin of the award should not review the award[135]. A second theory interprets the provision as only giving parties the freedom to choose the applicable law. Therefore, floating arbitration should find support in the applicable law in order to be capable of recognition or enforcement[136].

131. In three countries, denationalization of *awards* has been recognized, provided no local interests are involved. In Belgium, this has been implemented by a Statute of March 27, 1985 ousting the jurisdiction of Belgian courts for setting aside proceedings between parties who are not

134. See also infra Nos. 152-154.

135. *Cf.* DERAINS, Y., France as a place for international arbitration, 118; DAVID, R., L'arbitrage dans le commerce international, 207 and 501-502; FOUCHARD, P., L'arbitrage commercial international, 331-333; SCHLOSSER, P., Das Recht der internationalen privaten Schiedsgerichtsbarkeit, I, first edition, 569-570; SCHWAB, K.H., Kollisionsrechtliche Fragen des deutschen internationalen Schiedsverfahrensrechts, Festschrift für M. Luther, Munich, Beck, 1976, 168-169; BÄRMANN, J., Limits of arbitral jurisdiction, in International commercial arbitration, SCHMITTHOFF, C. (ed.), Dobbs Ferry, New York, Oceana, 1974, 61 and 72-80; SHINDLER, A., Arbitration still bound, L.Q.R., 1986, 504; FERRANTE, M., About the nature (national or international, contractual or jurisdictional) of ICC awards under the New York Convention, The art of arbitration, Essays on international arbitration, Liber amicorum Pieter Sanders, SCHULTSZ, J. and VAN DEN BERG, A.J., Deventer, Kluwer, 1982, 129 and 133-137; LUZZATO, R., International commercial arbitration and the municipal law of States, Academy of international law, 157 Collected Courses of The Hague, 1980, IV, 17 and 76-77.

136. *Cf.* KLEIN, F.E., The law to be applied by the arbitrators to the substance of the dispute, 205; SANDERS, P., Court decisions on the New York Convention 1958, Commentary, in Y.B.COM.ARB. I-1976, 207-208 and 215; SANDERS, P., Court decisions on the New York Convention 1958, Y.B.COM.ARB. VI-1981, 202 and 204-205; VAN DEN BERG, A.J., The New York Arbitration Convention of 1958, 28-43; VAN DEN BERG, A.J., Court decisions on the New York Convention 1958, Y.B.COM.ARB. VII-1982, 290 and 292-293; VAN DEN BERG, A.J., Should an international arbitrator apply the New York Convention of 1958 ?, in The art of arbitration, Essays on international arbitration, Liber amicorum Pieter Sanders, SCHULTSZ, J. and VAN DEN BERG, A.J., Deventer, Kluwer, 1982, 39 and 47-48; BÜLOW, A., La convention des parties relative à la procédure d'arbitrage visée à l'Art.V, par.1, litt.d) de la Convention de New York, Arbitrage commercial, Essais in memoriam Eugenio Minoli, Associazione italiana per l'arbitrato, Rome, 1974, 81 and 87-92; LALIVE, P., Problèmes relatifs à l'arbitrage international commercial, 573 and 644-645; GAYA, G., International commercial arbitration, New York Convention, Dobbs Ferry, New York, Oceana, I.A.3; ERNEMANN, A., Zur Anerkennung und Vollstreckung ausländischer Scheidssprüche nach § 1044 ZPO, Bielefeld, Gieseking, 1979, 94.

Belgian citizens or residents or corporations incorporated in Belgium or having a Belgian branch or center of activities. Similarly, article 192 of the Swiss Law on Conflict of Laws provides that the parties may exclude judicial review of awards provided they have no domicile, residence or center of activities in Switzerland[137]. Finally, in Sweden, a decision of the Supreme Court dated April 18, 1989 in the so-called *Uganda*-case, has also recognized the validity of exclusion agreements between non-Swedish parties[138]. These developments in Belgium, Switzerland and Sweden are not contrary to the New York Convention, which does not prescribe the extent to which judicial review should be available in the state of origin of the award[139].

132. It follows from the foregoing that most legal systems exercise some control or provide support for international commercial arbitrations provided there is some connection with their systems. To a certain extent, review has been limited in Belgium, Switzerland and Sweden. Some case law may be invoked to contest this conclusion but one may doubt whether these cases were correctly decided.

II.3.3.2 The conflict of laws system applicable before arbitral tribunals

133. There is at least one major difference between litigation before national courts and international commercial arbitration, as regards conflict of laws. National judges adjudicate transnational disputes on the basis of their conflict of laws system. For them, the conflict of laws of the *lex fori*

---

137. See infra Nos. 158-161.
138. HOBER, K., Arbitration and the Swedish courts, Swedish and international arbitration 1990, Yearbook of the Arbitration Institute of the Stockholm Chamber of Commerce, 1990, 56-59; PAULSSON, J., Arbitrage international et voies de recours : la Cour Suprême de Suède dans le sillage des solutions belge et helvétique, Clunet, 1990, 589-599.
139. DE LY, F., De liberalisering van de internationale arbitrage, 1044-1046; STORME, M., Belgium : a paradise for international commercial arbitration, INT'L BUS.LAWYER, 1986, 295; VAN HOUTTE, H., De Belgische wet van 27 maart 1985 inzake internationale arbitrage, 4 (but see VAN HOUTTE, H., Internationale arbitrage in België, Het scheidsgerecht, Brussels, Jeune Barreau, 1983, 107); MATRAY, L., La loi belge du 27 mars 1985 et ses répercussions sur l'arbitrage commercial international, Rev.Dr.Int.Comp., 1987, 256-262; VANDERELST, A., Increasing the appeal of Belgium as an international arbitration forum ? The Belgian law of March 27, 1985 concerning the annulment of arbitral awards, J.Int.Arb., 1986, 85-86; NELISSEN GRADE, J.M., The annulment of arbitral awards in Belgium, Int.Fin.L.Rev., November 1986, 36; GAILLARD, E., Introductory note, Belgium : Statute on the setting aside of arbitral awards, I.L.M., 1986, 726.

is applicable. In international commercial arbitration, the situation is quite different. Here, no conflict of laws system is immediately applicable. Rather, the question arises which conflict rules must be applied and where to find those rules. One may call this the question as to the applicable *arbitral conflict of laws*.

134. Often, this issue is referred to as the question of the *arbitral forum*[140]. One may criticize this expression for lack of precision and, therefore, for causing confusion. First, it may confuse the conflict issues raised before the arbitrators and those which eventually may be raised if national courts get involved in the arbitration process[141]. More important, the expression suggests that for international commercial arbitration, just as for litigation in national courts, a *forum* should be sought in order to solve the conflict issues[142]. From that perspective, international commercial arbitration should be localized in national law. However, one might take a broader perspective and rephrase the question in terms of the conflict methodology applicable before international commercial arbitrators. Quite rightly, some authors have thus rejected the notion of *arbitral forum*. From the absence of *forum*, they have made some deductions[143] which may be summarized as follows : 1) international commercial arbitrators are under no obligation to apply a national system of conflict of laws or national conflict rules[144]; 2) problems of qualification should not be solved

140. See I.C.C. case No. 1512, Clunet, 1974, 904, case note DERAINS, Y.; MAYER, P., Le mythe de l'"ordre juridique de base" (ou Grundlegung), 203; VON MEHREN, A.T., Limitations on party choice of the governing law : do they exist for international commercial arbitration ?, mimeographed paper, Tel Aviv, Mortimer and Raymond Sackler Institute of Advanced Studies, 1986, 19-21.

141. For that distinction, see JACQUET, J.M., Principe d'autonomie et contrats internationaux, 111.

142. *E.g.*, GENTINETTA, J., Die lex fori internationaler Handelsschiedsgerichte, 111; EISEMANN, F., La "lex fori" de l'arbitrage commercial international, Trav.com.fr.dr.int.privé, 1973-75, Paris, Dalloz, 1977, 189-206; *contra* KASSIS, A., Théorie générale des usages du commerce, 456.

143. *E.g.*, DERAINS, Y., Attente légitime des parties et droit applicable au fond en matière d'arbitrage commercial international, Trav.com.fr.dr.int.privé, 1984-85, Paris, CNRS, 1987, 87; DERAINS, Y., Détermination de la lex contractus, L'apport de la jurisprudence arbitrale, Paris, I.C.C.-publication No. 440/1, 1986, 12-13.

144. DEBY-GERARD, F., Le rôle de la règle de conflit dans le règlement des rapports internationaux, 202-203; VAN HOUTTE, H., La loi applicable à l'arbitrage commercial international, 296; LALIVE, P., Sur une notion de "contrat international", Multum non multa, 150; LOQUIN, E., Les pouvoirs des arbitres internationaux à la lumière de l'évolution récente du droit de l'arbitrage international, 302-303; JACQUET, J.M., Principe d'autonomie et contrats internationaux, 113; BUCHER, A., Transnationales Recht im ipr, 27.

by the law of the arbitral seat[145]; 3) international commercial arbitrators are under no obligation to review whether the applicable rules conflict with the public order of any national state or to apply mandatory laws of any national state[146]; or 4) international commercial arbitrators cannot sanction *fraude à la loi* since no national law may pretend that it should be applied by international commercial arbitrators[147]. It seems, however, that these conclusions do not necessarily follow from the absence of a *forum* in international commercial arbitration and, therefore, they must find further justification.

135. In many respects, the question of the arbitral conflict of laws might be relevant. It encompasses issues such as the applicable conflict rules, transnational substantive rules and their scope of application. Furthermore, the problems relating to qualification, *renvoi*, transitory law, *conflits mobiles* and *fraus legis* will be answered through the arbitral conflict system. Other questions such as public order, mandatory rules[148], the *ex officio*-application of conflict[149] and other rules[150] will also be determined by that system.

---

145. GOLDMAN, B., Les conflits de lois dans l'arbitrage international de droit privé, 422.
146. LOQUIN, E., Les pouvoirs des arbitres internationaux à la lumière de l'évolution récente du droit de l'arbitrage international, 340; LOQUIN, E., L'application de règles anationales dans l'arbitrage commercial international, L'apport de la jurisprudence arbitrale, Paris, I.C.C.-publication No. 440/1, 1986, 109; MAYER, P., L'interférence des lois de police, L'apport de la jurisprudence arbitrale, Paris, I.C.C.-publication No. 440/1, 1986, 46; *cf.* DUINTJER TEBBENS, H., A facelift for Dutch arbitration law, N.I.L.R., 1987, 156.
147. GOLDMAN, B., Les conflits de lois dans l'arbitrage international de droit privé, 444.
148. See DERAINS, Y., Attente légitime des parties et droit applicable au fond en matière d'arbitrage commercial international, 85-86 and PRIOUX, R., Le juge et l'arbitre face aux lois étrangères d'application immédiate dans les contrats internationaux : les nouvelles possibilités offertes par la loi du 14 juillet 1987, R.D.C., 1988, 251-295.
149. Bolard (Le nouveau droit français de l'arbitrage, 33) has argued for application of the law of the arbitral seat in order to determine this issue. However, in I.C.C. case No. 3540 (Clunet, 1981, 914, case note DERAINS, Y.), *ex officio*-application of a conflict rule was rejected without any reference to an applicable conflict of laws system.
150. See SANDROCK, O., Die Fortbildung des materiellen Rechts durch die Internationale Schiedsgerichtsbarkeit, 41-45; KASSIS, A., Théorie générale des usages du commerce, 470; *compare* VAN HOUTTE, H., Rechtsvinding bij transnationale handelsarbitrage, 39; LOQUIN, E., Les pouvoirs des arbitres internationaux à la lumière de l'évolution récente du droit de l'arbitrage international, 325; DERAINS, Y., case note I.C.C. case No. 1434, Clunet, 1976, 986-987; DERAINS, Y., Détermination de la lex contractus, 13.
In The Netherlands, article 1044 of the Code of Civil Procedure provides that the arbitrators may ask the President of the Hague District Court to collect information on foreign law as provided under article 3 of the European Convention signed in London on June 7, 1968.

136. Different opinions have been expressed as to the arbitral conflict of laws. Traditionally, there was a relation between the concept of arbitration[151] and the different theories on arbitral conflict of laws. One may doubt whether the nature of international commercial arbitration is after all relevant for determining the arbitral conflict of laws[152]. It seems that the law of international commercial arbitration has become too sophisticated in order to solve the problem of the arbitral conflict of laws simply by referring to the nature of arbitration. Furthermore, the relevance of the connecting elements may hardly be determined solely on the basis of the nature of arbitration. Factual as well as practical considerations may also come into play.

137. According to a traditional theory, the arbitral conflict of laws is the conflict of laws of the *arbitral seat*[153]. Arbitration rules sometimes follow this theory. A recent and important example may be found in article 4 of the Zurich International Arbitration Rules[154]. In many cases, this theory may have practical advantages[155]. Also, this theory assures that the arbitral conflict of laws is the same as the conflict of laws applied by national courts[156]. This may especially be relevant in relation to intervention of national courts during the arbitral process and the supervision of national courts regarding the arbitral award in the context of possible setting aside proceedings. In most countries, there exists agreement as to the rule that the courts of the state where the arbitral seat is located, have

---

151. A variety of conceptions exist. Distinctions have been made between procedural, contractual, mixed and *sui generis*-theories where respectively the procedural element, the contractual element, both the procedural and contractual or none of these elements were held to be characteristic of the arbitral process.

152. DAVID, R., L'arbitrage dans le commerce international, 112-115; LALIVE, P., Enforcing awards, International arbitration, 60 years of ICC arbitration, A look at the future, I.C.C.-publication No. 412, Paris, 1984, 326.

153. MANN, F.A., Internationale Schiedsgerichte und nationale Rechtsordnung, 113; MANN, F.A., Schiedsrichter und Recht, 598-601; MANN, F.A., State contracts and international arbitration, 4-5; JAFFEY, A.J.E., Arbitration of international commercial contracts : the law to be applied by the arbitrators, Current issues in international business law, PERROTT, D.L. and POGARNY, I. (ed.), Ausbury, Hants, 1988, 131 and 140; HIRSCH, A., The place of arbitration and the lex arbitri, ARB.J., 1979, No. 3, 43-48; SANDROCK, O., Zügigkeit und Leichtigkeit versus Gründlichkeit, JZ, 1986, 375.

In this respect, the term "*lex arbitri*" is often used. This concept does not refer to the law of the arbitrator's nationality, domicile or residence but to the law of the arbitral seat. "*Lex arbitrii*" or "*lex loci arbitralis*" would thus be better terms.

154. For criticism regarding this provision, see LALIVE, P., POUDRET, J.F. and REYMOND, C., Le droit de l'arbitrage interne et international en Suisse, 391-392.

155. MANN, F.A., Internationale Schiedsgerichte und nationale Rechtsordnung, 103.

156. MANN, F.A., Internationale Schiedsgerichte und nationale Rechtsordnung, 113.

jurisdiction to intervene and supervise international commercial arbitrations.

138. This theory has been criticized for practical and theoretical reasons. First, the concept of arbitral seat would be hard to define and determine. Should the place of the meetings or the place where the award was rendered, control[157] ? Especially in arbitrations where the arbitrators hardly meet or meet at different places or where the award is signed by the arbitrators at their respective domiciles, this may create practical problems. Further, the arbitral seat may well be unknown in advance[158] or may be changed before the start or during the proceedings.

These considerations should be taken care of. However, they are not so substantial since recent arbitrations laws, arbitration rules and practice have solved these problems. Basically, parties and, absent the parties, the arbitrators will determine the place of arbitration so that there hardly can be any misunderstandings regarding that place[159]. The main practical argument thus stems from the unpredictability of the arbitral place in the case that the parties have not stipulated that place in the arbitration agreement[160].

139. Criticism has also been expressed from a theoretical point of view. The choice for the place of the arbitral seat was thus considered to be quite arbitrary because in many international commercial arbitrations, there hardly is a connection between the dispute and that place. It has been argued that even when the parties did choose for arbitration in a neutral country, this choice did not imply that country's conflict of laws[161], except that a choice for the law of that country might be an indication to the contrary. Critics of the theory of the arbitral seat have furthermore insisted that that theory is reducing arbitration to litigation before national courts

157. In favour of the place of the first meeting, see the resolution of the Institute of international law (47 Annuaire, 1957, I, 481) and SAUSER-HALL, G., L'arbitrage en droit international privé, Institute of international law, 44 Annuaire, 1952, I, 539-541. In favour of the place where the award was rendered, see MANN, F.A., Lex facit arbitrum, 163.
158. LALIVE, P., Les règles de conflit de lois appliquées au fond du litige par l'arbitre international siégeant en Suisse, 80; JACQUET, J.M., Principe d'autonomie et contrats internationaux, 110.
159. For a discussion, see DE LY, F., The place of arbitration in the conflict of laws of international commercial arbitration : an exercise in arbitration planning, Nw J. INT'L L. & BUS. 1991, 53-61.
160. JACQUET, J.M., Principe d'autonomie et contrats internationaux, 110.
161. GOLDMAN, B., Les conflits de lois dans l'arbitrage international de droit privé, 372-373.

where the conflict of laws of the place where the judge seats, is applied. By analogy, in arbitration, the conflict of laws of the arbitral seat should be applied. According to these critics, this analogy must fail because arbitrators are not judges but entrusted by contracting parties with the task of resolving disputes[162]. Finally, the argument has been made that the theory of the arbitral seat makes choice of law dependent on the choice of an arbitration place which recognizes such choice[163].

These arguments are not totally convincing. Some practical considerations may go against but, as has been stated, others may be in favour of the theory of the arbitral seat. Also, the theory not necessarily reflects an outdated procedural conception of arbitration. The argument that the theory may lead to an unadequate localization of international commercial arbitration is of course serious. However, that statement may be overinclusive. For instance, some procedural elements may hardly be localized in another law than the law of the arbitral place. Furthermore, application of the conflict of laws of the arbitral place is not a final localization of the arbitration process since this will only be achieved through the conflict rules of that system of conflict laws. For instance, these conflict rules may authorize the parties or the arbitrators to choose the applicable law and thus, to provide for a more proper law[164]. In practice, parties may be advised to check their choice of law clauses with the law of the arbitral seat.

140. A second theory has stated that the arbitral conflict of laws should be the conflict of laws of the legal system applicable to the merits of the dispute[165]. This theory has serious flaws. First, as Goldman has pointed out, choice of law might hardly be extended outside the scope of contract

---

162. GOLDMAN, B., v° Arbitrage (droit international privé), 116; LOQUIN, E., Les pouvoirs des arbitres internationaux à la lumière de l'évolution récente du droit de l'arbitrage international, 298.

163. KLEIN, F.E., A propos de la jurisprudence du Tribunal fédéral suisse en matière d'arbitrage commercial international, Stabilité et dynamisme du droit dans la jurisprudence du Tribunal fédéral suisse, Basle, Helbing & Lichtenhahn, 1975, 493; LALIVE, P., Les règles de conflit de lois appliqués au fond du litige par l'arbitre international siégeant en Suisse, 82.

164. Also SANDROCK, O., Die Fortbildung des materiellen Rechts durch die Internationale Schiedsgerichtsbarkeit, 67-69 who argues that with respect to contractual issues, parties and arbitrators do have freedom, according to the conflict of laws of the arbitral seat, to determine the appropriate conflict rules.

165. KLEIN, F.E., Considérations sur l'arbitrage en droit international privé, Basle, Helbing & Lichtenhahn, 1955, 223; TALLON, D., The law applied by arbitration tribunals - II, 160; FRAGISTAS, C., Arbitrage étranger et arbitrage international en droit privé, R.C.D.I.P., 1960, 8-11.

law. The chosen law's conflict rules may thus not be applicable to non-contractual matters[166]. Furthermore, absent choice of law, one would need a conflict rule in order to determine the arbitral conflict of laws. Thus, this theory would lead to the strange conclusion that one should look first at a conflict rule which would in turn determine the conflict of laws system[167].

141. Other theories concerning the arbitral conflict of laws have been proposed which would localize on the basis of the nationality, domicile or residence of the arbitrators, the place of location of the arbitral institution, the nationality, domicile or residence of the parties or one of the parties, the place where the court having jurisdiction absent the arbitration agreement would be sitting or the enforcement place. These different theories have convincingly been refuted[168].

142. Apart from theories which would apply a *national* conflict of laws system to problems regarding international commercial arbitration, an *autonomous* theory has been developed. According to proponents of this theory, international commercial arbitration would be governed by an autonomous system of conflict of laws having specific conflict and transnational substantive rules. This theory was first advocated by Goldman[169] and endorsed by Fouchard, Lalive, Loquin and Von Mehren[170]. Similarly, Derains in his case notes to I.C.C. arbitral

166. V° Arbitrage (droit international privé), 116.
167. VAN HOUTTE, H., Rechtsvinding bij transnationale handelsarbitrage, 447; see also LALIVE, P., Les règles de conflit de lois appliqués au fond du litige par l'arbitre international siégeant en Suisse, 73-77.
168. VAN HOUTTE, H., Rechtsvinding bij transnationale handelsarbitrage, 447-451; LALIVE, P., Les règles de conflit de lois appliquées au fond du litige par l'arbitre international siégeant en Suisse, 67-72; CROFF, C., The applicable law in an international commercial arbitration : is it still a conflict of laws problem ?, INT'L LAW., 1982, 624-638.
169. GOLDMAN, B., Les conflits de lois dans l'arbitrage international de droit privé, 422-485; GOLDMAN, B., Arbitrage international et droit commun des nations, 116 and GOLDMAN, B., v° Arbitrage (droit international privé), 116.
170. FOUCHARD, P., L'arbitrage commercial international, 378-380; LALIVE, P., Les règles de conflit de lois appliqués au fond du litige par l'arbitre international siégeant en Suisse, 86-96; LOQUIN, E., L'amiable composition en droit comparé et international, 252-253; LOQUIN, E., Les pouvoirs des arbitres internationaux à la lumière de l'évolution récente du droit de l'arbitrage international, 304; VON MEHREN, A.T., To what extent is international commercial arbitration autonomous ?, 226-227. This theory has been rejected by Van Houtte (Rechtsvinding bij transnationale handelsarbitrage, 525).

awards has approved of developments in arbitral case law to apply general principles of conflict of laws rather than domestic conflict of laws[171].

143. The theory of an autonomous system of arbitral conflict of laws may first be found in article VII (1) of the European International Commercial Arbitration Convention which provides that the parties shall be free to determine the law to be applied by the arbitrators to the substance of the dispute. Failing any indication by the parties as to the applicable law, the arbitrators shall apply the proper law under the rule of conflict that they deem applicable[172].

As a preliminary remark, one may note that article VII (1) only applies as to the conflict issues arising in relation to the substance of the dispute. The scope of the provision may be broader than contractual elements[173] but matters relating to the agreement to arbitrate and the arbitral procedure will in principle not be dealt with under article VII (1).

Article VII (1) has led to different interpretations[174]. First, one has said that a *national* conflict rule should be chosen in order to apply *national* law[175]. A second theory argues that the broad wording of the article does permit to apply autonomous conflict rules and substantive non-national rules[176]. In any event, it is clear that article VII (1) no longer obliges to apply conflict rules of one predetermined legal system but rather authorizes arbitrators to apply any proper conflict rule[177]. In order to

---

171. Attente légitime des parties et droit applicable au fond en matière d'arbitrage commercial international, 89.

172. For a critical assessment, see MAIER, H., Europäisches Übereinkommen über die internationale Handelsschiedsgerichtsbarkeit und UN-Übereinkommen über die Anerkennung und Vollstreckung ausländischer Schiedssprüche, 19.

173. SCHWAB, K.H., Das Uncitral-model law und das deutsche Recht, Beiträge zum internationalen Verfahrensrecht und zur Schiedsgerichtsbarkeit, Festschrift für H. Nagel, Münster, Aschendorff, 1987, 438-439.
The same observation has been made in Switzerland (LALIVE, P., POUDRET, J.F. and REYMOND, C., Le droit de l'arbitrage interne et international en Suisse, 399).

174. See further LEW, J., Applicable law in international commercial arbitration, 300-347.

175. KOPELMANAS, L., La place de la convention européenne sur l'arbitrage commercial international du 21 avril 1961 dans l'évolution du droit international de l'arbitrage, Ann.fr.dr.int., 1961, 340; ROBERT, J., La convention européenne sur l'arbitrage commercial international signée à Genève le 21 avril 1961, 180; LANDO, O., The lex mercatoria in international commercial arbitration, 756.

176. GOLDMAN, B., v° arbitrage (droit international privé), 131-132; FOUCHARD, P., L'arbitrage commercial international, 384-385; LALIVE, P., Les règles de conflit de lois appliquées au fond du litige par l'arbitre international siégeant en Suisse, 91-92; RIGAUX, F., Droit international privé, II, 424.

177. LOQUIN, E., Les pouvoirs des arbitres internationaux à la lumière de l'évolution récente du droit de l'arbitrage international, 303.

assess the practical importance of this large freedom to apply appropriate conflict rules, one should know that only a limited number of West-, Central and East-European countries (20) have ratified or acceded to the European Convention. More important, certain important arbitration countries such as the United Kingdom, Switzerland, Sweden and The Netherlands are not contracting parties to the Convention.

144. Article VII (1) has inspired some important arbitration rules. For instance, article 13 (3) of the I.C.C. Arbitration Rules[178] and article 33 (1) of the Uncitral Arbitration Rules[179] have the same content as article VII (1). However, article 1 (2) of the Uncitral Arbitration Rules provides that the Rules do not prevail in case of a conflict with the law applicable to the arbitration from which the parties cannot derogate[180]. This provision makes clear that arbitration rules as such do not create law but for the

178. EISEMANN, F., Le nouveau règlement d'arbitrage de la Chambre de Commerce Internationale, 362; DERAINS, Y., case note I.C.C. case No. 3742, Clunet, 1984, 913; EISEMANN, F., The Court of arbitration : outline of its changes from inception to the present day, 398.

Some case law has accepted that article 13 (3) authorizes to depart from any national system of conflict of laws (Deutsche Schachtbau-und Tiefbohrgesellschaft mbH v. R'As Al Khaimah National Oil Co., [1987] 3 W.L.R. 1023 (Court of Appeal); I.C.C. case No. 3540, Clunet, 1981, 914, case note DERAINS, Y; *contra* Court of Appeal Frankfurt, October 26, 1983, RIW 1984, 400; LORENZ, W., Die Lex Mercatoria : eine internationale Rechtsquelle ?, 414-415).

For a sharp criticism, see MANN, F., England rejects "delocalized" contracts and arbitration, 196 and MANN, F., Private arbitration and public policy, 259 where the following citation is found : "Every practitioner is likely to confirm, only academics and the International Chamber of Commerce living in cloud cuckoo-land are likely to deny the legitimacy of legislation intended to afford parties the protection against abuse they need".

179. RAUH, K., Die Schieds- und Schlichtungsordnungen der Uncitral, Cologne, Heymanns, 1983, 138.

180. For a criticism on this provision which restricts the possibilities for an autonomous conflict of laws, see FOUCHARD, P., Les travaux de la CNUDCI, Le règlement d'arbitrage, Clunet, 1979, 824-825.

applicable law[181] which may review its provisions[182] and fill its gaps[183]. Arbitration Rules as such can, therefore, not be invoked as arguments in favour of the theory of an autonomous conflict of laws.

145. Also, article VII (1) of the European Convention has influenced recent arbitration laws such as the French, the Dutch and the Swiss laws as well as the Uncitral Model Law on International Commercial Arbitration. Thus, article 1496 N.C.P.C. and article 1054 of the Dutch Code of Civil Procedure provide that the arbitrators shall decide in accordance with the *rules of law* chosen by the parties. Failing such choice, the arbitral tribunal should make its award in accordance with the *rules of law* which it considers appropriate. Article 28 of the Uncitral Model Law provides that the parties may choose the *rules of law* applicable to the substance of the dispute. Failing any designation by the parties, the arbitral tribunal shall apply *the law* determined by the *conflict of laws rules* which it considers applicable. Finally, article 187 (1) of the Swiss Law on Conflict of Laws[184] states that the arbitral tribunal shall decide according to the *rules of law* agreed upon by the parties or, in the absence of a choice of law, by applying the *rules of law* with which the dispute has the *closest connection*[185].

---

181. Navierra Amazonica Peruana S.A. v. Compania Internacional de Seguros del Peru, [1988] 1 Lloyd's Rep. 120 (Court of Appeal); Court of Appeal Frankfurt, March 11, 1981, IPRax., 1982, 149; Court of Appeal Frankfurt, October 26, 1983, RIW, 1984, 400, case note DIELMANN, H. where the Court states: "Die Verfahrensordnung des Schiedsgerichtshof der ICC ist kein ausländisches Verfahrensrecht sondern ein Statut, das ein nationales Verfahrensrecht, in das die Verfahrensordnung als eingegliedert zu verstehen ist, nicht überflüssig macht."; VON HOFFMANN, B., Uncitral rules für internationale Schiedsverfahren, RIW, 1976, 4; *contra* LOQUIN, E., L'amiable composition en droit comparé et international, 120.
182. *E.g.*, article 11 I.C.C. Arbitration Rules, infra No. 154; article 21 I.C.C. Arbitration Rules, see DE LY, F., book review, BÖCKSTIEGEL, K.H. (ed.), Recht und Praxis der Schiedsgerichtsbarkeit der Internationalen Handelskammer, R.W., 1987-88, 164-165; DE LY, F., Gerechtelijke controle op besluiten van het IKK-Arbitragehof, Kanttekeningen bij Hof Brussel, 25 februari 1987, Tijdschrift voor Arbitrage, 1988, No. 4, 109-111.
183. *E.g.*, I.C.C. case No. 2730, Clunet, 1984, 915, case note DERAINS, Y.
184. As a matter of principle, the provisions of the new law will replace the Swiss Concordat of March 27, 1969 in relation to international commercial arbitrations. According to article 176 (2) of the Law, the Concordat may be applicable provided the provisions of Chapter 12 of the Law on Conflict of Laws relating to international arbitration have been excluded in writing and application of the Concordat is stipulated.
185. Originally, the Swiss draft bill had no provisions on the law applicable to the merits of the dispute, see LALIVE, P., Problèmes spécifiques de l'arbitrage international, Rev.Arb., 1980, 351.

146. However, substantial differences exist between these provisions and article VII (1) of the European Convention. First, the French and Dutch provisions no longer require that the arbitrators apply conflict rules in the adjudication process. The rules chosen by the parties or considered appropriate by the arbitrators, are being applied through a transnational substantive rule[186]. Arbitrators may therefore apply directly substantive rules without having to go through a conflict of laws analysis. Article 28 of the Uncitral Model Law did not go so far as the French and Dutch legislators. On the one hand, the Model Law follows the French and Dutch texts with regard to choice of law. In that case, no conflict rule is required and the arbitrators have to apply the rules (not necessarily a national law) chosen by the parties[187]. On the other hand and contrary to the French and Dutch examples, absent choice of law, the arbitrators have to apply conflict rules[188]. However, contrary to the European Convention, article 28 does not impose to apply one single law but authorizes to apply different rules of law[189]. Finally, a majority opinion in Switzerland argues that parties, under article 187 of the Law on Conflict of Laws, may choose non-national rules[190]. Failing choice of law, the Model Law approach has been followed. Thus, arbitrators not necessarily should apply national law but

---

186. *France* : BELLET, P. and MEZGER, E., L'arbitrage international dans le nouveau code de procédure civile, 631-632; FOUCHARD, P., La loi régissant les obligations contractuelles en droit international privé français, 111; FOUCHARD, P., L'arbitrage international en France après le décret du 12 mai 1981, 395-396 and 399; FOUCHARD, P., Le nouveau droit français de l'arbitrage, 1982, 45; PAULSSON, J., CRAIG, W. and PARK, W., French codification of a legal framework for international commercial arbitration : the decree of May 21, 1981, 596; *The Netherlands* : FRANX, J.P., Het ontwerp Boek IV van het Wetboek van Burgerlijke Rechtsvordering, 83; KOKKINI-IATRIDOU, D., Het Nederlandse arbitrage-wetsontwerp, 490; *contra* MEZGER, E., Kernpunkte der Reform des Rechts der internationalen Handelsschiedsgerichtsbarkeit in Frankreich, 514-515; PETER, W., Arbitration and renegotiation of international investment agreements. A study with particular reference to means of conflict avoidance under natural resources investment agreements, Dordrecht, Nijhoff, 1986, 178.

187. DORE, I., Arbitration and conciliation under the Uncitral rules : a textual analysis, 123 and 168-169; HOELLERING, A., The Uncitral model law on international commercial arbitration, INT'L LAW., 1986, 336.

188. FRANX, J.P., Het ontwerp Boek IV van het Wetboek van Burgerlijke Rechtsvordering, 66; JARVIN, S., La loi-type de la C.N.U.D.C.I. sur l'arbitrage commercial international, Rev.Arb., 1986, 522-523.

Implementing legislations in the Canadese provinces have amended article 28 in order to authorize arbitrators to depart from the conflict approach and to apply directly appropriate substantive rules, see infra No. 467.

189. DORE, I., Arbitration and conciliation under the Uncitral rules : a textual analysis, 168-169.

190. See No. 383.

they should localize the transaction and apply conflict rules which prevents them from directly applying appropriate substantive rules.

147. This review has shown that the theory of an autonomous arbitral conflict of laws may find some support in international texts and national laws but only in relation to the law applicable to the substance of the dispute. However, this does not establish the autonomy of an arbitral conflict of laws system since support for the theory is sought in international conventions, model laws and national law. Conflict of laws is then only autonomous by virtue of its endorsement by national law[191]. Therefore, further analysis is required to see whether an arbitral conflict system may be found outside national law.

II.3.3.3 Impact of national conflict rules

148. This section will analyze whether and to what extent autonomous conflict rules for arbitrators may be acceptable. Furthermore, their interaction with national legal systems should be discussed. The previous sections have already made clear that tendencies exist in order to free international commercial arbitration from national conflict systems. On the other hand, national legal systems, to varying degrees and under some conditions, might want to intervene and supervise international commercial arbitration. In that regard, national courts will also apply conflict rules. Thus, the question arises as to the compatibility of autonomous conflict rules with the national conflict rules. Theoretically, both come into play on different planes. In practice, the efficiency of autonomous conflict rules will be enhanced if they are compatible with national law[192]. If not, problems regarding the validity of the award, its recognition or enforcement[193] or the liability of arbitrators[194] may arise.

149. The foregoing analysis has been sometimes countered by the argument that most arbitral awards are being executed voluntarily. Consequently,

191. MANN, F.A., Internationale Schiedsgerichte und nationale Rechtsordnung, 102; LALIVE, P., Problèmes relatifs à l'arbitrage international commercial, 647; SANDROCK, O., Die Fortbildung des materiellen Rechts durch die Internationale Schiedsgerichtsbarkeit, 64.

192. BATIFFOL, H., L'arbitrage et les conflits de lois, Rev.Arb., 1957, 112; BATIFFOL, H., Problèmes de base de philosophie du droit, 106; JOLIDON, P., Commentaire du Concordat suisse sur l'arbitrage, Bern, Stämpfli, 1984, 455.

193. MANN, F.A., Internationale Schiedsgerichte und nationale Rechtsordnung, 113; VAN HOUTTE, H., La loi applicable à l'arbitrage commercial international, 1980, 287.

194. MANN, F.A., Private arbitration and public policy, 1985, 262.

there would be little interaction with national legal systems, and the law of the country where the award might be set aside or recognized or enforced, should not be taken into account. This element might well be considered in order to assess the practical impact of the discussion, but should not control the debate because one never can exclude challenges brought in court by a dissatisfied party[195], especially since the last decade has seen an increase in the number of challenges.

150. Interaction between international commercial arbitration and national systems takes place at different levels. Hereafter, this will be discussed in relation to 1) the arbitration agreement; 2) the arbitral procedure; 3) the judicial review of awards, basically in the context of setting aside proceedings; and 4) recognition and enforcement of the award.

151. First, national courts may be seized of disputes relating to the arbitration agreement when one of the parties challenges its formal or material validity[196]. This may relate to lack of capacity or representation. No uniform conflict rules exist in this regard; in some cases regarding state enterprises or entities, transnational substantive rules have been developed[197].

As to the formal validity of the arbitration agreement, different conflict rules also exist. However, the most important provision is here the uniform substantive rule of article II of the New York Convention, providing that an arbitration agreement in writing is to be recognized by Contracting States. Agreement in writing is defined as to include an arbitral clause in a contract or an arbitration agreement, signed by the parties or contained in an exchange of letters or telegrams.

---

195. EISEMANN, F., Die Incoterms im internationalen Warenkaufrecht, 52; KASSIS, A., Théorie générale des usages du commerce, 487; MUNZBERG, R., Die Schranken der Parteivereinbarungen in der privaten internationalen Schiedsgerichtbarkeit, 71; BONELL, M., The law applicable to international commercial contracts : the standpoint of Italian doctrine and case-law, 12.

196. See VON HÜLSEN, H.V., Die Gültigkeit von internationalen Schiedsvereinbarungen, Berlin, Schweizer, 1973, 167 pp. For a more extensive discussion, see DE LY, F., De Lex Mercatoria, Inleiding op de studie van het transnationaal handelsrecht, Antwerp, Maklu Publishers, 1989, 215-218.

197. The main example is the *Galakis*-case of the French Supreme Court dated May 2, 1966, R.C.D.I.P., 1967, 553, case note GOLDMAN, B.

Regarding the formation, the material validity and the consequences of the arbitration agreement, one often applies the *lex contractus*[198]. Article VI (2) of the European Convention and article 34 (2) (a) (i) of the Uncitral Model Law also take that position but, absent choice of law, they connect these issues to, respectively, the law of the place where the award is rendered and the place of the arbitral seat.

Different rules also apply in relation to the severance of the arbitral clause. This aspect might be solved by the *lex contractus*, but French case law in the *Gosset*-case has developed a transnational substantive rule providing for severance, irrespective of the applicable law[199]. A somewhat similar approach may be found in article 178 (3) of the Swiss Law on Conflict of Laws[200].

Finally, different opinions may exist as to the law applicable to the arbitrability of the subject matter where application of the *lex contractus*[201] or of the *lex fori*[202] have been proposed.

Autonomous conflict rules may depart from national conflict rules regarding the law applicable to the arbitration agreement. This is all the more so because even between national systems no uniformity can be found. National courts will then apply their own conflict rules and autonomous rules may be by-passed and remain without effect. If arbitrators take this into account, it will put a limit on their freedom to apply or develop autonomous conflict rules.

152. Second, autonomous conflict rules with regard to the arbitral procedure should be checked against national conflict rules. Basically, four systems exist as to the national law applicable to the arbitral procedure. A first theory proposes the law of the *arbitral seat* as law governing the arbitral procedure[203]. That law will then determine to what extent parties

---

198. RIGAUX, F., Droit international privé, II, 421; COING, H., Materielles Recht und Verfahrensrecht in der internationalen Schiedsgerichtsbarkeit, 18; SCHWAB, K.H., Kollisionsrechtliche Fragen des deutschen internationalen Schiedsverfahrensrechts, 166-167; *but see* article 178 (2) Swiss Law on Conflict of Laws. For a further discussion, see BUHMANN, J., Das auf den internationalen Handelsschiedsvertrag anzuwendende nationale Recht, 88-116.

199. French Supreme Court, May 7, 1963, J.C.P., 1963, 13405.

200. See also article 16 (1) Uncitral Model Law.

201. VAN HOUTTE, H., L'arbitrabilité de la résiliation des concessions de vente exclusive, in Mélanges offerts à Raymond Vander Elst, Volume 2, Brussels, Nemesis, 1986, 830-831.

202. Article VI (2) European Convention; article 34 (2) (b) (i) Uncitral Model Law.

203. SAUSER-HALL, G., L'arbitrage en droit international privé, Institute of international law, 44 Annuaire, 1952, I, 565-570; MANN, F.A., Lex facit arbitrum, 166; MANN, F.A., Schiedsrichter und Recht, 598-601.

may derogate from its provisions regarding arbitral proceedings. In this perspective, the parties only have freedom of contract but they may not localize the arbitration in another jurisdiction having different procedural rules[204]. This theory is prevailing in England[205]. It was clearly stated by LJ Kerr in the *Bank Mellat v. Helliniki Techniki SA* case that arbitration is not "floating in the transnational firmament unconnected with any municipal system of law". Thus, the arbitral procedure had to be connected to the law of the arbitral seat in order to determine whether the defendant had to provide security for costs, notwithstanding the provisions of the applicable I.C.C. Arbitration Rules[206]. However, in the Bank Mellat case, no such order for security was issued because the Court in its discretion thought that the case was insufficiently connected to England, but for the place of arbitration. In a more recent case with more connections to England, such order was issued[207]. A similar position also existed in Switzerland under the application of the Concordat[208]. Finally, article 19 of the Uncitral Model Law provides that the parties may agree on the procedure to be followed, subject to the provisions of the law.

153. A second theory has proposed allowing choice of law in relation to the arbitral procedure. According to this theory, parties have choice of law as

---

204. Under article V, §1, d of the New York Convention, although highly disputed, see KORNMEIER, U. and SANDROCK, O., Internationale Schiedsgerichtsvereinbarungen, Handbuch der internationalen Vertragsgestaltung, SANDROCK, O. (ed.), Volume 2, Heidelberg, Verlagsgesellschaft Recht und Wirtschaft, 1980, 975-976; under article IV (1)(b)(iii) of the European Convention, see MANN, F.A., Lex facit arbitrum, 165; under the Uncitral Model Law, see FRANX, J.P., Het ontwerp Boek IV van het Wetboek van Burgerlijke Rechtsvordering, 64; under the Dutch Arbitration Law, see FRANX, J.P., Het ontwerp Boek IV van het Wetboek van Burgerlijke Rechtsvordering, 82; SCHULTSZ, J.C., Legislation in the Netherlands and international arbitration, 11.

205. *But see* MUSTILL, M. and BOYD, S., The law and practice of commercial arbitration in England, 61.

206. [1983] 3 All E.R. 428, [1983] 3 W.L.R. 783, R.D.C., 1984, 488, case note VAN HOUTTE, H. (Court of Appeal); for a discussion, see MANN, F.A., England rejects "delocalized" contracts and arbitration, 198.

The Bank Mellat case was more recently confirmed in Naviera Amazonica Peruana S.A. v. Compania Internacional de Seguros del Peru, [1988] 1 Lloyd's Rep., 119.

207. K/S A/S Bani en K/S A/S Havbulk v. Korea Shipbuilding and Engineering Corp., Financial Times Law Reports, July 10, 1987, 9 (Court of Appeal).

208. See SCHWAB, K.H., ICC-Schiedsgerichtsbarkeit aus der Sicht des deutschen Rechts, Recht und Praxis der Schiedsgerichtsbarkeit der Internationalen Handelskammer, BÖCKSTIEGEL, K.H. (ed.), Cologne, Heymanns, 1986, 59.

that is understood in conflict of laws[209]. This means that they may derogate from the mandatory rules of procedure of the state of the arbitral seat and may opt for foreign procedural rules. Article 16 of the 1955 I.C.C. Arbitration Rules may be interpreted as expressing this theory[210].

154. A third view would give parties *complete autonomy*[211], which means that they may derogate from any national procedural rules. For instance, article 11 of the I.C.C. Arbitration Rules provides that gaps in these rules may be filled by any rules the parties of the arbitrators may settle, whether or not reference is thereby made to a municipal procedural law to be

---

209. Under article V,§ 1, a, d and e New York Convention : KLEIN, F.E., La Convention de New York pour la reconnaissance et l'exécution des sentences arbitrales étrangères, 247-248; KLEIN, F.E., La Convention européenne sur l'arbitrage commercial international, 634; FRAGISTAS, C., Arbitrage étranger et arbitrage international, 16-17; LALIVE, P., Problèmes relatifs à l'arbitrage international commercial, 644-645; also LOUSSOUARN, Y. and BREDIN, J.D., Droit du commerce international, 104; MEZGER, E., Das Europäische Übereinkommen über die Handelsschiedsgerichtsbarkeit, 256 and 275-276; SCHWAB, K.H., ICC-Schiedsgerichtsbarkeit aus der Sicht des deutschen Rechts, 59; WENGER, W., Die Rechtsmittel gegen schiedsrichterliche Entscheidungen, L'arbitrage international privé et la Suisse, Geneva, Georg, 1977, 25-26.

210. GOLDMAN, B., Arbitrage international et droit commun des nations, 115-116; BÖCKSTIEGEL, K.H., Die Bestimmung des anwendbaren Rechts in der Praxis internationaler Schiedsgerichtsverfahren, 445; BÖCKSTIEGEL, K.H., The legal rules applicable in international commercial arbitration involving States or state-controlled enterprises, 151.

211. Under article V,§ 1, d and e New York Convention and article IV European Convention : see Swiss Supreme Court, February 26, 1982, ATF 108 Ib 85, Ann.suisse Dr.Int., 1982, 344; MOTULSKY, H., L'évolution récente en matière d'arbitrage international, 302; MOTULSKY, H., Rapport au groupe de travail spécial sur l'arbitrage Commission Economique pour l'Europe, in MOTULSKY, H., Ecrits, études et notes sur l'arbitrage, Paris, Dalloz, 1974, 513; FOUCHARD, P., L'autonomie de l'arbitrage commercial international, Rev.Arb., 1965, 103-104; FOUCHARD, P., Länderbericht Frankreich, 38-39 and 43; RUBELLIN-DEVICHI, J., L'arbitrage, nature juridique, droit interne et droit international privé, 132 and 364; MAIER, H., Europäisches Übereinkommen über die internationale Handelsschiedsgerichtsbarkeit und UN-Übereinkommen über die Anerkennung und Vollstreckung ausländischer Schiedssprüche, 12; VON HOFFMANN, B., Internationale Handelsschiedsgerichtsbarkeit, 81-88; WETZMÜLLER, H., Der "internationale" Schiedsspruch im U.N.-Übereinkommen über die Anerkennung und Vollstreckung ausländischer Schiedssprüche vom 10.6.1958 von New York, 39-41 and 49; SCHLOSSER, P., Das internationale an der internationalen privaten Schiedsgerichtsbarkeit, 861; KITAGAWA, T., Contractual autonomy in international commercial arbitration including a Japanese perspective, International arbitration, Liber amicorum for Martin Domke, SANDERS, P. (ed.), The Hague, Nijhoff, 1967, 139; LANDO, O., The lex mercatoria in international commercial arbitration, 762-763.

applied to the arbitration[212]. The theory of complete autonomy may be surprising if compared to the general concept that contracts need some support in a legal system[213]. The view that arbitral proceedings should not find support in national law, dates back to the drafting history of article V, § 1, d) of the New York Convention[214]. Complete autonomy is thus based on an interpretation of an international convention which would authorize parties to derogate from national procedural law. It then derives its binding force from national law implementing the New York Convention.

155. Finally, a fourth system as to the applicable procedural rules may be found in articles 1493 and 1494 N.C.P.C. These provisions authorize the parties or, absent the parties, the arbitrators to settle directly, without relying on the applicable law, the nomination of the arbitrators as well as the arbitral procedure[215]. French law thus has created a *transnational substantive rule*[216]. Article 182 of the Swiss Law has followed the French example; parties or, absent the parties, the arbitrators may determine the procedure to be followed either directly or by reference to arbitration rules or national procedural law.

156. These different theories show that also at the procedural level, one has argued for liberalization from domestic law and application of non-national rules. To the extent that autonomy is based on international conventions or national law, its dependence from national law subsists. If autonomy is not, or not completely, recognized by the applicable law, conflicts may arise between the applicable law and the procedural rules applied by the arbitral tribunal in the course of proceedings before national courts. If arbitrators

---

212. EISEMANN, F., Le nouveau règlement d'arbitrage de la Chambre de Commerce Internationale, 361; EISEMANN, F., The Court of arbitration : outline of its changes from inception to the present day, 398; DERAINS, Y., case note I.C.C. case No. 2879, Clunet, 1979, 992; BÖCKSTIEGEL, K.H., Zu den Thesen von einer "delokalisierten" internationalen Schiedsgerichtsbarkeit, 3. In the *Gotaverken* case, the Paris Court of Appeal had refused to consider the award as a French award on the basis of article 11 of the I.C.C. Arbitration Rules. Hirsch (The place of arbitration and the lex arbitri, ARB.J., 1979, No. 3, 47) has doubted the validity of article 11 of the Arbitration Rules.

213. See supra No. 84.

214. See supra Nos. 152-153.

215. RIGAUX, F., Souveraineté des Etats et arbitrage transnational, 267; PAULSSON, J., CRAIG, W. and PARK, W., French codification of a legal framework for international commercial arbitration : the decree of May 21, 1981, 596.

216. FOUCHARD, P., L'arbitrage international en France après le décret du 12 mai 1981, 388. Other authors have proposed other interpretations of these provisions, see LEVEL, P., La procédure arbitrale, 56-58; MEZGER, E., Kernpunkte der Reform des Rechts der internationalen Handelsschiedsgerichtsbarkeit in Frankreich, 512.

anticipate court intervention or supervision, they will feel restrained in the development of non-national procedural rules.

II.3.3.4 Setting aside and review of the arbitral conflict rules regarding the substance of the dispute

157. Interaction between arbitral conflict rules and national laws may also exist in relation to setting aside proceedings against arbitral awards where the conflict rules applied to the substance of the dispute are being challenged[217]. This will be discussed in this section. First, attention will be paid to jurisdictions where judicial review has been or may be excluded. Second, judicial review in other jurisdictions will be considered. Finally, the impact of contractual clauses, trade usages and *amiable composition* will be discussed.

A. Exclusion of judicial review as to the merits of the dispute

158. Mention has been made already of the exclusion of judicial review which was introduced in Belgium, Switzerland and Sweden[218]. In this liberalization of the arbitral process, Belgium has gone the farthest since it is excluded by law to bring setting aside proceedings before Belgian courts if no local interests are involved. The state of origin of the award thus refuses to exercise any control over the award including the conflict rules applied by the arbitrators. This position implies that the only review left is shifted to the recognition or enforcement state[219]. The spiritual father of the Belgian reform, Marcel Storme, expressed this idea as follows :

> *"This is, in my opinion, an ideal approach for international arbitration; for as long as the procedure lasts, there is sense to the support of local courts. Once the procedure comes to an end, the award only needs the support of the courts in those countries where the award is to be enforced."* [220]

---

217. The applicable law will determine whether and to what extent, the parties may derogate from the review in the course of setting aside proceedings. In many countries, review is mandatory (*Germany* : see Supreme Court, September 26, 1985, NJW, 1986, 1436, JZ, 1986, 401, DB, 1986, 683; GOTTWALD, P., Die sachliche Kontrolle internationaler Schiedssprüche durch staatliche Gerichte, Beiträge zum internationalen Verfahrensrecht und zur Schiedsgerichtsbarkeit, Festschrift für H. Nagel, Münster, Aschendorff, 1987, 57).

218. See supra No. 131.

219. For criticism, see MUSTILL, M. and BOYD, S., The law and practice of commercial arbitration in England, first edition, 608.

220. STORME, M., Belgium : a paradise for international commercial arbitration, 1986, 295.

159. The Belgian reform may be assessed on several counts[221]. First, the reform may be criticized as to certain details and the way it was drafted[222]. More important, one may question the wisdom of excluding all judicial review in the origin state. It seems that here also the autonomist vision of international commercial arbitration was influential. Under the Belgian approach, the main risk might be that arbitrators would feel free to solve the dispute the way they like and would not be looking for a solid justification of their award from the conflicts perspective. On the one hand, the Belgian reform may thus indirectly contribute to the development of alternative methods to solve international business problems[223]. On the other hand, absent direct authorization in the law, there may be a risk of arbitrariness on the part of the arbitrators which cannot be sanctioned in Belgium but may create problems at the enforcement stage[224]. As to its consequences, the Belgian reform is thus characterized by a certain hybridity[225] due to the fact that these implications were insufficiently identified in its drafting history. In practice, however, this should not create too many problems, provided good arbitrators are chosen by the parties or appointing authorities and choice of law is made in the arbitration agreement for the rules to be applied to the substance of the dispute[226].

---

221. See generally, PAULSSON, J., Arbitration unbound in Belgium, ARB.INT'L, 1986, 68; REDFERN, A. and HUNTER, M., Law and practice of international commercial arbitration, first edition, 58-68; DERAINS, Y., Le choix du lieu de l'arbitrage, 114; VON HOFFMANN, B., Die Novellierung des deutschen Schiedsverfahrensrecht von 1986, IPRax, 1986, 340; GAILLARD, E., A foreign view of the new Swiss law on international arbitration, 30; GAILLARD, E., Centre International pour le règlement des différends relatifs aux investissements, Chronique des sentences arbitrales, Clunet, 1987, 185; FETTWEIS, A., La Belgique et l'arbitrage commercial international, Les particularités nationales de l'arbitrage commercial international, Lublin, 1987, 61; PARK, W., National law and commercial justice : safeguarding integrity in international arbitration, TUL.L.REV., 1989, 650, 658, 685-686 and 695; SMIT, H., A-national arbitration, 635-636.
222. See DE LY, F., De liberalisering van de internationale arbitrage, 1025-1050.
223. See infra No. 179 and IV.2 thru IV.4.
224. See infra Nos. 188-190 regarding enforcement abroad.

Enforcement in Belgium would imply that, under article 1710, 3° Code of Civil Procedure, review would be limited to the grounds of domestic public policy and arbitrability of the subject matter (see DE LY, F., De liberalisering van de internationale arbitrage, 1044). Violation of conflict or substantive rules would as a matter of principle fall outside the scope of such review.
225. See DE LY, F., Internationale arbitrage in België, Tijdschrift voor Arbitrage, 1989, 141-142.
226. Id. at 141-142.

160. Similarly, article 192 of the Swiss Law on Conflict of Laws has provided for the possibility of excluding judicial review of arbitral awards rendered in Switzerland, provided no local interests are involved[227]. Contrary to the Belgian reform, exclusion of judicial review under the Swiss law does not operate automatically but requires that the parties *expressly* waive the action for setting aside either in full or only with respect to one or several of the grounds for setting aside listed in the Law[228].

Finally, in Sweden, case law of the Supreme Court has also, in relation to non-Swedish parties, created the possibility for concluding *exclusion agreements*[229].

161. It follows from the foregoing that, for certain international commercial arbitrations which, but for the arbitral place, have no significant connection with Belgium, Switzerland and Sweden, judicial review is or may be excluded. This implies that these countries also exclude any possible review of arbitral awards with regard to the conflict methods applied by the arbitrators. However, outside these categories, setting aside review remains possible in these three countries. Hereafter, judicial review under setting aside proceedings will be discussed under French, Dutch, English and German law as well as, under the reservation set forth above, under Belgian and Swiss law.

B. Judicial review regarding the conflict rules applied to the substance of the dispute

162. Here again, article VII (1) of the European International Commercial Arbitration Convention is of utmost importance. Pursuant to this provision, the parties are free to determine the law to be applied by the arbitrators to the substance of the dispute and, failing such indication, the arbitrators may apply the proper law under the conflict rule that they deem applicable.

---

227. See supra No. 131. For a criticism, see HABSCHEID, W., Das neue schweizerische Recht der internationalen Schiedsgerichtsbarkeit nach dem Bundesgesetz über das Internationale Privatrecht, 772.

The Belgian and Swiss reforms are interrelated since the inspiration for the Belgian Statute was found in the Swiss draft Law on Conflict of Laws (Proposition de loi concernant l'annulation des sentences arbitrales, Documents parlementaires Sénat, 1980-81, No. 582/1).

228. Article 178 of a previous draft had provided that *exclusion agreements* could only be concluded after the composition of the arbitral tribunal.

229. See supra No. 131.

Given the freedom of parties and arbitrators under article VII (1)[230], review as to the conflict rules which have been applied, seems superfluous. Rather, non-application of the rules designated by the parties or of any conflict rule might be subject to review.

163. The same conclusion may also be reached under legislation which was influenced by article VII (1) of the European Convention. In France and The Netherlands, review regarding the law applied to the substance of the dispute seems barely possible since article 1496 N.C.P.C. and article 1054 Dutch Code of Civil Procedure authorize application of the rules chosen by the parties or, absent such choice, the rules the arbitral tribunal considers to be applicable. A majority opinion has argued that these provisions permit any conflict rule to be avoided[231]. Therefore, review of the conflict method applied by the arbitrators seems even more unlikely than under article VII (1) European Convention and the scope of the review seems to be limited to the question whether the rules chosen by the parties have been applied[232].

164. Article 28 Uncitral Model Law and article 187 (1) of the Swiss Law have taken a position somewhere between the European Convention and the French and Dutch Acts. Conflict rules may be departed from when parties have made a choice of law. Review might thus be possible as to the question whether arbitrators have applied the rules chosen by the parties. Absent choice of law, arbitrators have freedom to apply the conflict rule which they consider applicable (article 28 Uncitral Model Law) or with which the dispute is most closely connected (article 187 (1) Swiss Law)[233]. In this case, review seems to be limited to non-application of a conflict rule or, as in the case of the Swiss law, application of a conflict rule which would be incompatible with the open-ended rule of the closest connection.

165. Under Swiss law and under the Uncitral Model Law, possibilities for review in relation to the law applied to the substance of the dispute should be analyzed against the grounds for setting aside. Under article 36, f of the

---

230. See also article 13 (3) I.C.C. Arbitration Rules and article 33 (1) Uncitral Arbitration Rules.

231. See infra No. 467.

232. *France* : article 1502, 3° N.C.P.C.; ROBERT, J., case note Supreme Court, December 9, 1981, D., 1983, 240-241; FOUCHARD, P., case note Court of Appeal Paris, March 10, 1988, Rev.Arb., 1989, 274-275; *The Netherlands* : STEIN, P., De nieuwe arbitragewet, Deventer, Kluwer, 1986, 2 and 23.

233. TSCHANZ, P.Y., Le nouveau droit suisse de l'arbitrage international, R.D.A.I., 1988, 447.

Swiss Concordat, setting aside was possible if the award was arbitrary. Some authors have argued that application by the arbitrators of conflict rules, other than the Swiss, might be brought under this ground for setting aside, provided such application had some influence on the end result reached in the award[234]. Article 190 (2) of the Law on Conflict of Laws has limited the possibility for a review of the award on its merits to its compatibility with Swiss public policy[235]. In the absence of choice of law by the parties, review of the conflict rules applied by the arbitrators on the basis of exceeding authority seems impossible[236]. The main problem in Switzerland, then, seems to be whether non application by the arbitrators of the rules of law chosen by the parties may cause the award to be set aside. According to Lalive, Poudret and Reymond, violation of the choice of law clause would not amount to excess of jurisdiction and would only be subject to scrutiny under the public policy provision. In this regard, setting aside would depend upon a comparison between the award and the result which would have been reached if the choice of law clause had been applied. Setting aside would then ensue only if the award substantially deviated from the result the arbitrators ought to have reached[237].

166. Finally, under article 34 of the Uncitral Model Law, an award might be set aside if the arbitrators did not apply the rules of law chosen by the parties. This may be interpreted as a decision on matters beyond the scope of the submission to arbitration. It also has been argued that under article 34 of the Uncitral Model Law, no judicial review is possible as to the conflict rules applied by the arbitrators in the absence of a choice of law[238]. Here, the key issue seems to be whether the possibilities for review for violation of article 28 of the Model Law, may be interpreted as an attack against decisions by the arbitrators on matters beyond the scope of the submission to arbitration.

---

234. GOTTWALD, P., Die sachliche Kontrolle internationaler Schiedssprüche durch staatliche Gerichte, 58; *contra* BUCHER, A., Transnationales Recht im ipr, 30 and 33.

235. BLESSING, M., Das neue internationale Schiedsgerichtsrecht der Schweiz, 76-78; GAILLARD, E., A foreign view of the new Swiss law on international arbitration, ARB.INT'L, 1988, 30.

236. LALIVE, P., POUDRET, J.F. and REYMOND, C., Le droit de l'arbitrage interne et international en Suisse, 425, 431 and 173-174; *but see* HABSCHEID, W., Das neue schweizerische Recht der internationalen Schiedsgerichtsbarkeit nach dem Bundesgesetz über das Internationale Privatrecht, RIW, 1988, 770-772.

237. LALIVE, P., POUDRET, J.F. and REYMOND, C., Le droit de l'arbitrage interne et international en Suisse, 425, 431 and 173-174; *but see* BUCHER, A., Arbitrage international, 117 and Swiss Supreme Court, January 3, 1984, ATF 110 Ia 56 c. 1b.

238. BÖCKSTIEGEL, K.H., Zu den Thesen von einer "delokalisierten" internationalen Schiedsgerichtsbarkeit, 9.

167. Contrary to the liberal systems discussed above, review as to the merits seems more likely in England[239]. Primarily, this review aims to preserve unity and supremacy of English law[240]. In a 1922 Court of Appeal case, *Czarnikow v. Roth Schmidt and Co.*, the validity of a clause contained in the general conditions of the Refined Sugar Association which tended to exclude the review procedure called the *case stated* procedure, was challenged. The Court held the exclusion to be invalid[241]. The policy underlying the English position as to judicial review, was clearly stated in the opinion of Lord Justice Bankes :

> *"That they (commercial arbitrations FDL) will continue their present popularity I entertain no doubt, so long as the law retains sufficient hold over them to prevent and redress any injustice on the part of the arbitrator and to secure that the law that is administered by an arbitrator is in substance the law of the land and not some home-made law of the particular arbitrator or the particular association. To release real and effective control over commercial arbitrations is to allow the arbitrators, or the Arbitration Tribunal, to be a law unto himself, or themselves, to give him or them a free hand to decide according to law or not to law as he or they think fit, in other words to be outside the law ..."* [242].

In the same case, Lord Justice Scrutton stated :

> *"There must be no Alsatia in England where the Kings writ does not run"* [243].

Of course, when judicial review is so extensive that the case might be reviewed as to its substance, there will be little room for application of autonomous arbitral conflict rules.

168. The Arbitration Act 1979 has changed this traditional English position. The Act authorizes parties, in relation to non-domestic cases[244], to conclude *exclusion agreements*[245], (*i.e.*, clauses excluding the review of

239. Sections 1 and 2 Arbitration Act 1979.
240. MUSTILL, M. and BOYD, S., The law and practice of commercial arbitration in England, first edition, 400.
241. [1922] 2 K.B. 478.
242. Ibid., 484.
243. Ibid., 488. Alsatia is a London borough which used to be a refuge place for criminals.
244. As defined in Section 3 of the Act, see supra No. 36.
245. The existence of an *exclusion agreement* has been interpreted in a broad sense. It has been held that a boilerplate I.C.C. arbitration clause may be considered as an exclusion agreement since article 24 of the I.C.C. Arbitration Rules states that the parties are deemed to have waived their right from any form of appeal to the extent that such waiver can validly be made (Marine Contractors Inc. v. Shell Petroleum Development Company of Nigeria Ltd. [1984] 2 Lloyd's Rep. 77).

arbitral awards by the High Court)[246]. In section 4 of the Act, some restrictions have been inserted with regard to the use of exclusion agreements. For insurance contracts, some commodities transactions and maritime disputes, review by the High Court remains possible, notwithstanding any exclusion agreement, in order to preserve some unity of English law regarding these important sectors where arbitration in London is traditional and uniform interpretation of standard terms essential. That policy objective is absent in cases of *one-off contracts* where finality was deemed more important than uniformity of the law.

169. Under the 1979 Arbitration Act, exclusion of judicial review is not general[247]. Limited review remains possible under Sections 22 and 23 of the Arbitration Act 1950. Under Section 22, the High Court may remit the award or parts thereof to the reconsideration of the arbitrators if the award is uncertain, ambiguous or not capable of enforcement[248]. Under Section 23 (2), arbitral awards may be set aside on four grounds (*i.e.*, misconduct of the arbitrator, misconduct of the proceedings, improper procurement of the arbitration and improper procurement of the award), which have been construed restrictively. The question then arises whether non-application of conflict rules may be brought under one of these grounds. Particularly, misconduct of the arbitrator might be relevant. This ground has been held to encompass violation of due process or corruption but also a conscious refusal to apply a rule of law[249]. Some authors have interpreted this ground as including a violation of a fundamental element of the dispute, a manifest derogation from the applicable law, *ex officio* application of arguments and manifest lack of jurisdiction[250]. However, a gross error as to the facts or the application of the law cannot come under the scope

246. For a criticism, see MANN, F., Private arbitration and public policy, 257-267.

247. MUSTILL, M. and BOYD, S., The law and practice of commercial arbitration in England, first edition, 604.

248. LEW, J., The setting aside and enforcement of arbitration awards in the common law, Institute for National and International Arbitration Law, Ghent, mimeographed paper, 1987, 2.

249. MUSTILL, M. and BOYD, S., The law and practice of commercial arbitration in England, first edition, 503 and 602-603; Moran v. Lloyd's, [1983] 2 All E.R., 200, [1983] 1 Lloyd's Rep. 472 (Court of Appeal). A manifest error of law ("bad on its face") is, however, insufficient since Section 1 (1) of the Arbitration Act 1979 has abrogated this ground for review.

250. MUSTILL, M. and BOYD, S., The law and practice of commercial arbitration in England, first edition, 498; LEW, J., The setting aside and enforcement of arbitration awards in the common law, 3-4; RIEDBERG, P., Der amiable composition im internationalen privaten Schiedsgerichtsverfahren, Frankfurt, Metzner, 1962, 48.

of Sections 22 and 23 of the Arbitration Act 1950[251]. Furthermore, one may in this regard expect a narrow interpretation of both sections[252]. In the *Moran v.Lloyd's* case, the Court of Appeal has already indicated that Sections 22 and 23 cannot be used as a backdoor to reintroduce judicial review[253].

170. In Germany, a distinction is to be made between review as to motivation and as to the procedure. In the first case, the award may be reviewed for manifest errors in its motivation[254]. In the latter case, the procedure is reviewed with regard to its regularity[255]. It is unclear whether this may be interpreted as including a review as to the conflict rules applied by the arbitrators. In its decision of September 26, 1985, the German Supreme Court (*Bundesgerichtshof*) has endorsed this interpretation[256]. This review should clearly be distinguished from a full scale review on the merits. The German Supreme Court explicitly stated that an error in the application of the substantive law cannot lead to a setting aside of the award[257]. The same position had already been taken in 1962 by Riedberg[258].

---

251. Russell on the law of arbitration, 422-423.
252. See Bank Mellat v. GAA Development Construction Company, Financial Times Law Reports, Financial Times, January 22, 1987 (Commercial Court).
253. [1983] 2 All E.R. 200, [1983] 1 Lloyd's Rep. 472 (Court of Appeal); BERNSTEIN, R., General principles, Handbook of arbitration practice, BERNSTEIN, R. (ed.), London, Sweet & Maxwell, 1987, 148.
254. § 1041, I (5) ZPO. According to § 1041, II ZPO, parties may exclude this ground for setting aside.
255. § 1041, I (1) ZPO.
256. NJW 1986, 1436, JZ, 1986 401, DB 1986, 683; see also BAJONS, E.M., Zur Nationalität internationaler Schiedssachen, 27; SCHLOSSER, P., case note Court of Appeal Frankfurt, November 18, 1982, KTS, 1983, 670; ADEN, M., Die Anwendung materiellen Rechts durch den Schiedsrichter, RIW, 1984, 937-938; *but see* KAPPUS, A., "Conflict avoidance" durch "lex mercatoria" und UN-Kaufrecht 1980, 793; SANDROCK, O., Zügigkeit und Leichtigkeit versus Gründlichkeit, 375.

    It seems that such review should take account of article VII (1) of the European Convention, provided that Convention is applicable.

    The decision of September 26, 1985, may also be interpreted as providing a ground for setting aside when the arbitrators fail to apply the law chosen by the parties, see SCHLOSSER, P., Das Recht der internationalen privaten Schiedsgerichtsbarkeit, 627.
257. Sandrock and Böckstiegel have approved of this interpretation (see SANDROCK, O., Zügigkeit und Leichtigkeit versus Gründlichkeit, 374; BÖCKSTIEGEL, K.H., Zu den Thesen von einer "delokalisierten" internationalen Schiedsgerichtsbarkeit, 9).
258. RIEDBERG, P., Der amiable composition im internationalen privaten Schiedsgerichtsverfahren, 62-63.

171. In the *Norsolor*-arbitration, the Vienna Court of Appeal and the Austrian Supreme Court refused to interpret § 595, 6 ZPO, as it then was (providing that violation of mandatory rules may lead to setting aside), to include a review as to the conflict rules applied by the arbitrators[259]. However, the Court of Appeal decision also addressed the issue whether § 595, 5 ZPO ("excess of powers") had been violated. The Court held that it was because the arbitrators, contrary to article 13 (3) of the I.C.C. Arbitration Rules, had applied principles of loyalty and good faith belonging to the *lex mercatoria* and not the law applicable according to the conflict rule they deemed appropriate. The Supreme Court quashed the decision and argued that, after a review of the arbitration agreement and the award, the arbitrators had not decided beyond their mandate and no *ultra petita* decisions had been rendered[260]. The Court took a narrow formal view of § 595, 5 ZPO in order not to review arbitral conflict rules.

172. Under Belgian law and to the extent that judicial review is still possible, the question of review of the conflict rules applied by the arbitrators has hardly been analyzed. It seems that such review should be based on article 1704, 2°, d) of the Code of Civil Procedure providing for setting aside in case of excess of the arbitral tribunal's authority. In a case decided by the Brussels Court of Appeal, an error as to the applicable law was held not to imply that the award was rendered beyond the scope of the submission to arbitration, except if it would appear that the arbitral tribunal had not applied any rule of law[261].

173. In the preceding paragraphs, reference has been made on several occasions to setting aside on the basis of excess of powers by the arbitral

---

259. Vienna Court of Appeal, January 26, 1982, Rev.Arb., 1983, 516, AG, 1982, 165, case note DIELMANN, H.; Austrian Supreme Court, November 18, 1982, RIW, 1983, 868, case note SEIDL-HOHENVELDERN, I., Clunet, 1983, 645, case note SEIDL-HOHENVELDERN, I.; for a criticism, see BAJONS, E.M., Zur Nationalität internationaler Schiedssachen, Festschrift für W. Kralik, RECHBERGER, W. and WELSER, R. (ed.), Vienna, Manz, 1986, 22-35.

On these cases, see infra No. 393.

260. Supreme Court, November 18, 1982, RIW, 1983, 868, case note SEIDL-HOHENVELDERN, I., Clunet, 1983, 645, case note SEIDL-HOHENVELDERN, I.; *critical* BAJONS, E.M., Zur Nationalität internationaler Schiedssachen, 22-35.

261. December 30, 1969, Pas., 1970, II, 73. This case was decided under article 1028, 1° of the Code of Civil Procedure which was then in force and which contained language different from article 1704, 2° d) of the current Code.

Similarly to the position under German law, it seems that the liberal provision of article VII (1) of the European Convention will drastically reduce any possibilities for review.

tribunal. This ground may particularly be successful if the parties have chosen the applicable rules and these have not been applied by the arbitrators. However, the legal systems discussed above, apart from Germany and Belgium (to the extent that setting aside remains possible and the European International Commercial Arbitration Convention is not applicable), are much more hesitant to review awards as to the conflict rules applied by the arbitrators on the basis of excess of powers or similar grounds. Mostly, they take a narrow view whereby this ground is not applicable if the arbitral conflict system is not indicated in the arbitration agreement. Then, even if the arbitrators violate conflict rules, the award still remains within the submission to arbitration and the arbitrators have not exceeded their mandate, absent express provision in the agreement[262]. However, a more extensive view may also be taken. This may be illustrated by the arbitral award in the I.C.S.I.D. arbitration involving *Klöckner v. Republic Cameroon*. In this case, the award had applied French law and principles of equity. French law was applied on the assumption that the applicable law of West-Cameroon was still identical to French law applicable in that territory until its independence. Later, the annulment of the award was requested. An *ad hoc* Committee was formed under article 52 (3) C.S.I.D. which held that the award should be annulled because the arbitral tribunal manifestly had exceeded its powers as provided by article 52 (1) (b) C.S.I.D.[263]. The Committee decision has not given a narrow and procedural reading to *manifestly exceeded its powers* but has construed it in a substantive way which implies that violation of the obligation to adjudicate according to the law indicated in article 42 I.C.S.I.D. may constitute a ground for annulment[264]. However, an error as to the applicable law may not lead to annulment[265].

---

262. *But see* PARK, W., Control mechanisms in the development of a modern lex mercatoria, Lex mercatoria and arbitration, CARBONNEAU, T. (ed.), Dobbs Ferry, Transnational, 129-130 (who also refers to Federal Arbitration Act, 9 U.S.C § 10 (d) (1982) (excess of powers).

263. Decision of the *ad hoc* Committee of May 3, 1985, Clunet, 1987, 163, case note GAILLARD, E.

264. SCHLECHTRIEM, P., Zur Überprüfbarkeit von ICSID-Schiedssprüchen : die Aufhebungsentscheidung im Falle Klöckner/Kamerun, IPRax, 1986, 71; *critical* GAILLARD, E., Centre International pour le règlement des différends relatifs aux investissements, Chronique des sentences arbitrales, Clunet, 1987, 189. Redfern agrees with the Klöckner-decision, provided the ad hoc committee had stated that application of Cameroonian law would have led to a result other than by application of general principles of law (REDFERN, A., ICSID - Losing its appeal ?, ARB.INT'L, 1987, 108).

265. One may also add mistakes as to the applicable conflict rule (compare LAGARDE, P., case note Court of Appeal Paris, July 13, 1989, Rev.Arb., 1990, 668 and 673-674).

The conclusions which may be drawn from the *Klöckner* case have been affirmed in another I.C.S.I.D. procedure where an *ad hoc* Committee also annulled the award rendered in *Amco Asia Corp. v. Indonesia* since the arbitral tribunal had manifestly exceeded its powers by failing to apply Indonesian law[266].

One should be cautious in drawing conclusions from these I.C.S.I.D. cases, primarily because the wording of article 52 (1) (b) C.S.I.D. is different from conventions and some laws in the field of international commercial arbitration.

174. It follows from the preceding sections that judicial review regarding conflict rules applied to the substance of the dispute is very limited, apart from Germany and Belgium. The freedom for arbitrators to decide the conflict rules applicable to the substance of the dispute is thus great. In this respect, one also should analyze the function of contract clauses, trade usages and *amiable composition* in relation to the law applicable to the merits of the dispute.

C. Applicable law, contract clauses and trade usages

175. It is not very surprising that in international commercial dispute resolution attention has been paid to contract clauses and trade usages as possible dispute settlement rules. Article VII (1) of the European Convention has thus provided that the arbitrators shall take account of the terms of the contract and trade usages, whether or not the parties have indicated the applicable law[267].

As far as trade usages are concerned, different interpretations have been given to this provision[268]. A first theory argues that trade usages preempt the applicable national law, including its mandatory provisions[269]. According to a second theory, there is no such preemption and trade usages are thus applied by virtue of the applicable national law and, therefore, in cases of conflicts, priority should be given to mandatory rules

---

266. Decision of the *ad hoc* Committee of May 16, 1986, I.L.M., 1986, 1439-1465, Clunet, 1987, 174, critical note GAILLARD, E.
267. See also article 13 (5) I.C.C. Arbitration Rules. For the drafting history, see BENJAMIN, P., The European Convention on international commercial arbitration, Brit.Y.B.Int.L., 1961, 491-492.
268. See LOQUIN, E., L'amiable composition en droit comparé et international, 316-317.
269. KOPELMANAS, L., Quelques problèmes récents de l'arbitrage commercial international, Rev.Trim.Dr.Com., 1957, 892; GENTINETTA, J., Die lex fori internationaler Handelsschiedsgerichte, 330-331.

of that law[270]. Finally, some authors have taken the view that article VII (1) did not purport to take any decision as to the relation between trade usages and domestic laws[271].

176. Here also, article VII (1) has inspired article 1496 N.C.P.C. and article 1054 (4) of the Dutch Code of Civil Procedure[272]. Both provisions state that in all cases, arbitrators shall take trade usages into account. A majority opinion interprets these provisions as a reference to *lex mercatoria*[273]; according to a minority, trade usages are applicable by virtue of the applicable law[274]. Goldman has chosen a middle course between these opinions. If *lex mercatoria* is applicable, reference to trade usages is superfluous, since trade usages are a constituent part of *lex mercatoria*. If national law is applicable, reference to trade usages is very useful, in order to apply them instead of national law on the same subject[275]. Finally, it has been argued that application of trade usages is the only mandatory rule imposed upon the arbitrators[276].

---

270. KLEIN, F., L'arbitrage international de droit privé, Ann.suisse Dr.Int., 1963, 41; MEZGER, E., Das Europäische Übereinkommen über die Handelsschiedsgerichtsbarkeit, 280; MAIER, H., Europäisches Übereinkommen über die internationale Handelsschiedsgerichtsbarkeit und UN-Übereinkommen über die Anerkennung und Vollstreckung ausländischer Schiedssprüche, 19-20; LOQUIN, E., L'amiable composition en droit comparé et international, 314; BAJONS, E.M., Zur Nationalität internationaler Schiedssachen, 31.
271. VON HOFFMANN, B., Internationale Handelsschiedsgerichtsbarkeit, 124-125.
272. One author has argued that application of trade usages is not mandatory. This also prevents an award being set aside because of non-compliance by the arbitral tribunal of its mandate (SANDERS, P., Het nieuwe arbitragerecht, Deventer, Kluwer, 1987, 141).

    Kokkini-Iatridou (Het Nederlands arbitrage-wetsontwerp, 490) has wondered whether "applicable trade usages" refers to the scope of trade usages and whether "shall take into account" implies that trade usages also should be applied between non-businessmen and between a businessman and a non-businessman.
273. See infra Nos. 380-381.
274. DE BOISSESON, M., Le droit français de l'arbitrage, first edition, 420 and 423; SANDERS, P., Het nieuwe arbitragerecht, first edition, 140-141; VAN DELDEN, R., Lex mercatoria of ius commune ?, 18-23; *see also* Second Report to the Dutch Arbitration Bill, Tijdschrift voor Arbitrage, 1986, No. 2, 83-84.
275. Lex mercatoria, 14.
276. MEZGER, E., Kernpunkte der Reform des Rechts der internationalen Handelsschiedsgerichtsbarkeit in Frankreich, 514.

Under article 28 (4) of the Uncitral Model Law, the arbitral tribunal shall also take into account the usages of the trade applicable to the transaction[277].

Finally, no reference is made to trade usages in article 187 of the Swiss Law.

177. Article VII (1) of the European Convention also refers to the terms of the contract. No such reference is to be found in the French, Dutch and Swiss laws. Article 28 (4) of the Uncitral Model Law provides that the arbitral tribunal shall decide in accordance with the terms of the contract[278]. The provisions of the European Convention and the Model Law in relation to contract terms, have hardly been analyzed, apart from the relation between trade usages and contract terms. This problem has given rise to different interpretations[279]. According to Von Hoffmann, article VII (1) was not intended to solve this problem[280]. The wording of article 28 (4) of the Model Law ("*decide in accordance with* the terms of the contract and shall *take into account* the usages of the trade") may be interpreted to suggest that contract terms must prevail over conflicting trade usages[281].

178. Trade usages and contract clauses as substantive rules of international business law are discussed in Chapter III[282]. Here, it may be sufficient to note that both sources have been recognized in international commercial arbitration law and practice as important dispute settlement rules. However, it is not totally clear what their status might be in relation to the

---

277. Originally, pressure from developing countries led to the deletion from the draft Model Law of any reference to trade usages (BEGUIN, J., Le développement de la lex mercatoria menace-t-il l'ordre juridique international ?, 514). Finally, the reference was reinserted. Dore (Arbitration and conciliation under the Uncitral rules : a textual analysis, 123) has argued that trade usages are binding by virtue of the applicable law.

278. See also article 33 (3) Uncitral Arbitration Rules. Broches (A model law on international commercial arbitration ? A progress report on the work undertaken within the U.N. Commission on International Trade Law (Uncitral), GEO.WASH.J.INT'L L.& EC., 1984, 90-91) has criticized reference to contract terms since this may create problems if the contract conflicts with mandatory rules of the applicable law. Also, application of the terms of the contract may run counter to the real intentions of the parties.

279. See VON HOFFMANN, B., Internationale Handelsschiedsgerichtsbarkeit, 123.

280. Internationale Handelsschiedsgerichtsbarkeit, 124-125.

281. Sanders (Commentary on Uncitral arbitration rules, Y.B.COM.ARB. II-1977, 210-212) argues that the Uncitral Rules which were influential in the drafting history of the Model Law, has chosen preemption of contract terms over trade usages.

282. See infra III.1 and III.2.

applicable law and as between each other. In this respect, one might be faced with a situation where arbitrators and national judges sitting in setting aside proceedings have different opinions as to the nature of trade usages and contract terms. In many cases, this will hardly affect the setting aside proceedings. First, the liberal policies underlying the rules of international conventions, model laws and national laws, authorize or even compel arbitrators to apply contract terms and trade usages. Second, judicial review as to the application of contract terms and trade usages implies review on the merits which is limited. Only when mandatory rules are involved or when the arbitral tribunal is violating applicable conflict rules, review might be possible, provided a ground of review is available in the competent jurisdiction[283].

D. Applicable law and "amiable composition"

179. Finally, review of the law applied to the substance of the dispute should be analyzed in cases where the parties have mandated the arbitrators to decide *ex aequo et bono* or as *amiables compositeurs*[284]. This

283. See supra Nos. 173-174.

284. This authorizes but does not oblige the arbitrators to derogate from the applicable law, to the extent permitted by that law (Court of Appeal Paris, March 15, 1984, Rev.Arb., 1985, 285; Court of Appeal Paris, March 12, 1985, Rev.Arb., 1985, 299; SIMONT, L., Amiables compositeurs and their reasoning, International commercial arbitration, SCHMITTHOFF, C. (ed.), Dobbs Ferry, Oceana, 1974, 115). In this latter respect, confusion exists as to whether arbitrators may derogate from mandatory rules. If these rules are of a public order character, it is generally agreed that arbitrators may not derogate (GERARD, P., Le champ de la justice privée : aspects de la pratique de l'arbitrage en droit belge, 431; I.C.C. case No. 4265, Clunet, 1984, 922, case note DERAINS, Y.). However, a decision of the Swiss Supreme Court has taken the opposite view (April 8, 1981, ATF, 1981, 63; DERAINS, Y., Clunet, 1984, 924). On the contrary, different opinions exist in relation to mandatory rules, other than those of public policy (in favour of derogation : LOQUIN, E., Les pouvoirs des arbitres internationaux à la lumière de l'évolution récente du droit de l'arbitrage international, 316-317; SANDROCK, O., "Ex aequo et bono"- und "amiable composition"-Vereinbarungen : ihre Qualification, Anknüpfung und Wirkungen, Jahrbuch für die Praxis der Schiedsgerichtsbarkeit, Volume 2 (1988), Heidelberg, Verlag Recht und Wirtschaft, 1989, 130-131; GERARD, P., l.c., 431; VAN HOUTTE, H., Arbitrage, R.W., 1976-77, 2122; VAN HOUTTE, H., Rechtsvinding bij transnationale handelsarbitrage, 316; *contra* Belgien Supreme Court, February 2, 1973, R.C.J.B., 1975, 394, case note VAN GELDER, J. and LINSMEAU, J.; DEL MARMOL, C. and MATRAY, L., L'importance et l'interprétation du contrat, 195; MATRAY, L., L'amiable composition dans l'arbitrage interne et dans l'arbitrage international, 48; SCHULTSZ, J.C., Legislation in the Netherlands and international arbitration, 18).

Also, the question arises whether *amiables compositeurs* may derogate from the provisions of the contract (*negative* : DERAINS, Y., case note I.C.C. case No. 3267,

technique is not so frequently used in international commercial arbitration practice but is relevant in a study on the sources of international business law since it may be the lever for the application of dispute settlement rules such as general principles of law, trade usages and transnational substantive rules[285].

Amiable composition has been accepted favorably in many national laws, particularly of civil law countries. Recently, article 1497 N.C.P.C.[286], article 1054 (3) of the Dutch Code of Civil Procedure[287], article 187 (2) of the Swiss Law and article 28 (3) of the Uncitral Model Law have created a transnational substantive rule which recognizes *amiable composition*, provided parties had agreed and notwithstanding restrictions in the applicable law[288]. Thus, in these countries, restrictions as to *amiable composition* cannot be challenged in the course of a setting aside proce-

---

Clunet, 1980, 969; GERARD, P., ibid., 431; *positive* : BREDIN, J.D., L'amiable composition et le contrat, Rev.Arb., 1984, 266-267; SANDROCK, O., Ibid., 132-133; VAN HOUTTE, H., Arbitrage naar billijkheid in België, Tijdschrift voor arbitrage, 1983, No. 2, 36; BLESSING, M., Das neue internationale Schiedsgerichtsrecht der Schweiz, 71; SCHULTSZ, J.C., l.c., 18; I.C.C. case No. 3938, Clunet, 1984, 926, case note JARVIN, S.).

Finally, it is unclear whether *amiables compositeurs* may derogate from trade usages (for a negative answer under article VII (2) European Convention, see SANDERS, P., Trends in the field of international commercial arbitration, 246). Under French law, this might be possible, see FOUCHARD, P., L'arbitrage international en France après le décret du 12 mai 1981, 400). Article 1054 Dutch Code of Civil Procedure, article 13 I.C.C. Arbitration Rules and article 33 Uncitral Arbitration Rules proscribe such derogation (Tijdschrift voor arbitrage, 1984, No. 4, 40; SANDERS, P., Het nieuwe arbitragerecht, first edition, 140-141; KASSIS, A., Théorie générale des usages du commerce, 211).

285. FOUCHARD, P., Länderbericht Frankreich, 44. Other authors have argued that *amiable composition* may hinder the development of transnational rules for dispute settlement (KRINGS, E. and MATRAY, L., Le juge et l'arbitre, 239; MATRAY, L., L'amiable composition dans l'arbitrage interne et dans l'arbitrage international, 61-62).

286. Article 1497 N.C.P.C. is preempted by article VII (2) of the European Convention, if applicable (LOQUIN, E., Les pouvoirs des arbitres internationaux à la lumière de l'évolution récente du droit de l'arbitrage international, 321).

287. During the drafting of the Act, the question was asked whether the distinction between *amiable composition* and arbitration according to rules of law shouldn't be abolished (favorably : VAN DELDEN, R., Lex mercatoria of ius commune ?, 22). Finally, it was decided to keep it (Tijdschrift voor Arbitrage, 1986, No. 2, 83-84; SANDERS, P., Het nieuwe arbitragerecht, first edition, 137-138).

288. *France* : FOUCHARD, P., La loi régissant les obligations contractuelles en droit international privé français, 110; FOUCHARD, P., Le nouveau droit français de l'arbitrage, 45; LOQUIN, E., Les pouvoirs des arbitres internationaux à la lumière de l'évolution récente du droit de l'arbitrage international, 320; *The Netherlands* : FRANX, J.P., Het ontwerp Boek IV van het Wetboek van Burgerlijke Rechtsvordering, 50.

dure. Primarily, setting aside will be possible if arbitrators act as *amiables compositeurs* without party authorization. However, other jurisdictions do have restrictions on *amiable composition*[289] or are unfamiliar with this kind of arbitration[290]. In those jurisdictions, setting aside might be possible. Because of the different positions in national laws as to *amiable composition*, article VII (2) of the European Convention[291] has provided that the applicable law must authorize *amiable composition*[292].

---

289. *E.g., Belgium* : article 1700 Code of Civil Procedure proscribes *amiable composition* in an arbitral clause (but not once the dispute has arisen). Several techniques have been proposed to circumvent this prohibition (*i.e.*, 1) *dépeçage*, VAN HOUTTE, H., Arbitrage naar billijkheid in België, 36; 2) confirmation after the dispute has arisen; 3) conversion into normal arbitration under rules of law, see for Nos. 2) and 3), VAN HOUTTE, H., Arbitrage naar billijkheid in België, 36; VAN HOUTTE, H., Arbitrage, 2123; VAN HOUTTE, H., De "amiable composition" en de nieuwe arbitragewet, R.W., 1972-73, 739-740); and 4) choice of an arbitral place other than Belgium. This prohibition will, furthermore, hardly be effective when no Belgian interests are involved. In that case, Belgian courts cannot set aside awards and review is only possible at the enforcement place (see supra Nos. 158-159).

290. Originally, the arbitral tribunal was supposed to adjudicate on the basis of the applicable law leading to review under the *case stated* procedure (RIEDBERG, P., Der amiable composition im internationalen privaten Schiedsgerichtsverfahren, 45-47). Case law has, however, been confronted with *ex aequo et bono* clauses and has taken an ambivalent position. In *Orion Cia. Espanola de Seguros v. Belfort Maatschappij* ([1962] 2 Lloyd's Rep. 257 [Commercial Court]), such a clause in a reinsurance contract was held to be invalid since it purported to evade judicial review. However, in *Eagle Star Insurance Co.Ltd. v. Yuval Insurance Co.Ltd.* ([1978] 1 Lloyd's Rep. 357 [Court of Appeal]), the Court held that such a clause did not violate public policy. The latter case has been interpreted as an effort to limit the scope of the *case stated* procedure (MANN, F.A., Arbitration extra legem, L.Q.R., 1978, 486-488). The fate of these clauses has not yet been decided after the enactment of the 1979 Arbitration Act which abolished the *case state* procedure. One may assume that the liberal policy of the Act may favorably affect the validity of *amiable composition* and similar clauses under English law.

291. See RIEDBERG, P., Der amiable composition im internationalen privaten Schiedsgerichtsverfahren, 10 and 83-84; I.C.C. award, November 3, 1977, Rev.Arb., 1980, 560, case note SCHAPIRA, J.

    Kopelmanas (La place de la Convention européenne sur l'arbitrage commercial international du 21 avril 1961 dans l'évolution du droit international de l'arbitrage, 340) has argued that, absent choice of law, the arbitrators should apply a law that authorizes *amiable composition*.

292. Three theories regarding the law applicable to *amiable composition* have been proposed (*i.e.*, 1) the law applicable to the agreement to arbitrate (MATRAY, L., L'amiable composition dans l'arbitrage interne et dans l'arbitrage international, 60; SANDROCK, O., "Ex aequo et bono"- und "amiable composition"-Vereinbarungen : ihre Qualification, Anknüpfung und Wirkungen, 137-138); 2) the law of the arbitral place (LOQUIN, E., L'amiable composition en droit comparé et international, 184; I.C.C. award, November 3, 1977, Rev.Arb., 1980, 560, case note SCHAPIRA, J.); 3)

180. In this context, there is the issue whether violation of applicable conflict rules may not be interpreted as *amiable composition*[293]. In jurisdictions which give wide discretion to arbitrators, such as France and The Netherlands, this may not be used to reintroduce judicial review of the rules applied to the substance of the dispute[294]. In other jurisdictions, setting aside might be possible based on the argument that refusal to apply relevant conflict rules is equivalent to *amiable composition* arbitration. Since this requires party consent, arbitrators then go beyond the scope of the submission to arbitration when they act as *amiables compositeurs*. Setting aside might then follow under German and Belgian law[295]. In Switzerland, the matter is more disputed because of the restrictions in the Law on Conflict of Laws regarding the review of awards as to the law applied to the merits[296]. As to Belgium and Switzerland, one also should take the exclusion of review into account regarding awards rendered between foreigners.

181. In German case law, this problem has arisen in a case before the Court of Appeal in Frankfurt where the arbitrators had decided *in a common sense manner*, whereas the parties had chosen English law. Normally, the Court would have taken the position that this is *amiable*

---

cumulatively, the law applicable to the agreement and to the procedure (VAN HOUTTE, H., Rechtsvinding bij transnationale handelsarbitrage, 221).

293. *Positive* : MANN, F.A., Schiedsrichter und Recht, 615 (referring to article 1019 Code de procédure civile); SANDROCK, O., Die Fortbildung des materiellen Rechts durch die Internationale Schiedsgerichtsbarkeit, 79; VAN HOUTTE, H., Rechtsvinding bij transnationale handelsarbitrage, 482; HAAK, W.E., Preadvies, 7-11; BELLET, P. and MEZGER, E., L'arbitrage international dans le nouveau code de procédure civile, 632-633; LAGARDE, P., Approche critique de la lex mercatoria, 148-149; VON BAR, C., Internationales Privatrecht, Volume 1, 85-86; ROBERT, J., case note French Supreme Court, October 9, 1984, D., 1985, 104.

294. See for *The Netherlands* : SCHULTSZ, J.C., Legislation in the Netherlands and international arbitration, 21; SANDERS, P., Het nieuwe arbitragerecht, first edition, 185-186.

295. *In relation to German, English and Belgian law* see GOTTWALD, P., Die sachliche Kontrolle internationaler Schiedssprüche durch staatliche Gerichte, 61; *Belgium* : Court of Appeal Brussels, December 30, 1969, Pas., 1970, II, 73; *Germany* : SANDROCK, O., Zügigkeit und Leichtigkeit versus Gründlichkeit, 373-374; RIEDBERG, P., Der amiable compositeur im internationalen privaten Schiedsgerichtsverfahren, 45-46; SCHLOSSER, P., Das Recht der internationalen privaten Schiedsgerichtsbarkeit, first edition, 626.

296. *Positive* : BUCHER, A., Transnationales Recht im ipr, 50-51 and Le nouvel arbitrage international en Suisse, 117 with reference to the Swiss Supreme Court decision of January 3, 1984, ATF 110 Ia 56; *but see* LALIVE, P., POUDRET, J.F. and REY-MOND, C., Le droit de l'arbitrage interne et international en Suisse, 425, 431 and 173-174.

composition without party authorization and would have set aside the award. However, it saved the award by interpreting its precise meaning. Since the arbitrators had applied English law and had also referred to French and Dutch law, the Court was satisfied that the award was not solely based on equity or natural justice[297].

182. In order to assess the impact of *amiable composition* on arbitral conflict autonomy, the nature and development of *amiable composition* should be taken into account. Traditionally, *amiable composition* provided an equity correction as to the application of strict rules of law. Parties who give arbitrators the authority to act as *amiables compositeurs*, give them discretion as to the law applicable to the merits of the dispute. Therefore, provided the applicable law also authorizes *amiable composition*, this may be a vehicle to apply autonomous conflict rules or other conflict of laws methods. However, this does not necessarily imply that opposite conclusions may be drawn. This means that, failing party authorization permitted under the applicable law, arbitrators do not necessarily act as *amiables compositeurs* when they base their decisions on principles of fairness, equity and natural justice. This is so because, in many legal systems such as the Swiss, German and Dutch and to a lesser extent in French and Belgian law, the distinction between application of strict law and *amiable composition* has eroded due to the emergence of *open-ended rules* (*Generalklauseln, normes floues*)[298]. The law is therefore no longer as strict as it used to be and considerations of equity also are very important in its application. These developments may be seen in substantive law as well as in conflict of laws. Thus, the dispute settlement methods used by arbitrators should be reviewed against this development. Only when it appears that under rules of law, including open-ended rules, a certain conclusion could not have been drawn, the aforementioned problems relating to *amiable composition* not authorized by the parties or the applicable law, may be involved[299].

---

297. October 26, 1983, RIW, 1984, 400, case note DIELMANN, H., aff'd. Supreme Court, September 26, 1985, NJW 1986, 1436, JZ 1986, 401; *critical* ADEN, M., Die Anwendung materiellen Rechts durch den Schiedsrichter, 934-938.

298. See also BROGGINI, G., Réflexions sur l'équité dans l'arbitrage international, ASA Bull., 1991, 95-122.

299. The mere violation of the applicable conflict rule is thus insufficient; one should demonstrate that the arbitrators could not have come to their award if they had applied the correct conflict rule (BERGER, K.P., Internationale Wirtschaftsschiedsgerichtsbarkeit, 482-483). The Dutch Supreme Court has held otherwise (December 22, 1978, N.J., 1979, No. 521, opinion VAN OOSTEN, case note SANDERS, P.) but this case no longer applies as to the problem discussed here in view of the liberal provision

183. One may thus conclude that review might especially be available if the arbitrators act as *amiables compositeurs* without having been authorized to do so by the parties. Furthermore, in some jurisdictions, review might also be possible as to whether the applicable law authorizes *amiable composition*.

II.3.3.5 Impact of the recognition and enforcement procedure

184. There is interaction between conflict rules applied by the arbitrators and national legal systems also with respect to the recognition or enforcement of arbitral awards. Here, one may ask whether and to what extent the law of the place of recognition or enforcement should be taken into account by arbitrators applying conflict rules. Generally speaking, one might say that arbitrators do not account for the enforcement of the award. Consequently, they shouldn't take into account all laws of places where enforcement might be sought. Since enforcement depends upon the factual element of presence of assets, the place of enforcement is often not easy to determine and may be subject to change. In practice, however, it might be easier to determine what laws should be taken into account, for instance, because the place of arbitration has been chosen for enforcement purposes or because assets of the parties are located in a limited number of countries. This will also be the case with regard to recognition problems. Because of the large number of contracting states, the New York Convention will often be applicable. Also, the European Commercial Arbitration Convention and the Uncitral Model Law will be discussed[300].

185. Conflict rules are used in recognition or enforcement proceedings in order to determine the law which should be applied in order to assess whether the conditions for a ground for refusal of recognition or enforcement are met. Such rules may be found regarding the agreement to

---

of article 1054 Dutch Code of Civil Procedure. Furthermore, one may doubt, for reasons of efficiency, whether the position of the Court should be applied as to review on the conflict and substantive rules applied by the arbitrators.

300. Domestic law may be applicable under the more favourable treatment clause of article VII (1) of the New York Convention.

arbitrate[301], the capacity to conclude an agreement to arbitrate[302], the arbitrability of the subject matter[303] and the arbitral procedure[304].

186. Pursuant to article 2, c of the Geneva Convention of 1927, article V, § 1, c of the New York Convention, article IX (1), c of the European Convention and article 36 (1) (a) (iii) of the Uncitral Model Law, recognition or enforcement of the award may be refused if the award contains decisions as to matters beyond the scope of the submission to arbitration. The question may arise whether this applies if the arbitrators have not applied the law chosen by the parties. The answer may be positive. These grounds refer not only to an excess of powers in relation to the submission to arbitration but also to an excess as to the arbitrators' mandate[305]. The same provisions may, according to some authors, also be applied if arbitrators, absent party designated law, do not follow applicable conflict rules[306].

187. Also, interaction exists between the state of origin of the award and the state of recognition or enforcement. Article V, § 1, e of the New York Convention and article 36 (1) (a) (v) of the Uncitral Model Law provide that recognition or enforcement may be refused if the award has not yet become binding on the parties or has been set aside or suspended by a competent authority in the state of origin. Setting aside the award, on any grounds in the state of origin may thus automatically affect the recognition or enforcement of the award[307]. This has been changed under article IX (2) of the European Convention. If applicable, and between contracting states to the New York Convention, suspension or setting aside of the award may only lead to a refusal to recognize or enforce if the grounds for

---

301. Article V, § 1, a New York Convention, article IX (1), a European Convention and article 36 (1) (a) (i) Uncitral Model Law.
302. Article V, § 1, a New York Convention, article IX (1), a European Convention.
303. Article V, § 2, a New York Convention, article 36 (1) (b) (i) Uncitral Model Law.
304. Article V, § 1, d New York Convention, article 36 (1) (a) (iv) Uncitral Model Law, article IX (1), d European Convention. For the interpretations to which these provisions have led, see supra Nos. 152-154.
305. VAN DEN BERG, A.J., The New York Arbitration Convention of 1958, 314; TRIEBEL, V. and PETZOLD, E., Grenzen der lex mercatoria in der internationalen Schiedsgerichtsbarkeit, RIW, 1988, 250.
306. BÜLOW, A., Das UN-Übereinkommen über die Anerkennung und Vollstreckung ausländischer Schiedssprüche, KTS, 1959, 11; VON BAR, C., Internationales Privatrecht, Volume 1, 86.
307. MAIER, H., Europäisches Übereinkommen über die internationale Handelsschiedsgerichtsbarkeit und UN-Übereinkommen über die Anerkennung und Vollstreckung ausländischer Schiedssprüche, 21-22.

suspension or setting aside in the state of origin is at the same time a ground for refusal to recognize or enforce. Particular grounds for setting aside may thus only affect recognition or enforcement if these correspond to one of the grounds for refusal under the New York Convention. This system has loosened the link between state of origin and state of enforcement since application of the system may result in the recognition or enforcement of an award which has been suspended or set aside in the origin state. Recent arbitration laws have adopted the European Convention system[308].

188. Finally, article V, § 2, b of the New York Convention and article 36 (1) (b) (ii) of the Uncitral Model Law provide that recognition or enforcement of the award may have effects not contrary to international public policy of the recognition or enforcement forum[309].

189. Now, one may ask whether conflict rules applied by arbitrators may be reviewed in the course of recognition and enforcement proceedings[310].

---

308. Article 1502 N.C.P.C.; see BELLET, P. and MEZGER, E., L'arbitrage international dans le nouveau code de procédure civile, 648-649.

309. It has been argued that arbitral awards should be compatible with transnational public policy (see infra No. 446). Quite rightly, Kornblum has stated that this does not replace the reservation as to the compatibility with the international public policy of the enforcement forum (KORNBLUM, U., "Ordre public transnational", "ordre public international" und "ordre public interne" im Recht der privaten Schiedsgerichtsbarkeit, Beiträge zum internationalen Verfahrensrecht und zur Schiedsgerichtsbarkeit, Festschrift für H. Nagel, Münster, Aschendorff, 1987, 141-142).

Gottwald (Die sachliche Kontrolle internationaler Schiedssprüche durch staatliche Gerichte, 65) seems to exclude review of arbitral conflict rules by means of the public policy exception. Lalive (Les règles de conflit de lois appliquées au fond du litige par l'arbitre international siégeant en Suisse, 89) also denies review under the New York Convention.

For the U.S. where manifest disregard of the law may be considered contrary to public policy, see DE LA HOUSSAYE, I., Manifest disregard of the law in international commercial arbitrations, COL.J.TRANSNAT'L L. 1990, 449-472.

310. Goldman has argued that violation of a French conflict rule may not be challenged at the enforcement level (V° arbitrage (droit international privé), 134; also FRANCESCAKIS, P., v° jugement étranger, Répertoire Dalloz, Procédure civile, Paris, 1956, 244; *contra* NIBOYET, J.P., Traité de droit international privé français, VI, Paris, Sirey, 1950, 144-145).

Review as to conflict rules should be distinguished from review as to the substantive rules. A majority opinion stands for the proposition that the New York Convention does not authorize review as to the substantive law. This would imply that non-national rules may be applied (MAYER, P., Droit international privé, second edition, 557-558; VAN DEN BERG, A.J., Internationale arbitrage in Nederland en arbitrage buiten Nederland, 127; VON MEHREN, A., To what extent is international commercial

In this respect, one should discuss the decision of the English Court of Appeal in *Deutsche Schachtbau- und Tiefbohrgesellschaft mbh v. R'As Al Khamaih National Oil Company*[311]. This case involved an arbitral award rendered in connection with disputes arising out of an oil exploration contract. The award was in favour of Deutsche Schachtbau-und Tiefbohrgesellschaft, which sought enforcement in England. According to article 13 (3) of the I.C.C. Arbitration Rules, the Geneva-based arbitral tribunal had, absent party designated law, applied *internationally accepted principles of contract law*. The Court of Appeal granted enforcement of the award. In its opinion, enforcement was not contrary to public policy and application of internationally accepted principles of contract law was not beyond the scope of the mandate given to the arbitral tribunal by the parties to determine the proper law by means of the conflict rule the arbitrators deem appropriate. Under article 13 (3) of the I.C.C. Arbitration Rules, the parties had left it to the arbitrators to determine the applicable law and had not limited it to national legal systems. One may doubt whether the last part of this reasoning is correct, since not the arbitration rules, but the law of the enforcement forum must determine how to deal with application of non-national rules[312]. In any event, the *Deutsche Schachtbau*-case clearly indicates that English courts are willing to limit review in the course of enforcement proceedings[313].

190. It follows from the preceding analysis that enforcement review is generally limited. As to the merits of the dispute, hardly any review seems possible.

---

arbitration autonomous ?, 224; BÖCKSTIEGEL, K.H., Zu den Thesen von einer "delokalisierten" internationalen Schiedsgerichtsbarkeit, 9; GOTTWALD, P., Die sachliche Kontrolle internationaler Schiedssprüche durch staatliche Gerichte, 65; VAN DEN BERG, A.J., The New York Arbitration Convention of 1958, 313; *contra* but without motivation, BREDIN, J.D., La Convention de New-York du 10 juin 1958 pour la reconnaissance et l'exécution des sentences arbitrales étrangères, Clunet, 1960, 1022; LOUSSOUARN, Y. and BREDIN, J.D., Droit du commerce international, 115).

311. [1987] 3 W.L.R. 1023 (Court of Appeal), Financial Times Law Reports, March 31, 1987, 18.

312. *Compare* MUSTILL, M., The new lex mercatoria : the first twenty-five years, 171-172.

313. See also STEYN, J., Arbitration in England: the current issues, INT'L BUS.LAWYER, 1987, 434; HUNTER, M., Lex Mercatoria - Deutsche Schachtbau- und Tiefbohrgesellschaft mbh v. R'As Al Khaimah National Oil Co., Lloyd's Mar. & Com.L.Q., 1987, 277-280 and Arbitration, 1988, 58.

II.3.3.6 Conclusions

191. In many cases, parallelism between arbitral conflict rules and conflict rules of the competent jurisdiction will be necessary to guarantee the efficiency of the arbitral process[314]. In this respect, one may particularly refer to the conflict problems relating to the agreement to arbitrate and the arbitral procedure as well as to setting aside and enforcement litigation.

However, autonomous arbitral conflict rules may be accepted in relation to the law applicable to the substance of the dispute. Article VII (1) of the European Convention, the Uncitral Model Law and the provisions of the French, Dutch and Swiss laws have granted broad discretion regarding the dispute settlement rules. But also here, there is parallelism between what arbitrators do and what they are authorized to do under national law. Furthermore, review in the course of setting aside or enforcement proceedings is in this respect very limited so that arbitral conflict rules are generally not supervised unless arbitrators act contrary to the parties' choice of law (including *amiable composition* without party authorization). Thus, the question remains under what conditions one should recognize autonomous conflict rules applied by arbitrators to the substance of the dispute.

II.3.3.7 Requirements for application of autonomous conflict rules by arbitrators

192. To the extent that national law creates room for application of autonomous conflict rules, one should raise the question how such rules can be developed and whether they are not merely created by tolerance of national states. Bucher has proposed to base autonomous conflict rules on the general principle of choice of law. Since this principle is so generally accepted, it would no longer need support from international conventions or national laws in order to be applicable[315]. However, this principle is not as generally accepted as is often thought and it is so indefinite that autonomous conflict rules can hardly be based on it[316]. Absent choice of law, Bucher has recognized that application of transnational rules should be based on national conflict rules[317].

314. *Compare* LEW, J., Applicable law in international commercial arbitration, 252.
315. BUCHER, A., Transnationales Recht im ipr, 34.
316. See infra No. 426.
317. BUCHER, A., Transnationales Recht im ipr, 50-51.

193. When exploring the possibility of creating autonomous conflict rules, basic features of conflict rules should be taken into account. Traditionally, conflict rules were thought to be neutral from a substantive point of view, since they merely looked to geographical connections between transactions or situations and national states. Conflict of laws is then content-neutral and does not purport to achieve whatever social goals. From this perspective, it would hardly be relevant whether national or autonomous conflict rules are applicable, since no public or private interests have to be protected. Conflict of laws is open minded and willing also to apply foreign law. This implies that the mandatory rules of the *lex fori*, except for its *lois d'application immédiate*, are no longer applicable. This is acceptable since the mandatory rules of foreign law will then be applied. Application of autonomous conflict rules should have the same preoccupations. These conflict rules should lead to the application of legal rules which tend to offer at least minimal protection for some public and private interests[318]. If it were to lead to rules which have hardly any such protection, the openness of conflict of laws would be frustrated. Also, autonomous conflict rules should be embedded in a general framework for conflict rules which should be able to solve the problems related to the conflict method[319].

In addition, recent developments in conflict of laws make clear that in certain areas, conflict rules no longer are content-neutral but express some policy objectives. If arbitrators develop such autonomous conflict rules, one may ask where the underlying policy objectives have been found. One may, at this point of the analysis, assume that arbitrators find these policy objectives in an autonomous *system* of law[320].

Furthermore, gaps may be found as to the conflict rules to be applied. Again, an autonomous *system* should be capable of providing a mechanism to fill such gaps. Otherwise, arbitrators should have to fall back on national conflict rules which would prove the absence of a system of autonomous arbitral conflict rules.

194. Autonomy as to the applicable law may also be achieved through transnational substantive rules. Lalive has stated that the determination of the law applicable to the substance of the dispute is such a transnational

---

318. See CARBONNEAU, T., The remaking of arbitration : design and destiny, 13-19 and JUENGER, F., Afterword : the lex mercatoria and the conflict of laws, 222-223, both in Lex mercatoria and arbitration, CARBONNEAU, T. (ed.), Dobbs Ferry, Transnational 1990; JUENGER, F., Lex mercatoria und Eingriffsnormen, 245-249.

319. See supra No. 135.

320. Van Houtte has denied the existence of such system (Rechtsvinding bij transnationale handelsarbitrage, 525).

substantive rule. Furthermore, this rule would have a transnational origin[321]. But here also, an autonomous system should articulate this rule and determine its scope. This is all the more so because transnational substantive rules usually express liberal policies. It is thus necessary to find a transnational system containing these policies.

195. It follows from the foregoing that an autonomous system of arbitral conflict of laws should be available[322], containing autonomous conflict rules, transnational substantive rules, its own methodology and mandatory rules.

II.3.3.8 Conclusions

196. Absent an international court of arbitration which might adjudicate international business law disputes[323], national law still has a considerable impact on the conflict of laws techniques applied by international commercial arbitrators, provided the national court system at some point intervenes in the arbitral process. This impact is, however, much more limited as to the substance of the dispute. Absent authorization of the applicable national law, some conflict of laws system should be available which may be applied by the arbitrators. If not, problems may arise in the course of setting aside or enforcement proceedings where the arbitrators may be held to have exceeded their powers or to have acted as *amiables compositeurs*.

---

321. LALIVE, P., Les règles de conflit de lois appliquées au fond du litige par l'arbitre international siégeant en Suisse, 95; LOQUIN, E., Les pouvoirs des arbitres internationaux à la lumière de l'évolution récente du droit de l'arbitrage international, 303; see also LEW, J., Applicable law in international commercial arbitration, 96 and JACQUET, J.M., Principe d'autonomie et contrats internationaux, 115; *but see* WEISE, P.F., Lex mercatoria, 137-138.

322. See JACQUET, J.M., Principe d'autonomie et contrats internationaux, 103-112; RIGAUX, F., Examen de quelques questions laissées ouvertes par la Convention de Rome sur la loi applicable aux obligations contractuelles, 307-308 and 316.

323. COING, H., Materielles Recht und Verfahrensrecht in der internationalen Schiedsgerichtsbarkeit, 29-30; *contra* MOTULSKY, H., L'internationalisation du droit français de l'arbitrage, MOTULSKY, H., Ecrits, études et notes sur l'arbitrage, Paris, Dalloz, 1974, 325.

CHAPTER III

International Business Law and Substantive Law

197. In the previous chapter, the application of conflict rules to international business transactions by national courts and arbitration tribunals has been analyzed. In this chapter, the following sources of substantive law applied to international business law problems will be discussed : 1) international contracts, standard forms and general conditions; 2) international customs and trade usages; 3) self-regulatory rules of professional organizations; 4) general principles of law; 5) technical, professional and deontological standards and codes of conduct; 6) arbitral case law; and 7) international conventions. This discussion will focus primarily on the contribution that these sources may make to the law of international business transactions.

III.1 International contracts, standard forms and general conditions

198. Recent theories on international business law, and particularly the theory of *lex mercatoria*, have emphasized the important role of frequently used contract clauses and general conditions in international business life[1]. Contracts are indeed essential instruments of self-regulation. Post-war practice has seen the development of new sorts of contracts and of many innovative contract clauses. Furthermore, contract practice has to a certain extent been standardized by means of general conditions of contract. In many cases, international contract practice has taken the lead in these developments.

199. Apart from the practical relevance of contracts for international business, any reflection on international business law should also address the question how international contracts interact with and within national legal systems. The first question has been analyzed in Chapter II. The place of international business contracts within the applicable legal system may be tackled from a pragmatic and a jurisprudential perspective. Under the first perspective, questions as to the relation with statutory law and custom will be answered. A jurisprudential approach will, however, also put the

---

1. See infra IV.1.1.

question whether contracts do not by themselves create law. Any answer to this question will be faced with the distinction between rules of law (*droit objectif, Objektives Recht*) and rights derived from law (*droit subjectif, Subjektives Recht*). It is generally accepted that by virtue of and under the conditions set by law, contracts may create enforceable rights but do not create law[2]. For national contracts, self-regulation by contract is limited to those rules from which they are permitted by law to derogate. In international contracts, choice of law finds its limits in the mandatory rules of the chosen law[3].

200. A minority view has taken an opposite position, according to which the will of the parties may create law[4]. This conception is closely related to an individualistic jurisprudence. Similarly, in relation to general conditions, it has been argued that these create law[5]. One must admit that general conditions, like statutory law, have a general and almost mandatory character. However, this analogy seems to be insufficient to support the proposition.

III.2 International customs and trade usages

201. Post war theories on international business law also have pointed to the relevance of international custom and trade usages. From a legal point of view, repeated use of contract forms or clauses or repeated courses of action may have normative value. Hereafter, this will be discussed in domestic law and international conventions in order to be able to measure their relevance for international business transactions.

---

2. See article 1134, first paragraph Cc: VAN RYN, J., L'engagement par déclaration unilatérale de volonté, J.T., 1984, 130; JACQUET, J.M., Principe d'autonomie et contrats internationaux, 79; for other legal systems, see REIMANN, T., Zur Lehre vom "rechtsordnungslosen" Vertrag, 38-39, 47-50 and 65; KROPHOLLER, J., Internationales Einheitsrecht, Allgemeine Lehren, 120; SCHLOSSER, P., Das internationale an der internationalen privaten Schiedsgerichtsbarkeit, 866; DASSER, F., Internationale Schiedsgerichte und lex mercatoria, 84; DE CASTRO Y BRAVO, F., Les usages dans le projet de loi uniforme sur la vente internationale, Mélanges offerts à Jacques Maury, II, Paris, Dalloz, 1960, 85-86.
3. See supra No. 85.
4. ASSER-SCHOLTEN, Algemeen deel, second edition, Zwolle, Tjeenk Willink, 1934, 18-23; VERHEUL, J.P., Rechtsvinding in het internationaal privaatrecht, 107-108.
5. BERLIOZ, G., Le contrat d'adhésion, 167.

III.2.1 *International customs and trade usages in national legal systems*

202. The basic question in relation to customs and usages is to what extent the law should be open to recognize forms of spontaneous behaviour. Immediately, the relation between formalized law making processes and spontaneous rule making and rule formation is at stake. Also, this debate is obscured by the lack of precision of the terminology which is used. This terminological problem is due to the fact that various forms of spontaneous rule formation exist which cannot easily be converted under one heading. Custom and usage may, for instance, relate to a factual situation which is irrelevant from the legal point of view, to a factual situation which has been given certain effects by the law and to a legal rule[6]. The latter meaning will be used in the discussion below.

III.2.1.1 English law

203. English law does not know a clear distinction between custom and usage[7]. Only Allen and Wellwood have tried to identify both concepts. In their view, usages, contrary to customary law, are contractual and should not have existed for centuries in order to be binding. Also, they are preempted by mandatory rules of common law[8].

204. As to the requirements for custom, English law takes a very restrictive position. Custom should be constant, voluntary, certain, consistent and reasonable[9]. Furthermore, custom should meet the very harsh requirement of immemoriality (*i.e.*, custom should be proven to exist in 1189, when the reign of Richard I began)[10]. In practice, courts have relaxed this rule[11] and recognize custom if established by previous precedents[12]. Custom may

---

6. See KASSIS, A., Théorie générale des usages du commerce, 6; LEYMARIE, F., Les usages commerciaux, 57; PABBRUWE, H., Gebruik en gebruikelijk beding, Zwolle, Tjeenk Willink, 1961, 11-15.
7. ASKE, R., The law relating to custom and the usage of trade, London, Stevens & Sons, 1909, 13; HONNOLD, J., The influence of the law of international trade on the development and character of English and American commercial law, 79.
8. ALLEN, C., Law in the making, sixth edition, Oxford, Clarendon Press, 1958, 132; WELLWOOD, J., Custom and usage, in 12 Halsbury's laws of England, fourth edition, London, Butterworths, 1975, 4.
9. ASKE, R., The law relating to custom and the usages of trade, 48-74; ANSON'S LAW OF CONTRACT by A. GUEST, 26th edition, Oxford, Clarendon press, 1984, 128; CHITTY ON CONTRACTS, I, 25th edition, London, Sweet & Maxwell, 1983, 448.
10. ASKE, R., The law relating to custom and the usages of trade, 39-48.
11. See WELLWOOD, J., Custom and usage, 5.
12. WORTLEY, B., Mercantile usage and custom, RabelsZ, 1959, 261.

derogate from common law[13] but not from statutory law[14]. Finally, contract prevails over contrary custom[15].

205. On the other hand, usages are factual patterns of behaviour that are generally followed[16], are quite certain and have been in existence for some time[17]. Traditionally, they have been held binding on the basis of the presumed intentions of the parties[18]. From the second half of the nineteenth century, usages have been applied irrespective of whether the parties are aware of them[19]. In theory, usages were still deemed part of the contract as *implied terms*[20]. Scholars have criticized this, because knowledge and acceptance of usages is no longer required. At the same time, it has been emphasized that this situation leaves judges with wide discretion as to the application of usages[21].

206. Finally, Schmitthoff has given a very specific definition to international custom. He draws a line with the activities of international organizations who formulate international business rules aimed at unification of law. These rules are called international custom and are operative if accepted

---

13. ASKE, R.W., The law relating to custom and the usages of trade, 179-181.
14. ASKE, R.W., The law relating to custom and the usages of trade, 74-75 and 181-186.
15. ASKE, R., The law relating to custom and the usages of trade, 206-208; TREITEL, G., An outline of the law of contract, third edition, London, Butterworths, 1984, 68.
16. WELLWOOD, J., Custom and usage, 32; ASKE, R., The law relating to custom and the usages of the trade, 158-179; DEVLIN, P., The relation between commercial law and commercial practice, Mod.L.Rev., 1951, 251.
17. ASKE, R., The law relating to custom and the usages of the trade, 167-169.
18. ASKE, R., The law relating to custom and the usages of trade, 12 and 144.
19. WELLWOOD, J., Custom and usage, 44-45; ASKE, R., The law relating to custom and the usage of trade, 190-191; CHITTY ON CONTRACTS, I, 459; TREITEL, G., An outline of the law of contract, 65-66.
20. See WORTLEY, B., The relevance of courses of dealing, usages and customs in the interpretation of international commercial contracts, New directions in international trade law, Acts and proceedings of the second congress on private law held by Unidroit, I, Dobbs Ferry, New York, Oceana, 1977, 139.
21. CHITTY ON CONTRACTS, I, 451 and 459; SIMPSON, A., Historical introduction, GHESHIRE and FIFOOT, Law of contract, tenth edition, London, Butterworths, 1981, 13-14; ATIYAH, P., An introduction to the law of contract, third edition, Oxford, Clarendon Press, 1981, 166-167 and 176-183; TREITEL, G., An outline of the law of contract, 65-66; DAVID, R. and PUGSLEY, D., Les contrats en droit anglais, second edition, Paris, LGDJ, 1985, 199-200.

by the parties[22]. Thus, only a new description of international custom is given but no new theory on custom and usages is developed[23].

III.2.1.2 U.S.A. : the UCC

207. In the UCC, the distinction between custom and trade usages has been abandoned. In § 1-205, an extensive description regarding usages of trade and courses of dealing may be found. UCC § 1-205 (1) defines a course of dealing as a sequence of previous conduct between the parties to a particular transaction which is fairly to be regarded as establishing a common basis of understanding for interpreting their expressions and other conduct. § 1-205 (2) defines usages of trade as practices or methods of dealing having such regularity of observance in a place, vocation or trade as to justify an expectation that it will be observed[24]. One may note that under this provision, the parties need not consent to the application of a usage[25]. The Comment to § 1-205 (2) indicates that the requirements of English law as to the ancient, immemorial or universal character of custom are abandoned which may result in the recognition of new usages, usages currently observed by the great majority of dealers and usages agreed upon by merchants in trade codes[26]. Furthermore, one should no longer prove that a usage is reasonable. Rather, it is assumed that the acceptance of a usage makes a *prima facie* case of its reasonableness but the provisions of the UCC regarding unconscionable contracts and clauses may be used to review unconscionable or dishonest standard practices[27].

The legal status of courses of dealing and trade usages is determined by § 1-205 (3) UCC. It states that a course of dealing between parties and any usages of trade in the vocation of trade in which they are engaged or of which they are or should be aware give particular meaning to and

---

22. SCHMITTHOFF, C., International trade law and private international law, 267-268; SCHMITTHOFF, C., The law of international trade, its growth, formulation and operation, 16; SCHMITTHOFF, C., The unification of the law of international trade, 7; SCHMITTHOFF, C., Nature and evolution of the transnational law of commercial transactions, 24; SCHMITTHOFF, C., Commercial law in a changing economic climate, 23.
23. See infra No. 322.
24. According to Berman and Kaufman, § 1-205 (2) no longer has a psychological component (The law of international commercial transactions (lex mercatoria), 262-263).
25. BONELL, M., The relevance of courses of dealing, usages and customs in the interpretation of international commercial contracts, 111-112.
26. Comment 5 to UCC § 1-205.
27. Comment 6 to UCC § 1-205.

supplement or qualify terms of an agreement. Under that provision, they both have an interpretative as well as a supplementary function[28].

Finally, in § 1-205 (4), the hierarchy between contract terms, courses of dealing and trade usages is settled. In case of inconsistencies, express terms of an agreement control both course of dealing and trade usage and course of dealing controls usage of trade.

It follows from the foregoing that the UCC seems to indicate that the problem of custom and trade usage is not so much a question of sources of law or of contract terms but a question of contract construction.

III.2.1.3 German law

208. German law has four important provisions on custom and trade usages. First, article 2 of the Enactment Law of the Civil Code (*Einführungsgesetz zum Bürgerlichen Gesetzbuch*, "*EGBGB*") defines law as it is used in the BGB and EGBGB as including any rule of law[29]. Generally, one considers that custom is such rule of law and a genuine source of law[30]. In order to recognize custom, a psychological and a factual element are required. This means that there is custom if parties observe a certain constant pattern of behaviour while feeling bound by it[31].

209. Three provisions relate to trade usages (*Verkehrssitte*). These are defined as uniform patterns which have been observed for some time leading to a general conviction that they are applicable[32]. However,

---

28. BAINBRIDGE, S., Trade usages in international sales of goods : an analysis of the 1964 and 1980 Sales Convention, VA.J.INT'L L., 1984, 640; ANDERSON on the Uniform Commercial Code, Lawyers co-operative publishing company, Rochester, New York, 1970, 1, 175.
29. BROX, H., Allgemeiner Teil des Bürgerlichen Gesetzbuchs, fourth edition, Cologne, Heymanns, 1980, 6; BAHR, P., Grundzüge des bürgerlichen Rechts, fourth edition, Munich, Vahlen, 1983, 5.
30. LÖNING, G., Autonomes Recht der Wirtschaft, Mitteilungen des Jenaer Institut für Wissenschaftsrecht, Volume 20, 1930, 14; SCHMIDT, K., Handelsrecht, 19.
31. HUBNER, H., Allgemeiner Teil des Bürgerlichen Gesetzbuches, Berlin, de Gruyter, 1985, 19-20; HORN, N., Das Recht der internationalen Anleihen, 518; BÖCKSTIEGEL, K.H., Die Bestimmung des anwendbaren Rechts in der Praxis internationaler Schiedsgerichtsverfahren, 457-458.
32. German Supreme Court, May 2, 1984, WM, 1984, 1000; SONNENBERGER, H.J., Verkehrssitte im Schuldvertrag, Munich, Beck, 1969, 96-97; KROPHOLLER, J., Internationales Einheitsrecht, Allgemeine Lehren, 121.

contrary to custom, trade usages are not law since parties feel not bound by it[33]; rather they have specific functions in contract and commercial law.

210. First, the German Civil Code has two major open-ended rules. With regard to interpretation and performance of contracts, §§ 157 and 242 BGB refer to the notion of good faith (*Treu und Glauben*). Within this standard of good faith, express reference is made to usages which should be taken into account. In this process, it is irrelevant whether the parties knew the usages or consented to their application[34].

Usages have two functions[35]. Under § 157 BGB, they have an *interpretative* function[36]. In order to understand this function, it is necessary to know how interpretation operates under German law. Since contracts are formed upon the meeting of declarations (and not of the minds) (*Erklärungstheorie*), interpretation is aimed at constructing the declarations of the parties (and not their intentions). Thus, the interpretation process is *objective*[37]. This may be explained by the fact that German law looks more to the interests of the creditor than to the will of the debtor. This objective process is particularly clear when a declaration of a party may be supplemented according to standards of reasonableness and

33. SONNENBERGER, H.J., Verkehrssitte im Schuldvertrag, 107-108; FLUME, W., Allgemeiner Teil des Bürgerlichen Rechts, II, Das Rechtsgeschäft, second edition, Berlin, Springer, 1975, 312-313 and 325; LARENZ, K., Allgemeiner Teil des deutschen Bürgerlichen Rechts, sixth edition, Munich, Beck, 1983, 12; MünchKomm-MAYER-MALY, § 157, No. 15; LÖNING, G., Autonomes Recht der Wirtschaft, 14; BÖCKSTIEGEL, K.H., Die Bestimmung des anwendbaren Rechts in der Praxis internationaler Schiedsgerichtsverfahren, 457-458.

34. OERTMANN, P., Rechtsordnung und Verkehrssitte, 15 and 386; FLUME, W., Das Rechtsgeschäft, 313; MünchKomm-MAYER-MALY, § 157, Nos. 15-16; KROPHOLLER, J., Internationales Einheitsrecht, Allgemeine Lehren, 121; DUROUDIER, R. and KUHLEWEIN, R., De l'influence des usages commerciaux et des "conditions générales d'affaires" sur les contrats entre commerçants dans la loi allemande, Rev.Trim.Dr.Com., 1956, 36; EISEMANN, F., Die Incoterms in Handel und Verkehr, Vienna, GOF-Verlag Friedl, 1963, 18; EISEMANN, F., Die Incoterms im Recht der internationalen Warenhandels : Außerstaatliche Rechtsbildung oder Vertragsrecht ?, XII Yearbook of the school of law and economic science, Aristotelian University of Thessaloniki, Miscellany in honor of C. Fragistas, II, Thessaloniki, 1967, 331-333; EISEMANN, F., Die Incoterms im internationalen Warenkaufrecht, 47-49.

35. In practice, it is difficult to distinguish between these functions, see MünchKomm-ROTH, § 242, Nos. 83-85.

36. OERTMANN, P., Rechtsordnung und Verkehrssitte, 60-309.

37. OERTMANN, P., Rechtsordnung und Verkehrssitte, 71 and 74; RIEG, A., Le rôle de la volonté dans l'acte juridique en droit civil français et allemand, 358 and 368-377; ZWEIGERT, K. and KÖTZ, H., Einführung in die Rechtsvergleichung, II, 101-103; LOPEZ SANTA MARIA, J., Les systèmes d'interprétation des contrats, dissertation, Université de Paris, Faculté de droit et des sciences économiques, Paris, 1968, 182.

all circumstances surrounding the declaration (*ergänzende Auslegung*)[38]. Under the good faith rule of § 242 BGB, usages also have a *supplementary function* in relation to the performance of the contract[39].

211. The German Commercial Code (*Handelsgesetzbuch*, "*HGB*") has a provision similar to §§ 157 and 242 BGB. § 346 HGB states that in the construction of transactions among merchants[40], commercial custom and usages should be taken into account. Notwithstanding its reference to custom, § 346 HGB is generally considered as the application of §§ 157 and 242 BGB in commercial law. Therefore, trade usages have the same characteristics as usages in civil law[41].

212. Similar to the UCC, trade usages, under German law are not genuine sources of law nor implied contract terms[42]. More explicitly than under the UCC, they function as tools of contract construction applied by virtue of an open-ended rule[43].

213. Under German law, the hierarchy between usages and other rules is as follows. First, usages cannot derogate from contract terms[44]. Second, usages control statutory rules from which parties may derogate, with regard to the interpretation of declarations; their relation to these rules is debated in relation to the process of supplementing declarations and obligations[45].

---

38. FLOCKE, H.J., Risiken beim internationalen Anlagenvertrag, Heidelberg, Verlag Recht und Wirtschaft, 1986, 61.
39. OERTMANN, P., Rechtsordnung und Verkehrssitte, 310-475.
40. See SCHMIDT, K., Handelsrecht, 40-41.
41. OERTMANN, P., Rechtsordnung und Verkehrssitte, 34; REHME, P., Das heutige deutsche Handelsrecht, 273-275; SCHLEGELBERGER-HEFERMEHL, Handelsgesetzbuch, III, fourth edition, Berlin, Vahlen, 1965, 1511 and 1525; BAUMBACH/DUDEN/HOPT, Handelsgesetzbuch, twenty-fifth edition, Munich, Beck, 1983, 585; LUITHLEN, W., Einheitliches Kaufrecht und autonomes Handelsrecht, 46-48; ROTH, W.H., Internationales Versicherungsvertragsrecht, 544.
42. LUITHLEN, W., Einheitliches Kaufrecht und autonomes Handelsrecht, 42; JOKELA, H., The role of usages in the Uniform law on international sales, 85; JUNGE, W., in DÖLLE, H., Kommentar zum Einheitlichen Kaufrecht, 41.
43. OERTMANN, P., Rechtsordnung und Verkehrssitte, 314, 349-351, 364 and 367.
44. EISEMANN, F., Die Incoterms in Handel und Verkehr, 18.
45. SONNENBERGER, H.J., Verkehrssitte im Schuldvertrag, 120.

III.2.1.4 Swiss law

214. Article 1 (2) of the Swiss Civil Code provides that, absent statutory rules, a judge should apply customary law. This reference is interpreted as a recognition of custom as a genuine source of law[46].

215. Regarding usages, there is no general provision in the Swiss Code on Obligations. Sometimes, statutory provisions refer to usages which may derogate from non-mandatory rules (*gesetzesergänzende Verkehrssitte*)[47]. Also, Swiss law is familiar with the German *Verkehrssitte*[48] which are called *rechtsgeschäftliche Verkehrssitte*[49]. In the first place, these usages interpret contracts. Since Swiss law has a *subjective* theory on interpretation aimed at getting at the real intentions of the parties[50], one has to verify whether the parties intended to have a usage applied as an implied term of the contract. This requires that parties had actual or constructive

---

46. PACHE, A., La coutume et les usages dans le droit privé positif, Lausanne, 1938, 20 and 54-55.
47. GUHL/MERZ/KUMMER, Das schweizerische Obligationenrecht, sixth edition, Zurich, Schulthess, 1972, 28.
48. JÄGGI, P. and GAUCH, P., Zürcher Kommentar zum Schweizerischen Zivilgesetzbuch, Volume V 1 b, Zurich, Schulthess, 1980, 100-101 and 104; MERZ, H., Obligationenrecht, Allgemeiner Teil, Erster Teilband, Schweizerisches Privatrecht, VI/1, Basle, Helbing & Lichtenhahn, 1984, 44; ENGEL, P., Traité des obligations en droit suisse, Neuchâtel, Ides et Calendes, 1973, 169; VON TUHR, A. and PETER, H., Allgemeiner Teil des schweizerischen Obligationenrechts, I, third edition, Zurich, Schulthess, 1979, 7; BEGUELIN, M., Das Gewohnheitsrecht in der Praxis des Bundesgerichts, Bern, Lang, 1968, 13 and 113.
49. GUHL/MERZ/KUMMER, Das schweizerische Obligationenrecht, 28.
50. JÄGGI, P. and GAUCH, P., Zürcher Kommentar zum Schweizerischen Zivilgesetzbuch, Volume V 1 b, 3, 76, 78 and 89; LUITHLEN, W., Einheitliches Kaufrecht und autonomes Handelsrecht, 42; JOKELA, H., The role of usages in the Uniform law on international sales, 85; JUNGE, W., in DÖLLE, H., Kommentar zum Einheitlichen Kaufrecht, 41; *with more qualifications*, see MERZ, H., Obligationenrecht, 45; *contra* VON TUHR, A. and PETER, H., Allgemeiner Teil des schweizerischen Obligationenrechts, I, 288.

knowledge of that usage[51]. Second, usage may also have a supplementary function[52].

As to the hierarchy, contract terms control usage[53]. Statutory rules, whether mandatory or not, also seem to prevail over usage[54].

III.2.1.5 Austrian and Italian law

216. Austrian and Italian law are discussed here because some authors have suggested that under these legal systems, usages are genuine sources of law, which may be applied irrespective of parties' knowledge and consent[55].

As to Austrian law, this proposition was based on article 1 of the former Commercial Code (Allgemeines Handelsgesetzbuch, "AHGB")[56]. However, the AHGB was abolished in 1939 when, as a result of the *Anschluß*, the German HGB was introduced in Austria[57]. Article 1 AHGB provided that its gaps could be filled by trade usages and civil law. A majority opinion interpreted article 1 as a confirmation of the role of custom in commercial law[58]. Also, the AHGB in its article 279 had a provision similar to § 346 of the German HGB. From these provisions, one may hardly conclude that trade usages were recognized as a genuine source of law.

At present, Austrian law has some provisions on custom and usages. First, § 10 of the Civil Code (*Allgemeines Bürgerliches Gesetzbuch*, "*ABGB*") states that custom may only be taken into account if referred to by statute.

---

51. PACHE, A., La coutume et les usages dans le droit privé positif, 116-117 and 187-194; JÄGGI, P. and GAUCH, P., Zürcher Kommentar zum Schweizerischen Zivilgesetzbuch, Volume V 1 b, 102-104; ENGEL, P., Traité des obligations en droit suisse, 169-170; *with some qualification*, see DESCHENEAUX, H., Der Einleitungstitel, Schweizerisches Privatrecht, II, Basle, Helbing & Lichtenhahn, 1967, 170; *contra* VON TUHR, A. and PETER, H., Allgemeiner Teil des schweizerischen Obligationenrechts, I, 6-7 and 288.
52. JÄGGI, P. and GAUCH, P., Zürcher Kommentar zum Schweizerischen Zivilgesetzbuch, Volume V 1 b, 135; DESCHENAUX, H., Der Einleitungstitel, 173.
53. JÄGGI, P. and GAUCH, P., Zürcher Kommentar zum schweizerisches Zivilgesetzbuch, Volume V, 1 b, 89.
54. PACHE, A., La coutume et les usages dans le droit privé positif, 183-221.
55. LUITHLEN, W., Einheitliches Kaufrecht und autonomes Handelsrecht, 42; JOKELA, H., The role of usages in the Uniform law on international sales, 85; JUNGE, W., in DÖLLE, H., Kommentar zum Einheitlichen Kaufrecht, 41.
56. LUITHLEN, W., Einheitliches Kaufrecht und autonomes Handelsrecht, 45.
57. RUMMEL, P., Vertragsauslegung nach der Verkehrssitte, Vienna, Manzsche, 1972, 28.
58. See STAUB/PISKO, Kommentar zum allgemeinen deutschen Handelsgesetzbuch, I/1, Vienna, Manzsche, 1935, 7.

This is generally interpreted as referring to usages but not to custom[59]. Second, § 863 (2) ABGB refers to custom and usages in relation to the interpretation of the way in which the parties behave. Similarly, § 914 ABGB states that contracts should not be interpreted literally but in accordance with the intentions of the parties and usages. Austrian commercial law also has some provisions on custom and usage. Article 4 of the Enactment Decree of the HGB dated December 24, 1938, provided that civil law may only be applied in commercial matters if no custom is available. This is the recognition of custom as a genuine source of commercial law[60]. Furthermore, § 346 was introduced in Austria as part of the introduction of the German HGB. Trade usages thus have consequently the same status as under German law[61].

217. In Italy, article 1 of the Introductory Title to the Civil Code (*Codice civile*) recognizes custom as source of law while articles 1340, 1368 and 1374 relate to usages. In the section of the Code on consent, usual contract terms (*clausole d'uso*) are deemed to have been incorporated in the contract, unless otherwise agreed. In the section on interpretation, article 1368, first paragraph provides that ambiguous clauses should be interpreted according to general practice (*pratiche generali interpretative*) prevailing at the place where the contract was formed. As to usages (*usi negoziali o interpretativi*, referred to in articles 1340 and 1368 Cc), they are part of the contract by virtue of incorporation by the parties or by means of contract interpretation looking at the will of the parties[62]. Consequently, their knowledge and consent is required. On the contrary, article 1374 Cc provides that custom and equity also may create contractual obligations. This article refers to *usi normativi* which are applicable without party knowledge or consent[63].

---

59. KOZIOL, H. and WELSER, R., Grundriß des bürgerlichen Rechts, I, Allgemeiner Teil und Schuldrecht, seventh edition, Vienna, Manzsche, 1985, 33.
60. STRAUBE, M., Kommentar zum Handelsgesetzbuch, Vienna, Manzsche, 1987, 14-15.
61. RUMMEL, P., Vertragsauslegung nach der Verkehrssitte, 78-97; RUMMEL, P., ABGB-Kommentar, Volume 1, Vienna, Manzsche, 1983, 1037-1039; KRAMER, E., in STRAUBE, M., Kommentar zum Handelsgesetzbuch, 676, 678, 680-681 and 684.
62. MASSIMO BIANCA, C., Diritto civile, III, Milan, Giuffrè, 1984, 336-337 and 409-410.
63. BONELL, M., Le regole oggetive del commercio internazionale, 124-132; BONELL, M., The relevance of courses of dealing, usages and customs in the interpretation of international commercial contracts, 112-113; MASSIMO BIANCA, C., Diritto civile, III, 490-491.

III.2.1.6 Dutch law

218. On January 1, 1992, major parts of the Dutch New Civil Code (*Nieuw Burgerlijk Wetboek*, "*NBW*"), including law of obligations, entered into effect. Originally, it was intended to have an Introductory Title which would deal with sources of law. These provisions were criticized[64] and were repealed. This was motivated by the fact that codification regarding sources of law, was considered to be unnecessary and might unduly hinder judges in the application and creation of law. One may, however, not conclude that the NBW has changed the sources of Dutch law. For instance, custom is still regarded as a genuine source of law[65].

In contract law, article 248, Book 6 NBW provides that obligations are not limited to what the parties had agreed but also include those obligations which, taking into account the nature of the contract, follow from statutory law, custom or *reasonableness and equity*. This provision recognizes the supplementary function of custom[66].

Under the 1838 Civil Code, article 1383 stated that constantly used clauses (*bestendig gebruikelijke bedingen*) are implicit parts of the contract, even if not expressly indicated. This formulation slightly differs from article 1160 Cc[67] and has led to an interpretation in The Netherlands which is different from that in France and Belgium. Thus, usual clauses which are not customs may be brought into the contrat[68]. These usual clauses may be local or relate to a certain sector of industry or trade but also to clauses which have become usual as between contracting parties[69]. Similarly as

---

64. See PEL, J., De Inleidende Titel van het NBW, Zijn wetgevingsgeschiedenis alsmede de gevolgen daarvan voor de huidige Wet Algemene Bepalingen, Ars Aequi, 1986, 734-739.
65. ASSER-SCHOLTEN, Algemeen deel, 130-131 and 137-138; PITLO, A., Het systeem van het Nederlandse privaatrecht, second edition, Haarlem, Tjeenk Willink, 1964, 30-31.
66. It is the recodification of article 1375 of the 1838 Civil Code which is similar to article 1135 French Cc; see Report Meijers, Parliamentary history of the New Civil Code, Book 6, Deventer, Kluwer, 1981, 919.
    Article 1375 has been analyzed by PABBRUWE, H., Gebruik en gebruikelijk beding, 111-115.
67. According to this article, a contract should be supplemented with the usual clauses. Under French and Belgian law, this article has no meaning other than that of article 1135 Cc (see infra No. 220).
68. ASSER-RUTTEN-II (Algemene leer der overeenkomsten), fourth edition, Zwolle, Tjeenk Willink, 1975, 216.
69. DE KLERK-LEENEN, A., Aanvulling van de overeenkomst door wet, gebruik of bestendig gebruikelijk beding, IV-199; Supreme Court, September 21, 1990, N.J.B. 1990, 1387.

with custom, these clauses may supplement contracts[70]. Actual knowledge of the clause need not be established[71]. In the New Civil Code, article 1383 regarding usual clauses has not been recodified. This was considered unnecessary because usual clauses may be taken into account in the process of interpretation of the parties' expressed will and by means of the application of the theory of legitimate expectations (*vertrouwensbeginsel*)[72].

III.2.1.7 French and Belgian law[73]

219. The 1804 Civil Code (*Code civil*, "*Cc*") has a mixed attitude towards custom and usages. On the one hand, those were deeply embedded into legal tradition but, on the other hand, clearly recalled the *ancien régime*.

In contract law, one should look at articles 1135, 1159 and 1160 Cc. Under the first provision, contracting parties are not only obligated to what expressly has been agreed to but also to what follows from equity, *usage*[74] and statutory law. In the section on interpretation of contracts, article 1159 and 1160 Cc state that ambiguities should be interpreted according to *usage*[75]prevailing at the place where the contract was formed and that contracts should be supplemented with *usual clauses*[76].

220. As such, it is not very clear what the 1804 legislator meant with these provisions. For a better understanding, one should thus read pre-revolutionary authors and particularly Domat and Pothier who influenced these provisions. Domat formulated a rule akin to article 1135 Cc[77]. Sonnenberger has read this rule as the basis for the *supplementary function* of usages, irrespective of party intent[78]. However, one may also read the following in the work of Domat :

70. ASSER-RUTTEN-II (Algemene leer der overeenkomsten), 217-218; PITLO-BOLWEG, Verbintenissenrecht, Arnhem, Gouda Quint, 1979, 272-273.
71. DE KLERK-LEENEN, A., Aanvulling van de overeenkomst door wet, gebruik of bestendig gebruikelijk beding, IV-205; Supreme Court, September 21, 1990, N.J.B., 1990, 1387.
72. Parliamentary history of the New Civil Code, Book 6, 920.
73. Both legal systems have the same Civil Code which, in contract law, still to a large extent have the same provisions. For this reason, they are discussed together.
74. In French, the term *usage* is used and not custom (*coutume*).
75. Again, the Code does not speak of custom but of usage (in French, *ce qui est d'usage*).
76. In French, no reference is made to custom (*les clauses qui y sont d'usage*).
77. DOMAT, J., Les loix civiles dans leur ordre naturel, le droit public, et legum delectus, I, Paris, Brunet, 1723, 24.
78. SONNENBERGER, J., Verkehrssitte und Schuldvertrag, 127-129.

"Ainsi dans le louage d'une maison quelques coûtumes continuent le bail au-delà du terme pendant un certain temps, si les contractants n'y ont dérogé : Et toutes ces suites des conventions sont comme des pactes tacites, & sous-entendus, qui en font partie. Car les contractants consentent à tout ce qui est essentiel à leurs engagements."

A rule similar to article 1135 Cc cannot be found in the writings of Pothier. In his work, one may find two interpretation rules which have led to article 1159 and 1160 Cc[79]. Contrary to the opinion of Sonneberger[80], there seems to be no obvious difference of opinion between Pothier and Domat. Therefore, it is submitted that article 1160 Cc has no meaning different from article 1135 Cc[81].

221. Neither does the drafting history of article 1135 Cc give a complete answer as to its meaning. It seems that the provision was intended to be used as a criterion for interpreting the tacit will of the parties[82].

222. In the first period after codification, no hostile attitude existed against custom and usages[83]. As of 1841, the influence of political opinion and the *exegetic* method of interpretation changed that picture. Statute law is considered as the primary source of law and other sources receive less attention[84]. Custom is applied by virtue of the express or implied authorization of the state legislator. The rise of the *historical* method of interpretation did not change that situation and a more positive attitude was only brought about by the publication in 1899 of the work of Gény on statutory interpretation and sources of law[85] which deeply influenced French and Belgian law, also with respect to the role of customary law and usages.

223. In Gény's theory, one should distinguish between custom and usage. As to custom, it goes back to the tradition of Roman and canon law which

---

79. Oeuvres de POTHIER, Paris, I, 1827, 52.
80. SONNENBERGER, J., Verkehrssitte und Schuldvertrag, 127-130.
81. See also PABBRUWE, H., Gebruik en gebruikelijk beding, 88-91.
82. PABBRUWE, H., Gebruik en gebruikelijk beding, 75-76; SONNENBERGER, H.J., Verkehrssitten im Schuldvertrag, 128; *contra* VAN HOUTTE, H., Het gebruik ontstaan uit contract of verdrag, 2174.
    This is particularly clear from the meeting of the *Conseil d'Etat* of Brumaire II, year XII, see LOCRE, La législation civile, commerciale et criminelle de la France, XII, Paris, 1828, 140.
83. See TOULLIER, C., Le droit civil français, fifth edition, VI, Paris, 1830, 372-373.
84. LEBRUN, A., La coutume, 329-366.
85. GENY, F., Méthode d'interprétation et sources en droit privé positif, I, second edition, Paris, LGDJ, 1932, 446 pp.

required both a psychological and factual element[86]. Longstanding and constant observance of certain conduct does not suffice to constitute custom; it is also required that one feels legally bound to act in that way. Thus, custom is recognized as a genuine source of law, independent from statutory law. Up to the present, this conception has prevailed in France and Belgium.

224. However, Gény's theory has also come under attack. First, Lambert had argued that recognition of custom was dependent on the court system. Precedent and not custom would then create law[87]. However, custom may well create law in advance of court proceedings[88]. Second, Lebrun criticized Geny's theory for being too restrictive. According to Lebrun, not only spontaneous conduct but also articulated rules might create custom. Under this extensive conception, written usages, usual clauses, general conditions and judicial precedents also could qualify as customary law[89]. Finally, a Belgian author has proposed the abolition of custom as source of law. Custom would be important in tribal societies but unimportant in post-industrial life[90].

---

86. GENY, F., Méthode d'interprétation et sources en droit privé positif, I, 320 and 360-366.

These elements also led to theories where only the psychological or the factual element is required in order to form custom. There are hardly any proponents of such theories in France and Belgium. One may, however note, that Goldman argued that factual patterns of behaviour might create custom (see GOLDMAN, B., Rapport général, Le rôle de la pratique dans la formation du droit, Travaux de l'Association Henri Capitant, XXXIV, Paris, Economica, 1985, 169; see also EISEMANN, F., Die Incoterms im internationalen Warenkaufrecht, 38).

87. LAMBERT, E., La fonction du droit civil comparé, 814.

88. LEYMARIE, F., Les usages commerciaux, 61; PULBY, G., La coutume et son rôle en matière de compte courant, Paris, Larose, 1924, 22 and 172.

In a later publication, Lambert had come to qualify his theory, see LAMBERT, E., L'enseignement du droit comme science sociale et comme science internationale, Introduction, XLI-XLII.

89. LEBRUN, A., La coutume, 198-202 and 212-220; see also LEYMARIE, F., Les usages commerciaux, 36-37; GHESTIN, J. and GOUBEAUX, G., Introduction générale, second edition, Traité de droit civil, I, Paris, LGDJ, 1983, 398-400; FOUCHARD, P., L'Etat face aux usages du commerce international, 82; VAN GERVEN, W., Algemeen deel, 43 and 46.

90. BOUCKAERT, B., Gewoonterecht in de moderne samenleving : een fetisj ?, Liber amicorum Willy Calewaert, Antwerp, Kluwer, 1984, 40 and 47; see also BASEDOW, J., Handelsbräuche und AGB-Gesetz, Spontane Regelbildung im Zeitalter kodifizierter Usancen, ZHR 1986, 479-480; but see BASEDOW, J., Die Incoterms und der Container oder wie man kodifizierte Usancen reformiert, RabelsZ, 1979, 127.

225. Under Gény's prevailing theory, the requirements as to custom operate restrictively. As to its psychological element, it is often difficult to establish that parties feel legally bound by certain conduct or rules[91]. As to its factual element, certain conduct or the observance of certain rules should be voluntary, general, longstanding, constant, public and reasonable[92]. In commercial life, custom is particularly vulnerable as to its constant character. A pattern of behaviour may seem to be constant for some time but it may, ultimately, be tested in periods of crises (*e.g.*, a downturn in the market, great fluctuations in prices) where its customary nature may be challenged. Then, it often appears that the rules need adaptation[93]. Because of their restrictions, some requirements, especially that of the longstanding character of custom, have somewhat been relaxed. Thus, it has become accepted that custom be recognized after a shorter period since developments in society, particularly in commercial life, take place at a quicker pace[94].

226. In relation to usages, one also clearly notes the influence of Gény who made the distinction between custom or legal usages (*usages de droit*) and contractual usages (*usages volontaires*, *usages de fait*, *usages conventionnels* or *usages interprétatifs*). Usages referred to in articles 1135, 1159 and 1160 Cc are brought within the latter category[95]. These usages are binding since the parties had agreed as to their application. Therefore, parties feel bound by them only because they have incorporated them into their contract and not because they are *per se* binding[96]. These contractual usages can thus only be applied, provided parties knew them and intended their incorpora-

---

91. BRAECKMANS, H., De lex mercatoria, Zijn verhouding tot het nationaal recht en meer specifiek tot het internationaal privaatrecht, 2669-2670; BRAECKMANS, H., Juridische aspecten van consortiumkredieten in Eurodeviezen, 1985, 420; FIRSCHING, K., Internationales Schuldrecht, I, 358; DUNNWEBER, I., Vertrag zur Erstellung einer schlüsselfertigen Industrieanlage im internationalen Wirtschaftsverkehr, 168; HINSCH, C. and HORN, N., Das Vertragsrecht der internationalen Konsortialkredite und Projektfinanzierungen, 197-198.
92. LEBRUN, A., La coutume, 249-252.
93. *E.g.*, in relation to syndicated loans in eurocurrencies, BERLIOZ, G., La crise iranienne et les euro-crédits, Les euro-crédits, BLAISE, J.B., FOUCHARD, P. and KAHN, P. (ed.), Paris, Librairies Techniques, 1981, 600-601 and 610; BRAECKMANS, H., Juridische aspecten van consortiumkredieten in Eurodeviezen, 1985, 241-242, 246-248, 299, 425 and 436; HINSCH, C. and HORN, N., Das Vertragsrecht der internationalen Konsortialkredite und Projektfinanzierungen, 11.
94. VAN HOUTTE, H., Het gebruik ontstaan uit contract of verdrag, 2181.
95. GENY, F., Méthode d'interprétation et sources en droit privé positif, I, 418-419.
96. GENY, F., Méthode d'interprétation et sources en droit privé positif, I, 422-423.

tion into the contract[97]. Since the will of the parties is the cornerstone of the application of usages, Gény's theory has been called a *contractual* or *subjective* theory on usages[98]. This is consistent with the prevailing theory on contract interpretation in France and Belgium where the interpretation process is *subjective* (*i.e.*, aimed at getting at the intentions of the contracting parties)[99].

227. Recently, Kassis has reiterated Gény's theory. In his opinion, contractual usages never can develop into customary rules. This proposition is based upon the argument that parties always may derogate from contractual usages. Therefore, these usages would never be seen as rules of law which parties feel they have to observe as such[100]. One may doubt the correctness of the proposition since the issue is not whether parties may theoretically derogate from usage but whether they actually do. If not, no objections against formation of custom seem to exist[101].

Kassis' analysis also has paid attention to the process by which usages are incorporated into contracts by means of an express, tacit or presumed consent of the parties. Tacit consent may be troublesome because in French and Belgium law, consent by silence is generally not accepted unless proven by circumstantial evidence. For that reason, Kassis has introduced a presumption that the parties consented to any usages they knew or ought to have known[102]. A similar theory may be found in French commercial law where merchants are deemed to know trade usages and to contract under these usages[103].

---

97. See also VALERY, J., La coutume commerciale, Rev.Crit.Lég.Jur., 1924, 421 and 428; VAN ACKERE, C., Des usages commerciaux, Conférence française du Jeune Barreau de Gand, Ghent, Hoste, 1898, 23.
98. LUITHLEN, W., Einheitliches Kaufrecht und autonomes Handelsrecht, 41.
99. RIEG, A., Le rôle de la volonté dans l'acte juridique en droit civil français et allemand, 358-360; ZWEIGERT, K. and KÖTZ, H., Einführung in die Rechtsvergleichung, II, 99; LOPEZ SANTA MARIA, J., Les systèmes d'interprétation des contrats, dissertation, Université de Paris, Faculté de droit et des sciences économiques, Paris, 1968, 4, 7, 60 and 64; STORME, M. and STORME, M., De bindende derdenbeslissing naar Belgisch recht, T.P.R., 1985, 716.
100. KASSIS, A., Théorie générale des usages du commerce, 126-133 and 170.
101. See also GHESTIN, J. and GOUBEAUX, G., Introduction générale, 401; LEBRUN, A., La coutume, 314-315 who writes: "On semble croire que tous les usages interprétatifs de volonté s'appliquent par interprétation de volonté, ce qui est prendre l'effet pour la cause. ... Le fait qu'ils peuvent être écartés par une manifestation expresse de volonté contraire demeure indifférent et ne change pas leur nature.".
102. KASSIS, A., Théorie générale des usages du commerce, 125 and 133.
103. HOUIN, R., Usages commerciaux et loi en droit français, RabelsZ, 1959, 254; LEYMARIE, F., Les usages commerciaux, 39; STOUFFLET, J., L'oeuvre normative de la Chambre de Commerce Internationale dans le domaine bancaire, 367.

Consent by presumption relates to evidence. It means that the tacit will of the parties may be established by presumption[104]. According to article 1353 Cc, the presumptions should be certain, non-contradictory and important[105]. Thus, presumptive will should not be used too easily to compensate for absence of will.

228. Although many uncertainties exist, one might say that the case law of the Supreme Courts of France and Belgium seems to have endorsed the theory of Gény. The uncertainties relate to the difference between custom and contractual usage where it is unclear what the Supreme Courts are referring to. In any event, the proposition can be made that the Courts prefer to relate usage to the will of the parties[106]. On the other hand, the Belgian Supreme Court realizes that determining such a will may be conjectural and, therefore, some cases seem to indicate that by virtue of the provisions of the Civil Code, rather than through party incorporation, usages are deemed part of the contract[107].

---

104. DE PAGE, H., Traité élémentaire de droit civil belge, III, third edition, Brussels, Bruylant, 1967, 586-587.
105. DE CASTRO Y BRAVO, F., Les usages dans le projet de loi uniforme sur la vente internationale, 84; *cf.* LOQUIN, E., L'application de règles anationales dans l'arbitrage commercial international, 114-117.
106. French Supreme Court, January 14, 1959, Clunet, 1960, 476; Belgian Supreme Court, March 30, 1922, Pas., 1922, I, 223; Belgian Supreme Court, September 25, 1947, Bull.Cass., 1947, 290, R.C.J.B., 1948, case note HORION, P.; Belgian Supreme Court, March 29, 1976, Bull.Cass., 1976, 874, Pas., 1976, I, 833.
107. Supreme Court, May 29, 1947, Pas., 1947, I, 217, case note R.H., Bull.Cass., 1947, 171, R.W., 1947-48, 834; Supreme Court, February 24, 1966, Bull.Cass., 1966, 818, R.W., 1966-67, 209.; see also HANNEQUART, Y., La portée du contrat, Les Novelles, Droit civil, Volume IV, II, Brussels, Larcier, 1958, 66; *contra* VAN HOUTTE, H., Het gebruik ontstaan uit contract of verdrag, 2176.

229. The distinction between custom and usages has also been followed by scholars[108] but different interpretations of the articles 1135, 1159 and 1160 of the Civil Code have been proposed[109].

---

108. SALLE DE LA MARNIERRE, E., L'évolution technique du contrat et ses conséquences juridiques, 284; HOUIN, R., Usages commerciaux et loi en droit français, 253-258; PEDAMON, M., Y a-t-il lieu de distinguer les usages et les coutumes en droit commercial ?, 342; LEYMARIE, F., Les usages commerciaux, 29-30; MALINVERNI, P., Les conditions générales de vente et les contrats-types des chambres syndicales, Parijs, LGDJ, 1978, 83-84, 87 and 92; MAZEAUD, H., L. and J., Leçons de droit civil, I, Introduction à l'étude du droit, seventh edition by F. CHABAS, Paris, Montchrestien, 1983, 120-122; PIROVANO, A., Introduction critique au droit commercial contemporain, 257; VAN RYN, J. and HEENEN, J., Principes de droit commercial, I, second edition, 35.
109. SONNENBERGER, H.J., Verkehrssitten im Schuldvertrag, 16 and 31-32; BONELL, M., The relevance of courses of dealing, usages and customs in the interpretation of international commercial contracts, 111-112; LEYMARIE, F., Les usages commerciaux, 42; KRUITHOF, R., Overzicht van rechtspraak (1974-1980), Verbintenissen, 543 and 600; BRAECKMANS, H., De lex mercatoria, Zijn verhouding tot het nationaal recht en meer specifiek tot het internationaal privaatrecht, 2670; BRAECKMANS, H., Juridische aspecten van consortiumkredieten in Eurodeviezen, 1985, 424; BRAECKMANS, H., Paralegale normen en lex mercatoria, 37 and 60; GODFROID, M., L'étendue du contrôle exercé par la Cour de cassation sur les coutumes et usages en droit privé, R.G.D.C., 1990, 29.

230. However, some authors have come to reject Gény's theory on custom and usages[110]. They have proposed the elimination of the distinction and application of usages in contract law irrespective of party consent[111].

231. From a practical point of view, the distinction between custom and usage is to a certain extent relevant. First, custom is applied without the need for party consent while, according to a majority opinion, consent and knowledge are required for usages[112]. Under the prevailing view, party consent operates to protect contracting parties against usages which would be applied too easily. By contrast, this protective function is absent when customary law is involved. In that case, however, the strict requirements for custom will afford sufficient protection. Second, custom should not be proven and may be reviewed by the Supreme Court, while usage, only being a rule incorporated into the contract, must be established and cannot

---

110. *France* : MARTY, G., Rôle du juge dans l'interprétation des contrats, Travaux de l'Association Henri Capitant, V, Paris, Dalloz, 1950, 92; MARTY, G. and RAYNAUD, P., Droit civil, I, Introduction générale à l'étude du droit, second edition, Paris, Sirey, 1972, 204; DAVID, R., Sources of law, International Encyclopedia of Comparative law, Tubingen, Mohr, 1984, 106; DUPICHOT, J., Pour un retour aux textes : défense et illustration du "petit guide-âne" des articles 1156 à 1164 du Code civil, Etudes offertes à Jacques Flour, Paris, Répertoire du notariat Defrénois, 1979, 194-195; LE TOURNEAU, P., Quelques aspects de l'évolution des contrats, in Mélanges offerts à Pierre Raynaud, Parijs, Dalloz, 1985, 380; FOUCHARD, P., L'arbitrage commercial international, 414 and 545; FOUCHARD, P., L'Etat face aux usages du commerce international, 73, 78, 83 and 99; FOUCHARD, P., L'arbitrage international en France après le décret du 12 mai 1981, 399; FOUCHARD, P., Les usages, l'arbitre et le juge, A propos de quelques récents arrêts français, 66 and 78; FOUCHARD, P., La loi régissant les obligations contractuelles en droit international privé français, 108-109; BLAISE, J.B. and FOUCHARD, P., La valeur juridique de la syndication, in Les eurocrédits, BLAISE, J.B., FOUCHARD, P. and KAHN, P. (ed.), Paris, Libraries Techniques, 1981, 216-217; *Belgium* : FORIERS, P.A., Les contrats commerciaux, Chronique de jurisprudence (1976-1980), R.D.C., 1983, 126-129; VAN HOUTTE, H., Het gebruik ontstaan uit contract of verdrag, 2169 and 2179; VAN OMMESLAGHE, P., Examen de jurisprudence (1974 à 1982), Les obligations, R.C.J.B., 1986, 182-183.

111. DUPICHOT, J., Pour un retour aux textes: défense et illustration du "petit guide-âne" des articles 1156 à 1164 du Code civil, 194-195; DE CALLATAY, E., Etudes sur l'interprétation des conventions, Brussels, Bruylant, 1947, 136 and 138; BEGUIN, J., Le développement de la lex mercatoria menace-t-il l'ordre juridique international ?, 496-498.

112. BELLET, P. and MEZGER, E., L'arbitrage international dans le nouveau code de procédure civile, 623; BOUCOURECHLIEV, J., Usages commerciaux, usages professionnels : élaboration et formulation, 28; LE TOURNEAU, P., Quelques aspects de l'évolution des contrats, 380.

be reviewed[113]. Opponents of the Gény theory disagree, of course, as to these practical consequences[114]. Thirdly, the hierarchy of custom and usages as between each other and in relation to other sources should be discussed. As a preliminary point, one should first analyze whether there is a conflict between the different sources. This is primarily important regarding conflicts between mandatory rules of civil law and commercial custom. In that case, there is a false conflict since the commercial rule will preempt the rule of civil law[115]. In cases of true conflicts, mandatory statutory rules will preempt custom[116]. Custom will control non-mandatory rules, provided its rule is more specific[117] or of later date[118]. Last, parties may derogate from non-mandatory customs. As to usages, these are rules of contract which may not derogate from mandatory rules but control over statutory rules from which parties are authorized to derogate[119].

232. Both the majority view based on the theory of Gény and the minority view which would abolish the distinction between custom and usage, have major drawbacks. First, the majority view finds little support in the drafting history of the Civil Code and seems to be Gény's invention which does hardly convince. More important, the theory leads to either a restrictive application of usages or a very broad concept of party consent, which risks

---

113. GENY, F., Méthode d'interprétation et sources en droit privé positif, I, 425-427; SALLE DE LA MARNIERRE, E., L'évolution technique du contrat et ses conséquences juridiques, 293-294; LEYMARIE, F., Les usages commerciaux, 215, 222-232; LEBRUN, A., La coutume, 487-490 and 501-502; STORME, M., De bewijslast in het Belgisch privaatrecht, 288-290; GHESTIN, J. and GOUBEAUX, G., Introduction générale, 413.
114. LEVEL, P., Le contrat dit sans loi, 214; KAHN, P., Rapport français, Le rôle de la pratique dans la formation du droit, Travaux de l'Association Henri Capitant, XXXIV, Paris, Economica, 1985, 238; VAN HOUTTE, H., Het gebruik ontstaan uit contract of verdrag, 2179.
115. VAN RYN, J. and HEENEN, J., Principes de droit commercial, I, 34.
116. ESCARRA, J., De la valeur juridique de l'usage en droit commercial, 121; LIMPENS, J., De l'unification du droit civil et du droit commercial, 358.
117. PEDAMON, M., Y a-t-il lieu de distinguer les usages et les coutumes en droit commercial ?, 351.
118. LEBRUN, A., La coutume, 481-482.
119. SALLE DE LA MARNIERRE, E., L'évolution technique du contrat et ses conséquences juridiques, 291-292; LEYMARIE, F., Les usages commerciaux, 73-74; VAN RYN, J. and HEENEN, J., Principes de droit commercial, I, 36; LOQUIN, E., Les pouvoirs des arbitres internationaux à la lumière de l'évolution récente du droit de l'arbitrage international, 336-337; KASSIS, A., Théorie générale des usages du commerce, 213 and 221.

to be conjectural[120]. In a broader context, one may criticize French and Belgian law for being too consensual in contract law. This implies that contracts may hardly be supplemented except in accordance with the express or tacit agreement of the parties. Supplementing contracts, thus, operates through the interpretation process which is subjective and looks to the intentions of the parties. As with usages, either contracts are insufficiently supplemented if solutions remain within the logical boundaries of traditional theory, or satisfactory results are achieved outside the traditional theoretical framework.

On the other hand, the minority position takes an expansive view regarding spontaneous regulation under which custom, usage, usual clauses, general conditions and courses of dealing may create law. It does, however, not address the problem under what conditions this process must take place.

233. Party autonomy, consensualism and subjective interpretation are still major cornerstones of French contract law[121]. However, case law actually does supplement contracts[122] disguised as party intention. From a theoretical point of view, scholars have criticized the subjective interpretation theory[123] but no real theoretical alternative has been proposed.

The same criticisms may be found in Belgian scholarly writings. In contrast with France, from the beginning of the 1980's, a link has been made with the notion of *good faith* (*bonne foi*)[124]. Supreme Court cases contributed to this development. Limits on rights were traditionally based

---

120. RIEG, A., Le rôle de la volonté dans l'acte juridique en droit civil français et allemand, 362-363; VAN HOUTTE, H., Het gebruik ontstaan uit contract of verdrag, 2177.

121. RIEG, A., Le rôle de la volonté dans l'acte juridique en droit civil français et allemand, 396-406.

122. WEILL, A. and TERRE, F., Les obligations, fourth edition, Paris, Dalloz, 1986, 368-370; MALAURIE, P. and AYNES, L., Les obligations, Paris, Cujas, 1985, 286-289.

123. RIEG, A., Le rôle de la volonté dans l'acte juridique en droit civil français et allemand, 362-368 referring to Saleilles, Roubier, Gounot and Defreur; WEILL, A. and TERRE, F., Les obligations, 363-364.

124. BAERT, F., De goede trouw bij de uitvoering van overeenkomsten, R.W., 1956-57, 489-516; FONTAINE, MQ, Portée et limites du principe de la convention-loi, Les obligations contractuelles, Brussels, Jeune barreau, 1984, 170-177; PHILIPPE, D., Changement de circonstances et bouleversement de l'économie contractuelle, Brussels, Bruylant, 1986, 621-622; DE BONDT, W., Redelijkheid en billijkheid in het contractenrecht, T.P.R., 1984, 110-117; DUFRENE, S., case note Supreme Court, September 19, 1983, J.T., 1985, 56-59; DE BONDT, W., De leer der gekwalificeerde benadeling, Antwerp, Kluwer, 1985, 263-280; VAN GERVEN, W. and DEWAELE, A., Goede trouw en getrouw beeld, Liber amicorum Jan Ronse, Brussels, Story, 1986, 103-126; VAN OMMESLAGHE, P., L'exécution de bonne foi, principe général de droit ?, R.G.D.C., 1987, 101-110.

on tort law (*abus de droit-theory*) but the Court held in this period that abuse of contractual rights should be based on article 1134, third paragraph of the Civil Code which requires that contracts should be performed in good faith[125]. This has led to the revival of an almost forgotten provision of the Civil Code which may also be found in article 1135 of the Code stating that *equity* (*équité*) may also create obligations for the parties. Scholars have thus argued that article 1135 may provide a sound theoretical basis for supplementing contracts without a need to inquire into the intentions of the parties[126].

This development is important also from a policy point of view, since contracts no longer would contain only what parties have agreed expressly or tacitly, but also may be supplemented according to equity. Since this is basically an open-ended rule, contract law will be created by judicial decisions. In addition, this may lead to greater legal uncertainty than in the past. These policy considerations have yet to be analyzed.

Clearly, these developments in Belgian law are influenced by Dutch law. However, one may regret that inspiration is not directly sought in German law. This analysis would emphasize differences between the German and French traditions and the restrictions on reception of German solutions in legal systems based on French law. These tensions are, moreover, quite clear in Belgium where Dutch literature is much more sympathetic to the open-ended rule of good faith than the French speaking writers[127].

234. The supplementary function of the good faith provision of the Civil Code is also related to the legal force of usages. The latter problem has hardly been analyzed in this perspective. Only one author has argued that according to article 1135 Cc, usages, statutory law and equity can supplement contracts[128]. However, one may not forget that in the Civil Code, usages is used where non-codified custom is meant, since the drafters of the Code wanted to avoid reference to the codified customs of the *ancien régime*[129]. Therefore, one may argue that all Civil Code articles relate to

---

125. Supreme Court, September 19, 1983, Bull.Cass., 1983-84, 52, R.D.C., 1984, 276, case note RAUWS, W., J.T., 1985, 56, case note DUFRENE, S., R.C.J.B., 1986, 282, case note FAGNART, J.L.; Supreme Court, June 18, 1987, R.W., 1987-88, 503, J.T., 1988, 8; Supreme Court, November 20, 1987, R.W., 1987-88, 1099.

126. *But see* FAGNART, J.L., L'exécution de bonne foi des conventions : un principe en expansion, case note Supreme Court, September 19, 1983, R.C.J.B., 1986, 291-292; HANNEQUART, Y., La portée du contrat, 60-62.

127. FONTAINE, M., Portée et limites du principe de la convention-loi, 198.

128. DE BONDT, W., De leer der gekwalificeerde benadeling, 265.

129. LEBRUN, A., La coutume, 144.

custom. Article 1159 Cc gives custom an interpretative function while under article 1135 and 1160 Cc, it has a supplementary function[130]. This function was denied in the drafting process of the Code Civil[131] but one may question the wisdom of sticking to the drafting process if developments in society make clear that there is a need to supplement contracts. Thus, besides statutory law and equity, custom also may create contractual obligations. In this respect, parties are sufficiently protected by the strict rules regarding the recognition of custom.

235. As to other forms of spontaneous behaviour such as usual clauses, general conditions or courses of dealing, they also may have an *interpretative* function since they may clarify the intentions of the parties. If not, they still may have a *supplementary* function. Contrary to custom, this cannot be based directly on a provision of the Civil Code but rather indirectly through the equity clause of article 1135 Cc. As an open-ended rule, article 1135 Cc needs filling in. Forms of spontaneous conduct may just fulfill that purpose.

236. The difficult questions only begin when one has to determine to what extent contracts need to be supplemented and what criteria should be used in this regard. At this junction, the real tensions between freedom of contract and supplementing contracts become apparent. This has hardly been analyzed in Belgium. Only a small number of authors have identified the problem. First, Bouckaert has argued that contracts should be supplemented to the extent that the other contracting party might legitimately have so expected[132]. Other authors have argued for limits regarding the supplementary function of the good faith provision[133]. Finally, two authors have argued that contracts may be supplemented with any obligations that a reasonable contractant would have observed under the same circumstances (*bonus pater familias*)[134]. One may doubt whether this abstract notion is wholly consistent with French and Belgian law since

---

130. Interpretative and supplementary functions are defined taking into account the subjective interpretation theory in France and Belgium (see HANNEQUART, Y., La portée du contrat, 83-85). This interpretation theory may be subject to criticism (see in The Netherlands, VAN DUNNE, J., Normatieve uitlegging van rechtshandelingen, Deventer, Kluwer, 1972, 160 pp.) but should be kept in mind when comparing with legal systems based on German law.

131. See supra No. 221.

132. BOUCKAERT, B., Gewoonterecht in de moderne samenleving : een fetisj ?, 41.

133. VAN GERVEN, W. and DEWAELE, A., Goede trouw en getrouw beeld, 110-112 and 123.

134. DE BONDT, W., Redelijkheid en billijkheid in het contractenrecht, 112; VAN OEVELEN, A., case note Supreme Court, January 16, 1986, R.W., 1987-88, 1472.

it seems to be derived from German law where basic assumptions of contract law are different.

237. In this book, it is submitted, in accordance with the view of Bouckaert, that spontaneous observance of rules may create additional obligations if the counterparty in good faith could rely on that conduct (*théorie de l'apparence/confiance légitime*)[135]. This theoretical basis has the advantage that it remains close to basic notions of French and Belgian contract law, since the theory of *legitimate expectations* only operates as a correction to the real intentions of the parties. Starting from party intent seems justified since automatic application of usages might frustrate it. Finally, the theory of the real intentions of the parties clearly also operates as a protective device against unwanted clauses or usages. In this regard, the theory of legitimate expectations forms a compromise between views of contract law which are either too subjective (real intentions of the parties) or too objective (what reasonable contractants ought to have done in similar circumstances).

238. The theoretical basis for application of trade usages may be important in three respects. First, it might influence the question whether trade usages are applicable if the contractants come within the scope of these usages because they belong to the sector, region or profession where these usages are used. Under an objective standard, one will easily accept the incorporation of the usages under these circumstances. Under the theory of legitimate expectations, more will be required. One will have to show that the counterparty brought the other party to believe that the usages would be incorporated into the contract.

Second, the objective theory no longer requires that the parties knew about the usages and had accepted them. It suffices that reasonable contractants ought to have known that these usages were applicable. Consent is no longer required. Under the legitimate expectations theory, it is required that one party relied in good faith on the application of the usages caused by the false belief that the other party did know them and had accepted them[136].

Finally, usages which come to exist after contract formation may be incorporated under an objective criterion but will hardly be applicable

135. For this theory, see VAN GERVEN, W., Algemeen deel, 211-229; VAN OMMESLAGHE, P., L'apparence comme source autonome d'obligations et le droit belge, Rev.Dr.Int.Comp., 1983, 144-160; VAN OMMESLAGHE, P., Rechtsverwerking en afstand van recht, T.P.R., 1980, 789-791.

136. *E.g.*, Court of Appeal Brussels, November 2, 1972, E.T.L., 1973, 323.

under the theory of legitimate expectations, which is related to contract formation and not to contract construction or performance.

III.2.1.8 Conclusions

239. It follows from the foregoing analysis that the legal systems which have been discussed accept custom as a source of law. However, in most systems, requirements are hard to meet and few examples exist. For that reason, the status of usages is more important. However, it then appears that usages are not a formal source of law but are devices of contract construction. Here, several models exist. In Germany, Austria and in the U.S. under the UCC, an objective model is used where usages may supplement contracts without looking to party intent. In England, in practice the same position is taken, but in theory one still refers to party intent. In The Netherlands and Switzerland, a mixed model is used where usages may clarify the intentions of the parties but also supplement contracts. In France and Belgium, the subjective model has traditionally been followed. However, that theory has come under attack because it reduces usages to party intent and consequently, unduly restricts them, or because it artificially extends party intent. Thus, it has been proposed to base application of usages on good faith. This theory can be endorsed, but one may still wonder what criteria should be used under that theory in order to supplement contracts.

III.2.2 *Custom and usages in international conventions*

240. Apart from international texts on international commercial arbitration[137], one may look primarily to the unification efforts in international sales law for provisions on the legal status of custom and usages. First, both ULIS and ULFIS contain provisions regarding customs and usages. Article 9 (1) ULIS states that parties are bound by usages to which they expressly or implicitly have agreed and by any practices which they have established between themselves. Article 2 ULFIS has a similar provision, stating that the uniform law applies unless other rules prevail, by virtue of practices which the parties have established between themselves. Second, article 13 (1) ULFIS and article 9 (2) ULIS provide that parties are also bound by usages which reasonable persons in the same circumstances consider to apply to their contract or its formation. Finally, article 2 ULFIS and article

137. With regard to the European Convention on International Commercial Arbitration and the UNCITRAL Model Law on International Commercial Arbitration, see supra Nos. 175-178.

9 (2) ULIS provide that the uniform laws are preempted by usages, while article 8 ULIS states that the uniform law does not interfere with the problem of the validity of usages.

241. Article 2 ULFIS and article 9 (1) ULIS differ from article 13 (1) ULFIS and article 9 (2) ULIS since the former have an *interpretative* function, while the latter are *normative*, which implies that they are applied irrespective of the parties' knowledge or acceptance[138].

242. To a certain extent, the Hague Uniform Sales Laws also have addressed the issue of standard forms, general conditions and self-regulatory rules in international sales practice. Article 13 (2) ULFIS and article 9 (3) ULIS provide that terms, clauses or forms that are usually used in the trade should be interpreted according to the meaning which is common in that trade. These provisions are meant to stress the specific nature of the practice of international sales and to isolate it to a certain extent from interpretation which is too much inspired by notions of national law.

243. While the Hague Uniform Sales Laws left ample room for usages, CISG may be seen as a cutback. While article 9 (1) CISG also provides that parties are bound by usages to which they have agreed and by any practices which they have established between themselves, the difference between the 1964 and 1980 codifications of international sales law is found as with respect to other usages, where CISG has taken a more restrictive approach. Article 9 (2) CISG provides that usages are considered, unless

---

138. VON CAEMMERER, E., Die Haager Konferenz über die internationale Vereinheitlichung des Kaufrechts vom 2. bis 25. April 1964 : Die Ergebnisse der Konferenz hinsichtlich der Vereinheitlichung des Rechts des Abschlusses von Kaufverträgen, Gesammelte Schriften, I, Tubingen, Mohr, 1968, 109, originally published in RabelsZ 1965, 101 ff.; SCHLECHTRIEM, P., in DÖLLE, H., Kommentar zum Einheitlichen Kaufrecht, 757; DÖLLE, H., Bedeutung und Funktion der "Bräuche" im Einheitsgesetz über den internationalen Kauf beweglicher Sachen, 449; JUNGE, W., in DÖLLE, H., Kommentar zum Einheitlichen Kaufrecht, 42; MERTENS, H.J. and REHBINDER, E., Internationales Kaufrecht, Kommentar zu den einheitlichen Kaufgesetzen, 118-119; LUITHLEN, W., Einheitliches Kaufrecht und autonomes Handelsrecht, 22-23; JOKELA, H., The role of usages in the Uniform law on international sales, 88-91; BAINBRIDGE, S., Trade usages in international sales of goods : an analysis of the 1964 and 1980 Sales Convention, 633; GOLDSTAJN, A., Commercial usages as the source of the law of international trade, in XII Yearbook of the school of law and economic science, Aristotelian University of Thessaloniki, Miscellany in honor of C. Fragistas, II, Thessaloniki, 1967, 401; FOUCHARD, P., L'Etat face aux usages du commerce international, 83.

otherwise agreed, to be implicitly applicable to the contract or its formation. However, additional requirements have been imposed[139]. First, it is required that the parties knew or ought to have known these usages. Second, the usages should be widely known in international trade and regularly observed by parties to contracts of the type involved in the particular trade concerned. Contrary to ULFIS and ULIS, it no longer suffices that reasonable persons in the same circumstances might consider the usages to be applicable. Since more requirements have to be met than under ULFIS and ULIS, usages may be less frequently be applied under CISG. Also, the relevance of local and national usages has been limited[140].

According to Bonell, article 9 CISG has followed the system of the Hague Uniform Sales Laws in making a distinction between interpretative and normative usages. However, that distinction does not clearly appear from the wording of article 9 CISG and is contrary to the majority opinion in scholarly writing[141].

244. CISG also contains an interpretation rule in which reference is made to usages and practices. According to article 8 (3), in determining the intent of a party or the understanding a reasonable person would have had, due consideration is to be given to all relevant circumstances including the negotiations, any practices which the parties have established between themselves, usages and any subsequent conduct of the parties. In this context, the requirements as to usages of article 9 (2) CISG are not

---

139. BEGUIN, J., Le développement de la lex mercatoria menace-t-il l'ordre juridique international ?, 526.

140. BONELL, M., Die Bedeutung der Handelsbräuche im Wiener Kaufrechtsübereinkommen von 1980, Juristische Blätter, 1985, 390; SCHLECHTRIEM, P., Einheitliches UN-Kaufrecht, Das Übereinkommen der Vereinten Nationen über internationale Warenkaufverträge, Tubingen, Mohr, 1981, 27; BERMAN, H. and KAUFMAN, C., The law of international commercial transactions (lex mercatoria), 271-273; EÖRSI, G., General provisions, in International sales, The United Nations convention on contracts for the international sale of goods, GALSTON, N. and SMIT, H. (ed.), New York, Matthew Bender, 1984, 2-22 and 2-23.

141. BONELL, M., in BIANCA-BONELL, Commentary on the international sales law, Art. 9, Milan, Giuffrè, 1987, 105; *contra* HONNOLD, J., Uniform law for international sales under the 1980 United Nations Convention, 146-147; SCHLECHTRIEM, P., Einheitliches UN-Kaufrecht, 27; DE VRIES, H., The passing of risk in international sales under the Vienna Sales Convention 1980 as compared with traditional trade terms, E.T.L., 1982, 527; EÖRSI, G., General provisions, 2-24; GOLDSTAJN, A., Usages of trade and other autonomous rules of international trade according to the UN (1980) sales convention, in International sales of goods, New York, Oceana, 1986, 97.

applicable, which implies that local or national usages may be applied in the interpretation process[142].

Provisions similar to articles 13 (2) ULFIS and 9 (3) ULIS are absent from CISG. This is due to the opposition from some states against easy application of self-regulatory rules which were formed within trade organizations or institutions in which nationals from these states had not participated[143].

Similar to the Hague Uniform Sales Laws, usages preempt CISG because the provisions of CISG are not mandatory[144] and CISG also does not deal with the validity of usages (article 4, (a) CISG).

From the foregoing, it appears that CISG has some provisions on usages but does not directly deal with the nature of usages. According to Bonell, these problems should be determined *autonomously* (*i.e.*, solely on the basis of the Convention without relying on national law)[145]. However, Schlechtriem has argued that usages under CISG are binding on the basis of party intent[146].

245. Apart from international sales conventions, one may also refer to article 17 of the EEC Jurisdiction and Enforcement Convention which also contains a provision on international usages. Originally, the Brussels 1968 Convention did require that a jurisdiction clause be in writing or be evidenced in writing. Article 11 of the first Accession Convention[147] has modified article 17 and allows jurisdiction agreements in such form which in international trade accords with a usage of which the parties are or ought to have been aware. According to Kropholler, usages should not be

142. SCHLECHTRIEM, P., Einheitliches UN-Kaufrecht, 26; EÖRSI, G., General provisions, 2-17- 2-18.

143. BEGUIN, J., Le développement de la lex mercatoria menace-t-il l'ordre juridique international ?, 509; BONELL, M., in BIANCA-BONELL, Commentary on the international sales law, Art.9, 105-106.

144. BONELL, M., Die Bedeutung der Handelsbräuche im Wiener Kaufrechtsübereinkommen von 1980, 393; BONELL, M., in BIANCA-BONELL, Commentary on the international sales law, Art. 9, 104; SCHLECHTRIEM, P., Einheitliches UN-Kaufrecht, 28.

145. BONELL, M., Die Bedeutung der Handelsbräuche im Wiener Kaufrechtsübereinkommen von 1980, 390; BONELL, M., in BIANCA-BONELL, Commentary on the international sales law, Art. 9, 111.

146. SCHLECHTRIEM, P., Einheitliches UN-Kaufrecht, 27.

147. Convention on the accession of the Kingdom of Denmark, of Ireland and of the United Kingdom of Great Britain and Northern Ireland to the Convention on jurisdiction and the enforcement of judgments in civil and commercial matters and to the Protocol on its interpretation by the Court of Justice, signed on October 9, 1978. This convention has entered into effect on November 1, 1986 and applies between the first nine EEC Member States.

defined through national law but only by reference to the actual practices of transnational commerce[148].

The main principles of the EEC Jurisdiction and Enforcement mechanism have been adopted in relations between EEC- and EFTA-countries through the signing of the Lugano Convention[149]. Article 17 of the Lugano Convention differs in two respects from its counterpart in the EEC Jurisdiction Convention. First, article 17 of the Lugano Convention has added the provision that a jurisdiction clause also may be concluded in a form which accords with practices which the parties have established between themselves. Secondly, as to usual forms, the Lugano Convention adds that these forms should be widely known to and regularly observed by parties to contracts of the type involved in the particular trade or commerce concerned[150]. It is obvious that article 17 of the Lugano Convention has been inspired by article 9 CISG.

It was intended that differences between the Lugano Convention and the EEC Jurisdiction Convention would be abolished at the time of the accession of Spain and Portugal to the EEC Jurisdiction Convention. This has been realized by the Spanish-Portuguese Accession Convention done at San Sebastian[151]. With respect to article 17 of the EEC Jurisdiction Convention, article 7 of the Spanish-Portuguese Accession Convention has modified it so that it now is identical to article 17 of the Lugano Convention[152].

The Lugano Convention and the EEC Jurisdiction Convention as modified by the San Sebastian Convention have thus adopted the same

---

148. KROPHOLLER, J., Neues europäisches Zivilprozeßrecht, RIW 1986, 930.
149. Convention on jurisdiction and enforcement of judgments in civil and commercial matters done at Lugano on September 16, 1988, OJ 1988, L 319, 9.
150. JENARD, P. and MÖLLER, G., Report on the Convention on jurisdiction and the enforcement of judgments in civil and commercial matters done at Lugano on 16 September 1988, OJ, July 28, 1990, C 189, 77.
151. Convention on the accession of the Kingdom of Spain and the Portugese Republic to the Convention on jurisdiction and the enforcement of judgments in civil and commercial matters and to the Protocol on its interpretation by the Court of Justice with the adjustments made to them by the Convention on the accession of the Kingdom of Denmark, of Ireland and of the United Kingdom of Great Britain and Northern Ireland and the adjustments made to them by the Convention on the accession of the Hellenic Republic, done at Donostia-San Sebastion on May 26, 1989, OJ, 1989, L 285, 1. The San Sebastian Convention has entered into force on February 1, 1991 between Spain, France and The Netherlands.
152. DE ALMEIDA CRUZ, M., DESANTES REAL, M., and JENARD, P., Report on the Convention on the accession of the Kingdom of Spain and the Portugese Republic to the 1968 Convention on jurisdiction and the enforcement of judgments in civil and commercial matters, OJ, July 28, 1990, C 189, 47.

restrictive attitude as CISG with regard to the application of international trade usages.

246. In all these international conventions, one notes that custom is hardly ever mentioned. Rather, they only deal to a certain extent with usages. It then becomes clear that usages are not qualified as law-creating sources but as elements of contract interpretation (interpretative function). In ULFIS and ULIS, usages also had a supplementary function. To a certain extent, CISG seems to have come back on that position. It requires that parties knew or ought to have known usages and it also introduces new requirements for applying usages. The protective function which is characteristic for party intent was thought to be more important in a universal unification effort than in a regional one (such as the Hague Uniform Sales Laws) because parties from more diverse backgrounds might be brought together under the CISG system.

III.2.3 *Custom, usages and international business law*

247. From the analysis of custom and usages in national legal systems and international conventions, it appears that differences exist as to the conceptions of custom and usages[153]. Although one may give some credit to Rieg's observation that in practice and court decisions, these differences tend to be overcome[154], one may still be faced with practical implications which differ from jurisdiction to jurisdiction because of different theoretical bases for application of custom and usages.

248. In the context of international business transactions, one may thus have to decide which customs or usages to apply and which legal system to choose in order to determine the status of custom and usages[155]. In the contractual field, these questions will directly be applied by the law

153. See also BRAECKMANS, H., Juridische aspecten van consortiumkredieten in Eurodeviezen, 1983, 894-895.

154. RIEG, A., Le rôle de la volonté dans l'acte juridique en droit civil français et allemand, 420.

155. SCHMITTHOFF, C., International trade usages, I.C.C. publication No. 440/4, Paris, 1987, 22; ARMINJON, P., Précis de droit international privé commercial, Paris, Dalloz, 1948, 15; LAGARDE, P., Approche critique de la lex mercatoria, 143; MARTINY, D., Warenkauf, in REITHMANN, C., Internationales Vertragsrecht, third edition, Cologne, Schmidt, 1980, 274. In this respect, article 1054 Dutch Code of Civil Procedure provides that arbitrators should take account of *applicable trade usages*.

Some authors have taken the view that this question is of no practical relevance (GENTINETTA, J., Die lex fori internationaler Handelsschiedsgerichte, 148 and 292; DE VRIES, H., Preadvies, 77-78).

applicable to the contract or indirectly through that law by means of contract construction. This will be so for local and sector-related usages but also for *transnational* usages which have no apparent basis in one given country or are aimed at unification of law[156]. Finally, not only national courts but also international commercial arbitration tribunals adjudicating on the basis of rules of law (and not *ex aequo et bono*) will have to look for the law which has to determine the status of custom and usages[157].

III.3 Self-regulatory rules of professional organizations

249. Regulation is no monopoly of the state. Private organizations, both domestically and internationally, may also generate regulations. In this section, these self-regulatory rules will be analyzed with particular reference to transnational self-regulation and its nature as a formal or substantive source of law.

250. Article 1, 3) of the Italian Codice civile did recognize rules of organizations as a formal source of law. This was related to the corporatistic organization of the economy under Mussolini. After 1944, the Codice civile continued to refer to these self-regulatory rules but no such rules were promulgated[158].

In democratic societies, private organizations generally have no regulatory powers. This principle is based on equality among citizens and freedom of association[159]. Exceptionally, the legislative branch of government may provide that some organizations have the authority to organize a certain profession or trade. Absent legislative approval, one may wonder whether and under what conditions, private organizations can adopt binding regulation. Stoufflet has argued that in transnational business, the I.C.C. may be considered to have such authority notwithstanding the absence of legislative authority. He writes in this regard:

> *"Une conclusion s'impose quant à l'autorité des normes définies par la C.C.I. Celles-ci ne se confondent pas avec l'usage, même si elles ne s'en détachent pas entièrement, ni avec le mécanisme du contrat-type et des conditions-types. Elles*

156. LUITHLEN, W., Einheitliches Kaufrecht und autonomes Handelsrecht, 33-34.
157. KASSIS, A., Théorie générale des usages du commerce, 335.
158. BELTRAMO, M., LONGO, G. and MERRYMAN, J., The Italian civil code, Dobbs Ferry, New York, Oceana, 1969, xi-xii.
159. SIMON, J., Le commerce international des céréales, 312; PEDAMON, M., Y a-t-il lieu de distinguer les usages et les coutumes en droit commercial ?, 345; MALINVERNI, P., Les conditions générales de vente et les contrats-types des chambres syndicales, 8.

> *relèvent d'une autre catégorie de sources de droit originale. On est en présence de normes professionnelles dont l'autorité repose non pas sur le consentement des membres de cette profession mais sur l'aptitude reconnue à un organisme professionnel de traduire à la fois les besoins du commerce et la rationalité d'une opération. Ce type de norme est, d'une certaine manière, par le processus de sa formation, à l'opposé de l'usage. Il est, comme la loi, l'oeuvre d'une institution alors que l'usage se crée spontanément. Mais avec l'usage il a en commun d'être une source non étatique."* [160]

It is difficult to endorse this position since it is based on a sociological or pluralistic jurisprudence, in which certain groups in society may create law[161]. These conceptions, however, do not explain why rules adopted by private organizations would be binding. In this respect, an important distinction is to be made between the effects of these rules within the organization itself and *vis-à-vis* third parties. As to the internal effects of self-regulatory rules, the applicable law will determine under what conditions these rules are binding within the organization[162]. Often, it is stated that these rules are binding upon the members of the organization but this position is not well motivated.

251. Rules will generally be binding if their acceptance has been an explicit condition for membership. For instance, the *General Terms and Conditions* of the Belgian cooperative company, *Society for Worldwide Interbank Financial Telecommunications* ("*S.W.I.F.T.*") state that the Board of Directors must obtain an applicant's acceptance of these terms and conditions in order for the applicant to be eligible as a shareholder[163].

Sometimes, the articles of association explicitly oblige members to follow the duly adopted rules of the organization[164].

252. Absent explicit clauses, one may ask whether and how self-regulatory rules become binding upon members of the organization. French and Belgian law have rarely analyzed this problem. In Belgium, binding effect may be based on article 2 of the Law on Freedom of Association dated

---

160. STOUFFLET, J., L'oeuvre normative de la Chambre de Commerce Internationale dans le domaine bancaire, 369.

161. *E.g.*, FOUCHARD, P., L'arbitrage commercial international, 160; FOUCHARD, P., L'autonomie de l'arbitrage commercial international, 105; LOQUIN, E., L'amiable composition en droit comparé et international, 120 and 309.

162. OERTMANN, P., Rechtsordnung und Verkehrssitte, 11; BASEDOW, J., Die Industrie- und Handelskammern, Selbstverwaltung zwischen Staat und Verbandswesen, BB, 1977, 366-367.

163. Clause 3, first paragraph.

164. SIMON, J., Le commerce international des céréales, 322.

May 24, 1921 which provides that accession to organizations implies that one adheres to the regulations and decisions of the organization. On the other hand, this restriction on a member's freedom of action is offset by the fact that his freedom to leave the organization may not be restricted[165]. Case law still relies on the principle of *pacta sunt servanda* (article 1134 Cc) in order to explain the binding force of regulations upon members of organizations[166].

Some authors have made the distinction between articles of association and regulations[167]. To the extent permitted by law, articles of associations may derogate from statute law but regulations may not[168]. Regulations may thus only supplement the law or the articles of assocations[169].

253. In England too, little attention has been paid to the nature of self-regulatory rules developed by professional organizations. To the extent English law has done so, it primarily has followed a contractual approach. With respect to companies, Section 14 (1) of the Companies Consolidation Legislation 1985 provides that the *memorandum of association* and the *articles of association*[170] are binding upon the company and its shareholders as if they were signed by each shareholder. Section 14 (1) sets the binding character of memorandum and articles of association as between the company and its shareholders and between shareholders. In the first relation, the binding nature is based on contract; the theoretical justification in the relation between shareholders is not so clear[171]. More important for our analysis is the question as to the nature of rules developed outside the memorandum and articles of association. This has received little attention in England. Boyle and Bird state that directors may

165. 'T KINT, J., Les associations sans but lucratif, second edition, Brussels, Larcier, 1974, 42.
166. District Court Liège, October 7, 1949, Rev.Prat.Soc., 1950, 64; District Court Ghent, June 10, 1953, Rev.Prat.Soc., 1958, 26, case note BEYENS, E.
167. RESTEAU, C., Traité des sociétés anonymes, II, second edition, Brussels, Pée, 1933, 115; COLAES, J., Derdenwerking van grondrechten in private rechtsverhoudingen waarbij groeperingen betrokken zijn, in De toepasselijkheid van de grondrechten in private verhoudingen, RIMANQUE, K. (ed.), Antwerp, Kluwer, 1982, 268.
168. 'T KINT, J. and GODIN, M., Les sociétés coopératives, Brussels, Larcier, 1968, 125-126.
169. 'T KINT, J., Les associations sans but lucratif, 42-43; 'T KINT, J., Associations sans but lucratif, Répertoire notarial, Brussels, Larcier, 1987, 49-50; LINDEMANS, J., Verenigingen zonder winstoogmerk, A.P.R., Ghent, 1958, 166-167.
170. For the distinction, see Palmer's Company Law, I, London, Stevens & Sons, 1982, 72.
171. Palmer's Company Law, I, 162-167; Gower's principles of modern company law, fourth edition, London, Stevens & Sons, 1979, 315-318; Pennington's Company Law, 56-59; Boyle and Birds'Company Law, Bristol, Jordan & Sons, 1983, 44-47.

be authorized by the articles of association to adopt certain regulations ("bye-laws"[172]). A specific decision is required for any such rules in order to make them binding - by virtue of Section 7 of the Companies Consolidation Legislation 1985 - upon shareholders[173].

As to the English law of unincorporated associations, relations are also largely based on contract law[174]. Apart from *main rules* which are comparable to memoranda of association, *bye-laws* also exist. The main rules may thus authorize a certain committee to adopt certain rules which, if duly formed, are binding upon the members[175].

254. Self-regulatory rules have been analyzed somewhat better in The Netherlands, Germany and, to a lesser degree, Switzerland[176]. In The Netherlands, Book 2 of the New Civil Code had some impact on this issue. Corporate law has been seen much less from a contractual perspective[177] and articles of association and regulations would be binding within the

---

172. One may not confuse the term as it is used by Boyle and Bird with the similar term of art of American corporate law where it is used in its meaning of articles of association.

173. Boyle and Birds' Company Law, 49.

174. WARBURTON, J., Unincorporated associations : law and practice, London, Sweet & Maxwell, 1986, 3, 10 and 73.

175. WARBURTON, J., Unincorporated associations : law and practice, 16-17.

176. VON STEIGER, W., Gesellschaftsrecht, Allgemeiner Teil, 273-275; HEINI, A., Die Vereine, in Schweizerische Privatrecht, I, Basle, Helbing & Lichtenhahn, 1967, 542; RIEMER, H., Das Personenrecht, Volume I, 3 (3), Berner Kommentar, Bern, Stämpfli, 1981, 56, 67-68 and 71-72.

177. ASSER-VAN DER GRINTEN, II, De rechtspersoon, sixth edition, Zwolle, Tjeenk Willink, 1986, 192-195; POLAK, J.M., Inleiding tot het Nederlands rechtspersonenrecht, Groningen, Wolters, 1969, 45; SANDERS, P. and WESTBROEK, W., NV en BV, fourth edition, Deventer, Kluwer, 1985, 4.

organization irrespective of consent[178]. This does not, however, imply that they are a formal source of law[179].

255. As to the effects on third parties, Dutch law requires third parties to recognize articles of association, provided publication requirements fixed by law have been met[180], but articles of association cannot create rights or obligations for third parties. As to regulations outside articles of associations, their effects *vis-à-vis* third parties have rarely been discussed. Only one author has said that regulations would have no effect upon third parties[181].

256. Dutch law not only has rules on the effects of self-regulatory rules, it also makes distinctions between them and has analyzed their relation as between each other and with other sources of law. First, a distinction is made between articles of association containing essential rules and regulations where other problems may be regulated[182]. Regulations may create obligations for members, provided some authorization may be found in the articles of association[183].

---

178. ASSER-SCHOLTEN, Vertegenwoordiging en rechtspersoon, second edition, Zwolle, Tjeenk Willink, 1954, 152 and 159-161; VAN SCHILFGAARDE, P., Rechtspersonen, Algemeen deel, second edition, Deventer, Kluwer, 1979, 37-38; ASSER-VAN DER GRINTEN, II, De rechtspersoon, 34, 103 and 209-210; VAN DER HEIJDEN-VAN DER GRINTEN, Handboek voor de naamloze vennootschap naar Nederlands recht, eighth edition, Zwolle, Tjeenk Willink, 1968, 182; VAN DER VELDEN, P., De vereniging-rechtspersoon en haar leden, Deventer, Kluwer, 1969, 63-66; SLAGTER, W., Compendium van het ondernemingsrecht, third edition, Deventer, Kluwer, 1978, 112; VAN DER PLOEG, T., Het burgerlijk recht en de vrijwillige organisaties, Deventer, Kluwer, 1978, 95 and 98; VAN HENGSTUM, A. and VAN STEENDEREN, C., Het nieuwe verenigingsrecht, Deventer, Kluwer, 1979, 54; DEN TONKELAAR, J., Vrijheid en gebondenheid in het verenigingsrecht, Deventer, Kluwer, 1979, 173.

179. VAN DER HEIJDEN-VAN DER GRINTEN, Handboek voor de naamloze vennootschap, 182. For the notion of formal source of law, see SCHOBER, A., Die Vereinsautonomie, Cologne, Baun & Boden, 1936, 13-16 and 56-61.

180. VAN DER VELDEN, P., De vereniging-rechtspersoon en haar leden, 66-68; SLAGTER, W., Compendium van het ondernemingsrecht, 112.

181. DUYNSTEE, J., Beschouwingen over de stichting naar Nederlands privaatrecht, second edition, Deventer, Kluwer, 1978, 42.

182. ASSER-VAN DER GRINTEN, II, De rechtspersoon, 34; VAN DER VELDEN, P., De vereniging-rechtspersoon en haar leden, 75.

183. Artikel 34a, Book 2 Civil Code; see ASSER-VAN DER GRINTEN, II, De rechtspersoon, 216-217.

Regulations are preempted by mandatory rules of law, provisions of the articles of association and non-mandatory rules of law and may be set aside if contrary to good faith[184].

Notwithstanding this legal framework, authors apart from van der Velden hardly have applied it to self-regulatory efforts developed by organizations[185].

257. In Germany, three theories have been developed regarding corporations. Pursuant to Von Gierke's realistic theory on corporations[186], chartering an organization no longer was seen as a legal act and regulations developed within organizations were qualified as legal rules (*Normentheorie*)[187]. However, proponents of this theory also made clear that they did not imply that regulations by private organizations were formal sources of law[188]. A more traditional theory still puts emphasis on the fact that organizations come into existence through a legal act (*Rechtsgeschäftstheorie*)[189]. Finally, a mixed theory recognizes that organizations are formed through a legal act but, after coming into existence, are regulated by articles of association (*modifizierte Normentheorie*). Within the organization, self-regulation is then possible without the consent of all members[190].

The choice between these theories is relevant for the interpretation rules to be applied and as to the question whether the general rules of the BGB concerning legal acts are applicable[191].

258. German law makes clear that self-regulatory rules are not a formal source of law. Their binding force is derived from the applicable law in which one finds the principle of autonomy for the parties, within the boundaries of mandatory rules, to create their own rules to be applied

---

184. ASSER-VAN DER GRINTEN, II, De rechtspersoon, 210; VAN DER VELDEN, P., De vereniging-rechtspersoon en haar leden, 77; SLAGTER, W., Compendium van het ondernemingsrecht, 113-114; DAVIDS, W., Nieuwe spelregels voor verenigingen, Zwolle, Tjeenk Willink, 1977, 18.
185. VAN DER VELDEN, P., De vereniging-rechtspersoon en haar leden, 149-150.
186. VON GIERKE, O., Deutsches Privatrecht, I, Leipzig, 1895.
187. SCHOBER, A., Die Vereinsautonomie, 53-61 and WIEDEMANN, H., Gesellschaftsrecht, I, Munich, Beck, 1980, 160-161.
188. MünchKomm-Reuter § 25, No. 7.
189. WIEDEMANN, H., Gesellschaftsrecht, I, 162; Soergel-Hadding § 25 No. 17.
190. German Supreme Court, March 6, 1967, NJW, 1967, 1268; SAUTER, E. and SCHWEYER, G., Der eingetragene Verein, thirteenth edition, Munich, Beck, 1986, 18.
191. Soergel-Hadding § 25 No. 11.

within the organization. As such, this autonomy is similar to freedom of contract[192].

259. Similar to other legal systems, German law also knows the difference between fundamental provisions of the organization (*Satzung*) which should be stated in the articles of association, can only be amended according to strict procedures and require publication[193], and non-fundamental rules (*Geschäftsordnungen* or *Nebenordnungen*). The latter have been extensively analyzed by Kirberger[194]. The Annex to his dissertation contains references to hundreds examples of regulations, recommendations, codes and similar rules made by organizations in Germany which relate to a variety of problems such as organization, elections, finance or dispute resolution[195].

These regulations need some support in the organization's articles of association and cannot derogate from these[196]. They are only binding as between members of the associations or subparts of the association[197]. Requirements for this binding effect (*e.g.*, publication) have not extensively been analyzed[198]. In relations with third parties, these regulations will not be binding[199].

260. The picture which has been drawn above, does not dramatically change when arbitration is chosen to settle disputes which may arise within the organization. If the arbitration is conducted solely within the organization, abuses might be possible when a majority imposes its view on a minority or a dissident member. In that case, the dispute settlement mechanism no longer is impartial. On the other hand, there clearly may be

---

192. Soergel-Hadding Vor § 21 No. 79; KIRBERGER, W., Die Nebenordnungen im Vereins- und Verbandsrecht, 20-21.
193. Soergel-Hadding § 25 No. 8; KIRBERGER, W., Die Nebenordnungen im Vereins- und Verbandsrecht, 220-224.
194. KIRBERGER, W., Die Nebenordnungen im Vereins- und Verbandsrecht, 260 pp.
195. KIRBERGER, W., Die Nebenordnungen im Vereins- und Verbandsrecht, XX-XXXX and 47-196.
196. SAUTER, E. and SCHWEYER, G., Der eingetragene Verein, 100-101; Soergel-Hadding § 25 No. 8; STÖBER, K., Vereinsrecht, fifth edition, Baden-Baden, Nomos, 1988, 203.
197. MünchKomm-Reuter § 25 Nos. 15-17; Soergel-Hadding § 25 No. 8; KIRBERGER, W., Die Nebenordnungen im Vereins- und Verbandsrecht, 244-245; STÖBER, K., Vereinsrecht, 203.
198. See SAUTER, E. and SCHWEYER, G., Der eingetragene Verein, 101; Soergel-Hadding § 25 No. 8.
199. KIRBERGER, W., Die Nebenordnungen im Vereins- und Verbandsrecht, 246-249.

some advantages such as confidentiality or expertise, particularly regarding the self-regulatory rules developed within the organization.

The law applicable to the arbitration will generally provide the framework for arbitrations taking place within organizations. Sometimes specific provisions exist in arbitration laws which tend to promote these kind of arbitrations[200] or protect parties involved in these arbitrations[201].

261. It follows from the foregoing analysis, that self-regulatory rules of professional organizations are not formal sources of law. They are substantive rules which parties may create within the limits of the applicable law[202].

III.4 Examples of international contracts, standard forms, general conditions, custom, usages and self-regulatory rules

262. Rules of transnational practice may be binding by virtue of party consent, custom, usage or regulation of a trade organization. Since several of these grounds are often called upon simultaneously, they are discussed here together in relation to some important transnational rules. First, some codifications adopted by the I.C.C. will be discussed. Thereafter, a few other examples of rules of transnational practice will be analyzed.

---

200. *E.g.*, article 1020 Dutch Code of Civil Procedure.

201. *E.g.*, article 1678 (1) Belgian Code of Civil Procedure; article 1028 Dutch Code of Civil Procedure.

202. The law applicable to the corporation or organization generally will provide these answers.

III.4.1 *Codifications of the International Chamber of Commerce*

263. Since its inception after the first world war, the I.C.C.[203] has been working on unification of law. Some of its major achievements such as Incoterms, the Uniform Customs and Practice on Documentary Credits, the Uniform Rules on Collection and the Uniform Rules on Documentary Guarantees will be discussed hereafter. Less important rules such as the Uniform Rules for a document for combined transport[204], the I.C.C. Rules on Technical Expertise[205] and Adaptation of Contracts[206], the I.C.C. Rules for a pre-arbitral referee procedure[207] and non-normative I.C.C. Rules[208] will not be discussed.

III.4.1.1 International Commercial Terms (Incoterms)

264. Since the nineteen twenties, the I.C.C. has been concerned about the lack of uniformity among national legal systems and practices regarding *price-delivery terms* in transnational sales contracts. These terms fix the

---

203. The I.C.C. is an association under French law with national committees in 107 countries (Uncitral document A/CN. 9/303, March 2, 1988, 20).
204. I.C.C. publication No. 298, Paris, 1975. These rules were not so successful (BONELL, M., Le regole oggetive del commercio internazionale, 74) and are only applicable if incorporated by the parties (DAY, D., The law of international trade, 102; DELIERNEUX, M. and MARTIN, C., La "Révision 1983" des Règles et Usances Uniformes relatives aux crédits documentaires (R.U.U.), R.D.C., 1985, 515; STAUDINGER-HORN, Vorbem. zu §§ 765-778, in VON STAUDINGER, Kommentar zum bürgerlichen Gesetzbuch, twelfth edition, Berlin, Schweitzer Verlag, 1986, 325).
205. I.C.C. publication No. 307, Paris, 1977; see GLOSSNER, O., Contract adaptation through third party intervener, the referee arbitral, in Adaptation and renegotiation of contracts in international trade and finance, HORN, N. (ed.), Deventer, Kluwer, 1985, 195-196; DERAINS, Y., case note under I.C.C. case No. 2444, Clunet, 1977, 934-935.
206. I.C.C. publication No. 326, Paris, 1978; see HORN, N., The concept of adaptation and renegotiation in the law of transnational commercial contracts, in Adaptation and renegotiation of contracts, HORN, N. (ed.), Deventer, Kluwer, 1985, 8-9; SCHMITTHOFF, C., Extrajudicial dispute settlement, in Forum internationale, Deventer, Kluwer, 1985, 8.
207. I.C.C. publication No. 480, Paris, 1990; see ARNALDEZ, J.J. and SCHAFER, E., Le règlement pré-arbitral de la Chambre de Commerce Internationale (en vigueur depuis le 1er janvier 1990), Rev.Arb., 1990, 835-849; PAULSSON, J., A better mousetrap : 1990 I.C.C. Rules for a pre-arbitral referee procedure, INT'L BUS. LAWYER, 1990, 214-219.
208. *E.g.*, codes of conduct as the I.C.C. International Code of sales promotion practice and of advertising practice (I.C.C. publications Nos. 432A and 432B, Paris), bribery in business transactions (I.C.C. publication No. 315, Paris, 1978), Uniform Rules of Conduct for interchange of trade data by teletransmission, I.C.C. publication No. 452, Paris, 24 pp.

major obligations of buyer and seller through a simple formula. In 1923, the I.C.C. published Trade Terms in order to disseminate information on these divergent laws and practices[209].

265. In 1936, a first edition of International Commercial Terms ("*Incoterms*") was adopted. This codification effort was modest; it was aimed at proposing a limited number of price-delivery terms[210]. In 1953, a second revised edition with nine terms was published. The terms best known are probably "*fas*" (free alongside ship), "*fob*" (free on board) and "*cif*" (cost, insurance, freight). In 1967, 1976, 1980 and 1990, other terms have been added to these terms expressing new transport and delivery techniques[211].

266. The legal nature of Incoterms is controversial. Proponents of the theory of *lex mercatoria* saw it as a recognition of transnational customary law[212]. A more common view is that Incoterms have not yet developed into customary law[213]. Sometimes, they have been qualified as usage[214]. Other authors have stated that Incoterms may be applied in the process of supplementing contracts[215]. Finally, they are applicable if parties explicitly

---

209. EISEMANN, F., From "trade terms" to Incoterms, in Interpretation and application of international trade usages, I.C.C. publication No. 374, Paris, 45-49; VON WESTPHALEN, F., Rechtsprobleme der Exportfinanzierung, third edition, Heidelberg, Verlag Recht und Wirtschaft, 1987, 164-165.

210. BAKKERS, R., Rechtsgewoonte betreffende handelskoop, 10.

211. Incoterms 1990, I.C.C. publication No. 460, Paris, 1990. See also Guide to Incoterms, I.C.C. publication No. 461, Paris, 1991.

212. DEL MARMOL, C., Lex mercatoria, 165; DERAINS, Y., case note I.C.C. case No. 3202, Clunet, 1979, 1006; DERAINS, Y., case note I.C.C. case No. 3130, Clunet, 1981, 936; DERAINS, Y., case note I.C.C. case No. 3894, Clunet, 1982, 990; EISEMANN, F. and DERAINS, Y., La pratique des Incoterms, Paris, Jupiter, 1988, 33; KAHN, P., Rapport français, 241-242.

213. LEYMARIE, F., Les usages commerciaux, 322-323; BULCK, H., Betrachtungen über ein Völkerhandelsrecht, 167.

214. BASEDOW, J., Die Incoterms oder wie man kodifizierte Usancen reformiert, 125-127.

215. EISEMANN, F., Die Incoterms im internationalen Warenkaufrecht, 45-50; EISEMANN, F., Die Incoterms im Recht des internationalen Warenhandels: Außerstaatliche Rechtsbildung oder Vertragsrecht, 331-333; EISEMANN, F., Usages de la vente commerciale internationale, Incoterms aujourd'hui et demain, second edition, Paris, Jupiter, 1980, 43-44; LIESECKE, R., Die typische Klauseln des internationalen Handelsverkehrs in der neueren Praxis, WM, 1978, Annex No. 3, 26; LORENZ, W., Die Lex Mercatoria : eine internationale Rechtsquelle ?, 429; STAUB-GroßKomm-Koller, fourth edition, Berlin, de Gruyter, 1985, Vor § 373, No. 11.

or tacitly incorporated them into their contract[216]; sometimes, one has said that they are to be applied if parties did not exclude them[217].

In case law, few decisions have dealt with the nature of Incoterms. In a June 18, 1975 decision, the German Supreme Court held that a fob-clause also applied even if the parties did not expressly incorporate Incoterms in their contract[218]. The motivation of the decision is, however too brief in order to draw conclusions[219]. In some arbitral decisions, Incoterms have been applied irrespective of reference to them by the parties[220]. In I.C.C. arbitration No. 2438, Incoterms even have been identified as truly transnational sales customs. One should note that these arbitral decisions conflict greatly with the majority opinion in scholarly writing where Incoterms are basically seen as contractual rules.

267. Since national systems to a certain extent have different attitudes *vis-à-vis* trade usages, one can hardly give a universal opinion as to the legal status of Incoterms. Besides the need for a uniform interpretation, the applicable law may thus be an important factor in order to assess their position. Furthermore, their legal status cannot be determined as such but must be seen for each individual provision[221]. Some provisions have been in the Incoterms for long while others have recently been inserted so that the more recent ones may be more uncertain. Also, Incoterms not only

---

216. EISEMANN, F., Die Incoterms in Handel und Verkehr, 19; SCHEGELBERGER-HEFERMEHL, Handelsgesetzbuch, III, 1529; VON WESTPHALEN, F., Rechtsprobleme der Exportfinanzierung, 168-169; ZAHN, J., EBERDING, E. and EHRLICH, D., Zahlung und Zahlungssicherung im Außenhandel, sixth edition, Berlin, de Gruyter, 1986, 17; FIRSCHING, K., Internationales Schuldrecht, I, 355; SCHÜSSLER, C., Die Incoterms - Internationale Regeln für die Auslegung der handelsüblichen Vertragsformeln, DB, 1986, 1162; BEN ABDERRAHMANE, D., Le droit allemand des conditions générales des contrats dans les ventes commerciales franco-allemandes, 85; JADAUD, B. and PLAISANT, R., Droit du commerce international, 67; KAHN, P., La vente commerciale internationale, 226; SCHMITTHOFF, C. and SARRE, D., Charlesworth's mercantile law, fourteenth edition, London, Stevens & Sons, 1984, 373; BERMAN, H. and KAUFMAN, C., The law of international commercial transactions (lex mercatoria), 228-229; HONNOLD, J., Uniform law and uniform trade terms - two approaches to a common goal, in HORN, N. and SCHMITTHOFF, C., The transnational law of international commercial transactions, Deventer, Kluwer, 1982, 169.
217. KAHN, P., Rapport français, 242.
218. German Supreme Court, June 18, 1975, RIW, 1975, 578.
219. SCHÜSSLER, C., Die Incoterms - Internationale Regeln für die Auslegung der handelsüblichen Vertragsformeln, 1162. However, Goldman has interpreted it as recognition of the *lex mercatoria* (GOLDMAN, B., Lex mercatoria, 14).
220. I.C.C. case No. 2438, Clunet, 1976, 968, case note DERAINS, Y. and I.C.C. case No. 3894, Clunet, 1982, 987, case note DERAINS, Y.
221. See also SONNENBERGER, H.J., Verkehrssitte im Schuldvertrag, 79.

codified trade terms but also created some which may affect their nature[222].

The territorial scope of Incoterms should also be taken into account. Up to recently, they were barely used in the U.S.A. and by U.S. companies because the UCC and the *American Foreign Trade Definitions* were used. Quite recently, Incoterms seem to have prevailed over the American Foreign Trade Definitions and their application is now being recommended to American companies[223]. As to Article 2 UCC on sales, one should realize that its price-delivery terms which are sometimes different from those of Incoterms[224], may come to compete with Incoterms. It is then not evident that, absent express reference to Incoterms in the contract, these should prevail.

III.4.1.2 Uniform Customs and Practice for Documentary Credits

268. Since the second half of the nineteen twenties, the I.C.C. also has taken the lead codifying some principles regarding letters of credit (also called documentary credits). In 1933, a first edition of Uniform Customs and Practice for Documentary Credits ("*U.C.P.*") was published[225]. Revisions took place in 1951, 1962, 1974 and 1983[226]. A new revision (UCP No. 500) is under way and may be expected soon. The 1962 edition was particularly important because the British banks then agreed to accede to the U.C.P.[227]. The unification brought about by the U.C.P. was further

---

222. DERAINS, Y., Incoterms 1980 : from codification to formulation, in Interpretation and application of international trade usages, I.C.C. publication No. 374, Paris, 52; BASEDOW, J., Die Incoterms und der Container oder wie man kodifizierte Usancen reformiert, 124.

223. DERAINS, Y., Incoterms 1980 : from codification to formulation, 53; RAMBERG, J., Incoterms 1980, in The transnational law of international commercial transactions, HORN, N. and SCHMITTHOFF, C. (ed.), Deventer, Kluwer, 1982, 151.

224. See MICHIDA, S., Possible avenues to preparation of standard contracts for international trade on a global level, 255; DAY, D., The law of international trade, 42; WIJFFELS, R., Incoterms, 3; ZAHN, J., EBERDING, E. and EHRLICH, D., Zahlung und Zahlungssicherung im Außenhandel, 18.

225. See STOUFFLET, J., Le crédit documentaire, 101-105; CAHN, E., Het accreditief, Amsterdam, Paris, 1935, 10-11; DE VUYST, B., Documentaire kredieten, A.P.R., Ghent, Story, 1981, 10-11; DE ROOY, F., Documentaire kredieten, Deventer, Kluwer, 1980, 9-12.

226. I.C.C. publication No. 400, Paris, 1983.

227. ELLINGER, E., Letters of credit, in HORN, N. and SCHMITTHOFF, C., The transnational law of international commercial transactions, Deventer, Kluwer, 1982, 248-249.

supported through the publication of comments[228] and model forms for letters of credit[229] and the possibility to refer questions on the application or interpretation of the U.C.P. to the Banking Commission of the I.C.C., the special I.C.C. working group responsible for banking matters[230]. Finally, special mention should be made of the fact that Uncitral has recommended the use of the 1983 edition of the U.C.P.[231].

269. The U.C.P. are not an all-encompassing set of rules. Where there are gaps, reference to the applicable law may still be necessary[232].

270. The U.C.P. are applied by banks in countries where a Bankers' Association is active and acceded to the U.C.P. Absent a Bankers' Association, the U.C.P. will be acceded to by banks on an individual basis. The 1974 edition appears to have been endorsed by bankers' associations in more than 175 countries and in some twenty countries individual banks have acceded[233]. The 1983 edition has been accepted by bankers' associations in more than 84 countries and individual accessions from 63

---

228. UCP for documentary credits 1974/83 compared and explained, I.C.C. publication No. 411, Paris, 80 pp.; Guide to documentary credit operations, I.C.C. publication No. 415, Paris, 50 pp.; Case-studies on documentary credits, I.C.C. publication No. 459, Paris.

229. Standard forms and guidance notes for credit applicants, I.C.C. publication No. 416A, Paris, 24 pp. See ZAHN, J., EBERDING, E. and EHRLICH, D., Zahlung und Zahlungssicherung im Außenhandel, 15. This initiative was not so successful, see ELLINGER, E.P., Letters of credit, 255.

230. The decisions of the Banking Commission have been published, see Decisions (1975-1979) of the ICC Banking Commission, I.C.C. publication No. 371, Paris, 1981; Opinions (1980-1981) of the ICC Banking Commission, I.C.C. publication No. 399, Paris, 1982; Opinions of the Banking Commission (1982-1985), I.C.C. publication No. 434, Paris, 1987; Opinions of the I.C.C. Banking Commission (1987-1988), I.C.C. publication No. 469, Paris; see WHEBLE, B., Uniform customs and practice for documentary credits - 1974 revision, in Interpretation and application of international trade usages, I.C.C. publication No. 374, Paris, 59-60.

231. EISEMANN, F., BONTOUX, C. and ROWE, M., Le crédit documentaire dans le commerce extérieur, 4.

232. In the U.C.P., one provision (article 55 U.C.P.) refers to the applicable law. See further STOUFFLET, J., Le crédit documentaire, 112-113; EBERTH, R., Die Revision von 1983 der Einheitlichen Richtlinien und Gebräuche für Dokumenten-Akkreditive, WM, 1984, Annex No. 4, 20; EISEMANN, F., BONTOUX, C. and ROWE, M., Le crédit documentaire dans le commerce extérieur, 6; VAN HECKE, G., Le droit international privé des sûretés nouvelles issues de la pratique, in Les sûretés, FEDUCI, 1984, 454-455; EKELMANS, M., case note Court of Appeal Brussels, November 6, 1985, Rev.Banque, 1986, No. 6, 50-51.

233. DAVID, R., The international unification of private law, in International Encyclopedia of Comparative Law, Tubingen, Mohr, 1971, 59; DE VUYST, B., Documentaire kredieten, 12.

countries[234]. As between banks, the U.C.P. would be binding as a result of membership in a bankers' association which has acceded to the U.C.P. or of an individual accession[235].

271. The problems related to the nature of the U.C.P. thus involve banks which are not bound by them[236], account parties[237] and beneficiaries which are not an original party to the documentary credit[238].

The U.C.P. themselves tackle this problem. Article 1 provides that the U.C.P. are applicable to all documentary credits and are binding on all parties unless there is an express agreement to the contrary. In order to avoid problems regarding the application of the U.C.P., article 1 also imposes that the documentary credit should state that it is subject to the 1983 revision of the U.C.P.[239]. This provision accords with international practice; it appears that documentary credits almost always refer to the U.C.P.[240]. Also, documentary credits sent through the S.W.I.F.T.-network, are subject to the U.C.P. by virtue of S.W.I.F.T.- regulations[241].

---

234. Information Bulletin, Fédération des entreprises belges, 1988, 223.

235. STOUFFLET, J., Le crédit documentaire, 108; ROWE, M., The contribution of the ICC to the development of international trade law, in The transnational law of international commercial transactions, HORN, N. and SCHMITTHOFF, C. (ed.), Deventer, Kluwer, 1982, 53.

236. See STOUFFLET, J., Le crédit documentaire, 108; MATTOUT, J.P., Droit bancaire international, Paris, Banque, 1987, 302.

237. Exception is to be made for the case where the credit agreement between account party and issuer refers to the U.C.P.

238. STOUFFLET, J., Le crédit documentaire, 107; VAN RYN, J. and HEENEN, J., Principes de droit commercial, III, Brussels, Bruylant, 1960, 380-382.

239. WHEBLE, B., UCP 1974/1983 Revisions compared and explained, I.C.C. publication No. 411, Paris, 1984, 10.

240. See KURKELA, M., How banks treat commercial letters of credit, Int.Fin.Law Review, November 1984, 29.

241. S.W.I.F.T. User Handbook, Volume 6, Standards, Part 1, Section 7, Number 1.1 and 2.1; see WYMEERSCH, E., Règles professionnelles et règles standardisées dans les opérations financières, 69-70.

S.W.I.F.T.'s General Terms and Conditions are applicable by virtue of the members' acceptance at the time they were admitted. The General Terms and Conditions do not refer to the rules of the Handbook. Therefore, there is some doubt whether and how these rules are binding. Some scholars (WYMEERSCH, E., Règles professionnelles et règles standardisées dans les opérations financières, 70; BRAECKMANS, H., Paralegale normen en lex mercatoria, 12) have argued that the rules of the handbook have been accepted by the mere fact of the network's use. In practice, the problem of the binding effect of the handbook's rules has arisen in relation to third parties such as non-S.W.I.F.T. members and beneficiaries. An express reference is thus still useful (see Opinions of the ICC Banking Commission (1984-1986), Paris, I.C.C. publication No. 434, 1987, 21).

272. In most countries, the nature of the U.C.P. is controversial[242]. Proponents of the theory of the *lex mercatoria* have seen the U.C.P. as an example of transnational autonomous rules. This is not, however, a widespread opinion[243].

In Belgium, a minority view sees the U.C.P. as international custom[244]. A decision of the Brussels Commercial Court dated November 16, 1978 is often invoked for that position. In that case, the Court applied the U.C.P. as trade usages. The problem arose in relation to the beneficiary of the credit; the Court held that the U.C.P. also might apply against companies which regularly use documentary credits for their operations[245]. The decision remains unclear, however, as to whether the U.C.P. are to be applied as customary rules or as trade usages on the basis of the parties' consent. Therefore, it is an overstatement to say that in Belgium the U.C.P. are customary law[246].

The majority opinion sees the U.C.P. as trade usages which need the consent of the parties involved[247]. A decision of the Brussels Commercial

242. See KOZOLCHYK, G., Letters of credit, in International Encyclopedia of comparative law, Tubingen, Mohr, 1979, 17-18; WYMEERSCH, E., Règles professionnelles et règles standardisées dans les opérations financières, 62-63; RUEDIN, R., Rapport suisse, in Le rôle de la pratique dans la formation du droit, Travaux de l'Association Henri Capitant, XXXIV, Paris, Economica, 1985, 301-302.

243. See REIMANN, T., Zur Lehre vom "rechtsordnungslosen" Vertrag, 66.

244. DEL MARMOL, C., Lex mercatoria, 164; MERCHIERS, Y., Overzicht van rechtspraak (1977-1981), Bijzonder en afwijkend handelsrecht, T.P.R., 1982, 773; POULLET, Y., Le contrat de garantie, examen de quelques problèmes juridiques particuliers, in Les garanties bancaires dans les contrats internationaux, FEDUCI (ed.), Paris, Moniteur, 1981, 136.

245. Commercial Court Brussels, November 16, 1978, Rev.Banque, 1980, 249.

246. SCHMITTHOFF, C., Export trade, eight edition, 378, but see the ninth edition at 402.

247. DIERYCK, A., Les ouvertures de crédit, Brussels, Bruylant, 1945, 275; VAN MAELE, A., Droit bancaire, in Les Novelles, Brussels, Larcier, 1951, 250; FREDERICQ, L., Traité de droit commercial belge, IX, 305-306 and 319; FREDERICQ, L., Le crédit irrévocable transmissible, case note Commercial Court Brugge, June 10, 1952, R.C.J.B., 1953, 45-46; HEENEN, J., Le crédit irrévocable, Rev.Banque, 1952, 456; VAN RYN, J. and HEENEN, J., Principes de droit commercial, IV, second edition, Brussels, Bruylant, 1988, 471-472; HENRION, R., Aspects juridiques et économiques du crédit à court terme, Brussels, Editions de L'Université de Bruxelles, 1973, 164; SIMONT, L., Les garanties indépendantes, Rev.Banque, 1983, 607; SIMONT, L., Essai de classification des sûretés issues de la pratique et problèmes juridiques qu'elles posent, in Les sûretés, FEDUCI, Brussels, 1984, 300; SIMONT, L., De abstracte verbintenissen van de bankier naar Belgisch recht, T.P.R., 1985, 707; SIMONT, L., Misbruik bij documentair krediet, T.P.R., 1986, 100; MERCHIERS, Y., Overzicht van rechtspraak (1972-1976), Bijzonder en afwijkend handelsrecht, T.P.R., 1979, 104; LECHIEN, D. and REGOUT-MASSON, M., Chroniques : jurisprudence, Les sûretés internationales (Grande-Bretagne - Pays-Bas 1983-1984), R.D.A.I., 1985,

Court dated May 2, 1974 refused to apply the U.C.P. to the account party which had not been directly in touch with the issuer of the credit. The Court based its decision not so much on this factual element but stated that the U.C.P. were unilaterally codified by the banking community[248].

273. In France, a majority view sees the U.C.P. as international custom[249] or as applicable unless otherwise expressly agreed[250]. The theory of *lex mercatoria* clearly has influenced these positions. Recent Supreme Court decisions[251] have come to give more weight to these positions since they extend the scope of judicial review to the U.R.U. One has interpreted these decisions as indications that the Court considered the U.C.P. as legal rules[252]. A minority position sees the U.C.P. as a code of conduct[253], as self-regulatory rules of the I.C.C.[254] or as contractual trade usages[255].

879; EKELMANS, M., case note Court of Appeal Brussels, November 6, 1985, Rev.Banque, 1986, No. 6, 50-51.

248. J.T., 1975, 82, J.C.B., 1974, 325; for criticism, see DE ROOY, F., Documentaire kredieten, 16; DELIERNEUX, M. and MARTIN, C., La "Révision 1983" des Règles et Usances Uniformes relatives aux crédits documentaires (R.U.U.), 502; EISEMANN, F., BONTOUX, C. and ROWE, M., Le crédit documentaire dans le commerce extérieur, 7-8.

249. STOUFFLET, J., Le crédit documentaire, 110-111 (see also at 109); RODIERE, R. and RIVES-LANGE, J.L., Droit bancaire, third edition, Paris, Dalloz, 1980, 436; GOLDMAN, B., Le contrat international, 473; GOLDMAN, B., Rapport général, 167; LEYMARIE, F., Les usages commerciaux, 326; DERAINS, Y., case note I.C.C. case No. 3202, Clunet, 1979, 1006.

250. Commercial Court Paris, March 8, 1976, Dr.mar.fr., 1976, 558; HOUIN, R., Usages commerciaux et loi en droit français, 253; KAHN, P., Rapport français, 242.

251. Supreme Court, October 14, 1981, D., 1982, 301, case note VASSEUR, M., J.C.P., 1982, 19815, case note GAVALDA, C. and STOUFFLET, J., Rev. Banque, 1982, 681; see also two decisions of March 14, 1984 (D., 1985, I.R., Droit bancaire, 245).

252. GOLDMAN, B., Lex mercatoria, 14-15; DE LEVAL, G., Saisies et droit commercial, in Les créanciers et le droit de la faillite, COMMISSION DROIT ET VIE DES AFFAIRES (ed.), Brussels, Bruylant, 1983, 310; *contra* BEGUIN, J., Le développement de la lex mercatoria menace-t-il l'ordre juridique international ?, 508.

253. BONTOUX, C., La pratique du crédit documentaire : quelques problèmes particuliers, in Hommage à Frédéric Eisemann, I.C.C. publication No. 321, Paris, 1978, 162.

254. STOUFFLET, J., L'oeuvre normative de la Chambre de Commerce Internationale dans le domaine bancaire, 368-369; STOUFFLET, J., Banque et opérations de banque, conflits de lois, Jurisclasseur de droit commercial, 10.

255. STOUFFLET, J., Le crédit documentaire, 109; MARAIS, G., Du crédit confirmé en matière documentaire, Paris, LGDJ, 1945, 47; KASSIS, A., Théorie générale du commerce, 197, 310, 330 and 334.

274. In Germany, only a minority of authors takes the position that the U.C.P. are customary law[256]. A second opinion puts emphasis on the *sui generis* character of the U.C.P.[257]. Some authors have qualified the U.C.P. as trade usages as referred to in § 346 HGB[258]. However, the majority view sees the U.C.P. as general conditions which are subject to the Law on General Conditions (*Allgemeine Geschäftsbedingungengesetz*, "*AGBG*"); some provisions might also be trade usages[259]. One may note that the General Banking Conditions of the German banks explicitly refer to the U.C.P.[260]. This majority position implies that the mandatory provisions of the AGBG to a large extent apply to the U.C.P.[261].

275. In The Netherlands, on several occasions, the Supreme Court has been asked to set aside decisions based on wrongful application of the U.C.P. The Court always has declined jurisdiction since in its opinion the U.C.P.

---

256. *See* BULCK, H., Betrachtungen über ein Völkerhandelsrecht, 167.
257. EBERTH, R., The uniform customs and practice for documentary credits, in Current problems of international trade financing, CHINKIN, C.M., DAVIDSON, P.J. and RICQUIER, W. (ed.), Singapore, Faculty of Law, National University of Singapore, 1983, 29-34; EBERTH, R., Zur Rechtsnatur der Einheitlichen Richtlinien und Gebräuche für Dokumenten-Akkreditive, in Festschrift für Karl Neumayer, Baden-Baden, Nomos, 1985, 214-216.
258. HORN, N., Internationale Zahlungen und Akkreditive, in Dokumentenakkreditive und Bankgarantien im internationalen Zahlungsverkehr, Frhrr. MARSCHALL VON BIEBERSTEIN, W. (ed.), Frankfurt, Metzner, 1977, 13; STAUDINGER-HORN, Vorbem. zu §§ 765-778, in VON STAUDINGER, Kommentar zum bürgerlichen Gesetzbuch, twelfth edition, Berlin, Schweitzer Verlag, 1986, 325-326; EBERTH, R., Documentary credits in Germany and England, J.BUS.L., 1977, 30; ZAHN, J., EBERDING, E. and EHRLICH, D., Zahlung und Zahlungssicherung im Außenhandel, 10-14; German Supreme Court, February 14, 1958, WM, 1958, 456, AWD, 1958, 57.
259. SCHLEGELBERGER-HEFERMEHL, Handelsgesetzbuch, III, 1529; SCHÖNLE, H., Die Rechtsnatur der Einheitlichen Richtlinien und Gebräuche für Dokumentenakkreditive, NJW, 1968, 728-729; CANARIS, W., Bankvertragsrecht, second edition, Berlin, de Gruyter, 1981, 485-486; VON WESTPHALEN, F., Rechtsprobleme der Exportfinanzierung, 227-228; VON WESTPHALEN, F., Die Einheitliche Richtlinien und Gebräuche für Dokumentenakkreditive (1974) und die Einheitliche Richtlinien für Inkassi im Recht des AGB-Gesetzes, WM, 1980, 178-179; NIELSEN, J., Grundlagen des Akkreditivsgeschäfts, Revision 1983, Cologne, Bankverlag, 1985, 19; FIRSCHING, K., Internationales Schuldrecht, I, 355 and 577; SONNENBERGER, H., Verkehrssitten im Schuldvertrag, 87; RAITH, R., Das Recht des Dokumentenakkreditivs in den USA und in Deutschland, Bonn, Stollfuß, 1985, 39-43; MünchKomm-Hüffer, § 783, No. 85; PLAGEMANN, D., Rechtsprobleme bei der Arrestierung des Auszahlungsanspruches aus einem deferred payment-Akkreditiv, RIW, 1987, 27; BEN ABDERRAHMANE, D., Le droit allemand des conditions générales des contrats dans les ventes commerciales franco-allemandes, 84.
260. EBERTH, R., Documentary credits in Germany and England, 30.
261. See VON WESTPHALEN, F., Rechtsprobleme der Exportfinanzierung, 228-230.

are not customs. Since the Court by law can only review decisions for violation of formal sources of law, rules such as the U.C.P. which are not binding by themselves, cannot be reviewed[262]. Authors are divided; according to F. De Rooy, some provisions of the U.C.P. such as their general principles (*e.g.*, articles 3 through 6 U.C.P.) may be considered trade usages; the U.C.P. would, however, not constitute *lex mercatoria*[263]. In a recent dissertation, Boon has taken the opposite view; in her opinion, the U.C.P. would be part of the *lex mercatoria*[264].

276. In England, there is an almost unanimous consensus that the U.C.P. must be incorporated into the contract in order to be binding; the U.C.P. are not seen as trade usages[265].

277. The U.S.A. is one of the few countries with statutory rules, at state level, on letters of credit (Article 5 UCC). Of course, this creates the problem of the relation between these statutory rules and the U.C.P. This problem was especially relevant to the state of New York which, as an important commercial and financial center for international transactions, feared that the introduction of the UCC would hinder the long established practices regarding letters of credit which were handled under the U.C.P. Therefore, Article 5 UCC was amended in order to provide for preemption of the UCC by the U.C.P. if the letter of credit is in whole or in part subject to the U.C.P. by its wording, the agreement between the parties,

262. Dutch Supreme Court, March 12, 1982, N.J., 1982, No. 267; Dutch Supreme Court, October 28, 1983, N.J., 1985, No. 131, opinion Advocate General VAN SOEST and concurring note SCHULTSZ, J.; Dutch Supreme Court, April 26, 1985, N.J., 1985, No. 607, opinion Advocate General FRANX.

263. DE ROOY, F., Documentaire kredieten, 17-18; DE ROOY, F., Documentary credits, Deventer, Kluwer, 1984, 14-17; *contra* VAN DELDEN, R., Lex mercatoria of ius commune ?, 6 and 8.

264. See infra No. 361.

265. M. Golodetz & Co. Inc. v. Czarnikow-Rianda Co. Inc., [1979] 2 All E.R. 726 (Commercial Court); SCHMITTHOFF, C., Export trade, 338; SCHMITTHOFF, C., Conflict of laws issues relating to letters of credit : an English perspective, in Current problems of international trade financing, CHINKIN, C., DAVIDSON, P. and RICQUIER, N. (ed.), Singapore, Faculty of law, National University of Singapore, 1983, 145; SCHMITTHOFF, C., The new uniform customs for letters of credit, J.BUS.L., 1983, 193; GUTTERIDGE, H. and MEGRAH, M., The law of bankers' commercial credits, London, Europa publications, 1984, seventh edition, 6; HOYLE, M., The law of international trade, first edition, 98; OUSWORTH, J., International payment mechanisms, in International trade : law and practice, LEW, J. and STANBROOK, C. (ed.), London, Euromoney, 1983, 125; ROWE, M., Letters of credit : the ICC revises the rules, Int.Fin.Law Review, January 1983, 20; ROWE, M., Using letters of credit in trade, Int.Fin.Law Review, March 1986, 30.

practices or trade usages[266]. Alabama and Missouri have followed the New York example in amending their UCC[267].

278. A general answer to the legal nature of the U.C.P. is impossible. First, since national laws and international conventions have different views on custom and trade usages, this will be reflected in their positions regarding self-regulatory rules such as the U.C.P. In this respect, the applicable law might well still have a role to play[268]. Second, the U.C.P. have a variety of provisions which explains that the legal nature of the U.C.P. may not be determined in general but rather per provision[269]. Also, some provisions are new while others have long been in the U.C.P. Finally, some provisions codify trade patterns while other clauses create new rules in order to solve practical problems[270].

In any event, it is fair to say that the U.C.P. are far more binding than Incoterms. This is to a large extent due to the greater homogeneity of the international banking community. The fact that the U.C.P. are generally binding in interbank relations is in this respect a nice example. For other relations, the applicable law will determine whether a certain provision of the U.C.P. is binding as custom, usage, standard term or contract clause.

III.4.1.3 Uniform Rules for Collections

279. These rules were first adopted in 1956 and revised in 1967 and 1978[271]. They contain rules for collecting financial and trade docu-

---

266. N.Y. UCC § 5-102 (1).
267. LEACOCK, S., Fraud in the international transaction : enjoining payment of letters of credit in international transactions, VAND.J.TRANSNAT'L L., 1984, 905; DAVIDSON, P., The UCP and the need for amendment in the light of technological advances, in Current problems of international trade financing, CHINKIN, C., DAVIDSON, P. and RICQUIER, W. (ed.), Singapore, Faculty of law, National University of Singapore, 1983, 40.
268. See also VON BAR, C., Kollisionsrechtliche Aspekte der Vereinbarung und Inanspruchnahme von Dokumentenakkreditive, ZHR, 1988, 46.
269. STOUFFLET, J., Le crédit documentaire, 109.
270. STOUFFLET, J., L'oeuvre normative de la Chambre de Commerce Internationale dans le domaine bancaire, 367-368; EBERTH, R., Zur Rechtsnatur der Einheitlichen Richtlinien und Gebräuche für Dokumenten-Akkreditive, 203-205; NIELSEN, J., Grundlagen des Akkreditivsgeschäft, Revision 1983, 19.
271. I.C.C. publication No. 322, Paris, 1978; see BONELL, M., Le regole oggetive del commercio internazionale, 47-49.

ments[272]. Bankers' associations from more than 60 countries have acceded to these rules[273] and reference is often made to them[274]. As a whole, the Uniform Rules for Collections are not customs or trade usages[275]. They are primarily general conditions whose application must be stipulated by the parties[276]. Sometimes, they may be binding in interbank relations based upon self-regulatory rules of bankers' associations.

III.4.1.4 Uniform Rules for Contract Guarantees

280. These rules were made in 1978 and aimed to strike a fair balance between the interests of account parties, beneficiaries and issuers of bankers guarantees[277]. For that reason, the Uniform Rules only apply to

---

272. See GRAIGIE, C., The collection of bills in international trade, in Current problems of international trade financing, CHINKIN, C., DAVIDSON, P. and RICQUIER, W. (ed.), Singapore, Faculty of law, National University of Singapore, 1983, 100-133.
273. LEYMARIE, F., Les usages commerciaux, 339.
274. HORN, N., Uniformity and diversity in the law of international commercial contracts, 8-9; DAY, D., The law of international trade, 136; STOUFFLET, J., L'oeuvre normative de la Chambre de commerce internationale dans le domaine bancaire, 362-363.

    In the S.W.I.F.T. Network, the Uniform Rules for Collections are not applicable unless expressly referred to. The counterparty has to object to the incorporation of the Rules if he wants to avoid their application (S.W.I.F.T. User Handbook, Volume 6 - Standards - Part 2, Section 4, Number 1.1.; see WYMEERSCH, E., Règles professionnelles et règles standardisées dans les opérations financières, 69).
275. *But see* STOUFFLET, J., L'oeuvre normative de la Chambre de Commerce Internationale dans le domaine bancaire, 368-369; STOUFFLET, J., Banque et opérations de banque, conflits de lois, Jurisclasseur de droit commercial, 10 and ZAHN, J., EBERDING, E. and EHRLICH, D., Zahlung und Zahlungssicherung im Außenhandel, 16-17.
276. GRAIGIE, C., The collection of bills in international trade, 114; SCHMITTHOFF, C., Export trade, 332; DAY, D., The law of international trade, 136; KASSIS, A., Théorie générale des usages du commerce, 332 ("usage conventionnel"); SCHLEGELBERGER-HEFERMEHL, Handelsgesetzbuch, III, 1549; VON WESTPHALEN, F., Rechtsprobleme der Exportfinanzierung, 207-208; VON WESTPHALEN, F., Die Einheitlichen Richtlinien und Gebräuche für Dokumentenakkreditive (1974) und die Einheitlichen Richtlinien für Inkassi im Sicht des AGB-Gesetzes, 189; CANARIS, C.W., Bankvertragsrecht, second edition, 560.
277. I.C.C. publication No. 325, Paris, 1978; see also Model Forms for issuing contract guarantees, I.C.C. publication, No. 406, Paris, 16 pp.; see VON MARSCHALL, W., Recent developments in the field of standby letters of credit, bank guarantees and performance bonds, in Current problems of international trade financing, CHINKIN, C., DAVIDSON, P. and RICQUIER, W. (ed.), Singapore, Faculty of law, National University of Singapore, 1983, 271-274.

conditional bankers guarantees and not to on demand guarantees[278]. However, this restriction of the Rules' scope did not, at that time, correspond to market forces[279]. As a result of the first and second oil crises, the market had turned into a buyers' market where the beneficiaries contracted for on demand guarantees and thus the Uniform Rules were hardly ever applied[280]. Consequently, these Rules cannot be seen as transnational custom or usage[281]. Some case law indirectly took the Rules into account notwithstanding the fact that the parties had not referred to them[282].

---

278. Article 9 Uniform Rules.

279. MOREAU-MARGREVE, I., Evolution du droit et de la pratique en matière de sûretés, in Les créanciers et le droit de la faillite, COMMISSION DROIT ET VIE DES AFFAIRES (ed.), Brussels, Bruylant, 1983, 158; BRUYNEEL, A., Le droit bancaire, J.T., 1982, 356; BEGUIN, J., Le développement de la lex mercatoria menace-t-il l'ordre juridique international ?, 507; HORN, N., Uniformity and diversity in the law of international commercial contracts, 9; HORN, N., Securing international commercial transactions : standby letters of credit, bonds, guarantees, and similar sureties, in The transnational law of international commercial transactions, HORN, N. and SCHMITTHOFF, C. (ed.), Deventer, Kluwer, 1982, 286 and 289.

280. POULLET, Y., Les garanties contractuelles dans le commerce international, D.P.C.I., 1979, 394; PABBRUWE, H., De betekenis van de onafhankelijke bankgarantie, Deventer, Kluwer, 1984, 7; BOLL, J., Preadvies, in MIJNSSEN, F. and BOLL, J., De bankgarantie, Preadviezen van de Vereeniging Handelsrecht, Zwolle, Tjeenk Willink, 1984, 140; CANARIS, C.W., Bankvertragsrecht, second edition, 574; ZAHN, J., EBERDING, E. and EHRLICH, D., Zahlung und Zahlungssicherung im Außenhandel, 433-434; KURKELA, M., Letters of credit under international trade law : UCC, UCP and law merchant, 406.

However, some export credit agencies recommended the use of conditional guarantees (article 20.1 General Rules Belgian Export Credit Agency (652-1985), Contact No. 50, February 1985, 73 ff.).

281. WYMEERSCH, E., Bank guarantees on first demand in Belgian law, Bulletin Droit et Banque, Association luxembourgeoise des juristes de banque, 1987, No. 10, 17; MIJNSSEN, F., Preadvies, in MIJNSSEN, F. and BOLL, J., De bankgarantie, Preadviezen van de Vereeniging Handelsrecht, Zwolle, Tjeenk Willink, 1984, 12; KAHN, P., Rapport français, 242; KASSIS, A., Théorie générale des usages du commerce, 332; VON WESTPHALEN, F., Die Bankgarantie im internationalen Handelsverkehr, Heidelberg, Verlagsgesellschaft Recht und Wirtschaft, 1982, 329; TROST, U., Bankgarantien im Außenhandel: Die "Einheitlichen Richtlinien für Vertragsgarantien" der internationalen Handelskammer von 1978, Seggebruch, GFU-Verlagsgesellschaft, 1982, 184-185; ROESLE, E., Die internationale Vereinheitlichung des Rechts der Bankgarantien, Zurich, Schulthess, 1983, 161-162; DOHM, J., Bankgarantien im internationalen Handel, Bern, Stämpfli, 1985, 219.

282. President Commercial Court Brussels, April 6, 1982, Rev.Banque, 1982, 683; Court of Appeal Paris, December 13, 1984, D., I.R. Droit bancaire, 1985, 239, case note VASSEUR, M.; *contra* District Court Arnhem, October 14, 1982 and October 27, 1983, N.J., 1986, No. 79.

The I.C.C. then proceeded to the regulation of the practices regarding demand for payment under on demand guarantees. It was thought that a code of conduct might be an appropriate tool for such regulation[283]. These efforts have not succeeded and seem to have been abandoned. In 1983, at the occasion of the revision of the U.C.P., their scope has been extended to include *standby letters of credits*. This form of a letter of credit performs the same functions as bankers guarantees and has been used primarily in the U.S.A.[284]. At present, it is unclear whether and to what extent European banks have substituted bankers guarantees for standby letters of credit and to what extent the U.C.P. is thus applicable to standby letters of credit. Finally, some years ago, the I.C.C. again started unification work on bankers guarantees based on a model prepared by the British Bankers' Association. The final edition of new Uniform Rules may be expected in the near future.

III.4.2 *Other examples found in the banking, insurance, commodities, construction and maritime sectors*

281. Apart from the I.C.C., other organizations also have been active in the formulation of self-regulatory rules. Some of these rules are discussed below.

282. The *Economic Commission for Europe* ("*ECE*"), a regional organization of the United Nations, has been working, since the nineteen fifties on general conditions for specific sectors of the economy to be used in East-West transactions in Europe. Some twelve sets of general conditions have been adopted. Great interest was expressed in these general conditions[285]

283. STUMP, H. and ULLRICH, C., Die mißbräuchliche Inanspruchnahme von Bankgarantien im internationalen Geschäftsverkehr, RIW, 1984, 845; SION, G., La garantie bancaire internationale et les enseignements du droit américain, Rev.Banque, March 1984, 25; DE VUYST, B., Het documentair krediet als loutere waarborg : de standby letter of credit, T.P.R., 1984, 1030; DELIERNEUX, M. and MARTIN, C., La "Révision 1983" des Règles et Usances uniformes relatives aux crédits documentaires (R.U.U.), 505; ROWE, M., New rules for contract guarantees, Int.Fin.Law Review, December 1982, 41.

284. See DE LY, F., Garanties en standby letters of credit, R.D.C., 1986, 172-194.

285. Of some conditions, more than 1,5 million copies have been sold (BENJAMIN, P., The ECE General Conditions of Sale and Standard Forms of Contract, J.BUS.L., 1961, 131; JANSSEN, H., Totstandkoming van internationale handelskoop, 41-43; TUNC, A., L'élaboration de conditions générales de vente sous les auspices de la Commission Economique pour l'Europe, Rev.Int.Dr.Comp., 1960, 112; GOFFIN, R., Fourniture et montage à l'étranger de matériels d'équipement, in Contrats d'engineering, Rapport préliminaire du groupe de travail belge, COMMISSION DROIT ET VIE DES

and they have been used frequently in these sectors of the economy[286]. There is, however, little case law as to the ECE General Conditions[287]. A majority opinion clearly does not see them as transnational customs or usages of the trades concerned[288].

283. In the construction industry, the *Fédération Internationale des Ingénieurs-Conseils* ("*F.I.D.I.C.*")[289] has adopted a number of model contract forms[290]. These model contracts were influenced by English

---

AFFAIRES (ed.), Faculté de droit de l'Université de Liège, 1964, 120 and DEL MARMOL, C., Les clauses contractuelles types, facteur d'unification du droit commercial, 319).

286. LOUSSOUARN, Y. and BREDIN, J.D., Droit du commerce international, 586.

287. German Supreme Court, October 22, 1969, NJW, 1970, 383; French Supreme Court, November 26, 1980, Clunet, 1981, 355, case note KAHN, P. For arbitral decisions, see LEW, J., Applicable law in international commercial arbitration, 456-457.

288. DEL MARMOL, C., Lex mercatoria, 164; VAN DELDEN, R., Lex mercatoria of ius commune ?, 7; KAHN, P., case note French Supreme Court, November 26, 1980, Clunet, 1981, 357; BEN ABDERRAHMANE, D., Le droit allemand des conditions générales des contrats dans les ventes commerciales franco-allemandes, 86; SCHMITTHOFF, C., The risk of loss in transit in international sales, 178; LEW, J., Applicable law in international commercial arbitration, 455; MICHIDA, S., Possible avenues to preparation of standard contracts for international trade on a global level, 255 and 257; *contra* DELEUZE, J.M., Le contrat d'engineering, rapport général, in Nouvelles techniques contractuelles, Know-how - franchising - engineering - leasing, Actualités de droit de l'entreprise, Travaux de la faculté de droit et des sciences économiques de Montpellier, Librairies Techniques, 1971, 91; *cf.* GOLDMAN, B., Lex mercatoria, 6; KOPELMANAS, L., Quelques réflexions sur le colloque de Helsinki de l'Association internationale des sciences juridiques au sujet de la vente internationale, in Problèmes de l'inexécution et la force majeure dans les contrats de vente internationale, Institutum Iurisprudentiae comparativae Universitatis Helsingiensis, 1961, 304; KOPELMANAS, L., La codification des coutumes du commerce international dans le cadre des Commissions régionales des Nations Unies, Ann.fr.dr.int., 1955, 370-375.

289. F.I.D.I.C. is an international professional organization of national associations from 45 countries (Uncitral document A/CN. 9/303, March 2, 1988, 21).

290. Conditions of contract for works of civil engineering construction, two volumes ("Red Book"), fourth edition, 1987; Conditions of contract for electrical and mechanical works ("Yellow Book"), third edition, 1987; The FIDIC Client/Consultant model services agreement ("White Book").

law[291], and have been followed in common law countries[292] for large construction projects involving substantial engineering aspects. In other countries, the F.I.D.I.C. forms have been less successful[293]. Generally, they are not perceived as constituting custom or trade usage[294].

284. In the international commodities trades, numerous standard contract forms exist. Important examples have been the general conditions of the *London Corn Trade Association*[295] and the *London Cattle Food Trade Association*. When both organizations merged in 1971 to become the *Grain and Feed Trade Association* ("*GAFTA*"), new contract forms came into existence[296]. Another example are the standard contract forms of the *Federation of Oil Seeds and Fats Association*[297]. Other professional organizations of commodity traders which were formed primarily in London under the form of a company limited by guarantee[298], also have

291. BRABANT, A., Le contrat international de construction, 185; FLOCKE, H.J., Risiken beim internationalen Anlagenvertrag, 64; HORN, N., Standard clauses on contract adaptation in international commerce, in Adaptation and renegotiation of contracts in international trade and finance, HORN, N. (ed.), Deventer, Kluwer, 1985, 113-114; WESTRING, G., Construction and management contracts, in HORN, N. and SCHMITTHOFF, C., The transnational law of international commercial transactions, Deventer, Kluwer, 1982, 178.

292. HORN, N., Uniformity and diversity in the law of international commercial contracts, 9; SCHMITTHOFF, C., intervention during the discussions, in Basle symposium on the Law governing contractual obligations, KLEIN, F.E. and VISCHER, F. (ed.), Basle, Helbing & Lichtenhahn, 1983, 121 (stating that the F.I.D.I.C. Contract has been accepted by associations in 73 countries).

293. WESTRING, G., Construction and management contracts, 176 and 179.

294. SCHNEIDER, M., International construction contracts, D.P.C.I., 1983, 656; VAN DELDEN, R., Lex mercatoria of ius commune ?, 7.

295. See SCHWOB, G., Le contrat de la London Corn Trade Association, Paris, Rousseau, 1928, 21-80 and 353-354.

296. SIMON, J., Le commerce international des céréales, 313.

297. See MEINERTZHAGEN-LIMPENS, A., Quelques aspects des contrats en usage sur la place d'Anvers, in Quelques aspects des contrats standardisés, Brussels, Editions de l'Université de Bruxelles, 1982, 237.

298. SIMON, J., Le commerce international des céréales, 313-317.

adopted standard contracts[299]. The nature of these standard contracts is controversial; some have seen them as expressions of the *lex mercatoria*[300].

285. In the air transport sector, the need for unification of contract terms has also been felt. The *International Air Transport Association* ("*IATA*"), an organization with some hundred and sixty members[301], has primarily been active in this field and has adopted a uniform airway bill and standard contract forms. These models have been followed in different ways. On the one hand, the *conditions of contract* which are printed on the ticket have almost always been adopted by member airline companies. This does not hold true for the *conditions of carriage* which are not printed but referred to on the ticket. The conditions of carriage for transport of passengers only apply when two airline companies are involved. Furthermore, they are not applicable for transport of passengers to, from or within the United States or Canada. The conditions of carriage for transport of goods have never been adopted by IATA because of opposition from the United States; in practice, they are, however, used as a possible model[302].

The binding nature of these conditions may, as between IATA-members, be based on the self-regulatory system which IATA has put in place. As against non-IATA-members and the counterparty to the air transport contract, conditions modelled after the IATA standard forms remain general conditions of contract. They are not qualified as custom or usage[303]. A decision of the German Supreme Court dated January 20, 1983 clearly stated that the Lufthansa-conditions which conformed to IATA-recommendations, were general conditions of contract under § 1

---

299. Information on many of these organizations and standard contracts can be obtained from the competition law decisions of the EEC-Commission; see Decisions dated December 13, 1985, O.J. L 369, December 31, 1985, in cases IV/27.593 - London Rubber Terminal Market Association Limited, IV/27.592 - Coffee Terminal Market Association of London Limited, IV/27.590 - London Sugar Futures Market Limited, and IV/27.591 - London Cocoa Terminal Market Association Limited; Decision dated December 4, 1986, case IV/30.439 - International Petroleum Exchange of London Limited, O.J. L 3, January 6, 1987, 27; Decisions dated December 10, 1986, O.J. L 19, January 21, 1987 in cases IV/29.688 - London Grain Futures Market, IV/30.176 - London Potato Futures Association Limited, IV/31.614 - London Meat Futures Exchange Limited and IV/29.036 - GAFTA Soya Bean Meal Futures Association Limited; Decision dated July 13, 1987, case IV/31.764 - Baltic International Freight Futures Exchange Limited, O.J. L 222, August 10, 1987, 24.
300. SIMON, J., Le commerce international des céréales, 333-336.
301. Rev.fr.dr.aér., 1987, 226.
302. HONDIUS, E., Standaardvoorwaarden, 58-59; RODER, H., Speditions- und Transportverträge, in REITHMANN, C., Internationales Vertragsrecht, 372-373.
303. VERPLAETSE, J., Sources of private air law, INT'L & COMP.L.Q., 1958, 406; KROPHOLLER, J., Internationales Einheitsrecht, 91-92.

AGBG. The Court further held that the IATA-recommendations were only binding as between IATA-members and could not be seen as custom under international public law since IATA is a private organization. Then, the Court had to weigh the application of the AGBG which tends to protect consumers against the international unification of law brought about by the IATA-rules. In this process, the Court found unification of law no compelling reason not to offer consumers the benefit of protective German rules[304].

286. The maritime sector also has examples of international self-regulation. Already in 1877, the International Law Association made rules on *general average* in order to overcome the divergent rules on the subject which existed in various legal systems[305]. These rules are called the *York-Antwerp Rules* and their most recent edition was adopted by a resolution dated April 4, 1974 of the *Comité Maritime Internationale* ("*C.M.I.*").

These rules apply as of July 1, 1974 between the 44 National Associations for Maritime Law that are members of C.M.I.[306]. Their binding effect then, is based upon the C.M.I. self-regulatory system. The York-Antwerp Rules are commonly used through a clause in the bill of lading incorporating them. To a great extent, this leads to the exclusion of national rules on general average. The binding force of the York-Antwerp Rules, however, is still dependent upon party incorporation[307].

Standardization of contract terms may also be found with regard to charterparties and bills of lading but, in this context, one can hardly speak of transnational custom or trade usages[308].

---

304. German Supreme Court, January 20, 1983, E.T.L., 1984, 535.

305. HONDIUS, E., Standaardvoorwaarden, 55-57; SCHMITTHOFF, C., Export trade, 443-444.

306. Uncitral document A/CN. 9/303, March 2, 1988, 19.

307. SCHMITTHOFF, C., Export trade, 444; DAY, D., The law of international trade, 35; HOUIN, R., Usages commerciaux et loi en droit français, 253; DEMOGUE, R., L'unification internationale du droit privé, Paris, Rousseau, 1927, 32-36; *contra* VAN DELDEN, R., Lex mercatoria of ius commune ?, 8.

308. See KROPHOLLER, J., Internationales Einheitsrecht, 91; LORENZ-MEYER, G.C., Reeder und Charterer, Rechtsnatur der Zeitcharter und Haftung des Zeitcharterers gegenüber Dritten, Hamburg, 1961, Schiffahrtsverlag Hansa C. Schroedter, 60-62; LOPULSKI, J., Contrats maritimes internationaux et le problème de la liberté contractuelle, Dr.mar.fr., 1983, 410.

287. International standardization of contract terms and forms may also be found in the insurance sector[309]. As regards maritime insurance, the *Lloyd's S.G. Policy* was the model for a long time but has been replaced since January 1, 1982 by the *Lloyd's Marine Policy* and, in relation to the scope of the coverage, by the *Institute Cargo Clauses A, B and C*[310]. The co-insurance and reinsurance markets are by nature international; here also, model contracts are used but to a lesser extent than for maritime insurance. Standardization is, however, insufficient to state that in these sectors the clauses of these policies have turned into custom or usages[311].

288. In the field of financial services, many examples of self-regulatory rules may be found[312]. First, one may cite international factoring operations in which accounts receivable are transferred. Sometimes, an international group of companies is providing these services. The parent company will then set guidelines within the group for these international operations. If international factoring takes place outside an integrated group of companies, arrangements must be put in place between independent companies in various countries. One of these arrangements is *Factors Chain International*. This organization has made a *master agreement* to which companies may accede if they are accepted into the international network. This master agreement is a framework agreement setting rules for operations for the members of the network which may be supplemented by bilateral agreements among members. An I.C.C. arbitration has determined that the master agreement is purely contractual and cannot be seen as a code of good practices. Between the arbitrating parties, the 1967 edition of the master agreement applied which led the arbitral tribunal to rule that amendments to the agreement dating from 1976 to which the parties had not consented were inapplicable between them[313].

---

309. For a discussion on the system of the *green card* in the automobile insurance sector, see DE LY, F., De lex mercatoria, Inleiding op de studie van het transnationaal handelsrecht, 331-332.
310. SCHMITTHOFF, C., Export trade, 434-442; EISEMANN, F., BONTOUX, C. and ROWE, M., Le crédit documentaire dans le commerce extérieur, 43-44.
311. SCHÜTTE, E., Schiedsklauseln und "transnationales Recht", 223-225; ROTH, W.H., Internationales Versicherungsvertragsrecht, 542-559.
312. For a discussion on some international systems for retail banking (such as the Eurocheque-system, electronic payment systems for consumers and credit card operations), see DE LY, F., De lex mercatoria, Inleiding op de studie van het transnationaal handelsrecht, 333-335.
313. I.C.C. case No. 3202, Clunet, 1979, 1003.

289. As to crossborder foreign exchange (forex) transactions, the *Association Cambiste Internationale*, an association under French law, has adopted a code of conduct and a list of usual terms[314]. This voluntary code of conduct has been translated at the national level into several national codes. Notwithstanding the homogeneity of the forex-community[315], these codes do not constitute custom[316]. Sometimes, some of these rules or factual patterns of behaviour of the trade concerned may be taken into account in the application of some rules of contract or tort law[317].

290. In the secondary market for euro-bonds where the bonds are sold and bought (as opposed to the primary market where the bonds are placed with investors by the issuer), the *International Securities Market Association* ("*ISMA*")[318], an association under Swiss law, has adopted important rules of self-regulation[319]. These rules are binding as between ISMA members and may be binding against non-members through a reference to ISMA rules and recommendations inserted in the confirmation notes[320]. As a whole, ISMA rules and recommendations are not customary law. However, some provisions may have the character of custom as between professional dealers[321]. Seldom are these rules invoked before national courts. If disputes arise, conflicts are resolved through confidential arbitration. It seems that so far, only one arbitration has taken place and a second may be under way[322].

---

314. WYMEERSCH, E., Règles professionnelles et règles standardisées dans les opérations financières, 66; BRAECKMANS, H., Juridische aspecten van consortiumkredieten in Eurodeviezen, 1985, 316.
315. BRAECKMANS, H., Juridische aspecten van consortiumkredieten in Eurodeviezen, 1985, 414.
316. WYMEERSCH, E., Règles professionnelles et règles standardisées dans les opérations financières, 67-68.
317. See BRAECKMANS, H., Juridische aspecten van consortiumkredieten in Eurodeviezen, 1985, 417-418 and 424-425.
318. As of 1992, the Association has adopted this name. Up to then, it was called the *Association of International Bond Dealers* ("*AIBD*").
319. Association of International Bond Dealers, Statutes, by-laws, rules and recommendations, July 1986, Zurich, 43 pp.
320. WYMEERSCH, E., Règles professionnelles et règles standardisées dans les opérations financières, 87-91; BRAECKMANS, H., Paralegale normen en lex mercatoria, 17-19; WIGNY, D., AIBD : Une expérience d'auto-discipline, Rev.Banque, 1983, 255-260; OPPETIT, B., Le contrat d'émission d'euro-obligations, in Les euro-obligations, Paris, Librairies Techniques, 1972, 84-85; KAHN, P., Lex mercatoria et euro-obligations, 222-223; JACQUEMONT, A., L'émission des emprunts euro-obligataires, 48.
321. WYMEERSCH, E., Règles professionnelles et règles standardisées dans les opérations financières, 91-93; KAHN, P., Lex mercatoria et euro-obligations, 225 and 236.
322. Courtroom drama may shake AIBD, Euromoney, September 1987, 14.

291. Finally, deposition and compensation and settlement of euro-bonds is also subject to self-regulation which primarily runs through Euroclear and Cedel. Both organizations are companies each with some hundred shareholders-financial institutions. They both have developed an extensive self-regulatory scheme for their operations to which their shareholders/financial institutions are bound by contract[323]. Again, one may question whether these rules might be customs or usages.

III.5 Technical, professional and deontological standards and codes of conduct

292. Since this book deals with sources of law, rules which cannot be considered legal rules will not be discussed. However, the fact that these rules are not analyzed does not imply that they are not relevant for international business law. Indirectly, through some provision of law, these rules may prove to have some legal significance. In this regard, one might think of technical or professional standards (*e.g.*, International Standards Organization, International Accountancy Standards Committee), deontological rules or codes of conduct (*e.g.*, World Health Organization - International Code on Marketing of Breastmilk Substitutes, OECD-Guidelines for multinational enterprises, OECD-Guidelines on privacy protection and transborder data flow, International Labor Organization - Tripartite Declaration of principles concerning multinational enterprises and social policy, UN-Set of multilaterally agreed equitable principles and rules for the control of restrictive business practices)[324].

---

323. See WYMEERSCH, E., Règles professionnelles et règles standardisées dans les opérations financières, 83-87; ROELANTS, W., Le marché des euro-obligations, in Les crédits internationaux, Brussels, Chambre de Commerce de Bruxelles and Section de Bruxelles de l'Association belge des Banques, 1980, 86.

324. See Le droit des normes professionnelles et techniques, COMMISSION DROIT ET VIE DES AFFAIRES (ed.), Brussels, Bruylant, 1985, 514 pp.; Legal problems of codes of conduct for multinational enterprises, HORN, N. (ed.), Deventer, Kluwer, 1980, 509 pp.; HORN, N., Die Entwicklung des internationalen Wirtschaftsrechts durch Verhaltensrichtlinien, RabelsZ, 1980, 423-454; PEVTCHIN, G., Les codes de bon comportement, notamment dans la gestion des sociétés multinationales, in L'hypothèse du non-droit, COMMISSION DROIT ET VIE DES AFFAIRES (ed.), Liège, 1978, 43 ff.; SANDERS, P., Codes of conduct and sources of law, in Le droit des relations économiques internationales, Etudes offertes à Berthold Goldman, Paris, Litec, 1982, 281-298; FIKENTSCHER, W., United Nations Codes of Conduct : new paths in international law, AM.J.COMP.L., 1982, 577-604.

III.6 General principles of law

293. Legal positivism has been less important than it used to be. Also, many new problems have appeared for which the law had no ready made answers. These developments also have had their impact on international business law. After the second world war, some scholars have argued to free international business life from the strict rules of national law. In this context, they proposed that the sources of international business law should not only be found in national legal systems and self-regulation by interested circles but also in general principles of law.

294. First, a clear description of what is really meant by general principles of law is useful. Boulanger and Oppetit have quite rightly stated that the concept may have different meanings[325]. First, principles of law may be used in order to bring some system to legal rules. This is primarily the task of legal education and scholarly writing[326]. However, this does not necessarily imply that these principles are legal rules or are legally relevant.

295. In a transnational context, general principles of law may have a second meaning. Then, it might indicate that different legal systems have a similar rule of some abstraction which avoids the question as to what law to choose. Thus, general principles of law are not a formal source of law but a badly phrased way to refer to the *non-selection method* of conflict of laws which will be discussed below[327]. For instance, one may wonder whether the common law doctrine of estoppel and the similar rule in civil law countries of *venire contra factum proprium* should not be seen from this perspective rather than as a formal principle of law[328].

---

325. BOULANGER, J., Principes généraux du droit et droit positif, in Le droit privé français au milieu du XXe siècle, Etudes offertes à Georges Ripert, I, Paris, Pichon, 1950, 52; OPPETIT, B., case note French Supreme Court, October 13, 1981, Court of Appeal Paris, June 12, 1980 and French Supreme Court, December 9, 1981, Clunet, 1982, 937.

326. BOULANGER, J., Principes généraux du droit et droit positif, 54-55; OPPETIT, B., Les principes généraux en droit international privé, Arch.Phil.Dr., 1987, 180.

327. See infra Nos. 476 and 483 and REIMANN, T., Zur Lehre vom "rechtsordnungslosen" Vertrag, 81.

328. BÖCKSTIEGEL, K.H., Arbitration and state enterprises, Survey on the national and international state of law and practice, 43; *cf.* GAILLARD, E., L'interdiction de se contredire au détriment d'autrui comme principe général du droit du commerce international (le principe de l'estoppel dans quelques sentences arbitrales récentes), Rev.Arb., 1985, 241 and 253-254.

296. A third view sees general principles of law as a formal source of law. Apart from statute law and custom, general principles of law may also create legal rules. Especially in civil law jurisdictions where case law has only persuasive authority but no binding force of precedent, one may rely on general principles of law in order to fill some gaps in the legal systems created by the absence of statute or custom. Principles of law should then be sufficiently abstract in order to constitute a basis for deduction of more concrete rules[329].

297. Some authors have argued that general principles of law are not formal sources of law but constitute guiding principles within the legal system which may provide a basis for deduction of legal rules[330]. On the one hand, general principles of law should be distinguished from legal rules[331]. On the other hand, they do not overlap with principles of natural justice because they belong rather to a legal system and not to an ethical order[332]. General principles may apply throughout the legal system but they may also be restricted to one branch of the law[333] such as principles of criminal law, administrative law or civil procedure.

298. From the foregoing analysis, it appears that general principles of law may have a *structural* function within a legal system where they may provide tools for its development, particularly in relation to filling its gaps[334]. This

329. See KAHN, P., case note District Court Paris, March 4, 1981, Clunet, 1981, 842.
330. BUCH, H., La nature des principes généraux du droit, in Rapports belges au VIe Congrès international de droit comparé, CENTRE INTERUNIVERSITAIRE DE DROIT COMPARE (ed.), Brussels, Bruylant, 1962, 58 and 61; FORIERS, P., Les relations des sources écrites et non écrites du droit, in Rapports belges au VIIIe Congrès international de droit comparé, CENTRE INTERUNIVERSITAIRE DE DROIT COMPARE (ed.), Brussels, 1970, 53; DE WAARD, B.W.N., Beginselen van behoorlijke rechtspleging met name in het administratief procesrecht, Zwolle, Tjeenk Willink, 1987, 97.
331. BOULANGER, J., Principes généraux du droit et droit positif, 55-56; RIPERT, G., Les forces créatrices du droit, Paris, LGDJ, 1955, 330; GANSHOF VAN DER MEERSCH, W., Propos sur le texte de la loi et les principes généraux du droit, 567; SCHLESINGER, R. and BONASSIES, P., Le fonds commun des systèmes juridiques, Rev.Int.Dr.Comp., 1963, 516-517.
332. DABIN, J., Théorie générale du droit, Paris, Dalloz, 1969, 105; BEKAERT, H., Introduction à l'étude du droit, 173; MARTY, G. and RAYNAUD, P., Introduction générale à l'étude du droit, 234.
333. CANARIS, C.W., Systemdenken und Systembegriff in der Jurisprudenz, Berlin, Duncker & Humblot, 1969, 48.
334. BOULANGER, J, Principes généraux du droit et droit positif, 63; GHESTIN, J. and GOUBEAUX, G., Introduction générale, 366; VAN HOOF, G.J.H., Normvervaging en rechtsbeginsel, Zwolle, Tjeenk Willink, 1987, 15-20.

function to a large extent depends upon the density of available legal rules. For instance, in a study on *general maritime law*, Erades has shown that such a general maritime law used to be quite important until national shipping laws and maritime conventions were enacted[335]. Furthermore, general principles of law may also have an *ethical* function[336]. As for instance in criminal law, general principles of law may express some ethical standards inherent to any legal system.

299. In order to get a better view on general principles of law, they will be analyzed below under Belgian, French, Dutch and German law as well as under international law[337]. In Belgium, recent scholarly writings have recognized general principles of law as a formal source of law[338]. Case law of the Supreme Court was until the nineteen sixties reluctant to do so. Under the influence of Ganshof Van Der Meersch[339], the Court changed its position and from 1970 through 1976 many times applied general principles of law[340]. After 1976, the Court's attitude became more

---

335. ERADES, L., "General maritime law", in Recht door zee, Liber amicorum H. Schadee, Zwolle, Tjeenk Willink, 1980, 77-78.
336. See also SILANCE, L., Un moyen de combler les lacunes en droit : l'induction amplifiante, in Etudes de logique juridique, II, Droit et logique, les lacunes en droit, Brussels, Bruylant, 1967, 138; GHESTIN, J. and GOUBEAUX, G., Introduction générale, 363-364; DESCHENAUX, H., Der Einleitungstitel, 114.
337. Swiss law is akin to German law (see DESCHENAUX, H., Der Einleitungstitel, 113-114) and will for that reason not be discussed. In England, there is hardly any information on general principles of law (*principles of natural justice*) (see NEVILLE BROWN, L., General principles of law and the English legal system, in New perspectives for a common law of Europe, CAPPELLETTI, M. (ed.), European University Institute, 1978, 171-193). This is probably due to the common law system where case law may formally create legal rules and thus fill the gaps of the legal system.
338. GANSHOF VAN DER MEERSCH, W., Propos sur le texte de la loi et les principes généraux du droit, 567; BEKAERT, H., Introduction à l'étude du droit, 172; ORIANNE, P., Introduction au système juridique, 80 and 82; CEREXHE, E., HAUBERT, B. and REGNIER, J., Principes généraux et fondements du droit, Brussels, Larcier, 1977, 339-340; FORIERS, P., Les relations des sources écrites et non écrites du droit, 54; VAN ORSHOVEN, P., Non scripta, sed nata lex - Over het begrip en de plaats in de normenhiërarchie van de algemene rechtsbeginselen, R.W., 1989-90, 1380; *contra* STORME, M., Algemene inleiding tot het recht, 119; GIJSSELS, J., "Algemene rechtsbeginselen" zijn nog geen recht, R.W., 1988-89, 1105-1116.
339. Ganshof Van Der Meersch based this opinion on the tacit will of the legislative branch (Propos sur le texte de la loi et les principes généraux du droit, 568). This explanation is artificial (MARTY, G. and RAYNAUD, P., Introduction générale à l'étude du droit, 234).
340. CLAEYS BOUUAERT, P., Algemene beginselen van het recht, Vijftien jaar rechtspraak van het Hof van Cassatie, 914-915 and 996.

cautious. The Court's change in policy was motivated by the concern that inferior courts would rely too much on general principles of law and would thus be less careful in the motivation of their decisions[341].

An overview of the general principles of law which have been recognized by the Belgian Supreme Court would fall outside the scope of this book[342]. Research cited in the previous footnote has in this respect shown that, in substantive private law, the Court relied not too frequently on general principles of law. More important, the technique of general principles of law was mostly used to solve concrete problems; evident gaps in private law were filled by general principles of law which were created for that purpose[343]. This process has been called *induction amplifiante*[344]. Thus, in private law, the structural function of general principles of law is used, and hardly ever its ethical function. Furthermore, no very abstract principles such as *pacta sunt servanda*, good faith or abuse of rights are used.

300. In France, general principles of law are particularly important in administrative law[345]. In private law, their impact is more modest. Different theories have been developed in order to explain the way they operate. A first theory bases the binding force of general principles of law on an implicit will of the legislative branch[346]. According to Carbonnier, general principles of law would be customary rules developed by scholars[347]. Linking general principles of law to custom has the disadvantage of restricting the possible use of these principles. A third opinion reduces

341. See Belgian Supreme Court, December 12, 1980, Bull.Cass., 1980-81, 428; DUMON, F., opinion to Belgian Supreme Court, December 19, 1980, Bull.Cass., 1980-81, 452-453; see also CLAEYS BOUUAERT, P., Algemene beginselen van het recht, Vijftien jaar rechtspraak van het Hof van Cassatie, 996-997.

342. See DE LY, F., De lex mercatoria, Inleiding op de studie van het transnationaal handelsrecht, 341-343; CLAEYS BOUUAERT, P., Algemene beginselen van het recht, Vijftien jaar rechtspraak van het Hof van Cassatie, 913-934 and 977-998; SOETAERT, R., Rechtsbeginselen en marginale toetsing in cassatie, 51-66.

343. See also BOULANGER, J., Principes généraux du droit et droit positif, 63; GANSHOF VAN DER MEERSCH, W., Propos sur le texte de la loi et les principes généraux du droit, 568; WENGLER, W., Die allgemeinen Rechtsgrundsätze des internationalen Privatrechts und ihre Kollisionen, Z.öffentl.R., 1943, 474.

344. SILANCE, L., Un moyen de combler les lacunes en droit : l'induction amplifiante, 117-140; GHESTIN, J. and GOUBEAUX, G., Introduction générale, 363.

345. AUBY, J.M., case note Conseil d'Etat, October 4, 1974, D., 1975, 372; GHESTIN, J. and GOUBEAUX, G., Introduction générale, 359.

346. For a critical position, see MARTY, G. and RAYNAUD, P., Introduction générale à l'étude du droit, 234.

347. CARBONNIER, J., Droit civil, 1, Paris, Presses universitaires de France, 1974, 144-145.

general principles of law to scholarly activity[348] and immediately raises the question whether scholarly writing is a formal source of law. Finally, general principles of law have also been related to case law. Under that perspective, judges would create general principles of law in the process of dispute resolution[349]. One may wonder whether these principles do not pre-exist their application by judges. This may particularly be so regarding ethical standards[350]. The four theories above reflect some unease as to general principles of law because they try to reduce them to existing sources of law[351]. More recent scholarly writings have recognized this and accepted general principles of law as a formal source of law. At the same time, they are hesitant as to their significance and scope[352]. The case law of the French Supreme Court also refers to general principles of law but their meaning is not always clear[353]. Thus, one may say that French law is more hesitant than Belgian law to recognize general principles of law as a formal source of private law.

301. In The Netherlands, the draft New Civil Code had an Introductory Title which in article 5 (2) recognized general principles of law, provided statute did not directly solved the problem. However, Books 3, 5 and 6 N.B.W. entered into force on January 1, 1992 without the Introductory Title. It was thought that the New Code should not have provisions on sources of law because this might freeze further development in case law[354]. To a certain extent, some provisions of the Introductory Title have found another place in the New Code. As to contracts, article 248, Book 6 N.B.W. states that good faith (*redelijkheid en billijkheid*, reasonableness and equity) may supplement and correct contracts. In the application of

---

348. ROUBIER, P., L'ordre juridique et la théorie des sources du droit, in Le droit privé français au milieu du XXe siècle, Etudes offertes à Georges Ripert, I, Paris, LGDJ, 1950, 16-17 and 23-27.
349. GHESTIN, J. and GOUBEAUX, G., Introduction générale, 363; MARTY, G. and RAYNAUD, P., Introduction générale à l'étude du droit, 233-235; BELAID, S., Essai sur le pouvoir créateur et normatif du juge, Parijs, LGDJ, 1974, 308; *Belgium* : SILANCE, L., Un moyen de combler les lacunes en droit: l'induction amplifiante, 137-138; *cf.* OPPETIT, B., Les principes généraux en droit international privé, 184.
350. BOULANGER, J., Principes généraux du droit et droit positif, 67.
351. See also RODIERE, R., Les principes généraux du droit privé français, Bulletin de la Société de législation comparée, 1980, 313-317.
352. GHESTIN, J. and GOUBEAUX, G., Introduction générale, 361.
353. See the examples cited in BOULANGER, J., Principes généraux du droit et droit positif, 64; MARTY, G. and RAYNAUD, P., Introduction générale à l'étude du droit, 232-233; GHESTIN, J. and GOUBEAUX, G., Introduction générale, 361; OPPETIT, B., Le développement des règles matérielles, 12.
354. See supra No. 218.

these open-ended rules, the judge will find some support in article 12, Book 3 N.B.W. which provides that reasonableness and equity encompass *generally accepted principles of law*, conceptions of law prevailing in The Netherlands and the public and personal interests which are at stake.

These provisions make clear that the New Civil Code has recognized the importance of principles of law in the elaboration of legal rules, particularly regarding contracts. As such, it has taken a pragmatic approach in affirming the substantive value of general principles of law without addressing their formal character.

302. Case law in The Netherlands frequently seems to apply general principles of law. In many cases, this process is indirect through application of open-ended rules. The same tendency may be found in scholarly writings. Traditionally, a strict distinction was made between principles and rules of law[355]. Because open-ended rules have become increasingly important in private law, the distinction has lost much of its attraction and the interaction between principles and rules has been emphasized[356]. Principles may thus provide an interpretative background for legal rules and may supplement them in case of gaps[357]. In this perspective, general principles of law are seen less as possible sources of law but as a method for judicial dispute resolution.

303. The development which has just been pictured for The Netherlands, also applies to Germany where general principles of law have been analyzed much more from the perspective of law creation by judges than from the perspective of sources of law. The *Begriffsjurisprudenz* which merely applied legal rules in a deductive way, has been abandoned by many authors who, amongst other methods placed legal rules within their system (*Systemdenken*). Within such system, ethical standards[358] and, more important, logical and conceptual principles[359] may be found. The latter

---

355. SCHOLTEN, P., Rechtsbeginselen, in Verzamelde geschriften, I, Zwolle, Tjeenk Willink, 1949, 403.
356. SCHOLTEN, G., Rechtsbeginselen en rechtsregels, Scheiden schaadt, 3.
357. SCHOLTEN, G., Rechtsbeginselen en rechtsregels, Scheiden schaadt, 6-8; NIEUWENHUIS, J., Drie beginselen van contractenrecht, 38-39.
358. ESSER, J., Grundsatz und Norm, second edition, Tubingen, Mohr, 1964, 91-92; CANARIS, C.W., Systemdenken und Systembegriff in der Jurisprudenz, 69-72; ESSER, J., Vorverständnis und Methodenwahl in der Rechtsfindung, Frankfurt, Athenäum Verlag, 1972, 38 ff.
359. CANARIS, C.W., Systemdenken und Systembegriff, 68.

are induced from legal rules[360]. Both ethical standards and principles of law have a function in the law creation process[361]. However, they are not legal rules which are readily applicable but may well lead to deduction of less abstract principles (*Unterbegriffe*) and concrete rules[362].

General principles of law are in this perspective not formal source of law but are elements of system formation[363] and development which, from a methodological point of view, are important in case law. This systematic approach does not take place within a closed system[364]. Since principles are subject to change and system and applications interact, one is confronted with an open-ended system[365]. These theories have influenced the German scholars who have analyzed the problem of the sources of international business law and the role of general principles in that law[366].

304. General principles of law are also important in international law. The most important provision is probably article 38 of the Statute of the International Court of Justice stating the sources for adjudication by the Court. This provision includes the general principles of law recognized by civilized nations. Two interpretations exist as to the meaning of the provision. According to a public international law conception, article 38 only refers to principles of international law. A majority view has taken a comparative view; the drafting history of article 38 might indicate that the provision refers to principles of law of national states[367].

---

360. CANARIS, C.W., Systemdenken und Systembegriff in der Jurisprudenz, 68; LARENZ, K., Methodenlehre der Rechtswissenschaft, fourth edition, Berlin, Springer, 1979, 366 and 411.
361. ESSER, J., Vorverständnis und Methodenwahl in der Rechtsfindung, 10, 31 and 43.
362. CANARIS, C.W., Systemdenken und Systembegriff in der Jurisprudenz, 57; LARENZ, K., Methodenlehre der Rechtswissenschaft, 277 and 458.
363. CANARIS, C.W., Systemdenken und Systembegriff in der Jurisprudenz, 47.
364. LARENZ, K., Methodenlehre der Rechtswissenschaft, 159 and 459; PENSKI, U., Rechtsgrundsätze und Rechtsregeln, JZ, 1989, 105-114.
365. ESSER, J., Grundsatz und Norm, 132-140.
366. VON HOFFMANN, B., "Lex mercatoria" vor internationalen Schiedsgerichten, 107; STOLL, J., Vereinbarungen zwischen Staat und ausländischem Investor, 33 and 38-39; ERNEMANN, A., Zur Anerkennung und Vollstreckung ausländischer Schiedssprüche nach § 1044 ZPO, 105-107; KREUZER, K., Einheitsrecht als Ersatzrecht, Zur Frage der Nichtermittelbarkeit fremden Rechts, 1945-1946.
367. VERDROSS, A., Les principes généraux du droit comme source du droit des gens, in Recueil d'études sur les sources du droit en l'honneur de François Gény, III, Paris, Sirey, s.d., 386-387; RIPERT, G., Les règles du droit civil applicables aux rapports internationaux, Academy of international law, 44 Collected Courses of The Hague, 1933, II, 579-580; CHENG, B., General principles of law as applied by international courts and tribunals, London, Stevens & Sons, 1953, 23; SCHLESINGER, R. and BONASSIES, P., Le fonds commun des systèmes juridiques, 513-514; RIGAUX, F.,

305. In some instances, EEC law also refers to general principles of law. Article 215, second paragraph of the Treaty of Rome sets the standard for liability in tort of the Community; this liability is to be determined in accordance with the general principles common to the legal systems of the Member States[368]. In other cases too, general principles have been applied in EEC law. The Court of Justice at several occasions has referred to principles common to the Member States, general principles of law, the general principles of the Community treaties and the principles of the treaties to which the Member States have acceded[369].

Also, the Court of Justice, in the process of the interpretation of the Jurisdiction and Enforcement Convention, has relied on the general principles of the laws of the Member States in those cases where an autonomous interpretation was followed and no reference to the applicable law was made[370]. Comparative study is, however, seldom done in order to find these common principles[371].

Finally, article 7 of the 1970 proposal for a Statute for a European Company[372] referred to the general principles of the laws of the Member States in order to avoid the automatic application of the *lex fori*[373]. Comparative analysis was called upon to provide for these principles[374]. The latest proposal has dropped the reference to the principles of the laws

---

Droit public et droit privé dans les relations internationales, 118-119; RIGAUX, F., Le droit comparé comme science appliquée, Rev.Dr.Int.Comp., 1978, 67-68; VIRALLY, M., Un tiers droit ?, Réflexions théoriques, 381.

368. See VAN GERVEN, W., De niet-contractuele aansprakelijkheid van de Gemeenschap wegens normatieve handelingen, S.E.W., 1976, 8-9; CORNELIS, L., De extra-contractuele aansprakelijkheid van de Gemeenschap (1976-1982), S.E.W., 1984, 10-11; NEVILLE BROWN, L., General principles of law and the English legal system, 171-174.

369. CEREXHE, E., HAUBERT, B. and REGNIER, J., Principes généraux et fondements du droit, 343-344.

370. VAN GYSEL, A.C., Le concept de "notion autonome" dans la Convention du 27 septembre 1968 et le droit international conventionnel en général, in Mélanges offerts à Raymond Vander Elst, II, Brussels, Nemesis, 1986, 801-810; KÖHLER, C., La jurisprudence de la Cour de Justice des Communautés européennes sur la Convention (CEE) du 28 septembre 1968 concernant la compétence judiciaire et l'exécution des décisions en matière civile et commerciale, Ann.Dr., 1983, 177-217; RIGAUX, F., Le droit comparé comme science appliquée, 70-71.

371. RIGAUX, F., Le droit comparé comme science appliquée, 75.

372. O.J. C 124, October 10, 1970.

373. FICKER, H.C., "Hilfsweise geltendes Recht" für "Europäische Aktiengesellschaften" ?, in Quo vadis, ius societatum ?, Liber amicorum Pieter Sanders, ZONDERLAND, P. (ed.), Deventer, Kluwer, 1972, 45.

374. FICKER, H.C., "Hilfsweise geltendes Recht" für "Europäische Aktiengesellschaften" ?, 46.

of the Member States; general principles on which the Regulation is based should now govern the matters dealt with by the Regulation but not expressly settled by it[375].

306. Finally, international sales law also refers to general principles of law. Article 17 ULIS stated that matters which are not expressly settled by the uniform law, shall be governed in conformity with the general principles on which the uniform law is based. One should read article 17 in conjunction with article 2 ULIS stating that rules of conflict of laws are excluded for the purposes of the application of the uniform law. Gaps in the uniform law must thus be settled within its own system without referring to national law[376].

Article 17 ULIS has led to different interpretations. A minority view holds that article 17 has only interpretative force but does not allow for gap-filling[377]. A majority position gives article 17 ULIS both interpretative and supplementary functions[378]. Within the majority view, differences still exist as to whether or not conflict of laws is totally excluded. Some authors prefer to stick with the total ban on conflict of laws[379] while others would still use it as a fall back method[380].

307. More recent conventions have come back on the exclusion of conflict of laws and the *intro-interpretation*[381] and provide more room for conflict of laws. For instance, article 7 of the Sales Limitation Period Convention provides that in the interpretation and application of the Convention,

---

375. Article 7 (1) Proposal for a Council Regulation on the Statute for a European Company, O.J., C 263, October 16, 1989, 41.

376. Nadelmann has compared the problems caused by article 17 ULIS with those involved in the development of a *federal common law* in the United States (The conflicts problems of the uniform law on the international sale of goods, AM.J.COMP.L., 1965, 239-240; see also VON BAR, C., Typen des internationalen Einheitsrecht und das internationale Privatrecht, 23-24).

377. MANN, F., Einheitliches Kaufgesetz und internationales Privatrecht, JZ, 1975, 14-18 and 248.

378. WAHL, E., Art. 17 : Verweisung auf die allgemeinen Grundsätze des Gesetzes, in DÖLLE, H., Kommentar zum Einheitlichen Kaufrecht, 122-123; KROPHOLLER, J., Der "Ausschluß" des internationalen Privatrechts im Einheitlichen Kaufgesetz, RabelsZ, 1974, 380-385; VAN DER VELDEN, F., De eenvormige koopwetten 1964, 53.

379. MERTENS, H.J. and REHBINDER, E., Internationales Kaufrecht, 144.

380. VAN ROOIY, R., Overzicht der Nederlandse rechtspraak, Internationaal privaatrecht, W.P.N.R., 1977, 277-278; KROPHOLLER, J., Der "Ausschluß" des internationalen Privatrechts im Einheitlichen Kaufgesetz, 382-385.

381. The expression comes from LOEWE, R., Anwendungsgebiet, Auslegung, Lücken, Handelsgebräuche, in Convention de Vienne de 1980 sur la vente internationale de marchandises, Zurich, Schulthess, 1985, 18.

regard shall be had to its international character and the need to promote uniformity[382]. Article 7 (2) CISG is more explicit; matters governed by the Convention which are not expressly settled by it are to be settled in conformity with the general principles on which it is based[383] and, in the absence of such principles, in conformity with the law applicable by virtue of the rules of conflict of laws[384].

308. After the analysis of general principles of law under national and international law, one should complete the picture with the question which principles to apply in an international context. Van Houtte rightly has stated that a general principle of law should be applied through a conflict rule[385]. More generally, one might say that some conflict of law technique must be used to determine which general principle of law to apply[386].

III.7 Arbitral case law

309. Literature on international business law has emphasized the role of arbitral case law for the development of the law of international trade. Proponents of the theory of *lex mercatoria* have come to argue that arbitral case law might be considered a genuine source of law[387] but this has barely been analyzed.

310. Other authors have rejected the idea of arbitral precedents as a formal source of law on several grounds. First, there is no hierarchy among international commercial arbitration tribunals, since no such system has

382. See also article 18 EEC Convention on the law applicable to contractual obligations and article 16 of the Hague 1985 Convention on the law applicable to international sales.
383. See BONELL, M., in BIANCA-BONELL, Commentary on the international sales law, Art. 7, 81-82.
384. ROHWER, C. and COE, J., The 1980 Vienna Convention on the international sale of goods and the UCC - Peaceful coexistence ?, in Legal aspects of international business transactions, CAMPBELL, D. and ROHWER, C. (ed.), Amsterdam, North Holland, 1984, 233.
385. VAN HOUTTE, H., Rechtsvinding bij transnationale handelsarbitrage, 351; see also STOLL, J., Vereinbarungen zwischen Staat und ausländischem Investor, 41.
386. VON HOFFMANN, B., Internationale Handelsschiedsgerichtsbarkeit, 117; WENGLER, W., Les principes généraux du droit en tant que loi du contrat, 487.
387. GOLDMAN, B., Lex mercatoria, 19; GOLDMAN, B., Rapport général, 164; FOUCHARD, P., L'arbitrage commercial international, 46.

been set up by treaty[388]. Therefore, it is very hard to achieve uniformity between arbitral awards[389] and, more important, there seems to be no reason to give previous arbitral awards the benefit of binding force of precedent. Rather, such awards may have persuasive force of precedent based upon their merits. As such, they may be an important substantive source of international business law. Also, another major problem with seeing arbitral case law as a formal source of law is to be found in the secrecy of the arbitral process. Generally, arbitral awards are not published, which makes it hardly possible to know them and to use them as binding precedents[390]. Only extracts from I.C.C. arbitral awards have been published for some time, which in certain cases has had some influence on later I.C.C. awards.

III.8 International conventions

311. Finally, one may see international conventions as an important source of international business law. Recent theories on international trade law have confirmed this view. Schmitthoff has particularly emphasized the central role of international conventions for international business law as they express a more transnational approach. Such conventions include conflict of laws conventions, unification conventions, conventions containing uniform or model laws and conventions on international commercial arbitration.

312. From a pragmatic point of view, these conventions are very important since they reduce differences between national systems and thus make the legal regulation of international business life less complex, which in turn may encourage international commercial flows. From a more theoretical perspective, these conventions regulate international business transactions

---

388. SCHMITTHOFF, C., Das neue Recht des Welthandels, 71; FIRSCHING, K., Internationales Schuldrecht, I, 351; KASSIS, A., Théorie générale des usages du commerce, 509; BEGUIN, J., Le développement de la lex mercatoria menace-t-il l'ordre juridique international ?, 501-502; COING, H., Materielles Recht und Verfahrensrecht in der internationalen Schiedsgerichtsbarkeit, 29-30.

389. REDFERN, A. and HUNTER, M., Law and practice of international commercial arbitration, first edition, 92; FOUCHARD, P., L'arbitrage commercial international, 446.

390. REDFERN, A. and HUNTER, M., Law and practice of international commercial arbitration, first edition, 92; KROPHOLLER, J., Internationales Einheitsrecht, 148; BAJONS, E.M., Zur Nationalität internationaler Schiedssachen, 34; FOUCHARD, P., L'arbitrage commercial international, 446; LOQUIN, E., L'amiable composition en droit comparé et international, 371.

only partially which implies that no universal or regional international trade law exists. Consequently, international business law must still be understood as a complex set of rules involving interaction between national laws, international conventions and self-regulatory rules. Also, these international conventions prove that no sharp distinction can be made between national and international transactions since some of these conventions also apply or have been extended to domestic transactions[391].

313. The interaction between these international conventions and national law is sometimes confirmed by these conventions which have settled their relation with rules of national law. This is particularly so when the role of conflict of laws is defined in these conventions. The Hague Uniform Sales Laws have made an attempt to exclude conflict of laws from the application of these laws (article 1 (9) ULFIS and article 2 ULIS). One may doubt whether any such attempt can be successful, because conflict of laws problems may arise as a result of different interpretations given in different countries to uniform law texts[392]. Article 7 (2) CISG has not gone as far as ULFIS and ULIS in excluding conflict of laws; it provides that gaps in the convention may be filled in conformity with the law applicable by virtue of conflict of laws, provided no solution is found in the general principles on which the convention is based.

314. Interaction may also take place in the interpretation of international conventions. Article 17 ULIS refers to the general principles on which the uniform law is based. Article 7 of the Sales Limitation Period Convention, article 7 (1) CISG, article 18 of the EEC Convention on the law applicable to contractual obligations and article 16 of the Hague 1986 Convention on the law applicable to international sales of goods provide that in the

---

391. See supra No. 38 and LOUSSOUARN, Y., Cours général de droit international privé, 292.

392. KROPHOLLER, J., Der "Ausschluß" des internationalen Privatrechts im Einheitlichen Kaufgesetz, 380-385; LOUSSOUARN, Y., Cours général de droit international privé, 299; DEL MARMOL, C. and MATRAY, L., L'importance et l'interprétation du contrat, 165; RIGAUX, F. and VANDER ELST, R., Relations juridiques transnationales ou dialogue sur un autre droit, 231.

A *school* example is the *Hocke* decision of the French Supreme Court dated March 4, 1963 (J.C.P., 1963, II, 13376, R.C.D.I.P., 1964, 264) involving the interpretation of article 31, fourth paragraph of the Geneva Convention of June 7, 1930 on a uniform law on bills of exchange and promissory notes which provides that *aval* is deemed to have been given for the drawer. Proof to the contrary is not allowed in France whereas it is possible in Germany. Courts faced with this problem in Franco-German relations are thus faced with the question whether to follow the French or the German interpretation of a uniform text.

interpretation of these conventions regard shall be had to their international character and to the need to promote uniformity in their application.

Absent interpretation rules stated in the conventions, national courts and arbitral tribunals should develop their own interpretation rules. For instance, Belgian and English courts have refused to rely on national interpretation rules and have created specific rules for the interpretation of conventions[393]. On the other hand, French case law seems to use more often national interpretation rules[394].

315. Finally, the question should be answered whether international conventions are formal sources of international business law. Since individuals and companies for which the rules of international business law conventions have been written, are generally not subjects under public international law, these rules will have to be implemented into legal systems which make them binding upon individuals and companies. In most cases, the international convention is incorporated in a national legal system through the process of approval, ratification or accession[395] which makes the international convention a formal source of national law. However, the international origin of the text distinguishes it from other sources. A separate category is formed by supranational legal systems (such as the EEC), which by virtue of the treaty establishing it has received legislative powers which make incorporation of supranational texts into national systems unnecessary. These texts are then formal sources of both the supranational and national systems.

---

393. *Belgium* : Supreme Court, January 27, 1977, Bull.Cass., 1977, 574, Pas., 1977, I, 574, opinion DELANGE; *England* : Fothergill v. Monarch Airlines, [1980] 2 All E.R. 696 (House of Lords).

394. French Supreme Court, December 5, 1967, J.C.P., 1968, II, 15350, Rev.dr.aér., 1968, 184, contrary opinion Adv.Gen. LINDON.

395. See WAELBROECK, M., Portée et critères de l'applicabilité directe des traités internationaux, case note under Belgian Supreme Court, April 21, 1983, R.C.J.B., 1985, 41.

CHAPTER IV

Recent Theories on the Sources of International Business Law

316. This chapter gives an overview of post-war theories on international business law. Since the theory of *lex mercatoria* has received most attention, a substantial part of this chapter will be devoted to a discussion and assessment of this theory (IV.1). Thereafter, other theories will be discussed (IV.2 - IV.4).

IV.1 The theory of the lex mercatoria

317. This section will discuss and assess the origin and development of the theory of *lex mercatoria* in scholarly writings, legislation, international conventions, case law and transnational practice. The analysis of the theory itself is important because this has not yet been done in a comprehensive way[1]. Such analysis is necessary in order better to understand the theory's presuppositions and the different interpretations which have been given to it.

318. By way of introduction, the use of the term *lex mercatoria* should be explained. Historically, the term *lex mercatoria* was used in an English collection called the *Fleta* in which customs had been written down around 1290[2] as well as in the book *Consuetudo vel lex mercatoria*, written by Malynes in 1622. The term *lex mercatoria* may, however, be criticized because it does not reflect the international nature of international business law and because many more sources than statutory law are relevant for international business transactions. On the other hand, one cannot ignore

---

1. In my dissertation, *De lex mercatoria, Inleiding op de studie van het transnationaal handelsrecht*, an extensive review of the theory has been made. In this book, where the sources of international business law, as opposed to the *lex mercatoria* itself are discussed, only the most important elements of the dissertation's analysis will be used.
2. POHLMANN, H., Die Quellen des Handelsrechts, in Handbuch der Quellen und Literatur der neueren Europäischen Privatrechtsgeschichte, I, COING, H. (ed.), Munich, Beck, 1973, 814; BÜLCK, H., Betrachtungen über ein Völkerhandelsrecht, ZHR, 1968, 159.

the fact that the term *lex mercatoria* is now so well settled that introducing a new concept such as, for instance, *ius mercatorum* might only increase terminological confusion.

IV.1.1 *Lex mercatoria in legal literature*

319. In this section, the emergence and development of the theory of *lex mercatoria* will be discussed.

IV.1.1.1 International business law and the emergence of a new lex mercatoria

320. The theory of *lex mercatoria* can be traced back to four authors who have developed new ideas about the sources of international business law. These authors are Edouard Lambert (theory of *droit corporatif international*), Clive Schmitthoff (theory of the *new law merchant*), Berthold Goldman (theory of *lex mercatoria*) and Philippe Kahn (theory of the *société internationale des commerçants*).

321. At the end of the nineteen twenties, Edouard Lambert came to realize that international trade is not only governed by national law and courts but that interested business circles, to a certain extent, had made a law on their own through the combination of general conditions, trade usages and arbitration[3]. Lambert called this the *droit corporatif international*[4]. Driven by market forces, unification of the law at the level of a given trade or profession is achieved[5] and may even lead to more universal forms of unification[6].

---

3. Lambert's theory has been followed in Belgium by Del Marmol, see DEL MARMOL, C., Le droit corporatif de la vente commerciale, Rev.Dr.Int. Lég.Comp., 1936, 60; DEL MARMOL, C., Les clauses contractuelles types, facteur d'unification du droit commercial, Liber amicorum L. Frédéricq, Ghent, Story, 1966, 308.
4. LAMBERT, E., Sources du droit comparé ou supranational, Législation uniforme et jurisprudence comparative, 499; LAMBERT, E., Preface, in ISHIZAKI, M., Le droit corporatif international de la vente de soies, XXVII, XXVIII and XXX.
5. LAMBERT, E., Sources du droit comparé ou supranational, Législation uniforme et jurisprudence comparative, 498.
6. LAMBERT, E., Sources du droit comparé ou supranational, Législation uniforme et jurisprudence comparative, 500-501.

322. From 1954 on, Clive Schmitthoff[7] had developed his influential theory on the *new law merchant*. Schmitthoff emphasized the specific character of international business law, where international conventions, uniform laws and usages have a prominent place[8]. As to usages, Schmitthoff did point out that usages are no longer solely created by spontaneous behaviour but also are formulated by international organizations such as the I.C.C., the E.C.E. or international professional organizations[9]. Unless imposed by these organizations[10], the binding effect of the rules still depends on party incorporation[11].

323. The relation between these sources of international business law and national legal systems has somewhat been obscured by the fact that Schmitthoff referred to international business law as an *autonomous* legal system. In his opinion, this does not mean that international business law exists outside national legal systems but only that, within national systems,

---

7. For a collection from the writings of Clive Schmitthoff, see Clive M. Schmitthoff's select essays on international trade law, CHIA-JUI CHENG (ed.), Dordrecht, Martinus Nijhoff, 1988, 802 p.
8. SCHMITTHOFF, C., International business law: a new law merchant, 149; SCHMITTHOFF, C., The law of international trade, its growth, formulation and operation, 16-18; SCHMITTHOFF, C., The unification of the law of international trade, 27 Gothenburg School of Economics and Business Administration Publications, 1964, 7; SCHMITTHOFF, C.,International trade law and private international law, 267; SCHMITTHOFF, C., The sale of goods, second edition, London, Stevens & Sons, 1966, 204 and 214; SCHMITTHOFF, C., The risk of loss in transit in international sales, in Unification of the law governing international sales of goods, HONNOLD, J., (ed.), Paris, Dalloz, 1966, 170; SCHMITTHOFF, C., The unification of the law of international trade, J.BUS.L., 1968, 109; SCHMITTHOFF, C., The legal organisation of commerce and its relation to the social conditions, in The legal organisation of commerce and its relation to the social conditions, Aarhus, Provinsbanken, 1979, 17; SCHMITTHOFF, C., Commercial law in a changing economic climate, 22; SCHMITTHOFF, C., Nature and evolution of the transnational law of commercial transactions, in The transnational law of international commercial transactions, HORN, N. and SCHMITTHOFF, C. (ed.), Deventer, Kluwer, 1982, 23.
9. SCHMITTHOFF, C., The law of international trade, its growth, formulation and operation, 16; SCHMITTHOFF, C., Das neue Recht des Welthandels, 75; SCHMITTHOFF, C., Nature and evolution of the transnational law of commercial transactions, 24.
10. SCHMITTHOFF, C., The law of international trade, its growth, formulation and operation, 17.
11. SCHMITTHOFF, C., The law of international trade, its growth, formulation and operation, 16-18; SCHMITTHOFF, C., International trade law and private international law, 267-268; SCHMITTHOFF, C., Das neue Recht des Welthandels, 64; SCHMITTHOFF, C., The unification or harmonization of laws by means of standard contracts and general conditions, in L'unification du droit, Yearbook 1967-1968, II, Rome, Unidroit, 1969, 97.

it has some features of its own[12]. Thus, Schmitthoff basically combines two elements in his theory. First, he stresses the importance of the international origin of some rules for the application and interpretation of international business law. Second, because of its international character, it leads to uniformity of international business law[13].

324. Schmitthoff sees the place of international business law within national legal systems from a pragmatic point of view. The following citation is self-evident :

> *"We have to face the fact that the new law merchant which is emerging before our eyes is an entirely new phenomenon. When trying to understand it we must forget the victorian predilection of orderliness but take it as what it was in the Middle Ages and what it will be again: unsystematic, complex and multiform, but of bewildering vigour, realism and originality."* [14]

However, one may also wonder whether one cannot extrapolate from Schmitthoff's position and see international business law as a more or less independent branch of national law[15].

325. During the same period as Schmitthoff, Berthold Goldman developed his theory on *lex mercatoria*. To discuss Goldman's theory, one might distinguish between his analyses regarding substantive transnational rules, custom and usages, contracts, general principles of law and international commercial arbitration. As to substantive transnational rules, Goldman analyzed, in many case notes, French case law, which created such rules. First, Goldman seemed to integrate these rules into French law[16]. In a

---

12. SCHMITTHOFF, C., intervention during the discussions, in Basle symposium on the law governing contractual obligations, 188-189; SCHMITTHOFF, C., Finality of arbitral awards and judicial review, 232.
13. SCHMITTHOFF, C., International trade law and private international law, 257-258; SCHMITTHOFF, C., Agency in international trade, 115-116; SCHMITTHOFF, C., Das neue Recht des Welthandels, 59; SCHMITTHOFF, C., Nature and evolution of the transnational law of commercial transactions, 21-22.

    The idea of unification of law through *lex mercatoria* had a great impact upon Kappus (see KAPPUS, A., "Conflict avoidance" durch "lex mercatoria" und UN-Kaufrecht 1980, RIW 1990, 788-794).
14. SCHMITTHOFF, C., The unification of the law of international trade, J.BUS.L., 1968, 112.
15. See infra IV.1.5.2.
16. GOLDMAN, B., Arbitrage international et droit commun des nations, 115; GOLDMAN, B., Règles de conflit, règles d'application immédiate et règles matérielles dans l'arbitrage commercial international, Trav.com.fr.dr.int.privé, 1966-69, Paris, Dalloz, 1970, 121, 135-136; GOLDMAN, B., case note French Supreme Court, January

second stage, these transnational substantive rules no longer seem to appear within French law but as supranational rules[17]. Finally, notwithstanding some hesitation[18], Goldman returned to his original position and qualified transnational substantive rules as French rules[19] which are specifically tailored to international situations and may be followed by other jurisdictions[20].

326. Second, Goldman has pointed to the importance of codified usages[21], general conditions as well as international conventions and bye-laws regarding international companies[22]. These are considered to be formal sources of international business law because these rules are sufficiently general, are made by legitimate authorities and effectively enforced[23]. At first, Goldman thought that customary law is not that relevant for international business law since general consensus on established trade practices will be absent[24]. In a second stage, Goldman did away with the

---

24, 1956, Clunet, 1956, 1012.

17. GOLDMAN, B., case note Commercial Court Paris, March 24, 1957, Clunet, 1958, 1002; GOLDMAN, B., case note Court of Appeal Paris, April 10, 1957, Clunet, 1958, 1014.
18. GOLDMAN, B., case note French Supreme Court, May 2, 1966, R.C.D.I.P., 1967, 556-557; GOLDMAN, B., case note Court of Appeal Paris, June 19, 1970, J.C.P., 1971, 16927.
19. GOLDMAN, B., case note French Supreme Court, May 7, 1963, J.C.P., 1963, 13405; GOLDMAN, B., case note French Supreme Court, October 29, 1964, Clunet, 1965, 641; GOLDMAN, B., Preface, in DEBY-GERARD, F., Le rôle de la règle de conflit dans le règlement des rapports internationaux, Paris, Dalloz, 1973, IX; GOLDMAN, B., Les problèmes spécifiques de l'arbitrage international, Rev.Arb., 1980, 330.
20. GOLDMAN, B., Le contrat international, in Renaissance du phénomène contractuel, COMMISSION DROIT ET VIE DES AFFAIRES (ed.), The Hague, Nijhoff, 1971, 470.
21. GOLDMAN, B., La volonté des parties et le rôle de l'arbitre dans l'arbitrage international, Rev.Arb., 1981, 484; GOLDMAN, B., La nouvelle réglementation française de l'arbitrage international, in The art of arbitration, Essays on international arbitration, Liber amicorum Pieter Sanders, SCHULTSZ, J. and VAN DEN BERG, A.J. (ed.), Deventer, Kluwer, 1982, 165.
22. Generally, other international conventions are, in Goldman's theory, no formal sources of the *lex mercatoria* (see GOLDMAN, B., Un "conflictualiste" d'esprit international : Mr.Henri Batiffol, 331; GOLDMAN, B., Le contrat international, 474; GOLDMAN, B., La lex mercatoria dans les contrats et l'arbitrage internationaux : réalité et perspectives, 477-478 and 498 and GOLDMAN, B., Les travaux de la Commission des Nations Unies pour le Droit Commercial International, Clunet, 1979, 748 and 753).
23. GOLDMAN, B., Les conflits de lois dans l'arbitrage international de droit privé, Academy for international law, 109 Collected Courses of The Hague, 1963, II, 475-477; GOLDMAN, B., Frontières du droit et "lex mercatoria", 180 and 188-192; GOLDMAN, B., V° Arbitrage (droit international privé), 132.
24. GOLDMAN, B., Frontières du droit et "lex mercatoria", 190.

psychological element in the formation of custom; the fact that traders repeatedly act in a certain way is, according to Goldman, sufficient evidence that they feel bound by the rules of behaviour that they observe[25]. Under that perspective, usual contract clauses such as *force majeure* clauses or hardship clauses and new contract forms such as turnkey contracts or euro-bond issues may be qualified as customary[26]. Finally, it seems that Goldman has abandoned the distinction between custom and usages altogether. Both are now considered to be formal sources of law and no longer dependent on acceptance by the parties[27].

327. Third, Goldman has referred to the role of general principles of law in international contracts and arbitral awards. These principles are common to all or many states which participate in international commerce[28] or are specific to international commerce[29]. These principles are genuine sources of the *lex mercatoria*[30] because they are effectively used in international trade[31]. Their function is primarily to fill any gaps which other sources may have left.

328. International commercial arbitration also is an important element in Goldman's theory on *lex mercatoria*. First, Goldman referred to the 1955 edition of the I.C.C. Arbitration Rules where the Arbitration Rules were, in principle, self-sufficient unless some gaps had to be filled, in which case the procedural law chosen by the parties or the law of the arbitral seat were to be applied[32]. Goldman's major contribution to international commercial arbitration law were his lectures before the Hague Academy

25. GOLDMAN, B., La lex mercatoria dans les contrats et l'arbitrage internationaux : réalité et perspectives, 501; GOLDMAN, B., La volonté des parties et le rôle de l'arbitre dans l'arbitrage international, 484; GOLDMAN, B., La nouvelle réglementation française de l'arbitrage international, 165; GOLDMAN, B., Rapport général, in Le rôle de la pratique dans la formation du droit, 169.
26. GOLDMAN, B., La lex mercatoria dans les contrats et l'arbitrage internationaux : réalité et perspectives, 487-491.
27. GOLDMAN, B., Lex mercatoria, 14; GOLDMAN, B., Rapport général, in Le rôle de la pratique dans la formation du droit, 164 and 175-177.
28. GOLDMAN, B., Les conflits de lois dans l'arbitrage international de droit privé, 477-480; GOLDMAN, B., Le contrat international, 471-472.
29. GOLDMAN, B., The applicable law : general principles of law - lex mercatoria, in Contemporary problems in international arbitration, LEW, J. (ed.), London, School of international arbitration, Queen Mary College, 1986, 115.
30. GOLDMAN, B., La lex mercatoria dans les contrats et l'arbitrage internationaux : réalité et perspectives, 487.
31. GOLDMAN, B., La lex mercatoria dens les contrats et l'arbitrage internationaux : réalité et perspectives, 501.
32. GOLDMAN, B., Arbitrage international et droit commun des nations, 115-116.

for International Law. There, Goldman stressed the need to develop autonomous conflict rules for international commercial arbitrations in order to avoid the unsatisfactory results stemming from application of the conflict rules of the state of the arbitral place and the state whose law was applicable to the merits of the dispute[33]. Also, autonomous conflict rules were needed for arbitrations which were governed only by arbitration rules and where the *lex mercatoria* was applicable to the substance of the dispute[34]. Goldman then made an extensive research as to the contents of such an autonomous conflict system drawing from international conventions, arbitration rules, general conditions and arbitral case law. Although no uniform answers are available from these sources, Goldman concluded that they do not exclude the possibility of an autonomous arbitral conflict system[35].

329. Originally, Goldman did see the *lex mercatoria* as an uncompleted development process[36] which had not led yet to the formation of a legal system[37]. Thereafter, Goldman became more hesitant[38], but finally Goldman stated that, in his opinion, the *lex mercatoria* was a legal system, albeit incomplete[39].

---

33. GOLDMAN, B., Les conflits de lois dans l'arbitrage international de droit privé, 367-380.
34. Ibid., 379.
35. Ibid., 380-414.
36. GOLDMAN, B., Les conflits de lois dans l'arbitrage international de droit privé, 379, 452 and 479; GOLDMAN, B., Frontières du droit et "lex mercatoria", 189; GOLDMAN, B., V° Arbitrage (droit international privé), 121-122 and 131; GOLDMAN, B., La lex mercatoria dans les contrats et l'arbitrage internationaux : réalité et perspectives, 479-480; GOLDMAN, B., Une bataille judiciaire autour de la lex mercatoria, Rev.Arb., 1983, 407.
37. GOLDMAN, B., Frontières du droit et "lex mercatoria", 189 and GOLDMAN, B., Règles de conflit, règles d'application immédiate et règles matérielles dans l'arbitrage commercial international, 136.
38. GOLDMAN, B., La lex mercatoria dans les contrats et l'arbitrage internationaux : réalité et perspectives, 502 and GOLDMAN, B., intervention during the discussions, in Basle symposium on the law governing contractual obligations, 167.
39. GOLDMAN, B., Lex mercatoria, 22 and GOLDMAN, B., Une bataille judiciaire autour de la lex mercatoria, 407.

330. From the foregoing analysis, one may deduce that, contrary to Schmitthoff, Goldman uses a formal conception of law-creating sources[40]. These sources are binding on themselves and are not binding by virtue of national law[41]. As non-national sources, they create a non-national, autonomous legal system. Contracts in which reference is made to the rules of the *lex mercatoria*, and arbitral awards which apply such rules are thus not without law but only without a national law.

331. The formal autonomy of the *lex mercatoria* raises the question of its relation with national law. First, Goldman does not give the *lex mercatoria* monopoly status in resolving transnational business disputes. National laws and public international law may as well have their say in this process[42]. Also, to a certain extent, the *lex mercatoria* may need the support of national law, especially regarding the enforcement of awards which have applied some of its rules[43]. Finally, Goldman puts the *lex mercatoria* on the same footing as foreign law. Before national courts, *lex mercatoria* may be applied by virtue of a choice of law for the *lex mercatoria* or a transnational substantive rule[44]. In case of choice of law, this implies that this may, just as for choice of law for a foreign law, lead to the exclusion of mandatory rules of the *lex fori*. However, application of rules of *lex mercatoria* may not violate the international public policy of the *lex fori* nor

---

40. See GOLDMAN, B., intervention during the discussions, in Basle symposium on the law governing contractual obligations, 195; GOLDMAN, B., Lex mercatoria, 5-6; GOLDMAN, B., The applicable law : general principles of law - lex mercatoria, 113-114 and 116.

The difference between the Schmitthoff and Goldman conceptions regarding *lex mercatoria* have only quite recently become apparent (see also DASSER, F., Internationale Scheidsgerichte und lex mercatoria, 43-64; MUNZBERG, R., Die Schranken der Parteivereinbarungen in der privaten internationalen Schiedsgerichtsbarkeit, Berlin, Duncker & Humblot, 1970, 74; GRIGERA NAON, H., The UN Convention on contracts for the international sale of goods, in The transnational law of international commercial transactions, HORN, N. and SCHMITTHOFF, C. (ed.), Deventer, Kluwer, 1982, 90 and 93; VAN HECKE, G., Contracts subject to international or transnational law, in Miscellanea Georges Van Hecke, Antwerp, Kluwer, 1985, 305-306, International contracts, New York, Matthew Bender, 1981, 25 ff.).

41. GOLDMAN, B., Frontières du droit et "lex mercatoria", 189.

42. GOLDMAN, B., Le contrat international, 474; GOLDMAN, B., La lex mercatoria dans les contrats et l'arbitrage internationaux: réalité et perspectives, 498; GOLDMAN, B., Lex mercatoria, 22-23; GOLDMAN, B., Une bataille judiciaire autour de la lex mercatoria, 408-409.

43. GOLDMAN, B., Lex mercatoria, 22; GOLDMAN, B., Une bataille judiciaire autour de la lex mercatoria, 408.

44. GOLDMAN, B., intervention during the discussions, in Basle symposium on the law governing contractual obligations, 129.

may they preempt *règles d'application immédiate*[45] of the *lex fori*[46]. In the course of international commercial arbitrations, the rules of the *lex mercatoria* will only be reviewed against a truly transnational public policy (other than international public policy of national states)[47]. Conflicts between transnational public policy and national conceptions of international public policy may arise but should be solved in favour of transnational public policy, except in the state whose international public policy is involved[48].

332. Notwithstanding the influence of Goldman on Philippe Kahn, the latter deserves special discussion because he has stressed the sociological dimension of international business law in which the international business community would create its own rules. In his dissertation, Kahn has analyzed this particularly with regard to the international community of buyers and sellers which is well organized and has sufficient homogeneity and solidarity[49]. Similar tendencies may be observed in other markets as for instance within the banking community which is active on the euro-bond markets[50]. The self-regulatory rules of subsections of the international business community consist of usages, general conditions, usual contract

---

45. GOLDMAN, B., intervention during the discussions, in Basle symposium on the law governing contractual obligations, 168-170.
46. Goldman has not taken position as to application of *règles d'application immédiate* of countries, other than that of the *lex fori* (GOLDMAN, B., intervention during the discussions, in Basle symposium on the law governing contractual obligations, 170).
47. Ibid., 170 and 196; GOLDMAN, B., Lex mercatoria, 22.
48. GOLDMAN, B., La lex mercatoria et les contrats et l'arbitrage internationaux : réalité et perspectives, 490.
49. KAHN, P., La vente commerciale internationale, Paris, Sirey, 1961, 2 and 15; KAHN, P., La Convention de La Haye du 1er juillet 1964 portant loi uniforme sur la vente internationale des objets mobiliers corporels, Rev.Trim.Dr.Com., 1964, 700; KAHN, P., L'essor du non-droit dans les relations commerciales internationales et le contrat sans loi, in L'hypothèse du non-droit, COMMISSION DROIT ET VIE DES AFFAIRES (ed.), Liège, 1978, 234.
50. KAHN, P., Lex mercatoria et euro-obligations, 224-225 and KAHN, P., Lex mercatoria et pratique des contrats internationaux : l'expérience française, in Le contrat économique international, Travaux des VIIes Journées d'études Jean Dabin, Brussels, Bruylant, 1975, 173-176.

clauses[51] and general principles of law[52]. Under a sociological conception of law in which any organized community may create legal rules, these rules are then seen as legal rules[53] which apply to the traders belonging to the international business community or to a subsection thereof[54]. Under Goldman's influence, these rules are also called *lex mercatoria*.

The autonomy of the rules of the international business community may be jeopardized if litigation is brought before national courts. These will apply national law and review the self-regulation of international traders against that law[55]. For that reason, international commercial arbitration seems to be more appropriate in order to have these self-regulatory rules applied[56]. However, Kahn recognizes that the autonomy of the *lex mercatoria* is not absolute[57] and that international public policy and the *ius cogens* of public international law may restrict its application[58].

---

51. KAHN, P., Lex mercatoria et pratique des contrats internationaux : l'expérience française, 179, 189, 193 and 198; KAHN, P., Force majeure et contrats internationaux de longue durée, Clunet, 1975, 474 and 485; KAHN, P., L'interprétation des contrats internationaux, Clunet, 1981, 26.
52. KAHN, P., case note District Court Paris, March 4, 1981, Clunet, 1981, 842; KAHN, P., Droit international économique, droit du développement, lex mercatoria : concept unique ou pluralisme des ordres juridiques ?, in Le droit des relations économiques internationales, Etudes offertes à Berthold Goldman, Paris, Litec, 1982, 100-101.
53. KAHN, P., La vente commerciale internationale, 36 and 42; KAHN, P., L'essor du non-droit dans les relations commerciales internationales et le contrat sans loi, 1978, 231.
54. KAHN, P., Lex mercatoria et euro-obligations, 224.
55. KAHN, P., La vente commerciale internationale, 232-236.
56. KAHN, P., La Convention de La Haye sur la loi applicable aux ventes à caractère international d'objets mobiliers corporels, Clunet, 1966, 325-326; KAHN, P., Lex mercatoria et pratique des contrats internationaux : l'expérience française, 209; KAHN, P., Force majeure et contrats internationaux de longue durée, 485.
57. KAHN, P., L'essor du non-droit dans les relations commerciales internationales et le contrat sans loi, 265-266.
58. KAHN, P., Lex mercatoria et euro-obligations, 240; KAHN, P., Lex mercatoria et pratique des contrats internationaux : l'expérience française, 210-211; KAHN, P., L'essor du non-droit dans les relations commerciales internationales et le contrat sans loi, 266.

IV.1.1.2 The development of the theory of the lex mercatoria

333. After its emergence, the theory of *lex mercatoria* soon became widely known in legal literature. The main events of this development will hereafter briefly be discussed per country[59].

---

59. A complete overview falls outside the scope of this book. For *proponents* of the theory of the *lex mercatoria*, see HONNOLD, J., The influence of the law of international trade on the development and character of English and American commercial law, in The sources of the law of international trade, SCHMITTHOFF, C. (ed.), International Association of Legal Science, London, Stevens & Sons, 1964, 87; CRAIG, W., PARK, W. and PAULSSON, J., International Chamber of Commerce Arbitration, New York, Oceana, 1985, 35, 1-13; CREMADES, B., Multinational companies and international commercial arbitration, in Legal problems of codes of conduct for multinational enterprises, HORN, N. (ed.), Deventer, Kluwer, 1980, 85-87; CREMADES, B., The impact of international arbitration on the development of business law, AM.J.COMP.L., 1983, 526; CREMADES, B. and PLEHN, S., The new law merchant and the harmonization of the laws of international commercial transactions, B.U.INT'L L.J., 1984, 317; LANDO, O., Länderbericht Nordische Staaten, in Materielles Recht und Verfahrensrecht in der internationalen Schiedsgerichtsbarkeit, COING, H. (ed.), Frankfurt, Metzner, 1972, 106-107; LANDO, O., The lex mercatoria in international commercial arbitration, INT'L & COMP.L.Q., 1985, 747; LANDO, O., The law applicable to the merits of the dispute, in Contemporary problems in international arbitration, LEW, J. (ed.), London, School of international arbitration, Queen Mary College, 1986, 104; HAYES, L., A modern lex mercatoria : political rhetoric or substantive progress ?, BROOKLYN J.INT'L L., 1977, 210-232; GAL, I., The commercial law of nations and the law of international trade, CORNELL INT'L L.J., 1972, 55-75; BAXTER, I., International conflict of laws and international business, INT'L & COMP.L.Q., 1985, 538-562; General principles of law in international commercial arbitration, HARV.L.REV. 1988, 1819; GIARDINA, A., Arbitrato transnazionale e lex mercatoria di fronte alla Corte di Cassazione, Riv.Dir.Int.Priv.Proc., 1982, 754; RAMBERG, J., Les Incoterms demain, in EISEMANN, F., Usages de la vente commerciale internationale, second edition, Paris, Jupiter, 1980, 245; SCHINNERER, E., Um ein Recht des internationalen Handels, ZfRV 1968, 185-213; MICHIDA, S., Possible avenues to preparation of standard contracts for international trade on a global level, in Unification of the law governing international sales of goods, HONNOLD, J. (ed.), Paris, Dalloz, 1966, 251; KITAGAWA, T., Contractual autonomy in international commercial arbitration including a Japanese perspective, in International arbitration, Liber amicorum for Martin Domke, SANDERS, P. (ed.), The Hague, Martinus Nijhoff, 1967, 140-141; KRISHNAMURTHI, N., Some thoughts on a new convention on international arbitration, Liber amicorum Pieter Sanders, SCHULTSZ, J. and VAN DEN BERG, A.J. (ed.), Deventer, Kluwer, 1982, 211-212; CARBONNEAU, T., Etude historique et comparée de l'arbitrage : vers un droit matériel de l'arbitrage international fondé sur la motivation des sentences, Rev.Int.Dr.Comp., 1984, 760, TEX.INT'L L.J., 1984, 33 ff.; CARBONNEAU, T., The remaking of arbitration : design and destiny, 1-19; KURKELA, M., Letters of credit under international trade law : UCC, UCP and law merchant, Dobbs Ferry, New York, Oceana, 1985, 12, 25 and 28; PRUJINER, A., La gestion des arbitrages commerciaux internationaux : l'exemple de

334. In England, authors have been divided as to the merits of the theory of *lex mercatoria*. Three tendencies exist. First, some authors are sympathetic to Schmitthoff's theory on *lex mercatoria*[60]. Other authors have

---

la Cour d'arbitrage de la CCI, Clunet, 1988, 717-718; FOX, W.F., International commercial agreements, Deventer, Kluwer, 1988, 31; CROFF, C., The applicable law in an international commercial arbitration : is it still a conflict of laws problem ?, INT'L LAW., 1982, 642-645; GOLDSTAJN, A., The new law merchant, J.BUS.L., 1961,12; GOLDSTAJN, A., International conventions and standard contracts as means of escaping from the application of municipal law - I, in The sources of the law of international trade, SCHMITTHOFF, C. (ed.), London, Stevens & Sons, 1964, 106; GOLDSTAJN, A., Commercial usages as the source of the law of international trade, in XII Yearbook of the School of law and economic science, Aristotelian University of Thessaloniki, Miscellany in honor of C. Fragistas, Deel II, Thessaloniki, 1967, 393-394; GOLDSTAJN, A., The new law merchant reconsidered, in Law and international trade, Recht und internationaler Handel, Festschrift für Clive M. Schmitthoff, FABRICIUS, F. (ed.), Frankfurt, Athenäum Verlag, 1973, 174-183; GOLDSTAJN, A., Usages of trade and other autonomous rules of international trade according to the UN (1980) sales convention, in International sales of goods, Dubrovnik lectures, New York, Oceana, 1986, 55-110; GOLDSTAJN, A., Reflections on the structure of the modern law of international trade, International contracts and conflicts of laws, SARCEVIC, P., (ed.), London, Graham & Trotman, 1990, 14-35; JAKUBOWSKI, J., The autonomy of international trade law and its influence on the interpretation and application of its rules, in Law and international trade, Recht und internationaler Handel, Festschrift für Clive M. Schmitthoff, FABRICIUS, F. (ed.), Frankfurt, Athenäum Verslag, 1973, 209; MADL, F., Lex mercatoria, unification of law, the Hague conventions and Hungary, in Conflicts and harmonization, Mélanges en l'honneur d'Alfred E. Von Overbeck, Editions universitaires Fribourg, 1990, 298-301.

For *opponents* of the theory, see POCAR, F. and VITTA, F., interventions during the discussions, Basle symposium on the law governing contractual obligations, KLEIN, F.E. and VISCHER, F. (ed.), Basle, Helbing & Lichtenhahn, 1983, at respectively 189 and 158; DRAETTA, U., La cosidetta lex mercatoria, Foro Padano, 1987, II, 53 ff.; GRIGERA NAON, H., Transnational enterprises under the Pacto Andino and national laws of Latin America, in Legal problems of codes of conduct for multinational enterprises, HORN, N. (ed.), Deventer, Kluwer, 1980, 261; DELAUME, G., Comparative analysis as a basis of law in State contracts : the myth of the lex mercatoria, TUL.L.REV., 1989, 575-611; HIGHET, K., The enigma of the lex mercatoria, TUL.L.REV., 1989, 613-628; CAPATINA, O., Doctrine et pratique du droit socialiste roumain en matière de contrat international, in Le contrat économique international, Travaux des VIIes Journées d'études juridiques Jean Dabin, Brussels, Bruylant, 1975, 252-253; POPESCU, T., Le droit du commerce international: une nouvelle tâche pour les législateurs nationaux ou une nouvelle "lex mercatoria" ?, in New directions in international trade law, Acts and proceedings of the second congress on private law held by Unidroit, I, Dobbs Ferry, New York, Oceana, 1977, 44-45; TSCHIKVADSE, V. and RUBANOV, A., Some aspects of the unification of the law of sales, in Unification of the law governing international sales of goods, HONNOLD, J. (ed.), Paris, Dalloz, 1966, 348.

60. LEW, J., Applicable law in international commercial arbitration, Dobbs Ferry, New York, Oceana, 1978, 437-438.

expressed the importance of general principles of law, international usages and international commercial arbitration for the law of international trade without, however, taking an explicit position as to Goldman's theory on *lex mercatoria*[61]. Second, some other authors remain rather sceptical as to the *lex mercatoria*[62]. Third, there is Francis Mann who has led a sole opposition against the *lex mercatoria*, particularly in so far as its application in international commercial arbitration is concerned. According to Mann, there necessarily should be a link between international commercial arbitration and the place of arbitration. Arbitrators should look into the law of the arbitral place for conflict and procedural rules[63]. Thus, Goldman's

---

61. ROWE, M., The contribution of the ICC to the development of international trade law, in The transnational law of international commercial transactions, HORN, N. and SCHMITTHOFF, C. (ed.), Deventer, Kluwer, 1982, 52-53; HOYLE, M., The law of international trade, first edition, 2; BAGNER, H., Dispute settlement, in International trade : law and practice, LEW, J. and STANBROOK, C. (ed.), London, Euromoney, 1983, 180; REDFERN, A. and HUNTER, M., Law and practice of international commercial arbitration, first edition, 90-92; Mc LAGHLAN, C., The new Hague sales convention and the limits of the choice of law process, 102 L.Q.R., 1986, 597, 604 and 617.
62. GRAVESON, R., COHN, E. and GRAVESON, D., The uniform laws on international sales act 1967, London, Butterworths, 1968, 28; MUSTILL, M. and BOYD, S., The law and practice of commercial arbitration in England, first edition, 612; MUSTILL, M., Transnational arbitration in English law, Current legal problems, 1984, 150; BOYD, S., The role of national law and the national courts in England, in Contemporary problems in international arbitration, LEW, J. (ed.), London, School of international arbitration, Queen Mary College, 1986, 148; MUSTILL, M., The new lex mercatoria : the first twenty-five years, in Liber amicorum for Lord Wilberforce, BOS, M. and BROWNLIE, I. (ed.), Oxford, Clarendon Press, 1987, 149-182; WOOD, P., Law and practice of international finance, London, Sweet & Maxwell, 1980, 20; SLATER, R., The transnational law of syndicated loans - a hopeless case ?, in HORN, N. and SCHMITTHOFF, C. (ed.), The transnational law of international commercial transactions, Deventer, Kluwer, 1982, 330; COLLINS, L., Arbitration and the law governing contractual relations : an introductory report on the position in England, Basle symposium on the law governing contractual obligations, KLEIN, F.E. and VISCHER, F. (ed.), Basle, Helbing & Lichtenhahn, 1983, 70-73; COLLINS, L., The law governing the agreement and procedure in international arbitration in England, in Contemporary problems in international arbitration, LEW, J. (ed.), London, School of international arbitration, Queen Mary College, 1986, 136-138.

    For a rejection of Goldman's theory, see GOODE, R., The adaptation of English law to international commercial arbitration, ARB., 1992, 26-27.
63. MANN, F.A., Internationale Schiedsgerichte und nationale Rechtsordnung, ZHR, 1968, 97 ff., also published as Lex facit arbitrum, in International arbitration, Liber amicorum for Martin Domke, SANDERS, P. (ed.), The Hague, Martinus Nijhoff, 1967, 157 ff.; MANN, F.A., State contracts and international arbitration, Brit.Y.B.Int.L., 1967, 4-6; MANN, F.A., Schiedsrichter und Recht, Festschrift für Werner Flume, JAKOBS, H. (ed.), Cologne, Verlag Schmidt, 1978, 593 ff.; MANN, F.A., intervention during the discussions, Basle symposium on the law governing contractual obligations,

suggestion to apply autonomous conflict rules is categorically rejected[64] and arbitrations in which Goldman's theory would be followed, would lead to *ex aequo et bono* awards rendered without having been authorized to do so by the parties[65]. In this perspective, there is of course hardly any room to apply a formally autonomous *lex mercatoria*.

335. In France, the theory of the *lex mercatoria* has received ample attention. For a long time, proponents of the theory were clearly in a majority position. More recently, opponents have become more and more important. This development will hereafter be discussed.

336. At the University of Dijon where Goldman and Kahn have worked, their theories specifically[66] influenced Motulsky[67], Stoufflet[68], Fouchard,

---

KLEIN, F.E. and VISCHER, F. (ed.), Basle, Helbing & Lichtenhahn, 1983, 124-125; MANN, F.A., England rejects "delocalized" contracts and arbitration, INT'L & COMP.L.Q., 1984, 198.

64. MANN, F.A., Internationale Schiedsgerichte und nationale Rechtsordung, 104; MANN, F.A., Schiedsrichter und Recht, 615; MANN, F.A., Private arbitration and public policy, Civil Justice Quarterly, 1985, 264.
65. MANN, F.A., Schiedsrichter und Recht, 615; MANN, F.A., Staatsunternehmen in internationalen Handelsbeziehungen, RIW, 1987, 193; MANN, F.A., The proper law in the conflict of laws, INT'L & COMP.L.Q., 1987, 448.
66. See also SALEM, M. and SANSON-HERMITTE, M.A., Les contrats "clé en main" et les contrats "produit en main", Université de Dijon, Travaux du centre de recherche sur le droit des marchés et des investissements internationaux, Volume 5, Paris, Librairies techniques, 1979, 203; SANSON-HERMITTE, M.A., La notion de source de droit à l'épreuve du droit européen de la concurrence, in Le droit des relations économiques internationales, Etudes offertes à Berthold Goldman, Paris, Litec, 1982, 302.
67. MOTULSKY, H., L'internationalisation du droit français de l'arbitrage, in MOTULSKY, H., Ecrits, études et notes sur l'arbitrage, Paris, Dalloz, 1974, 325 and Rev.Arb., 1963, 110 ff.; MOTULSKY, H., L'exequatur des sentences étrangères non motivées, in MOTULSKY, H., Ecrits, études et notes sur l'arbitrage, Paris, Dalloz, 1974, 408 and Rev.Arb., 1967, 103 ff.
68. STOUFFLET, J., L'oeuvre normative de la Chambre de commerce internationale dans le domaine bancaire, 367-371; STOUFFLET, J., Payment and transfer in documentary letters of credit : interaction between the French general law of obligations and the uniform customs and practice, ARIZ.L.REV., 1982, 267-268.

Jacquemont[69], Loquin and Jehl[70]. Only the views of Fouchard and Loquin will here summarily be analyzed.

337. In his dissertation, Fouchard discussed the relation between the international business community's needs and international commercial arbitration[71]. He also found an anational legal system[72] which exists outside national legal systems[73]. This *lex mercatoria* consists of self-regulatory rules of professional organizations, usages, customs, general conditions, usual contractual clauses and techniques, arbitration rules, arbitral case law[74], general principles of private law and general principles of conflict of laws[75]. In two more respects, Fouchard has made an innovative contribution to the theory of the *lex mercatoria*. First, he has analyzed the distinction between custom and usages. In his opinion, the distinction is solely made because of procedural reasons; national courts cannot know all usages and parties must thus provide evidence as to their existence. Customs as rules of law should, on the contrary, not be proven and may also be reviewed by supreme courts. In international commercial arbitration, this rationale no longer applies. Arbitrators are presumed to know the usages of the trade and, for them, there would be no substantial difference between custom and usage[76]. Also, Fouchard has pointed out

---

69. JACQUEMONT, A., L'émission des emprunts euro-obligataires, Pouvoir bancaire et souverainetés étatiques, Université de Dijon, Travaux du centre de recherche sur le droit des marchés et des investissements internationaux, Volume 3, Paris, Librairies Techniques, 1976, 178-180 and 185. Jacquemont's major contribution has been to have shown that self-regulation at the international plane not only takes place in private law but also in the field of economic regulation (Ibid., 347).
70. JEHL, J., Le commerce international de la technologie, Approche juridique, Université de Dijon, Travaux du centre sur le droit des marchés et des investissements internationaux, Volume 10, Paris, Librairies Techniques, 1985, 105, 107-108 and 492.
71. FOUCHARD, P., L'arbitrage commercial international, Paris, Dalloz, 1965, 24-25, 48, 403 and 506.
72. FOUCHARD, P., L'arbitrage commercial international, 401-402.
73. FOUCHARD, P., L'arbitrage commercial international, 48.
74. FOUCHARD, P., L'arbitrage commercial international, 46 and 446.
75. FOUCHARD, P., La loi régissant les obligations contractuelles en droit international privé français, 105; FOUCHARD, P., L'arbitrage international en France après le décret du 12 mai 1981, 395-396; FOUCHARD, P., Le nouveau droit français de l'arbitrage, 45; FOUCHARD, P., L'arbitrage Elf Aquitaine Iran c/ National Iranian Oil Company, Une nouvelle contribution au droit international de l'arbitrage, Rev.Arb., 1984, 354-355.
76. FOUCHARD, P., L'arbitrage commercial international, 414; FOUCHARD, P., L'Etat face aux usages du commerce international, Trav.com.fr.dr.int.privé, 1973-75, Paris, Dalloz, 1977, 73; FOUCHARD, P., La loi régissant les obligations contractuelles en droit international privé français, 109.

that usages are applied irrespective of party acceptance under French[77], American, German, Italian and Swiss law and under article 13 ULFIS, article 9 ULIS and article 9 GISG[78]. Second, Fouchard has analyzed the process of applying general principles of law. He has suggested that only a limited number of legal systems would be compared from which a common position may be deduced. Faced with problems in finding such a common denominator, he would prefer to apply the rule which is most suited to solve the problem[79].

338. Another original contribution to the theory of the *lex mercatoria* was made by Loquin who analyzed *ex aequo et bono* arbitration (*amiable composition*) in a comparative and transnational setting[80]. Loquin made the link between *lex mercatoria* and amiable composition. If the parties have chosen the applicable law, the rules of the *lex mercatoria* may only be applied by virtue of the chosen law[81]. If the applicable law was not chosen, *amiable composition* may authorize the arbitrators directly to apply rules of the *lex mercatoria* without having to go through a conflict of laws analysis[82]. In a later publication, Loquin has stated that one cannot deny that in international commercial arbitration practice, anational customs and general principles of law are often applied. Under the perspective that not only the state but also other groups in society may create law (the so-called jurisprudence of legal pluralism), Loquin has expressed his willingness to see the *lex mercatoria* as an anational legal system[83].

---

77. Fouchard bases this view on article 1135 Cc (FOUCHARD, P., L'Etat face aux usages du commerce international, 83 and 99; FOUCHARD, P., La loi régissant les obligations contractuelles en droit international privé français, 201-202; FOUCHARD, P., L'arbitrage international en France après le décret du 12 mai 1981, 399; FOUCHARD, P., Les usages, l'arbitre et le juge, 66-67 and 78-79). Fouchard recognizes that this is not the prevailing point of view of French case law (FOUCHARD, P., L'Etat face aux usages du commerce international, 83-84).
78. FOUCHARD, P., L'Etat face aux usages du commerce international, 78-79 and 83.
79. FOUCHARD, P., L'arbitrage commercial international, 424.
80. LOQUIN, E., L'amiable composition en droit comparé et international, Contribution à l'étude du non-droit dans l'arbitrage commercial, Université de Dijon, Travaux du centre sur le droit des marchés et des investissements internationaux, Volume 7, Paris, Librairies techniques, 1980, 381 pp.
81. Ibid., 314.
82. Ibid., 325-331.
83. LOQUIN, E., L'application de règles anationales dans l'arbitrage commercial international, in L'apport de la jurisprudence arbitrale, INSTITUTE OF INTERNATIONAL BUSINESS LAW AND PRACTICE (ed.), Paris, I.C.C. publication No. 440/1, 1986, 73-75 and 113-119.

339. Other French authors also have endorsed the theory of the lex mercatoria[84]. One may particularly mention René David[85],

84. *E.g.*, KOPELMANAS, L., L'adaptation des règles juridiques du commerce international aux relations particulières entre les pays industrialisés et les pays en voie de développement, in Droit économique, Institut des Hautes Etudes Internationales de Paris, Paris, Pedone, 1978, 133; PEYREFITTE, L., Le problème du contrat dit "sans loi", D., 1965, 113; SCHAPIRA, J., Le droit international des affaires, Paris, Presses Universitaires de France, 1972, 11 and 14; JADAUD, B. and PLAISANT, R., Droit du commerce international, Paris, Dalloz, 1976, 54; LEVEL, P., Le contrat dit sans loi, Trav.com.fr.dr.int.privé, 1964-66, Paris, Dalloz, 1967, 212-213; LEVEL, P., La réforme de l'arbitrage international, J.C.P. éd.C.I., 1981, 246; LEVEL, P., case note French Supreme Court, December 9, 1981, J.C.P., 1983, 19971; GAUDEMET-TALLON, H., Réflexions comparatives sur certaines tendances nouvelles en matière de compétence internationale des juges et des arbitres, in Mélanges dédiés à Gabriël Marty, Université des sciences sociales de Toulouse, 1978, 548; LEDOUBLE, J., L'entreprise et le contrat, Paris, Librairies Techniques, 1980, 276-280; LE TOURNEAU, P., Quelques aspects de l'évolution des contrats, in Mélanges offerts à Pierre Raynaud, Paris, Dalloz, 1985, 379; Quel droit des affaires pour demain ?, Essai de prospective juridique, SAYAG, A. (ed.), Paris, Librairies Techniques, 1984, 74; GAILLARD, E., L'interdiction de se contredire au détriment d'autrui comme principe général du droit du commerce international, Rev.Arb., 1985, 241-242; GAILLARD, E., Centre International pour le règlement des différends relatifs aux investissements, Chronique des sentences arbitrales, Clunet, 1987, 141-143 and 156-157; GAILLARD, E., La distinction des principes généraux du droit et des usages du commerce international, Etudes offertes à Pierre Bellet, Paris, Litec, 1991, 203-217; DIENER, M., Contrats internationaux de propriété industrielle, Paris, Litec, 1986, 52, 56, 72 and 258-260; VASSEUR, M., Droit bancaire, D., Informations rapides, 1984, 201; MOULY, C., La doctrine, source d'unification internationale du droit, Rev.Int.Dr.Comp., 1986, 363; RANOUIL, V., Remarques sur le droit applicable aux contrats de développement, Gaz.Pal., 27-28 juni 1986, 4; MALAURIE, P., Le droit monétaire dans relations privées internationales, Academy for international law, 160 Collected Courses of The Hague, 1978, II, 280-281; AUDIT, B., Le caractère fonctionnel de la règle de conflit, Academy for international law, 186 Collected Courses of The Hague, 1984 III, 259; THIEFFRY, J. and GRANIER, C., La vente internationale, Paris, Centre français du commerce extérieur, 1985, 60-62.

85. DAVID, R., L'avenir de l'arbitrage, in International arbitration, Liber amicorum for Martin Domke, SANDERS, P. (ed.), The Hague, Martinus Nijhoff, 1967, 59; DAVID, R., Arbitrage et droit comparé, Rev.Int.Dr.Comp., 1959, 13; DAVID, R., Conception française et conception anglaise de l'arbitrage, in Miscellanea W.J. Ganshof Van Der Meersch, II, Brussels, Bruylant, 1972, 775; DAVID, R., Sources of law, in International Encyclopedia of Comparative Law, Tubingen, Mohr, 1984, 106 and 178; DAVID, R., Les méthodes de l'unification, in Le droit comparé, droits d'hier, droits de demain, Paris, Economica, 1982, 314 and AM.J.COMP.L., 1968, 13-27; DAVID, R., L'arbitrage dans le commerce international, Paris, Economica, 1982, 7, 106, 386, 431, 484-485 and 555; DAVID, R., The legal systems of the world, their comparison and unification, the international unification of private law, in International Encyclopedia of Comparative Law, Tubingen, Mohr, 1971, 66; DAVID, R., Le droit du commerce international : une nouvelle tâche pour les législateurs nationaux ou une nouvelle "lex

Loussouarn[86], Rubellin-Devichi[87], Toubiana[88], Deby-Gérard[89], Leymarie[90], Leboulanger[91], Simon[92], Oppetit, Jacquet, and Derains. Only the latter three authors will hereafter be discussed.

340. To a large extent, Oppetit may be counted among the proponents of the theory of the *lex mercatoria* as developed by Goldman[93]. His contribu-

---

mercatoria" ?, in New directions in international trade law, Acts and proceedings of the second congress on private law held by Unidroit, I, Dobbs Ferry, New York, Oceana, 1977, 16-19; DAVID, R., Unification du droit et arbitrage, in Le droit comparé, droits d'hier, droits de demain, Paris, Economica, 1982, 345, 349 and 351; DAVID, R., Renaissance de l'idée de ius gentium : une proposition française, in Le droit comparé, droits d'hier, droits de demain, 319-331; DAVID, R., Le droit du commerce international, Paris, Economica, 1988, 152 pp.

86. LOUSSOUARN, Y. and BREDIN, J.D., Droit du commerce international, Paris, Sirey, 1969, 11; LOUSSOUARN, Y., Cours général de droit international privé, Academy for international law, Collected Courses of The Hague, 1973, II, 287; LOUSSOUARN, Y. and BOUREL, P., Droit international privé, Paris, Dalloz, 1978, 75-76; LOUSSOUARN, Y., Le rôle de la méthode comparative en droit international privé français, R.C.D.I.P., 1979, 338-339; LOUSSOUARN, Y., intervention during the discussions, Basle symposium on the law governing contractual obligations, KLEIN, F.E. and VISCHER, F. (ed.), Basle, Helbing & Lichtenhahn, 1983, 131-132 and 183-185; LOUSSOUARN, Y., Arbitrage commercial international et droit du commerce international, J.T., 1982, 170.
87. RUBELLIN-DEVICHI, J., L'arbitrage, nature juridique, droit interne et droit international privé, Paris, LGDJ, 1965, 126-128.
88. TOUBIANA, A., Le domaine de la loi du contrat en droit international privé, Paris, Dalloz, 1972, 2 and 155.
89. DEBY-GERARD, F., Le rôle de la règle de conflit dans le règlement des rapports internationaux, Paris, Dalloz, 1973, 177 and 212.
90. LEYMARIE, F., Les usages commerciaux, dissertation, Bordeaux, 1970, 20 and 272.
91. LEBOULANGER, P., Les contrats entre Etats et entreprises étrangères, Paris, Economica, 1985, 221-225; LEBOULANGER, P., case note under French Supreme Court, January 6, 1987, Rev.Arb., 1987, 477.
92. SIMON, J., Le commerce international des céréales - Pouvoirs étatiques, pouvoirs économiques privés, dissertation, Paris II, 1982, 321-338 and 345.
93. OPPETIT, B., L'engagement d'honneur, D., 1979, 114; OPPETIT, B., La notion de source du droit et le droit du commerce international, Arch.Phil.Dr., 1982, 50-51; OPPETIT, B., Le développement des règles matérielles, Com.fr.dr.int.privé, meeting of November 23, 1985, mimeograph, Paris, 1985, 8-9 and 14; OPPETIT, B., Le paradoxe de la corruption à l'épreuve du droit du commerce international, Clunet, 1987, 16 and 18; OPPETIT, B., Eléments pour une sociologie de l'arbitrage, L'année sociologique, 1976, 194-195; OPPETIT, B., Le contrat d'émission d'euro-obligations, in Les euro-obligations, Université de Dijon, Travaux du centre de recherche sur le droit des marchés et des investissements internationaux, Volume 1, Paris, Librairies Techniques, 1972, 86-87; OPPETIT, B., Le trust dans le droit du commerce international, R.C.D.I.P., 1973, 6; OPPETIT, B., case note French Supreme Court, July 4, 1972, Clunet, 1972, 846 ; OPPETIT, B., case note Court of Appeal Paris, December 13, 1975, R.C.D.I.P., 1976, 514; OPPETIT, B., case note French Supreme Court, October 13,

tion to the theory of the *lex mercatoria* may be found in his analysis of general principles of law as a possible source of *lex mercatoria*. First, Oppetit distinguishes between non-legal principles, conceptual principles and legal principles[94]. Second, the distinction is made between principles of public international law, general principles of law applicable in transnational commerce and general principles common to the legal systems connected to the dispute[95].

341. In Jacquet's dissertation[96], the application of the *lex mercatoria* in international commercial arbitrations is explained against the background of the freedom of arbitrators to apply substantive rules without going through the conflict of laws process[97]. In this context, Jacquet acknowledges that some rules of the *lex mercatoria* may be applicable as substantive legal rules[98]. However, since the *lex mercatoria* still has many gaps and cannot be considered an autonomous legal system, the *lex mercatoria* cannot be identified with foreign law and, thus, conflicts with rules of legal systems could not be solved by a conflict rule[99].

342. Since 1974, extracts from I.C.C. arbitral awards have been published anually and many of these extracts have been commented by Yves Derains. In these notes, Derains has particularly noted that in international commercial arbitration specific dispute settlement methods and rules (such as those of the *lex mercatoria*) are being used. Application of the *lex mercatoria* is, in this perspective, welcome when the dispute is connected to more than two legal systems, because localization in a national legal system might then be rather arbitrary. Also, some international commercial transactions can hardly be localized in national law and, for multinational companies, it might be inconvenient to have a variety of national laws applied to their intra-group transactions. In both cases, application of the *lex mercatoria* might bring the solution[100]. This process is direct, without

---

1981, Court of Appeal Paris, June 12, 1980 and French Supreme Court, December 9, 1981, Clunet, 1982, 940.

94. Case note French Supreme Court, October 13, 1981, Paris, June 12, 1980 and French Supreme Court, December 9, 1981, Clunet, 1982, 937.
95. OPPETIT, B., Arbitrage et contrats d'Etat, L'arbitrage Framatome et autres c/ Atomic Energy organization of Iran, Clunet, 1984, 41 and 44-45.
96. JACQUET, J.M., Principe d'autonomie et contrats internationaux, Paris, Economica, 1983, 342 pp.
97. Ibid., 128-129.
98. Ibid., 125.
99. Ibid., 125-127.
100. DERAINS, Y., case note I.C.C. case No. 2375, Clunet, 1976, 976.

the need to look for a conflict rule[101]. Thus, one might apply as rules of the *lex mercatoria* usages[102], general principles of law[103] and mandatory rules forming a transnational public policy[104]. In this respect, some restraint should be exercised in applying national mandatory rules and the exception of international public policy of the applicable national law since this may frustrate the parties' legitimate expectations[105].

343. Until recently, only a small number of French authors was critical of the theory of the *lex mercatoria*[106]. In recent publications, some authors

---

101. DERAINS, Y., case note I.C.C. case Nos. 2745 and 2762, Clunet, 1978, 995.
102. DERAINS, Y., case note I.C.C. case Nos. 2745 and 2762, Clunet, 1978, 995; DERAINS, Y., case note I.C.C. case No. 2438, Clunet, 1976, 972; DERAINS, Y., case note I.C.C. case No. 3130, Clunet, 1981, 936 and DERAINS, Y., case note I.C.C. case No. 3894, Clunet, 1982, 990; DERAINS, Y., case note I.C.C. case No. 3202, Clunet, 1979, 1006.
103. DERAINS, Y., case note I.C.C. case No. 2291, Clunet, 1976, 989; DERAINS, Y., case note I.C.C. case No. 2520, Clunet, 1976, 993-994; DERAINS, Y., case note I.C.C. case No. 2404, Clunet, 1976, 996-997; DERAINS, Y., case note I.C.C. case No. 2508, Clunet, 1977, 943; DERAINS, Y., case note I.C.C. case No. 3380, Clunet, 1981, 931.
104. DERAINS, Y., case note I.C.C. case No. 2521, Clunet, 1976, 999; DERAINS, Y., case note I.C.C. case No. 3267, Clunet, 1980, 969; DERAINS, Y., case note I.C.C. case No. 3327, Clunet, 1982, 977; DERAINS, Y., case note I.C.C. case No. 3344, Clunet, 1982, 986-987.
105. DERAINS, Y., L'ordre public et le droit applicable au fond du litige dans l'arbitrage international, Rev.Arb., 1986, 381-383 and 390-392.
106. SALLE DE LA MARNIERRE, E., L'évolution technique du contrat et ses conséquences juridiques, Paris, Rousseau, 1930, 300; FRANCESCAKIS, P., Le principe jurisprudentiel de l'autonomie de l'accord compromissoire après l'arrêt Hecht de la Cour de Cassation, Rev.Arb., 1974, 84; MEZGER, E., intervention during the discussions, in Materielles Recht und Verfahrensrecht in der internationalen Schiedsgerichtsbarkeit, COING, H. (ed.), Frankfurt, Metzner, 1972, 51; BREDIN, J.D., La Convention de New-York du 10 juin 1958 pour la reconnaissance et l'exécution des sentences arbitrales étrangères, Clunet, 1960, 1026; BREDIN, J.D., La loi du juge, in Le droit des relations économiques internationales, Etudes offertes à Berthold Goldman, Paris, Litec, 1982, 26-27; BREDIN, J.D., L'amiable composition et le contrat, Rev.Arb., 1984, 270; DELAUME, G.R., Les stipulations de droit applicable dans les accords de prêt et de développement économique et de leur rôle, R.B.D.I., 1968, 363; EISEMANN, F., Die Incoterms im internationalen Warenkaufrecht, Stuttgart, Enke Verlag, 1967, 31, 51 and 64-65; EISEMANN, F., Die Incoterms in Handel und Verkehr, Wenen, GOF-Verlag Friedl, 1963, 19; EISEMANN, F., Die Incoterms im Recht des internationalen Warenhandels : Außerstaatliche Rechtsbildung oder Vertragsrecht, in XII Yearbook of the School of law and economic science, Aristotelian University of Thessaloniki, Miscellany in honor of C. Fragistas, Deel II, Thessaloniki, 1967, 329; EISEMANN, F., La clause d'arbitrage pathologique, in Arbitrage commercial, Essais in memoriam Eugenio Minoli, Associazione italiana per l'arbitrato, Rome, 1974, 146; *but see* EISEMANN, F., Le phénomène de l'arbitrage, son utilité, ses avantages et son rôle, Rev.Dr.Int.Comp., 1976, 106; EISEMANN, F., Le nouveau règlement d'arbitrage

have strongly opposed the theory of the *lex mercatoria* as developed by Goldman. Hereafter, the opinions of Batiffol, Lagarde, Mayer, Béguin and Kassis will shortly be discussed[107].

344. Batiffol has expressed his scepticism regarding the theory of the *lex mercatoria*, but cannot truly be considered an outspoken opponent of it. The main reason for Batiffol's scepticism is his distrust for self-regulation if the public interest and private interests, other than those of a given community, are not sufficiently considered[108]. However, if that condition is met, some general conditions or some transactions which are difficult to localize, might be governed by the *lex mercatoria*. This process should not, however, be extended to all kinds of contracts or all contractual problems[109] because the predictability of international business law might be put at risk[110]. The main disadvantages of the *lex mercatoria* are its lack of coherence and autonomy. As to the former, Batiffol has doubted whether

---

de la Chambre de Commerce internationale, D.P.C.I., 1975, 362; EISEMANN, F., The Court of arbitration : outline of its changes from inception to the present day, in International arbitration, 60 years of ICC arbitration, A look at the future, International Chamber of Commerce, publication No. 412, Paris, 1984, 398.

107. Other authors, recently, have joined these critics, see BELLET, P., intervention during the discussions, Basle symposium on the law governing contractual obligations, KLEIN, F.E. and VISCHER, F. (ed.), Basle, Helbing & Lichtenhahn, 1983, 133-134; BELLET, P. and MEZGER, E., L'arbitrage international dans le nouveau code de procédure civile, R.C.D.I.P., 1981, 633; MERCADAL, B., Les caractéristiques juridiques des contrats internationaux de coopération industrielle, D.P.C.I., 1984, 328; BAPTISTA, L. and DURAND-BARTHEZ, P., Les associations d'entreprises (joint ventures) dans le commerce international, Paris, Feduci, LGDJ, 1986, III and 88; BEN ABDERRAHMANE, D., Le droit allemand des conditions générales des contrats dans les ventes commerciales franco-allemandes, Paris, LGDJ, 1985, 82-83; ZAKI, M.S., Le formalisme conventionnel, Illustration de la notion de contrat-cadre, Rev.Int.Dr.Comp., 1986, 1089; HOLLEAUX, D., FOYER, J. and DE GEOUFFRE DE LA PRADELLE, G., Droit international privé, Paris, Masson, 1987, 343; LESGUILLONS, H., Contrats internationaux, Paris, Lamy, Volume 1, Division 2, Articles 274-284; ROBERT, J., Le phénomène transnational, Paris, LGDJ, 1988, 23-34.

108. BATIFFOL, H., Réflexions sur la coordination des systèmes nationaux, Academy for international lw, 120 Collected Courses of The Hague, 1967, I, 172; BATIFFOL, H. and LAGARDE, P., Droit international privé, II, seventh edition, Paris, LGDJ, 1983, 288.

109. BATIFFOL, H., L'état du droit international privé en France et dans l'Europe continentale de l'Ouest, Clunet, 1973, 31; BATIFFOL, H., Le pluralisme des méthodes en droit international privé, 123-124; BATIFFOL, H., Problèmes de base de philosophie du droit, 109.

110. BATIFFOL, H., Aspects philosophiques du droit international privé, Paris, Dalloz, 1956, 70-77; BATIFFOL, H., Conflict avoidance in European law, LAW & CONTEMP.PROBS., 1956, 580; BATIFFOL, H., Les contrats en droit international privé comparé, Mc Gill University, 1981, 83-84.

general principles of law may fill the gaps of the *lex mercatoria* in the absence of an authority with competence to determine these principles[111]. As to autonomy, judicial review by national authorities cannot be excluded[112], even regarding arbitral awards[113], which implies that national rules may still have their say in the resolution of international business litigation.

345. Lagarde is much more critical than Batiffol. In Lagarde's opinion, no single international business community exists, but rather many subcommunities have developed their own rules. There is not one single *lex mercatoria* but rather many *leges mercatoriae* coexist[114] which excludes that the *lex mercatoria* may be seen as a single legal system[115]. Also, national courts cannot apply the *lex mercatoria* since they have to follow their own conflict rules. Since the *lex mercatoria* pretends to be directly applicable to international business transactions, its application by national courts would entail a violation of their conflict rules[116].

Lagarde also fiercely attacked the sources of the *lex mercatoria.* International conventions and international substantive rules are not sources of the *lex mercatoria* but sources of public international law and national law[117]. Neither are contract clauses and techniques sources of the *lex mercatoria,* since they are based on the principle of freedom of contract contained in the applicable national law[118]. Finally, general principles of law are sources of public international law or are derived from national law which implies that they may barely be seen as sources of the *lex mercatoria*[119].

---

111. BATIFFOL, H., Les contrats en droit international privé comparé, 153; BATIFFOL, H. and LAGARDE, P., Droit international privé, I, 405 and II, 287.
112. BATIFFOL, H., Problèmes de base de philosophie du droit, 109.
113. BATIFFOL, H., L'arbitrage et les conflits de lois, Rev.Arb., 1957, 112; BATIFFOL, H., Le pluralisme des méthodes en droit international privé, Academy of international law, 139 Collected Courses of The Hague, 1973, II, 125; BATIFFOL, H., Problèmes de base de philosophie du droit, Paris, LGDJ, 1979, 108 and 110.
114. LAGARDE, P., Approche critique de la lex mercatoria, in Le droit des relations économiques internationales, Etudes offertes à Berthold Goldman, Paris, Litec, 1982, 135-136, 139.
115. Ibid., 138-139.
116. Ibid., 144-146.
117. Ibid., 128.
118. Ibid., 129-130.
119. Ibid., 131-132.

346. A similar criticism has been expressed by Mayer[120], who argued that usages[121] and general conditions are dependent on the will of the parties which is determined by the applicable law[122]. In a recent publication, Mayer made the link between the theory of the *lex mercatoria* and jurisprudence. He noted that the theory of the *lex mercatoria* had failed to clearly admit that arbitrators are not so much applying transnational legal rules of *lex mercatoria* but are rather creating these rules. This autonomous process of arbitral adjudication is an essential feature of the arbitral process and is not derived from any municipal law giving binding effect to this process[123].

347. In an extensive article, Béguin has made an intelligent analysis of the assumptions on which the theory of the *lex mercatoria* is based. The success of the theory is not only explained by the fact that it meets the wish to have international business problems regulated by more appropriate rules but is also due to the desire within the international business community for self-regulation[124]. These two elements are clearly reflected in the theory of the *lex mercatoria*. The assumptions are thus that international business life has a sufficient degree of specificity which implies that it would need specific rules, other than those which apply to national transactions, and that self-regulation should not unduly be restricted[125]. Even it the first assumption were correct, it would not necessarily need a regulation outside national law[126]. As to the second assumption, it is stated by Béguin that self-regulation is not a law in itself and needs the support of the applicable national law[127].

348. The most outspoken critic of the theory of the *lex mercatoria* is Kassis, the Syrian lawyer living in France, who did research as to the legal status of trade usages. Kassis comes to the conclusion that trade usages are not a formal source of law and depend upon the will of the parties[128].

---

120. MAYER, P., Droit international privé, second edition, Paris, Montchrestien, 1983, 20.
121. Ibid., 558.
122. Ibid., 19.
123. MAYER, P., L'autonomie de l'arbitre international dans l'appréciation de sa propre compétence, Academy of international law, 217 Collected Course of The Hague, 1989, V, 392 and 453-454.
124. BEGUIN, J., Le développement de la lex mercatoria menace-t-il l'ordre juridique international ?, Mc GILL L.J., 1985, 485.
125. Ibid., 494.
126. Ibid., 494-495.
127. Ibid., 498.
128. KASSIS, A., Théorie générale des usages du commerce, Paris, LGDJ, 1984, 125, 129, 133, 310, 330.

Because the parties may always derogate from usages, no customs may be formed. Therefore, the mere fact that the parties know that they may contract out of usages would, according to Kassis, imply that these usages are never seen as legal rules that have to be observed. Thus, the psychological element in the formation of custom is always lacking[129]. Since trade usages are not formal sources of law, they cannot be considered a genuine source of the *lex mercatoria*[130].

349. In Switzerland, the theory of the *lex mercatoria* also received attention, although not on the same scale as in France. Contrary to France, there is no prevailing view in Switzerland. Proponents and opponents of the theory are in balance. Hereafter, only the most important authors will briefly be discussed[131].

350. The most important Swiss proponent of the theory of the *lex mercatoria* is Pierre Lalive who has accepted that non-national conflict rules exist according to which parties may choose the rules which are applicable to their relation and may, thus, choose not to have national law applied[132]. Also, Lalive has argued that in international commercial arbitration, the question is not so important to know whether the *lex*

---

129. Ibid., 160-177.

130. Ibid., 300, 381-384, 399-400, 423-424; KASSIS, A., L'arbitre, les conflits de lois et la lex mercatoria, in Proceedings of the first international commercial arbitration conference, ANTAKI, N. and PRUJINER, A. (ed.), Université Laval, Wilson & Lafleur, Montréal, 1986, 133-143.

131. *Proponents* : SCHNITZER, A., Die Einordnung der internationalen Sachverhalte in das Rechtssystem, in Internationales Recht und Wirtschaftsordnung, Festschrift für F.A. Mann, Munich, Beck, 1977, 300-301; GENTINETTA, J., Die lex fori internationaler Handelsschiedsgerichte, Bern, Stämpfli, 1973, 148 and 192; BUCHER, A., Transnationales Recht im ipr, in Aktuelle Fragen aus der Sicht in- und ausländischer Gelehrter, SCHWIND, F. (ed.), Vienna, 1986, 48-51; BUCHER, A., Le nouvel arbitrage international en Suisse, Basle, Helbing & Lichtenhahn, 1988, 97-103; BUCHER, A. and TSCHANZ, P.Y., International arbitration in Switzerland, Basle, Helbing & Lichtenhahn, 1988, 113-120; BLESSING, M., Das neue internationale Schiedsgerichtsrecht der Schweiz, in Die internationale Schiedsgerichtsbarkeit in der Schweiz (II), BÖCKSTIEGEL, K.H., (ed.), Cologne, Heymanns, 1989, 69; *opponents* : LUITHLEN, W., Einheitliches Kaufrecht und autonomes Handelsrecht, Freiburg, Universitätsverlag, 1956, 20; RIESE, O., Über die methoden der internationalen Vereinheitlichung des Privatrechts, Zschwr 1967, I, 12-14; PETER, W., Arbitration and renegotiation of international investment agreements, Dordrecht, Nijhoff, 1986, 176.

132. LALIVE, P., Problèmes relatifs à l'arbitrage international commercial, Academy of international law, 120 Collected Courses of The Hague, 1967, I, 649; LALIVE, P., Les règles de conflit de lois appliquées au fond du litige par l'arbitre international siégeant en Suisse, in L'arbitrage international privé et la Suisse, Geneva, Librairie Georg, 1977, 95; LALIVE, P., Sur une notion de contrat "international", 1980, 148.

mercatoria is a legal system, because arbitrators are mostly concerned with specific problems asking for specific solutions. Finally, Lalive is optimistic as to the predictability of dispute resolution taking place through the application of the *lex mercatoria* (including its general principles of law). In his opinion, conflict rules and application of foreign law do not necessarily create less uncertainty in international business litigation[133].

351. Klein and Vischer have remained sceptical as to the theory of the *lex mercatoria*, which is considered uncertain and full of gaps. In Klein's opinion, the theory is too indebted to a jurisprudence influenced by principles of natural justice and the *lex mercatoria* also is preempted by mandatory provisions of national law or dependent on national law for its enforcement[134]. Vischer has stressed the fact that the *lex mercatoria* does not guarantee protection of so-called weaker parties and, at the most, can be incorporated by the parties into their contract[135].

---

133. LALIVE, P., Problèmes relatifs à l'arbitrage international commercial, 643; LALIVE, P., intervention during the discussions, Basle symposium on the law governing contractual obligations, KLEIN, F.E. and VISCHER, F. (ed.), Basle, Helbing & Lichtenhahn, 1983, 135 and 200; LALIVE, P., On the neutrality of the arbitrator and of the place of arbitration, in Recueil de travaux suisses sur l'arbitrage international, REYMOND, C. and BUCHER, E. (ed.), Zurich, Schulthess, 1984, 28; LALIVE, P., Sur la bonne foi dans l'exécution des contrats d'état, in Mélanges offerts à Raymond Vander Elst, Volume 1, Brussels, Nemesis, 1986, 436.

134. KLEIN, F.E., La Convention de New York pour la reconnaissance et l'exécution des sentences arbitrales étrangères, Schweizerische Juristenzeitung, 1961, 230; KLEIN, F.E., Internationale Schiedsverfahren und nationale Rechtsordnungen, Ann. suisse Dr.Int., 1967, 98; KLEIN, F.E., De l'autorité de la loi dans les rapports commerciaux internationaux, in Internationales Recht und Wirtschaftsordnung, Festschrift für F.A. Mann, Munich, Beck, 1977, 632-633; KLEIN, F.E., Die internationale Schiedsgerichtsbarkeit und die schweizerische Rechtsordnung, in Die internationale Schiedsgerichtbarkeit in der Schweiz, BÖCKSTIEGEL, K.H. (ed.), Cologne, Heymanns, 1979, 45; KLEIN, F.E., intervention during the discussions, Basle symposium on the law governing contractual obligations, KLEIN, F.E. and VISCHER, F. (ed.), Basle, Helbing & Lichtenhahn, 1983, 171-172; KLEIN, F.E., The law to be applied by the arbitrators to the substance of the dispute, in The art of arbitration, Essays on international arbitration, Liber amicorum Pieter Sanders, SCHULTSZ, J.C. and VAN DEN BERG, A.J. (ed.), Deventer, Kluwer, 1982, 196.

135. VISCHER, F., intervention during the discussions, in Basle symposium on the law governing contractual obligations, KLEIN, F.E. and VISCHER, F.(ed.), Basle, Helbing & Lichtenhahn, 1983, 137-138 and 181; see also HEINI, A., Die Rechtswahl im Vertragsrecht und das neue IPR-Gesetz, Beiträge zum neuen IPR des Sachen-, Schuld- und Gesellschaftsrechts, Festschrift für Rudolf Moser, SCHWANDER, I. (ed.), Zurich, Schulthess, 1987, 72 and SCHWANDER, I., Lois d'application immédiate, Sonderanknüpfung, IPR-Sachnormen und andere Ausnahmen von der gewöhnlichen Anknüpfung im internationalen Privatrecht, Zurich, Schulthess, 1975, 397-399.

352. In his recent dissertation on the theory of the *lex mercatoria* as applied in international commercial arbitrations[136], Felix Dasser has reviewed the autonomist conception of the theory as it was developed by Goldman in France. He concludes that the *lex mercatoria* should not be seen as a legal system, but rather as autonomous rules consisting of trade usages and general principles of law, which are applied in international commercial arbitrations. However, other sources such as general conditions, codes of conduct, international conventions, public international law or arbitral case law, may not be qualified as genuine sources of the *lex mercatoria*. In international commercial arbitration practice, the impact of the *lex mercatoria* is, according to Dasser, important because it may be applied without national courts being able to review the award at all on its merits. On the other hand, Dasser has doubted whether choice of law by the parties for the *lex mercatoria* may be a very sensible approach.

353. In Germany, much attention has been paid to the theory of the *lex mercatoria*. In contrast with other countries, both the conceptions of Schmitthoff and Goldman have been analyzed. The prevailing theory in Germany is sceptical and even opposed to Goldman's autonomist theory on the *lex mercatoria*; only a minority view has endorsed Goldman's conception. The most important elements of these positions will hereafter

---

136. DASSER, F., Internationale Schiedsgerichte und lex mercatoria, Rechtsvergleichender Beitrag zur Diskussion über ein nichtstaatliches Handelsrecht, Zurich, Schulthess, 1989, 408 pp.; for a more extensive review of this dissertation, see DE LY, F., book review, AM.J.COMP.L. 1991, 601-603; *adde* DASSER, F., Lex mercatoria : Werkzeug der Praktiker oder Spielzeug der Lehre, Schweizerische Zeitschrift für internationales und europäisches Recht, 1991, 299-323.

be mentioned[137]; a complete review would fall outside the scope of this book[138].

---

137. Many authors also have noted the disputes without taking a position; see DROBNIG, U., intervention during the discussions, Basle symposium on the law governing contractual obligations, KLEIN, F.E. and VISCHER, F. (ed.), Basle, Helbing & Lichtenhahn, 1983, 146-147; BARTELS, M., Contractual adaptation and conflict resolution, Deventer, Kluwer, 1985, 125; GLOSSNER, O., The influence of the International Chamber of Commerce upon modern arbitration, in International arbitration, 60 years of ICC arbitration, A look to the future, International Chamber of Commerce, Publication No. 412, Paris, 1984, 402-403; GLOSSNER, O., Die lex mercatoria - Vision oder Wirklichkeit, RIW, 1984, 350; JOERGES, C., Vorüberlegungen zu einer Theorie des internationalen Wirtschaftsrechts, RabelsZ, 1979, 6; SCHLECHTRIEM, P., Einheitliches UN-Kaufrecht, Tubingen, Mohr, 1981, 2; TRIEBEL, V. and VIERTEL, B., Die Bundesrepublik Deutschland wird als Schiedsgerichtsort im internationalen Schiedsverfahren gemieden, BB 1986, 1169; PETERSMANN, E., "Entwicklungsvölkerrecht", "Droit international du développement", "International economic development law" : Mythos oder Wirklichkeit ?, Jahrbuch für internationales Recht, Berlin, Duncker & Humblot, 1975, 172-173; SCHLESINGER, R. and GUNDISCH, H.J., Allgemeine Rechtsgrundsätze als Sachnormen in Schiedsgerichtsverfahren, RabelsZ, 1964, 45.
138. *Opponents* : VON CAEMMERER, E., The influence of the law of international trade on the development and character of the commercial law in the civil law countries, in The sources of the law of international trade, SCHMITTHOFF, C. (ed.), London, Stevens & Sons, 1964, 88 ff., Gesammelte Schriften, I, Tubingen, Mohr, 1968, 11 ff.; VON CAEMMERER, E., Measures for unifying the rules on choice of law, in Unification of the law governing international sales of goods, HONNOLD, J. (ed.), Paris, Dalloz, 1966, 323; BÄRMANN, J., Ist internationales Handelsrecht kodifizierbar ?, in Internationales Recht und Wirtschaftsordnung, Festschrift für F.A. Mann, Munich, Beck, 1977, 553, 564 and 569; LORENZ, W., Formularpraxis und Rechtsvereinheitlichung im internationalen Kaufrecht, ZHR, 1964, 152; WENGLER, W., Les principes généraux du droit en tant que loi du contrat, R.C.D.I.P., 1982, 496; WENGLER, W., BGB-RGRK, twelfth edition, Volume VI/II, Berlin, de Gruyter, 1981, 1301; MULLER-FREIENFELS, W., intervention during the discussions, Basle symposium on the law governing contractual obligations, KLEIN, F.E. and VISCHER, F. (ed.), Basle, Helbing & Lichtenhahn, 1983, 149-150; GOERKE, E., Kollisionsrechtliche Probleme internationaler Garantien, Konstanz, Universitätsverlag, 1982, 61-62; KONIG, A., Die internationalprivatrechtliche Anknüpfung von syndicated loan agreements, Konstanz, Universitätsverlag, 1984, 115-117; PFAFF, D., International licensing contracts, transfer of technology and transnational law, in The transnational law of international commercial transactions, HORN, N. and SCHMITTHOFF, C. (ed.), Deventer, Kluwer, 1982, 209; STOLL, J., Vereinbarungen zwischen Staat und ausländischem Investor, 46-50; VON BREITENSTEIN, D., Die internationale Arbitrage im französischen Recht, in Schiedsgerichtsbarkeit in Frankreich, BÖCKSTIEGEL, K.H. (ed.), Cologne, Heymanns, 1983, 39, 40 and 43; EBENROTH, C., Das Vertragsrecht der internationalen Konsortialkredite und Projektfinanzierungen, JZ, 1986, 735.

354. The most important German proponent of the *lex mercatoria* as developed by Schmitthoff, is Norbert Horn. In order to understand international business law, account should be taken of customary rules and practices existing within sufficiently organized communities[139]. These rules are still growing in the euro-bond markets[140] and also, as has been shown by empirical research conducted under Horn's supervision by Hinsch, Dunnweber and Schlüter in relation to the euroloan markets, turnkey projects and management- and advice contracts[141]. This transnational law has two main characteristics; it is uniform[142] and autonomous[143]. Just like Schmitthoff, autonomy is used in a specific meaning and related to the substantive sources of international business law. However, it does not intend to suggest that international business law would exist outside national legal systems. Gaps still have to be filled by national law and enforcement of self-regulatory rules may also depend on national legal systems[144]. Finally, Horn has pointed out that one has to realize that transnational custom developed by the business community or subparts

---

139. HORN, N., Das Recht der internationalen Anleihen, 519-521 and 529; HORN, N., Das neue luxemburgische Recht der représentation fiduciaire für obligationäre, in Recht und Wirtschaft in Geschichte und Gegenwart, Festschrift für Johannes Bärmann, Munich, Beck, 1975, 506.
140. HORN, N., Das Recht der internationalen Anleihen, 531-532.
141. HINSCH, C. and HORN, N., Das Vertragsrecht der internationalen Konsortialkredite und Projektfinanzierungen, Berlin, de Gruyter, 1985, 196-198; DUNNWEBER, I., Vertrag zur Erstellung einer schlüsselfertigen Industrieanlage im internationalen Wirtschaftsverkehr, Berlin, de Gruyter, 1984, 167-168; SCHLÜTER, A., Management- und Consultingverträge, Berlin, de Gruyter, 1987, 5-7 and 214.
142. HORN, N., Uniformity and diversity in the law of international commercial contracts, in The transnational law of international commercial transactions, HORN, N. and SCHMITTHOFF, C. (ed.), Deventer, Kluwer, 1982, 13-15; see also KAPPUS, A., "lex mercatoria" in Europa und Wiener Kaufrechtskonvention 1980, Frankfurt, Lang, 1990, 133 and 156.
143. Ibid., 15-16; HORN, N., Die Anpassung langfristiger Verträge im internationalen Wirtschaftsverkehr, in Die Anpassung langfristiger Verträge, KÖTZ, H. and Frhr. MARSCHALL VON BIEBERSTEIN, W. (ed.), Frankfurt, Metzner, 1984, 45-46; HORN, N., Das chinesische Außenwirtschaftsvertragsgesetz von 1985, RIW, 1985, 691.
144. HORN, N., Das Recht der internationalen Anleihen, 535; HORN, N., Der Einfluß monetärer Risiken auf den internationalen Handel und Kapitalverkehr und die Möglichkeit rechtlicher und wirtschaftlicher Risikokontrollen, in Monetäre Probleme im internationalen Handel und Kapitalverkehr, HORN, N. (ed.), Baden-Baden, Nomos, 1976, 29; HORN, N., Die Entwicklung des internationalen Wirtschaftsrechts durch Verhaltensrichtlinien, RabelsZ, 1980, 450-451.

thereof may not sufficiently encompass ethical rules to be observed in international trade[145].

355. Kurt Siehr developed a conception of the *lex mercatoria* which comes very close to Schmitthoff's and Horn's. In his opinion, the *lex mercatoria* is a part of national law where parties may find sufficient freedom to make self-regulatory rules and which may provide for rules which are adapted to international trade and correspond to similar rules in other jurisdictions[146]. There is, however, one major difference between Siehr and Schmitthoff/Horn. Contrary to the latter, Siehr does not restrict the sources of the *lex mercatoria* to international sources, since statutory law and national case law containing specific rules for transnational commerce are included in his definition of the *lex mercatoria*[147]. Moreover, Siehr rejects a conception in which this uniform law would be restricted to business law and has pleaded for uniform rules applicable to all private relations (and not merely applicable to commercial transactions)[148].

356. Few German authors have defended Goldman's theory on the *lex mercatoria*[149]. One notable exception is Weise who, to a certain extent, argued in favour of Goldman's theory. He uses an extensive definition of the *lex mercatoria* encompassing custom, trade usages, international conventions, model laws, general conditions, general principles of law and arbitral case law. These are considered as forming a legal system which might be applied in the context of arbitration. Their application depends, however, upon a choice of law in favour of the *lex mercatoria*, an *amiable*

---

145. HORN, N., Codes of conduct for MNEs and transnational lex mercatoria : an international process of learning and law making, 61; HORN, N., Die Entwicklung des internationalen Wirtschaftsrechts durch Verhaltensrichtlinien, 450-451.

146. SIEHR, K., Sachrecht im IPR, transnationales Recht und lex mercatoria, in Internationales Privatrecht, internationales Wirtschaftsrecht, HOLL, W. and KLINKE, U. (ed.), Cologne, Heymanns, 1985, 115-117; KELLER, M. and SIEHR, K., Allgemeine Lehren des internationalen Privatrechts, Zurich, Schulthess, 1986, 101-102.

147. SIEHR, K., Sachrecht im IPR, transnationales Recht und lex mercatoria, 118-122 and 125.

148. SIEHR, K., Sachrecht im IPR, transnationales Recht und lex mercatoria, 125; see also JUENGER, F., Afterword : the lex mercatoria and the conflict of laws, 221-222.

149. See COING, H., La détermination de la loi contractuelle en droit international privé allemand, Basle symposium on the law governing contractual obligations, KLEIN, F.E. and VISCHER, F. (ed.), Basle, Helbing & Lichtenhahn, 1983, 50-53; LORENZ, E., Die Rechtswahlfreiheit im internationalen Schuldvertragsrecht, RIW, 1987, 569-584; BERGER, K.P., Internationale Wirtschaftsschiedsgerichtsbarkeit, 369 ff.

composition-clause or specific factors which point to application of non-national rules[150].

357. One of the first German critics of the theory of the *lex mercatoria* has been Langen. Langen had emphasized the role of general conditions and arbitration for international commercial transactions[151] but refused to give these autonomous status[152]. On the other hand, the traditional conflict method also is unsatisfactory[153]. As an alternative, Langen then proposes a *transnational method* which will be discussed later[154].

358. Most German conflict of laws and comparative law scholars have rejected Goldman's autonomist conception of the *lex mercatoria*. The arguments may be summarized as follows. First, there is a widespread belief that choice of law is imbedded in national law. Thus, parties may only choose the law to be applied to their contract to the extent permitted under the applicable law. A choice of non-national rules, self-regulatory rules, general principles of law or the *lex mercatoria* will depend upon the applicable national law[155]. Any such choice is, therefore, not a choice on

---

150. WEISE, P.F., Lex mercatoria, Materielles Recht vor der internationalen Handelsschiedsgerichtsbarkeit, Frankfurt, Lang, 1990, 111-116 and 137-142.

151. LANGEN, E., Studien zum internationalen Wirtschaftsrecht, Munich, Beck, 1963, 9.

152. LANGEN, E., Transnational commercial law, Leyden, Sijthoff, 1973, IX and 11-12; LANGEN, E., Transnationales Recht, Heidelberg, Verlagsgesellschaft Recht und Wirtschaft, 1981, 39; LANGEN, E., Vom internationalen Privatrecht zum transnationalen Handelsrecht, N.J.W., 1969, 358-359.

153. LANGEN, E., Vom internationalen Privatrecht zum transnationalen Handelsrecht, 358; LANGEN, E., Transnational commercial law, IX.

154. See infra No. 471.

155. STEINDORFF, E., Autonomy of contracting parties in international commerce - an economic evaluation, in New directions in international trade law, Acts and proceedings of the second congress on private law held by Unidroit, I, Dobbs Ferry, New York, Oceana, 1977, 87 ff.; KEGEL, G., The crisis of conflict of laws, Academy of international law, Collected Courses of The Hague, 1964, II, 260-261; KEGEL, G., Internationales Privatrecht, fifth edition, Munich, Beck, 1985, 61; KEGEL, G., Zum heutigen Stand des internationalen Privatrechts : Theorie und Rechtspolitik, in Internationales Privatrecht, internationales Wirtschaftsrecht, HOLL, W. and KLINKE, U. (ed.), Cologne, Heymanns, 1985, 10-11; FIRSCHING, K., Internationales Schuldrecht I, in VON STAUDINGER, Kommentar zum BGB, Internationales Privatrecht, Berlin, Schweitzer, 1978, 350-351 and 357; VON BAR, C., Internationales Privatrecht, Volume 1, Munich, Beck, 1987, 79-81; VON BAR, C., Typen des internationalen Einheitsrecht und das internationale Privatrecht, in Recht und Wirtschaft, Osnabrücker Rechtswissenschaftliche Abhandlungen, Volume 1, Cologne, Heymanns, 1985, 28-33; MünchKomm-Sonnenberger, IPR Einleitung, Munich, Beck, 1983, 48-49; KROPHOLLER, J., Internationales Einheitsrecht, Allgemeine Lehren, Tubingen, Mohr, 1975,121-122; KROPHOLLER, J., Die Wissenschaft als Quelle der

the conflict of laws level but at the substantive level (*materiellrechtliche Verweisung*). This implies that parties may only incorporate these non-national rules into their contract but cannot isolate the contract from the applicable national law[156].

Second, some authors have emphasized the fact that the *lex mercatoria* is not an autonomous legal system because it has no mechanism to fill gaps. General principles of law are, in this respect, too indefinite and incomplete[157] to assume a gap filling function. Also, they are mostly derived from national law[158].

359. German specialists on international commercial arbitration law have, in general, also been sceptical towards the theory of the *lex mercatoria*[159].

---

internationalen Rechtsvereinheitlichung, Zvglrwiss 1986, 153; KREUZER, K., Einheitsrecht als Ersatzrecht, Zur Frage der Nichtermittelbarkeit fremden Rechts, NJW, 1983, 1947; SANDROCK, O. and STEINSCHULTE, F.P., Grundfragen des internationalen Vertragsrecht : die kollisionsrechtliche Anknüpfung von Schuldverträgen, in SANDROCK, O. (ed.), Handbuch der internationalen Vertragsgestaltung, Volume 1, Heidelberg, Verlagsgesellschaft Recht und Wirtschaft, 1980, 101-102; SANDROCK, O., Choice of law and choice of forum in civil law jurisdictions, in Drafting and enforcing contracts in civil and common law jurisdictions, Deventer, Kluwer, 1986, 162-165; SANDROCK, O., Die Fortbildung des materiellen Rechts durch die Internationale Schiedsgerichtsbarkeit, in Fortbildung durch die Internationale Schiedsgerichtsbarkeit, BÖCKSTIEGEL, K.H. (ed.), Cologne, Heymanns, 1989, 53-54 and 77-80; OTTO, H.H., Allgemeine Geschäftsbedingungen und internationales Privatrecht, 152; SCHURIG, K., Kollisionsnorm und Sachrecht, 331-332; ROTH, W.H., Internationales Versicherungsvertragsrecht, Tubingen, Mohr, 1985, 542-557.

156. BÖCKSTIEGEL, K.H., Der Staat als Vertragspartner ausländischer Privatunternehmen, 141-142 and 375; MünchKomm-Martiny, Vor Art.12, Munich, Beck, 1983, 540; TROST, U., Bankgarantien im Außenhandel: Die "Einheitlichen Richtlinien für Vertragsgarantien" der internationalen Handelskammer von 1978, Seggebruch, GFU-Verlagsgesellschaft, 1982, 154-156 and 171.

157. *E.g.*, formation of contracts, vices of consent, interpretation and statute of limitations cited and analyzed in REIMANN, T., Zur Lehre vom "rechtsordnungslosen" Vertrag, Bonn, Röhrscheid Verlag, 1970, 80-94; see also LORENZ, W., Die Lex Mercatoria : eine internationale Rechtsquelle ?, in Festschrift für K. Neumayer, Baden-Baden, Nomos, 1985, 428-429; LORENZ, W., Vom alten zum neuen internationalen Schuldvertragsrecht, IPRax, 1987, 272.

158. REIMANN, T., Zur Lehre vom "rechtsordnungslosen" Vertrag, 30-31, 50 and 53.

159. SCHLOSSER, P., Das Recht der internationalen privaten Schiedsgerichtsbarkeit, I, second edition, Tubingen, Mohr, 1989, 149-154; SCHLOSSER, P., Das internationale an der internationalen privaten Schiedsgerichtsbarkeit, RIW, 1982, 857 and 867; MUNZBERG, R., Die Schranken der Parteivereinbarungen in der privaten internationalen Schiedsgerichtsbarkeit, 74-76; VON HOFFMANN, B., Internationale Handelsschiedsgerichtsbarkeit, Die Bestimmung des Maßgeblichen Rechts, Frankfurt, Metzner, 1970, 26; VON HOFFMANN, B., Zur Auslegung von Formularbedingungen des internationalen Handelsverkehrs, AWD, 1970, 248 and 250.

According to Von Hoffmann, arbitrators cannot apply general principles of law without the consent of the parties because these principles are not universal, but are merely principles common to the legal systems connected to the dispute[160].

360. In The Netherlands, the theory of the *lex mercatoria* has only more recently been analyzed. Both proponents and opponents have emerged. Only the most important contributions to the debate will be discussed hereafter[161]. Undoubtedly, Pieter Sanders has been the first proponent of the *lex mercatoria* in The Netherlands. The principle of *pacta sunt servanda*, trade usages and general principles of law are the building blocks of this international business law[162]. Sanders made an important contribution to the theory of the *lex mercatoria* when he analyzed the legal status of codes of conduct. Rules contained in codes of conduct may, in his opinion, be

---

160. VON HOFFMANN, B., "Lex mercatoria" vor internationalen Schiedsgerichten, IPRax., 1984, 107-108; VON HOFFMANN, B., Internationale Handelsschiedsgerichtsbarkeit, 117; VON HOFFMANN, B., Grundsätzliches zur Anwendung der "lex mercatoria" durch internationale Schiedsgerichte, in Festschrift für Gerhard Kegel, Stuttgart, Kohlhammer, 1987, 215-233.
161. A more extensive review may be found in DE LY, F., De lex mercatoria, Inleiding op de studie van het transnationaal handelsrecht, 68-71. For proponents, see DE VRIES, H., Preadvies, in DE VRIES, H., MEIJER, R.S. and DEN DRIJVER, G.M.M., Internationale koop van roerende zaken naar materieel en internationaal privaatrecht, Reports to the Dutch Association of Commercial Law, Zwolle, Tjeenk Willink, 1982, 77-78; VAN DEN BERG, A.J., The New York Arbitration Convention of 1958, Deventer, Kluwer, 1981, 1, 33 and 208; VAN DEN BERG, A.J., Wetsontwerp Nieuwe Arbitragewet, Tijdschrift voor Arbitrage, 1984, No. 6, 200; *for opponents*, see KOLLEWIJN, R.D., De conventies voor eenvormig internationaal kooprecht en het internationaal privaatrecht, N.J.B., 1964, 150; JANSSEN, H., Totstandkoming van internationale handelskoop, Groningen, Wolters-Noordhoff, 1970, 36; HAAK, W.E., Preadvies, in Internationaal overeenkomstenrecht, Mededelingen van de Nederlandse Vereniging voor Internationaal Recht, Deventer, Kluwer, 1975, 7-11; SCHULTSZ, J.C., intervention during the discussions, Basle symposium on the law governing contractual obligations, KLEIN, F.E. and VISCHER, F. (ed.), Basle, Helbing & Lichtenhahn, 1983, 154-156.
162. SANDERS, P., Ecafe rules for international commercial arbitration, in International arbitration, Liber amicorum for Martin Domke, SANDERS, P. (ed.), The Hague, Martinus Nijhoff, 1967, 254 and 263-264; SANDERS, P., International commercial arbitration, N.T.I.R., 1973, 50; SANDERS, P., International commercial arbitration, in Arbitrage commercial, Essais in memoriam Eugenio Minoli, Rome, Associazioni italiana per l'arbitrato, 1974, 484-485; SANDERS, P., Trends in the field of international commercial arbitration, Academy of international law, 145 Collected Courses of The Hague, 1975, II, 262-264; SANDERS, P., Aspects de l'arbitrage international, Rev.Dr.Int.Comp., 1976, 131 and 137; SANDERS, P., Codes of conduct and sources of law, in Le droit des relations économiques internationales, Etudes offertes à Berthold Goldman, Paris, Litec, 1982, 298.

part of the *lex mercatoria* provided they are generally observed and accepted as transnational custom or generally accepted as principles of law[163].

361. Another Dutch proponent of the *lex mercatoria* is Wery who defined it very broadly. Wery argued that gaps in the applicable rules should, in international business problems, not be solved through conflict and substantive rules of national legal systems but by judicial decisions that are based on *comparative research*[164].

362. Dutch law is also interesting because the application of the *lex mercatoria* to company law problems has been analyzed. The basic problem is that internationally operating companies are treated as national companies under national laws. Struycken and Vlas have in this respect come to the conclusion that there is no alternative to national law, absent a more elaborated *lex mercatoria* on these issues[165]. More generally, one should note that Struycken is sceptical as to the *lex mercatoria* to the extent that self-regulation would imply that the international business communities do not assume their responsibilities as to values which transcend their own interests[166].

363. Finally, Van Delden also took a critical stance against the *lex mercatoria*. After empirical research, he notes that there are hardly any examples of general conditions or trade usages which may be seen as genuine sources of law[167]. Also, no universal principles or rules of law may be found which may form an autonomous *lex mercatoria*. At the most,

---

163. SANDERS, P., Codes of conduct and sources of law, 297-298.

164. WERY, P., De autonomie van het eenvormig privaatrecht, Deventer, Kluwer, 1971, 7 and 10-11; WERY, P., intervention during the discussions, proceedings of the annual meeting of the Dutch Association for Commercial law, Zwolle, Tjeenk Willink, 1988, 32-38; *but see* MIJNSSEN, F., ibid., 60-61. Wery's opinions strongly influenced Boon's dissertation on the U.C.P., see BOON, M.N., Het documentaire accreditief, De rechtspositie van de opdrachtgever ingevolge de UCP, Amsterdam, Nederlands Instituut voor Bank- en Effectenbedrijf, 1988, 120-121 and 160-161.

165. STRUYCKEN, A.V.M., Verenigingen als wereldburgers: "Qua patet orbis", in Goed en trouw, Opstellen aangeboden aan Prof.mr. W.C.L.van der Grinten, Zwolle, Tjeenk Willink, 1984, 289; VLAS, P., "Apatride" associations, Aspects of private international law, 47-48 and 60.

166. STRUYCKEN, A.V.M., Verenigingen als wereldburgers: "Qua patet orbis", 282 and 287-288; STRUYCKEN, A.V.M., La lex mercatoria dans le droit des contrats internationaux, in L'évolution contemporaine du droit des contrats, Journées René Savatier, Paris, P.U.F., 1986, 225.

167. VAN DELDEN, R., Lex mercatoria of ius commune?, Deventer, Kluwer, 1986, 6-9.

these phenomena may be interpreted as a very modest beginning of a new *ius commune* which could not be restricted to commercial law[168].

364. In Belgium, the theory of the *lex mercatoria* has been mentioned and discussed by many authors[169]. Both proponents and opponents are present but no position clearly prevailed. One can note that French speaking authors by and large have endorsed Goldman's theory while in the Dutch speaking part of the country, the opponents seem to be in the majority.

365. One of the major Belgian proponents of the *lex mercatoria* is François Rigaux. However, in order to understand Rigaux' position, one should be aware that Rigaux sees the *lex mercatoria* from the perspective of *legal pluralism*, a jurisprudential theory according to which any community may create legal rules. This is coupled with the perception that international business relations take place at a transnational plane where powerful companies operate and where public international law and national laws through the conflict of laws, hardly regulate anything[170]. Therefore, there seems to be something like a no-man's land where there is room for self-regulation[171] and where parties may avoid mandatory provisions of national law as well as uncertainties stemming from the conflict of laws by

168. Ibid., 18; VAN DELDEN, R., in Arbitragerecht, VAN DEN BERG, A.J., VAN DELDEN, R. and SNIJDERS, H.J., Zwolle, Tjeenk Willink, 1988, 100-101.

169. Only the major developments will be discussed in this book; for a more complete review, see DE LY, F., De lex mercatoria, Inleiding op de studie van het transnationaal handelsrecht, 71-81; see DABIN, J., Théorie générale du droit, 26-27; HUYS, M. and KEUTGEN, G., L'arbitrage en droit belge et international, Brussels, Bruylant, 1981, 243 and 594-595; VAN OMMESLAGHE, P., Les clauses de force majeure et d'imprévision (hardship) dans les contrats internationaux, Rev.Dr.Int.Comp., 1980, 14; FONTAINE, M., Introduction, in Le contrat économique international, Travaux des VIIes Journées d'études juridiques Jean Dabin, Brussels, Bruylant, 1975, 37; FONTAINE, M., Les clauses de force majeure dans les contrats internationaux, D.P.C.I., 1979, 494-495.

170. RIGAUX, F., Droit public et droit privé dans les relations internationales, Paris, Pedone, 1977, 3-4, 344-345, 399 and 423; RIGAUX, F., Droit international privé, I, Brussels, Larcier, 1977, 108-111; RIGAUX, F., Pour un autre ordre international, in Droit économique, Volume 2, Institut des Hautes Etudes Internationales de Paris, Paris, Pedone, 1979, 291 and 293; RIGAUX, F. and VANDER ELST, F., Relations juridiques transnationales ou dialogue sur un autre droit, J.T., 1982, 231.

171. RIGAUX, F., L'harmonisation des règles de conflits de lois et de jurisdiction dans les divers groupes régionaux d'Etats, in Rapports belges au VIe Congrès international de droit comparé, CENTRE INTERUNIVERSITAIRE DE DROIT COMPARE (ed.), Brussels, Bruylant, 1962, 175-176; RIGAUX, F., L'évolution du droit et de la pratique des contrats internationaux en Belgique : Essai de synthèse, in Le contrat économique international, 446.

way of choice of law and arbitration clauses[172]. The theory of the *lex mercatoria* adequately reflects these realities of international life[173] and, from a perspective of *legal pluralism*, the *lex mercatoria* may be considered to be a legal system[174]. However, Rigaux remains sceptical about some elements of the *lex mercatoria*. First, it is an incomplete legal system[175]. Second, Rigaux doubts whether trade usages and general principles of law may be seen as formal sources of law[176] and, thus, they should be applied by virtue of the applicable law[177].

366. Edouard Lambert's conception about the *lex mercatoria*[178], influenced Del Marmol who in turn had great impact on many scholars and practitioners affiliated with the University of Liège[179]. In this respect, special mention should be made of Lambert Matray who based the *lex mercatoria*

---

172. RIGAUX, F., Droit public et droit privé dans les relations internationales, 350 and 399; RIGAUX, F. and VANDER ELST, F., Relations juridiques transnationales ou dialogue sur un autre droit, 230.
173. RIGAUX, F., Droit public et droit privé dans les relations internationales, 399 and 413.
174. Ibid., 437-438; RIGAUX, F., Droit international privé, I, 114-115; RIGAUX, F., Pour un autre ordre international, 371.
175. RIGAUX, F. and VANDER ELST, F., Relations juridiques transnationales ou dialogue sur un autre droit, 231 and 233; RIGAUX, F., L'internationalisation du droit étatique, Rev.Dr.Int.Comp., 1983, 97.
176. RIGAUX, F., Le rôle de la comparaison dans la préparation de la réglementation juridique internationale, in Rapports belges au Xe Congrès international de droit comparé, CENTRE INTERUNIVERSITAIRE DE DROIT COMPARE (ed.), Brussels, Bruylant, 1978, 348; RIGAUX, F., Droit international privé, II, Brussels, Larcier, 1979, 425; RIGAUX, F., Le droit comparé comme science appliquée, Rev.Dr.Int.Comp., 1978, 68, 73, 74 and 76-77; RIGAUX, F., Souveraineté des Etats et arbitrage transnational, in Le droit des relations économiques internationales, Etudes offertes à Berthold Goldman, Paris, Litec, 1982, 277-278; RIGAUX, F. and VANDER ELST, F., Relations juridiques transnationales ou dialogue sur un autre droit, 232.
177. RIGAUX, F., Examen de quelques questions laissées ouvertes par la Convention de Rome sur la loi applicable aux obligations contractuelles, Cah.Dr.Eur., 1988, 318-319.
178. See supra No. 321.
179. DABIN, L., Preface, in HUBERT, A., Le contrat d'ingénierie-conseil, Paris, Masson, 1980, 5; DABIN, L., Les structures de coopération et les contraintes nées du droit des sociétés, D.P.C.I., 1984, 515-517; DELEUZE, J.M., Les contrats d'engineering, in Ekonomisch en financieel recht vandaag, II, SCHRANS, G. and FLAMME, J. (ed.), Ghent, Gakko, 1973, 394; DELEUZE, J.M., Le contrat de transfert de processus technologique, Paris, Masson, 1976, 41-42; HUBERT, A., Evolution des conventions de consulting engineering, D.P.C.I., 1977, 631; HUBERT, A., Le contrat d'ingénierie-conseil, 40-41, 52 and 156; BOON, J.A. and GOFFIN, R., Les contrats "clé en main", Paris, Masson, 1981, 144-145.

on trade usages and general principles of law[180]. Matray's major contribution to the debate on the *lex mercatoria* consisted in raising the question whether the *lex mercatoria* shouldn't have mandatory rules[181], apart from the application of the exception of a truly transnational public policy[182].

367. Dutch speaking authors were more critical regarding Goldman's theory of the *lex mercatoria*. Van Hecke attacked the *lex mercatoria* on three grounds. First, as far as general conditions are concerned, one may acknowledge that they may lead to unification of law but they remain subject to national law with regard to mandatory rules and their interpretation which may be different in different countries and create conflict problems[183]. Second, some so-called sources of the *lex mercatoria* have become national law because of their integration into the national legal system or their application by national courts[184]. Finally, the *lex mercatoria* has no mandatory rules, creating gaps as to the validity of contracts or the protection of weaker parties[185]. However, Van Hecke had to admit that, in the course of international commercial arbitration, non-national rules may well be applied but he rather opposed this development because of its lack of predictability and the risk of arbitrary decisions[186]. Thus, Van Hecke sees the *lex mercatoria* as non-national rules which parties may

---

180. MATRAY, L., Arbitrage et ordre public transnational, in The art of arbitration, Essays on international arbitration, Liber amicorum Pieter Sanders, SCHULTSZ, J. and VAN DEN BERG, A.J. (ed.), Deventer, Kluwer, 1982, 243-244; MATRAY, L., L'amiable composition dans l'arbitrage interne et dans l'arbitrage international, in Het scheidsgerecht, Brussels, Jeune Barreau, 1983, 57; MATRAY, L., Quelques problèmes de l'arbitrage commercial international (doctrine et jurisprudence), Travaux offerts au Professeur A. Fettweis, Brussels, Story-Scientia, 1989, 313-319; MATRAY, L., Rédaction d'une clause d'arbitrage et choix d'arbitres compétents en matière internationale, Rev.Dr.Int.Comp., 1979, 64; DEL MARMOL, C. and MATRAY, L., L'importance et l'interprétation du contrat, Rev.Dr.Int.Comp., 202-203.
181. MATRAY, L., Arbitrage et ordre public transnational, 244.
182. DEL MARMOL, C. and MATRAY, L., L'importance et l'interprétation du contrat, 194.
183. VAN HECKE, G., Principes et méthodes de solution des conflits de lois, Academy of international law, 126 Collected Courses of The Hague, 1970, I, 465.
184. VAN HECKE, G., Contracts subject to international or transnational law, 305-306.
185. Ibid., 311; VAN HECKE, G., Internationaal privaatrecht, first edition, Ghent, Story, 1986, 360.
186. VAN HECKE, G., Principes et méthodes de solution des conflits de lois, 466; VAN HECKE, G., Contracts subject to international or transnational law, 305-306; VAN HECKE, G., Internationaal privaatrecht, 316.

incorporate into their contract but which does not detach these contracts from their base in the applicable national law[187].

368. In his dissertation, Van Houtte rejected the existence of one single *lex mercatoria*[188]. Also, general principles of law and equity may not provide sufficient support to solve concrete disputes[189]. Furthermore, the *lex mercatoria* cannot fill its own gaps[190]. Finally, no system of anational conflict rules exists which may be applied in international commercial arbitration. Although some conflict rules may be created, so far, no system has emerged[191].

369. Limpens has emphasized that the repeated and international use of general conditions clearly has unifying effects[192] but he was quite reluctant to relate this tendency to the *lex mercatoria*[193].

Wymeersch has expressed a similar reluctance. In his opinion, enforceable legal rules may only be created within the boundaries of national law. Within these limits, self-regulatory rules may develop and be applied[194]. Wymeersch made an important contribution to the empirical verification of the hypothesis of the *lex mercatoria* with respect to the financial sector. In a study on professional rules and standards, he concluded that few usages have already developed[195].

370. In his dissertation on syndicated euro-loans and subsequent publications, Braeckmans extensively analyzed the theory of the *lex mercatoria*. He

---

187. VAN HECKE, G., intervention during the discussions, Basle symposium on the law governing contractual obligations, KLEIN, F.E. and VISCHER, F. (ed.), Basle, Helbing & Lichtenhahn, 1983, 136.

188. VAN HOUTTE, H., Rechtsvinding bij transnationale handelsarbitrage, dissertation, Leuven, 1977, 286-287; see also VAN HOUTTE, H., Het gebruik ontstaan uit contract of verdrag, R.W., 1985-86, 2182.

189. VAN HOUTTE, H., Rechtsvinding bij transnationale handelsarbitrage, 287.

190. Ibid., 287.

191. Ibid., 524-525.

192. LIMPENS, J., La vente en droit belge, Brussels, Bruylant, 1960, 537-538; LIMPENS, J., Les facteurs propices à l'éclosion et au développement d'un droit commun européen, in New perspectives for a common law of Europe, CAPPELLETTI, M. (ed.), European University Institute, 1978, 78-80.

193. LIMPENS, J., Les facteurs propices à l'éclosion et au développement d'un droit commun européen, 76.

194. WYMEERSCH, E., Preface, in BRAECKMANS, H., Juridische aspecten van consortiumkredieten in Eurodeviezen, Antwerp, Maklu Uitgevers, 1985, II.

195. WYMEERSCH, E., Règles professionnelles et règles standardisées dans les opérations financières, in Le droit des normes professionnelles et techniques, COMMISSION DROIT ET VIE DES AFFAIRES (ed.), Brussels, Bruylant, 1985, 62-63, 67 and 91.

defined the *lex mercatoria* as a set of rules which attempts to regulate international business transactions apart from national law. The *lex mercatoria* primarily consists of self-regulatory rules but international conventions may also form part of it[196], provided they are an expression of self-regulatory rules. However, they are no longer of the essence of the *lex mercatoria* because they have been incorporated into national law[197]. Self-regulatory rules consist of customs, trade usages, general conditions, usual contract clauses and arbitral case law[198]. Usual contract clauses do not qualify as formal sources of law because they depend on the will of the parties and the applicable law[199]. Also, few transnational customs exist. Most usages only recently came into existence, the international business communities in many cases are insufficiently homogeneous, usages are not public and observance is hard to control[200]. As regards syndicated loans in euro-currencies, the criteria for the formation of custom have not yet been met and, therefore, there is not yet any *lex mercatoria* on the euro-loans markets[201]. Furthermore, established contractual clauses have a contractual nature and are also not a formal source of the *lex mercatoria*[202].

Braeckmans also compared the *lex mercatoria* with other forms of regulation which may be found at the national level. These phenomena are called forms of *paralegal regulation*. The *lex mercatoria* and other forms of paralegal regulation are based on the same principles which exist within

196. BRAECKMANS, H., Juridische aspecten van consortiumkredieten in Eurodeviezen, 1985, 407; BRAECKMANS, H., De lex mercatoria. Zijn verhouding tot het nationaal recht en meer specifiek tot het internationaal privaatrecht, 2655; BRAECKMANS, H., Paralegale normen en lex mercatoria, T.P.R., 1986, 50-51, Aktuele problemen van handels-, economisch en financieel recht, Postuniversitaire cyclus Willy Delva 1985-86, STORME, M. and FREDERICQ, S. (ed.), Ghent, 1986, 50-51.
197. BRAECKMANS, H., Juridische aspecten van consortiumkredieten in Eurodeviezen, 1985, 407; BRAECKMANS, H., De lex mercatoria. Zijn verhouding tot het nationaal recht en meer specifiek tot het internationaal privaatrecht, 2655.
198. BRAECKMANS, H., Juridische aspecten van consortiumkredieten in Eurodeviezen, 1985, 408; BRAECKMANS, H., De lex mercatoria. Zijn verhouding tot het nationaal recht en meer specifiek tot het internationaal privaatrecht, 2657.
199. BRAECKMANS, H., De lex mercatoria. Zijn verhouding tot het nationaal recht en meer specifiek tot het internationaal privaatrecht, 2667-2668 and 2670-2671; BRAECKMANS, H., Paralegale normen en lex mercatoria, 37 and 59-61.
200. BRAECKMANS, H., De lex mercatoria. Zijn verhouding tot het nationaal recht en meer specifiek tot het internationaal privaatrecht, 2669; BRAECKMANS, H., Paralegale normen en lex mercatoria, 59-60.
201. BRAECKMANS, H., Juridische aspecten van consortiumkredieten in Eurodeviezen, 1985, 424.
202. Ibid., 423-424, 427 and 463; BRAECKMANS, H., De lex mercatoria. Zijn verhouding tot het nationaal recht en meer specifiek tot het internationaal privaatrecht, 2670.

national legal systems. These principles are for instance the principle of freedom of contract and open-ended rules of contract, company[203] or tort law by virtue of which the *lex mercatoria* and other paralegal forms of regulation may be applied.

From the foregoing, it results that Braeckmans rejects the notion of a formally autonomous *lex mercatoria* and that he sees the rules of the *lex mercatoria* within national legal systems[204]. In his view, the *lex mercatoria* does not determine its own scope and can only be applied by virtue of a conflict rule of the *lex fori*[205]. Even if disputes are settled by arbitration, national courts might still intervene in the course of the enforcement proceedings[206].

At this point, it should be noted that Braeckmans' theory may have one major disadvantage. In putting the *lex mercatoria* and national forms of paralegal regulation on the same footing, there is a risk that national rules will be too easily applied to fill gaps[207]. The transnational nature and characteristics of the rules of the *lex mercatoria* may be neglected if national law is automatically applied to these gaps.

371. In addition to the discussion of the development of the theory of the *lex mercatoria* in England, France, Switzerland, Germany, The Netherlands and Belgium, a less systematic analysis of the contribution of some other important authors will be given below.

372. Inspired by Schmitthoff, Berman and Trakman have stressed the role of transnational usages and unification conventions for transnational

---

203. BRAECKMANS, H., Paralegale normen en lex mercatoria, 36, 38, 41 and 61-62. In this article, Braeckmans is pointing to company law techniques and multi-party contracts as means of regulation.

204. BRAECKMANS, H., Juridische aspecten van consortiumkredieten in Eurodeviezen, 1985, 433; BRAECKMANS, H., De lex mercatoria. Zijn verhouding tot het nationaal recht en meer specifiek tot het internationaal privaatrecht, 2672-2676; BRAECKMANS, H., Paralegale normen en lex mercatoria, 57-58 and 61-63.

205. BRAECKMANS, H., De lex mercatoria. Zijn verhouding tot het nationaal recht en meer specifiek tot het internationaal privaatrecht, 2677-2681; BRAECKMANS, H., Paralegale normen en lex mercatoria, 63-67.

206. BRAECKMANS, H., De lex mercatoria. Zijn verhouding tot het nationaal recht en meer specifiek tot het internationaal privaatrecht, 2680; BRAECKMANS, H., Paralegale normen en lex mercatoria, 67.

207. This seems to be Braeckmans' position, see BRAECKMANS, H., De lex mercatoria. Zijn verhouding tot het nationaal recht en meer specifiek tot het internationaal privaatrecht, 2680; BRAECKMANS, H., Paralegale normen en lex mercatoria, 67.

commerce[208]. As to usages, Berman and Trakman refer to § 1-205 UCC in arguing that a shift has taken place from normative custom to behavioral custom. The factual element would thus prevail over the psychological requirement; factual observance of certain rules would be sufficient evidence of the parties' conviction that they have to observe these rules[209]. The status of the *lex mercatoria* is, however, unclear. On the one hand, it is argued that the *lex mercatoria* is more than merely factual identity or uniformity between national systems[210]. On the other hand and contrary to Schmitthoff's theory, the application of rules of the *lex mercatoria* through a rule of national law is hardly emphasized[211].

373. Ole Lando should briefly be discussed because he made - similarly to Pierre Mayer - the link between the theory of the *lex mercatoria* and the judicial function. If the function of the judiciary and of arbitration panels is seen from an exegetic point of view, they can only apply legal rules but not create them. Under that perspective, one should look for formal sources of law, other than case law, in order to explain the creation of new legal rules and the development of a legal system. Many efforts by the proponents of an autonomist vision on the *lex mercatoria* to have trade usages, general conditions, contractual clauses, professional rules or general principles of law recognized as formal sources of law must be seen in that perspective. When one acknowledges that in the process of judicial and arbitral adjudication, solutions should be found and new rules may gradually develop, the key issue is no longer on formal sources of law and building a legal system but on methods of dispute resolution and adjudica-

---

208. BERMAN, H., Criteria of comparison of contract law in planned and market economies, in Hulde aan René Dekkers, Brussels, Bruylant, 1982, 267; TRAKMAN, L., The evolution of the Law Merchant : our commercial heritage, J.MAR.L.& COM., 1981, 153-182; TRAKMAN, L., book review, KURKELA, M., Letters of credit under international trade law, UCC, UCP and law merchant, AM.J.COMP.L., 1986, 145; see also BENSON, B., The spontaneous evolution of commercial law : what the other invisible hand is doing !, Florida State University, Tallahassee, Florida, 39 pp.

209. BERMAN, H. and KAUFMAN, C., The law of international commercial transactions (lex mercatoria), HARV.INT'L.L.J., 1978, 262-263 and 274; TRAKMAN, L., The evolution of the Law Merchant : our commercial heritage, J.MAR.L.& COM., 1981, 166. See also BERMAN, H. and DASSER, F., The "new" law merchant and the "old" : sources, content and legitimacy, Lex mercatoria and arbitration, CARBONNEAU, T. (ed.), Dobbs Ferry, Transnational, 1990, 29.

210. BERMAN, H. and KAUFMAN, C., The law of international commercial transactions (lex mercatoria), 273.

211. Ibid., 273.

tion. Under the latter perspective, reference to *lex mercatoria* does not imply application of legal rules but relates to adjudication processes[212].

374. Lowenfeld cannot be considered as a proponent of the lex mercatoria, but certainly sympathises with its analyses. The doctrine of *lex mercatoria* should in his view be seen as an effort to explain the practice of international arbitral adjudication, which to a large extent avoids conflict of law principles. To that extent, the theory expresses the freedom of arbitrators from the law (including the conflict of law rules) of the place of arbitration[213] and may provide a basis for alternative dispute resolution in which the needs of international trade are better taken care of[214].

375. A.T. Von Mehren has doubted whether it is advisable to have non-national substantive rules applied in international commercial arbitration awards. Arbitrators will tend to apply pre-existing rules and not aim at *ad hoc* adjudication. However, on the level of conflict rules, Von Mehren endorses Goldman's efforts to create a *lex mercatoria* of autonomous conflict rules[215].

376. In a recent article, Paulsson has opposed the ideas of the *lex mercatoria* as an autonomous legal system or as a set of self-sufficient contractual rules. However, this does not imply that Paulsson objects to application of the *lex mercatoria* with regard to international commercial arbitration. On the contrary, Paulsson develops a third conception about lex

---

212. LANDO, O., The law applicable to the merits of the dispute, Essays on international commercial arbitration, SARCEVIC, P. (ed.), London, Graham & Trotman, 1989, 141, 143 and 147-148.
213. LOWENFELD, A., The two-way mirror : international arbitration as comparative procedure, in International Chamber of Commerce Arbitration, CRAIG, W., PARK, W. and PAULSSON, J., Dobbs Ferry, New York, Issue November 1986, Appendix VII, 206-208.
214. LOWENFELD, A., Lex mercatoria : an arbitrator's view, Lex mercatoria and arbitration, CARBONNEAU, T. (ed.), Dobbs Ferry, Transnational, 1990, 50-51.
215. VON MEHREN, A., To what extent is international commercial arbitration autonomous ?, in Le droit des relations économiques internationales, Etudes offertes à Berthold Goldman, Paris, Litec, 1982, 226-227; VON MEHREN, A.T., Limitations on party choice of the governing law : do they exist for international commercial arbitration ?, Tel Aviv, Mortimer and Raymond Sackler Institute of Advanced Studies, 1986, 7-8 and 21-22.

mercatoria in which it is seen as the expression of trade usages and general principles of law which may be applied in arbitral adjudication[216].

377. In a series of writings, Bonell, on several grounds, has rejected the theory of the *lex mercatoria* as an autonomous system[217]. First, review of the *lex mercatoria* in the course of enforcement procedures is always possible. Second, the theory of the *lex mercatoria* confuses incorporation of non-national rules with the question of the national law to be applied to the substance of the dispute. Third, the public interest and the interests of weaker parties are not well handled[218]. Finally, one may doubt whether trade usages are formal sources of law[219]. Absent satisfactory results in the application of conflict of laws or the *lex mercatoria*, Bonell develops a *substantive* or *transnational method* which is discussed below[220].

IV.1.2 *The lex mercatoria in legislation*

378. Attention to the sources of international business law and *lex mercatoria* has not been limited to legal literature but recently also had some impact on statutory law in some countries and on international conventions. These will be discussed below.

---

216. PAULSSON, J., La lex mercatoria dans l'arbitrage C.C.I., Rev.Arb., 1990, 60-77; CRAIG, W., PARK, W. and PAULSSON, J., International Chamber of Commerce Arbitration, Chapter 35 (issue January 1990), in International commercial arbitration, Dobbs Ferry, Oceana.
217. BONELL, M., Le regole oggetive del commercio internazionale, 4.
218. BONELL, M., Le regole oggetive del commercio internazionale, 155-179; BONELL, M., The relevance of courses of dealing, usages and customs in the interpretation of international commercial contracts, 119-120 and 128-129; BONELL, M., Das autonome Recht des Welthandels - rechtsdogmatische und rechtspolitische Aspekte, 495 and 505; BONELL, M., The law applicable to international commercial contracts : the standpoint of Italian doctrine and case-law, Basle symposium on the law governing contractual obligations, KLEIN, F.E. and VISCHER, F. (ed.), Basle, Helbing & Lichtenhahn, 1983, 16-20 and 23; BONELL, M., La nouvelle Convention des Nations-Unies sur les contrats de vente internationale des marchandises, D.P.C.I., 1981, 16.
219. BONELL, M., Le regole oggetive del commercio internazionale, 103-104.
220. BONELL, M., The relevance of courses of dealing, usages and customs in the interpretation of international commercial contracts, 128-129; BONELL, M., Das autonome Recht des Welthandels - rechtsdogmatische und rechtspolitische Aspekte, 496-505; BONELL, M., Some critical reflections on the new Uncitral draft convention on international sales, UNIF.L.REV., 1978, II, 7-11; BONELL, M., The law applicable to international commercial contracts : the standpoint of Italian doctrine and case-law, 21-27; BONELL, M., La nouvelle Convention des Nations-Unies sur les contrats de vente internationale de marchandises, 14.
    For the transnational method, see infra Nos. 472-474.

IV.1.2.1 The lex mercatoria in statutory law

379. In this section, the influence of the theory of the *lex mercatoria* on statutory law of some European countries will be analyzed[221]. France, The Netherlands, Belgium, Switzerland, Spain and Portugal will be discussed; no references to the *lex mercatoria* could be found in statutes in England and Germany.

380. In France, the proponents of the *lex mercatoria* clearly have influenced the reform of French law on international commercial arbitration. A new section on international commercial arbitration has been created within the New Code of Civil Procedure in which article 1496 N.C.P.C. provides that in arbitrations involving the interests of international commerce, the arbitrators apply the rules of law chosen by the parties. Absent such a choice, they may apply the rules they consider appropriate. Furthermore, trade usages should be taken into account.

Although no express reference to the *lex mercatoria* may be found in article 1496 N.C.P.C. nor in the Report to the Prime Minister[222], a majority of writers have interpreted the provision as a recognition of the *lex mercatoria* by French legislation which authorizes the arbitral tribunal only to apply the *lex mercatoria* in transnational arbitral dispute resolution[223]. Some authors, however, still argue that the arbitrators should use

---

221. For other countries, see for instance article 5.3 of the Chinese Statute of March 21, 1985 on Transnational Economic Contracts which refers to general principles of transnational commerce as the applicable rules, absent choice of law. Horn has interpreted this provision as a reference to the *lex mercatoria* (HORN, N., Das chinesische Außenwirtschaftsvertragsgesetz von 1985, RIW, 1985, 691).

222. Annexe to the J.C.P. of June 3, 1981.

223. GOLDMAN, B., Lex mercatoria, 13 (based on the drafting history of the provision); GOLDMAN, B., The applicable law : general principles of law - lex mercatoria, 118-119; KAHN, P., Rapport français, 247; FOUCHARD, P., La loi régissant les obligations contractuelles en droit international privé français, 111; FOUCHARD, P., L'arbitrage international en France après le décret du 12 mai 1981, 399; FOUCHARD, P., Le nouveau droit français de l'arbitrage, 45; LOUSSOUARN, Y., intervention during the discussions, in La réforme de l'arbitrage international en France, Rev.Arb., 1981, 496; LOUSSOUARN, Y., Arbitrage commercial international et droit du commerce international, 170-171; ROBERT, J., L'arbitrage en matière internationale, 213; ROBERT, J., L'arbitrage, droit interne, droit international privé, 290; BEGUIN, J., Le développement de la lex mercatoria menace-t-il l'ordre juridique international ?, 515; DERAINS, Y., La sentence arbitrale, in Droit et pratique de l'arbitrage international en France, s.l., Feduci, 1984, 75; VON BREITENSTEIN, D., Die internationale arbitrage im französischen Recht, in Schiedsgerichtsbarkeit in Frankreich, BÖCKSTIEGEL, K.H. (ed.), Cologne, Heymanns, 1983, 40; FUNCK-BRENTANO, R., Die "amiable composition", in Schiedsgerichtsbarkeit in

a conflict rule in order to determine the applicable law[224]. It is obvious that this dispute is closely related to the conceptions on the *lex mercatoria*; proponents will give article 1496 N.C.P.C. an extensive interpretation while opponents will take an opposite view as to its interpretation[225].

381. Under the influence of the French international commercial arbitration reform and the ideas of Pieter Sanders on the *lex mercatoria*, the 1986 Dutch Arbitration Act of July 2, 1986 inserted a new section on arbitration into the Dutch Code of Civil Procedure. Article 1054 of that Code deals with the law to be applied to the merits of the dispute and is phrased in the same way as article 1496 N.C.P.C.[226]. The explanatory report to the arbitration bill confirmed explicitly that arbitrators in international cases may apply the *lex mercatoria*, provided they have been authorized by the parties or failing choice of law by the parties. Under reference to Goldman, the report defines the *lex mercatoria* as generally accepted usages in international trade, which are autonomous from national law[227].

Article 1054 Dutch Code of Civil Procedure was received with some scepticism[228]. Van Delden explicitly argued that the debate regarding the *lex mercatoria* is not over and, therefore, the legislator shouldn't yet take any position[229]. In its second report in the parliamentary process, the Dutch government responded to the criticism of Van Delden by extending

---

Frankreich, BÖCKSTIEGEL, K.H. (ed.), Cologne, Heymanns, 1983, 101; BOLARD, G., Le nouveau droit français de l'arbitrage, in Les particularités nationales de l'arbitrage commercial international, Lublin, 1987, 41.

224. BELLET, P. and MEZGER, E., L'arbitrage international dans le nouveau code de procédure civile, R.C.D.I.P., 1981, 631-633; MEZGER, E., Kernpunkte der Reform des Rechts der internationalen Handelsschiedsgerichtsbarkeit in Frankreich, RIW, 1981, 514-515; LAGARDE, P., Approche critique de la lex mercatoria, 148-149; DE BOISSESON, M., Le droit français de l'arbitrage, first edition, Paris, Joly, 1983, 418-423.
225. For a personal interpretation, see infra Nos. 448 and 490-491.
226. Statute of July 2, 1986 on new rules on arbitration to be inserted into the Code of Civil Procedure, Official Gazette, 1986, 372, Tijdschrift voor Arbitrage, 1986, No. 5, 213 ff.
227. Explanatory Report, Document No. 18464, Tijdschrift voor Arbitrage, 1984, No. 4, 40.
228. KOKKINI-IATRIDOU, D., Het Nederlands arbitrage-wetsontwerp, Ars Aequi-katern, 1985, 488-490; BROCHES, A., The 1985 Uncitral model law on international commercial arbitration : an exercise in international legislation, N.Y.B.Int.L., 1987, 46; *but see* SILLEVIS SMITT, J., Iets over rechtskeuze en aanverwante problemen in de nieuwe arbitragewet, Enkele kanttekeningen bij artikel 1054 Rv., in Feestbundel ter gelegenheid van het vijfentwintigjarig bestaan van de Studiekring Prof. Mr. J. Offerhaus, Deventer, Kluwer, 1987, 164; VAN DEN BERG, A.J., Wetsontwerp Nieuwe Arbitragewet, Tijdschrift voor Arbitrage, 1984, No. 6, 200.
229. VAN DELDEN, R., Lex mercatoria of ius commune ?, 18-23.

the notion of the *lex mercatoria* which was now also thought to encompass transnational rules and principles of law[230].

382. In Belgium, Verhoeven has argued that the Belgian Statute of March 27, 1985 which has deregulated international commercial arbitral awards rendered in Belgium to the extent that setting aside is no longer possible, may be seen as a recognition of the *lex mercatoria*[231]. However, neither the parliamentary process nor the commentaries on the law support this argument.

383. In Switzerland, article 187 (1) of the Law on Conflict of Laws provides that the arbitral tribunal shall decide according to the rules of law agreed upon by the parties or, in the absence of a choice of law, by applying the rules of law with which the dispute has the closest connection. From the drafting history of the Law and the French text (*règles de droit*), a majority opinion has concluded that the parties and the arbitrators may apply the *lex mercatoria*[232]. It would, however, go too far to see article 187 (1) as a recognition of the *lex mercatoria*. One may be more tempted to interpret that provision as a policy to give the parties and the arbitrators discretion as to the substantive rules of the dispute resolution process.

384. Finally, mention should be made of Spain and Portugal's recent moves to liberalize their arbitration laws. However, in both countries, non-traditional methods of arbitral adjudication were met with some scepticism[233]. In Spain, the legislator opposed the tendency to denationalize arbitration proceedings conducted in Spain. In this respect, article 62 of the Law of December 5, 1988 remained within classical conflict of law boun-

230. Second Report, Tijdschrift voor Arbitrage, 1986, No. 2, 83-84.

231. VERHOEVEN, J., Arbitrage entre Etats et entreprises étrangères : des règles spécifiques ?, 630-631.

232. BLESSING, M., Das neue internationale Schiedsgerichtsrecht der Schweiz, 64-68; LALIVE, P., The new Swiss law on international arbitration, ARB.INT'L, 1988, 14; LALIVE, P., POUDRET, J.F. and REYMOND, C., Le droit de l'arbitrage interne et international en Suisse, 393-394 and 399-400; GAILLARD, E., A foreign view of the new Swiss law on international arbitration, ARB.INT'L, 1988, 29-30; VON OVERBECK, A., Das neue schweizerische Bundesgesetz über das Internationale Privatrecht, IPRax., 1988, 332; BUCHER, A., Das Kapitel 11 des IPR-Gesetzes über die internationale Schiedsgerichtsbarkeit, in Beiträge zum neuen IPR des Sachen-, Schuld- und Gesellschaftsrechts, Festschrift für Rudolf Moser, Zurich, Schulthess, 1987, 217.

233. See KOKKINI-IATRIDOU, D., Twee recente arbitrageregelingen : Portugal en Spanje, in Eenvormig en vergelijkend privaatrecht 1990, Molengrafica, Lelystad, Vermande, 1990, 396-397 and 404.

daries and did not open the door to application of non-national legal systems such as the *lex mercatoria*[234]. A similar stance was taken in Portugal where, notwithstanding the liberal provision of article 33-2 of the Law of August 29, 1986 which authorizes arbitrators to apply the law they consider appropriate absent choice of law, the drafters of the new arbitration law seem to have excluded the possibility of referring to the *lex mercatoria* in relation to the law to be applied to the merits of the dispute[235].

IV.1.2.2 The lex mercatoria in international conventions and uniform laws[236]

385. Some authors have taken the position that some international conventions and uniform laws referred to the *lex mercatoria* or were attempts to encourage its development[237]. In this respect, reference is made to article 9 ULIS, article 9 CISG, artikel VII (1) of the European International Commercial Arbitration Convention, article 42 C.S.I.D. and article V of the Algiers Agreements between the U.S.A. and Iran of January 19, 1981 regarding the resolution of the Iranian-U.S. disputes[238].

386. In Schmitthoff's theory, one can see the importance of these conventions for the unification of international business law and the development of the *lex mercatoria*. In Goldman's perspective, one may first note that

---

234. CREMADES, B., L'Espagne étrenne une nouvelle loi sur l'arbitrage, Rev.Arb., 1989, 192.

235. MOURA VICENTE, D., L'évolution récente du droit de l'arbitrage au Portugal, Rev.Arb., 1991, 436-437.

236. The 1991 Basle Resolution of the Institute of International Law regarding choice of law in international contracts did not take a position as to the issue of the *lex mercatoria* (preamble and article 1 (1) of the Resolution, see JAYME, E., Die Parteiautonomie im internationalen Vertragsrecht auf dem Prüfstand - 65. Sitzung des Institut de Droit International in Basel, IPRax., 1991, 429).

237. SCHMITTHOFF, C., The sale of goods, 324; LEVEL, P., Le contrat dit sans loi, Trav.com.fr.dr.int.privé, 1964-66, Paris, Dalloz, 1967, 212-213; BRAECKMANS, H., Juridische aspecten van consortiumkredieten in Eurodeviezen, 407; BRAECKMANS, H., De lex mercatoria. Zijn verhouding tot het nationaal recht en meer specifiek tot het internationaal privaatrecht, 2656; BRAECKMANS, H., Paralegale normen en lex mercatoria, 51-52; KAHN, P., case note District Court Paris, March 4, 1981, Clunet, 1981, 841; SEIDL-HOHENVELDERN, I., Le règlement du contentieux irano-américain par les accords d'Alger du 19 janvier 1981, in Le droit des relations économiques internationales, Etudes offertes à Berthold Goldman, Paris, Litec, 1982, 353; OPPETIT, B., La notion de source du droit et le droit du commerce international, 51-52.

238. I.L.M., 1981, 229.

these conventions are not formal sources of the *lex mercatoria*[239]. Thus, these conventions may only give persuasive authority to his theory on the *lex mercatoria*. However, one may doubt whether international conventions may give such authority. First, the conventions mentioned above, do not explicitly refer to the *lex mercatoria*[240]. A mere reference to trade usages may not be interpreted as an endorsement of the theory of an autonomous *lex mercatoria* since these references say nothing about the sources of the *lex mercatoria* or its relation to national law. Also, the drafting histories of these conventions do not indicate the intent of their drafters in relation to their views on the *lex mercatoria*. This is quite evident for those conventions, such as ULIS, which antedate the theory of the *lex mercatoria*. As to CISG, one may interpret article 9 as an indication that developing countries wanted to cut back on self-regulatory rules developed by the business communities of developed countries[241]. As to C.S.I.D. and the Algiers Agreements, one may doubt whether generalizations may be drawn from these specific instruments regulating the Iran-U.S. crisis or investment problems between private investors and public entities from the country in which the investment is made.

387. More recently, Schmitthoff has argued that article 28 of the Uncitral Model Law on International Commercial Arbitration has recognized the *lex mercatoria*. Since article 28 (1) authorizes arbitrators to apply the rules of law chosen by the parties, one no longer has to apply a given national law and, thus, the *lex mercatoria*, if chosen by the parties, may be applied[242]. In Schmitthoff's theory on the *lex mercatoria*, this interpretation does not create problems. However, one may hardly interpret article 28 of the Model Law as support for Goldman's theory. First, article 28 (2) has somewhat restricted the freedom for arbitrators since they are bound by a conflict rule. Failing a choice by the parties, they have to apply the law determined by the conflict rule which they consider applicable. The reference to a conflict rule seems at first glance to imply that national law should be applied. Furthermore, the drafting history of the Model Law does not provide answers as to the question whether the parties can choose the *lex mercatoria* to be applied to the merits of the dispute nor as to the

---

239. See supra No. 326.

240. *But see* BRAECKMANS, H., De lex mercatoria. Zijn verhouding tot het nationaal recht en meer specifiek tot het internationaal privaatrecht, 2656; KAHN, P., case note District Court Paris, March 4, 1981, Clunet, 1981, 841.

241. See supra No. 243.

242. SCHMITTHOFF, C., International trade usages, I.C.C. publication No. 440/4, Paris, 1987, 48-49.

nature of the *lex mercatoria*. One author has stated that the *lex mercatoria* could only apply as rules incorporated by the parties into their contract but not as the law applicable to the contract[243]. This would imply that article 28 of the Model Law cannot be seen as a recognition of Goldman's theory on *lex mercatoria* since its rules are subject to the applicable law.

388. The only international convention where the *lex mercatoria* seems to have been addressed explicitly, is the 1986 Hague Convention on the law applicable to international sales of goods. In the drafting process, the question was raised whether the convention should allow for general principles of law or the *lex mercatoria* as the applicable law. Finally, votes on this issue were divided and the Convention ultimately did not get an explicit provision on this question[244]. From the 1986 Convention, one can thus not deduce a clear position as to the *lex mercatoria*.

IV.1.3 *The lex mercatoria in case law*

389. Quite recently, case law of national courts and arbitration tribunals has been faced with cases in which some rules of the *lex mercatoria* were raised.

---

243. STALEV, Z., Das neue bulgarische Gesetz über die internationale Handelsschiedsgerichtsbarkeit, in Jahrbuch für die Praxis der Schiedsgerichtsbarkeit, Volume 2 (1988), Heidelberg, Verlag Recht und Wirtschaft, 1989, 212.

244. Minutes and working documents of the first commission, Hague Conference on private international law, Proceedings of the extraordinary session, Diplomatic Conference on the law applicable to contracts for the international sale of goods, Minutes No. 12, 477-483; Explanatory report by Arthur Taylor Von Mehren, Hague Conference on private international law, Proceedings of the extraordinary session, Diplomatic Conference on the law applicable to contracts for the international sale of goods, 745-747; VON MEHREN, A., Limitations on party choice of the governing law : do they exist for international commercial arbitration ?, 10-11; Mc LACHLAN, C., The new Hague sales convention and the limits of the choice of law process, 604.

IV.1.3.1 Case law of national courts

390. Recently, in litigation in France, Austria, Italy, Germany and Belgium, national courts have been confronted with the *lex mercatoria* in the course of setting aside or enforcement proceedings regarding arbitral awards[245].

A first French case involved a dispute between the French company *Fougerolle* and a Lebanese bank concerning commission fees. The bank had been an intermediary for Fougerolle in relation to public works to be made in Syria under a public procurement procedure. The contract between Fougerolle and the bank provided that it would end if no contract with the Syrian state were concluded before June 30, 1976. Notwithstanding the lapse of this period without a contract being formed, commission fees were claimed. An arbitral tribunal was constituted and the arbitrators awarded the bank some fees, based on a ratio between the actual and the original estimated contract term. The award was not based on any specific legal principle but the arbitrators had relied on general principles of contract law as those are applied in transnational commerce. The enforcement of the award was granted but opposed by Fougerolle. The case was thus brought before the Paris Court of Appeal which confirmed the enforcement order. The Court stated that the arbitrators had by implication applied a transnational usage according to which fees, in case of contract termination, are to be computed on the basis of actual and expected revenue from the contract[246]. The case was subsequently brought before the French Supreme Court on the ground that the arbitrators had violated due process in applying a general principle although parties had not invoked or discussed it. The Supreme Court confirmed the appellate decision because the arbitrators had only been determining the applicable law and had stayed within their jurisdiction[247]. In interpreting this case, one first notes that the *lex mercatoria* is not explicitly involved. Second, one might say that the case only raised due process problems regarding the *ex officio*

245. In Switzerland, the Court of Appeal of Zurich in its decision of May 9, 1985 (BlZürchRspr., 1986, No. 23, 44) referred to the *lex mercatoria* in relation to the interpretation of an on demand bank guarantee. It is unclear, however, whether the Court in this case applied a rule of *lex mercatoria* or merely referred to it to give a transnational interpretation of the bank guarantee.

246. Court of Appeal Paris, June 12, 1980, Clunet, 1982, 933, case note OPPETIT, B., Rev.Arb., 1981, 292, case note COUCHEZ, G.

247. French Supreme Court, December 9, 1981, D., 1983, 239, case note ROBERT, J., Clunet, 1982, 935, case note OPPETIT, B., Rev.Arb., 1982, 183, case note COUCHEZ, G., J.C.P., 1983, 19771, case note LEVEL, P.

application of a general principle of law without the parties being heard[248]. However, such a restrictive reading would not explain why the case was confirmed[249]. One is thus left with the interpretation that the Fougerolle case might be seen as a first modest step towards considering the *lex mercatoria* as the *lex fori* for transnational commercial arbitrations, which might explain why the arbitrators could have applied it without hearing the parties[250].

391. A second French case concerned the termination of an agency agreement between the French company *Norsolor* and her Turkish agent Pabalk Ticaret Limited Sirketi regarding late payment of commission fees and an indemnity for contract termination. The arbitrators were faced with the difficulty of determining the applicable law and, thus, given the transnational nature of the contract, decided to apply the *lex mercatoria* on the issue of the contract termination. Based upon the principle of good faith, the arbitrators held Norsolor accountable for the contract termination and awarded Pabalk a termination indemnity[251]. Norsolor then applied for the setting aside of the award in Austria where the arbitral tribunal had its seat and opposed its enforcement in France.

392. The enforcement of the award was first granted by the President of the Paris District Court and, notwithstanding Norsolor's opposition, affirmed by the Court itself. In the Court's opinion, the arbitrators had applied a law (*i.e.*, general principles of law as generally observed in

---

248. COUCHEZ, G., case note French Supreme Court, December 9, 1981, Rev.Arb., 1982, 189.

249. See also BELLET, P., Le rôle des usages en matière d'arbitrage international suivant la jurisprudence française, Journées de la Société de législation comparée, 1985, 240-241; ROBERT, J., case note French Supreme Court, December 9, 1981, D., 1983, 241; LEVEL, P., case note French Supreme Court, December 9, 1981, J.C.P., 1983, 19971.

250. ROBERT, J., case note under French Supreme Court, December 9, 1981, D., 1983, 214-242. In a subsequent case note, Robert expressed his criticism regarding the Fougerolle decision (see ROBERT, J., case note French Supreme Court, October 9, 1984, D., 1985, 101).

Goldman, Level, Jehl and Diener have interpreted the Fougerolle case as a recognition of the *lex mercatoria* (GOLDMAN, B., Lex mercatoria, 15; GOLDMAN, B., Une bataille judiciaire autour de la lex mercatoria, 400-401; GOLDMAN, B., The applicable law : general principles of law - lex mercatoria, 120; LEVEL, P., La procédure arbitrale, in Droit et pratique de l'arbitrage international en France, s.l., Feduci, 1984, 58; JEHL, J., Le commerce international de la technologie, Approche juridique, 102; DIENER, M., Contrats internationaux de propriété industrielle, 258-260).

251. I.C.C. case No. 3131, Rev.Arb., 1983, 525, Y.B.COM.ARB., IX-1984, 109.

international commerce) in accordance with article 13 of the I.C.C. Arbitration Rules. Since rules of law are used as a settlement method, one cannot speak of arbitrators acting as *amiables compositeurs* without being authorized by the parties and subject to refusal of enforcement on the basis of excess of authority[252]. The decision of the Paris District Court seems to be quite clear since it accepts that the *lex mercatoria* is a set of legal rules which may be applied, even if the parties have not authorized the arbitral tribunal to act as *amiables compositeurs*[253].

393. In the Austrian procedure for the setting aside of the award, the Vienna Commercial Court upheld the award since no mandatory rules of Austrian law had been violated. The arbitrators had been adjudicating according to rules of law and not as *amiables compositeurs* and the application of a non-national legal system could not be reviewed in the course of setting aside proceedings[254]. However, the Vienna Court of Appeal reversed the decision. The Appeal Court stated that a general principle such as good faith, does not enable arbitrators to settle concrete cases and, therefore, implies that arbitrators make personal value judgments as to the equitable results of the decision. Thus, they had exceeded their jurisdiction and the award was set aside with regard to the termination indemnity[255]. Finally, the Austrian Supreme Court reversed the appellate decision. The Supreme Court's motivation by and large is identical to that of the Commercial Court; the award had not violated mandatory rules and the arbitrators had not exceeded the scope of their mandate[256]. Contrary to the Court of Appeal's decision, the Supreme

---

252. District Court Paris, March 4, 1981, Clunet, 1981, 836, case note KAHN, P., Rev.Arb., 1983, 466.

253. KAHN, P., case note District Court Paris, March 4, 1981, Clunet, 1981, 841; GOLDMAN, B., Lex mercatoria, 17; GOLDMAN, B., Une bataille judiciaire autour de la lex mercatoria, 396; KAHN, P., Rapport français, 248-249; OPPETIT, B., La notion de source du droit et le droit du commerce international, 52; JEHL, J., Le commerce international de la technologie, Approche juridique, 102.

254. Vienna Commercial Court, June 29, 1981, Rev.Arb., 1983, 514.

255. Vienna Court of Appeal, January 26, 1982, Rev.Arb., 1983, 516, AG, 1982, 165, case note DIELMANN, H.

256. Austrian Supreme Court, November 18, 1982, RIW, 1983, 868, case note SEIDL-HOHENVELDERN, I., Rev.Arb., 1983, 519, Clunet, 1983, 645, case note SEIDL-HOHENVELDERN, I., IPRax., 1984, 97, case note VON HOFFMANN, B., ibid., 106, Y.B.COM.ARB., IX-1984, 159, KTS, 1983, 666, case note SCHLOSSER, P.; see also D.T., The lex mercatoria in Paris and Vienna, Journal of world trade law, 1983, 358. For a criticism of the decision, see BAJONS, E.M., Zur Nationalität internationaler Schiedssachen, Festschrift für W. Kralik, RECHBERGER, W.H. and WELSER, R. (ed.), Vienna, Manz, 1986, 25-27.

Court decision did not take a position regarding the *lex mercatoria* since the Court gave a restrictive interpretation to excess of jurisdiction (*i.e.*, limited to *ultra petita* decisions). Under this restrictive line of thought, the question whether non-national rules may be applied no longer arises. Contrary to the Paris District Court decision, one can hardly attach precedential force to the Austrian Supreme Court decision as far as the *lex mercatoria* is concerned[257].

394. In Italy, the Supreme Court in its decision of February 8, 1982, was faced with an enforcement procedure regarding an arbitral award which was rendered in London and which was not motivated[258]. On that ground, the Court refused to grant the enforcement of the award. However, non-motivation of awards is permitted under the applicable procedural law (*i.e.*, English law). The Court then made a construction whereby reference was made to article VIII of the European International Commercial Arbitration Convention. Under that article, parties may generally ask for reasoned awards. However, the Convention was not so much applied as such (the parties belonging to Contracting States but the award being rendered in a non-Contracting State) but as incorporated into the contract. Since this contractual right was then not respected, enforcement of the award was refused under article V, § 1, d of the New York Convention.

---

257. VON HOFFMANN, B., "Lex mercatoria" vor internationalen Schiedsgerichten, IPRax., 1984, 108; SCHLOSSER, P., case note Austrian Supreme Court, November 18, 1982, KTS, 1983, 669; VAN DELDEN, R., Lex mercatoria of ius commune ?, 16-17; MELIS, W., case note Austrian Supreme Court, November 18, 1982, Y.B.COM.ARB., IX-1984, 163; D.T., The lex mercatoria in Paris and Vienna, Journal of world trade law, 1983, 362; THOMPSON, D., case note French Supreme Court, October 3, 1984, J.INT.ARB., 75; HUNTER, M., Lex Mercatoria - Deutsche Schachtbau- und Tiefbohrgesellschaft mbh v R/As Al Khaimah National Oil Co., Lloyd's Mar. & Com.L.Q., 1987, 277-280, Arbitration, 1988, 58.

Other authors, on the contrary, have seen the Norsolor case of the Austrian Supreme Court as recognition of the *lex mercatoria* (SEIDL-HOHENVELDERN, I., case note Austrian Supreme Court, November 18, 1982, RIW, 1983, 871 and Clunet, 1983, 649; GOLDMAN, B., Lex mercatoria, 17; GOLDMAN, B., Une bataille judiciaire autour de la lex mercatoria, 399; GOLDMAN, B., The applicable law : general principles of law - lex mercatoria, 121-122; LANDO, O., The lex mercatoria in international commercial arbitration, 757; BÖCKSTIEGEL, K.H., The legal rules applicable in international commercial arbitration involving States or state-controlled enterprises, in International arbitration, 60 years of ICC arbitration, A look at the future, International Chamber of Commerce, publication No. 412, Paris, 1984, 169; JEHL, J., Le commerce international de la technologie, Approche juridique, 102; KAPPUS, A., "Conflict avoidance" durch "lex mercatoria" und UN-Kaufrecht 1980, 792).

258. Riv.Dir.Int.Priv.Proc., 1982, 829, Y.B.COM.ARB., IX- 1984, 418.

The strange element in this case is, of course, the incorporation of the European Convention into the agreement of the parties. The Court argues that the Convention attempts to encourage international commercial arbitration between parties from different Contracting States, irrespective of the arbitral place and the nationality of the arbitrators. In this perspective, the Court refers to an autonomous transnational law that exists within an international business community through the accession of merchants to that community and their acceptance and observance of its rules. Differences between the rules of these communities may exist depending on the degree of their organization. As regards enforcement, these communities still depend on national law. Since parties may be expected to have contracted under the perspective of the application of the European Convention and not English law, there should not be a link between the state of origin of the award and the state of enforcement, but motivation might have been expected under the Convention[259]. Doubts have been expressed as to the relevance[260] and the logic[261] of the reference to the *lex mercatoria*. Furthermore, one may oppose the application of the Convention to awards rendered in non-contracting States[262]. Finally, the major element of criticism is that the rules of the Convention, having been incorporated into the contract, preempt the law of the arbitral seat[263] and, foremost, the arbitral rules under which the arbitration was conducted[264]. Notwithstanding these critical reflections, one cannot deny the importance of the Court's observations regarding the *lex mercatoria*.

---

259. See VAN DELDEN, R., Lex mercatoria of ius commune ?, 17; MANN, F.A., England rejects "delocalized" contracts and arbitration, INT'L & COMP.L.Q., 1984, 196; GOLDMAN, B., Lex mercatoria, 20-22; GOLDMAN, B., Une bataille judiciaire autour de la lex mercatoria, 401.
260. MANN, F.A., England rejects "delocalized" contracts and arbitration, 196; MANN, F.A., Private arbitration and public policy, 265; GOLDMAN, B., Lex mercatoria, 21.
261. GIARDINA, A., Arbitrato transnazionale e lex mercatoria, Di fronte alla Corte di Cassazione, 759.
262. GIARDINA, A., Arbitrato transnazionale e lex mercatoria, 762-764; VAN DEN BERGH, A.J., New York Convention 1958, Commentary cases, Y.B.COM.ARB., IX-1984, 383.
263. MANN, F.A., England rejects "delocalized" contracts and arbitration, 196; *but see* SCHLOSSER, P., Das deutsche Recht der Schiedsgerichtsbarkeit und seine Bedeutung für deutsch-englischen Wirtschaftsbeziehungen, in Handelsschiedsgerichtsbarkeit in England und in der Bundesrepublik Deutschland, BÖCKSTIEGEL, K.H. (ed.), Cologne, Heymanns, 1987, 55-58.
264. GIARDINA, A., Arbitrato transnazionale e lex mercatoria, 761.

395. In Germany, the theory of the *lex mercatoria* was indirectly raised in a setting aside proceeding against an arbitral award which had not only applied English law as the law chosen by the parties but also had referred to French and Dutch law and to *common sense*. The Frankfurt Court of Appeal refused to set the award aside; the procedure that had been followed, had been regular[265] since the award was not merely based on equity or justice. To this, the Court added :

> *"Der Schiedsvertrag ist damit auch nicht auf ein vom nationalen Recht losgelöstes, gewohnheitsrechtlich begründetes Welthandelsrecht, die sog. "lex mercatoria" gestützt worden."* [266]

However, an explicit position of the Court as to the *lex mercatoria* may not be read into this decision.

396. In Belgium, the Brussels District Court and Court of Appeal were faced with the *lex mercatoria* in the course of enforcement proceedings related to an arbitral award between a Belgian manufacturer and its British distributor involving the termination of the distributorship agreement for Great-Britain and Ireland. The arbitrators were authorized to act as *amiables compositeurs* and had applied the *lex mercatoria* to the substance of the dispute[267]. The enforcement was granted because the application of the *lex mercatoria* did not cause any problems because of the *amiable composition* clause[268]. Because of its close relation to *amiable composition*, these Belgian cases may hardly be interpreted as a recognition of the *lex mercatoria* by Belgian courts.

397. The English courts have seldom been expressly confronted with the *lex mercatoria* but in one recent case, transnational rules did arise before them. In *Deutsche Schachtbau- und Tiefbohrgesellschaft mbh v. R'As Al Khamaih*

---

265. § 1041, I (1) ZPO.
266. Court of Appeal Frankfurt, October 26, 1983, RIW, 1984, 400, case note DIELMANN, H. aff'd German Supreme Court, September 26, 1985, NJW, 1986, 1436, JZ, 1986, 401; see ADEN, M., Die Anwendung materiellen Rechts durch den Schiedsrichter, RIW, 1984, 934-938; SANDROCK, O., Zügigkeit und Leichtigkeit versus Gründlichkeit, JZ, 1986, 370-378.
267. I.C.C. award, November 3, 1977, Rev.Arb., 1980, 560, case note SCHAPIRA, J., Y.B.COM.ARB., VII-1982, 77.
268. District Court Brussels, December 12, 1978 and Court of Appeal Brussels, October 14, 1980, *S.A. Mines, minérais et métaux v. Mechema Ltd.*, case 374/79, Y.B.COM.ARB., VII-1982, 316; see MANN, F.A., intervention during the discussions, Basle symposium on the law governing contractual obligations, KLEIN, F.E. and VISCHER, F. (ed.), Basle, Helbing & Lichtenhahn, 1983, 174-175.

National Oil Company[269], enforcement of an award rendered in Switzerland was sought in England. In the absence of a party-designated law, the arbitrators had applied *internationally accepted principles of contract law* to the merits of the dispute. The Court of Appeal did grant the enforcement of the award and refused to review the conflict of laws method used by the arbitrators in the course of enforcement proceedings. In the aftermath of this litigation, further proceedings took place which led to a decision of the House of Lords[270]. One author has read the House of Lords decision as an implied endorsement of the lex mercatoria[271]. However, the House did not have to decide upon this aspect of the Court of Appeal decision. Furthermore, it should again be noted that the lex mercatoria was not expressly raised in this case and that the English courts, as the enforcement forum under the 1958 New York Convention, could only exercise a limited review over the award.

398. Finally, the Court of Appeal of Paris in its decision *Compania Valenciana de Cementos Portland S.A. v. Primary Coal Inc.* refused to set an I.C.C. award aside on the ground that it had applied the lex mercatoria[272]. In this case, in an interim award dated September 1, 1988[273], the arbitrator refused to apply Spanish, New York or English law and chose to apply the *lex mercatoria*, a set of usages which constitute a truly international business law. The award was challenged before the Paris Court of Appeal basically on the ground of article 1502, 3° N.C.P.C. alleging that the arbitrator had exceeded his authority in applying the *lex mercatoria*. The Court dismissed the case. In its opinion, arbitrators are not under article 13 (3) of the I.C.C. Arbitration Rules bound by any domestic conflict rule. The court then concluded that application of the *lex mercatoria* was consistent with the terms of reference because the arbitrator had applied the proper law, having indicated that Spanish, New York and English law would frustrate the contracting parties' tacit will. Furthermore, the Court seems to have referred to article 1496 N.C.P.C. to justify its qualification

---

269. [1987] 3 W.L.R. 1023 (Court of Appeal); Financial Times Law Reports, March 31, 1987, 18.
270. Deutsche Schachtbau- und Tiefbohrgesellschaft mbh and Shell International Petroleum Co. Ltd., [1988] 2 All E.R. 883, [1988] 3 W.L.R. 230 (House of Lords).
271. KAPPUS, A., Einzug der "lex mercatoria" in das englische House of Lords, IPRax., 1990, 135.
272. Court of Appeal Paris, July 13, 1989, Mealey's International Arbitration Report, December 1989, B-1, Clunet, 1990, 430, case note GOLDMAN, B., R.C.D.I.P., 1990, 305, case note OPPETIT, B., Rev.Arb., 1990, 663, case note LAGARDE, P.
273. I.C.C. case No. 5953, Rev.Arb., 1990, 701; the final award was published in Clunet, 1990, 1056, case note DERAINS, Y.

of the *lex mercatoria* as the proper law. However, faced with an I.C.C. arbitration, one may wonder whether more weight should not be given to article 13 (3) of the I.C.C. Arbitration Rules than to article 1496 N.C.P.C. Consequently, the award should have indicated what conflict rule it applied and whether and why the *lex mercatoria* might have been the proper law of the contract. Notwithstanding this criticism regarding the *Valenciana* decision, it is a clear indication of the French courts' restraint in setting aside awards based upon the *lex mercatoria* even in cases falling outside the scope of article 1496 N.C.P.C.

IV.1.3.2 Arbitral case law

399. A review of the *lex mercatoria* in arbitral case law is complicated by the fact that most arbitral awards are not published. Therefore, generalizations are hard to make. In this respect, Schlosser has noted that the *lex mercatoria* cannot be found in the arbitral awards of the (former) arbitration commissions affiliated with the Chambers of Commerce in Central and Eastern European countries. Also, arbitrators from common law countries would not feel a need to apply the *lex mercatoria*[274].

400. These restrictions are less valid with regard to I.C.C. arbitral awards, some of which have been published by extract since 1975. The selection of these awards is, of course, important. It appears that the application of non-national rules has been one of the major selection criteria[275]. The publication of these awards thus gives an incomplete and somewhat distorted picture of the actual practice in I.C.C. arbitrations and the frequency of application of transnational rules.

401. First, some I.C.C. arbitrations have applied the *lex mercatoria* or transnational rules and have led to litigation before national courts. These awards have been discussed above[276].

---

274. SCHLOSSER, P., Das internationale an der internationalen privaten Schiedsgerichtsbarkeit, 866.

275. THOMPSON, R. and DERAINS, Y., Cour d'Arbitrage de la Chambre de Commerce Internationale, Chronique des sentences arbitrales, Clunet, 1974, 878; DERAINS, Y. and JARVIN, S., Cour d'Arbitrage de la Chambre de Commerce Internationale, Chronique des sentences arbitrales, Clunet, 1983, 889.

276. See the Fougerolle- , Norsolor- and Valenciana-cases as well as the November 3, 1977 arbitral award leading to the decisions of the Brussels District Court and Court of Appeal (see supra Nos. 390, 391-393, 396 and 398).

402. In I.C.C. case No. 2291, the arbitral tribunal expressly applied the *lex mercatoria*. The tribunal revised freight tariffs on the basis of the principle of the *lex mercatoria* of *rebus sic stantibus* and according to which in international commercial transactions a certain contractual balance should exist between the mutual obligations of the parties. However, the tribunal only applied this principle in relation to the goods which were not specified at the time of the conclusion of the contract. For goods specified at that time, the freight was not revised since, under French law which was applicable, revision was not possible under those circumstances[277]. Thus, one might interpret this award as a cumulative application of French law and the *lex mercatoria* to the extent that both coexist. When they conflict, French law seems to prevail over the *lex mercatoria*.

403. In I.C.C. case No. 3267 involving a dispute between a Mexican subcontractor and a syndicate of contractors, the arbitrators were authorized to act as *amiables compositeurs* and decided to apply general principles of law as accepted in transnational commerce, without further reference to national law[278]. However, it seems that the arbitrators applied primarily contract clauses.

404. In I.C.C. case No. 3327 dealing with a dispute between a French company and an African state, the *amiables compositeurs* decided that the state was, according to the general principles of law of the *lex mercatoria*, precluded from raising the defence that its law required that, unless otherwise provided by contract, contracts concluded by the state should have been approved through a specific procedure organized by the state's constitution[279].

405. In I.C.C. case No. 3540, the arbitrators had to resolve a dispute between a French company and a Yugoslav subcontractor. The arbitrators were *amiables compositeurs* and referred expressly to the *lex mercatoria* in which they found the principle of set-off between a debt come due and a debt which hasn't yet come due, provided some connection exists between the two debts[280]. However, the arbitrators, at the same time, reviewed the

277. I.C.C. case No. 2291, Clunet, 1976, 989, case note DERAINS, Y.
278. I.C.C. case No. 3267, Clunet, 1980, 962, case note DERAINS, Y., Y.B.COM.ARB., VII-1982, 96.
279. I.C.C. case No. 3327, Clunet, 1982, 971, case note DERAINS, Y.
280. I.C.C. case No. 3540, Clunet, 1981, 914, case note DERAINS, Y., Y.B.COM.ARB., VII-1982, 124.

legal systems that the parties had invoked in order to see whether the same solutions applied in those systems.

406. In I.C.C. case No. 5721, the issue was raised whether an arbitral clause could be invoked against an officer of an American company who had signed contracts for the account of its Egyptian subsidiary which was in the process of incorporation. The arbitral tribunal pierced the corporate veil under reference to the *lex mercatoria*. Good faith in the conduct of international business and trade usages would authorize such a piercing of the corporate veil. The tribunal stated also that it was authorized to rely on the *lex mercatoria* and not solely on Egyptian law as the law applicable to the substance of the dispute because of the principle of the severability of the arbitral clause[281]. Finally, one should note that the arbitrators were *amiables compositeurs* and that they also based the piercing of the corporate veil on a brief comparative analysis of the legal systems connected to the dispute.

407. Sometimes, indirect references to the *lex mercatoria* may be found in I.C.C. cases. First, in I.C.C. case No. 2438, the arbitral tribunal asked whether a national law applies at all to the contractual relations between the litigating parties[282]. Since this question is answered positively, no implicit recognition of the *lex mercatoria* may be read into this award[283]. In a similar vein, I.C.C. case No. 2375 states that the transnational business community may escape the control of national legal systems but the arbitrators limited themselves to the application of contract clauses[284]. Thus, also in this award, the *lex mercatoria* was not applied.

408. In I.C.C. case No. 4761, the *lex mercatoria* was applied expressly but by virtue of an express clause of a preliminary award on agreed terms regarding the law to be applied to the substance of the dispute[285]. The parties provided in that clause that the arbitrators had to apply the *lex mercatoria* if Lybian law was unsettled or not proved with regard to some points of law. A similar setting was found in I.C.C. case No. 5904 where the parties had entrusted the arbitrator with the adjudication according to principles and usages generally applicable in international commerce.

---

281. I.C.C. case No. 5721, Clunet, 1990, 1019, case note DERAINS, Y.
282. I.C.C. case No. 2438, Clunet, 1976, 969, case note DERAINS, Y.
283. *But see* DERAINS, Y., case note under I.C.C. case No. 2438, Clunet, 1976, 971.
284. I.C.C. case No. 2375, Clunet, 1976, 973, case note DERAINS, Y.
285. I.C.C. case No. 4761, Clunet, 1986, 1137, case note JARVIN, S., Clunet, 1987, 1012, case note JARVIN, S.

Therefore, the arbitrator was not bound to look for a national legal system applicable by virtue of a conflict of laws rule. However, having found no specific rules of lex mercatoria with regard to the applicable interest rate, the arbitrator fell back on national legal rules[286].

409. Apart from express references to the *lex mercatoria* or principles of law generally applied in transnational commerce, I.C.C. awards also often refer to transnational trade usages or general principles of law[287]. One may wonder how these references should be interpreted. However, this depends upon the final assessment to be given to the sources and the nature of the *lex mercatoria*, which will be given below[288].

410. Some I.C.C. awards are critical as to the *lex mercatoria*. In I.C.C. case No. 4237, the arbitral tribunal refused to apply the *lex mercatoria* because the parties had invoked application of national law. In an *obiter dictum*, the arbitrator referred to the uncertain contents of the *lex mercatoria*[289]. An analogous situation was presented in I.C.C. case No. 4650 where the arbitral tribunal refused to apply the lex mercatoria in the absence of agreement between the litigating parties as to its application[290].

411. In the context of the Convention on the Settlement of Investment Disputes, arbitrations are held within the I.C.S.I.D. framework. So far, no I.C.S.I.D. awards have expressly used the *lex mercatoria* as applicable law. In some cases, general principles of law have been applied[291]. The question whether these references to principles of law may be interpreted

---

286. I.C.C. case No. 5904, Clunet, 1989, 1107.

287. See the I.C.C. awards cited by FOUCHARD, P., L'arbitrage commercial international, 401 ff.; DEBY-GERARD, F., Le rôle de la règle de conflit dans le règlement des rapports internationaux, 207; LEW, J., Applicable law in international commercial arbitration, 468-472 and VAN HOUTTE, H., Rechtsvinding bij transnationale handelsarbitrage, 265 ff. and 326 ff.; I.C.C. case No. 1397, Clunet, 1974, 879; I.C.C. case No. 1422, Clunet, 1974, 884; I.C.C. case No. 1641, Clunet, 1974, 888; I.C.C. case No. 2375, Clunet, 1976, 973; I.C.C. case No. 2801, cited by DERAINS, Y., case note I.C.C. case No. 2735, Clunet, 1977, 949; I.C.C. case No. 3380, Clunet, 1981, 927, Y.B.COM.ARB., VII-1982, 116; I.C.C. case No. 4131, Clunet, 1983, 899, Y.B.COM.ARB., IX-1984, 131; I.C.C. case No. 2730, Clunet, 1985, 914.

288. See infra IV.1.5.3.D.

289. I.C.C. case No. 4237, February 17, 1984, Y.B.COM.ARB., X-1985, 52.

290. I.C.C. case No. 4650, Y.B.COM.ARB. XII-1987, 111.

291. I.C.S.I.D. award Klöckner belge S.A. and Klöckner Handelsmaatschappij v. Cameron Republic and Société camerounaise des engrais (Clunet, 1987, 137) and I.C.S.I.D. award Amco Asia Corp. v. Republic Indonesia (Clunet, 1986, 201 and Clunet, 1987, 145).

as a recognition of the *lex mercatoria* will be discussed below[292]. At this point, one may already note that the arbitral award in the Klöckner case was set aside under article 52 (1) (b) C.S.I.D. (*manifest excess of powers*) by a decision of an ad hoc Committee dated May 3, 1985. The Committee which was instituted under article 52 (3) C.S.I.D., decided that the arbitral tribunal had manifestly exceeded its powers in imposing upon Klöckner a general obligation to provide adequate and sufficient information without reference to the applicable law that should determine the conditions, scope and consequences of such an obligation. The arbitral tribunal had thus violated article 42 (1) C.S.I.D.(which requires, absent choice of law, that the law of the State, party to the dispute be applied) because it hadn't based its award on that law but on considerations of equity and justice. Thus, it had acted *ex aequo et bono* without authorization from the parties, as provided in article 42 (3) C.S.I.D.[293]. It follows from the decision of the ad hoc Committee that article 42 C.S.I.D. - absent choice of law - leaves scant room for the application of the *lex mercatoria*.

412. From this section, it appears that the *lex mercatoria* has not frequently been applied. Only a very small number of cases decided by state courts, primarily in France and Italy, may be interpreted as a recognition of the *lex mercatoria* theory of Goldman. The same holds true for I.C.C. arbitrations[294] and I.C.S.I.D. awards. With regard to I.C.C. case law, one may note that some cases are based on a party choice for the *lex mercatoria* or on *amiable composition*. Notwithstanding these infrequent references to the *lex mercatoria*, one cannot ignore the role that trade usages and general principles of law play in international business law and particularly in international commercial arbitral adjudication. This will be analyzed below[295].

---

292. Goldman, who also was the president of the I.C.S.I.D. arbitration panel in the case Amco Asia Corp. v. Republic Indonesia, has argued that this case has recognized the *lex mercatoria* (see GOLDMAN, B., The applicable law : general principles of law - lex mercatoria, 122).

293. Clunet, 1987, 167-168.

294. See also BÖCKSTIEGEL, K.H., Die Bestimmung des anwendbaren Rechts in der Praxis internationaler Schiedsgerichtsverfahren, 457; SCHLOSSER, P., Das internationale an der internationalen privaten Schiedsgerichtsbarkeit, 866; BRAECKMANS, H., De lex mercatoria. Zijn verhouding tot het nationaal recht en meer specifiek tot het internationaal privaatrecht, 2664; BRAECKMANS, H., Paralegale normen en lex mercatoria, 56; JARVIN, S., case note I.C.C. case No. 4761, Clunet, 1986, 1138; *but see* GOLDMAN, B., Lex mercatoria, 8-10.

295. See infra Nos. 450 and 466 ff.

IV.1.4 *The lex mercatoria in transnational practice*

413. It is very difficult to measure the impact of the theory of the *lex mercatoria* on transnational practice because of the difficulties involved in finding documents used in transnational practice and the incomplete character of any inventory of that practice. Here, only some indications will be given.

Transnational practice consists of many forms of documents used in international trade to regulate the conduct of its participants. It includes transnational contracts, general conditions, arbitration rules, codes of conduct and codifications of trade usages and other rules. Some of these documents make reference to usages or general principles accepted in international trade[296] and have been interpreted by some authors as references to the *lex mercatoria*[297]. However, one should be careful not to read one's own perceptions about the *lex mercatoria* into the contract. These clauses might, however, also be construed in a sensible way if one is not a proponent of Goldman's theory on the *lex mercatoria*.

Explicit references to the *lex mercatoria* are, on the other hand, highly relevant for its analysis. However, any such clauses are rare. An analysis of 452 I.C.C. arbitration clauses has for instance shown that no references to lex mercatoria were found while parties chose a given national law in 75%

---

296. Article 13 (5) I.C.C. Arbitration Rules (I.C.C. publication No. 447, Paris, 1987), article 33 Uncitral Arbitration Rules.

Scant empirical research has been done in this area, see, however, VERWILGHEN, M. and RAVET-GOBBE, A.F., Une enquête sur la pratique du contrat international dans les milieus d'affaires belges, and DE DONCKER, C., JONGLET, J., LAMBRECHT, M., LEMAIRE, M. and LENOBLE, J., Analyse de clauses contenues dans des contrats internationaux conclus entre entrepreneurs belges et étrangers, in Le contrat économique international, Travaux des VIIes Journées d'études juridiques Jean Dabin, Brussels, Bruylant, 1975, 313 and 361 and ROBERT, J., Le phénomène transnational, Paris, LGDJ, 1988, 39-41 on the contract practices of twelve major French companies engaged in international commerce.

297. GOLDMAN, B., La lex mercatoria dans les contrats et l'arbitrage internationaux : réalité et perspectives, 479; GOLDMAN, B., intervention during the discussions, Basle symposium on the law governing contractual obligations, KLEIN, F.E. and VISCHER, F. (ed.), Basle, Helbing & Lichtenhahn, 1983, 127; HORN, N., Die Anpassung langfristiger Verträge internationalen Wirtschaftsverkehr, Vertragsklauseln und Schiedspraxis, 59; LANDO, O., Conflict-of-law rules for arbitrators, 167; CRAIG, W., PARK, W. and PAULSSON, J., International Chamber of Commerce Arbitration, Dobbs Ferry, New York, Oceana, 1985, 13; *but see* KASSIS, A., Théorie générale des usages du commerce, 430-432; CHAPELLE, A., case note Court of Appeal Paris, October 21, 1983, Rev.Arb., 1984, 106.

and 66% of these contracts[298]. An explicit reference to the *lex mercatoria* could be found in only one document. In its comments to article 21 of its Rules of Operation, the Belgian State Credit Insurance Agency (*Office National du Ducroire*), requires that a tender for a procurement contract should make a reservation against clauses which would derogate from transnational usages. Absent such a clause, the Agency might refuse to intervene under its cover relating to a request for payment under a bid bond, provided the demand under the bid bond is related to the non-conclusion of the contract. In turn, the non-formation of the contract should have been caused by the refusal of the Export Credit Agency to give cover under the contract because of clauses which derogate from international trade usages. The comments to the Operational Rules in this regard provide that the exporters are deemed to know the lex mercatoria and are obliged to conclude contracts which are consistent with international usages[299].

414. Finally, in order to assess the importance of the lex mercatoria for transnational practice, one may refer to the opinions of practitioners who have taken different positions as to the lex mercatoria[300].

IV.1.5 *Assessment of the theory of the lex mercatoria*

415. From the analysis above, it has become clear that two basic conceptions on the theory of the *lex mercatoria* should be distinguished. To assess the theory, this distinction should be kept in mind. Thus, hereafter, the theories of Schmitthoff and Goldman will be discussed separately.

IV.1.5.1 Assessment of Schmitthoff's theory of the lex mercatoria

416. The theory of Clive Schmitthoff emphasizes the importance of international sources (particularly international conventions and international usages) for the law of international trade. However, these sources of international origin are to be situated within the applicable national law. Other authors among which Kurt Siehr, have endorsed this position but

298. BOND, S., How to draft an arbitration clause (revisited), The ICC International Court of Arbitration Bulletin, 1990, No. 2, 19; BOND, S., How to draft an arbitration clause, 6 J.INT.ARB. 1989, 74.

299. National Credit Export Agency, Rules of Operation (652-1985), Contact No. 50, February 1985, 96; see SIMONT, L., Les mécanismes financiers des contrats internationaux, Rev.Dr.Int.Comp., 1980, 279.

300. See supra Nos. 333-334.

have argued that sources of national origin also form part of the *lex mercatoria*[301].

417. The underlying policy in Schmitthoff's theory is by and large the idea of unification of law. In this respect, one can easily understand why international conventions on the unification of law and uniform international practice play such a crucial role in his theory. Of course, one may approve of Schmitthoff's efforts to point to the importance of international conventions and self-regulation for the unification of the law which might ultimately lead to a reduction of national differences and elements of regional or universal law. Also, from both a practical and theoretical perspective, one cannot operate in international business life and understand international business law without some understanding of the mechanisms of transnational self-regulation. However, sources of national origin (statutory law, case law of national courts) are also important for international business law. From the unification perspective, Schmitthoff's intuition led him to believe that sources of international origin might be better instruments of unification. One may wonder whether this is a sufficient justification for not studying unifying effects which take place at the level of the sources of national origin (*e.g.*, comparative research for preparation of legislation or in case law). Consequently, one may doubt whether the restriction to sources of international origin can be upheld.

IV.1.5.2 Extrapolation of Schmitthoff's theory : the lex mercatoria as an independent branch of national law

418. In Schmitthoff's view, the *lex mercatoria* is a complex and unsystematic set of rules[302]. One might extrapolate from this position and wonder whether the *lex mercatoria* or (to avoid confusion) international business law is a branch of national law with a sufficient degree of autonomy or whether, as in Schmitthoff's view, it is just a name to group different rules applicable to international business transactions. Since systematization is more important in civil than in common law jurisdictions, the discussion below seems to be more relevant in civil law countries.

419. Generally, one cannot say when certain rules have developed sufficient features of their own to be considered an independent branch of the law.

---

301. See supra No. 355.

302. SCHMITTHOFF, C., The unification of the law of international trade, J.BUS.L., 1968, 112.

This process is a dynamic one. Furthermore, autonomy within a national legal system never is absolute but rather gradual[303].

420. Autonomy within national legal systems may be analyzed from two angles. On the one hand, one might look to the sources, the contents and the structure of international business law. On the other hand, one also might determine the relation between international business law and other branches of national law[304]. To put it in other words, the question arises whether international business law has both *internal* and *external* autonomy within a given national legal system. Reimann has formulated this as follows :

> *"Zum zweiten kann mit dem Wort Eigengesetzlichkeit die inhaltliche, materielle Unabhängigkeit und Eigenständigkeit von Normen gemeint sein. Autonom wäre danach ein Recht, das seine Prinzipien und deren Ausgestaltung nicht von anderen Rechtsgebieten entlehnt, sondern neue, eigene Lösungen für seine speziellen Problemstellungen entwickelt."* [305]

421. From the notions of internal and external autonomy, it follows that international business law should have a sufficient number of specific[306] rules and principles[307] which may give it an internal consistency[308] and that, to a certain extent, it should be self-sufficient in its relation to civil and commercial law, conflict of laws and arbitration law. In this respect, international business law should have a scope of application of its own and

---

303. *Compare* GASSIN, R., Lois spéciales et droit commun, D., 1961, 93-97.
304. See GASSIN, R., Lois spéciales et droit commun, 97.
305. REIMANN, T., Zur Lehre vom "rechtsordnungslosen" Vertrag, 30.
306. The specificity of international business law may be one of the justifications for specific rules. Some authors have argued that the international character of trade and the need for uniform law are insufficient to have a commercial law, apart from civil law (FREDERICQ, S., De eenmaking van het burgerlijk recht en het handelsrecht, 118-123; WERY, P., De autonomie van het eenvormig privaatrecht, 7). A fortiori, one might say that there is no need for an international business law, apart from general private law.
307. These rules and principles may derogate from the rules of national law which might otherwise be applicable (*compare* KASSIS, A., Théorie générale des usages du commerce, 236-237) or may supplement these rules (*compare* FREDERICQ, S., De eenmaking van het burgerlijk recht en het handelsrecht, 553).
308. *Compare* VIANDIER, A., Actes de commerce, commerçants, activité commerciale, 22; ROZMARYN, S., intervention during the discussions, in GODWIN SARRE, D., A note on the discussions of the colloquium, in The sources of the law of international trade, SCHMITTHOFF, C. (ed.), London, Stevens & Sons, 1964, 260; BURIN DES ROZIERS, H., La distinction du droit civil et du droit commercial et le droit anglais, Paris, LGDJ, 1959, 13-14; GASSIN, R., Lois spéciales et droit commun, 97.

a technique to have its gaps filled, other than merely referring the solution back to other branches of the law[309].

422. As to its scope, Chapter I has made clear that international business law has no uniform scope of application. Different conceptions exist as to the definition of its international and business character and no uniform territorial scope may be found.

As to its sources, these also exist within other fields of national law and are generally not different for international business problems. In this respect, international business law, in contrast with for instance, public international law or EEC law, seems too much embedded in national law in order to develop its own sources. However, this does not imply that national law should always control these issues; in its application regard should be had to the international character of the transaction.

As to its contents, the analysis has made clear that few transnational customs or general principles of law exist from which international business law might be further developed. Trade usages, self-regulatory rules, codes of conduct and professional and other standards are to a large extent influenced by the applicable contract law which will determine their status. Finally, rules in international conventions are too heterogeneous in order to be very useful for international business law. Also, conflict of laws and the applicable substantive law are still relevant in the process of interpretation and gap filling of these conventions.

Finally, as to its relation with other fields of national law, international business law seems to have an insufficient methodology to independently solve interpretation and gap filling problems. Thus, frequently, recourse is to be had to other rules of the applicable national law.

423. From this analysis, the conclusion may be drawn that, at the present time, one can hardly say that international business law is an independent field of national law with its own rules which may be applied without frequent reference to other fields of that law. The hypothesis of an extrapolation from Schmitthoff's theory must thus fail. Therefore, one might say that international business law consists of a mix of rules of national law from various sources (national, international, self-regulatory) relating to conflict of laws, substantive law and civil procedure in which the interplay between these rules is of paramount importance.

---

309. *Compare* BURIN DES ROZIERS, H., La distinction du droit civil et du droit commercial et le droit anglais, 13-14; VIANDIER, A., Actes de commerce, commerçants, activité commerciale, 22; GASSIN, R., Lois spéciales et droit commun, 97; REIMANN, T., Zur Lehre vom "rechtsordnungslosen" Vertrag, 31.

IV.1.5.3 Assessment of the theory of the lex mercatoria as an autonomous legal system

424. In this subsection, Goldman's theory on the *lex mercatoria* will be assessed. As stated in Chapter II[310], conflict of laws regarding international contracts is so pragmatic that the *lex mercatoria* might be applicable before national courts, provided it can be characterized as a legal system. This implies that it should have its own scope, sources, contents and mandatory rules. In relation to international commercial arbitration where choice of law methodology is even more relaxed, the *lex mercatoria* should have its own conflict of laws system which can determine its application. These requirements are discussed below. First, the application of the *lex mercatoria* before national courts and arbitral tribunals will be discussed. Furthermore, the substantive sources of the *lex mercatoria* will be analyzed. Finally, an assessment of the theory will be given.

A. The lex mercatoria as chosen or proper law before national courts

425. The way national courts look at international contracts has been discussed in Chapter II.2. In this section, that analysis will be applied in relation to the theory of the *lex mercatoria.* The basic issue is whether national courts might apply the *lex mercatoria* as law chosen by the parties or as the proper law of the contract, absent any such choice.

426. In all cases and whatever the theoretical explanation, national courts use their own conflict rules to determine the applicable law. As to the *lex mercatoria*, Lagarde has made it very clear that application before national courts of the *lex mercatoria* through a transnational substantive rule would violate the conflict rule applicable for the court having jurisdiction over the case[311]. However, the proponents of the *lex mercatoria* have not argued that it would be applicable without the support of a rule of the conflict system of the *lex fori*. They have proposed to base its application on a conflict rule or a transnational substantive rule of the *lex fori*[312].

---

310. See supra Nos. 192-194.

311. Approche critique de la lex mercatoria, 144-146; see also BRAECKMANS, H., Juridische aspecten van consortiumkredieten in Eurodeviezen, 1983, 938; BRAECKMANS, H., De lex mercatoria. Zijn verhouding tot het nationaal recht en meer specifiek tot het internationaal privaatrecht, 2677-2680; BRAECKMANS, H., Paralegale normen en lex mercatoria, 66-67.

312. In favour of a transnational substantive rule, see LOUSSOUARN, Y., intervention during the discussions, Basle symposium on the law governing contractual obligations, KLEIN, F.E. and VISCHER, F. (ed.), Basle, Helbing & Lichtenhahn, 1983, 131.

This is very important. The *lex fori* will thus determine whether and how the *lex mercatoria* might be applied. The scope and limits on its application by national courts are set by the *lex fori*. This implies that the requirements which one may find in the *lex fori* will be applied. The analysis of Chapter II.2 is then applicable to the integration of the *lex mercatoria* in its application by national courts. Consequently, this integration process may differ from country to country, and in its application by national courts, uniformity is not guaranteed[313]. For instance, Diener has argued that the parties should prove the contents of the *lex mercatoria*[314]. This might have been correct under French law but one should realize that jurisdictions take different positions as to the evidence of foreign law[315].

B. The lex mercatoria as applicable law in international commercial arbitration

427. In Chapter II.3, the different theories about the conflict system to be applied by the arbitrators have been discussed. Some of these theories the most important of which is the arbitral seat theory, connect the arbitral conflict system to a national system of conflict of laws[316]. Because national conflict rules are applied, there are hardly any differences from

---

313. It is an overstatement to consider the principle of choice of law for international contracts as a general principle of law. Furthermore, in its concrete applications, differences between jurisdictions appear (*compare* FRANCESCAKIS, P., case note Commission arbitrale soviétique pour le commerce extérieur, R.C.D.I.P., 1971, 494-495; YNTEMA, H., "Autonomy" in choice of law, AM.J.COMP.L., 1952, 350-351; BERVOETS, T., Rechtskeuze, Een rechtstheoretisch onderzoek van het beginsel der rechtskeuze, 40).

314. DIENER, M., Contrats internationaux de propriété industrielle, 72.
A recent French Supreme Court case states that the Court should not review the principles and usages of international trade (French Supreme Court, January 6, 1987, Clunet, 1987, 638, case note GOLDMAN, B., Rev.Arb., 1987, 469, case note LEBOULANGER, P.). One might interpret this case as an indication that the principles and usages of international trade are set on the same footing as foreign law which, up to that date, was not reviewed by the Supreme Court.

315. In Belgium, Germany, The Netherlands and Switzerland, courts are assumed to look into the contents of foreign law, see Belgian Supreme Court, October 9, 1980, Pas., 1981, I, 159, J.T., 1981, 70, opinion KRINGS, E. and case note VANDER ELST, R., R.W., 1981-82, 1471, case note ERAUW, J., R.C.J.B., 1982, 8, case note RIGAUX, F.; SAUVEPLANNE, G., Elementair internationaal privaatreht, 126-127; KEGEL, G., Die Ermittlung ausländischen Rechts, 166-167 and article 16 Swiss Law on Conflict of Laws. In England, the opposite position prevails, see CHESHIRE, G. and NORTH, P., Private international law, 125.

316. See supra Nos. 137-141.

litigation in national courts. Thus, the choice of the dispute settlement mechanism does not change the conflict of laws process in its relation to non-national rules since national conflict rules are applicable. The elements of the analysis pertaining to the *lex mercatoria* before national courts, are *mutatis mutandis* applicable under these theories[317].

428. That being said, the relation between the theory of the *lex mercatoria* and the theory of autonomous conflict rules[318] becomes apparent. In order to avoid the impact of national conflict rules on the application of the *lex mercatoria*[319], non-national conflict rules are created. Autonomous conflict rules may, then, within the framework of transnational commercial arbitration, lead to the application of the *lex mercatoria*. However, it remains unclear whether the proponents of the *lex mercatoria* would include an autonomous arbitral conflict system within that same *lex mercatoria*. Under such a perspective, the *lex mercatoria* would include conflict and substantive rules. An opposite view may also exist. Under that view, autonomous conflict rules would only free arbitrators from national conflict rules but would still oblige them to apply national substantive law. Both views are discussed below.

429. The desire to be freed from national conflict rules and to give arbitrators more freedom in arbitral conflict of laws adjudication, might well be seen as distinct from the tendency to detach international business transactions from national law. The former policy consideration is related to conflict of laws while the latter one is situated at the level of substantive law. If only the former one is followed, arbitrators might have authority to choose the applicable law but that choice would be limited to national legal systems and could not include a choice of the *lex mercatoria*. Thus, there only is a question as to the possibility of autonomous conflict rules but not as to the application of the substantive provisions of the *lex mercatoria*. This theory may raise some problems because it seems unclear where conflict rules or transnational substantive rules should be found and where one should look for answers to methodological problems[320]. To a certain extent, conflict of laws and substantive law are interrelated and, therefore,

317. See supra Nos. 88, 92 and 103.
318. See supra No. 142.
319. See supra No. 135.
320. *E.g.*, qualification, *renvoi*, preliminary questions, evidence of law, *ex officio* application of conflict rules, *fraude à la loi*, exception of international public policy, mandatory rules.

substantive law might influence conflict of laws and thus, reduce the autonomy of arbitral conflict rules.

430. The other view is to see autonomous conflict rules as constituent parts of the *lex mercatoria*[321] which will determine the conflict of laws issues raised in international commercial arbitrations. For instance, autonomous rules would have to determine what connecting factors should exist between the *lex mercatoria* and an international business transaction. The main problem is that the *lex mercatoria* cannot be localized geographically. Bucher has argued that the will of the parties might be such a factor; the parties should then be able to choose the *lex mercatoria* as the law of the transnational business community, notwithstanding the fact that it cannot be localized geographically[322]. Absent choice of law, *lex mercatoria* might, according to Weise, exceptionally be applicable if the circumstances of the case or the nature of the contract indicate that the parties intended to have their contract governed by non-national legal rules[323].

A further question is whether these rules may also refer to national law if the autonomous rule localizes the transaction not in the *lex mercatoria* but in national law. In that case, the further question is whether the concrete application of national law should not be reviewed against fundamental values of the *lex mercatoria*. The proponents of the *lex mercatoria* have argued that it would have a *truly international or transnational public policy*[324].

Among the rules of the arbitral autonomous system, one may find transnational substantive rules. Some authors have argued that the *lex mercatoria* should be applied through such a transnational rule[325]. The question then arises as to the scope and the limits of such a rule. Mostly, this rule is understood as an almost unlimited freedom for parties and arbitrators to determine the applicable substantive rules. Seldom, attention has been paid by the proponents of the theory of the *lex mercatoria* to

---

321. This theory has been rejected by Klein and Stoecker (KLEIN, F.E., La Convention européenne sur l'arbitrage commercial international, 634; KLEIN, F.E., L'arbitrage international de droit privé, Réalités et perspectives, Ann.suisse Dr.Int., 1963, 55-57; STOECKER, C., The lex mercatoria : to what extent does it exist ?, 109-113).

322. BUCHER, A., Transnationales Recht im ipr, 48.

323. WEISE, P.F., Lex mercatoria, 137-142.

324. GOLDMAN, B., Arbitrage international et droit commun des nations, 116; see also infra No. 446.

In a similar vein, one might argue that *fraude à la loi* might be sanctioned, provided rules of the *lex mercatoria* are evaded.

325. See supra No. 106; WEISE, P.F., Lex mercatoria, 137-138 seems to be hesitant to apply the *lex mercatoria* through a substantive rather than through a conflict rule.

develop, within such a unilateral perspective, a set of transnational mandatory rules which might protect the public interest and private interests. For instance, Bucher stated that recognition of the *lex mercatoria* is not dependent on it having transnational mandatory rules; he thought that the exception of international public policy might be sufficient[326].

431. By way of summary, one can say that, because of its international character, a conflict of laws technique must be used in order to apply the *lex mercatoria* in the course of international commercial arbitrations. A national conflict rule would either lead to the application of national law or, if the *lex mercatoria* might be applied, to a certain extent *nationalize* the *lex mercatoria*. For that reason and in order to free arbitrators from national conflict of laws, autonomous conflict rules are proposed. The question is where these may come from and how their contents, scope and objectives are to be determined.

432. These rules might be found in custom or general principles of law. It is hard to believe that customary conflict rules exist. Thus, one primarily has to rely on general principles of conflict of laws[327]. As has been seen in the general overview on general principles of law[328], these principles generally are not legal rules but rather act as guidelines which need further development and concretization. One may thus doubt whether an autonomous system of conflict of laws exists and whether general principles of conflict of laws can be applied in the course of international commercial arbitration. For instance, the principle of choice of law in contracts is neither universal in all its effects nor sufficiently concrete in its application[329]. Other principles are hard to recognize.

---

326. BUCHER, A., Transnationales Recht im ipr, 39.
327. DERAINS, Y., Attente légitime des parties et droit applicable au fond en matière d'arbitrage commercial international, 84-85.
328. See supra III.6.
329. STOLL, J., Vereinbarungen zwischen Staat und ausländischem Investor, 69-70.

C. The substantive[330] rules of the lex mercatoria

433. In Chapter III, the various sources of international business law have been discussed. To some extent, these sources are also the sources of the *lex mercatoria*. From the analysis in Chapter III, it was clear that general conditions, standard contracts, usual contract clauses, professional and other standards, codes of conduct, arbitral case law[331] and international conventions are not, in Goldman's theory, genuine sources of the *lex mercatoria*. Hereafter, customs and usages, self-regulatory rules and general principles of law are discussed in their relation to the *lex mercatoria*.

434. As to usages, some authors have stated that, in international commercial arbitration, their force should not be determined according to national law. Their legal status would be autonomous[332]; they would be applicable through a transnational substantive rule rather than through a conflict rule[333]. This position has far reaching consequences; it implies that usages should be applied, irrespective of the applicable law and thus, maybe even

---

330. One may also wonder whether the *lex mercatoria* contains procedural rules. Proponents of the *lex mercatoria* have argued for a complete autonomy with respect to the arbitral procedure but have rarely made clear whether autonomous procedural rules were part of the *lex mercatoria*. Here again, one may question whether this might be left completely to the parties and the arbitrators or whether some gap filling mechanisms and mandatory rules should be present (DAVID, R., L'arbitrage dans le commerce international, 105-106 and 431). In the latter case, these elements should be sought in the *lex mercatoria* itself since it is seen as an autonomous legal system. Since only customs and general principles of law are genuine sources (see infra Nos. 434-445) and hardly any procedural customs exists, procedural rules should primarily be sought in general principles of law. However, few such procedural principles seem to exist as a formal source (see also STOECKER, C., The lex mercatoria : to what extent does it exist ?, 113-118).

331. Although arbitral case law has not been characterized as a formal source of law, its publication may be important for the development of the *lex mercatoria*. Thus, proponents of the *lex mercatoria* have argued for a relaxation of the confidential nature of arbitration, see GAILLARD, E., Le principe de confidentialité de l'arbitrage commercial international, D., 1987, 153.

332. VAN HOUTTE, H., Het gebruik ontstaan uit contract of verdrag, 2181-2182; *compare* VAN HOUTTE, H., Rechtsvinding bij transnationale handelsarbitrage, 278-279. Schmitthoff (International trade usages, 46) reported this as follows: "In Belgium, according to a comment of Professor Van Houtte in the Belgian report, the conflict of laws allows the arbitrator to apply international trade custom directly as they are the law of the legal environment with which the issue is most closely connected.". It seems that the statement as to Belgian law expresses more a personal opinion of Van Houtte than a general consensus of Belgian writers.

333. DERAINS, Y., case note I.C.C. case No. 2745 and 2762, Clunet, 1978, 989; LOQUIN, E., La réalité des usages du commerce international, R.I.D.E., 1989, 164.

contrary to the applicable law. The status of usages under the applicable law is then irrelevant; requirements, nature, hierarchy with other rules and evidence under the applicable law are not taken into account. In this respect, Derains has argued that usages, in some cases, may even preempt an express or tacit will of the parties, irrespective of the applicable law[334]. One may doubt whether this is correct. ULIS and ULFIS have also not settled this problem and left that to the applicable law, notwithstanding the general distrust in both uniform sales laws for conflict of laws.

Often, the transnational substantive rule that usages should be applied irrespective of the applicable law, is based on the argument that parties by submitting their dispute to international commercial arbitration tacitly have chosen the application of the usages of the trade[335]. The argument falls back on a fictitious will of the parties.

One may thus wonder whether the transnational substantive rule developed by some authors is after all such a good idea and whether the traditional conflict rule might not be a better solution. However, one should note that international conventions, model laws and national statutes have given a special status to usages as dispute settlement rules in international commercial arbitrations but that this is not an argument in relation to the debate on an autonomous *lex mercatoria*[336]. Finally, a transnational substantive rule is not necessary in order to have the *lex mercatoria* applied; it may as well be applicable through a conflict rule.

435. A transnational substantive rule which provides for the application of usages, does not make much sense if the legal status of these usages is not determined by the *lex mercatoria*. In the analysis in the previous chapter[337], the different conceptions of national laws regarding usages have been shown. It is unclear what conception the *lex mercatoria* would follow. Since none of the legal systems or international conventions which have been analyzed qualifies usages as genuine sources of law, it is hard to see why the *lex mercatoria* would take such a position. Transnational usages are, thus, not a formal source of the *lex mercatoria*. Furthermore, it seems that the *lex mercatoria* has hardly any rules on the status of usages. One may thus question whether it is sensible to have the *lex mercatoria* applied

334. DERAINS, Y., case note I.C.C. case No. 2708, Clunet, 1977, 947.

335. See VAN HOUTTE, H., Rechtsvinding bij transnationale handelsarbitrage, 276-277; for a recent example regarding a national arbitration, see Court of Appeal Paris, March 3, 1981, Rev.Arb., 1982, 298, case note FOUCHARD, P.

336. See supra No. 147.

337. See supra III.2.1.

through a substantive or conflict rule if it has fewer answers than national law regarding usages.

Finally, one might say that there is a clear impression that transnational arbitral tribunals create new legal rules rather than applying transnational usages[338].

436. On the other hand, custom is a formal source of national law and may thus well be a source of the *lex mercatoria*. However, it is uncertain what requirements the *lex mercatoria* would impose for the formation of custom and what the relation would be between custom and its other sources. Again, one might prefer to apply national law with longer standing regarding these issues than the *lex mercatoria*. Also, the analysis in Chapter III made clear that in commercial life few customs exist.

437. Self-regulatory rules are as yet no genuine sources of law[339]. Their force is determined through the applicable law. Thus, these rules are not a formal source of the *lex mercatoria* but, eventually, they might be applied by virtue of a transnational company law. One may doubt whether such a law exists at the present time[340].

438. Finally, one might consider whether general principles of law are formal sources of the *lex mercatoria*. These principles are not the ones found in applicable national laws but, in order to denationalize the *lex mercatoria* from national law, transnational principles should be found which are common to several legal systems or really transnational. Here, the proponents of the *lex mercatoria* seem to have been confused by the fact that the notion of general principles of law may have many meanings. On the one hand, it has been stated that international trade has its own principles which should be distinguished from a *comparative method* which analyzes national laws in order to find principles common to these systems[341]. On the other hand, one notes that national rules are also

338. VAN RYN, J. and HEENEN, J., Principes de droit commercial, I, 1976, 53.

339. See supra III.3.

340. See supra No. 56.

341. GOLDMAN, B., intervention during the discussions, in Les accords entre un Etat et une personne privée étrangère, Institute of international law, 58 Annuaire, 1979, II, 54; *compare* LOQUIN, E., L'application de règles anationales dans l'arbitrage commercial international, 117-118; BEGUIN, J., Le développement de la lex mercatoria menace-t-il l'ordre juridique international ?, 484 and 517.

compared in order to solve a transnational business dispute[342]. The attitude of the proponents of the *lex mercatoria* towards the method of finding general principles of law is thus ambivalent. In this respect, Roth has observed that principles which have been found through a comparative process are, to a large extent, influenced by the national systems from which they have been drawn and, therefore, do not necessarily offer better solutions for international business disputes than national law[343]. Similarly, Lagarde argued that general principles of law are either sources of public international law or of national law and thus, cannot be formal sources of the *lex mercatoria*[344]. Other authors have doubted whether it makes sense to apply general principles after all[345], whether one should authorize some parts of the international business community to create their own rules[346], or whether one might create general principles of law through an inductive process[347].

439. These arguments need further analysis. First, there is a general consensus that universal general principles of law hardly exist[348]. However, unanimity does not seem to be a requirement for transnational principles[349]. Thus, a selective process takes place when general principles are being chosen or developed[350]. The key issue is then how this selection

---

342. FOUCHARD, P., L'arbitrage commercial international, 423-424; OPPETIT, B., Arbitrage et contrats d'Etat, L'arbitrage Framatone et autres c/ Atomic Energy Organization of Iran, Clunet, 1984, 45; GAILLARD, E., Centre International pour le règlement des différends relatifs aux investissements, Chronique des sentences arbitrales, Clunet, 1987, 156-157; LANDO, O., Conflict-of-law rules for arbitrators, 167-168.
343. ROTH, W.H., Internationale Versicherungsvertragsrecht, 556-557.
344. LAGARDE, P., Approche critique de la lex mercatoria, 131-132.
345. REDFERN, A. and HUNTER, M., Law and practice of international commercial arbitration, first edition, 86-87.
346. MAYER, P., Droit international privé, second edition, 20.
347. RIGAUX, F. and VANDER ELST, R., Relations juridiques transnationales ou dialogue sur un autre droit, 232.
348. EBERT, K., Rechtsvergleichung, Einführung in die Grundlagen, Bern, Stämpfli, 1978, 183; SALMON, J., Les principes généraux du droit, Une insaisissable source du droit applicable aux contrats d'état, 741-742.
349. MANN, F.A., Reflections on a commercial law of nations, 38-39; LORENZ, W., Rechtsvergleichung als Methode zur Konkretisierung der allgemeinen Grundsätze des Rechts, JZ, 1962, 270; GENTINETTA, J., Die lex fori internationaler Handelsschiedsgerichte, 146.
350. DASSER, F., Internationale Schiedsgerichte und lex mercatoria, 114-115.

is done. In order to avoid arbitrary decisions, there should be some method to guide this process[351].

440. In choosing a general principle, quantitative and qualitative criteria have been proposed. As to the quantitative criterion, one generally agrees that general principles of law are not a common denominator of rules of many legal systems[352]. For instance, Fouchard proposed that only a small number of similar legal systems should be analyzed[353]. As to the qualitative criterion which is applicable if no common solution among national systems may be found, various solutions have been suggested. One position argues for the most reasonable solution[354]. Fouchard proposed application of the most appropriate rule[355]. Finally, Kropholler and Huys/Keutgen would prefer to look for a solution which may be found in international conventions and uniform laws[356].

441. Comparative law may be an important method in the formation of general principles of law[357]. This method has been described by Rigaux. The method consists of four stages. First, information is collected, then the legal systems are compared. In a third stage, the similarities are identified and, finally, a general principle is induced from these similar rules[358].

---

351. BATIFFOL, H. and LAGARDE, P., Droit international privé, I, 405; SUMAMPOUW, M., case note Swiss Supreme Court, March 23, 1965, RabelsZ, 1966, 348; CRAIG, W., PARK, W. and PAULSSON, J., International Chamber of Commerce arbitration, § 35, 10; BAJONS, E.M., Zur Nationalität internationaler Schiedssachen, 25; FOUCHARD, P., L'arbitrage commercial international, 423; FOUCHARD, P., L'autonomie de l'arbitrage commercial international, 106.
352. VAN HOUTTE, H., Rechtsvinding bij transnationale handelsarbitrage, 346.
353. FOUCHARD, P., L'arbitrage commercial international, 424.
354. COING, H., La détermination de la loi contractuelle en droit international privé allemand, 51.
355. FOUCHARD, P., L'arbitrage commercial international, 424.
356. KROPHOLLER, J., Internationales Einheitsrecht, 162-163; HUYS, M. and KEUTGEN, G., L'arbitrage en droit belge et international, 594.
357. SCHLESINGER, R. and GUNDISCH, H.J., Allgemeine Rechtsgrundsätze als Sachnormen in Schiedsgerichtsverfahren, 31; KROPHOLLER, J., Internationales Einheitsreht, 159-161; EBERT, K., Rechtsvergleichung, 185; REIMANN, T., Zur Lehre vom "rechtsordnungslosen" Vertrag, 73-76; GAILLARD, E., Centre International pour le règlement des différends relatifs aux investissements, Chronique des sentences arbitrales, 142-143.
358. RIGAUX, F., Le rôle de la comparaison dans la préparation de la réglementation juridique internationale, 334 and 346; see also SCHLESINGER, R., The common core of legal systems, An emerging subject of comparative study, in XXth Century comparative and conflicts law, Legal essays in honor of Hessel E. Yntema, Leyden, Sijthoff, 1961, 65-79.

However, one notes that in transnational practice, scant comparative research has been done. This is probably due to the practical problems in doing comparative research in relation to concrete dispute resolution such as time and cost constraints, lack of information or of adequate comparative knowledge. These practical problems have been insufficiently stressed[359]. A direct consequence is, however, that this method leaves judges and arbitrators with great freedom in their search for and creation of general principles[360].

442. Some transnational general principles of law have been discussed in case law and legal literature[361]. First, the proponents of the *lex mercatoria* have generally characterized the principle of *pacta sunt servanda* as a transnational principle[362]. However, that principle is vague and will hardly be able to solve the dispute; in many cases the dispute will rather focus on the requirements, limits and consequences of such a principle[363]. This

---

359. See VON HOFFMANN, B., "Lex mercatoria" vor internationalen Schiedsgerichten, 107.
360. RIGAUX, F., Droit public et droit privé dans les relations internationales, 400; RIGAUX, F., Le rôle de la comparaison dans la préparation de la réglementation juridique internationale, in Rapports belges au Xe Congrès international de droit comparé, Brussels, Bruylant, 1978, 348; RIGAUX, F., Le droit comparé comme science appliquée, 73 and 76-77; VERHOEVEN, J., Arbitrage entre Etats et entreprises étrangères : des règles spécifiques ?, 625; SALMON, J., Les principes généraux du droit, Une insaisissable source du droit applicable aux contrats d'état, 740; VAN HOUTTE, H., Rechtsvinding bij transnationale handelsarbitrage, 340; PERRIN, G., Réflexions sur le rôle des principes généraux dans l'ordre juridique international, 515; LORENZ, W., Die Lex Mercatoria : eine internationale Rechtsquelle ?, 413-414.
361. MUSTILL, M., The new lex mercatoria : the first twenty-five years, 149-182; BERGER, K.P., Internationale Wirtschaftsschiedsgerichtsbarkeit, 374-382; General principles of law in international commercial arbitration, HARV.L.REV. 1988, 1823-1833; DEL MARMOL, C. and MATRAY, L., L'importance et l'interprétation du contrat, 196-204; VAN DELDEN, R., Lex mercatoria of ius commune ?, 10-15; CRAIG, W., PARK, W. and PAULSSON, J., International Chamber of Commerce arbitration, § 35, 10-12; HUYS, M. and KEUTGEN, G., L'arbitrage en droit belge et international, 595-597; KAHN, P., case note District Court Paris, March 4, 1981, Clunet, 1981, 842; I.C.C. case No. 5065, Clunet, 1987, 1039, case note DERAINS, Y.; DELAUME, G., Comparative analysis as a basis of law in State contracts : the myth of the lex mercatoria, TUL.L.REV. 1989, 595-609.
362. COING, H., La détermination de la loi contractuelle en droit international privé allemand, 51-52; SANDERS, P., Trends in the field of international commercial arbitration, 263.
363. RIGAUX, F., Le droit comparé comme science appliquée, 74; STOLL, J., Vereinbarungen zwischen Staat und ausländischem Investor, 33; VIRALLY, M., Un tiers droit ?, Réflexions théoriques, 381.

becomes already apparent when the principle is confronted with the rule of *rebus sic stantibus* (hardship). Proponents of the *lex mercatoria* have taken different views as to the acceptance of *rebus sic stantibus* in international business transactions but a majority has rejected it[364]. Similarly, one may ask whether the obligation to mitigate damages is a general principle of law[365] and, if so, what its relation with the principle of *pacta sunt servanda* might be.

In other cases, contracts have been held void because corruption or bribery were involved. These cases were based on a general principle of law common to all civilized nations according to which corruption and bribery is prohibited[366].

443. The most important survey on transnational principles of law has been done by Reimann who was sceptical as to the existence of such principles in view of the diversity of national laws regarding contract formation, vices of consent, interpretation of contracts and statute of limitations[367].

444. From the foregoing discussion, one may conclude that few transnational principles of law exist. Moreover, in order to be a formal source of the *lex mercatoria*, these principles should be sufficiently precise to be practicable. Otherwise, they are mere guidelines operating as interpretative elements within a legal system[368]. One gets the impression that principles of law cited by proponents of the *lex mercatoria* belong to that category. General principles of law may thus well be a formal source of the *lex mercatoria*; in many cases they will, however, be mere interpretative

---

364. PHILIPPE, D., "Pacta sunt servanda" et "rebus sic stantibus", in L'apport de la jurisprudence arbitrale, INSTITUTE OF INTERNATIONAL BUSINESS LAW AND PRACTICE (ed.), Paris, I.C.C. publication No. 440/1, 1986, 234; BATIFFOL, H., Subjectivisme et objectivisme dans le droit international privé des contrats, 259; BÖCKSTIEGEL, K.H., Hardship, force majeure and special risks clauses in international contracts, in Adaptation and renegotiation of contracts in international trade and finance, HORN, N. (ed.), Deventer, Kluwer, 1985, 161-162; CARBONNEAU, T., Arbitral adjudication : a comparative assessment of its remedial and substantive status in transnational commerce, 106.

365. For a negative answer, see GOLDMAN, B., intervention during the discussions, Basle symposium on the law governing contractual obligations, KLEIN, F.E. and VISCHER, F. (ed.), Basle, Helbing & Lichtenhahn, 1983, 170-171; CARBONNEAU, T., Arbitral adjudication : a comparative assessment of its remedial and substantive status in transnational commerce, 106.

366. I.C.C. case No. 3916, Clunet, 1984, 930, case note JARVIN, S.; I.C.C. case No. 2730, Clunet, 1984, 915, case note DERAINS, Y.

367. REIMANN, T., Zur Lehre vom "rechtsordnungslosen" Vertrag, 80-94.

368. See supra III.6.

guidelines. Also, few examples exist of any such transnational principles[369]. Finally, one may wonder whether general principles of law are not much more expression of a *comparative method* used in arbitral adjudication[370] than a formal source of the *lex mercatoria*.

445. The mere fact that general principles of law may to a certain extent, be a formal source of the *lex mercatoria* is, however, insufficient for the *lex mercatoria* which also needs other sources[371]. The fact that, apart from transnational custom of which few examples exist, general principles of law are the only source left, places a great burden on that source. One thus notes that frequently, recourse is sought in general principles of law. However, as we have seen, few such principles exist as legally enforceable rules. These elements together may cast some doubt upon the theory of the *lex mercatoria* itself[372].

446. Finally, the question should be addressed whether mandatory rules exist within the *lex mercatoria*. Here, two techniques should be distinguished. First, the proponents of the *lex mercatoria* have relied on international public policy as an exception to the application of national law on the basis of its incompatibility with fundamental notions of the *lex mercatoria*. This international public policy is that of the *lex mercatoria* and should be distinguished from the international public policy of the national court having jurisdiction over a case. In order to reflect this distinction, the terms of *truly international public policy* or *transnational public policy* have been introduced[373]. In practice, this exception frequently works differently

---

369. In relation to the effects of the application of general principles of law on the predictability of dispute resolution, see LALIVE, P., intervention during the discussions, Basle symposium on the law governing contractual obligations, KLEIN, F.E. and VISCHER, F. (ed.), Basle, Helbing & Lichtenhahn, 1983, 200; LALIVE, P., Sur la bonne foi dans l'exécution des contrats d'état, in Mélanges offerts à Raymond Vander Elst, Volume 1, Brussels, Nemesis, 1986, 436.

370. See infra IV.3.

371. MANN, F.A., Reflections on a commercial law of nations, 38; REIMANN, T., Zur Lehre vom "rechtsordnungslosen" Vertrag, 77-79; RIGAUX, F., Souveraineté des Etats et arbitrage transnational, 277-278; VAN HOUTTE, H., Rechtsvinding bij transnationale handelsarbitrage, 352.

372. VON HOFFMANN, B., Internationale Handelsschiedsgerichtsbarkeit, 117; VERHOEVEN, J., Contrats entre Etats et ressortissants d'autres Etats, 143.

373. GOLDMAN, B., Lex mercatoria, 22; GOLDMAN, B., case note Court of Appeal Paris, July 12, 1984, Clunet, 1985, 154; GOLDMAN, B., intervention during the discussions, Basle symposium on the law governing contractual obligations, KLEIN, F.E. and VISCHER, F. (ed.), Basle, Helbing & Lichtenhahn, 1983, 170 and 196; DEL MARMOL, C. and MATRAY, L., L'importance et l'interprétation du contrat, 194; MATRAY, L., Arbitrage et ordre public transnational, 244; LEW, J., La loi applicable

than before national courts. While national courts apply the exception most often in order not to apply a more favourable provision of foreign law, the exception is mostly used in international commercial arbitration in order to avoid restrictive provisions of national law[374].

The contents of the international public policy of the *lex mercatoria* are, however, far from clear[375]. Since the *lex mercatoria* has barely any sources and rules of its own, one may wonder how the transnational public policy of the *lex mercatoria* should be defined. Also, it is unclear whether transnational public policy refers to an exception to the application of national law or to transnational mandatory rules[376] (*règles d'application immédiate*).

Second, one may construe mandatory rules within the *lex mercatoria*[377]. Bucher has opposed this idea. If parties choose the *lex mercatoria* as applicable law, such a choice should not depend upon the requirement that the legal system thus chosen should have mandatory rules[378]. Apart from the authors just cited, proponents of the *lex mercatoria* have barely paid attention to this problem. One might conclude from this gap in the

---

aux contrats internationaux dans la jurisprudence des tribunaux arbitraux, 154 and 166; LALIVE, P., Ordre public transnational (ou réellement international) et arbitrage international, Rev.Arb., 1986, 329-373, Transnational (or truly international) public policy and international arbitration, in Comparative arbitration practice and public policy in arbitration, SANDERS, P. (ed.), International Council for Commercial Arbitration, Deventer, Kluwer, 1987, 257-318; KORNBLUM, U., "Ordre public transnational", "ordre public international" und "ordre public interne" im Recht der privaten Schiedsgerichtsbarkeit, 140-156; ROLIN, H., Vers un ordre public réellement international, in Hommage d'une génération de juristes au Président Basdevant, Paris, Pedone, 1960, 442-448.

374. *E.g.*, DERAINS, Y., case note I.C.C. case No. 1526, Clunet, 1974, 919; DERAINS, Y., case note I.C.C. case No. 2521, Clunet, 1976, 999; DERAINS, Y., case note I.C.C. case No. 2708, Clunet, 1977, 947; DERAINS, Y., case note I.C.C. case No. 3267, Clunet, 1980, 969; DERAINS, Y., case note I.C.C. case No. 3327, Clunet, 1982, 977; DERAINS, Y., case note I.C.C. case No. 3344, Clunet, 1982, 986; DERAINS, Y., case note I.C.C. case No. 4381, Clunet, 1986, 1111-1112.

375. According to Vander Elst, a universal international public policy does not exist (VANDER ELST, R., Ordre public international, lois de police et lois d'application immédiate, 658-659). In Loquin's opinion, transnational public policy coincides with the international public policies of the national legal systems (LOQUIN, E., L'amiable composition en droit comparé et international, 269; LOQUIN, E., Les pouvoirs des arbitres internationaux à la lumière de l'évolution récente du droit de l'arbitrage international, 340-341).

376. For the latter, see JUENGER, F., Lex mercatoria une Eingriffsnormen, 245-249.

377. MATRAY, L., Arbitrage et ordre public transnational, 244; MOITRY, J.H., Arbitrage international et droit de la concurrence : vers un ordre public de la lex mercatoria ?, Rev.Arb., 1989, 33-36.

378. BUCHER, A., Transnationales Recht im ipr, 39.

theory of the *lex mercatoria* that protection of the public interest and private interests does not seem to be a priority of the theory. This is presumably based on the assumption that international business players have equal bargaining power or are sufficiently sophisticated that protection is hardly needed.

The conclusion may thus be drawn that the theory of the *lex mercatoria* in its relation to mandatory rules primarily seeks to limit the scope and effects of mandatory rules of national law. However, an autonomous mandatory regulation regarding interests which might need protection is absent.

D. Final assessment of Goldman's theory on the lex mercatoria

447. From Chapter I, it had become clear that the *lex mercatoria* could hardly define its own scope regarding the international and commercial character of the transaction as well as its territorial application[379]. Section IV.1.5.3.C led to the conclusion that few sources and rules of the *lex mercatoria* may be identified. Also, it has hardly any mandatory rules to protect public and private interests. For these reasons, the *lex mercatoria* does not yet seem to constitute a legal system which might be able to solve international business problems independently, fill the gaps of its own regulation and protect some interests. One cannot then accept that national courts might apply the *lex mercatoria* as applicable law. In relation to international commercial arbitration, there is no autonomous system of conflict of laws which might provide for its application.

448. More than thirty years of controversy about the theory of the *lex mercatoria* seems almost to have served no purpose. This has resulted in little other theoretical research on the sources of international business law[380]. However, one cannot escape the conclusion that, as has been shown in IV.1.2 thru 4, the theory of the *lex mercatoria* has influenced transnational practice, international conventions, national statutes and case law of national courts and arbitral tribunals. As far as these developments are necessarily linked to the theory of the *lex mercatoria*, one might question them. Most of these influences can be seen independently from the *lex mercatoria*. Article 1496 N.C.P.C. and article 1054 of the Dutch Code of Civil Procedure may, for instance, be interpreted as indications that the parties and arbitrators have great discretion in the choice of the rules to be applied to the dispute rather than as references to the *lex*

379. See supra I.3.
380. But see the theories in IV.2 thru IV.4.

mercatoria. This point of view better clarifies the practical choices to be made. It makes it obvious that the parties should decide whether they want such discretion themselves, or want to give it to arbitrators.

449. One may wonder why the theory of the *lex mercatoria* had such a deep influence on post war international business law. First, the theory corresponded with the need of the international business community for self-regulation[381]. To a certain extent, it is very liberal and favourable to a *laisser faire* economy. One might see this in the jurisprudential theories which have served as a basis for the *lex mercatoria*. First, a sociological theory was prominent in stressing the identity of the international business community. Also, some natural justice influences were present. More recently, the *lex mercatoria* has been based on legal pluralism[382].

The theory also flourished in a favourable period of economic recovery after the second world war and economic expansion in which international trade expanded in the post war order of international economic regulation. Such periods are quite receptive to internationalistic ideas[383].

Another cause is the complexity of the problem of the sources of international business law where a mix of substantive law, conflict of laws, arbitration law and self-regulatory rules is applied. These complexities have for long obscured the debate on the *lex mercatoria*.

450. Although one can hardly endorse Goldman's theory of the *lex mercatoria*, the theory of the *lex mercatoria* has had great merits from a broader perspective. First, it constantly drew attention to legal problems of international business and particularly led to analysis of self-regulatory instruments. In this respect, the theory has rightly emphasized the importance of the substantive sources discussed in Chapter III, for international business law. In practice, these substantive rules are frequently much more important than the rules of national law which are only applied

---

381. BEGUIN, J., Le développement de la lex mercatoria menace-t-il l'ordre juridique international ?, 485; RIGAUX, F., Droit public et droit privé dans les relations internationales, 3-4 and 399; BONELL, M., The law applicable to international commercial contracts : the standpoint of Italian doctrine and case-law, 19; FIRSCHING, K., Internationales Schuldrecht, I, 351.

382. See LOQUIN, E., L'application de règles anationales dans l'arbitrage commercial international, 118-119.

383. See OLY, G., Algemene beschouwingen over de eenvormige wet op de internationale koop van goederen in historisch perspectief, 26.

in the absence of such substantive rules[384]. In this context, the theory has pointed out that these substantive rules may be important tools of unification of law. Furthermore, the theory also has implications for national transactions since the self-regulatory mechanisms which may be found in international business transactions may apply *mutatis mutandis* to domestic transactions. Finally, the theory's assumption that conflict of laws and national substantive laws may be inappropriate to regulate international business law, remains valid to a certain extent, and at least should be a warning for legislators and judges that in the development and application of international business law account should be taken of the particularities of international business life[385].

E. Implications of the rejection of Goldman's theory

451. Notwithstanding the rejection of the theory of the *lex mercatoria* as an autonomous legal system, one is still left with the question of the legal implications of references to the *lex mercatoria*, international trade usages or international general principles of law which may be found in transnational practice. The main problem with clauses referring to the *lex mercatoria* or transnational rules is to be found in their ambiguity[386]. As has been stated, *lex mercatoria* has in Schmitthoff's or Goldman's theory a different meaning and it may therefore be unclear whether parties intended their contract to be governed by an autonomous lex mercatoria or by substantive international trade law sources. Also, these clauses may be interpreted as an expression of the parties' intent to have transnational rules incorporated in the contract, as *amiable composition* clauses or authorizing the arbitrators to experiment with conflict of law methodology[387]. The latter four options do not create specific problems.

---

384. RIGAUX, F., Droit public et droit privé dans les relations internationales, 413; RIGAUX, F., Pour un autre droit international, 371, PETERSMANN, E., "Entwicklungsvölkerrecht", "Droit international du développement", "International Economic Development Law" : Mythos oder Wirklichkeit ?, 172; KAHN, P., Rapport français, in Le rôle de la pratique dans la formation du droit, 238; LÖNING, G., Autonomes Recht der Wirtschaft, 20; KROPHOLLER, J., Internationales Einheitsrecht, 122; HORN, N., Codes of conduct for MNEs and transnational lex mercatoria : an international process of learning and law making, 60; DAVID, R., Les méthodes de l'unification, 313-314; BEGUIN, J., Le développement de la lex mercatoria menace-t-il l'ordre juridique international ?, 500.

385. See infra IV.2.2. and IV.4.

386. See also LAGARDE, P., case note Court of Appeal Paris, July 13, 1989, Rev.Arb., 1990, 669.

387. See infra IV.2.2 and IV.3.

However, when references are to be construed as indicating an autonomous *lex mercatoria*, they should be understood as incorporating transnational rules in the contract[388]. Because an autonomous *lex mercatoria* does not exist, the choice of law cannot be put into practice, even contrary to the parties' will. To give their intention maximal effect, transnational rules may be applied as far as possible as incorporated contractual rules, provided they do not conflict with the applicable national law and do not need further support from that law as, for instance, in relation to gap filling and interpretation. If this is not the case, the impact of national rules upon the contract will be minimal.

The scope of these incorporated rules is, however, not unlimited. In relation to litigation before national courts, the *lex fori* will determine in what fields choice of transnational rules may exist. Although recently arguments have been made to extend choice of law to other field than contract law[389], one may be somewhat sceptical as to a generalization of choice of law in the conflict of laws. One may wonder whether the correct position is not that where the parties are not authorized by the applicable law to choose the applicable law, conflict rules are mandatory and clauses to the contrary will be dependent upon the applicable law[390]. The rationale of this principle has been discussed already; since choice of law is a legitimate method of avoiding the mandatory rules of the otherwise applicable law, there are few problems in authorizing choice of laws in those fields of law such as contract law, where few mandatory provisions exist. In other fields with a greater density of mandatory rules, choice of law is more problematic. For international business problems, one might for instance think of company law, property law or bankruptcy law.

452. The same analysis may also be applied to arbitration clauses referring to lex mercatoria. These clauses give arbitrators broad discretion to apply transnational rules. Generally, the scope for choice of law is broader in arbitration than in court litigation. In the latter, it is limited to contract law while in international commercial arbitration, it applies to the substance of the dispute.However, since the *lex mercatoria* does not exist as an autonomous legal system, its application in the course of arbitral adjudica-

388. See supra Nos. 351, 358 and 367 as well as SANDROCK, O., Die Fortbildung des materiellen Rechts durch die Internationale Schiedsgerichtsbarkeit, 53-54.

389. In Belgium, only one author has proposed such an extension, see DE FOER, L., Over de samenloop van de lex loci delicti en de Belgische arbeidsongevallenwetgeving bij een buitenlands ongeval en over de cassatiecontrole op de ambtshalve toepassing van de verwijzingsregel, case note Belgian Supreme Court, November 17, 1983, R.W., 1984-85, 2192. In The Netherlands, a similar development is taking place.

390. MANN, F.A., Schiedsrichter und Recht, 613; MANN, F.A., Lex facit arbitrum, 166.

tion should be analyzed in order to assess the implications of such clauses. First, there is no problem if arbitrators apply substantive rules within the applicable national law. However, if these rules are applied as autonomous rules, one may wonder whether this may in any way be sanctioned, particularly by national courts seized of the award during setting aside or enforcement proceedings[391]. Schlosser, Samuel and Berger have stated that these clauses should be respected by the arbitral tribunal and could not be challenged in court[392]. Under the reservation set forth above, this view may be endorsed. Moreover, this reservation will work differently in international commercial arbitrations than in national court litigation since review of arbitral awards in the course of setting aside or enforcement proceedings generally will not pertain to the application of the substantive rules or the characterization of the choice of law clause.

453. A further question is whether and how application of the *lex mercatoria* by the arbitrators which runs counter to the choice of law made by the parties can be sanctioned. Setting aside of such an award may be possible under the Uncitral Model Law and national law because the arbitrators then act beyond their authority[393]. Recognition and enforcement may also be refused on the same ground under the 1927 Geneva Convention, the 1958 New York Convention, the 1961 European Convention and the Uncitral Model Law[394].

454. In the absence of a choice of law, the arbitrators may apply the *lex mercatoria* without being authorized by the arbitral conflict of laws rules. In many jurisdictions, this violation of the arbitral conflict of laws system which may be characterized as excess of power does not, however, seem to be a ground for setting aside or refusal of enforcement[395]. Indirectly though, setting aside or refusal of enforcement may ensue if the application of the *lex mercatoria* might be characterized as *amiable composition*. However, it has already been argued that this argument may only be made if under the applicable law and its open-ended rules a different result had

---

391. The liability of the arbitrators as a possible sanction will not be discussed (see VON BAR, C., Internationales Privatrecht, Volume 1, 86-87).
392. SCHLOSSER, P., Das Recht der internationalen privaten Schiedsgerichtsbarkeit, first edition, 532-533; SAMUEL, A., Jurisdictional problems in international commercial arbitration : a study of Belgian, Dutch, English, French, Swedish, Swiss, U.S. and West German law, Zurich, Schulthess, 1989, 237; BERGER, K.P., Internationale Wirtschaftsschiedsgerichtsbarkeit, 483.
393. See supra Nos. 173-174.
394. See supra Nos. 189-190.
395. See supra Nos. 173-174.

been reached[396]. Finally, one may doubt whether recognition and enforcement may be refused if the arbitrators had applied the *lex mercatoria* without having been authorized by the applicable conflict rule[397]. Eventually, the award might not be recognized or enforced if it is contrary to the international public policy of the recognition or enforcement forum[398].

455. From the foregoing, it appears that awards may risk being set aside or refused enforcement if the law designated by the parties has not been applied. However, it is more difficult to attack an award where the *lex mercatoria* is applied notwithstanding the arbitral conflict system.

IV.2 Substantive methods

456. Apart from the theory of the *lex mercatoria*, other theories regarding the sources of international business law have been proposed. One way to look to international business problems is not to their localization but to the substance of the dispute. In this respect, transnational substantive rules have been developed as well as a direct method for arbitral adjudication.

IV.2.1 *The unilateral method of transnational substantive rules*[399]

457. The method of transnational substantive rules has already been mentioned. Under this method, a substantive rule is applied directly (unilaterally) to transnational situations not by virtue of a conflict rule but

396. See supra Nos. 180-182; *but see* DASSER, F., Internationale Schiedsgerichte und lex mercatoria, 152-153, 278-281 and 358-359 and BERGER, K.P., Internationale Wirtschaftsschiedsgerichtsbarkeit, 484 who refuse to identify *lex mercatoria* and *amiable composition*.

397. See supra Nos. 189-190.

398. Gottwald (Die sachliche Kontrolle internationaler Schiedssprüche durch staatliche Gerichte, 65) seems to exclude this as regards Germany. Lalive (Les règles de conflit de lois appliquées au fond du litige par l'arbitre international siégeant en Suisse, 89) stated that the New York Convention does not allow any review as to the conflict rules applied. For the U.S., where manifest disregard of the law may be considered contrary to public policy, see DE LA HOUSSAYE, I., Manifest disregard of the law in international commercial arbitrations, COL.J.TRANSNAT'L L. 1990, 449-472.

399. In France, these rules are called *règles de droit international privé matérielles*; in Germany, they are called *Sachnormen*.

by means of a scope rule[400]. This is an example of unilateral methods in post-war conflict of laws[401].

458. Transnational substantive rules may be found in international conventions, statutes and case law[402]. In unification instruments relating to substantive law, the scope of substantive rules may or may not be limited to transnational situations. In the former case, transnational substantive rules have been created. In most cases, the restriction to international situations is motivated by political considerations rather than by the specific features of such situations[403].

459. In statutory law, some examples exist of transnational substantive rules which contain specific rules for transnational situations. For instance, many provisions of the N.C.P.C. regarding international arbitration and of the arbitration chapter of the Swiss Law on Conflict of Laws may be characterized as transnational substantive rules[404]. In these countries, the deregulation of international arbitration has, to a certain extent, taken place through application of transnational substantive rules.

However, in market economies, few examples of transnational substantive rules exist. The rules which apply to national transactions also apply, as a matter of principle, to transnational transactions because national and international trade are basically guided by the same economic principles. Thus, there is not an urgent need to have specific rules tailored

---

400. Controversy exists as to the question whether transnational substantive rules still depend upon the *lex fori* or not, see OPPETIT, B., Le développement des règles matérielles, 7; SIMON-DEPITRE, M., Les règles matérielles dans le conflit de lois, R.C.D.I.P., 1974, 599-600; VERWILGHEN, M., Les règles de droit délimitant leur propre domaine d'application en droit international privé belge, 342; RIGAUX, F. and VERWILGHEN, M., Le champ d'application dans l'espace des règles uniformes de droit privé matériel, 228-232.

401. See KEGEL, G., The crisis of conflict of laws, 95-263; STEINDORFF, E., Sachnormen im internationalen Privatrecht, Frankfurt, Klostermann, 1958, 288 pp.; SCHURIG, K., Kollisionsnorm und Sachrecht, 19-23 and 279-281.

402. LOUSSOUARN, Y., Cours général de droit international privé, 292.

403. See supra No. 38.

404. *France* : LOUSSOUARN, Y., Les arbitres, Droit et pratique de l'arbitrage international en France, FEDUCI (ed.), s.l., 1984, 42; BEGUIN, J., La logique du régime des voies de recours en matière d'arbitrage commercial international, Etudes offertes à Roger Houin, Paris, Dalloz, 1985, 253 and 256; GOLDMAN, B., The complementary roles of judges and arbitrators in ensuring that international commercial arbitration is effective, International arbitration, 60 years of ICC arbitration, A look at the future, International Chamber of Commerce, publication No. 412, Paris, 1984, 263; *Switzerland*: DUTOIT, B., KNOEPFLER, F., LALIVE, P. and MERCIER, P., Répertoire de droit international privé suisse, Volume 1, 269.

to international trade transactions[405]. In centrally planned economies, the picture is different. National commercial transactions are governed by economic regulation which sets the trading terms and conditions. In order to enter world markets, countries with centrally planned economies have to adapt to market forces and competition. Thus, specific rules for transnational commercial transactions must be created.

460. In case law too, transnational substantive rules have been created. In the absence of international conventions and statutes, case law might create such rules in order to adapt national rules to the specificity of international trade or the needs of international commerce[406]. Particularly in France, case law has been quite inventive in creating transnational substantive rules[407]. Before the second world war, the French Supreme Court held that gold clauses were valid in transnational payments despite their prohibition in relation to national payments. Also, in international commercial arbitrations, arbitral clauses were held enforceable between merchants despite their prohibition in national arbitration[408]. Thus, specific rules were created for transnational situations.

After the second world war, the same method was also applied on several occasions. In the *Gosset* case, the French Supreme Court held that an arbitral clause was severable in international commercial arbitrations. The clause was held to be valid notwithstanding the fact that the main contract was null and void[409]. However, the autonomy of the arbitral clause vis-à-vis the main contract did not exist in French arbitration law. Second, in the *Galakis* case, the Court held that the French state was precluded from raising the defence that under French law it was not authorized to conclude an arbitration agreement, since a transnational transaction was involved where such clauses are usual[410]. This transnation-

---

405. FOUCHARD, P., La loi régissant les obligations contractuelles en droit international privé français, 96-98.

406. Some German authors would seem to endorse such judicial creativity, see RAHMANN, D., Ausschluß staatlicher Gerichtszuständigkeit, Cologne, Heymanns, 1984, 165-167; VON WINTERFELD, A., Noch einmal : der deutsche ordre public in der internationalen Schiedsgerichtsbarkeit, NJW, 1987, 3061.

407. See VON MEHREN, A., International commercial arbitration : the contribution of the French jurisprudence, LA.L.REV., 1986, 1050-1056.

408. See supra No. 33.

409. French Supreme Court, May 7, 1963, J.C.P., 1963, 13405, case note GOLDMAN, B., R.C.D.I.P., 1963, 615, D., 1963, 545, case note ROBERT, J., Clunet, 1964, 82, case note BREDIN, J.D.

410. French Supreme Court, May 2, 1966, R.C.D.I.P., 1967, 553, case note GOLDMAN, B., Clunet, 1966, 648, case note LEVEL, P.

al substantive rule is applied irrespective of the applicable law. This implies that it might also be raised against foreign states[411].

In the *Hecht* case, in contrast to the *Gosset* case, the validity of the arbitral clause itself was attacked. Under French domestic law, the clause would have been null and void. The Supreme Court, however, held that the prohibition on arbitral clauses in disputes regarding non-merchants was not applicable in transnational relations[412]. Thus, international commercial arbitrators may determine whether they have jurisdiction over the case, notwithstanding the fact that one of the parties claims the incompetence of the arbitral tribunal as a result the arbitral clause's invalidity.

In all these cases, a restrictive provision of French law was set aside as far as international commercial transactions or arbitrations are concerned[413]. National rules of the applicable law were thought to be unfit for international commercial relations and were not applied. Thus, a new, more permissible transnational substantive rule was created by judicial act. In the absence of legislative reform, judges created new rules and adapted national law to the needs and realities of international business life. For political reasons, this was not done for national transactions, although the need was there too[414], but limited to international commercial transactions.

---

411. LOQUIN, E., case note Court of Appeal Paris, January 20, 1987, Clunet, 1987, 964.

412. French Supreme Court, July 4, 1972, Clunet, 1972, 843, case note OPPETIT, B., R.C.D.I.P., 1974, case note LEVEL, P.
The scope of the *Hecht* rule is still somewhat unclear, see BOURDIN, R., La convention d'arbitrage international en droit français depuis le décret du 12 mai 1981, in Droit et pratique de l'arbitrage international en France, FEDUCI, s.l., 1984, 17-18; MAYER, P., L'insertion de la sentence dans l'ordre juridique français, in Droit et pratique de l'arbitrage international en France, FEDUCI, s.l., 1984, 93; SYNVET, H., case note Court of Appeal Toulouse, October 26, 1982, Clunet, 1984, 611-612.

413. In other contexts too, legal writers and case law have proposed this technique in order to avoid restrictions of the applicable law, see Court of Appeal Paris, April 11, 1972, Clunet, 1974, 620, case note AUDIT, B.; JACQUEMONT, A., L'émission des emprunts euro-obligataires, 323-325 (restrictions on indexation clauses); MAZZONI, A., Les clauses d'exigibilité anticipée et de paiement tardif, in Les euro-crédits: expériences continentales, BELLIS, M. (ed.), FEDUCI, Paris, Moniteur, 1982, 156-157 (restrictions as to accrued interest).

414. BREDIN, J.D., case note French Supreme Court, May 7, 1963 and Court of Appeal Paris, May 30, 1963, Clunet, 1964, 89; BOURDIN, R., La convention d'arbitrage international en droit français depuis le décret du 12 mai 1981, 16; *but see* MOTULSKY, H., case note French Supreme Court, May 7, 1963, in MOTULSKY, H., Ecrits, études et notes sur l'arbitrage, Paris, Dalloz, 1974, 349, R.C.D.I.P., 1963, 615 ff.; MOTULSKY, H., L'internationalisation du droit français de l'arbitrage, 326; KASSIS, A., Théorie générale des usages du commerce, 497.

461. Transnational substantive rules should not necessarily have liberalizing effects. In the *British Leyland* case of June 6, 1978, the French Supreme Court refused to apply the applicable law and created a transnational rule whereby the plaintiff who sued before the French courts, despite the existence of an arbitration agreement, was not only estopped from raising the argument that the court was incompetent but also from using the same defence against the counterclaims[415]. Contrary to the applicable law, the French courts were thus also competent as to the counterclaims[416] which had a restrictive effect on international arbitration but seemed to have been inspired by concerns of litigation economics.

462. Apart from France, only in the U.S. does there seem to have been major examples of the use of transnational substantive rules. In *The Bremen v. Zapata Off-Shore Co.*[417], the U.S. Supreme Court refused to apply the *forum non conveniens* theory to a jurisdiction clause in a transnational contract. In *Scherk v. Alberto-Culver Co.*[418] and *Mitsubishi Motors Corp. v. Soler Chrysler-Plymouth Inc.*[419], the Court refused to intervene in the international commercial arbitration process through the application of, respectively, securities regulation and anti-trust law. However, *Sherk v. Alberto Culver Co.* may, as a transnational substantive rule, be reinterpreted since *Shearson/American Express Inc. v. McMahon*[420], in which the Supreme Court held that securities regulation disputes may well be arbitrable. This case implies that the distinction between international and national disputes no longer exists and that *Sherk* may no longer be characterized as a transnational substantive rule[421].

463. A problem with respect to the development of transnational substantive rules by case law is whether case law may create such rules. One might expect that in civil law countries courts will feel more restrained in the creation of such rules because they are more bound by codified law than

415. Clunet, 1978, 907, case note OPPETIT, B., Rev.Arb., 1979, 230, case note LEVEL, P.
416. OPPETIT, B., case note French Supreme Court, June 6, 1978, Clunet, 1978, 914; FOUCHARD, P., La loi régissant les obligations contractuelles en droit international privé français, 103; PONSARD, A., La jurisprudence de la Cour de cassation et le droit commercial international, Le droit des relations économiques internationales, Etudes offertes à Berthold Goldman, Paris, Litec, 1982, 252-254.
417. 407 U.S. 1 [1972].
418. 417 U.S. 506 [1974].
419. 105 S.Ct. 3346 [1985].
420. 107 S.Ct. 2332 [1987].
421. See also CARBONNEAU, T., L'arbitrage en droit américain, Rev.Arb., 1988, 40 and 42.

in common law jurisdictions. However, one notes that transnational substantive rules have primarily been developed in France and in the U.S. In the abovementioned examples, French courts felt that statutory rules were not an obstacle to the creation of new rules which derogated from existing statutory rules. Specific exceptions to statutory rules were created by case law. As to the U.S., the Supreme Court also refined the law in order better to adapt it to transnational commerce.

If, for various reasons, superior courts are willing to create transnational substantive rules, this judicial activism may hardly be sanctioned, except by the legislator who might overrule precedents by statute. Most superior courts are, however, not willing to create such rules. For instance, the Swiss Supreme Court stated in two cases that there were no reasons to give the *Concordat* a different interpretation depending upon its transnational or national character[422]. Inferior courts will be tempted to follow the position of the superior courts. Since all countries but France and the U.S., are taking a restrictive view as to the creation of transnational substantive rules by case law, this method seems to have a limited scope in international business law.

That might be different in international commercial arbitrations[423]. If the arbitrators are not authorized to act as *amiables compositeurs* or to adjudicate with great discretion by virtue of the will of the parties, one may doubt whether they easily might create transnational substantive rules[424]. However, some national statutes authorize the arbitrators not to follow a conflict rule[425] which opens up possibilities to apply transnational substantive rules. Also, violation of a conflict rule may hardly be sanctioned in court, except if the award were rendered *ex aequo et bono* and the result might not have been achieved through the applicable law[426]. In the practice of I.C.C. arbitration, some examples of arbitral creation of transnational substantive rules may be found[427].

464. A major issue regarding transnational substantive rules is their relation to conflict rules. As these rules are applied as soon as a transnational

---

422. JOLIDON, P., Commentaire du Concordat suisse sur l'arbitrage, 52; *compare* DUTOIT, B., KNOEPFLER, F., LALIVE, P. and MERCIER, P., Répertoire de droit international privé suisse, Volume 1, 256.
423. LOWENFELD, A., Lex mercatoria : an arbitrator's view, 50 and 53.
424. LOUSSOUARN, Y. and BREDIN, J.D., Droit du commerce international, 44-45.
425. See supra Nos. 143 ff.
426. See supra Nos. 180-182.
427. I.C.C. case No. 1526, Clunet, 1974, 915, case note DERAINS, Y.; I.C.C. case No. 1507, Clunet, 1974, 913, case note DERAINS, Y.; DERAINS, Y., case note I.C.C. case No. 2478, Clunet, 1975, 928; I.C.C. award, September 23, 1982, Rev.Arb., 1984, 137.

situation exists, they might seem to exclude conflict rules and to have a universal scope. These rules will be applied unilaterally by national courts as part of the *lex fori* and by arbitration tribunals by virtue of the applicable law, although only minor links might exist with the country of the *lex fori* or of the applicable law[428]. In this respect, these rules have been characterized as imperialistic. Because of their unilateral character, foreign courts also will be very reluctant to apply these foreign transnational substantive rules as such. Rather they might only consider applying them through a conflict rule. If the applicable law determined by virtue of the conflict rule of the *lex fori*, is the law of a jurisdiction in which transnational substantive rules exist, these rules might be applied not directly (since they are foreign rules), but through a conflict rule. In the absence of sufficient connection with that jurisdiction, foreign transnational substantive rules are unlikely to be applied[429]. Because of these objections related to the unilateral character of these rules, some transnational substantive rules have been drafted not in terms of scope rules but are made dependent on a conflict rule in order to make sure that they are only applied if sufficient links exist between the international transaction and the country whose transnational substantive rules are to be applied[430].

One may doubt whether transnational substantive rules exclude conflict rules altogether. Since many of these transnational substantive rules are very broadly phrased, it may be preferable to have some elements still determined by virtue of a conflict rule. For instance, if choice of law is seen as a transnational substantive rule[431], one might still rely on a conflict rule as to the problem of vices of consent or the interpretation of clauses authorizing one of the parties to determine or change the applicable law after the contract was formed[432]. Certainly when national systems offer different solutions to a problem, one may prefer to apply a content-neutral conflict rule rather than a unilateral substantive rule.

Finally, transnational substantive rules may create conflicts because of their unilateral character. Their application by a national court may conflict with other legal systems or the conflict may arise with the setting aside or enforcement *forum* in the case of application by arbitral tribunals. In the

428. DEBY-GERARD, F., Le rôle de la règle de conflit dans le règlement des rapports internationaux, 130.

429. GOLDMAN, B., Le contrat international, 469; SCHLOSSER, P., Das internationale an der internationalen privaten Schiedsgerichtsbarkeit, 864.

430. LOUSSOUARN, Y., Cours général de droit international privé, 293; DEBY-GERARD, F., Le rôle de la règle de conflit dans le règlement des rapports internationaux, 123-126; GOLDMAN, B., Le contrat international, 448.

431. See supra II.2.1.3.C.

432. *Compare* MAYER, P., Droit international privé, second edition, 556.

former case, these problems are not too important if enforcement is governed by international conventions which generally limit review of the merits of the dispute, provided no conflicts with applicable mandatory rules or the international public policy of the enforcement forum arise[433]. This is even more so with regard to review of arbitral awards in setting aside or enforcement proceedings where review does not seem to extend to the merits of the dispute, even if arbitrators are creating transnational substantive rules, irrespective of any national law, provided the award cannot be characterized as rendered *ex aequo et bono*[434].

465. By way of conclusion, one may wonder whether the method of transnational substantive rules may be a substitute method for the resolution of international business law problems or whether it may rather function as a supplementary method which may supplement or correct the conflict method. The answer to this question may be deduced from the fact that a general system of transnational substantive rules does not exist, but rather disparate elements have been formed in international conventions, statutes and case law. In the latter case, their scope is limited to the case at hand[435] and they clearly function as a correction to the conflict method[436]. Thus, conflict rules and transnational substantive rules seem to be complementary tools for the resolution of international business problems[437].

IV.2.2 *The direct method in arbitral adjudication*

466. Some arbitral cases and some writers have argued that the arbitral tribunal may directly apply a substantive rule. This method has been called the *direct method*. Faced with a true conflict, arbitrators would be authorized to choose which substantive rule to apply. Consensus exists as to the point that the direct method implies that the arbitrators are not

433. See FOUCHARD, P., Le nouveau droit français de l'arbitrage, 42.
434. See supra Nos. 180-182.
435. BELLET, P. and MEZGER, E., L'arbitrage international dans le nouveau code de procédure civile, 613-614.
436. BATIFFOL, H., Les contrats en droit international privé comparé, 15; LEREBOURS-PIGEONNIERE, P., A propos du contrat international, 14.
437. BATIFFOL, H., La loi appropriée au contrat, 11-12; LOUSSOUARN, Y., Cours général de droit international privé, 316; VAN HECKE, G., Principes et méthodes de solution des conflits de lois, 475.

bound by the arbitral conflict system[438]. However, differences of opinion exist as to whether the direct method authorizes the application of no conflict rule at all or to choose whichever conflict rule is appropriate. In the former case, the direct method is a mandate given to the arbitral tribunal to depart from any conflict rule as to the law applicable to the merits of the dispute and to apply the *better law*. A substantive criterion and not a connecting factor will then determine the applicable law. As such, the method would be unilateral. Also, the method would be direct since the substantive law is applied directly without going indirectly through the conflict of laws method[439]. However, other authors have argued that the direct method is based upon the conflict rule of the proper law or of the closest connection[440]. In this respect, it would only confirm the principle of autonomous conflict rules which has been recognized in the aftermath of article VII (1) of the 1961 European Convention[441] and would add hardly anything to existing methodology. Thus, it seems that the better view regarding the direct method is the substantive view rather than the conflict view. The substantive conception will thus be discussed below.

467. According to a majority opinion, article 1496 N.C.P.C. and article 1054 of the Dutch Code of Civil Procedure authorize a departure from conflict rules and a direct application of the most appropriate rules of law[442].

---

438. I.C.C. case No. 3540, Clunet, 1981, 914, case note DERAINS, Y.; DERAINS, Y., Attente légitime des parties et droit applicable au fond en matière d'arbitrage commercial international, 85.

439. See also JUENGER, F., Afterword : the lex mercatoria and the conflict of laws, 215.

440. DASSER, F., Internationale Schiedsgerichte und lex mercatoria, 177; General principles of law in international commercial arbitration, HARV.L.REV. 1988, 1822; KOKKINI-IATRIDOU, D., Twee recente arbitrageregelingen : Portugal en Spanje, 396; MOURA VICENTE, D., L'évolution récente du droit de l'arbitrage au Portugal, Rev.Arb., 1991, 438-439.

441. See supra Nos. 143 ff.

442. *France* : GOLDMAN, B., Lex mercatoria, 13 relying on the drafting history of article 1496 N.C.P.C.; GOLDMAN, B., The applicable law : general principles of law - lex mercatoria, 118-119; KAHN, P., Rapport français, in Le rôle de la pratique dans la formation du droit, 247; FOUCHARD, P., La loi régissant les obligations contractuelles en droit international privé français, 111; FOUCHARD, P., L'arbitrage international en France après le décret du 12 mai 1981, 399; FOUCHARD, P., Le nouveau droit français de l'arbitrage, 45; LOUSSOUARN, Y., intervention during the discussions, La réforme de l'arbitrage international en France, Rev.Arb., 1981, 496; LOUSSOUARN, Y., Arbitrage commercial international et droit du commerce international, 170-171; ROBERT, J., L'arbitrage en matière internationale, 213; ROBERT, J., L'arbitrage, droit interne, droit international privé, 290; BEGUIN, J., Le développement de la lex mercatoria menace-t-il l'ordre juridique international ?, 515; VERHOEVEN, J., Arbitrage entre Etats et entreprises étrangères : des règles

However, not all recent arbitration texts follow the direct method. Article 28 of the Uncitral Model Law[443] and article 187 of the Swiss Law on Conflict of Laws impose a conflict rule which seems to exclude the direct method. With regard to the Uncitral Model Law, the direct method was reintroduced in Canada through an amendment to the Model law at the time it was adopted[444]. Finally, it seems that the direct method cannot be followed under article 13 I.C.C Arbitration Rules and article 33 Uncitral Arbitration Rules[445].

468. One may wonder whether the direct method can be used in the absence of authorization drawn from the applicable law. First, the parties may authorize the arbitrators to use the direct method. If the applicable law authorizes *amiable composition*, parties should also be able to empower arbitrators to apply the better law. In the absence of a contractual mandate to apply the direct method, its application may be more troublesome since

---

spécifiques ?, 630-631; DERAINS, Y., La sentence arbitrale, in Droit et pratique de l'arbitrage international en France, s.l., Feduci, 1984, 75; VON BREITENSTEIN, D., Die internationale arbitrage im französischen Recht, in Schiedsgerichtsbarkeit in Frankreich, BÖCKSTIEGEL, K.H. (ed.), Cologne, Heymanns, 1983, 40; FUNCK-BRENTANO, R., Die "amiable composition", in Schiedsgerichtsbarkeit in Frankreich, BÖCKSTIEGEL, K.H. (ed.), Cologne, Heymanns, 1983, 101; REDFERN, A. and HUNTER, M., Law and practice of international commercial arbitration, first edition, 96-97; BOLARD, G., Le nouveau droit français de l'arbitrage, in Les particularités nationales de l'arbitrage commercial international, Lublin, 1987, 41; *but see* BELLET, P. and MEZGER, E., L'arbitrage international dans le nouveau code de procédure civile, R.C.D.I.P., 1981, 631-633; MEZGER, E., Kernpunkte der Reform des Rechts der internationalen Handelsschiedsgerichtsbarkeit in Frankreich, RIW, 1981, 514-515; LAGARDE, P., Approche critique de la lex mercatoria, 148-149; DE BOISSESON, M., Le droit français de l'arbitrage, first edition, 418-423; *The Netherlands* : SANDERS, P. and VAN DEN BERG, A.J., The Netherlands Arbitration Act, note 67; *but see* SCHULTSZ, J., Legislation in the Netherlands and international arbitration, 20; SCHULTSZ, J., Les nouvelles dispositions de la législation néerlandaise en matière d'arbitrage, Rev.Arb., 1988, 222; DUINTJER TEBBENS, H., A facelift for Dutch arbitration law, N.I.L.R., 1987, 155.

443. For criticism of this position, see DERAINS, Y., Possible conflict of law rules and the rules applicable to the substance of the dispute, in Uncitral's project for a model law on international commercial arbitration, Deventer, Kluwer, 1984, 192; DERAINS, Y. and JARVIN, S., case note I.C.C. case No. 3880, Clunet, 1983, 899; DERAINS, Y., case note I.C.C. case No. 4381, Clunet, 1986, 1110.

444. JARVIN, S., La loi-type de la C.N.U.D.C.I. sur l'arbitrage commercial international, Rev.Arb., 1986, 527; BROCHES, A., The 1985 Uncitral model law on international commercial arbitration : an exercise in international legislation, 54; NÖCKER, T., Das neue Schiedsverfahrensrecht in Kanada, RIW, 1988, 364.

445. FRANX, J.P., Het ontwerp Boek IV van het Wetboek van Burgerlijke Rechtsvordering, Zwolle, Tjeenk Willink, 1985, 35-36.

the arbitrators are bound by the arbitral conflict system[446]. The freedom to experiment with new conflict of laws techniques such as the direct method, should thus be found within that system. However, application of the direct method despite a lack of authorization from the applicable law may be hard to sanction since review by national courts over arbitral awards is limited. Only when the award is rendered *ex aequo et bono* and cannot be upheld under the applicable law, setting aside or refusal of enforcement might ensue[447].

469. Some authors have attacked the direct method because it would give arbitrators too much discretion and arbitrary decisions might follow[448]. At first glance, this might seem correct. However, this objection is more related to the lack of elaboration of the method than to the method itself. In applying the direct method, arbitrators are not looking for just any rule of law which might be appropriate for the resolution of the dispute. Rather, they no longer have to go through a conflict of laws process. Thus, within the direct method, there clearly is room for the substantive comparative methods which will be discussed below[449]. Also, the contents of the laws might be taken into account in order to determine what rule to apply. While traditional conflict of laws, to a large extent, is content-neutral, the direct method authorizes regard for underlying policies. Thus, it might be

---

446. Court of Appeal Frankfurt, October 26, 1983, RIW, 1984, 400, case note DIELMANN, H.; DAVID, R., L'arbitrage dans le commerce international, 551; EISEMANN, F., Le phénomène de l'arbitrage, son utilité, ses avantages et son rôle, 106; RIGAUX, F., Souveraineté des Etats et arbitrage transnational, 263; BUCHER, A., Transnationales Recht im ipr, 36; SCHLOSSER, P., Das internationale an der internationalen privaten Schiedsgerichtsbarkeit, 857. Leo Raape (Internationales Privatrecht, 520) wrote in this regard :

> *"Die Parteien erstreben mit dem Schiedsspruch eine rechtliche Wirkung. Diese aber können sie nie auf Grund einer positiven Rechtsordnung erziehen. Diese Einsicht is der feste Ausgangspunkt für das Folgende. Die Parteien müssen sich also bei dem Schiedsverfahren auf den Boden einer bestimmten Rechtsordnung stellen. Das Schiedsgericht thront nicht über die Erde, es schwebt nicht in der Luft, es muß irgendwo landen, irgendwo 'erden'."*

447. See supra Nos. 180-182.

448. BUCHER, A., Transnationales Recht im ipr, 36; TSCHANZ, P.Y., Le nouveau droit suisse de l'arbitrage international, R.D.A.I., 1988, 447; GAILLARD, E., A foreign view of the new Swiss law on international arbitration, ARB.INT'L, 1988, 29; CALAVROS, C., Das UNCITRAL-Modellgesetz über die internationale Handelsschiedsgerichtsbarkeit, Bielefeld, Gieseking, 1988, 127-128.

449. See infra IV.3.; see also JUENGER, F., Afterword : the lex mercatoria and the conflict of laws, 215-216.

more value-oriented than the conflict method. Finally, it remains unclear which laws should be taken into account in which the better rule should be sought.

Also, the direct method has been identified with *amiable composition*. Since under article 1496 N.C.P.C., the direct method does not require an authorization from the parties while article 1497 does with regard to *amiable composition*, these two provisions would be incompatible[450]. The question arises whether the identification of the direct method and *amiable composition* is correct. As has been stated, the direct method is no excuse for arbitrariness or *ad hoc* decisions based on concrete elements which would allow for a derogation from an abstract rule. The latter is precisely one of the possibilities open to *amiables compositeurs*. The direct method is rather a substantive method to look for a better rule of law, irrespective of conflict rules. The distinction remains tenuous, like the distinction between *amiable composition* and arbitration according to rules of law[451].

IV.3 Comparative methods

470. One of the preoccupations of theories on the sources of international business law has been to reduce the impact of national law. This can be done by promoting international conventions and self-regulation (Schmitthoff's theory on the *lex mercatoria*), developing anational rules (Goldman's theory of the *lex mercatoria*) or creating specific rules for transnational transactions (the method of transnational substantive rules). One also might want to develop general principles of substantive law or of conflict of laws based on comparative analysis. This has already been discussed in relation to the formal sources of the *lex mercatoria*[452]. In this section, such a comparative analysis is discussed from a different angle. Here, the perspective is not to create legal rules but to use the comparative method for dispute resolution purposes. In this perspective, the comparative methods of Langen, Bonell and Rubino-Sammartano will be discussed. Also, the comparative methods which are often used in international commercial arbitration practice, will be analyzed. A distinction should in

---

450. BELLET, P. and MEZGER, E., L'arbitrage international dans le nouveau code de procédure civile, 632-633; MEZGER, E., Kernpunkte der Reform des Rechts der internationalen Handelsschiedsgerichtsbarkeit in Frankreich, 514-515; DE BOISSESON, M., Le droit français de l'arbitrage, first edition, 423.

451. See supra No. 182.

452. See supra Nos. 438-445.

this regard be made between substantive comparative methods and comparative methods at the conflict of laws level. Both are discussed below.

IV.3.1 *Substantive comparative methods*

471. Langen created his comparative method in 1969 as a middleway between the application of conflict of laws and the application of the *lex mercatoria*. To a large extent, this method is *comparative*. It would apply general principles of law applicable in international commerce in cases where the conflict of laws would lead to unsatisfactory results[453]. These principles or rules should be found in the laws of the countries which are connected to the international transaction in relation to which a dispute has arisen[454]. If application of the legal systems involved lead to the same conclusions (*false conflicts*), the solution of the *lex fori* may be applied. If the solutions are mutually exclusive (*true conflicts*) and mandatory rules of one legal system are at stake, the solution of that legal system must prevail. If no mandatory rules are involved, the judge should consider the contradictory rules and should, taking all circumstances into account apply the *better law*[455]. The reactions to Langen's method have generally been sceptical[456].

472. Bonell also has argued in favour of a transnational substantive method based on comparative law. Judges and arbitrators should apply universally accepted principles and rules or principles and rules that do not contradict the national legal systems that are connected to the transaction[457]. Thus, Bonell seems to limit his method to the *false conflict* problem which might avoid many problems.

---

453. LANGEN, E., Vom internationalen Privatrecht zum transnationalen Handelsrecht, 359-360. The substantivists of the American conflicts crisis (Currie, Cavers, Ehrenzweig) have clearly influenced Langen's method.

454. LANGEN, E., Transnationales Handelsrecht, 2229-2230.

455. LANGEN, E., Transnational commercial law, 33 and 50; LANGEN, E., Transnationales Recht, 13.

456. See LANGEN, E., Transnationales Recht, 13-28; KASSIS, A., Théorie générale des usages du commerce, 557-561; KROPHOLLER, J., Die Wissenschaft als Quelle der internationalen Rechtsvereinheitlichung, 153-154; VON BAR, C., Internationales Privatrecht, Volume 1, 90-92.

457. BONELL, M., Le regole oggetive del commercio internazionale, 217-247; BONELL, M., The law applicable to international commercial contracts : the standpoint of Italian doctrine and case-law, 22.

To illustrate his method, Bonell refers to international conventions in which such a transnational method also is being applied[458]. In this respect, article 17 ULIS, article 7 CISG as well as the autonomous interpretation of the EEC Jurisdiction and Enforcement Convention by the EEC Court of Justice are cited[459]. The transnational method may, according to Bonell, have three advantages. First, rules of national law which are inappropriate to international business transactions may be avoided. Second, it leads to unification of law through case law and, third, there no longer is a need to rely on the theory of the *lex mercatoria*[460].

473. The examples of the transnational method which Bonell cites, are useful in order to be able to assess the transnational method. First, the autonomous interpretation of the EEC Convention by the Court of Justice is not at all applicable in all cases. In fields other than the definition of the Convention's scope, the Court frequently refers back to national law in order to interpret it[461]. Moreover, it is hard to make generalizations as to a transnational method to be applied by national courts and arbitrators, from the interpretation of an international convention by a supranational court. As to article 17 ULIS, this provision does not totally exclude the conflict of laws. Article 7 CISG has confirmed this point of view and even increased the importance of the conflict of laws[462]. In both cases, a transnational method is a lot easier since they are unification instruments which are easier subject to uniform interpretation than national laws which have a different content.

474. However, Bonell also has referred to national case law in France, Italy and Germany which has applied the transnational method. As to France, the transnational substantive rules developed by the case law of the French Supreme Court and which were discussed above[463], were cited. However, these rules are unilateral adaptations of French domestic law to international situations and do not primarily aim to unify the law. Their content but not the underlying policy are transnational.

The Italian case law referred to by Bonell, is related to the form of arbitral clauses. First, in the Italian Supreme Court's decision of May 2,

---

458. BONELL, M., The law applicable to international commercial contracts : the standpoint of Italian doctrine and case-law, 23-25.
459. See supra No. 305.
460. BONELL, M., The law applicable to international commercial contracts : the standpoint of Italian doctrine and case-law, 23.
461. See supra No. 305.
462. See supra No. 307.
463. See supra IV.2.

1960[464], the Court held that the form of arbitral clauses are no longer governed by the *lex fori* but by the law applicable to the contract. The impact of the decision was that arbitral clauses in general conditions and other standard forms which were subject to foreign law, were valid notwithstanding article 1341 Codice civile which requires express acceptance in writing[465]. However, this case seems to change the characterization of the form of arbitral clauses rather than to apply the transnational method. Bonell also cites Italian case law of lower courts where article 1341 Codice civile is no longer applied when the protection offered by that provision is not needed (*i.e.*, in relations between contracting parties with comparable bargaining power)[466]. These cases are also applicable in national transactions and, therefore, are not an application of the transnational method.

Finally, German case law involving the acceptance of general conditions in international trade is invoked. This case law intended to protect the party against whom the general conditions were used. If the general conditions contained a choice of law clause, the law thus chosen would in principle apply to the contrat, including its formation. Thus, the user of the general conditions, under the applicable law which is favourable to acceptance by silence, might bind the other party to a contract to which the latter did not agree, notwithstanding the fact that the law of the latter's residence rejects acceptance by silence. The German Supreme Court has offered that party protection; the user of the general conditions cannot hold the other party to the contract if the latter hadn't agreed as determined by the law of his residence[467]. In these cases, the German Supreme Court seems to make a correction to a conflict rule and not to apply a transnational method.

475. Another comparative method has been developed by Rubino-Sammartano. According to this author, transnational problems may be solved by reference to the *tronc commun* of the legal systems involved (*i.e.*, application of principles common to these legal systems). This process can be based upon the parties' express will or be inferred from an implied will.

---

464. Foro it., 1960, I, 736.

465. BONELL, M., The law applicable to international commercial contracts : the standpoint of Italian doctrine and case-law, 21.

466. BONELL, M., The law applicable to international commercial contracts : the standpoint of Italian doctrine and case-law, 21.

467. German Supreme Court, September 22, 1971, NJW, 1972, 391 and July 13, 1973, NJW, 1973, 2154. This rule has been codified in article 8, § 2 of the EEC Convention on the law applicable to contractual obligations, see DE LY, F., Formulierenstrijd en totstandkoming van contracten, 1329-1333 and supra No. 91.

In this regard, the *lex mercatoria* would only apply to the extent that the application of the *tronc commun* method does not lead to practical results[468].

This theory has been criticized by Ancel. Quite rightly, Ancel points out that Rubino-Sammartano departs from two assumptions which may be subject to criticism. First, *tronc commun* assumes that the parties intended to exclude their respective legal systems to the extent that differences exist. Second, the theory assumes that the parties intended to apply the provisions common to their respective legal systems and not any other national legal system[469]. The basic flaw of the theory is thus its intention-guessing character.

476. In international commercial arbitration, one also often notes that arbitrators do not apply one single national law but base their award on several laws[470]. Comparative research of these laws is done in order to find a common solution. The substantive provisions of these laws are then applied cumulatively. In The Netherlands, this method has been called the *non-selection method* or the *conflict avoidance method*[471]. In cases of false conflicts, this does not create so many problems. In relation to true conflicts, a decision is needed in order to prefer one law over the others or the method should be abandoned in order to apply a conflict rule to determine the applicable law. In the latter case, one notes that the conflict avoidance rule complements the conflict of laws method rather than replaces it.

There are a few reasons for the use of comparative methods in international commercial arbitration. Apart from the concerns about the arbitrariness of some conflict rules and the wish to denationalize the arbitral process, other factors may also be cited. First, arbitrators might feel the need to convince litigating parties about the correctness and fairness of the award and, thus, may want not to base the award in one national legal system but in various systems connected to the dispute,

---

468. RUBINO-SAMMARTANO, M., Le "tronc commun" des lois nationales en présence (réflexions sur le droit applicable par l'arbitre international), Rev.Arb., 1987, 133-138; RUBINO-SAMMARTANO, M., International arbitration law, Deventer, Kluwer Law & Taxation, 1990, 269-280.

469. ANCEL, B., The Tronc Commun doctrine : logics and experience in international arbitration, J.INT. ARB., 1990, 65-72.

470. *E.g.*, I.C.C. case No. 3916, Clunet, 1984, 930, case note JARVIN, S.; I.C.C. case No. 5103, Clunet, 1988, 1206, case note AQUILAR ALVAREZ, G. and the cases referred to in Nos. 395 and 405.

471. JESSURUN D'OLIVEIRA, H.U., De antikiesregel, Deventer, Kluwer, 1971; see also VON BAR, C., Internationales Privatrecht, Volume 1, 88.

eventually under reference to authoritative texts such as international conventions. Another factor is the deliberation process in multi-arbitrators' tribunals[472]. In order to form a majority or to arrive at a unanimous opinion, concessions must sometimes be made or parallel motivations applied. This may particularly be so in arbitrations with party-appointed arbitrators.

477. The comparative methods developed by Langen, Bonell and Rubino-Sammartano and applied in international commercial arbitrations, may be assessed together because of their similarities. Undoubtedly, the method gives judges and arbitrators great discretion[473]. One may ask whether the burden placed on judges and arbitrators may generally not be too high in terms of knowledge of comparative law, availability of information on different legal systems and demands of time and money[474]. Furthermore, comparative methods frequently might violate the conflict rules of the *lex fori* or of the arbitral conflict system[475]. In both cases, one may wonder whether this is possible without authorization by the parties[476] or by the applicable law. In the absence of such an authorization, application of the comparative method might lead to review by superior courts in case of litigation pending before national courts. Since this review is mostly a full scale review including the motivation of the decision, courts which exclusively use the comparative method may well be forced, even in the case of *false conflicts* where the laws of the countries connected to the dispute have the same contents, also to base their decisions convincingly on the applicable national law. In case of arbitration proceedings, review is much more limited and attacks against the award on the basis of use of the comparative method seems more difficult, unless the arbitrators may be held to have acted as *amiables compositeurs*[477]. This might be so in cases of *true conflicts* where Langen would have to apply his better law approach, unless the same result may be reached under open-ended and escape clauses of the arbitral conflict system. Finally, the comparative method might increase unpredictability in international business law. Langen has refuted this argument by arguing that this would be offset by a better

---

472. BREDIN, J.D., La loi du juge, 15-27.
473. See LANGEN, E., Transnational commercial law, 203.
474. See also No. 441 where the same argument was made regarding transnational principles of law.
475. KASSIS, A., Théorie générale des usages du commerce, 558-559.
476. This is probably the reason why Rubino-Sammartano based his comparative method on the will of the parties.
477. See supra Nos. 180-182.

adjudicatory process[478]. This might be overoptimistic and it seems that in international business law greater attention should be given to predictability of the dispute resolution process in order not to frustrate party intent and the economic realities behind international commercial transactions.

It thus looks as if the substantive comparative methods developed in arbitration practice and by Langen, Bonell and Rubino-Sammartano cannot function as a complete alternative to traditional techniques such as conflict of laws with regard to the resolution of international business disputes. These methods seem to be useful mainly in false conflict situations. Finally, one cannot but regret that these comparative methods have not been more elaborated. For instance, the analyses on transnational principles of law and their relation to comparative law[479] have insufficiently been related to the comparative method.

IV.3.2 *Comparative methods at the conflict of laws level*

478. Conflict of law methodology has particularly flourished in international commercial arbitration where arbitrators have shown great creativity. The reasons for this creativity have already been indicated above[480].

Apart from previously discussed methods, the following methods will be discussed below[481] : (1) the application of general principles of conflict of laws; and (2) the cumulative application of conflict rules.

479. Contrary to national courts which apply the conflict rules of the *lex fori,* arbitrators are faced in international commercial arbitration with the problem of what conflict rules to apply. This problem has already been analyzed. According to some theories, national conflict rules should be applied; according to the autonomous theory, autonomous conflict rules may be chosen[482]. In the latter perspective, one is still faced with the question of where these autonomous conflict rules should come from. In

---

478. LANGEN, E., Transnationales Handelsrecht, 2229-2230.
479. See supra No. 441.
480. See supra No. 476.
481. See LANDO, O., The law applicable to the merits of the dispute, in Essays on international commercial arbitration, SARCEVIC, P. (ed.), London, Graham & Trotman, 1989, 138-140. Other methods are also used and referred to in Lando's article but will not be discussed. First, awards often contain references to uniform law or international conventions, even if these are not applicable to the dispute. These references may be interpreted as persuasive authority in support of some arguments (*e.g.*, I.C.C. case No. 6281, Clunet, 1991, 1054, case note HASCHER, D.). Also, the conflict of laws system in which the conflict rule was found, is sometimes not indicated in the award, probably in order not to nationalize the arbitral process.
482. See supra Nos. 136 ff.

relation to the theory of the *lex mercatoria*, it had been argued that its application was sometimes based on general principles of conflict of laws[483]. General principles of conflict of laws and the *lex mercatoria* are closely related. In order to uphold the theory of an autonomous *lex mercatoria*, its proponents had to base its application on an autonomous basis since it could not be applicable by virtue of a national conflict rule. General principles of conflict of laws are then one of the possible bases for an autonomous application. As has been stated, such principles hardly exist as a formal source of law and, thus, are of no help for the theory of the *lex mercatoria*[484].

480. General principles of conflict of laws may also be conceived as guiding principles of interpretation[485]. Without being a genuine source of law, they may guide the arbitrators in finding an appropriate conflict rule. In this respect, they should be dissociated from the theory of an autonomous *lex mercatoria*. The question then arises how these interpretative principles may be applied. Clearly, they may function within the autonomy given to the parties and to the arbitrators under international conventions and national laws[486]. As such, arbitrators may find in these principles a source for autonomous conflict of laws adjudication and arbitrary decisions may be avoided. Also, these principles allow for a more transnational approach to conflict of laws problems regarding the merits of the dispute as is intended by conventions and national laws. If no authority may be found in these texts for autonomous conflict rules, application of general principles of conflict of laws may be more risky since the award may then be attacked in the course of setting aside or enforcement proceedings[487].

481. If one no longer sees general principles of conflict of laws as genuine sources of law but as a method to solve the problem of the arbitral conflict of laws, the similarity becomes apparent between that method and the

---

483. DERAINS, Y., Attente légitime des parties et droit applicable au fond en matière d'arbitrage commercial international, 89; DEBY-GERARD, F., Le rôle de la règle de conflit dans le règlement des rapports internationaux, 204-205; LALIVE, P., Les règles de conflit de lois appliquées au fond du litige par l'arbitre international siégeant en Suisse, 93-95; JARVIN, S., Aus der Praxis des ICC Schiedsgerichtshofes, Recht und Praxis der Schiedsgerichtsbarkeit der Internationalen Handelskammer, BÖCKSTIEGEL, K.H. (ed.), Cologne, Heymanns, 1986, 24.

484. See supra No. 432.

485. See supra Nos. 444-445.

486. See supra No. 156.

487. See supra Nos.173-174 and 180-182.

method of the *cumulative application of conflict rules*[488]. Under the latter method, arbitrators might want not to apply one single system, but all systems of conflicts which are connected to the transaction. The same considerations which were expressed above in relation to the comparative method[489], may also apply here. Since arbitral autonomy is more generally recognized in relation to conflict of laws than to substantive law, the method of applying conflict rules of different jurisdictions cumulatively, may be one way for arbitrators to motivate their award as to the issue of the law applicable to the merits of the dispute.

As to its practical operation, the cumulative conflict method does not create problems if the conflict rules are identical or lead to the same results (false conflict). If a real conflict exists between the conflict rules (true conflict), a choice will have to be made. Otherwise the cumulative application of conflict rules might not be workable or might prove to be very restrictive[490]. If the applicable law authorizes the arbitrators to apply the most appropriate conflict rule, a choice of the better conflict rule might be possible. If not, arbitrators should be aware that national courts might have limited review to see whether their award was not rendered ex aequo et bono[491].

---

488. See I.C.C. case No. 1512, Clunet, 1974, 904, case note DERAINS, Y.; I.C.C. case No. 5118, Clunet, 1987, 1027, case note JARVIN, S., I.C.C. case No. 6281, Clunet, 1991, 1054, case note HASCHER, D.; DERAINS, Y., L'application cumulative par l'arbitre des systèmes de conflit de lois intéressés au litige, Rev.Arb., 1972, 99-121; SANDROCK, O., Die Fortbildung des materiellen Rechts durch die Internationale Schiedsgerichtsbarkeit, 65-66; General principles of law in international commercial arbitration, HARV.L.REV. 1988, 1822.

489. See supra No. 476.

490. LOQUIN, E., Les pouvoirs des arbitres internationaux à la lumière de l'évolution récente du droit de l'arbitrage international, 339; SCHULTSZ, J.C., Legislation in the Netherlands and international arbitration, Mededelingen van de Nederlandse Vereniging voor Internationaal Recht, No. 93, Deventer, Kluwer, 1986, 20; TSCHANZ, P.Y., Le nouveau droit suisse de l'arbitrage international, R.D.A.I., 1988, 447; CROFF, C., The applicable law in an international commercial arbitration : is it still a conflict of laws problem ?, 630.

For an example, see I.C.C. case No. 4996, Clunet, 1986, 1132, case note DERAINS, Y.

491. See supra Nos. 180-182.

IV.4 National conflict rules and substantive law

482. The previous sections have made clear that national law may still play an important role in international business law. This will be discussed below in relation to conflict of laws and substantive law.

483. The proponents of the *lex mercatoria* have generally been critical as to conflict of laws[492]. However, conflicts are often avoided through choice of law clauses or extensive contractual or other forms of self-regulation[493]. Conflicts may also be avoided once the dispute has arisen. The non-selection or conflict avoidance method which has been discussed in relation to international commercial arbitration[494], is also available for court litigation[495]. Also, one may not exaggerate the complexity of the conflict method. One may wonder whether other methods (substantive or comparative) are much simpler. Also, in relation to contracts, one may note a diminution of the technicalities of conflict law inspired by pragmatism[496]. Too often, the conflict of laws is also seen as a set of rules which automatically through a hard and fast rule refers to the applicable law. However, the conflict of laws also has open-ended rules and escape clauses which allow for a more flexible approach[497]. Also, judges and arbitrators may create new conflict rules and thus develop conflict of laws. Finally, traditional conflict of laws is content-neutral and may, thus, be blind to the interests and policies underlying international commercial transactions. Sometimes, efforts are made, however, to take these considerations into

---

492. See supra II.1.

493. SCHMITTHOFF, C., Conflict avoidance in practice and theory, 430 and 453; SCHMITTHOFF, C., International trade law and private international law, 261 and 265; RABEL, E., The conflict of laws, A comparative study, I, second edition, Ann Arbor, University of Michigan Law School, 1958, 20; JOERGES, C., Vorüberlegungen zu einer Theorie des internationalen Wirtschaftsrechts, 40; DELAUME, G., Issues of applicable law in the context of the World Bank's operations, in The transnational law of international commercial transactions, HORN, N. and SCHMITTHOFF, C. (ed.), Deventer, Kluwer, 1982, 325-326.

494. See supra No. 476.

495. JESSURUN D'OLIVEIRA, H.U., De antikiesregel, Deventer, Kluwer, 1971; VON BAR, C., Internationales Privatrecht, Volume 1, 88. *E.g.*, Court of Appeal Brussels, February 25, 1982, R.D.C., 1982, 351.

496. See supra II.2.1.3.

497. See supra No. 102.

account. In this respect, one might refer to conflict rules with substantive features and recent theories on legitimate expectations[498].

484. The criticism regarding the conflict of laws should thus be seen against the background of the aforementioned elements. Obviously, conflict of laws always should wonder about its method in order to adapt it to the specific characteristics and needs of international business life. The main issue is in this respect to what extent national courts will be willing to make any adjustments. This is an issue not specific to international business law; it is related to the question of the role of the judiciary in society[499]. Since arbitrators have generally more discretion than judges and review of awards is more limited than that of judgments, experimentation with national conflict of laws is easier for arbitrators.

485. As to substantive law, the proponents of the *lex mercatoria* also have pointed to the unproven assertion that national substantive law is inappropriate to regulate international business transactions. This statement also is insufficiently qualified. Although centrally planned economies have different rules for domestic and international transactions, free market and mixed market economies have only exceptionally created specific rules for international business transactions. Also, conventions on the unification of the law often apply as well to national as to international transactions. These elements may indicate that national law is not *per se* inappropriate for international business transactions.

486. Apart from the applicable law, foreign rules may be incorporated into the contract. In the interpretation of these rules, regard should be had to the foreign law from which they are drawn[500]. As to the applicable law, various techniques exist to take account of the transnational nature of business transactions[501]. First, in interpreting contracts, their transnational character may be taken into account. General conditions or self-regulatory rules which have been drafted at the transnational level or which are used

498. See JOBARD-BACHELLIER, M.N., L'apparence en droit international privé, Essai sur le rôle des représentations individuelles en droit international privé, Paris, LGDJ, 1984, 425 pp.; OPPETIT, B., Le développement des règles matérielles, 20-21.

499. See infra No. 490.

500. *E.g.*, Amin Rasheed Shipping Corporation v. Kuwait Insurance Co., [1983] 2 All E.R. 894, [1984] AC 50 (House of Lords); Commercial Court Brussels, June 21, 1985, R.G.A.R., 1987, 11242.

501. ROTH, W.H., Internationales Versicherungsvertragsrecht, 547.

transnationally, may be interpreted in the light of that origin or use[502]. Although there is no general interpretative rule that interpretation should tend to promote international commerce and its unification, it may still be an element or guideline in the interpretative process. German literature has proposed such an interpretation in relation to the U.C.P.[503].

487. In the absence of contractual clauses, the provisions of the applicable law should in principle be applied. One may, however, wonder whether one may derogate from such provisions under open-ended rules of the applicable law if that is justified by the specific nature of the transaction[504]. As to mandatory rules, any such derogations may be more difficult. Case law may also take a more flexible approach to international business problems in view of the needs and features of international trade. This will by and large depend upon the interpretation methods used in the different countries. In England, because of the strict rule of precedent, few examples of such a flexible approach may be found[505]. In the U.S., the *stare decisis* rule is not so stringent and thus more flexibility towards international trade problems may be encountered[506]. In European continental systems, the more dogmatic and less empirical approach is

502. WENGLER, W., Die Anknüpfung des zwingenden Schuldrechts im internationalen Privatrecht, Zvglrwiss, 1941, 209-210; WENGLER, W., Die Funktion des richterlichen Entscheidung über internationale Rechtsverhältnisse, Feststellung und Gestaltung im internationalen Privatrecht, RabelsZ, 1951, 15; FIRSCHING, K., Internationales Schuldrecht, I, 357; ISHIZAKI, M., Le droit corporatif international de la vente de soies, 352; SCHMITTHOFF, C., The law of international trade, its growth, formulation and operation, 33-35; SCHMITTHOFF, C., Das neue Recht des Welthandels, 68-69.

503. STEINDORFF, E., Das Akkreditiv im internationalen Privatrecht der Schuldverträge, Festschrift für Von Caemmerer, 1978, 765; CANARIS, C.W., Bankvertragsrecht, second edition, 488-489; HORN, N., Internationale Zahlungen und Akkreditiv, 13-14; STAUDINGER-HORN, Vorbem. zu §§ 765-778, 326; EBERTH, R., The uniform customs and practice for documentary credits, 34; EBERTH, R., Die Revision von 1983 der Einheitlichen Richtlinien und Gebräuche für Dokumenten-Akkreditive, 20; *but see* VON WESTPHALEN, F., Rechtsprobleme der Exportfinanzierungen, 230-231.

504. SANDROCK, O., Zur ergänzenden Vertragsauslegung im materiellen und internationalen Schuldvertragsrecht, 13-14, 87 and 263; RUMMEL, P., Vertragsauslegung nach der Verkehrssitte, 68 ff.

505. *But see* Power Curber International Ltd. v. National Bank of Kuwait SAK, [1981] 3 All E.R. 607 (Court of Appeal); SCHWANK, F., Documentary letters of credit - recent cases, Int.Fin.Law Review, May 1982, 11; BRABANT, A., Le contrat international de construction, 279.

506. BERMAN, H. and KAUFMAN, C., The law of international commercial transactions (lex mercatoria), 254-264; TRAKMAN, L., The evolution of the law merchant : our commercial heritage, 163-171.

accountable for less pragmatism in international business dispute resolution[507].

488. In the absence of contractual, statutory or case law rules providing for specific solutions to international business problems, the applicable law might still have methods to have regard to the transnational nature of the transaction[508]. In this perspective, open-ended rules may be used as a tool for a more transnational approach. These rules such as good faith, reasonable conduct or rules of art are vague and need further elaboration. Within that process, there is ample room to take account of a transaction's transnational character[509]. Some authors have, for instance, referred to common understandings in international commerce[510]. In Chapter III, it has been demonstrated that transnational usages may be applied by virtue of the good faith notion which may be found in civil law jurisdictions[511].

IV.5 Conclusions

489. From this chapter, the conclusion may be drawn that Goldman's theory of the *lex mercatoria* should be rejected. Schmitthoff's theory may be approved but it is hard to see why the sources of international business law should be limited to international sources. Other theories and methods such as the substantive and comparative methods discussed above certainly have their merits but also their limitations. Consequently, recourse still should be had to national substantive law and national conflict of laws in which tools might be available for more transnational approaches.

---

507. For exceptions, see ZAHN, J., Nationale Rechtselemente im Widerstreit mit der internationalen Praxis des Außenhandels, Festschrift für Rittershausen, 1968, 260; District Court Rotterdam, January 12, 1979, N.J., 1982, No. 267; German Supreme Court, May 15, 1986, RIW, 1986, 816, NJW, 1986, 3027, WM, 1986, 982, DB, 1986, 2178; POULLET, Y., Les incertitudes relatives à la nature juridique de l'assurance-caution, Bull.Ass., 1979, 29; POULLET, Y., case note Court of Appeal Antwerp, October 13, 1982, R.D.C., 1982, 662; VELU-SPREUTELS, S., DELIERNEUX, M. and LEVY MORELLE, J., Les garanties payables à première demande, in Les sûretés issues de la pratique, Brussels, PUB, Volume 3, I.63.
508. SANDROCK, O. and STEINSCHULTE, F.P., Grundfragen des internationalen Vertragsrecht : die kollisionsrechtliche Anknüpfung von Schuldverträgen, in Handbuch der internationalen Vertragsgestaltung, Volume 1, 100.
509. HORN, N., Die Anpassung langfristiger Verträge im internationalen Wirtschaftsverkehr, Vertragsklauseln und Schiedspraxis, 45-46.
510. BOLL, J., Preadvies, in MIJNSSEN, F. and BOLL, J., De bankgarantie, 82, 96 and 125; Staub-Großkomm-Koller, Vor § 373, No. 11.
511. See supra Nos. 233-238.

490. In this regard, one may approve Lando's analysis of arbitral case law as a creative judicial process[512]. One might even generalize and note that the problem of the sources of international business law is related to *judicial and arbitral adjudication*. However, one may doubt whether such a process should be linked to concepts such as the *lex mercatoria*. In all the theories and methods discussed above, the key issue does not seem to be whether the international business community has autonomous rules of its own and how these rules should be translated in formal sources of law. Rather, the issue is how judges should operate with international business problems and how arbitrators should use the discretion given to them by international instruments and national statutes. Thus, the attention shifts from formal sources of law to adjudicatory methodology. The distinction between formal and substantive sources of law is then no longer so important but rather the issue is what judges and arbitrators actually do with any source, whatever its nature. This is particularly so for usages as elements of contract construction and general principles of law as interpretative guidelines. Within that perspective, focus is on the role of the judiciary and arbitrators as rule makers, entrusted with the creation and development of international business law. In this process, they should take account of policies set by international and national legislators as well as by the originators of transnational self-regulation. One should add that, in relation to arbitration, arbitrators are not solely rule appliers and makers but also dispute settlors which implies that the development of international business law is not their only preoccupation. They also should try to find solutions which facilitate the dispute resolution process. Arbitral adjudication methods discussed in Chapter IV, seem to confirm this.

491. In international business dispute resolution and particularly in international commercial arbitration, adjudicators have received wider powers to operate with conflict rules and substantive rules. This might have its price in terms of a decrease in predictability of the outcome of a case. In practice, one is thus faced with the question what to do in the light of these developments. In this respect, parties may choose litigation in national courts of jurisdictions where little judicial activism is encountered. As to arbitration, one might want to arbitrate under Arbitration Rules which limit arbitral discretion[513] or in countries whose law may provide

512. LANDO, O., The law applicable to the merits of the dispute, 141, 143 and 147-148; see also BREDIN, J.D., La loi du juge, 15-27.

513. This may be illustrated by article 4 of the Zurich Chambre of Commerce International Arbitration Rules which provide for application of Swiss conflict rules (as the conflict of laws system of the arbitral seat) and seem to proscribe application of autonomous

for more extensive review than generally is the case. More important, a choice of law clause may limit judicial and arbitral activism. This is particularly relevant in those jurisdictions such as France or The Netherlands where the arbitration laws are very liberal as to the conflict methodology[514].

conflict rules. Thus, a contradiction with article 187 (1) of the Swiss Law on Conflict of Laws was created. Presumably, the drafters of the Zurich Rules wanted to limit arbitral discretion as authorized under the Law. Some authors have argued that article 4 should be disregarded because it is contrary to the will of the parties and article 187 (1) of the Law (LALIVE, P., On the conflict rules applicable by the international arbitrator, ASA Bull. 1989, 27-37; *but see* SAMUEL, A., A critical look at the reform of Swiss Arbitration Law, ARB. INT'L, 1991, 47).

514. VON BREITENSTEIN, D., Die internationale Arbitrage im französischen Recht, Schiedsgerichtsbarkeit in Frankreich, BÖCKSTIEGEL, K.H. (ed.), Cologne, Heymanns, 1983, 39-40.

GENERAL CONCLUSIONS

492. After the second world war, many theories emerged on the sources of international business law. In this book, an attempt was made to discuss and assess these theories. Prior to this discussion, the theories on the sources of international business law have been put in a historical perspective. Also, the scope of international business law has been discussed. Finally, an overview was given of the role of conflict of laws in international business litigation and arbitration as well as of the sources of international business law. In light of these elements, recent theories were analyzed.

493. First, historical antecedents to present-day international business law were discussed. From this analysis, it appeared that the *ius gentium* of Roman law and the medieval law merchant are not comparable to present-day international business law. Moreover, recent theories on international business law have emphasized the need for self-regulation and unification of law. However, these elements seem to be lacking in the *ius gentium* and the medieval law merchant. Both existed within their respective legal systems and were not autonomous. Also, their sources were not exclusively international and, thus, formed an impediment to unification.

494. In order to understand the sources of international business law, one should be able clearly to define their scope. A uniform definition of the *lex mercatoria*'s international and business character is, however, extremely difficult. Analysis of international conventions, national law and transnational practice made clear that such a uniform definition is not possible. Also, the territorial scope of international business law has been discussed. In this respect, a universal worldwide law does not seem possible. Rather, attempts should be made to encourage uniformity at the regional level.

495. International business problems create conflict of laws problems. National courts or arbitrators must look for the applicable law. The traditional answer is that national law should be applied by virtue of a conflict of laws rule. Recent theories, however, have proposed not to apply national rules or to develop new methods in conflict of laws. The question then arises whether and to what extent national conflict of laws systems regarding international business contracts and international commercial arbitration law might authorize application of anational rules and new conflict methods.

The conflict of laws regarding contracts is in many countries very pragmatic. Particularly when parties have chosen the applicable law, there are few limits. Within this perspective, there may be room for application of transnational rules or conflict of laws experimentation. However, some minimal requirements must be met. Some gap filling mechanism should be available and some mandatory rules should exist in the application of transnational rules. Thus, one might say that transnational rules may be applied provided they form a legal system. If not, they might only be applicable within the applicable national law. In the absence of a choice of law clause, application of transnational rules or new conflict methods will be more difficult since national courts are then, as a matter of principle, bound by their own conflict rules. It seems that only within these limits, transnational rules and other methods may be used. Both in the case of choice of law and in the absence thereof, the application of transnational rules or new conflict methods will depend upon and be influenced by the *lex fori*.

496. These elements might be different in international commercial arbitration. Here, the arbitrators are faced with the problem which system of conflict of laws to apply. If such system is a national system, the analysis set forth above would apply *mutatis mutandis*. However, in order to minimize the impact of national law or to develop an autonomous law of international trade which is independent from national law, autonomous conflict rules must be sought. Here also, within such autonomous conflict rules, some system should be available which might regulate the conflict method, fill gaps and provide conflict rules. Generally, review of arbitral awards will be limited and will not extend to the merits of the dispute or the conflict method applied. One may note one exception; the arbitrators should respect the choice of law made by the parties and cannot act *ex aequo et bono* without having been duly authorized to do so. Otherwise, setting aside and enforcement problems might ensue based on the argument that the arbitrators went beyond the scope of their mandate or rendered an award *ultra petita*. This seems to be a key issue in recent theories on arbitral adjudication and might prove to be their *Achilles' heel*. Here, the practical implications of these theories become apparent.

497. As to the sources of international business law, it has been noted that general conditions, trade usages, self-regulatory rules, arbitral case law and international conventions are major substantive sources of international business law. They are of paramount importance for its understanding and practice. However, if we look to international business law from the perspective of building an autonomous law, independent from national law, only custom and, to a certain extent, general principles of law may be seen as genuine sources of such a law. In this respect, one also notes that few such customs or principles exist.

498. The elements of the analysis must now be applied to the recent theories on the sources of international business law. The most influential theory has been the theory of the *lex mercatoria*. The theory was, until recently, prevailing in France. Apart from French speaking authors in Belgium, the theory had a mixed reception in Switzerland, The Netherlands, Germany, England and by Dutch speaking authors in Belgium. In these countries, proponents and opponents of the theory kept each other in balance.

The theory also influenced legislation and case law. In the French and Dutch arbitration laws, the influence of the theory may clearly be found. On the other hand, other legislation or international conventions hardly have directly been influenced by the theory. As to case law, the *lex mercatoria* has only been recognized in a very limited number of cases. Other cases where the *lex mercatoria* was raised, may be interpreted on different grounds but not necessarily imply that the *lex mercatoria* was recognized. Finally, few examples exist in which transnational practice expressly referred to the *lex mercatoria*.

499. In order to get a better understanding of the theory of the *lex mercatoria*, the theory itself has been discussed at some length. From this analysis, the conclusion may be drawn that there are basically two different conceptions of the *lex mercatoria*. The first conception which is much indebted to Clive Schmitthoff, sees the *lex mercatoria* as a set of rules within national legal systems which have been created at the international level (basically international conventions and international usages) and may promote the unification of international business law. According to the second view which primarily has been inspired by Berthold Goldman, the *lex mercatoria* is a set of autonomous rules (such as general conditions, trade usages, self-regulatory rules, general principles of law) which exist outside national legal systems and are an attempt better to regulate international business transactions, without much interference from national legal systems. Since these conceptions are fundamentally different, one clearly should distinguish them in a debate on the *lex mercatoria*.

500. Schmitthoff's conception on the *lex mercatoria* may generally be endorsed. Indeed, international conventions and usages make important contributions to the unification of international business law. However, one may criticize the theory of Schmitthoff for having limited these unifying effects to international sources.

It seems that an extrapolation from Schmitthoff's theory whereby international business law is an independent branch of national law, must fail. International business law has insufficient rules which may allow for systematization and is also too dependent on substantive law and conflict of laws.

501. Goldman's theory on the *lex mercatoria* also fails. The *lex mercatoria* has insufficient rules of its own (including conflict rules), cannot define its own scope, has hardly any sources, cannot fill its own gaps and has hardly any mandatory rules. Thus, it is not a legal system which may be chosen under any conflict of laws method. References to *lex mercatoria*, transnational usages and principles may thus be interpreted as rules incorporated into the contract which may be applied by virtue of the applicable national law. All this does not intend to suggest that the theories regarding the *lex mercatoria* have no merits. Their main virtue has been that they have emphasized that international business law cannot be understood or practiced without adequate knowledge of transnational practice, self-regulation and the methodology of arbitral adjudication.

502. Apart from the theory of the *lex mercatoria*, other theories or methods have been developed. Basically, these methods are substantive or comparative. They seem to be unable to replace traditional conflict rules but may be useful as a supplementary method. They are used particularly in international commercial arbitration because international conventions and national statutes give wide discretion to the parties and the arbitrators as to the methods to be applied to the merits of the dispute. Even absent such an authorization, review is generally limited, except for *amiable composition*. The comparative methods are primarily attractive in false conflict situations since it thus enhances the authority of the award which is based on the laws of the different countries involved and it expresses more a transnational approach. Substantive methods may also be attractive in cases where the content-neutrality of a conflict rule would need correction or where the application of the conflict rule would be arbitrary.

503. All theories or methods do not completely exclude national law, both substantive and conflict of laws. Any theory which would like to take account of the transnational nature of business relations, will be faced with integrating this element into national law. This will be easier in factual determinations than in the development of legal rules. With regard to the latter, general problems involving the relation between legislator and judiciary are involved. Judges might feel restraint in creating new rules for international business transactions, especially when statutory rules are applicable to the problem. Open-ended conflict and substantive rules may in this regard be helpful. In international commercial arbitration, adaptation of national law is easier since review is more limited, except as to *amiable composition*.

504. In all cases, one notes that the problem of the sources of international business law is related to *judicial and arbitral adjudication*. The key issue is not whether the international business community has autonomous rules of its own and how these rules should be translated in formal sources of law. Rather, the issue is how judges should operate with international business problems and how arbitrators should use the discretion given to them by international instruments and national statutes. Thus, the attention shifts from formal sources of law to the application of formal and substantive sources and to adjudicatory methodology. Within that perspective, focus is on a traditional debate on the role of the judiciary and arbitrators as rule makers, entrusted with the creation and development of international business law. In this process, they should take account of policies set by international and national legislators as well as by the originators of transnational self-regulation. One should add that arbitrators are not solely rule appliers and makers but also dispute settlors which implies that the development of international business law is not their only preoccupation. They also should try to find solutions which facilitate the dispute resolution process. Arbitral adjudication methods discussed in Chapter IV, seem to confirm this.

BIBLIOGRAPHY

This bibliography only contains titles and articles which have been cited more than once throughout the book. Other bibliographical data may be found in the footnotes of the respective chapters.

- Adaptation and renegotiation of contracts in international trade and finance, HORN, N. (ed.), Deventer, Kluwer, 1985, 421 pp.;
- ADEN, M., Die Anwendung materiellen Rechts durch den Schiedsrichter, RIW, 1984, 934-938;
- AGUILAR ALVAREZ, G., Cour d'Arbitrage de la Chambre de Commerce Internationale, Chronique des sentences arbitrales, Clunet, 1989, 1097-1120;
- L'apport de la jurisprudence arbitrale, INSTITUT DU DROIT ET DES PRATIQUES DES AFFAIRES INTERNATIONALES (ed.), Paris, I.C.C.-publication No. 440/1, 1986, 260 pp.;
- ASKE, R.W., The law relating to custom and the usages of trade, London, Stevens & Sons, 1909, 448 pp.;
- ASSER-RUTTEN-II (Algemene leer der overeenkomsten), fourth edition, Zwolle, Tjeenk Willink, 1975, 398 pp.;
- ASSER-SCHOLTEN, Algemeen deel, second edition, Zwolle, Tjeenk Willink, 1934, 264 pp.;
- ASSER-VAN DER GRINTEN, II, De rechtspersoon, sixth edition, Zwolle, Tjeenk Willink, 1986, 395 pp.;
- AUBERT, J.F., Les contrats internationaux dans la doctrine et la jurisprudence suisse, R.C.D.I.P., 1962, 19-52;
- AUDIT, B., A national codification of international commercial arbitration : the French Decree of May 12, 1981, in Resolving transnational disputes through international arbitration, CARBONNEAU, T. (ed.), Charlottesville, University Press of Virginia, 1984, 117-145;

- BAERT, F., De goede trouw bij de uitvoering van overeenkomsten, R.W., 1956-57, 489-516;
- BAINBRIDGE, S., Trade usages in international sales of goods : an analysis of the 1964 and 1980 sales conventions, 24 VA J. INT'L L., 1984, 619-665;
- BAJONS, E.M., Zur Nationalität internationaler Schiedssachen, Festschrift für W. Kralik, RECHBERGER, W.H. and WELSER, K. (ed.), Vienna, Manz, 1986, 3-35;
- BAKER, J.H., The law merchant and the common law before 1700, Cambridge Law Journal, 1979, 295-322;
- BAKKERS, R., Rechtsgewoonten betreffende handelskoop, Amsterdam, Noord-Hollandsche Uitgevers Maatschappij, 1961, 326 pp.;
- BÄRMANN, J., Ist internationales Handelsrecht kodifizierbar ?, in Internationales Recht und Wirtschaftsordnung, Festschrift für F.A. Mann, Munich, Beck, 1977, 547-573;
- BARON, J., Peregrinenrecht und ius gentium, Festschrift für Von Jhering, Leipzig, Duncker & Humblot, 1892, 40 pp.;
- BASEDOW, J., Die Incoterms und der Container oder wie man kodifizierte Usancen reformiert, RabelsZ, 1979, 116-146;
- Basle symposium on the law governing contractual obligations, KLEIN, F.E. and VISCHER, F. (ed.), Basle, Helbing & Lichtenhahn, 1983, 248 pp.;

- BATIFFOL, H., Les conflits de lois en matière de contrats, Paris, Sirey, 1938, 500 pp.;
- BATIFFOL, H., Aspects philosophiques du droit international privé, Paris, Dalloz, 1956, 346 pp.;
- BATIFFOL, H., Conflict avoidance in European law, 21 LAW & CONTEMP. PROBS., 1956, 571-580;
- BATIFFOL, H., Subjectivisme et objectivisme dans le droit international privé des contrats, Mélanges Jacques Maury, Paris, Dalloz, 1960, I, 39, reprint in BATIFFOL, H., Choix d'articles, Paris, LGDJ, 1976, 249-263;
- BATIFFOL, H.i Réflexions sur la coordination des systèmes nationaux, Academy of international law, 120 Collected courses of The Hague, 1967, I, 165-190;
- BATIFFOL, H., Le pluralisme des méthodes en droit international privé, Academy of international law, 139 Collected courses of The Hague, 1973, II, 75-147;
- BATIFFOL, H., L'état du droit international privé en France et dans l'Europe continentale de l'Ouest, Clunet, 1973, 22-45;
- BATIFFOL, H., Problèmes de base de philosophie du droit, Paris, LGDJ, 1979, 519 pp.;
- BATIFFOL, H. and LAGARDE, P., Droit international privé, Volume I, seventh edition, Paris, LGDJ, 1981;
- BATIFFOL, H., Les contrats en droit international privé comparé, McGill University, 1981, 166 pp.;
- BATIFFOL, H., La loi appropriée au contrat, in Le droit des relations économiques internationales, Etudes offertes à Berthold Goldman, Paris, Litec, 1982, 1-13;
- BATIFFOL, H., and LAGARDE, P., Droit international privé, Volume II, seventh edition, Paris, LGDJ, 1983, 692 pp.;
- BAXTER, I., International conflict of laws and international business, INT'L & COMP.L.Q., 1985, 538-562;
- BEGUIN, J., Le développement de la lex mercatoria menace-t-il l'ordre juridique international ?, 30 Mc GILL L.J., 1985, 478-538;
- BEGUIN, J., La logique du régime des voies de recours en matière d'arbitrage commercial international, in Etudes offertes à Roger Houin, Paris, Dalloz, 1985, 241-262;
- BEKAERT, H., Introduction à l'étude du droit, Brussels, Bruylant, 1973, 550 pp.;
- BELLET, P. and MEZGER, E., L'arbitrage international dans le nouveau code de procédure civile, R.C.D.I.P., 1981, 611-656;
- BELLET, P., Le rôle des usages en matière d'arbitrage international suivant la jurisprudence française, Journées de la société de législation comparée, 1985, 231-241;
- BEN ABDERRAHMANE, D., Le droit allemand des conditions générales des contrats dans les ventes commerciales franco-allemandes, Paris, LGDJ, 1985, 392 pp.;
- BENJAMIN, P., The European Convention on international commercial arbitration, 37 Brit. Y.B. Int.L., 1961, 478-495;
- BENJAMIN, P., The ECE general conditions of sale and standard forms of contract, J.BUS.L., 1961, 113-131;
- BERGER, K.P., Internationale Wirtschaftsschiedsgerichtsbarkeit, Berlin, de Gruyter, 1992, 687 pp.;
- BERLIOZ, G., Le contrat d'adhésion, Paris, LGDJ, 1973, 204 pp.;
- BERMAN, H. and KAUFMAN, C., The law of international commercial transactions (lex mercatoria), 19 HARV. INT'L L.J., 1978, 221-277; third edition published in 2 EMORY J.INT'L DISP.RES. 1988, 235-310;
- BERMAN, H. and DASSER, F., The "new" law merchant and the "old": sources, content, and legitimacy, in Lex mercatoria and arbitration, CARBONNEAU, T. (ed.), Dobbs Ferry, Transnational, 1990, 21-36;

- BERVOETS, T.M., Rechtskeuze, Een rechtstheoretisch onderzoek van het beginsel der rechtskeuze, in Partij-invloed in het internationaal privaatrecht, Deventer, Kluwer, 1974, 31-45;
- BEWES, W., The romance of the law merchant, Being an introduction to the study of international and commercial law, London, Sweet & Maxwell, 1923, 141 pp.;
- BIERZANEK, R., Quelques remarques sur le statut juridique des étrangers à Rome, IVRA, Rivista internazionale di diritto romano e antico, 1962, 89-109;
- BLESSING, M., Das neue internationale Schiedsgerichtsrecht der Schweiz -Ein Fortschritt oder ein Rückschritt ?, in Die internationale Schiedsgerichtsbarkeit in der Schweiz (II), BÖCKSTIEGEL,K.H. (ed.), Cologne, Heymanns, 1989, 13-87;
- BÖCKSTIEGEL, K.H., Der Staat als Vertragspartner ausländischer Privatunternehmen, Frankfurt, Athenäum Verlag, 1971, 432 pp.;
- BÖCKSTIEGEL, K.H., Die Bestimmung des anwendbaren Rechts in der Praxis internationaler Schiedsgerichtsverfahren, in Festschrift für G. Beitzke, Berlin, de Gruyter, 1979, 443-458;
- BÖCKSTIEGEL, K.H., The legal rules applicable in international commercial arbitration involving States and state-controlled enterprises, in International arbitration, 60 years of ICC arbitration, A look at the future, International Chamber of Commerce, publication No. 412, Paris, 1984, 117-176;
- BÖCKSTIEGEL, K.H., ICC-Schiedsgerichtsbarkeit aus der Sicht eines Schiedsrichters, in Recht und Praxis der Schiedsgerichtsbarkeit der Internationalen Handelskammer, BÖCKSTIEGEL, K.H. (ed.), Cologne, Heymanns, 1986, 75-88;
- BÖCKSTIEGEL, K.H., Zu den Thesen von einer "delokalisierten" internationalen Schiedsgerichtsbarkeit, in Festschrift für W. Oppenhoff, Munich, Beck, 1986, 1-10;
- BOLARD, G., Le nouveau droit français de l'arbitrage, in Les particularités nationales de l'arbitrage commercial international, Lublin, 1987, 29-47;
- BOLL, J., Preadvies, in MIJNSSEN,F. and BOLL, J., De bankgarantie, Preadviezen van de Vereeniging Handelsrecht, Zwolle, Tjeenk Willink, 1984, 77-142;
- BONELL, M., Le regole oggettive del commercio internazionale, Milan, Giuffrè, 1976, 314 pp.;
- BONELL, M., The relevance of courses of dealing, usages and customs in the interpretation of international commercial contracts, in New Directions in international trade law, Acts and proceedings of the 2nd congress on private law held by Unidroit, I, Dobbs Ferry, New York, Oceana, 1977, 109 ff.;
- BONELL, M., Das autonome Recht des Welthandels - rechtsdogmatische und rechtspolitische Aspekte, RabelsZ, 1978, 485-506;
- BONELL, M., Some critical reflections on the new Uncitral draft convention on international sales, UNIF.L.REV., 1978, II, 5-12;
- BONELL, M., La nouvelle Convention des Nations-Unies sur les contrats de vente internationale de marchandises, D.P.C.I., 1981, 7-35;
- BONELL, M., The law applicable to international commercial contracts : the standpoint of Italian doctrine and case-law, in Basle symposium on the law governing contractual obligations, KLEIN, F.E. and VISCHER, F. (ed.), Basle, Helbing & Lichtenhahn, 1983, 13-27;
- BONELL, M., Die Bedeutung der Handelsbräuche im Wiener Kaufrechtsübereinkommen von 1980, Juristische Blätter, 1985, 385-395;
- BONELL, M., in BIANCA-BONELL, Commentary on the international sales law, Art. 9, Milan, Giuffrè, 1987, 103-115;
- BOON, M.N., Het documentaire accreditief, De rechtspositie van de opdrachtgever ingevolge de UCP, Amsterdam, NIBE, 1988, 613 pp.;
- BOUCKAERT, B., De exegetische school, Antwerp, Kluwer, 1981, 527 p.;

- BOUCKAERT, B., Gewoonterecht in de moderne samenleving : een fetisj ?, in Liber Amicorum Willy Calewaert, Antwerp, Kluwer, 1984, 23-48;
- BOUCOURECHLIEV, J., Usages commerciaux, usages professionnels : élaboration et formulation, in Dix ans de droit de l'entreprise, Paris, Litec, 1978, 19-30;
- BOULANGER, J., Principes généraux du droit et droit positif, in Le droit privé français au milieu du XXe siècle, Etudes offertes à Georges Ripert, I, Paris, Pichon, 1950, 51-74;
- BOURDIN, R., La convention d'arbitrage international en droit français depuis le décret du 12 mai 1981, in Droit et pratique de l'arbitrage international en France, FEDUCI, s.l., 1984, 11-36;
- BOURGIGNON, P, L'autonomie de la volonté dans le système belge de droit international privé, Rev.Dr.Int.Comp., 1950, special issue, 42-56;
- Boyle and Birds' Company Law, Bristol, Jordan & Sons, 1983, 838 pp.;
- BRABANT, A., Le contrat international de construction, Brussels, Bruylant, 1981, 479 pp.;
- BRAECKMANS, H., Juridische aspecten van consortiumkredieten in Eurodeviezen, dissertation University Antwerp, Wilrijk, 1983, 1044 pp.;
- BRAECKMANS, H., De lex mercatoria, zijn verhouding tot het nationaal recht en meer specifiek tot het internationaal privaatrecht, R.W., 1983-84, 2651-2682;
- BRAECKMANS, H., Juridische aspecten van consortiumkredieten in Eurodeviezen, Antwerp, Maklu, 1985, 538 pp.;
- BRAECKMANS, H., Paralegale normen en lex mercatoria, in Aktuele problemen van handels-, economisch en financieel recht, Postuniversitaire cyclus Willy Delva 1985-86, STORME, M. and FREDERICQ, S. (ed.), Ghent, 1986, 1 -70 and T.P.R., 1986, 1-70;
- BREDIN, J.D., La Convention de New-York du 10 juin 1958 pour la reconnaissance et l'exécution des sentences arbitrales étrangères, Clunet, 1960, 1002-1029;
- BREDIN, J.D., L'amiable composition et le contrat, Rev.Arb., 1984, 259-271;
- BREDIN, J.D., La loi du juge, in le droit des relations économiques internationals, Etudes offertes à Berthold Goldman, Paris, Litec, 1982, 15-27;
- BRIGGS, A., The validity of "floating" choice of law and jurisdiction clauses, Lloyd's Mar.& Com.L.Q., 1986, 508-518;
- BROCHES, A., A model law on international commercial arbitration ? A progress report on the work undertaken within the U.N. Commission on international trade law (Uncitral), 18 GEO.WASH.J.INT'L L.& EC., 1984, 79-95;
- BROCHES, A., The 1985 Uncitral model law on international commercial arbitration : an exercise in international legislation, N.Y.B.Int.L., 1987, 3-67;
- BRUNING, G., Die Bedeutung von Gewohnheitsrecht, Handelsbräuche und Verkehrssitte für die Anwendung der allgemeinen deutschen Spediteurbedingungen, Hamburg, 1963, 175 pp.;
- BUCHER, A., Transnationales Recht im ipr, in Actuelle Fragen aus der Sicht in- und ausländischer Gelehrter, SCHWIND F. (ed.), Vienna, 1986, 11-59;
- BUCHER, A., Le nouvel arbitrage international en Suisse, Basle, Helbing & Lichtenhahn, 1988, 203 pp., an English edition was published by BUCHER,A. and TSCHANZ, P., International arbitration in Switzerland, Basle, Helbing & Lichtenhahn, 1988, 230 pp.;
- BUHMANN, J., Das auf den internationalen Handelsschiedsvertrag anzuwendende nationales Recht, dissertation, Regensburg, 1970, 143 pp.;
- BULCK, H., Betrachtungen über ein Völkerhandelsrecht, ZHR, 1968, 150-173;
- BÜLOW, A., Das U.N.-Übereinkommen über die Anerkennung und Volkstreckung ausländischer Schiedssprüche, KTS, 1959, 1-17;
- BÜLOW, A., Europäische Übereinkommen über die internationale Handelsschiedsgerichtsbarkeit, AWD, 1961, 144-145;
- BURIN DES ROZIERS, H., La distinction du droit civil et du droit commercial et le droit anglais, Paris, LGDJ, 1959, 194 pp.;

- CANARIS, C.W., Systemdenken und Systembegriff in der Jurisprudenz, Berlin, Duncker & Humblot, 1969, 169 pp.;
- CANARIS, C.W., Bankvertragsrecht, Volume I, fourth edition, Berlin, de Gruyter, 1988, 792 pp.;
- CAPATINA, O., Doctrine et pratique du droit socialiste roumain en matière de contrat international, in Le contrat économique international, Travaux des VIIes Journées d'études Jean Dabin, Brussels, Bruylant, 1975, 231-283;
- CARBONNEAU, T., Arbitral adjudication : a comparative assessment of its remedial and substantive status in transnational commerce, 19 TEX.INT'L L.J., 1984, 33-114;
- CARBONNEAU, T., Rendering arbitral awards with reasons : the elaboration of a common law of international transactions, 23 COL. J. TRANSNAT'L L., 1985, 579-614, published in French as Etude historique et comparé de l'arbitrage : vers un droit matériel de l'arbitrage commercial international fondé sur la motivation des sentences, Rev.Int.Dr.Comp., 1984, 727-781;
- CARBONNEAU, T., The remaking of arbitration,: design and destiny, in Lex mercatoria and arbitration, CARBONNEAU,T. (ed.), Dobbs Ferry, Transnational, 1990, 1-19;
- CARTER, A., Early history of the law merchant in England, L.Q.R., 1901, 232-251;
- CEREXHE, E., HAUBERT, B. and REGNIER, J., Principes généraux et fondements du droit, Brussels, Larcier, 1977, 547 pp.;
- CHESHIRE, G. and NORTH, P., Private international law, eleventh edition, London, Butterworths, 1987, 940 pp.;
- CHIA-JUI CHENG, Clive M. Schmitthoff's select essays on international trade law, Dordrecht, Nijhoff, 1988, 802 pp.;
- CHITTY ON CONTRACTS, I, 25th edition, London, Sweet & Maxwell, 1983, 902 pp.;
- CLAEYS BOUUAERT, P., Algemene beginselen van het recht, Vijftien jaar rechtspraak van het Hof van Cassatie, R.W., 1986-87, 913-934 and 977-998;
- COING, H., Materielles Recht und Verfahrensrecht in der internationalen Schiedsgerichtsbarkeit, Einführendes Referat, in Materielles Recht und Verfahrensrecht in der internationalen Schiedsgerichtsbarkeit, COING,H. (ed.), Frankfurt, Metzner, 1972, 9-23;
- COING, H., Materielles Recht und Verfahrensrecht in der internationalen Schiedsgerichtsbarkeit, in Law and international trade, Festschrift für Clive M. Schmitthoff, FABRICIUS, F. (ed.), Frankfurt, Athenäum Verlag, 1973, 19-32;
- COING, H., La détermination de la loi contractuelle en droit international privé allemand, in Basle symposium on the law governing contractual obligations, KLEIN, F.E. and VISCHER, F. (ed.), Basle, Helbing & Lichtenhahn, 1983, 29-53;
- COLAES, J., Derdenwerking van grondrechten in private rechtsverhoudingen waarbij groeperingen betrokken zijn, in De toepasselijkheid van de grondrechten in private verhoudingen, RIMANQUE, K. (ed.), Antwerp, Kluwer, 1982, 243-277;
- COLLINS, L., Arbitration and the law governing contractual relations : an introductory report on the position in England, in Basle Symposium on the law governing contractual obligations, KLEIN, F.E. and VISCHER, F. (ed.), Basle, Helbing & Lichtenhahn, 1983, 55-79;
- Contemporary problems in international arbitration, LEW, J.(ed.), London, School of International Arbitration, Queen Mary College, 1986, 380 p.;
- Le contrat économique international, Travaux des VIIes Journées d'études juridiques Jean Dabin, Brussels, Bruylant, 1975, 586 pp.;
- CORNIL, H., The ECE general conditions of sale, Journal of World Trade Law, 1969, 390-412;
- CRAIG, W., PARK, W., and PAULSSON, J., International Chamber of Commerce Arbitration, I.C.C.-Publication No 414, Paris/Dobbs Ferry, I.C.C. Publishing and Oceana, second edition, 1988, 704 pp.;

- CREMADES, B. and PLEHN, S., The new lex mercatoria and the harmonization of the laws of international commercial transactions, 2 B.U.INT'L L.J., 1984, 317-348;
- CROFF, C., The applicable law in an international commercial arbitration: is it still a conflict of laws problem?, INT'L LAW., 1982, 613-645;

- DABIN, J., Théorie générale du droit, third edition, Paris, Dalloz, 1969, 424 pp.;
- DAL, G.A., L'eurochèque, in La banque dans la vie quotidienne, Brussels, Editions du jeune barreau, 1986, 287-344;
- DALHUISEN, J., Wat is vreemd recht ?, Deventer, Kluwer, 1991, 30 pp.
- DANILOWICZ, V., The choice of applicable law in international arbitration, 9 HASTINGS INT'L & COMP. L. REV., 1986, 235-284;
- DASSER, F., Internationale Schiedsgerichte und lex mercatoria, Zurich, Schulthess, 1989, 408 pp.;
- DASSER, F., Lex mercatoria: Werkzeug der Praktiker oder Spielzeug der Lehre ?, Schweizerische Zeitschrift für internationaler und europäischer Recht, 1991, 299-323;
- DAVID, R., Arbitrage et droit comparé, Rev.Int.Dr.Comp., 1959, 5-18;
- DAVID, R., Les méthodes de l'unification, The methods of unification, 16 AM.J.COMP.L., 1968, 19-27; also published in DAVID, R., Le droit comparé, droits d'hier, droits de demain, Paris, Economica, 1982, 304-318;
- DAVID, R., The international unification of private law, in International Encyclopedia of Comparative Law, Tubingen, Mohr, 1971, 218 pp.;
- DAVID, R., Renaissance de l'idée de ius gentium : une proposition française, in Le droit comparé, droits d'hier, droits de demain, Paris, Economica, 1982, 319-331;
- DAVID, R., Le droit du commerce international : une nouvelle tâche pour les législateurs nationaux ou une nouvelle "lex mercatoria" ?, in New directions in international trade law, Acts and Proceedings of the 2nd Congress on Private law held by Unidroit, I, Dobbs Ferry, New York, Oceana, 1977, 5 ff.;
- DAVID, R., Unification du droit et arbitrage, in Le droit comparé, droits d'hier, droits de demain, Paris, Economica, 1982, 339-353;
- DAVID, R., L'arbitrage dans le commerce international, Paris, Economica, 1982, 613 pp., translated as DAVID, R., Arbitration in international trade, Deventer, Kluwer, 1985, 482 pp.;
- DAVID, R., Sources of law, in International Encyclopedia of comparative law, Tubingen, Mohr, 1984, 209 pp.;
- DAVID, R., Le droit du commerce international, Réflexions d'un comparatiste sur le droit international privé, Paris, Economica, 1987, 152 pp.;
- DAY, D.M., The law of international trade, London, Butterworths, 1981, 254 pp.;
- DE BOER, T.M., Subjectieve verwijzing : anomalie of grondbeginsel ?, in Partij-invloed in het internationaal privaatrecht, Deventer, Kluwer, 1974, 47-72;
- DE BOISSESON, M., Le droit français de l'arbitrage interne et international, Paris, GLN Joly Editions, Second edition, 1990, 1132 pp.;
- DE BONDT, W., De leer der gekwalificeerde benadeling, Antwerp, Kluwer, 1986, 316 pp.;
- DEBY-GERARD, F., Le rôle de la règle de conflit dans le règlement des rapports internationaux, Paris, Dalloz, 1973, 457 pp.;
- DE CALLATAY, E., Etudes sur l'interprétation des conventions, Brussels, Bruylant, 1947, 175 pp.;
- DE CASTRO Y BRAVO, F., Les usages dans le projet de loi uniforme sur la vente internationale, in Mélanges offerts à Jacques Maury, II, Paris, Dalloz, 1960, 81-96;
- DECLAREUIL, J., Rome et l'organisation du droit, Paris, Albin Michel, 1924, 452 pp.;
- DE DONCKER, C., JONGLET, J., LAMBRECHT, M., LEMAIRE, M. and LENOBLE, J., Analyse de clauses contenues dans des contrats internationaux conclus entre

entrepreneurs belges et étrangers, in Le contrat économique international, Travaux des VIIes Journées d'études Jean Dabin, Brussels, Bruylant, 1975, 361-394;
- DEELEN, J.E., Rechtskeuze in het Nederlands internationaal contractenrecht, Amsterdam, Scheltema & Holkema, 1965, 302 pp.;
- DE KEYSER, L., De eenvormige wetten inzake de internationale koop van roerende lichamelijke zaken en inzake de totstandkoming daarvan, R.W., 1971-72, 449-460;
- DE KLERK-LEENEN, A., Aanvulling van de overeenkomst door wet, gebruik of bestendig gebruikelijk beding, in Contractenrecht, BLOEMBERGEN, A. and KLEYN, W. (ed.), Deventer, Kluwer, loose-leaf;
- DELAUME, G., What is an international contract ?, An American and a Gallic dilemma, INT'L & COMP.L.Q., 1979, 258-279;
- DELAUME, G., L'arbitrage transnational et les tribunaux nationaux, Clunet, 1984, 521-547;
- DELAUME, G., The proper law of State contracts and the lex mercatoria: a reappraisal, 3 ICSID REV., 1988, 79-106;
- DELAUME, G., Law and practice of transnational contracts, Dobbs Ferry, New York, Oceana, 1988, 409 pp.;
- DELAUME, G., Comparative analysis as a basis of law in State contracts: the myth of the lex mercatoria, 63 TUL.L.REV., 1989, 575-611, reprint as The myth of the lex mercatoria and state contracts, in Lex mercatoria and arbitration, CARBONNEAU, T. (ed.), Dobbs Ferry, Transnational, 1990, 77-98;
- DELEUZE, J.M., Le contrat de transfert de processus technologique, Paris, Masson, 1976, 223 pp.;
- DELIERNEUX, M. and MARTIN, C., La "Révision 1983" des règles et usances uniformes relatives aux crédits documentaires (R.U.U.), R.D.C., 1985, 501-530;
- DEL MARMOL, C., Le droit corporatif de la vente commerciale, Rev.Dr.Int. Lég.Comp., 1936, 601-632;
- DEL MARMOL, C., Les clauses contractuelles types, facteur d'unification du droit commercial, Liber Amicorum L. Frédéricq, I, Ghent, Story, 1966, 307-321;
- DEL MARMOL, C., Réflexions sur l'utilisation des techniques contractuelles dans la vie des affaires, J.T., 1973, 69-75, Economisch en financieel recht vandaag, SCHRANS, G. and FLAMME, J. (ed.), Ghent, Gakko, 1973, 305-323;
- DEL MARMOL, C., Rédaction d'une clause d'arbitrage et choix d'arbitres compétents, D.P.C.I., 1977, 277-304;
- DEL MARMOL, C., Droit commercial terrestre, Cahier N° 1, Introduction générale, Liège, Librairie Gothier, 1981, 51 pp.;
- DEL MARMOL, C., Lex mercatoria, J.T., 1982, 164-167;
- DE LY, F., De liberalisering van de internationale arbitrage, T.P.R., 1986, 1025-1050;
- DE LY, F., Formulierenstrijd en totstandkoming van contracten, R.W., 1986-87, 1313-1334;
- DE LY, F. and BALLON, G., Elektronische bank- en koperskaarten, Juridische aspecten naar Belgisch-Frans recht, in Juridische aspecten van moderne betaalmiddelen, Preadviezen van de Vereeniging Handelsrecht, Zwolle, Tjeenk Willink, 1987, 93-229;
- DE LY, F., De lex mercatoria, Inleiding op de studie van het transnationaal handelsrecht, Antwerp, Maklu Publishers, 1989, 389 pp.;
- DE LY, F., The place of arbitration in the conflict of laws of international commercial arbitration: an exercise in arbitration planning, Nw.J.INT'L L.& BUS., 1991, 48-85;
- DE PAGE, H., Traité élémentaire de droit civil belge, Brussels, Bruylant;
- DERAINS, Y., L'application cumulative par l'arbitre des systèmes de conflit de lois intéressés au litige, Rev.Arb., 1972, 99-121;
- DERAINS, Y., Le statut des usages du commerce international devant les juridictions arbitrales, Rev.Arb., 1973, 122-149;

- DERAINS, Y., Incoterms 1980; from codification to formulation, in Interpretation and application of international trade usages, I.C.C.-publication No.374, Paris, 51-55;
- DERAINS, Y., New trends in the practical application of the ICC Rules of arbitration, 3 Nw.J.INT'L L. & BUS., 1981, 39-55;
- DERAINS, Y., France as a place for international arbitration, in The art of arbitration, Essays on international arbitration, Liber amicorum Pieter Sanders, SCHULTSZ, J. and VAN DEN BERG, A.J. (ed.), Deventer, Kluwer, 1982, 111-119;
- DERAINS, Y., Les normes d'application immédiate dans la jurisprudence arbitrale internationale, in Le droit de relations économiques internationales, Etudes offertes à Berthold Goldman, Paris, Litec, 1982, 29-46;
- DERAINS, Y., Sources et domaine d'application du droit français de l'arbitrage international, in Droit et pratique de l'arbitrage international en France, FEDUCI, s.l., 1984, 1-10;
- DERAINS, Y., La sentence arbitrale, in Droit et pratique de l'arbitrage international en France, FEDUCI, s.l., 1984, 69-80;
- DERAINS, Y., Possible conflict of law rules and the rules applicable to the substance of the dispute, in Uncitral's project for a model law on international commercial arbitration, Deventer, Kluwer, 1984, 169-195;
- DERAINS, Y., Attente légitime des parties et droit applicable au fond en matière d'arbitrage commercial international, Trav.com.fr.dr.int.privé, 1984-85, Paris, Editions du Centre national de recherche scientifique, 1987, 81-92;
- DERAINS, Y., Détermination de la lex contractus, in L'apport de la jurisprudence arbitrale, INSTITUT DU DROIT ET DES PRATIQUES DES AFFAIRES INTERNATIONALES (ed.), Paris, I.C.C.-publication No. 440/1, 1986, 7-30;
- DERAINS, Y., L'ordre public et le droit applicable au fond du litige dans l'arbitrage international, Rev.Arb., 1986, 375-413, also published as Public policy and the law applicable to the dispute in international arbitration, in Comparative arbitration practice and public policy in arbitration, SANDERS, P. (ed.), International Council for Commercial Arbitration, Deventer, Kluwer, 1987, 227-256;
- DERAINS, Y., Le choix du lieu d'arbitrage, R.D.A.I., 1986, 109-116;
- DERAINS, Y., Cour d'Arbitrage de la Chambre de Commerce Internationale, Chronique des sentences arbitrales, Clunet, 1975, 916-944;
- DERAINS, Y., Cour d'Arbitrage de la Chambre de Commerce Internationale, Chronique des sentences arbitrales, Clunet, 1976, 968-999;
- DERAINS, Y., Cour d'Arbitrage de la Chambre de Commerce Internationale, Chronique des sentences arbitrales, Clunet, 1977, 931-957;
- DERAINS, Y., Cour d'Arbitrage de la Chambre de Commerce Internationale, Chronique des sentences arbitrales, Clunet, 1978, 976-1004;
- DERAINS, Y., Cour d'Arbitrage de la Chambre de Commerce Internationale, Chronique des sentences arbitrales, Clunet, 1979, 982-1006;
- DERAINS, Y., Cour d'Arbitrage de la Chambre de Commerce Internationale, Chronique des sentences arbitrales, Clunet, 1980, 949-983;
- DERAINS, Y., Cour d'Arbitrage de la Chambre de Commerce Internationale, Chronique des sentences arbitrales, Clunet, 1981, 913-943;
- DERAINS, Y., Cour d'Arbitrage de la Chambre de Commerce Internationale, Chronique des sentences arbitrales, Clunet, 1982, 969-993;
- DERAINS, Y. and JARVIN, S., Cour d'Arbitrage de la Chambre de Commerce Internationale, Chronique des sentences arbitrales, Clunet, 1983, 889-919;
- DERAINS, Y. and JARVIN, S., Cour d'Arbitrage de la Chambre de Commerce Internationale, Chronique des sentences arbitrales, Clunet, 1984, 907-957;

- DERAINS, Y. and JARVIN, S., Cour d'Arbitrage de la Chambre de Commerce Internationale, Chronique des sentences arbitrales, Clunet, 1985, 961-990;
- DERAINS, Y. and JARVIN, S., Cour d'Arbitrage de la Chambre de Commerce Internationale, Chronique des sentences arbitrales, Clunet, 1986, 1093-1141;
- DERAINS, Y. and JARVIN, S., Cour d'Arbitrage de la Chambre de Commerce Internationale, Chronique des sentences arbitrales, Clunet, 1987, 1009-1061;
- DERAINS, Y. and AGUILAR ALVAREZ, G., Cour d'Arbitrage de la Chambre de Commerce Internationale, Chronique des sentences arbitrales, Clunet, 1988, 1195-1224;
- DERAINS, Y., Cour Internationale d'Arbitrage de la Chambre de Commerce Internationale, Chronique des sentences arbitrales, Clunet, 1990, 1017-1063;
- DERAINS, Y., HASCHER, D. and ARNALDEZ, J.J., Court Internationale d'Arbitrage de la Chambre de Commerce Internationale, Chronique des sentences arbitrales, Clunet, 1991, 1043-1073;
- DERMINE, L., L'exequatur des sentences arbitrales étrangères en Belgique, in Le contrat économique international, Travaux des VIIes Journées d'études juridiques Jean Dabin, Brussels, Bruylant, 1975, 413-431;
- DE ROOY, F., Documentary credits, Deventer, Kluwer, 1984, 266 pp.;
- DESCHENEAUX, H., Der Einleitungstitel, in Schweizerisches Privatrecht, II, Basle, Helbing & Lichtenhahn, 1967, 1-281;
- DE VRIES, H., Preadvies, in DE VRIES, H., MEIJER, R.S. and DEN DRIJVER, G.M.M., Internationale koop van roerende zaken naar materieel en internationaal privaatrecht, Preadviezen uitgebracht voor de Vereeniging "Handelsrecht", Zwolle, Tjeenk Willink, 1982, 1-100;
- DE VUYST, B., Documentaire kredieten, in A.P.R., Ghent, Story, 1981, 124 pp.;
- DICEY, A. and MORRIS, J., The conflict of laws, tenth edition, Volume 2, London, Stevens & Sons, 1980, 519-1351;
- DIENER, M., Contrats internationaux de propriété industrielle, Paris, Litec, 1986, 347 pp.;
- DIJK, P. and VAN DER PLOEG, T., Van de vereniging en de stichting, Arnhem, Gouda Quint, 1982, 393 pp.;
- DÖLLE, H., Bedeutung und Funktion der "Bräuche" im Einheitsgesetz über den internationalen Kauf beweglicher Sachen, in Ius Privatum Gentium, Festschrift für Max Rheinstein, I, Tubingen, Mohr, 1969, 447-453;
- DÖLLE, H., Kommentar zum Einheitlichen Kaufrecht, Munich, Beck, 1976, 840 pp.;
- DOMAT, J., Les loix civiles dans leur ordre naturel, le droit public, et legum delectus, I, Paris, Brunet, 1723, 522 pp.;
- DORE, I., Arbitration and conciliation under the Uncitral rules : a textual analysis, Dordrecht, Nijhoff, 1986, 246 pp.;
- DROBNIG, U., Internationale Schiedsgerichtsbarkeit und wirtschaftsrechtliche Eingriffsnormen, in Festschrift für G.Kegel, Stuttgart, Kohlhammer, 1987, 95-118;
- Le droit des normes professionnelles et techniques, COMMISSION DROIT ET VIE DES AFFAIRES, Brussels, Bruglant, 1985, 514 pp.;
- Le droit des relations économiques internationales, Etudes offertes à Berthold Goldman, Paris, Litec, 1982, 427 pp.;
- Droit et pratique de l'arbitrage international en France, FEDUCI, s.l., 1984, 107 pp.;
- D.T., The lex mercatoria in Paris and Vienna, Journal of world trade law, 1983, 358-365;
- DULCKEIT/SCHWARZ, Römische Rechtsgeschichte, fifth edition, Munich, Beck, 1970, 331 pp.;
- DUNNWEBER, I., Vertrag zur Erstellung einer schlüsselfertigen Industrieanlage im internationalen Wirtschaftsverkehr, Berlin, de Gruyter, 1984, 317 pp.;

- DUPICHOT, J., Pour un retour aux textes, défense et illustration du "petit guide-âne" des articles 1156 à 1164 du Code Civil, in Etudes offertes à Jacques Flour, Répertoire du Notariat Defrénois, Paris, 1979, 179;
- DUROUDIER, R. and KUHLEWEIN, R., De l'influence des usages commerciaux et des "conditions générales d'affaires" sur les contrats entre commerçants dans la loi allemande, Rev.Trim.Dr.Com., 1956, 35-40;
- DUTOIT, B., KNOEPFLER, F., LALIVE, P. and MERCIER, P., Répertoire de droit international privé suisse, Volume 1, Bern, Stämpfli, 1982, 407 pp.;

- EBERT, K., Rechtsvergleichung, Einführung in die Grundlagen, Bern, Stämpfli, 1978, 230 pp.;
- EBERTH, R., Documentary credits in Germany and England, J.BUS.L., 1977, 29-43;
- EBERTH, R., The uniform customs and practice for documentary credits, in Current problems of international trade financing, CHINKIN,C.M., DAVIDSON, P.J. and RICQUIER, W.J.M. (ed.), Singapore, Faculty of law, National University of Singapore, 1983, 21-37;
- EBERTH, R., Die Revision von 1983 der Einheitlichen Richtlinien und Gebräuche für Dokumenten-Akkreditive, WM, 1984, Annex No. 4, 20 pp.;
- EBERTH, R., Zur Rechtnatur der Einheitlichen Richtlinien und Gebräuche für Dokumenten-Akkreditive, in Festschrift für Karl Neumayer, Baden-Baden, Nomos, 1985, 199-216;
- EISEMANN, F., Die Incoterms in Handel und Verkehr, Vienna, G0F-Verlag Friedl, 1963, 190 pp.;
- EISEMANN, F., Incoterms and the British Export Trade, J.BUS.L., 1965, 114-122;
- EISEMANN, F., Die Incoterms im Recht des internationalen Warenhandels : Außerstaatliche Rechtsbildung oder Vertragsrecht, in XII Yearbook of the School of law and economic science, Aristotelian University of Thessaloniki, Miscellany in honor of C. Fragistas, Volume II, Thessaloniki, 1967, 325-335;
- EISEMANN, F., Die Incoterms im internationalen Warenkaufrecht, Stuttgart, Enke Verlag, 1967, 77 pp.;
- EISEMANN, F., Considérations sur les règles et usances uniformes relatives aux crédits documentaires, in Recht und Wirtschaft in Geschichte und Gegenwart, Festschrift für Johannes Bärmann, Munich, Beck, 1975, 265-284;
- EISEMANN, F., Le nouveau règlement d'arbitrage de la Chambre de Commerce Internationale, D.P.C.I., 1975, 355-365;
- EISEMANN, F. and BONTOUX, C., Le crédit documentaire dans le commerce extérieur, Paris, Jupiter, 1976, 217 pp.;
- EISEMANN, F., Le phénomène de l'arbitrage, son utilité, ses avantages et son rôle, Rev.Dr.Int.Comp., 1976, 106-115;
- EISEMANN, F., Usages de la vente commerciale internationale, Incoterms aujourd'hui et demain, second edition, Paris, Jupiter, 1980, 363 pp.;
- EISEMANN, F., The Court of arbitration : outline of its changes from inception to the present day, in International arbitration, 60 years of ICC arbitration, A look at the future, International Chamber of Commerce, publication No. 412, Paris, 1984, 391-398;
- EISEMANN, F., BONTOUX, C. and ROWE, M., Le crédit documentaire dans le commerce extérieur, Paris, Jupiter, 1985, 211 pp.;
- EISEMANN, F. and SCHÜTZE, R., Das Dokumentenakkreditiv im internationalen Handelsverkehr, Heidelberg, Verlagsgesellschaft Recht und Wirtschaft, third edition, 1989, 336 pp.;

- EKELMANS, M., Le dépeçage du contrat dans la Convention de Rome du 19 juin 1980 sur la loi applicable aux obligations contractuelles, in Mélanges offerts à Raymond Vander Elst, Volume 1, Brussels, Nemesis, 1986, 243-253;
- ELLINGER, E.P., Letters of credit, in The transnational law of international commercial transactions, HORN, N. and SCHMITTHOFF, C. (ed.), Studies in transnational economic law, Volume 2, Deventer, Kluwer, 1982, 241-273;
- ELLINGER, E.P., The Uniform Customs - their nature and the 1983 revision, Lloyd's Mar. & Com. L.Q., 1984, 578-606;
- ENDERLEIN, F., La réglementation juridique des relations économiques internationales en République démocratique allemande, Clunet, 1977, 390-417;
- ENGEL, P., Traité des obligations en droit suisse, Neuchâtel, Ides et Calendes, 1973, 667 pp.;
- EÖRSI, G., General provisions, in International sales, The United Nations convention on contracts for the international sale of goods, GALSTON, N. and SMIT, H. (ed.), New York, Matthew Bender, 1984, 2-1 - 2-36;
- ERADES, L., "General maritime law", in Recht door zee, Liber amicorum H.Schadee, Zwolle, Tjeenk Willink, 1980, 67-78;
- ERAUW, J., Beginselen van internationaal privaatrecht, Ghent, Story, 1985, 334 pp.;
- ERNEMANN, A., Zur Anerkennung und Vollstreckung ausländischer Schiedssprüche nach § 1044 ZPO, Bielefeld, Gieseking, 1979, 132 pp.;
- ESCARRA, J., De la valeur juridique de l'usage en droit commercial, Ann.Dr.Comm., 1910, 97-123;
- ESSER, J., Grundsatz und Norm, second edition, Tubingen, Mohr, 1964, 394 pp.;
- Les Euro-crédits, Un instrument du système bancaire pour le financement international, BLAISE, J.B., FOUCHARD, P. and KAHN, P. (ed.), Université de Dijon, Institut de relations internationales, Travaux du centre de recherche sur le droit des marchés et des investissements internationaux, Volume 8, Paris, Librairies Techniques, 1981, 764 pp.;
- Les Euro-crédits : expériences continentales, BELLIS, M. (ed.), FEDUCI, Paris, Moniteur, 1982, 295 pp.;

- FALLON, M., Lettres de patronage et droit international privé, in Les lettres de patronage, Travaux de la faculté de droit de Namur and Feduci, 1984, 333-369;
- FEUER, G. and CASSAN, H., Droit international du développement, Paris, Dalloz, 1985, 644 pp.;
- FICKER, H.C., "Hilfsweise geltendes Recht" für "Europäische Aktiengesellschaften" ?, in Quo vadis, ius societatum ?, Liber amicorum Pieter Sanders, ZONDERLAND, P. (ed.), Deventer, Kluwer, 1972, 37-48;
- FIRSCHING, K., Internationales Schuldrecht, I, in VON STAUDINGER, Kommentar zum BGB, Internationales Privatrecht, Berlin, Schweitzer Verlag, 1978, 727 pp.;
- FLOCKE, H.J., Risiken beim internationalen Anlagenvertrag, Heidelberg, Verlag Recht und Wirtschaft, 1986, 167 pp.;
- FLUME, W., Allgemeiner Teil des bürgerlichen Rechts, II, Das Rechtsgeschäft, second edition, Berlin, Springer, 1975, 985 pp.;
- FONTAINE, M., Introduction, in Le contrat économique international, Travaux des VIIes Journées d'études juridiques Jean Dabin, Brussels, Bruylant, 1975, 17-37;
- FONTAINE, M., Les clauses de force majeure dans les contrats internationaux, D.P.C.I., 1979, 469-506;
- FONTAINE, M., Portée et limites du principe de la convention-loi, in Les obligations contractuelles, Brussels, Jeune barreau, 1984, 165-198;

- FORIERS, P., Les relations des sources écrites et non écrites du droit, in Rapports belges au VIIIe Congrès international de droit comparé, CENTRE INTERUNIVERSITAIRE DE DROIT COMPARE (ed.), Brussels, 1970, 39-60;
- FORIERS, P.A., Les contrats commerciaux, Chronique de jurisprudence (1970-1980), R.D.C., 1983, 105-184;
- FOUCHARD, P., L'arbitrage commercial international, Paris, Dalloz, 1965, 611 pp.;
- FOUCHARD, P., L'autonomie de l'arbitrage commercial international, Rev.Arb., 1965, 99-110;
- FOUCHARD, P., Quand un arbitrage est-il international ?, Rev.Arb., 1970, 59-77;
- FOUCHARD, P., Länderbericht Frankreich, in Materielles Recht und Verfahrensrecht in der internationalen Schiedsgerichtsbarkeit, COING,H. (ed.), Frankfurt, Metzner, 1972, 35-45;
- FOUCHARD, P., L'Etat face aux usages du commerce international, Trav.com.fr.dr.int.privé, 1973-75, Paris, Dalloz, 1977, 71-91;
- FOUCHARD, P., Les travaux de la CNUDCI, Le règlement d'arbitrage, Clunet, 1979, 816-845;
- FOUCHARD, P., Introduction : spécificité de l'arbitrage international, in La réforme de l'arbitrage international en France, Rev.Arb., 1981, 449-467;
- FOUCHARD, P., Le nouveau droit français de l'arbitrage, Rev.Dr.Int.Comp., 1982, 29-49;
- FOUCHARD, P., L'arbitrage international en France après le décret du 12 mai 1981, Clunet, 1982, 374-420;
- FOUCHARD, P., Les usages, l'arbitre et le juge, A propos de quelques récents arrêts français, in Le droit des relations économiques internationales, Etudes offertes à Berthold Goldman, Paris, Litec, 1982, 67-87;
- FOUCHARD, P., La loi régissant les obligations contractuelles en droit international privé français, in Basle symposium on the law governing contractual obligations, KLEIN, F.E. and VISCHER, F. (ed.), Basle, Helbing & Lichtenhahn, 1983, 81-114;
- FRAGISTAS, C., Arbitrage étranger et arbitrage international en droit privé, R.C.D.I.P., 1960, 1-20;
- FRANCESCAKIS, P., Le principe jurisprudentiel de l'autonomie de l'accord compromissoire après l'arrêt Hecht de la Cour de Cassation, Rev.Arb., 1974, 67-87;
- FRANX, J.P., Het ontwerp Boek IV van het Wetboek van Burgerlijke Rechtsvordering, Zwolle, Tjeenk Willink, 1985, 106 pp.;
- FREDERICQ, L., Traité de droit commercial belge, Ghent, Fecheyr;
- FREDERICQ, L., La vente de droit international privé (quelques conventions récentes), Académie de droit international, 93 Recueil des cours, 1958, I, 5-116;
- FREDERICQ, S., De eenmaking van het burgerlijk recht en het handelsrecht, dissertation, Law Faculty, University Ghent, 1957, 577 pp.;
- FUSINATO, G., Le droit international de la république romaine, Les étrangers, les récupérateurs, les fétiaux, Rev.Dr.Int.Lég.Comp., 1885, 278-296;

- GAILLARD, E., Centre International pour le règlement des différends relatifs aux investissements, Chronique des sentences arbitrales, Clunet, 1988, 135-191;
- GAILLARD, E., A foreign view of the new Swiss law on international arbitration, ARB.INT'L, 1988, 25-31;
- GAILLARD, E., La distinction des principes généraux du droit et des usages du commerce international, Etudes offertes à Pierre Bellet, Paris, Litec, 1991, 203-217;
- GAMILLSCHEG, F., Rechtswahl, Schwerpunkt und mutmaßlicher Parteiwille im internationalen Vertragsrecht, AcP, 1958-59, 303-341;
- GANSHOF VAN DER MEERSCH, W., Propos sur le texte de la loi et les principes généraux du droit, J.T., 1970, 557-573 and 581-596;

- GASSIN, R., Lois spéciales et droit commun, D., 1961, 91-98;
- GAUDEMET-TALLON, H., Réflexions comparatives sur certaines tendances nouvelles en matière de compétence internationale des juges et des arbitres, in Mélanges dédiés à Gabriël Marty, Université des sciences sociales de Toulouse, 1978, 531-568;
- GENTINETTA, J., Die lex fori internationaler Handelsschiedsgerichte, Bern, Stämpfli, 1973, 511 pp.;
- GENY, F., Méthode d'interprétation et sources en droit privé positif, I, second edition, Paris, LGDJ, 1932, 446 pp.;
- GERARD, P., Le champ de la justice privée : aspects de la pratique de l'arbitrage en droit belge, in Fonction de juger et pouvoir judiciaire, transformations et déplacements, GERARD, P., VAN DE KERCKHOVE, A. and OST, F. (ed.), Publications des Facultés Universitaires Saint-Louis No.30, Brussels, 1983, 419-446;
- GHESTIN, J. and GOUBEAUX, G., Introduction générale, second edition, in Traité de droit civil, I, Paris, LGDJ, 1983, 757 pp.;
- GIARDINA, A., Arbitrato transnazionale e lex mercatoria di fronte alla Corte di Cassazione, Riv.Dir.Int.Priv.Proc., 1982, 754-765;
- GOLDMAN, B., Arbitrage international et droit commun des nations, Rev.Arb., 1956, 115-116;
- GOLDMAN, B., Les conflits de lois dans l'arbitrage international de droit privé, Académie de droit international, 109 Recueil des cours, 1963, II, 347-483;
- GOLDMAN, B., Le droit des sociétés internationales, Clunet, 1963, 320-389;
- GOLDMAN, B., Frontières du droit et "lex mercatoria", Arch.Phil.Dr., 1964, 177-192;
- GOLDMAN, B., Règles de conflit, règles d'application immédiate et règles matérielles dans l'arbitrage commercial international, Trav.com.fr.dr.int.privé, 1966-69, Paris, Dalloz, 1970, 119-136;
- GOLDMAN, B., V° Arbitrage (droit international privé), in Répertoire de droit international, FRANCESCAKIS, P. (ed.), Volume I, Paris, Dalloz, 1968, 111-138;
- GOLDMAN, B., Un "conflictualiste" d'esprit international : M.Henri Batiffol, Clunet, 1968, 327-331;
- GOLDMAN, B., Le contrat international, in Renaissance du phénomène contractuel, COMMISSION DROIT ET VIE DES AFFAIRES (ed.), Faculté de Droit de Liège, The Hague, Martinus Nijhoff, 1971, 443-485;
- GOLDMAN, B., Les travaux de la Commission des Nations Unies pour le Droit Commercial International, Clunet, 1979, 747-754;
- GOLDMAN, B., Les problèmes spécifiques de l'arbitrage international, in Le juge et l'arbitre, XIe Colloque des instituts d'études judiciaires, Rev.Arb., 1980, 323-339;
- GOLDMAN, B., La lex mercatoria dans les contrats et l'arbitrage internationaux : réalité et perspectives, Clunet, 1979, 475-505; also published in Trav.com.fr.dr.int.privé, 1977-1979, Paris, Dalloz, 221-259, and under the title "La lex mercatoria et l'arbitrage international" in L'influence des Communautés européennes sur le droit international privé des Etats-membres, Brussels, Larcier, 1981, 209-240;
- GOLDMAN, B., La volonté des parties et le rôle de l'arbitre dans l'arbitrage international, in La réforme de l'arbitrage international en France, Rev.Arb., 1981, 469-486;
- GOLDMAN, B., La nouvellle réglementation française de l'arbitrage international, in The art of arbitration, Essays on international arbitration, Liber amicorum Pieter Sanders, SCHULTSZ, J. and VAN DEN BERG, A.J. (ed.), Deventer, Kluwer, 1982, 153-174;
- GOLDMAN, B., Une bataille judiciaire autour de la lex mercatoria, Rev.Arb., 1983, 379-409;
- GOLDMAN, B., Rapport général, in Le rôle de la pratique dans la formation du droit, Travaux de l'Association Henri Capitant XXXIV, 1983, Paris, Economica, 1985, 163-180;

- GOLDMAN, B., Lex mercatoria, Forum internationale No. 3, November 1983, Deventer, Kluwer, s.d., 24 pp.;
- GOLDMAN, B., The complementary roles of judges and arbitrators in ensuring that international commercial arbitration is effective, in International arbitration, 60 years of ICC arbitration, A look at the future, International Chamber of Commerce, publication No. 412, Paris, 1984, 257-285;
- GOLDMAN, B., The applicable law : general principles of law - lex mercatoria, in Contemporary problems in international arbitration, LEW,J. (ed.), London, School of international arbitration, Queen Mary College, 1986, 113-125;
- GOLDSMITH, L., Universalgeschichte des Handelsrecht, I, Aalen, Scientia, 1957, 468 pp.;
- GOLDSTAJN, A., The new law merchant, J.BUS.L., 1961, 12-17;
- GOLDSTAJN, A., International conventions and standard contracts as means of escaping from the application of municipal law - I, in The sources of the law of international trade, SCHMITTHOFF, C. (ed.), International Association of Legal Science, London, Stevens & Sons, 1964, 103-117;
- GOLDSTAJN, A., Reflections on the structure of the modern law of international trade, International contracts and conflict of laws, SARVEVIC, P. (ed.), London, Graham & Trotman, 1990, 14-35;
- GOODE, R., The adaptation of English law to international commercial arbitration, ARB., 1992, 21-28;
- GORLE, F., BOURGEOIS, G. and BOCKEN, H., Rechtsvergelijking, Ghent, Story, 1985, 415 pp.;
- GOTTWALD, P., Die sachliche Kontrolle internationaler Schiedssprüche durch staatliche Gerichte, in Beiträge zum internationalen Verfahrensrecht und zur Schiedsgerichtbarkeit, Festschrift für H.Nagel, Munster, Aschendorff, 1987, 54-69;
- GRAIGIE, C., The collection of bills in international trade, in Current problems of international trade financing, CHINKIN, C., DAVIDSON, P. and RICQUIER, N. (ed.), Singapore, Faculty of law, National University of Singapore, 1983, 100-133;
- GRIGERA NAON, H., Transnational enterprise under the Pacto Andino and national laws of Latin America, in Legal problems of codes of conduct for multinational enterprises, HORN, N. (ed.), Studies in transnational economic law, Volume 1, Deventer, Kluwer, 1980, 237-273;
- GUHL/MERZ/KUMMER, Das schweizerische Obligationenrecht, sixth edition, Zurich, Schulthess, 1972, 948 pp.;
- GÜTERBOCK, K., Zur Geschichte des Handelsrecht in England, ZHR, 1861, 13-29;

- HAAK, K., De aansprakelijkheid van de vervoerder ingevolge de CMR, The Hague, Stichting Vervoeradres, 1984, 474 pp.;
- HAAK, W.E., Preadvies, in Internationaal overeenkomstenrecht, Mededelingen van de Nederlandse Vereniging voor Internationaal Recht, Deventer, Kluwer, 1975, 1-70;
- HABSCHEID, W., Das neue schweizerische Recht der internationalen Schiedsgerichtsbarkeit nach dem Bundesgesetz über das Internationale Privatrecht, RIW, 1988, 766-772;
- HANNEQUART, Y., La portée du contrat, in Les Novelles, Droit civil, Volume IV, II, Brussels, Larcier, 1958;
- HARTKAMP, A., Het Weense Koopverdrag, Deventer, Kluwer, 1980, 73 pp.;
- HAYES, L., A modern lex mercatoria : political rhetoric or substantive progress ?, 3 BROOKLYN J.INT'L L., 1977, 210-232;
- HELLEMA, A., Beschouwingen over de aanknopingsleer in het internationaal privaatrecht, Deventer, Kluwer, 1969, 200 pp.;
- HERBER, R., Anwendungsbereich des Gesetzes, in Kommentar zum einheitlichen Kaufrecht, DÖLLE, H. (ed.), Munich, Beck, 1976, 1-37;

- HEUZE, V., La réglementation française des contrats internationaux, Etude critique des méthodes, Paris, GLN Editions, 1990, 392 pp.;
- HIGHET, K., The enigma of the lex mercatoria, 63 TUL.L.REV., 1989, 613-628, reprint in Lex mercatoria and arbitration, CARBONNEAU,T. (ed.), Dobbs Ferry, Transnational, 1990, 99-108;
- HILAIRE, J., Introduction historique au droit commercial, Paris, P.U.F., 1986, 355 pp.;
- HINSCH, C. and HORN, N., Das Vertragsrecht der internationalen Konsortialkredite und Projektfinanzierungen, Berlin, de Gruyter, 1985, 337 pp.;
- HOLDSWORTH, W., A history of English law, London, Methuen;
- HONDIUS, E., Standaardvoorwaarden, Deventer, Kluwer, 1978, 956 pp.;
- HONDIUS, E., Naar een wettelijke regeling van algemene voorwaarden, Handelingen 1979 der Nederlandse Juristen-Vereniging, Volume 1, first part, Zwolle, Tjeenk Willink, 91-290;
- HONNOLD, J., The influence of the law of international trade on the development and character of English and American commercial law, in The sources of the law of international trade, SCHMITTHOFF, C. (ed.), International Association of Legal Science, London, Stevens & Sons, 1964, 70-87;
- HONNOLD, J., Uniform Law for International Sales under the 1980 United Nations Convention, Deventer, Kluwer, 1982, 586 pp.;
- HORN, N., Das Recht der internationalen Anleihen, Frankfurt, Athenäum Verlag, 1972, 572 pp.;
- HORN, N., Internationale Zahlungen und Akkreditive, in Dokumentenakkreditive und Bankgarantien im internationalen Zahlungsverkehr, Frhr. MARSCHALL VON BIEBERSTEIN, W. (ed.), Frankfurt, Metzner, 1977, 9-25;
- HORN, N., Codes of conduct for MNEs and transnational lex mercatoria : an international process of learning and law making, in Legal problems of codes of conduct for multinational enterprises, HORN, N. (ed.), Studies in transnational economic law, Volume 1, Deventer, Kluwer, 1980, 45-81;
- HORN, N., Die Entwicklung des internationalen Wirtschaftsrecht durch Verhaltensrichtlinien, RabelsZ, 1980, 423-454;
- HORN, N., Uniformity and diversity in the law of international commercial contracts, in HORN, N. and SCHMITTHOFF, C., The transnational law of international commercial transactions, Studies in transnational economic law, Volume 2, Deventer, Kluwer, 1982, 3-31;
- HORN, N., Normative problems of a new international economic order, Journal of world trade law, 1983, 338-351;
- HORN, N., Die Anpassung langfristiger Verträge im internationalen Wirtschaftsverkehr : Vertragsklauseln und Schiedspraxis, in Die Anpassung langfristiger Verträge, KÖTZ, H. and Frhr. MARSCHALL VON BIEBERSTEIN, W. (ed.), Frankfurt, Metzner, 1984, 9-71;
- HORN, N., Das chinesische Außenwirtschaftsverkehrgesetz von 1985, RIW, 1985, 688-693;
- HORSMANS, G. and VERWILGHEN, M., Stabilité et évolution du contrat économique international, in Le contrat économique international, Travaux des VIIes Journées d'études Jean Dabin, Brussels, Bruylant, 1975, 449-473;
- HOUIN, R., Usages commerciaux et loi en droit français, RabelsZ 1959, 252-258;
- HOYLE, M., The law of international trade, second edition, London, CCH, 1985, 518 pp.;
- HUBERT, A., Le contrat d'ingénierie-conseil, Paris, Masson, 1980, 227 pp.;
- HÜBNER, H., Allgemeiner Teil des Bürgerlichen Gesetzbuches, Berlin, de Gruyter, 1985, 559 pp.;
- HUNTER, M., Lex Mercatoria - Deutsche Schachtbau- und Tiefbohrgesellschaft mbh v. R'As Al Khaimah National Oil Co., Lloyd's Mar. & Com.L.Q., 1987, 277-280 and ARB., 1988, 55-67;

- HUVELIN, P., Essai historique sur le droit des marchés et des foires, Paris, Rousseau, 1897, 620 pp.;
- HUVELIN, P., L'histoire du droit commercial, Paris, Librairie Cerf, 1904, 115 pp.;
- HUVELIN, P., Etudes d'histoire du droit commercial romain, Paris, Sirey, 1929, 298 pp.;
- HUYS, M. and KEUTGEN, G., L'arbitrage en droit belge et international, Brussels, Bruylant, 1981, 812 pp.;

- ISHIZAKI, M., Le droit corporatif international de la vente de soies, Bibliothèque de l'institut de droit comparé de Lyon, Volume 18, 19 and 20, Paris, Giard, 1928, 344, 363 and 264 pp.;
- ISHIZAKI, M., De la récente évolution du droit corporatif dans le commerce des soies, in Introduction à l'étude du droit comparé, Recueil d'études en l'honneur d'Edouard Lambert, I, Paris, LGDJ, 1938, 494-510;

- JACQUEMONT, A., L'émission des emprunts euro-obligataires, Pouvoir bancaire et souverainetés étatiques, Université de Dijon, Institut de relations internationales, Travaux du centre de recherche sur le droit des marchés et des investissements internationaux, Volume 3, Paris, Librairies Techniques, 1976, 509 pp.;
- JACQUEMONT, A., Le contrat d'euro-crédit : un contrat à contenu variable, Clunet, 1979, 34-78;
- JACQUET, J.M., Principe d'autonomie et contrats internationaux, Paris, Economica, 1983, 342 pp.;
- JADAUD, B. and PLAISANT, R., Droit du commerce international, Paris, Dalloz, 1987, 203 pp.;
- JAFFEY, A.J.E., Arbitration of international commercial contracts : the law to be applied by the arbitrators, in Current issues in international business law, PERROTT, D.L. and POGARNY, I. (ed.), Ausbury, Hants, 1988, 129-151;
- JÄGGI, P. and GAUCH, P., Zürcher Kommentar zum Schweizerischen Zivilgesetzbuch, Volume V 1 b, Zurich, Schulthess, 1980, 208 pp.;
- JAKUBOWSKI, J., The autonomy of international trade law and its influence on the interpretation and application of its rules, in Law and international trade, Festschrift für Clive M. Schmitthoff, FABRICIUS,F. (ed.), Frankfurt, Athenäum Verlag, 1973, 209-214;
- JANSSEN, H., Totstandkoming van internationale handelskoop, Groningen, Wolters, 1970, 216 pp.;
- JARVIN, S. and DERAINS, Y., Collection of ICC arbitral awards 1974-85, ICC Publications N°. 433, Deventer/Paris, Kluwer Law & Taxation/ICC Publishing, 1990, 581 pp.;
- JEHL, J., Le commerce international de la technologie, Approche juridique, Université de Dijon, Travaux du Centre de recherche sur le droit des marchés et des investissements internationaux, Volume 10, Paris, Librairies Techniques, 1985, 502 pp.;
- JOERGES, C., Vorüberlegungen zu einer Theorie des internationalen Wirtschaftsrecht, RabelsZ, 1979, 6-79;
- JOKELA, H., The role of usages in the uniform law on international sales, 10 Scand.Stud.L., 1966, 81-96;
- JOLIDON, P., Commentaire du Concordat suisse sur l'arbitrage, Bern, Stämpfli, 1984, 563 pp.;
- JOLOWICZ, H. and NICHOLAS, B., Historical introduction to the study of Roman law, third edition, Cambridge, University Press, 1972, 528 pp.;
- JÖRS, P., Römisches Privatrecht, third edition by KUNKEL, W., Berlin, Springer, 1949, 434 pp.;

- JUENGER, F., The lex mercatoria and the conflict of laws, in Lex mercatoria and arbitration, CARBONNEAU, T. (ed.), Dobbs Ferry, Transnational, 1990, 213-224;
- JUENGER, F., Lex mercatoria und Eingriffsnormen, Beiträge zum Handels- und Wirtschaftsrecht, Festschrift für Fritz Rittner, Munich, Beck, 1991, 233-249;

- KAHN, P., La vente commerciale internationale, Paris, Sirey, 1961, 465 pp.;
- KAHN, P., La convention de La Haye du 1er juillet 1964 portant loi uniforme sur la vente internationale des objets mobiliers corporels, Rev.Trim.Dr.Com., 1964, 689-727;
- KAHN, P., La convention de La Haye sur la loi applicable aux ventes à caractère international d'objets mobiliers corporels, Clunet, 1966, 301-355;
- KAHN, P., International companies, A study of companies having international legal studies, Journal of world trade law, 1969, 498-521;
- KAHN, P., Lex mercatoria et euro-obligations, in Law and international trade, Festschrift für Clive M.Schmitthoff, FABRICIUS,F. (ed.), Frankfurt, Athenäum Verlag, 1973, 215-241;
- KAHN, P., Etude de quelques problèmes juridiques de la vente international de gaz, in Les hydrocarbures gazeux et le développement des pays producteurs, Université de Dijon, Institut de relations internationales, Travaux du centre de recherche sur le droit des marchés et des investissements internationaux, Volume 2, Paris, Librairies Techniques, 1974, 235-286;
- KAHN, P., Lex mercatoria et pratique des contrats internationaux : l'expérience française, in Le contrat économique international, Travaux des VIIes Journées d'études juridiques Jean Dabin, Brussels, Bruylant, 1975, 171-211;
- KAHN, P., Force majeure et contrats internationaux de longue durée, Clunet, 1975, 467-485;
- KAHN, P., L'essor du non-droit dans les relations commerciales internationales et le contrat sans loi, in L'hypothèse du non-droit, COMMISSION DROIT ET VIE DES AFFAIRES (ed.), Liège, 1978, 231-266;
- KAHN, P., La Convention de Vienne du 11 avril 1980 sur les contrats de vente international de marchandises, Rev.Int.Dr.Comp., 1981, 951-986;
- KAHN, P., Droit international économique, droit du développement, lex mercatoria : concept unique ou pluralisme des ordres juridiques ?, in Le droit des relations économiques internationales, Etudes offertes à Berthold Goldman, Paris, Litec, 1982, 97-107;
- KAHN, P., Aspects récents du droit de la vente commerciale internationale, Trav.com.fr.dr.int.privé, 1980-81, Volume 2, Paris, Editions du Centre National de la Recherche Scientifique, 1983, 69-82;
- KAHN, P., Rapport français, in Le rôle de la pratique dans la formation du droit, Travaux de l'Association Henri Capitant, XXXIV, 1983, Paris, Economica, 1985, 237-261;
- KAHN, P., Les principes généraux du droit devant les arbitres du commerce international, Clunet, 1989, 305-327;
- KAPPUS, A., "Conflict avoidance" durch "lex mercatoria" und UN-Kaufrecht 1980, RIW, 1990, 788-794;
- KAPPUS, A., Lex mercatoria in Europa und Wiener UN-Kaufrechtskonvention 1980, Frankfurt, Lang, 1990, 232 pp.;
- KASER, M., Das römische Privatrecht, I, Munich, Beck, 1955, 651 pp.;
- KASSIS, A., Théorie générale des usages du commerce, Paris, LGDJ, 1984, 602 pp.;
- KEGEL, G., The crisis of conflict of laws, Académie de droit international, Recueil des cours, 1964, II, 95-268;
- KEGEL, G., Die Ermittlung ausländischen Rechts, in Die Anwendung ausländischen Rechts im internationalen Privatrecht, Berlin, de Gruyter, 1968, 159;
- KEGEL, G., Internationales Privatrecht, fifth edition, Munich, Beck, 1985, 735 pp.;

- KEGEL, G., Zum heutigen Stand des internationalen Privatrechts : Theorie und Rechtspolitik, in Internationales Privatrecht, internationales Wirtschaftsrecht, HOLL, W. and KLINKE, U. (ed.), Cologne, Heymanns, 1985, 1-24;
- KELLER, M. and SIEHR, K., Allgemeine Lehren des internationalen Privatrechts, Zurich, Schulthess, 1986, 714 pp.;
- KERR, M., International arbitration v.litigation, J.BUS.L., 1980, 164-180;
- KEUTGEN, G. and HUYS, M., Chronique de jurisprudence, L'arbitrage (1950 à 1975), J.T., 1976, 53-64;
- KEUTGEN, G. and HUYS, M., Chronique de jurisprudence, L'arbitrage (1975 à 1982), J.T., 1984, 53-59;
- KIPP, T., Das Römische Recht, II, Berlin, Georg Stilke, s.d., 314 pp.;
- KIRBERGER, W., Die Nebenordnungen im Vereins- und Verbandsrecht, dissertation, Marburg, 1981, 260 pp.;
- KISCH, I., Rechtsvergelijking en handelsrecht, in Uitgelezen opstellen, Een bloemlezing uit het werk van Prof.mr.I.Kisch, Zwolle, Tjeenk Willink, 1981, 119-135;
- KLEIN, F.E., Considérations sur l'arbitrage en droit international privé, Basle, Helbing & Lichtenhahn, 1955, 320 pp.;
- KLEIN, F.E., Autonomie de la volonté et arbitrage, R.C.D.I.P., 1958, 255-284 and 479-494;
- KLEIN, F.E., La convention de New York pour la reconnaissance et l'exécution des sentences arbitrales étrangères, Schweizerische Juristenzeitung, 1961, 229-235 and 247-252;
- KLEIN, F.E., La Convention européenne sur l'arbitrage commercial international, R.C.D.I.P., 1962, 621-640;
- KLEIN, F.E., L'arbitrage international de droit privé, Réalités et perspectives, Ann.suisse Dr.Int., 1963, 41-62;
- KLEIN, F.E., Internationale Schiedsverfahren und nationale Rechtsordnungen, Ann.suisse Dr.Int., 1967, 87-118;
- KLEIN, F.E., A propos de la jurisprudence du tribunal fédéral suisse en matière d'arbitrage commercial international, in Stabilité et dynamisme du droit dans la jurisprudence du tribunal fédéral suisse, Recueil offert au tribunal fédéral à l'occasion de son centenaire par les facultés de droit suisses, Basle, Helbing & Lichtenhahn, 1975, 487-506;
- KLEIN, F.E., De l'autorité de la loi dans les rapports commerciaux internationaux, in Internationales Recht und Wirtschaftsordnung, Festschrift für F.A. Mann, Munich, Beck, 1977, 617-638;
- KLEIN, F.E., Die internationale Schiedsgerichtsbarkeit und die schweizerische Rechtsordnung, in Die internationale Schiedsgerichtsbarkeit in der Schweiz, BÖCKSTIEGEL, K.H. (ed.), Cologne, Heymanns, 1979, 33-51;
- KLEIN, F.E., The law to be applied by the arbitrators to the substance of the dispute, in The art of arbitration, Essays on international arbitration, Liber amicorum Pieter Sanders, SCHULTSZ, J. and VAN DEN BERG, A.J. (ed.), Deventer, Kluwer, 1982, 189-206;
- KOKKINI-IATRIDOU, D., Het Nederlands arbitragewetsontwerp, Ars Aequi, 1985, 488-491;
- KOKKINI-IATRIDOU, D., Twee recente arbitrageregelingen: Portugal en Spanje, Eenvormig en vergelijkend privaatrecht 1990, Molengrafica, Lelystad, Vermande, 1990, 357-424;
- KOLLEWIJN, R.D., De conventies voor eenvormig internationaal kooprecht en het internationaal privaatrecht, N.J.B., 1965, 149-159, N.I.L.R., 1964, 271;
- KOPELMANAS, L., La codification des coutumes du commerce international dans le cadre des commissions régionales des Nations Unies, Ann.fr.dr.int., 1955, 370-375;
- KOPELMANAS, L., Quelques problèmes récents de l'arbitrage commercial international, Rev.Trim.Dr.Com., 1957, 879-911;

- KOPELMANAS, L., La place de la Convention européenne sur l'arbitrage commercial international du 21 avril 1961 dans l'évolution du droit international de l'arbitrage, Ann.fr.dr.int., 1961, 331;
- KORNBLUM, U., "Ordre public transnational", "ordre public international" und "ordre public interne" im Recht der privaten Schiedsgerichtsbarkeit, in Beiträge zum internationalen Verfahrensrecht and zur Schiedsgerichtsbarkeit, Festschrift für H.Nagel, Munster, Aschendorff, 1987, 140-156;
- KORNMEIER, U. and SANDROCK, O., Internationale Schiedsgerichtsvereinbarungen, in SANDROCK, O. (ed.), Handbuch des internationalen Vertragsgestaltung, Volume 2, Heidelberg, Verlagsgesellschaft Recht und Wirtschaft, 1980, 885-990;
- KOZIOL, H. and WELSER, R., Grundriß des bürgerlichen Rechts, I, Allgemeiner Teil und Schuldrecht, seventh edition, Vienna, Manzsche, 1985, 478 pp.;
- KREUZER, K., Einheitsrecht als Ersatzrecht, Zur Frage der Nichtermittelbarkeit fremden Rechts, NJW, 1983, 1943-1948;
- KRINGS, E. and MATRAY, L., Le juge et l'arbitre, Rev.Dr.Int.Comp., 1982, 227-260;
- KRONSTEIN, H., The law of international cartels, Ithaca, Cornell University Press, 1973, 489 pp.;
- KROPHOLLER, J., Der "Ausschluss" des internationalen Privatrechts im einheitlichen Kaufgesetz, RabelsZ, 1974, 372-387;
- KROPHOLLER, J., Internationales Einheitsrecht, Allgemeine Lehren, Tubingen, Mohr, 1975, 386 pp.;
- KROPHOLLER, J., Die Wissenschaft als Quelle des internationalen Rechtsvereinheitlichung, Zvglrwiss, 1986, 143-163;
- KROPHOLLER, J., Neues europäisches Zivilprozeßrecht, RIW, 1986, 929-935;
- KRUITHOF, R., Overzicht van rechtspraak (1974-1980), Verbintenissen, T.P.R., 1983, 495-717;
- KRUITHOF, R., Contractuele aansprakelijkheidsregelingen, in Verbintenissenrecht, STORME, M. and BOCKEN, H. (ed.), Ghent, 1984, 233-298 and T.P.R., 1984, 233-298;
- KUNKEL, W., Römische Rechtsgeschichte, sixth edition, Cologne, Böhlau Verlag, 1972, 209 pp.;
- KURKELA, M., Letters of credit under international trade law : UCC, UCP and law merchant, Dobbs Ferry, New York, Oceana, 1985, 517 pp.;

- LABORDERIE, P., Essai sur l'histoire du droit international privé, L'application des droits pérégrins dans le monde romain, Revue générale du droit, de la législation et de la jurisprudence en France et à l'étranger, 1910, 41-48;
- LAGARDE, P., Approche critique de la lex mercatoria, in Le droit des relations économiques internationales, Etudes offertes à Berthold Goldman, Paris, Litec, 1982, 125-150;
- LALIVE, P., Problèmes relatifs à l'arbitrage international commercial, Académie de droit international, 120 Recueil des cours, 1967, I, 569-714;
- LALIVE, P., Les règles de conflit de lois appliquées au fond du litige par l'arbitre international siégeant en Suisse, in L'arbitrage international privé et la Suisse, Geneva, Librairie de l'Université Georg, 1977, 57-113 and Rev.Arb., 1976, 155-185;
- LALIVE, P., Problèmes spécifiques de l'arbitrage international, in Le juge et l'arbitre, XIe Colloque des Instituts d'études judiciaires, Rev.Arb., 1980, 341-372;
- LALIVE, P., Sur une notion de "contrat international", in Multum non multa, Festschrift für Kurt Lipstein, Heidelberg, Müller Verlag, 1980, 135-155;
- LALIVE, P., Codification et arbitrage international, in Le droit des relations économiques internationales, Etudes offertes à Berthold Goldman, Paris, Litec, 1982, 151-166;

- LALIVE, P., Sur la bonne foi dans l'exécution des contrats d'état, in Mélanges offerts à Raymond Vander Elst, Volume 1, Brussels, Nemesis, 1986, 425-451;
- LALIVE, P., Ordre public transnational (ou réellement international) et arbitrage international, Rev.Arb., 1986, 329-373; also published as Transnational (or truly international) public policy and international arbitration, in Comparative arbitration practice and public policy in arbitration, SANDERS, P. (ed.), Deventer, Kluwer, 1987, 257-318;
- LALIVE, P., Arbitrage en Suisse et "Lex Mercatoria", ASA Bull., 1987, 165-173;
- LALIVE, P., POUDRET, J.F. and REYMOND, C., Le droit de l'arbitrage interne et international en Suisse, Lausanne, Payot, 1989, 508 pp.;
- LAMBERT, E., La fonction du droit civil comparé, Paris, Giard & Brière, 1903, 927 pp.;
- LAMBERT, E., L'enseignement du droit comme science sociale et comme science internationale, Introduction, in VALEUR, R., L'enseignement du droit en France et aux Etats-Unis, Bibliothèque de l'Institut de droit comparé de Lyon, Volume 23, Paris, Marcel Giard, 1928, 122 pp.;
- LAMBERT, E., Un parère de jurisprudence comparative, Bibliothèque de l'Institut de droit comparé de Lyon, Volume 33, Paris, Marcel Giard, 1934, 221 pp.;
- LAMBERT, E., Sources du droit comparé ou supranational, Législation uniforme et jurisprudence comparative, in Recueil d'études sur les sources du droit en l'honneur de François Gény, III, Paris, Sirey, 1934, 478-510;
- LANDO, O., Conflict-of-law rules for arbitrators, in Festschrift für Konrad Zweigert, Tubingen, Mohr, 1981, 157-178;
- LANDO, O., The lex mercatoria in international commercial arbitration, INT'L & COMP.L.Q., 1985, 747-768;
- LANDO, O., The law applicable to the merits of the dispute, in Essays on international commercial arbitration, SARCEVIC, P. (ed.), London, Graham & Trotman, 1989, 129-159;
- LANGEN, E., Studien zum internationalen Wirtschaftsrecht, Munich, Beck, 1963, 132 pp.;
- LANGEN, E., Vom internationalen Privatrecht zum transnationalen Handelsrecht, NJW, 1969, 358-360;
- LANGEN, E., Transnationales Handelsrecht, NJW, 1969, 2229-2233;
- LANGEN, E., Transnational commercial law, Leyden, Sijthoff, 1973, 280 pp.;
- LANGEN, E., Transnationales Recht, Heidelberg, Verlagsgesellschaft Recht und Wirtschaft, 1981, 241 pp.;
- LARENZ, K., Methodenlehre der Rechtswissenschaft, fourth edition, Berlin, Springer, 1979, 525 pp.;
- LEBOULANGER, P., Les contrats entre Etats et entreprises étrangères, Paris, Economica, 1985, 354 pp.;
- LEBRUN, A., La coutume, Paris, LGDJ, 1932, 556 pp.;
- LEE, R., The elements of Roman law, London, Sweet & Maxwell, 1952, 489 pp.;
- LEMAIRE, W., Nederlands internationaal privaatrecht (Hoofdlijnen), Leyden, Sijthoff, 1968, 453 pp.;
- LEMHÖFER, B., Die Beschränkung der Rechtsvereinheitlichung auf internationale Sachverhalte, RabelsZ, 1960, 401-455;
- LEQUETTE, Y., L'évolution des sources nationales et conventionnelles du droit des contrats internationaux, in L'évolution contemporaire du droit des contrats, Journées René Savatier, Paris, P.U.F., 1986, 185-204;
- LEREBOURS-PIGEONNIERE, P., A propos du contrat international, Clunet, 1951, 4-28;
- LE TOURNEAU, P., Quelques aspects de l'évolution des contrats, in Mélanges offerts à Pierre Raynaud, Paris, Dalloz, 1985, 349-370;
- LEVEL, P., Le contrat dit sans loi, Trav.com.fr.dr.int.privé, 1964-66, Paris, Dalloz, 1967, 209-231;

- LEVEL, P., La procédure arbitrale, in Droit et pratique de l'arbitrage international en France, FEDUCI, s.l., 1984, 51-67;
- LEW, J., La loi applicable aux contrats internationaux dans la jurisprudence des tribunaux arbitraux, in Le contrat économique international, Travaux des VIIes Journées d'études juridiques Jean Dabin, Brussels, Bruylant, 1975, 151-167;
- LEW, J., Applicable law in international commercial arbitration, Dobbs Ferry, New York, Oceana, 1978, 633 pp.;
- LEW, J., The setting aside and enforcement of arbitration awards in the common law, Instituut voor nationale en internationale arbitrage, Ghent, mimeograph, 1987, 15 pp.;
- Lex mercatoria and arbitration, A discussion of the New Law Merchant, CARBONNEAU, T.E. (ed.), Dobbs Ferry, Transnational, 1990, 227 pp.;
- LEYMARIE, F., Les usages commerciaux, dissertation, Bordeaux, 1970, 406 pp.;
- LIBOUTON, J., Chronique de jurisprudence, Les transports routiers internationaux, J.T., 1972, 381-386 and 397-406;
- LIBOUTON, J., Chronique de jurisprudence, Les transports routiers internationaux, J.T., 1982, 693-704 and 713-725;
- LIMPENS, J., De l'unification du droit civil et du droit commercial, J.T., 1953, 353-359;
- LIMPENS, J., Unificatie van het nationaal en het internationaal privaatrecht, R.W., 1957-58, 1729-1746;
- LIMPENS, J., Les facteurs propices à l'éclosion et au développement d'un droit commun européen, in New perspectives for a common law of Europe, CAPPELLETTI, M. (ed.), European University Institute, Leyden, Sijthoff, 1978, 75-94;
- LINDEMANS, J., Verenigingen zonder winstoogmerk, in A.P.R., Ghent, 1958, 252 pp.;
- LINDEMANS, J., De verenigingen zonder winstoogmerk, Brussels, Licap, 1982, 111 pp.;
- LINSMEAU, J. and VAN GELDER, J., La nouvelle loi sur l'arbitrage volontaire, J.T., 1973, 205-219;
- LOEWE, R., Note explicative sur la convention au contrat de transport international de marchandises par route (CMR) du 19 mai 1956, E.T.L., 1976, 407-501;
- LÖNING, G., Autonomes Recht der Wirtschaft, Mitteilungen des Jenaer Instituts für Wissenschaftsrecht, Volume 20, 1930, 13-20;
- LOQUIN, E., L'amiable composition en droit comparé et international, Contribution à l'étude du non-droit dans l'arbitrage commercial, Université de Dijon, Institut de relations internationales, Travaux du centre de recherche sur le droit des marchés et des investissements internationaux, Volume 7, Paris, Librairies Techniques, 1980, 381 pp.;
- LOQUIN, E., Les pouvoirs des arbitres internationaux à la lumière de l'évolution récente du droit de l'arbitrage international, Clunet, 1983, 293-345;
- LOQUIN, E., L'application de règles anationales dans l'arbitrage commercial international, in L'apport de la jurisprudence arbitrale, INSTITUT DU DROIT ET DES PRATIQUES DES AFFAIRES INTERNATIONALES (ed.), Paris, I.C.C.-publication No. 440/1, 1986, 67-122;
- LOQUIN, E., La réalité des usages du commerce international, R.I.D.E., 1989, 163-195;
- LORENZ, E., Die Rechtswahlfreiheit im internationalen Schuldvertragsrecht, RIW, 1987, 569-584;
- LORENZ, W., Die Lex Mercatoria : eine internationale Rechtsquelle ?, in Festschrift für Karl N.Neumayer, Baden-Baden, Nomos, 1985, 407-429;
- LORENZ, W., Vom alten zum neuen internationalen Schuldvertragsrecht, IPRax, 1987, 269-276;
- LOUSSOUARN, Y. and BREDIN, J.D., Droit du commerce international, Paris, Sirey, 1969, 1033 pp.;
- LOUSSOUARN, Y., Cours général de droit international privé, Académie de droit international, Recueil des cours, 1973, II, 270-385;

- LOUSSOUARN, Y. and BOUREL, P., Droit international privé, Paris, Dalloz, third edition, 1988, 1004 pp.;
- LOUSSOUARN, Y., Arbitrage commercial international et droit du commerce international, J.T., 1982, 167-171;
- LOWENFELD, A., Lex mercatoria: an arbitrator's view, in Lex mercatoria and arbitration, CARBONNEAU, T. (ed.), Dobbs Ferry, Transnational, 1990, 37-57, reprint in ARB.INT'L 1990, 133-150;
- LUITHLEN, W., Einheitliches Kaufrecht und autonomes Handelsrecht, Universitätsverlag Freiburg, 1956, 71 pp.;

- MAIER, H.J., Europäische Übereinkommen über die internationale Handelsschiedsgerichtsbarkeit und UN-Übereinkommen über die Anerkennung und Vollstreckung ausländischer Schiedssprüche, Cologne, Deutsches Wirtschaftsdienst, 1966, 47 pp.;
- MALINVERNI, P., Les conditions générales de vente et les contrats-types des chambres syndicales, Paris, LGDJ, 1978, 380 pp.;
- MANN, F.A., Reflections on a commercial law of nations, 33 Brit.Y.B.Int.L., 1958, 20-51;
- MANN, F.A., Lex facit arbitrum, in International arbitration, Liber amicorum for Martin Domke, SANDERS, P. (ed.), The Hague, Martinus Nijhoff, 1967, 157, also published as Internationale Schiedsgerichte und nationale Rechtsordnung, ZHR, 1968, 97-129, reprint in Arbitration International 1986, 241-261;
- MANN, F.A., State contracts and international arbitration, 42 Brit.Y.B.Int.L., 1967, 1-37;
- MANN, F.A., International corporations and national law, 42 Brit.Y.B.Int.L., 1967, 145-174;
- MANN, F.A., Arbitration extra legem, L.Q.R., 1978, 486-488;
- MANN, F.A., Schiedsrichter und Recht, in Festschrift für Werner Flume, JAKOBS, H (ed.), Cologne, 1978, 593-619;
- MANN, F.A., England rejects "delocalised" contracts and arbitration, INT'L & COMP.L.Q., 1984, 193-198;
- MANN, F.A., Zur Nationalität des Schiedsspruchs, Festschrift für Oppenhoff, Munich, Beck, 1985, 215-226;
- MANN, F.A., Private arbitration and public policy, Civil Justice Quarterly, 1985, 257-267;
- MARTINY, D., Bestimmung des Schuldstatuts, in REITHMANN, C., Internationales Vertragsrecht, fourth edition, Cologne, Schmidt, 1988, 1-143;
- MARTY, G. and RAYNAUD, P., Droit civil, I, Introduction générale à l'étude du droit, second edition, Paris, Sirey, 1972, 532 pp.;
- MASKOW, D., Organisation et droit du commerce extérieur de la République démocratique allemande, D.P.C.I., 1984, 67-94;
- MATRAY, L., Rédaction d'une clause d'arbitrage et choix d'arbitres compétents en matière internationale, Rev.Dr.Int.Comp., 1979, 51-78;
- MATRAY, L. and DEL MARMOL, Ch., L'importance et l'interprétation du contrat, Rev.Dr.Int.Comp., 1980, 158-208;
- MATRAY, L., Arbitrage et ordre public transnational, in The art of arbitration, Essays on international arbitration, Liber amicorum Pieter Sanders, SCHULTSZ, J. and VAN DEN BERG, A.J. (ed.), Deventer, Kluwer, 1982, 241-251;
- MATRAY, L., L'amiable composition dans l'arbitrage interne et dans l'arbitrage international, in Het scheidsgerecht, Brussels, Jeune barreau, 1983, 39-61;
- MATRAY, L., La loi belge du 27 mars 1985 et ses répercussions sur l'arbitrage commercial international, Rev.Dr.Int.Comp., 1987, 243-262;
- MAY, G., Eléments de droit romain, fourteenth edition, Paris, Sirey, 1922, 737 pp.;
- MAYER, P., Le mythe de l'"ordre juridique de base" (ou Grundlegung), in Le droit des relations économiques internationales, Etudes offertes à Berthold Goldman, Paris, Litec, 1982, 199-216;

- MAYER, P., L'insertion de la sentence dans l'ordre juridique français, in Droit et pratique de l'arbitrage international en France, FEDUCI, s.l., 1984, 81-104;
- MAYER, P., Droit international privé, third edition, Paris, Montchrestien, 1987, 653 pp.;
- MAYER, P., L'autonomie de l'arbitre international dans l'appréciation de sa propre compétence, 217 Collected Courses of The Hague, Academy of International Law, 1989, V, 319-454;
- Mc LACHLAN, C., The new Hague sales convention and the limits of the choice of law process, L.Q.R., 1986, 591-627;
- MEIJER, R., Uncitral en het nieuwe verdrag inzake de internationale handelskoop, N.J.B., 1980, 1021-1040;
- MEINERTZHAGEN-LIMPENS, A., Quelques aspects des contrats en usage sur la place d'Anvers, in Quelques aspects des contrats standardisés, Brussels, Editions de l'Université de Bruxelles, 1982, 231-272;
- MERCADAL, B. and JANIN, P., Les contrats de coopération inter-entreprises, Paris, Editions juridiques Lefebvre, 1974;
- MERTENS, H.J. and REHBINDER, E., Internationales Kaufrecht, Kommentar zu dem einheitlichen Kaufgesetzen, Frankfurt, Metzner Verlag, 1975, 407 pp.;
- MEZGER, E., Das Europäische Übereinkommen über die Handelsschiedsgerichtsbarkeit, RabelsZ, 1965, 231-301;
- MEZGER, E., Kernpunkte der Reform des Rechts der internationalen Handelsschiedsgerichtsbarkeit in Frankreich, RIW, 1981, 511-517;
- MICHIDA, S., Possible avenues to preparation of standard contracts for international trade on a global level, in Unification of the law governing international sale of goods, HONNOLD, J. (ed.), International Association of Legal Science, Paris, Dalloz, 1966, 251-291;
- MODDERMAN, W., Handboek voor het Romeinse recht, I, fifth edition by TICHELAAR, P., Groningen, Wolters, 1913, 332 pp.;
- MOENS, S., Kontrakten tussen Staten en vreemde private investeerders met het oog op de ekonomische ontwikkeling van de Staat, Iura Falc., 1974-75, 403-418;
- MOSER, R., Vertragsabschluß, Vertragsgültigkeit und Parteiwille im internationalen Obligationenrecht, St.Gallen, Verlag der Fehr'schen Buchhandlung, 1948, 253 pp.;
- MOTULSKY, H., L'évolution récente en matière d'arbitrage international, Rev.Arb., 1959, 3, reprint in MOTULSKY, H., Ecrits, études et notes sur l'arbitrage, Paris, Dalloz, 1974, 295-303;
- MOTULSKY, H., L'internationalisation du droit français de l'arbitrage, Rev. Arb., 1963, 110, reprint in MOTULSKY,H., Ecrits, études et notes sur l'arbitrage, Paris, Dalloz, 1974, 319-331;
- MOURA VICENTE, D., L'évolution récente du droit de l'arbitrage au Portugal, Rev.Arb., 1991, 434-439;
- MUNZBERG, R., Die Schranken der Parteivereinbarungen in der privaten internationalen Schiedsgerichtsbarkeit, Berlin, Duncker & Humblot, 1970, 190 pp.;
- MUSTILL, M., Transnational arbitration in English law, Current legal problems, 1984, 133-152;
- MUSTILL, M., The new lex mercatoria : the first twenty-five years, in Liber amicorum for Lord Wilberforce, BOS, M. and BROWNLIE, I. (ed.), Oxford, Clarendon Press, 1987, 149-182;
- MUSTILL, M. and BOYD, S., The law and practice of commercial arbitration in England, second edition, London, Butterworths, 1989, 835 pp.;

- NEUHAUS, P.H., Die Grundbegriffe des internationalen Privatrechts, second edition, Tubingen, Mohr, 1976, 488 pp.;

- NEVILLE BROWN, L., General principles of law and the English legal system, in New perspectives for a common law of Europe, CAPPELLETTI, M. (ed.), European University Institute, Leyden, Sijthoff, 1978, 171-193;
- NIELSEN, J., Grundlagen des Akkreditivsgeschäfts, Revision 1983, Cologne, Bankverlag, 1985, 205 pp.;
- NIEUWENHUIS, J., Drie beginselen van contractenrecht, Deventer, Kluwer, 1979, 264 pp.;

- OERTMANN, P., Rechtsordnung und Verkehrssitte, Leipzig, Deichert'sche Verlagsbuchhandlung, 1914, 526 pp.;
- OLY, G., Algemene beschouwingen over de eenvormige wet op de internationale koop van goederen in historisch perspectief, Deventer, Kluwer, 1982, 212 pp.;
- OPDEBEEK, I., De aansprakelijkheid van de luchtvervoerder voor de door hem vervoerde reizigers zoals geregeld in het Verdrag van Warschau, R.W., 1985-86, 1393-1418;
- OPPETIT, B., L'engagement d'honneur, D., 1979, 107-116;
- OPPETIT, B., La notion de source du droit et le droit du commerce international, Arch.Phil.Dr., 1982, 43-53;
- OPPETIT, B., Le développement des règles matérielles, Trav.com.fr.dr. int.privé, Paris, CNRS, 1988, 121-134;
- OPPETIT, B., Les principes généraux en droit international privé, Arch.Phil.Dr., 1987, 179-187;
- ORIANNE, P., Introduction au système juridique, Brussels, Bruylant, 1982, 353 pp.;
- OTTO, H.H., Allgemeine Geschäftsbedingungen und internationales Privatrecht, Göttingen, Verlagsgesellschaft für Wirtschafts- und Steurrecht, 1984, 255 pp.;

- PABBRUWE, H., Gebruik en gebruikelijke beding, Zwolle, Tjeenk Willink, 1961, 219 pp.;
- PACHE, A., La coutume et les usages dans le droit privé positif, Lausanne, Bovard-Giddey, 1938, 288 pp.;
- PADIS, P., La vente commerciale internationale par contrats types et incoterms, Gaz.Pal., September 4, 1970, 91-104;
- PADIS, P., L'affrontement des économies socialistes et capitalistes dans le monde ou l'arbitrage international en 1972, Gaz.Pal., May 20-22, 1973, 6;
- Palmer's Company Law, I, London, Stevens & Sons, 1987, 1857 pp.;
- PARK, W., Control mechanisms in the development of a modern lex mercatoria, in Lex mercatoria and arbitration, CARBONNEAU,T. (ed.), Dobbs Ferry, Transnational, 1990, 109-138;
- PATOCCHI, P.A., Règles de rattachement localisatrices et règles de rattachement à caractère substantiel, Geneva, Georg, 1985, 376 pp.;
- PAULSSON, J., CRAIG, W. and PARK, W., French codification of a legal framework for international commercial arbitration : the decree of May 21, 1981, D.P.C.I., 1981, 589-602;
- PAULSSON, J., Le tiers monde et l'arbitrage commercial international, Rev.Arb., 1983, 3-45;
- PAULSSON, J., La lex mercatoria dans l'arbitrage C.C.I., Rev.Arb., 1990, 55-100;
- PEDAMON, M., Y a-t-il lieu de distinguer les usages et les coutumes en droit commercial ?, Rev.Trim.Dr.Com., 1959, 335-357;
- Pennington's Company Law, fourth edition, London, Butterworths, 1979, 874 pp.;
- PERRIN, G., Réflexions sur le rôle des principes généraux dans l'ordre juridique international, in Mélanges Guy Flattet, Lausanne, Payot, 1985, 509-522;
- PETERSMANN, E., "Entwicklungsvölkerrecht", "Droit international du développement", "International Economic Development Law" : Mythos oder Wirklichkeit ?, 17 Jahrbuch für internationales Recht, Berlin, Duncker & Humblot, 1975, 145-176;
- PEYREFITTE, L., Le problème du contrat dit "sans loi", D., 1965, 113-120;

- PIERCE, D., Post-formation choice of law in contract, Mod.L.Rev., 1987, 176-201;
- PIROVANO, A., Introduction critique au droit commercial contemporain, Rev.Trim Dr.Com., 1985, 219-263;
- PLUCKNETT, T., A concise history of the common law, London, Butterworths, fifth edition, 1956, 746 pp.;
- POLAK, J.M., Inleiding tot het Nederlands rechtspersonenrecht, Groningen, Wolters, 1969, 108 pp.;
- POHLMANN, H., Die Quellen des Handelsrecht, in Handbuch der Quellen und Literatur der neueren Europäischen Privatrechtsgeschichte, I, COING, H. (ed.), Munich, Beck, 1973, 801-834;
- PULBY, G., La coutume et son rôle en matière de compte courant, Paris, Emile Larose, 1924, 188 pp.;

- RAAPE, L., Internationales Privatrecht, fourth edition, Berlin, Vahlen, 1955, 672 pp.;
- RAJSKI, J., Les principes du droit commercial international de certains pays socialistes européens, Académie de droit international, Recueil des cours, 1982, I, 9-105;
- REDFERN, A. and HUNTER, M., Law and practice of international commercial arbitration, London, Sweet & Maxwell, 1986, 462 pp.;
- REHME, P., Geschichte des Handelsrechtes, in EHRENBERG, V., Handbuch des gesamten Handelsrecht, I, Leipzig, Reisland, 1913, 28-259;
- REHME, P., Das heutige deutsche Handelsrecht, in EHRENBERG, V., Handbch des gesamten Handelsrecht, I, Leipzig, Reisland, 1913, 260-285;
- REIMANN, T., Zur Lehre vom "rechtsordnungslosen" Vertrag, Bonn, Röhrscheid Verlag, 1970, 108 pp.;
- REITHMANN, C. (ed.), Internationales Vertragsrecht, Das internationale Privatrecht der Schuldverträge, fourth edition, Cologne, Verlag Schmidt, 1988, 1183 pp.;
- RENGGLI, P., Die Grenzen der Parteifreiheit im internationalen privatrechtlichen Schiedsverfahren, Bern, Stämpfli, 1955, 75 pp.;
- RIEDBERG, P., Der amiable compositeur im internationalen privaten Schiedsgerichtsverfahren, Frankfurt, Metzner, 1962, 94 pp.;
- RIEG, A., Le rôle de la volonté dans l'acte juridique en droit civil français et allemand, Paris, LGDJ, 1961, 589 pp.;
- RIGAUX, F. and VERWILGHEN, M., Le champ d'application dans l'espace des règles uniformes de droit matériel, in Rapports belges au VIIIe Congrès international de droit comparé, CENTRE INTERUNIVERSITAIRE DE DROIT COMPARE (ed.), Brussels, 1970, 217-289;
- RIGAUX, F., Le domaine d'application de la loi uniforme sur la vente internationale des objets mobiliers corporels et la loi uniforme sur la formation de ces contrats de vente, in Le contrat économique international, Travaux des VIIes Journées d'études juridiques Jean Dabin, Brussels, Bruylant, 1975, 67-113, also published in J.T., 1972, 561-572;
- RIGAUX, F., Droit public et droit privé dans les relations internationales, Paris, Pedone, 1977, 486 pp.;
- RIGAUX, F., Le droit comparé comme science appliquée, Rev.Dr.Int.Comp. 1978, 65-77;
- RIGAUX, F., Le rôle de la comparaison dans la préparation de la réglementation juridique internationale, in Rapports belges au Xe Congrès international de droit comparé, Brussels, Bruylant, 1978, 331-348;
- RIGAUX, F., Pour un autre ordre international, in Droit Economique, Volume 2, Institut des Hautes Etudes Internationales de Paris, Paris, Pedone, 1979, 269-426;
- RIGAUX, F., Droit international privé, II, Brussels, Larcier, 1979, 678 pp.;
- RIGAUX, F. and VANDER ELST, R., Relations juridiques transnationales ou dialogue sur un autre droit, J.T., 1982, 230-234;

- RIGAUX, F., Souveraineté des Etats et arbitrage transnational, in Le droit des relations économiques internationales, Etudes offertes à Berthold Goldman, Paris, Litec, 1982, 261-279;
- RIGAUX, F., Droit international privé, I, Brussels, Larcier, second edition, 1987, 386 pp.;
- RIGAUX, F., Examen de quelques questions laissées ouvertes par la Convention de Rome sur la loi applicable aux obligations contractuelles, Cah.Dr.Eur., 1988, 306-321;
- RIPERT, G., Les forces créatrices du droit, Paris, LGDJ, 1955, 431 pp.;
- ROBERT, J., La convention européenne sur l'arbitrage commercial international signée à Genève le 21 avril 1961, D., 1961, 173-184;
- ROBERT, J., Exposé introductif et général sur l'arbitrage, Ann.Fac.Dr.Liège, 1964, 29-37;
- ROBERT, J., L'arbitrage en matière internationale, D., 1981, 209-216;
- ROBERT, J., De la règle de conflit à la règle matérielle en matière d'arbitrage international (spécialement en droit international privé français), in The art of arbitration, Essays on international arbitration, Liber amicorum Pieter Sanders, SCHULTSZ, J. and VAN DEN BERG, A.J. (ed.), Deventer, Kluwer, 1982, 273-284;
- ROBERT, J., L'arbitrage, droit interne, droit international privé, fifth edition, Paris, Dalloz, 1983, 478 pp.;
- ROBERT, J. and CARBONNEAU, T.E., The French law of arbitration, New York, Matthew Bender, 1983;
- ROBERT, J., Le phénomène transnational, Paris, LGDJ, 1988, 60 pp.;
- ROTH, W.H., Internationales Versicherungsvertragsrecht, Tubingen, Mohr, 1985, 817 pp.;
- ROWE, M., The contribution of the ICC to the development of international trade law, in HORN, N. and SCHMiTTHOFF, C., The transnational law of international commercial transactions, Studies in transnational economic law, Volume 2, Deventer, Kluwer, 1982, 51-60;
- RUBELLIN-DEVICHI, J., L'arbitrage, nature juridique, droit interne et droit international privé, Paris, LGDJ, 1965, 412 pp.;
- RUBINO-SAMMARTANO, M., International arbitration law, Deventer, Kluwer, 1989, 537 pp.
- RUMMEL, P., Vertragsauslegung nach der Verkehrssitte, Vienna, Manzsche Verlags- und Universitätsbuchhandlung, 1972, 127 pp.;
- RUSSELL on the law of arbitration, door WALTON, A. and VITORIA, A., twentieth edition, London, Stevens & Sons, 1982, 602 pp.;

- SALEM, M. and SANSON-HERMITTE, M.A., Les contrats "clé en main" et les contrats "produit en main", Université de Dijon, Institut de relations internationales, Travaux du centre de recherche sur le droit des marchés et des investissements internationaux, Paris, Librairies Techniques, 1979, 212 pp.;
- SALLE DE LA MARNIERRE, E., L'évolution technique du contrat et ses conséquences juridiques, Paris, Rousseau, 1930, 352 pp.;
- SALMON, J., Les principes généraux du droit, Une insaisissable source du droit applicable aux contrats d'état, in Mélanges offerts à Raymond Vander Elst, Volume 2, Brussels, Nemesis, 1986, 717-754;
- SAMUEL, A., Jurisdictional problems in international commercial arbitration: a study of Belgian, Dutch, English, French, Swedish, Swiss, U.S. and West German law, Zurich, Schulthess, 1989, 333 pp.;
- SAMUEL, A., A critical look at the reform of Swiss arbitration law, ARB.INT'L, 1991, 27-56;
- SANDERS, P., Ecafe rules for international commercial arbitration, in International arbitration, Liber amicorum for Martin Domke, SANDERS, P. (ed.), The Hague, Nijhoff, 1967, 252 ff.;

- SANDERS, P., International commercial arbitration, in Arbitrage commercial, Essais in memoriam Eugenio Minoli, Associazione italiano per l'arbitrato, Rome, 1974, 467-485;
- SANDERS, P., Trends in the field of international commercial arbitration, Academy of international law, 145 Collected courses of The Hague, 1975, II, 205-296;
- SANDERS, P., Aspects de l'arbitrage international, Rev.Dr.Int.Comp. 1976, 129-139;
- SANDERS, P., Codes of conduct and sources of law, in Le droit des relations économiques internationales, Etudes offertes à Berthold Goldman, Paris, Litec, 1982, 281-298;
- SANDERS, P., Het nieuwe arbitragerecht, Deventer, Kluwer, 1987, first edition, 250 pp.;
- SANDERS, P. and VAN DEN BERG, A.J., The Netherlands Arbitration Act 1986, Deventer, Kluwer, 1987, 190 pp.;
- SANDROCK, O., Zur ergänzenden Vertragsauslegung im materiellen und internationalen Schuldvertragsrecht, Cologne, Westdeutscher Verlag, 1966, 318 pp.;
- SANDROCK, O. and STEINSCHULTE, F.P., Grundfragen des internationalen Vertragsrechts : die kollisionsrechtliche Anknüpfung von Schuldverträgen, in SANDROCK, O. (ed), Handbuch der internationalen Vertragsgestaltung, Volume 1, Heidelberg, Verlagsgesellschaft Recht und Wirtschaft, 1980, 1-258;
- SANDROCK, O., Die Bedeutung des Gesetzes zur Neuregelung des internationalen Privatrechts für die Unternehmenspraxis, RIW, 1986, 841-855;
- SANDROCK, O., Choice of law and choice of forum in civil law jurisdictions, in Drafting and enforcing contracts in civil and common law jurisdictions, Deventer, Kluwer, 1986, 145-207;
- SANDROCK, O., Zügigkeit und Leichtigkeit versus Gründlichkeit JZ, 1986, 370-378;
- SANDROCK, O., Die Fortbildung des materiellen Rechts durch die Internationale Schiedsgerichtsbarkeit, in Fortbildung durch die Internationale Schiedsgerichtsbarkeit, BÖCKSTIEGEL, K.H. (ed.), Cologne, Heymanns, 1989, 21-81;
- SANDROCK, O., "Ex aequo et bono"- und "amiable composition"-Vereinbarungen: ihre Qualification, Anknüpfung und Wirkungen, Jahrbuch für die Praxis der Schiedsgerichtsbarkeit, Volume 2 (1988), Heidelberg, Verlag Recht und Wirtschaft, 1989, 120-140;
- SAUSER-HALL, G., L'arbitrage en droit international privé, report, 44 Annuaire de l'Institut de Droit International, Sienna Session, 1952, I, 469-613;
- SAUTER, E. and SCHWEYER, G., Der eingetragene Verein, thirteenth edition, Munich, Beck, 1986, 392 pp.;
- SAUVEPLANNE, G., Elementair internationaal privaatrecht, ninth edition, Deventer, Kluwer, 1989, 170 pp.;
- SCHAPIRA, J., Le droit international des affaires, Paris, Presses Universitaires de France, 1972, 124 pp.;
- SCHILLER, A., Roman law, The Hague, Mouton Publishers, 1978, 606 p.;
- SCHINNERER, E., Um ein Recht des internationalen Handels, ZfRV, 1968, 185-213;
- SCHLECHTRIEM, P., Einheitliches U.N.-Kaufrecht, Das Übereinkommen der Vereinten Nationen über internationale Warenkaufverträge, Tubingen, Mohr, 1981, 167 pp.;
- SCHLEGELBERGER-HEFERMEHL, Handelsgesetzbuch, III, fourth edition, Berlin, Vahlen, 1965, 2200 pp.;
- SCHLESINGER, R. and BONASSIES, P., Le fonds commun des systèmes juridiques, Rev.Int.Dr.Comp., 1963, 501-540;
- SCHLESINGER, R. and GUNDISCH, H.J., Allgemeine Rechtsgrundsätze als Sachnormen in Schiedsgerichtsverfahren, RabelsZ, 1964, 4-46;
- SCHLOSSER, P., Entwicklungstendenzen in Recht und Praxis der internationalen privaten Schiedsgerichtsbarkeit, Karlsruhe, Müller Verlag, 1976, 79 pp.;
- SCHLOSSER, P., Das internationale an der internationalen privaten Schiedsgerichtsbarkeit, RIW, 1982, 857-867;

- SCHLOSSER, P., Das Recht der internationalen privaten Schiedsgerichtsbarkeit, second edition, Tubingen, Mohr, 1989, 791 pp.;
- SCHMIDT, K., Handelsrecht, second edition, Cologne, Heymanns, 1982, 782 pp.;
- SCHMITTHOFF, C., The English conflict of laws, third edition, London, Stevens & Sons, 1954, 514 pp.;
- SCHMITTHOFF, C., Conflict avoidance in practice and theory, 21 LAW & CONTEMP.PROBS., 1956, 429-462;
- SCHMITTHOFF, C., Modern trends in English commercial law, in Tidskrift av. Juridiska Förreningen i Finland, 1957, 349-364;
- SCHMITTHOFF, C., International business law : a new law merchant, Current law and social problems, University Western Ontario, 1961, 129-153;
- SCHMITTHOFF, C., International law and private international law, in Vom deutschen zum europäischen Recht, Festschrift für Hans Dölle, II, VON CAEMMERER, E., NIKISCH, A. and ZWEIGERT, K. (ed.), Tubingen, Mohr, 1963, 257-272;
- SCHMITTHOFF, C., Das neue Recht des Welthandels, RabelsZ, 1964, 47-77;
- SCHMITTHOFF, C., The unification of the law of international trade, 27 Gothenburg School of Economics and Business Administration Publications, 1964, 5-28;
- SCHMITTHOFF, C., The law of international trade, its growth, formulation and operation, in The sources of the law of international trade, SCHMITTHOFF, C. (ed.), International Association of Legal Science, London, Stevens & Sons, 1964, 3-38;
- SCHMITTHOFF, C., The sale of goods, second edition, London, Stevens & Sons, 1966, 381 pp.;
- SCHMITTHOFF, C., The risk of loss in transit in international sales, in Unification of the law governing international sales of goods, HONNOLD, J. (ed.), International Association of Legal Science, Paris, Dalloz, 1966, 169-199;
- SCHMITTHOFF, C., The unification or harmonization of laws by means of standard contracts and general conditions, in L'unification du droit, Annuaire 1967-1968, II, Unidroit, Rome, 1969, 93-117, INT. & COMP.L.Q., 1968, 551-570;
- SCHMITTHOFF, C., The unification of the law of international trade, J.BUS.L., 1968, 105-119;
- SCHMITTHOFF, C., Agency in international trade, Academy of international law, 129 Collected courses of The Hague, 1970, I, 107-203;
- SCHMITTHOFF, C. and SIMMONDS, K., International economic and trade law, Universal and regional unification, Leyden, Sijthoff, 1976, 252 pp.;
- SCHMITTHOFF, C., Standard contracts and the protection of the weaker party in international trade relations, in New directions in international trade law, Acts and Proceedings of the 2nd Congress on private law held by Unidroit, I, Dobbs Ferry, New York, Oceana, 1977, 177 ff.;
- SCHMITTHOFF, C., Commercial law in a changing economic climate, second edition, London, Sweet & Maxwell, 1981, 78 pp.;
- SCHMITTHOFF, C., Interpretation and application of international trade usages, in Interpretation and application of international trade usages, I.C.C.-publication No. 374, Paris, 1981, 21-44;
- SCHMITTHOFF, C., Nature and evolution of the transnational law of commercial transactions, in HORN, N. and SCHMITTHOFF, C., The transnational law of international commercial transactions, Studies in transnational economic law, Volume 2, Deventer, Kluwer, 1982, 19-31;
- SCHMITTHOFF, C. and SARRE, D., Charlesworth's Mercantile Law, fourteenth edition, London, Stevens & Sons, 1984, 733 pp.;
- SCHMITTHOFF, C., The codification of the law of international trade, J.BUS.L., 1985, 34-44;

- SCHMITTHOFF, C., Extrajudicial dispute settlement, in Forum internationale, Deventer, Kluwer, 1985, 18 pp.;
- SCHMITTHOFF, C., Schmitthoff's export trade, The law and practice of international trade, ninth edition, London, Stevens & Sons, 1990, 798 pp.;
- SCHMITTHOFF, C., International trade usages, I.C.C.- publication No. 440/4, Paris, 1987, 75 pp.;
- SCHNITZER, A., Die Einordnung der internationalen Sachverhalte in das Rechtssystem, in Internationales Recht und Wirtschaftsordnung, Festschrift für F.A. Mann, Munich, Beck, 1977, 289-305;
- SCHNYDER, A.K., Das neue IPR-Gesetz, Zurich, Schulthess, 1988, 161 pp.;
- SCHOBER, A., Die Vereinsautonomie, Cologne, Baun & Boden, 1936, 84 pp.;
- SCHOLTEN, G., Rechtsbeginselen en rechtsregels, Scheiden schaadt, in Rechtsbeginselen, SCHOLTEN, G., SCHELTENS, D. and VAN EIKEMA HOMMES, H. (ed.), Encyclopedie der rechtswetenschap, Zwolle, Tjeenk Willink, 1980, 1-14;
- SCHÖNBAUER, E., Studien zum Personalitätsprinzip im antiken Rechte, 49 Z.Savigny-Stiftung für Rechtsgeschichte, Romanistische Abteilung, 1929, 345-403;
- SCHÖNENBERGER, W., Kommentar zum schweizerischen Zivilgesetzbuch, Volume V, 1a, Allgemeine Einleitung, Zurich, Schulthess, 1973, 1-142;
- SCHRANS, G., Poging tot omschrijving van de onderneming als rechtssubject, R.W., 1979-80, 2379-2396;
- SCHRANS, G., Levend en herlevend recht rond het winstoogmerk, in Aktuele problemen van handels-, economisch en financieel recht, Postuniversitaire cyclus Willy Delva, 1985, STORME, M. and FREDERICQ, S. (ed.), Ghent, 669-701 and T.P.R., 1986, 669-701;
- SCHULTSZ, J.C., Legislation in the Netherlands and international arbitration, Mededelingen van de Nederlandse Vereniging voor Internationaal Recht No. 93, Deventer, Kluwer, 1986, 1-48;
- SCHULZ, F., History of Roman legal science, Oxford, Clarendon Press, 1967, 358 pp.;
- SCHULZE, C., Die Kodifikation des Vertragsstatuts im internationalen Privatrecht, Basle, Helbing & Lichtenhahn, 1980, 232 pp.;
- SCHURIG, K., Kollisionsnormen und Sachrecht, Berlin, Duncker & Humblot, 1981, 392 pp.;
- SCHÜSSLER, C., Die Incoterms - Internationale Regeln für die Auslegung der handelsüblichen Vertragsformeln, DB, 1986, 1161-1166;
- SCHÜTTE, E., Schiedsklauseln und "transnationales Recht", VersR, 1982, 223-225;
- SCHWAB, K.H., Kollisionsrechtliche Fragen des deutschen internationalen Schiedsverfahrensrechts, in Festschrift für M.Luther, Munich, Beck, 1976, 163-178;
- SCHWAB, K.H., Die Schiedsgerichtsbarkeit der Internationalen Handelskammer aus der Sicht des deutschen Rechts, Festschrift für W.Kralik, RECHBERGER, W. and WELSER, R. (ed.), Vienna, Manzsche, 1986, 317-327, also published as ICC-Schiedsgerichtsbarkeit aus der Sicht des deutschen Rechts, in Recht und Praxis der Schiedsgerichtsbarkeit der Internationalen Handelskammer, BÖCKSTIEGEL, K.H. (ed.), Cologne, Heymanns, 1986, 53-64;
- SCHWANDER, I., Zur Rechtswahl im IPR des Schuldvertragsrecht, Festschrift für Max Keller, Zurich, Schulthess, 1989, 473-484;
- SCHWIND, F., Römisches Recht, I, Vienna, Springer, 1950, 410 pp.;
- SIEHR, K., Sachrecht im IPR, transnationales Recht und lex mercatoria, in Internationales Privatrecht, internationales Wirtschaftrecht, HOLL, W. and KLINKE, U. (ed.), Cologne, Heymanns, 1985, 103-126;
- SIEHR, K., Die Parteiautonomie im internationalen Privatrecht, Festschrift für Max Keller, Zurich, Schulthess, 1989, 485-510;

- SILANCE, L., Un moyen de combler les lacunes en droit : l'induction amplifiante, in Etudes de logique juridique, II, Droit et logique, Les lacunes en droit, Brussels, Bruylant, 1967, 117-140;
- SIMON, J., Le commerce international des céréales, Pouvoirs étatiques, pouvoirs économiques privés, dissertation, Paris II, 1982, 1230 pp.;
- SIMONT, L., Amiables compositeurs and their reasoning, in International commercial arbitration, SCHMITTHOFF, C. (ed.), Dobbs Ferry, New York, Oceana, 1974, 109-135;
- SIMONT, L., Les mécanismes financiers des contrats internationaux, Rev.Dr.Int.Comp., 1980, 267-284;
- SLAGTER, W., Compendium van het ondernemingsrecht, fourth edition, Deventer, Kluwer, 1985, 510 pp.;
- SLATER, R., The transnational law of syndicated loans - a hopeless case ?, in The transnational law of international commercial transactions, HORN,N. and SCHMITTHOFF, C. (ed.), Studies in transnational economic law, Volume 2, Deventer, Kluwer, 1982, 329-352;
- SMIT, H., A-national arbitration, 63 TUL.L.REV., 1989, 629-645; reprint as Proper choice of law and the lex mercatoria arbitralis, in Lex mercatoria and arbitration, CARBONNEAU, T. (ed.), Dobbs Ferry, Transnational, 1990, 59-75;
- SOETAERT, R., Rechtsbeginselen en marginale toetsing in cassatie, in Liber amicorum Jan Ronse, Brussels, Story, 1986, 51-66;
- SOHM, R., Institutionen, Geschichte und System des römischen Privatrechts, seventeenth edition by MITTEIS,L., Munich, Duncker & Humblot, 1923, 756 pp.;
- SONNENBERGER, H.J., Verkehrssitten im Schuldvertrag, Munich, Beck, 1969, 323 pp.;
- MünchKomm-Sonnenberger, IPR Einleitung, Munich, Beck, 1983, 5-202;
- SPRUIT, J.E., Enrichidium, Overzicht van de geschiedenis van het Romeins privaatrecht, second edition, Deventer, Kluwer, 1977, 298 pp.;
- STAUDINGER-HORN, Vorbem. zu §§ 765-778, Von Staudinger Kommentar zum bürgerlichen Gesetzbuch, twelfth edition, Berlin, Schweitzer verlag, 1986, 325-326;
- STEIN, P.A., De nieuwe arbitragewet, Deventer, Kluwer, 1986, 55 pp.;
- STÖBER, K., Vereinsrecht, fifth edition, Baden-Baden, Nomos, 1988, 401 pp.;
- STOECKER, C., The lex mercatoria: to what extent does it exist ?, J.INT.ARB., 1990, 101-125;
- STOLL, J., Vereinbarungen zwischen Staat und ausländischem Investor, Berlin, Springer, 1982, 166 pp.;
- STORME, M., De bewijslast in het Belgisch privaatrecht, dissertation, Ghent, Law Faculty, 1962, 465 pp.;
- STORME, M., Algemene inleiding tot het recht, Antwerp, Kluwer, 1978, 233 pp.;
- STORME, M., Aspects importants du droit arbitral belge, Rev.Dr.Int.Comp. 1976, 116-128;
- STORME, M., Belgium: a paradise for international commercial arbitration, INT'L BUS.LAWYER, 1986, 296-295;
- STOUFFLET, J., Le crédit documentaire, Paris, Librairies Techniques, 1957, 411 pp.;
- STOUFFLET, J., L'oeuvre normative de la Chambre de commerce internationale dans le domaine bancaire, in Le droit des relations économiques internationales, Etudes offertes à Berthold Goldman, Paris, Litec, 1982, 361-371;
- STRAUBE, M., Kommentar zum Handelsgesetzbuch, Vienna, Manzsche, 1987, 1302 pp.;
- STRUYCKEN, A., Internationaal privaatrecht, in Contractenrecht, VI, BLOEM-BERGEN, A. and KLEYN, W. (ed.), Deventer, Kluwer, loose-leaf;
- STRUYCKEN, A., Verenigingen als wereldburger : "qua patet orbis", in Goed en trouw, Opstellen aangeboden aan Prof.mr.W.C.L. van der Grinten, Zwolle, Tjeenk Willink, 1984, 267-289;

- STRUYCKEN, A., La lex mercatoria dans le droit des contrats internationaux, in L'évolution contemporaire du droit des contrats, Journées René Savatier, Paris, P.U.F., 1986, 207- 229;
- STUART SUTHERLAND, L., The Law Merchant in England in the seventeenth and eighteenth centuries, Royal Historical Society's Transactions, (4th series), XVII, 1934, 149-176;

- TALLON, D., The law applied by arbitration tribunals - II, in The sources of the law of international trade, SCHMITTHOFF, C. (ed.), International Association of Legal Science, London, Stevens & Sons, 1964, 154-166;
- THOMPSON, R. and DERAINS, Y., Cour d'Arbitrage de la Chambre de Commerce internationale, Chronique des sentences arbitrales, Clunet, 1974, 876-921;
- 'T KINT, J., Les associations sans but lucratif, second edition, Brussels, Larcier, 1974, 367 pp.;
- 'T KINT, J., Associations sans but lucratif, Répertoire notarial, Brussels, Larcier, 1987, 139 pp.;
- TRAKMAN, L., The evolution of the Law Merchant : our commercial heritage, 12 J.MAR.L.& COM., 1980, 1-24;
- TRAKMAN, L., The evolution of the Law Merchant : our commercial heritage, 12 J.MAR.L.& COM., 1981, 153-182;
- TRAKMAN, L., The law merchant : the evolution of commercial law, Littleton, Colorado, Rothman, 1983, 195 pp.;
- TREITEL, G., An outline of the law of contract, third edition, London, Butterworths, 1984, 366 pp.;
- TREVES, T., Les clauses monétaires dans les émissions d'euro-obligations, in Les euro-obligations, Université de Dijon, Institut de relations internationales, Travaux du centre de recherche sur le droit des marchés et des investissements internationaux, Volume 1, Paris, Librairies Techniques, 1972;
- TRIEBEL, V. and PETZOLD, E., Grenzen der lex mercatoria in der internationalen Schiedsgerichtsbarkeit, RIW, 1988, 245-250;
- TSCHIKVADSE, V. and RUBANOV, A., Some aspects of the unification of the law of sales, in Unification of the law governing international sales of goods, HONNOLD, J. (ed.), International Association of Legal Science, Paris, Dalloz, 1966, 333-361;

- Unification of the law governing international sales of goods, HONNOLD, J. (ed.), International Association of Legal Science, Paris, Dalloz, 1966, 425 pp.;

- VAN ACKERE, C., Des usages commerciaux, Conférence française du jeune barreau de Gand, Ghent, Hoste, 1898, 52 pp.;
- VAN BEMMELEN, P., Het Romeinsche jus gentium benevens het jus naturale en de naturalis obligatio, in III Rechtsgeleerde bijdragen en bijblad, 1888, Afdeeling D, Amsterdam, Müller, 1889, 14-65;
- VAN BOGAERT, E., Volkenrecht, Antwerp, Kluwer, 1982, 648 pp.;
- VAN DELDEN, R., Lex mercatoria of ius commune ?, Deventer, Kluwer, 1986, 24 pp.;
- VAN DEN BERG, A.J., L'arbitrage commercial en Amérique latine, Rev.Arb., 1979, 124-203;
- VAN DEN BERG, A.J., The New York arbitration convention of 1958, Towards a uniform judicial interpretation, Deventer, Kluwer 1981, 480 pp.;
- VANDER ELST, R., L'autonomie de la volonté en droit international privé français et belge, in Liber amicorum L. Frédéricq, II, Ghent, Story, 1965, 977-997;

- VANDER ELST, R., Conflits de lois, in VANDER ELST, R. and WESER, M., Droit international privé belge et droit conventionnel international, I, Brussels, Bruylant, 1983, 391 pp.;
- VANDER ELST, R., Ordre public international, lois de police et lois d'application immédiate, in Mélanges offerts à Robert Legros, Brussels, Editions de l'Université de Bruxelles, 653-667;
- VAN DER HEIJDEN-VAN DER GRINTEN, Handboek voor de naamloze vennootschap naar Nederlands recht, eleventh edition, Zwolle, Tjeenk Willink, 1989, 893 pp.;
- VAN DER VELDEN, F., De eenvormige koopwetten van 1964, Deventer, Kluwer, 1979, 339 pp.;
- VAN DER VELDEN, P., De vereniging-rechtspersoon en haar leden, Deventer, Kluwer, 1969, 228 pp.;
- VAN GERVEN, W., Algemeen Deel, in Beginselen van Belgisch Privaatrecht, DILLEMANS, R. and VAN GERVEN, W. (ed.), Antwerp, Standaard, 1973, 519 pp.;
- VAN GERVEN, W., Handels- en economisch recht, in Beginselen van Belgisch Privaatrecht, DILLEMANS,R. and VAN GERVEN,W. (ed.), Antwerp, Standaard, 1975, 584 pp.;
- VAN GERVEN, W. and DEWAELE, A., Goede trouw en getrouw beeld, in Liber amicorum Jan Ronse, Brussels, Story, 1986, 103-126;
- VAN HECKE, G., Signification et limites du principe de l'autonomie de la volonté dans les contrats internationaux, Rev.Dr.Int.Comp., 1955, 81-91;
- VAN HECKE, G., Problèmes juridiques des emprunts internationaux, second edition, Leyden, E.J.Brill, 1964, 332 pp.;
- VAN HECKE, G., Principes et méthodes de solution des conflits de lois, Academy of international law, 126 Collected courses of The Hague, 1969, I, 399-569;
- VAN HECKE, G., Contracts subject to international or transnational law, International contracts, New York, Matthew Bender, 1981, 25-49, reprint in Miscellanea Georges Van Hecke, Antwerp, Kluwer, 1985, 299-312;
- VAN HECKE, G. and LENAERTS, K., Internationaal privaatrecht, in A.P.R., Brussels, Story, second edition, 1989, 435 pp.;
- VAN HOF, J., Commentary on the UNCITRAL Arbitration Rules, The application by the Iran-U.S. Claims Tribunal, The Hague, T.M.C. Asser Instituut, 1991;
- VAN HOUTTE, H., L'arbitrage : son territoire et ses frontières, Rev.Dr.Int.Comp. 1976, 140-151;
- VAN HOUTTE, H., Arbitrage, R.W., 1976-77, 2113-2142;
- VAN HOUTTE, H., Rechtsvinding bij transnationale handelsarbitrage, dissertation University Leuven, 1977, 556 pp.;
- VAN HOUTTE, H., La loi applicable à l'arbitrage commercial international, Rev.Dr.Int.Comp., 1980, 285-300, translated as Arbitrage en toepasselijk recht, T.P.R., 1982, 703-719;
- VAN HOUTTE, H., Internationale arbitrage in België, in Het scheidsgerecht, Brussels, Jeune barreau, 1983, 91-108;
- VAN HOUTTE, H., Arbitrage naar billijkheid in België, Tijdschrift voor arbitrage, 1984, No. 2, 36;
- VAN HOUTTE, H., Het gebruik ontstaan uit contract of verdrag, R.W., 1985-86, 2169-2186;
- VAN HOUTTE, H., De Belgische wet van 27 maart 1985 inzake internationale arbitrage, Tijdschrift voor Arbitrage, 1986, No. 1, 1-6;
- VAN HOUTTE, H., La loi belge du 27 mars 1985 sur l'arbitrage international, Rev.Arb., 1986, 29-42;

- VAN OMMESLAGHE, P., Examen de jurisprudence (1974 à 1982), Les obligations, R.C.J.B., 1986, 33-259;
- VAN OMMESLAGHE, P., L'exécution de bonne foi, principe général de droit ?, R.G.D.C., 1987, 101-112;
- VAN OVEN, J.C., Leerboek van Romeinsch privaatrecht, third edition, Leyden, Brill, 1948, 594 pp.;
- VAN RYN, J. and HEENEN, J., Principes de droit commercial, Brussels, Bruylant, four volumes;
- VAN SCHILFGAARDE, P., Rechtspersonen, Algemeen deel, second edition, Deventer, Kluwer, 1979, 292 pp.;
- VERHEUL, J.P., Rechtsvinding in het internationaal privaatrecht, Preadvies Calvinistische Juristenvereniging, 1973, 81-152;
- VERHOEVEN, J., Contrats entre Etats et ressortissants d'autres Etats, in Le contrat économique international, Travaux des VIIes Journées d'études juridiques Jean Dabin, Brussels, Bruylant, 1975, 115-150;
- VERHOEVEN, J., Arbitrage entre Etats et entreprises étrangères : des règles spécifiques ?, in Hommage à Jean Robert, Les Etats et l'arbitrage international, Rev.Arb., 1985, 609-640;
- VERWILGHEN, M. and RAVET-GOBBE, A.F., Une enquête sur la pratique du contrat international dans les milieux d'affaires belges, in Le contrat économique international, Travaux des VIIes Journées d'études Jean Dabin, Brussels, Bruylant, 1975, 313-360;
- VERWILGHEN, M., Les règles de droit limitant leur propre domaine d'application en droit international privé belge, in Rapports belges au XIième Congrès de l'Académie Internationale de droit comparé, Antwerp, Kluwer, 1982, 333-368;
- VIANDIER, A., Actes de commerce, commerçants, activité commerciale, Paris, P.U.F., 1986, 312 pp.;
- VIRALLY, A., Un tiers droit ?, Réflexions théoriques, in Le droit des relations économiques internationales, Etudes offertes à Berthold Goldman, Paris, Litec, 1982, 373-385;
- VISCHER, F., Internationales Vertragsrecht, Bern, Stämpfli, 1962, 275 pp.;
- VLAS, P., Rechtspersonen in het internationaal privaatrecht, Deventer, Kluwer, 1982, 215 pp.;
- VLAS, P., "Apatride" associations, Aspects of private international law, N.I.L.R., 1990, 37-70;
- VON BAR, C., Typen des internationalen Einheitsrecht und das internationale Privatrecht, in Recht und Wirtschaft, Osnabrücker Rechtswissenschaftliche Abhandlungen, Volume 1, Cologne, Heymanns, 1985, 19-36;
- VON BAR, C., Internationales Privatrecht, Volume 1, Munich, Beck, 1987, 565 pp.;
- VON BREITENSTEIN, D., Die internationale Arbitrage im französischen Recht, in Schiedsgerichtsbarkeit in Frankreich, BÖCKSTIEGEL,K.H. (ed.), Cologne, Heymanns, 1983, 15-44;
- VON CAEMMERER, E., The influence of the law of international trade on the development and character of the commercial law in the civil law countries, in The sources of the law of international trade, SCHMITTHOFF, C. (ed.), International Association of Legal Science, London, Stevens & Sons, 1964, 88-100, also published in Gesammelte Schriften, I, Tubingen, Mohr, 1968, 11-25;
- VON CAEMMERER, E., Measures for unifying the rules on choice of law, in Unification of the law governing international sales of goods, HONNOLD, J. (ed.), International Association of Legal Science, Paris, Dalloz, 1966, 313 ff.;
- VON CZYHLARZ, K., Lehrbuch der Institutionen des römischen Rechts, eighteenth edition by SAN NICOLO, M., Vienna, Hölder, 1924, 504 pp.;

- VON HOFFMANN, B., Internationale Handelsschiedsgerichtbarkeit, Die Bestimmung des massgeblichen Rechts, Frankfurt, Metzner Verlag, 1970, 143 pp.;
- VON HOFFMANN, B., Zur Auslegung von Formularbedingungen des internationalen Handelsverkehrs, AWD, 1970, 247-253;
- VON HOFFMANN, B., Uncitral Rules für internationale Schiedsverfahren, RIW, 1976, 1-7;
- VON HOFFMANN, B., Zur Nationalität internationaler Schiedssprüche, IPRax, 1981, 30-32;
- VON HOFFMANN, B., "Lex mercatoria" vor internationalen Schiedsgerichten, IPRax, 1984, 106-108;
- VON MEHREN, A.T., To what extent is international commercial arbitration autonomous ?, in Le droit des relations économiques internationales, Etudes offertes à Berthold Goldman, Paris, Litec, 1982, 217-227;
- VON MEHREN, A.T., Limitations on party choice of the governing law : do they exist for international commercial arbitration ?, Tel Aviv, Mortimer and Raymond Sackler Institute of Advanced Studies, mimeograph, 1986, 27 pp.;
- VON OVERBECK, A., Das neue schweizerische Bundesgesetz über das Internationale Privatrecht, IPRax, 1988, 329-334;
- VON STEIGER, W., Gesellschaftsrecht, Allgemeiner Teil, in Schweizerisches Privatrecht, VIII/1, Basle, Helbing & Lichtenhahn, 1976, 213-313;
- VON TUHR, A. and PETER, H., Allgemeiner Teil des schweizerischen Obligationenrecht, I, third edition, Zurich, Schulthess, 1979, 524 pp.;
- VON WESTPHALEN, F., Die Einheitlichen Richtlinien und Gebräuche für Dokumentenakkreditive und die Einheitlichen Richtlinien für Inkassi im Licht des AGB-Gesetzes, WM, 1980, 178-191;
- VON WESTPHALEN, F., Rechtsprobleme der Exportfinanzierung, third edition, Heidelberg, Verlag Recht und Wirtschaft, 1987, 589 pp.;

- WALTON, F.P., Historical introduction to the Roman law, second edition, Edinburgh, Green & Sons, 1912, 391 pp.;
- WARBURTON, J., Unincorporated associations : law and practice, London, Sweet & Maxwell, 1986, 145 pp.;
- WEILL, A. and TERRE, F., Les obligations, fourth edition, Paris, Dalloz, 1986, 1069 pp.;
- WEISE, P.F., Lex mercatoria, Materielles Recht vor der internationalen Handelsschiedsgerichtsbarkeit, Frankfurt, Lang, 1990, 182 pp.;
- WEISS, E., V° Ius gentium, in Paulys Real-Encyclopädie der classischen Altertumswissenschaft, Volume 19, Stuttgart, Metzler, 1917, 1218-1231;
- WELLWOOD, J., Custom and usage, in 12 Halsbury's laws of England, fourth edition, London, Butterworths, 1975, 1-60;
- WENGLER, W., Die Anknüpfung des zwingenden Schuldrechts im internationalen Privatrecht, Zvglrwiss, 1941, 168-212;
- WENGLER, W., Die Funktion des richterlichen Entscheidung über internationale Rechtsverhältnisse, Feststellung und Gestaltung im internationalen Privatrecht, RabelsZ, 1951, 1-31;
- WENGLER, W., Les principes généraux du droit en tant que loi du contrat, R.C.D.I.P., 1982, 467-501, also published as Allgemeine Rechtsgrundsätze als wählbares Geschäftsstatut ?, ZfRV, 1982, 28 ff.;
- WERY, P., De autonomie van het eenvormig privaatrecht, Deventer, Kluwer, 1971, 40 pp.;
- WETZMÜLLER, H., Der "internationale" Schiedsspruch im U.N.- Übereinkommen über die Anerkennung und Vollstreckung ausländischer Schiedssprüche vom 10.6.1958 von New York, dissertation, Mainz, 1966, 95 pp.;

- WIEDEMANN, H., Gesellschaftsrecht, I, Munich, Beck, 1980, 905 pp.;
- WIGNY, P., La règle de conflit applicable aux contrats, Une solution transactionnelle, Rev.Dr.Int.Lég.Comp., 1933, 676-703;
- WIJFFELS, R., Incoterms, E.T.L., 1987, 3-15;
- WILINSKI, A., Das römische Recht, Leipzig, Teubner Verlagsgesellschaft, 1966, 117 pp.;
- WOOD, P., Law and practice of international finance, London, Sweet & Maxwell, 1980, 462 pp.;
- WYMEERSCH, E., Règles professionnelles et règles standardisées dans les opérations financières, in le droit des normes professionnelles et techniques, COMMISSION DROIT ET VIE DES AFFAIRES (ed.), Brussels, Bruylant, 1985, 47-110;

- YAHIA-BACHA, M., Sociétés transnationales et nouvel ordre économique international, in Revue algérienne des sciences juridiques, économiques et politiques, 1982, 273-289;

- ZAHN, J., EBERDING, E. and EHRLICH, D., Zahlung und Zahlungssicherung im Außenhandel, sixth edition, Berlin, de Gruyter, 1986, 502 pp.;
- ZWEIGERT, K., Verträge zwischen staatlichen und nichtstaatlichen Partnern, in Berichte der deutschen Gesellschaft für Völkerrecht, Volume 5, Karlsruhe, Müller, 1964, 194-214;
- ZWEIGERT, K. and KÖTZ, H., Einführung in die Rechtsvergleichung, II, second edition, Tubingen, Mohr, 1984, 490 pp.

KEYWORD INDEX

References are to paragraph numbers and not to pages.